EDUCATIONAL
and
PSYCHOLOGICAL RESEARCH

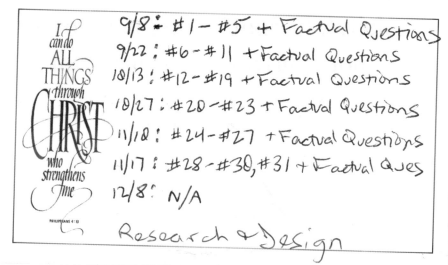

I can do ALL THINGS through CHRIST who strengthens me

PHILIPPIANS 4:13

9/8: #1 - #5 + Factual Questions
9/22: #6 - #11 + Factual Questions
10/13: #12 - #19 + Factual Questions
10/27: #20 - #23 + Factual Questions
11/10: #24 - #27 + Factual Questions
11/17: #28 - #30, #31 + Factual Ques
12/8: N/A

Research & Design

Mildred L. Patten

Pyrczak Publishing
P.O. Box 39731
Los Angeles, CA 90039

Editorial assistance provided by Virginia Iorio, Robert E. King, Ralph Carroll, and Randall R. Bruce.

Cover design by Mario Sanchez.

Printed in the United States of America.

ISBN 1-884585-03-5

CONTENTS

Continued →

True Experimental Research

Quasi-Experimental Research

Pre-Experimental Research

Program Evaluation

Meta-Analysis

Appendices

Introduction to the Second Edition

In this edition, you will find an entirely new set of research articles that illustrate a wide variety of approaches to research. By analyzing and evaluating them, you will become a skilled consumer of research. In addition, by studying them, you will learn how to conduct basic research and write research reports.

Like the first edition, this one emphasizes research articles that employ straightforward research designs, emphasize basic statistics, and are on topics of interest to students in the social and behavioral sciences, with an emphasis on education and psychology.

I believe that all of the articles in this collection provide valuable information. Note that some are reports on pilot studies in which researchers were trying out new methods, exploring new ideas on a small-scale basis, etc. Such pilot studies are valuable because they suggest promising hypotheses that may be explored later in more definitive studies.

From article to article, you will probably spot different weaknesses in research methodology. This should not surprise you because each investigator conducts research under a different set of limitations—such as limited financial support, access to subjects, availability of appropriate measuring tools, and so on. When applying evaluation criteria to the articles, keep in mind that your goal is to evaluate the methodology—not the researchers.

Answering the Questions in This Book

At the end of each article, there are two sets of questions. The *Factual Questions* help draw your attention to important methodological details. Field tests indicate that there is only one correct answer for each of these questions. The *Questions for Discussion*, on the other hand, are designed to stimulate classroom discussions. Each of these questions may have more than one defensible answer.

The paragraphs in each article are sequentially numbered. Keeping track of the paragraph numbers on which you base your answers will prove helpful when you discuss your answers with your instructor and other students.

About the Appendices

Appendix A contains a brief introduction to reading research articles. For those of you who have not read journal articles extensively, this appendix is a good place to start in this book.

Appendix B is a reprint of a classic article by Harry F. Harlow. His tongue-in-cheek discussion of the preparation of research articles from the perspective of a journal editor is both enjoyable and informative.

Appendices C and D provide research criteria that you can apply when evaluating the articles. In addition, your main textbook may contain a list of criteria. Your instructor will inform you which, if any, of these sets of criteria you are to apply.

NOTES

LEARNING ON THE JOB: AN ANALYSIS OF THE ACQUISITION OF A TEACHER'S KNOWLEDGE

Paul G. Schempp   *The University of Georgia*

This study analyzed the criteria used by an experienced teacher to acquire the knowledge necessary to teach. An interpretive analytic framework and case study methodology were used in this yearlong project with a midcareer high school teacher. Data were collected using a variety of ethnographic techniques including: nonparticipant observations, artifact and document analysis, stimulated recall from videotapes, and formal and informal interviews. Data analysis followed the conventions described by Glaser and Strauss (1967). Five distinct knowledge categories were identified, each with unique selection criteria. These knowledge forms included: class organization and operation, teaching behavior, subject matter, pedagogical content knowledge (Shulman, 1986), and external conditions. In matters of class organization and operation, Bob (the teacher) looked to his experience for those things that worked (i.e., insured classroom order). The acquisition of instructional behavior came largely from observations of other teachers (e.g., cooperating teacher, peers) or from experience. Bob selected subject matter knowledge based upon previous knowledge, current personal interests, resource availability, and student interest. Pedagogical content knowledge was comprised in three phases: demonstrations, drills, and activities. External conditions were influences outside the classroom (e.g., laws, school policy). Years of occupational service have left Bob with a well-developed set of criteria upon which he acquires the knowledge to teach.

1.   A distinguishing characteristic of any profession is the body of knowledge for practicing that profession. Professionals are called into service because they bring a unique understanding and critical insight to a situation that is inaccessible to the uninitiated. It is the body of professional knowledge that explains what those in a particular occupation do and why (Schon, 1983). The body of knowledge currently used in a profession is, therefore, of major concern to those practicing the profession and preparing future practitioners.

2.   Contemporary literature on teaching lacks substantive information on the knowledge base teachers use in their professional practice. As Shulman (1986) noted, important questions such as "Where do teacher explanations come from? How do teachers decide what to teach, how to represent it and how to deal with problems of misunderstanding?" (p. 8) have gone unanswered. There has been a growing recognition in teacher education that the understanding of the knowledge used by teachers will lead to a better understanding of pedagogical practice.

3.   Within the last decade, educational researchers have studied rules and principles used in teacher thinking (Elbaz, 1983), teachers' classroom images (Clandinin, 1985), the experience of classroom cycles and rhythms (Clandinin & Connelly, 1986), subject matter expertise (Leinhardt & Smith, 1985), and pedagogical content knowledge (Grossman, 1989; Gudmundsdottir & Kristjansdottir, 1989). These studies, and other similar work, represent the start of a growing trend in research into what teachers know and how they use that knowledge in their classrooms. This study continues that line of inquiry by offering a glimpse into the world of an experienced high school teacher. Specifically, this case study examines the criteria one teacher employed in acquiring the knowledge he found necessary for his professional practice.

Method

Teacher

4.   Robert Halstop has taught high school physical education for the past 14 years at Hillcrest High School (HHS). Over those years, Bob has coached many sports and been involved in numerous school clubs, groups, and projects. At the time of this study, he was coaching the girls' varsity basketball team. Besides teaching and coaching, he performed normal student counseling activities and other school duties assigned by the administrators. Bob worked at a local lumber mill during the summers, but did not work outside the school during the academic year. Bob's school day officially began at 7:30 a.m. and ended at 3:30 p.m., but he was usually in school much earlier and it was common for him to stay later. There were seven instructional periods in the day. Bob was assigned six classes, one planning period, and had a 30 minute lunch break. Bob was presented with an initial draft of this report for his review and comment. His comments were incorporated into subsequent drafts and used to validate the accuracy of the events and quotes reported.

Setting

5.   Hillcrest is a small, rural community in the Pacific Northwest. Education was held in high esteem as evidenced by the town having one of the highest tax bases in the state. Hillcrest High School enrolled approximately 470 students. Two years before this study, HHS received an educational excellence award from the United States Department of Education. All first-year students were required to take physical education for one year and could elect physical education after that. The freshman physical education classes were separated by gender and were taught as a survey course to cover many subject areas. The other physical education classes were coeducational and defined by student interest (e.g., recreational sports, weight training). HHS had two physical education teachers: one for boys (Bob) and one for girls (Kathy).

Data Collection

6.   Data were collected and analyzed using a variety of qualitative techniques. Among these techniques were nonparticipant observation, artifact and document analyses, stimulated recall using videotaped classes, and both formal and informal interviews. Besides Bob, Kathy and other school personnel (e.g., students, teachers, administrators) were also interviewed. Field notes were recorded during and after observations and a summary statement was made off site after each day of data collection. Data

Schempp, P. G. (1995). Learning on the job: An analysis of the acquisition of a teacher's knowledge. *Journal of Research and Development in Education, 28*, 237-244. Copyright © 1995 by College of Education, The University of Georgia. Reprinted by permission.

collection began 2 days before the start of school and officially ended just before the Christmas break. I was present in the school on a daily basis for the first month of the study and made field trips twice a week on average after that.

Data Analyses

7.   Data analysis began on the first day of the study and ended approximately 1 year later. Concurrently collecting and analyzing data allowed me to develop data summary themes and check the emerging themes against recurring field activities. Analyzing data during the study also allowed data collection techniques to be tailored to gather data that were amenable to testing and understanding the emerging themes. Specific strategies employed to insure data trustworthiness included triangulation of methods, member checks (particularly the use of key informants and the constant use of follow-up interviews to check consistency of responses), disconfirming case analyses (the investigation of responses and/or occurrences that were incompatible with emerging themes), and cultivating reactions from the case-study teacher to the themes, categories, and events to be included in the final report.

8.   My key informant was Bob's teaching colleague, Kathy. At the time of this study, Kathy and Bob had been teaching physical education together at Hillcrest for 3 years. Kathy was particularly helpful in cross-checking stories and events described by Bob. In cases where discrepant information occurred (e.g., differences between what Bob told me and what I observed) Kathy often provided valuable insights.

9.   Data analysis involved summarizing data into themes and categories using procedures recommended by Miles and Huberman (1984), Goetz and LeCompte (1984), and Patton (1980). The construction of these categories was influenced by Shulman's (1987) theory of a knowledge base for teaching. He identified seven categories of teachers' knowledge: subject matter, general pedagogical, curriculum, pedagogical content, learners, contexts, and purposes. As themes emerged and clustered into categories, these categories were checked against Shulman's propositions. Four of Shulman's seven categories were ultimately used to describe the forms of knowledge Bob acquired in pursuit of his professional practice: subject matter, general pedagogical (renamed teaching behavior), pedagogical content, and context (renamed external conditions). Classroom organization and operation was a category constructed independent of Shulman's theory as it appeared to better describe a dominant form of Bob's knowledge.

10.   The themes and categories identified forms of knowledge as well as the criteria Bob used in acquiring pedagogical knowledge. The categories allowed the data to be summarized and reported in a succinct, yet accurate, manner. The first step was to review the collected data to determine tentative categories. Next, the data were coded using the tentative scheme. The category scheme underwent revisions until the data were able to be classified within the scheme with no redundancy of categories. The constant comparison method of analysis (Glaser & Strauss, 1967) was used to identify these patterns and relationships.

11.   The final step of the analytic procedure was to present a copy of the report to Bob for his comments and reactions. The findings were brought back to the case study teacher so that he could: (a) check the accuracy of the data (reliability), and (b) validate the findings of the report. This procedure was considered a critical component for establishing the validity and trustworthiness of the study's findings (Lather, 1986). Additional revisions were then made based on the responses and reactions from the teacher. Events contained in the report seen by Bob as either inaccurate or threatening to confidentiality were rechecked and eliminated where appropriate. Bob's comments and additional supporting evidence were incorporated into the final draft of the report to lend strength to the propositions put forth.

Findings

12.   From years of contact with many sources of occupationally useful information, Bob had constructed a comfortable set of criteria for evaluating and selecting knowledge necessary for his day-to-day classroom operation. He seemed to have a clear sense of both the expectations others held for him, and his own purpose for being in the school. These criteria formed a screen through which all potential pedagogical knowledge passed. Bob's knowledge acquisition represented an intersection between the demands of his day-to-day practice and the knowledge available to meet those demands. Thus, Bob appropriated knowledge based upon his perception of the power and quality of its source, and his perception of its potential to solve a recurring problem or improve a current practice.

13.   In analyzing the data, five knowledge categories emerged: (a) classroom organization and operation, (b) teaching behavior, (c) subject matter, (d) pedagogical content knowledge, and (e) external conditions. Each category was unique in terms of the problems it addressed, the sources from which it came, and the criteria

that determined knowledge selection and rejection.

Class Organization and Operation

14.   Like many teachers (West, 1975; Yinger, 1980), classroom order and control were predominant concerns for Bob. The concern for classroom organization and controlled operation rose from Bob's belief that, if order was not established and the classroom not operated in the manner he needed, little could be accomplished. In his own words,

> I'm going to get across more to kids in a structured setting. Otherwise kids are pretty much allowed to go where they want to and pick and choose what they want to take and what they don't want to take. . . . I have more kids working at a higher level than I would otherwise.

15.   Although he had spent much time formulating, writing, and explaining his operational policies and procedures, the complex and fluid nature of his classes required constant interpretation and reevaluation of the codes of operation and organization. The variety of students with varying levels of interest, responsibilities, motivations, and attitudes demanded adaptations in the organization and management of the class. Similarly, different subject matter, teaching stations, or equipment would also signal a change in class organization and operation. Bob, like many teachers (Clandinin, 1985; Clandinin & Connelly, 1986), relied on practical rules and principles, routines, and habits to guide classroom operation rather than inflexible standards or absolute rules.

16.   Bob perceived the ability to organize and operate a class to be a fundamental and critical responsibility of a teacher. When asked "What would you look for in a high school teacher to determine if they were a good teacher?" he responded with a list of criteria heavily skewed toward organizational and operational concerns. His list included: (a) the kids are paying attention; (b) gives directions clearly and the kids respond to directions showing that they heard; (c) what he said made good sense; (d) organized drills, organized calisthenics, lesson didn't get bogged down; (e) didn't let a few kids take over the lesson; and (f) didn't get distracted from where he wanted to go.

17.   Bob relied upon few resources in deciding the organizational and operational patterns of his classes. It was, perhaps, the improvisational character of a classroom that forced Bob to look primarily to his experience and beliefs in crafting his operational procedures and organizational patterns (Doyle, 1986; Kelsay, 1991; Leinhardt & Greeno, 1986). He explained that

> There have been so many times I have had a structured program and then something comes

along and changes it at the last second. . . . So you just, I guess it is out of necessity or survival, you just make do. Some things work and some don't and you just throw out the things that don't and you go to something else.

The fundamental criterion for evaluating his class organization and operation knowledge was Bob's satisfaction with the results of the policy, rule, or procedure. If it worked all was well, for the problem had been solved. The level of evaluation did not go any further.

18. Outside influence over his operation and organization came on two fronts. The first influence was over his teaching stations. Other members of the school had a greater influence over Bob's teaching station than he. In my time with Bob, I observed the nurse usurp the gymnasium to conduct health screening exams, the custodians claim the football field so that they could mow it for that evening's contest, and the building principal threaten to reallocate the all-purpose room Bob and Kathy used as a teaching station for a student lounge.

19. The second area of influence that held consequence for Bob's organization and class operation dealt with the consequences for student misconduct. He could set all of the rules he cared to set. There were no formal guidelines or recommendations. How he enforced those rules was another matter. Parents and administrators took a strong interest in the consequences Bob dealt students for misbehavior. Bob explained it this way:

You've gotta have the right administration, the administrator that is willing to go along with what you see as important, what your values are, a disciplined structured program, and back you up on that because if you don't . . . the kids are going to start complaining, which in turn, the parents start complaining. Parents are going to the administration. If the administrator will support you and back you up, then you can.

20. Bob seemed unaware of an existence of a "shared technical culture" (Lortie, 1975) for matters of classroom operation and organization. The approval of others usually seemed unnecessary. For example, Bob's policy of required student showers was disliked by the students and Kathy alike. He believed that Kathy was entitled to her opinion, but his students conformed to his opinion. Bob accommodated opinions from parents and administrators when he had no choice, but he did not see their views as more important than his own. As he was fond of telling his students, "In this class, it's my way or the highway."

Teaching Behavior

21. A significant portion of Bob's everyday actions and activities were devoted to the task of instructing students. Knowledge for meeting these demands was classified by Shulman (1987) as general pedagogical knowledge, for this knowledge transcended a particular subject content. Much of Bob's teaching behavior was characterized by well-rehearsed, time-worn rituals. Every class began with student-led exercises while Bob took attendance. Then Bob informed the students of the day's activities. A brief skill demonstration or explanation was followed by a drill. Most classes closed with a game or culminating activity. Sometimes, a game was played for the entire class period. The practices that defined Bob's teaching behavior were largely composed of comfortable habits and familiar routines. In crafting a teaching style, comfort does not appear to be an uncommon criterion among teachers (Lange & Burroughs-Lange, 1994; Russell & Johnston, 1988).

22. Bob did not actively pursue knowledge that directly affected his instructional practices. The roots of this perspective can be traced to his undergraduate days. "When I was going through college," he said, "they didn't have any methods classes. None. Zero." The fundamental criteria used to determine the success of a lesson was, therefore, not so much what students learned, but rather their level of enjoyment. During one interview Bob told me that "they really seem to enjoy it (the activity). They develop certain skills. The more skill they develop, the more they seem to enjoy it."

23. While he did not actively seek effective teaching strategies, Bob recognized its lacking in his repertoire of skills. He told me, "I hear in some cases, teachers drop the ball and let them play. You know, I'm guilty of a little bit of that too, at times, you know." He went on to say "That's one thing I could upgrade my program with, some more creative drill work that would teach the skills I want them to learn and at the same time give them some fun and enjoyment."

24. Bob's teaching behavior was a nonissue with almost everybody in the school. The structure of the school provided him with no feedback on his teaching behavior, nor was there visible encouragement for him to stimulate greater student achievement. Students, for example, appeared to have little regard for their learning in physical education. Upon seeing Bob before class, students would invariably ask "What are we gonna play?" "Do we have to dress down?" or "Are we gonna do anything today?" No student ever thanked Bob for something they learned or requested to learn a particular skill or concept.

25. Although student learning was a concern in Bob's occupational activity, it was not the driving force behind his pedagogical practices. He harbored a stronger concern for maintaining control over the collective social behavior of the students. He showed far greater frustration when there was a breach of order than when students failed to make significant learning gains. The concern for classroom control over educational substance has been a consistent finding in research on physical education teachers' conceptions of their occupational duties and responsibilities (Placek, 1983; Schempp, 1985, 1986).

26. The immediate and multiple demands placed on Bob's time in school often relegated the learning of his approximately 130 students to the back burner of his priorities. During one observation, Bob and I were in his office between classes and I remarked, "I can't believe all the things you have to attend to." His comment was

Yeah, there's a lot going on. Right now I'm trying to get a test set up, get the equipment I need for that, worry about the two kids who are on their way to the counselors' office to drop the class, answer kids' questions about what we're doing today, think about that indoor soccer ball for next period, I have two home counseling visits coming up, remember to read the announcements this period, and I have an executive school meeting.

He rose out of his chair, picked up his roster book, glanced over a tardy note pushed into his hand by a late student, and was on his way to take roll and begin another class.

27. Time that could be used to evaluate and improve his instructional practices is consumed by the competing requirements of his coaching responsibilities and the many mundane activities he continually has to attend to (e.g., lost locks, attendance records, clean towel supply, field preparation, equipment maintenance). One morning every free moment before and between classes was used to locate a popcorn machine for the concessions that evening at the boys basketball game. His work environment conspired to inform Bob that the operation of the school as a system took precedent over student learning in a physical education class.

28. Additionally, there was little incentive for Bob to improve his teaching behavior to stimulate increases in student learning. Administrators held a greater concern for the operation of the school than they did for achievement of students in physical education. Parents were more concerned with how their children were treated than what they learned. Students wanted to play, not learn. Whether students learned in his class or not was a concern that was, from my observations, held only by Bob. And because of the lack of concern from others, it was often not even at the forefront of Bob's concerns. He received no rewards if learning was increased, and there were no consequences for a lack of student achievement.

Subject Matter

29. The content of Bob's classes was described and detailed in a curriculum guide he had compiled. Objectives for each program were identified and the policies used to conduct the program were also described. The largest portion of the guide was composed of the specific subject-matter units. When asked about the resources used to complete the guide, Bob told me that most of the units came from an undergraduate curriculum course assignment. He has added to the guide materials and resources gathered at in-service programs.

30. Although the guide was a 148-page document and included an outline of each subject taught, it was used sparingly. Over the course of my time with Bob, I observed him using the guide perhaps a half dozen times, mostly to review teaching points for an upcoming lesson or remind himself of game rules. The guide did not hold the majority of subject matter Bob taught, for experience has taught him that he must "keep most of the (subject matter) knowledge organized in my head and I can't write it down because everything is situation specific."

31. Bob acquired new subject-matter knowledge based upon these criteria: (a) perceptions of his own competence in teaching the subject, (b) personal interest in the subject matter, (c) perceptions of student interest, (d) actual student demand as demonstrated by elective class enrollments, (e) time investment necessary to teach or prepare to teach the subject, (f) the novelty of the subject, and (g) facility and equipment constraints.

32. Bob reported that gymnastics and outdoor education were two content areas recently dropped. Gymnastics was no longer offered because Bob did not like teaching it and had a concern for liability. Outdoor education was no longer part of the curriculum because the individual who taught the course had left the school and Bob did not want to give up his weekends for the activities. Weight training was a new subject added to the course offerings because of student demand, Bob's personal interest in teaching the subject, and the availability of an adequate facility. Personal understanding and meaning of subject matter plays an important role in Bob's acquisition and use of content knowledge. Teachers in other subject areas also appear to rely on personal understanding in selecting content (Wilson & Wineburg, 1988).

33. By his own admission, Bob is not an expert in many of the areas he teaches. Rather, he knows enough to teach a 10-day unit in the selected subject. He would draw from the subject areas in which he had expertise to bolster areas that were unfamiliar. For example, soccer drills were structured very much like basketball drills. Bob was required to teach over 23 different units in any given year. It would be difficult for any teacher to be knowledgeable in so many different subjects.

34. Bob gave this example of how and why new subject knowledge was selected:

> I had never heard of pickleball until last year. I happened to be looking through a magazine and it looked like a neat game. So I wrote to them and I cheated a bit. It said, "We'll give you some free materials if you order a program." And I wrote to them and said we didn't receive our teaching sheets and they sent me one. Once I saw what it was all about, I wanted to implement it in our program. I wrote back and got the equipment.

The company supplied both the equipment necessary for instruction as well as the content to be taught. Bob was able to incorporate the content immediately into his program with no prior knowledge of the subject. Because the game strongly resembled tennis, a subject he had taught for many years, Bob used the same drills and skill demonstrations he used in his tennis unit. Thus, the combination of his previous experience and information from an equipment manufacturer supplied all the content knowledge necessary for a new instructional unit.

35. Perhaps it was the lack of expertise in subject matter that provided the flexibility that allowed Bob to change content so readily and amenably. It is also the lack of expert knowledge in these areas that forces Bob to use noneducational rationales in selecting subject matter for his classes. "They got some enjoyment out of it. . . . They wanted to keep playing it (pickleball) forever, but I said 'Hey, we gotta stop and go on to something else . . .' but that was a success."

Pedagogical Content Knowledge

36. Shulman (1986) defines pedagogical content knowledge as content knowledge "which goes beyond knowledge of subject matter per se to the dimension of subject matter for teaching" (p. 9). Years of experience have forged a mode of operation, a routine, which frames the knowledge Bob imparts to his students. Bob seeks curricular content that fits his teaching style. In pedagogical practice, he teaches an activity in terms of its essential skills by giving brief explanations and sometimes demonstrations, then has students practice these skills through drills, and after varying amounts of practice the students are then given the rules and play the game. These procedures have been used for years by Bob with all varieties of subject matter. He is, therefore, more inclined to select new activities that fit his mode of operation than he is to look for new ways to teach old subject matter. Further, Bob was less likely to teach subject matter in depth and more likely to teach many activities at the introductory level. The more new information conveniently fits into familiar routines, the more likely it would be incorporated.

37. Bob's content knowledge appeared to not only influence what he teaches, but how he teaches. Activities, particularly skill drills, were borrowed from better-known subject lessons and adapted and applied in lesser-known subject areas. In concept explanations, metaphors and images were drawn from parallel concepts in better-known subjects and used to help explain subject concepts that he did not know well. Bob does not appear unique in this regard. Teachers of mathematics (Leinhardt & Smith, 1985; Marks, 1990), social studies (Gudmundsdottir & Shulman, 1987), and English (Grossman, 1989, 1990; Gudmundsdottir, 1991) all seem to follow this process in acquiring and developing pedagogical content knowledge.

38. As Bob screened new content knowledge for his pedagogical practice, he used the term *practical* to identify acceptable pedagogical content knowledge. For example, in explaining why he takes few university courses, he stated he had "a great deal of difficulty finding coursework of relevance for a teacher in my situation. A lot of philosophy, theory, etc., but not many practical, time-proven methods which I can use in my class." Another time, he identified coaching clinics as more worthwhile than teaching workshops because the clinics "offer practical information that can be directly implemented into our program." Content that could be incorporated into the existing classroom routines and rituals was highly valued. Previous research reveals that Bob is not alone in his regard for knowledge that is easily imported into existing classroom practices (Alexander, Muir, & Chant, 1992; Elbaz, 1983).

External Conditions

39. Conditions originating outside the classroom, and removed from Bob's immediate control, came to bear on several pedagogical decisions. These conditions include local regulations and requirements that were imposed by the administration and school board as well as regulations and laws handed down from state and federal agencies. Therefore, the wishes and demands of administrators, students, parents, and state agencies factored into Bob's procurement of knowledge. The influence of administrators, parents, and students on Bob's knowledge was discussed above. School and state regulations also influenced him, but to a far lesser degree.

40. Bob passively resisted school and state imperatives that ran counter to his personal beliefs and his interpretation of the community moral standards. For example, in discussing coed classes, he reported that:

> We used to (have coed classes) but it was a hassle. . . . We had a lot of nondressers and got a lot of complaints from parents. It just wasn't worth it. So we have boys and girls separate the first year and together after that. We got a little pressure from the state about Title IX, but I think we're in compliance.

41. When he and I discussed the new state curricular guidelines, Bob expressed frustration that change seems to negate previous work. To him, it was not so much that the new ideas were better or worse than old ones, but that all his previous work on curriculum development was for naught. He felt frustrated that the amount of work that had gone into developing his curriculum was ignored by those in state agencies. "Hillcrest has always prided themselves on being a leader. Now we'll have to throw them (present guidelines) out for no apparent reason or justification." As he had in the past, he would continue as before making only token modifications to existing practice. External conditions were only a minor consideration in Bob's acquisition of knowledge.

Conclusion

42. After years of service, Bob had a well-developed set of criteria to guide his acquisition of occupational knowledge. These criteria allowed Bob to identify gaps in his knowledge and to assess new knowledge in light of its potential contribution to his teaching. Contrary to the belief of many students, administrators, and colleagues, Bob continually reviewed and screened new information and then made attempts to integrate this knowledge into his professional practice. Because the criteria used in acquiring new knowledge were primarily comprised of experiences, interests, values, beliefs, and orientations, Bob's professional knowledge appeared personal and idiosyncratic (Carter, 1990; Zeichner, Tabachnick, & Densmore, 1987). Bob was, by his own admission, set in his ways. Therefore, the changes and alterations he did make were neither dramatic nor overtly visible. In short, little changed in the observable practices of Bob's day-to-day activities as a teacher and he became fairly predictable in his course of action.

43. Classroom order and operation held the highest priority in Bob's pedagogical knowledge. Subject matter that fit his personal interests, workplace conditions, and would result in student enjoyment had the greatest chance of penetrating the curriculum. New knowledge that conformed to his well-worn classroom practices passed Bob's test of valued professional knowledge. He acknowledged a lack of information regarding effective teaching behavior, and given his workplace conditions, this situation appears to have little chance to change. Will Bob ever change? He is, in fact, always changing as new information comes to him and is incorporated into his professional knowledge base. In the final analysis, however, Bob's time in service has made him well aware of who he is, what he does, why he does it, and what knowledge is required for him to meet the demands of teaching in a public school.

References

Alexander, D., Muir, D., & Chant, D. (1992). Interrogating stories: How teachers think they learn to teach. *Teaching and Teacher Education, 8*, 59-68.

Carter, K. (1990). Teachers' knowledge and learning to teach. In W. R. Houston (Ed.) *Handbook of Research on Teacher Education* (pp. 291-330). New York: Macmillan.

Clandinin, D. J. (1985). Personal practical knowledge: A study of teachers' classroom images. *Curriculum Inquiry, 15*, 361-385.

Clandinin, D. J., & Connelly, F. M. (1986). Rhythms in teaching: The narrative study of teachers' personal practical knowledge of classrooms. *Teaching and Teacher Education, 2*, 377-387.

Doyle, W. (1986). Classroom organization and management (pp. 392-431). In M. Wittrock (Ed.) *Handbook of Research on Teaching* (3rd ed.). New York: Macmillan.

Elbaz, F. (1983). *Teacher thinking: A study of practical knowledge.* London: Croom Helm.

Glaser, B., & Strauss, A. (1967). *The discovery of grounded theory: Strategies for qualitative research.* Chicago: Aldine.

Goetz, J. P., & LeCompte, M. D. (1984). *Ethnography and qualitative design in educational research.* Orlando: Academic Press.

Grossman, P. (1989). A study of contrast: Sources of pedagogical content knowledge for secondary English. *Journal of Teacher Education, 40*, 24-32.

Grossman, P. (1990). *The making of a teacher: Teacher knowledge and teacher education.* New York: Teachers College Press.

Gudmundsdottir, S. (1991). Ways of seeing are ways of knowing: The pedagogical content of an expert English teacher. *Journal of Curriculum Studies, 23*, 207-218.

Gudmundsdottir, S., & Kristjansdottir, E. (1989, March). *The concern of pedagogical content knowledge: Case studies of learning to teach.* Paper presented at the American Educational Research Association Annual Meeting, San Francisco, CA.

Gudmundsdottir, S., & Schulman, L. (1987). Pedagogical content knowledge in social studies. *Scandinavian Journal of Educational Research, 31*, 59-70.

Kelsay, K. L. (1991). When experience is the best teacher: The teacher as researcher. *Action in Teacher Education, 13*, 14-21.

Lange, J. D., & Burroughs-Lange, S. G. (1994). Professional uncertainty and professional growth: A case study of experienced teachers. *Teaching and Teacher Education, 10*, 617-631.

Lather, P. (1986). Issues of validity in openly ideological research: Between a rock and a soft place. *Interchange, 17*, 63-84.

Leinhardt, G., & Greeno, J. (1986). The cognitive skill of teaching. *Journal of Educational Psychology, 78*, 75-95.

Leinhardt, G., & Smith, D. A. (1985). Expertise in mathematics instruction: Subject matter knowledge. *Journal of Educational Psychology, 77*, 247-271.

Lortie, D. C. (1975). *Schoolteacher: A sociological study.* Chicago: University of Chicago Press.

Marks, R. (1990). Pedagogical content knowledge: From a mathematical case to a modified conception. *Journal of Teacher Education, 41*, 3-11.

Miles, M. B., & Huberman, A. M. (1984). *Qualitative data analysis: A sourcebook of new methods.* Beverly Hills: Sage Publications.

Patton, M. (1980). *Qualitative evaluation methods.* Beverly Hills: Sage Publications.

Placek, J. (1983). Conceptions of success in teaching: Happy, busy and good? In T. Templin & J. Olson (Eds.) *Teaching in Physical Education* (pp. 46-56). Champaign, IL: Human Kinetics.

Russell, T., & Johnston, P. (1988, April). *Teachers' learning from experiences of teaching: Analysis based on metaphor and reflection.* Paper presented at the annual meeting of the American Education Research Association, New Orleans, LA.

Schempp, P. G. (1985). Becoming a better teacher: An analysis of the student teaching experience. *Journal of Teaching in Physical Education, 4*, 158-166.

Schempp, P. G. (1986). Physical education student teachers' beliefs in their control over student learning. *Journal of Teaching in Physical Education, 5*, 198-203.

Schon, D. A. (1983). *The reflective practitioner.* New York: Basic Books.

Shulman, L. S. (1986). Those who understand: Knowledge growth in teaching. *Educational Researcher, 15*, 4-14.

Shulman, L. S. (1987). Knowledge and teaching: Foundations of the new reform. *Harvard Educational Review, 57*, 1-22.

West, W. G. (1975). Participant observation research on the social construction of everyday classroom order. *Interchange, 6(4)*, 35-43.

Wilson, S., & Wineburg, S. (1988). Peering at history through different lenses: The role of disciplinary perspectives in teaching history. *Teachers' College Record, 89*, 525-539.

Yinger, R. J. (1980). A study of teacher planning. *Elementary School Journal, 80*, 107-127.

Zeichner, K., Tabachnick, R., & Densmore, K. (1987). Individual, institutional and cultural influences on the development of teachers' craft knowledge. In J. Calderhead (Ed.) *Exploring teachers' thinking* (pp. 21-59). London: Cassell.

Factual Questions

1. How long had Robert Halstop taught high school physical education at Hillcrest High School?

2. When were summary statements made by the researcher?

3. After the first month, how often did the researcher visit the school?

4. How is "disconfirming case analyses" defined?

5. Who was the key informant in this study?

6. How many knowledge categories emerged from the data analysis?

7. Why was gymnastics no longer taught?

8. How does Shulman define pedagogical content knowledge?

Questions for Discussion

9. In which paragraph is the purpose of this study most clearly stated?

10. If you were selecting a single teacher for a study of this type, what kind of teacher would you select?

11. In your opinion, are there advantages and disadvantages of analyzing data during the study? (See paragraph 7. Note: This is often done in qualitative research. Typically, in quantitative research, all the data are collected before the analysis is undertaken.)

12. Is the method of data analysis described in sufficient detail? Could you replicate it in a future study? Explain.

13. What is your opinion on the final step in the analytic procedure? (See paragraph 11.)

14. How important are the quotations in helping you understand the findings? Would you like to see more quotations? Explain.

15. Is the finding that "Bob's teaching behavior was a nonissue with almost everybody in the school" surprising to you? (See especially paragraphs 24 and 28.)

16. The author points out parallels between his findings and the findings of others reported in the literature. (See, for example, paragraphs 14, 25, and 38.) Is this important? Explain.

17. In your opinion, what are the implications of this study for other teachers? For the teaching profession?

18. Do you believe that it would be valuable to do a series of studies such as this one using a number of other teachers? Why? Why not?

Quality Ratings

DIRECTIONS: Indicate your level of agreement with each of the following statements by circling a number from 5 for strongly agree (SA) to 1 for strongly disagree (SD). If you believe that an item is not applicable to this research article, leave it blank. Be prepared to explain your ratings.

A. The introduction establishes the importance of the research topic.
   SA   5   4   3   2   1   SD

B. The literature review establishes the context for the study.
   SA   5   4   3   2   1   SD

C. The research purpose, question, or hypothesis is clearly stated.
   SA   5   4   3   2   1   SD

D. The method of sampling is sound.
   SA   5   4   3   2   1   SD

E. Relevant demographics (for example, age, gender, and ethnicity) are described.
   SA   5   4   3   2   1   SD

F. Measurement procedures are adequate.
   SA   5   4   3   2   1   SD

G. The results are clearly described.
   SA   5   4   3   2   1   SD

H. The discussion/conclusion is appropriate.
   SA   5   4   3   2   1   SD

I. Despite any flaws noted above, the report is worthy of publication.
   SA   5   4   3   2   1   SD

PARENTS WHO ABDUCT: A QUALITATIVE STUDY WITH IMPLICATIONS FOR PRACTICE

Geoffrey L. Greif   *University of Maryland at Baltimore*
Rebecca L. Hegar   *University of Maryland at Baltimore*

Little is known about parents' motivations for abducting their children and going into hiding. In-depth interviews were conducted with 17 parents (nine fathers and eight mothers) to learn of their relevant experiences. Reported reasons for abduction included unsatisfactory contact with court-related professionals, revenge, and fear for the child's safety. Some abductors, after the abduction had been resolved, had increased contact with their children.

1. If we conceptualize custody decisions between divorcing parents on a continuum from the harmonious to the acrimonious, at the latter extreme would be those that result in parental abduction. Parental abduction has been defined as "the taking, retention, or concealment of a child or children by a parent, other family member, or their agent, in derogation of the custody rights . . . of another parent or family member" (Girdner & Hoff, 1992, p. 1). When a parent snatches his or her child with the intent of going into hiding, the parent is depriving the child not only of contact with the other parent but with the child's accustomed surroundings (home, toys, school, neighborhood), as well as friends and family members. Because these children are typically young, with almost 40% being five or younger (Finkelhor, Hotaling, & Sedlak, 1991), such disjunctures, even for a relatively short period of time, can be harmful to the child's emotional development (Greif & Hegar, 1992). As abductions often occur at a time of high family conflict, that is, during a custody battle or as a marriage is breaking up, they can have an additive effect on the level of stress for all family members. Particularly with an abduction of significant duration, the suffering on the part of the adults and the child involved can be enormous.

2. Abductions have become recognized as a significant social problem. The United States Justice Department has allocated millions of dollars since the late 1980s to study and develop programs to cope with them (see, for example, Office of Juvenile Justice and Delinquency Prevention, 1993). Estimates of family-related abductions have ranged as high as 350,000 annually (Finkelhor et al., 1991). Given that such an event affects three people at a minimum (two parents and a child) and potentially many more (other family members, agents of the Federal Bureau of Investigation [FBI], court-related resources, and international governments), abductions merit extensive research. Despite the emotional, financial, and intellectual resources that have been expended on this issue, little is known about the abducting parent's perspective on the circumstances leading up to and stemming from such actions.

3. The dialogue about parental abduction has been dominated by the so-called "searching," or left-behind parent. It is he or she who contacts the police, the FBI, private investigators, lawyers, and missing children's organizations in attempts to locate the missing child. Searching parents are also willing to participate in studies. Many believe, whether they have recovered their children or not, that their participation in studies geared toward understanding the phenomenon of parental abduction will help themselves as well as others (Greif & Hegar, 1993). By contrast, abductors, after the location and return of the children, have been difficult to find and often refuse requests to be interviewed. They are difficult to locate because the searching parent, who is usually the contact person, must first agree to give researchers the name of the abductor. Searching parents are often loathe to do this, as it may inflame an already tenuous relationship. Abductors, if they are found, are reluctant to participate when contacted because they are often distrustful of someone contacting them through the searching parent and are suspicious of government-funded research. Although the total number of abductions is substantial, few court jurisdictions handle enough cases to make court-based research fruitful, and such local data have other inherent biases, such as the manner in which abductions are reported and the idiosyncrasies of the bench in that jurisdiction or of the laws of the state.

4. The purpose of this article is to present the findings from qualitative interviews with 17 parents who abducted their children. The reasons abductors gave for their actions are highlighted. This study begins to fill a void in our understanding of what can be a life-changing and, occasionally, life-threatening event.

Review of Relevant Literature Concerning Abductors

5. What is known about abductors and their motivations has been drawn largely from case records, the searching parents' reports, the abducted children, and a handful of anecdotal interviews with abductors. Sagatun and Barrett's (1990) description of 43 abductors (25 mothers and 18 fathers) was derived from interviews with counselors and analysis of court files in one Los Angeles court. Sagatun and Barrett conclude that abductions occur for purposes of revenge against the other parent, because the abducting parent wished to be pursued by the searching parent as had occurred during courtship, and because the abductors have psychologically merged with the child to an unhealthy degree. In the latter situation, the child assumes a disproportionately important role in the abducting parent's life. In addition, some abductions occur because of fear for the child's safety.

6. Agopian (1980, 1981), in a review of 91 California cases in which children had been parentally abducted, also reported a history of criminal activity among the abductors. The offenders tended to be male, in the 27-to-35-year old range, and employed. In one case, Agopian suggests that the father was justified in

Greif, G. L., & Hegar, R. L. (1994). Parents who abduct: A qualitative study with implications for practice. *Family Relations, 43,* 283-288. Copyright © 1994 by the National Council on Family Relations, 3989 Central Ave. NE, Suite 550, Minneapolis, MN 55421. Reprinted by permission.

This research was supported by funds to the authors from the Office of Juvenile Justice and Delinquency Prevention, U.S. Department of Justice, under contract #OJP-92-196M.

Geoffrey L. Greif is Associate Professor and Rebecca L. Hegar is Associate Dean at the School of Social Work, University of Maryland at Baltimore, 525 W. Redwood Street, Baltimore, MD 21201.

abducting his child because of the mother's drug-abusing behavior and sexual acting out in front of the child.

7.   Janvier, McCormick, and Donaldson (1990) analyzed responses from 65 searching parents identified from a survey of five missing children's organizations. Abducting mothers tended to kidnap domestically, while abducting fathers tended to cross international borders. At the time of abduction, joint custody was in effect in one third of the cases, with a similar number of mothers having sole custody. Court-ordered custody arrangements were not in effect in most of the other cases. Abductors were believed to have rarely acted alone and to have made prior threats in almost half of the cases.

8.   The parents left behind, when asked to choose descriptors of the abductors from a list, tended to indicate that the abductors were impulsive, revengeful, manipulating, and controlling (Janvier et al., 1990). The abductors were also frequently described as having mental problems and having been products of dysfunctional families (these descriptors should be considered in light of the parent-left-behind's potential bias). About one-quarter of the abductors had abused drugs and alcohol, and domestic violence characterized 60% of the pre-abduction relationships.

9.   Long, Forehand, and Zogg (1991) reviewed telephone transcripts from 86 parents who telephoned a national hotline that was established to prevent child abduction. Domestic violence was present in about half of the marriages. Callers were split evenly between mothers and fathers, with mothers more apt to have custody at the time of the call. The parents provided up to four reasons for considering abduction: protection of the child (54%), a desire to be with the child (46%), the other parent's refusal to comply with the visitation order (32%), and dissatisfaction with court-ordered visitation (21%). Of the parents who gave protection of the child as a reason, 63% were concerned about emotional abuse, 32% about physical abuse, 26% about the other parent's abusing drugs, 21% about alcohol, and 11% about sexual abuse (multiple responses were possible).

10.   Johnston, Sagatun-Edwards, and Girdner (1993) are currently gathering data about risk factors for family abduction from 630 cases in two California counties. In a preliminary analysis, they found that families where parents have had prior "contact with the criminal justice system, are unmarried, have little income and education, and have concerns about the well-being of their child with the other parent" (p. 6) were most at risk for abduction. Psychological factors did not appear to play a significant role in differentiating families where there was an abduction from those where there was a divorce but no abduction.

11.   Greif and Hegar (1993) gathered information about abductors through two methods. The first method was similar to that of other researchers, asking parents left behind for their descriptions. The second method, unused in other research, involved interviewing four abductors in depth over the telephone or in person. Three hundred seventy-one searching parents had responded to a survey mailed from 15 missing children's organizations throughout the United States and Canada. A slight majority (55%) of the abductors were male, 84% were white, and 87% were born in the U.S. Half were described by the searching parents as having been raised in a home with a substance-abusing parent, one third had been physically abused, and one fifth had been sexually abused. At the time of the abduction, half of the abductors were said to have been unemployed, and 40% had some education past high school. Over half the marriages were characterized by domestic violence, with left-behind parents saying they were the sole victims in almost all cases.

12.   When asked about the abductor's level of involvement with the children during the marriage, almost half were depicted by the left-behind parents as being "involved" or "very involved" with the children's physical care, with females depicted as being more involved than males. An even higher percentage was described by the left-behind parents as being close emotionally with the children. Preabduction visitation between the abducted child and the abductor was fairly frequent, with two thirds seeing the child at least once every other week.

13.   The reasons the left-behind parent gave for the abductions (they could give more than one) tended to focus on revenge motives; 77% believed the abduction occurred to hurt the searching parent. Less frequently given reasons included: "anger over the breakup (23%); a desire to be with the child (16%); pressure from others (13%); dissatisfaction with visitation (13%); and the new marriage or relationship of the parent left behind (9%)" (Greif & Hegar, 1993, p. 34).

14.   Four case studies based on in-depth interviews with abductors show a different side to the issue (Greif & Hegar, 1993). Two of the abductors, one with custody and one without it at the time of the abduction, reported that they were spurred on by the unresponsiveness of the court system and concerns about sexual abuse. Three of the four were concerned with how the children were being raised: in one case as recluses, in another to hate their mother, and in a third to deal with life passively rather than actively. One mother acted because she also feared that her children were going to repeat her own experience of having been raised without a mother.

15.   The literature provides a portrait of abductors that is varied and complex. Searching parents frequently describe abductors as revengeful and angry, while the few abductors who have been interviewed say that they are concerned about their children and find that the courts are unresponsive to their concerns. This retrospective study attempted to learn from parental abductors who were no longer in violation of a court order related to their abducting behavior their reasons for their actions and their experiences while in hiding.

Methodology

16.   Recruiting a reasonably sized sample was difficult. Respondents were gathered from a variety of sources. First, searching parents who had participated in a previous study (Greif & Hegar, 1993) and who had located their children were contacted for permission to telephone the abductors. Out of approximately 180 parents who had recovered their missing children, 25 eventually gave us the telephone numbers of the abductors. Out of the 25, some numbers were no longer valid. In other cases, the abductor refused to be interviewed because either the abductor wanted to put the experience behind him or her, did not trust us to maintain confidentiality, or was angry at the searching parent for revealing the telephone number. This left a pool of 13. Four more respondents were found from contacts with missing children's organizations and from personal contacts arranged through speaking engagements.

17.   The respondents were interviewed for between 90 minutes and 3 hours using a semi-structured interview schedule that sought information about a range of the abductors' experiences from early childhood, courtship and marital history, relationships with children, successful instances of coping, and other events leading up to and stemming from the abduction. Standardized scales (Beck Depression Inventory, Trait Anger Scale, Attachment Scale) were also administered during the interview. Respondents were paid $50 for their participation.

18.   Given the difficulty in locating a sample, the lack of representativeness, and the time that had expired since the abductions, generalizability to other abducting parents must be undertaken with great caution. Rather what these parents offer are 17 views of parental abductors' behavior, a seldom heard, yet important, perspective. Qualitative interviews were the best method to use in beginning to formulate new hypotheses about this difficult-to-locate-and-interview population.

19. The 17 abductors (nine males and eight females) ranged in age from 20 to 50 years old and had kidnapped 26 children who were between 1 and 13 years old. With the exception of one woman born in Puerto Rico, they were U.S.-born Caucasians with a variety of religious backgrounds. Sixteen of the parents were residing in the U.S. at the time of the survey, with the seventeenth a resident of a Central American country. The abductors' educational levels varied greatly from 10th grade to the doctoral level, with 10 having some education past high school. Income varied accordingly, with two women receiving welfare at the time of the interviews and one man earning over $80,000. When they abducted, most were unemployed or marginally employed in work that could be easily transferred to another location. Only the holder of the doctorate, a professor who never went into hiding, was employed at a level commensurate with his educational level.

20. The parents hid for between 1 week and 11 years, with the mean duration being almost 2 years. The time since the abductor had been located also varied greatly, from 9 months to 11 years, with the mean being 6-1/2 years. At the time of the abduction, eight abductors did not have custody, seven had joint or shared custody, one had sole custody, and one's child was in foster care.

Findings

Early, Marital, and Abductor-Child History

21. We wondered whether abduction-related activity, which can be considered in some cases to be impulsive and abusive, would be linked to early childhood events, such as abuse and trauma, being a member of a divorced family, or witnessing parental domestic violence or substance abuse. Although the parental abduction literature is equivocal on the effects of early upbringing on later behavior, much of the research has not considered early familial factors in depth. Johnston et al. (1993), whose research is still in progress, did not find a link between early upbringing and later behavior, but Janvier et al. (1990) reported that a substantial proportion of abductors (over 70%) were described as coming from dysfunctional families. Other studies have established the potential link between: (a) being a victim of abuse as a child and having a greater potential for abusing a child as an adult and (b) witnessing violence between parents and later being abusive as an adult (Gelles & Cornell, 1985; Saunders, 1994). In addition, anecdotal reports establish the potential link between being abused as a child and using violence against a partner when an adult (Browne, 1987). Although people who grow up in families where alcohol has been abused often come to abuse alcohol (Kaufman, 1985), there is no clear link between alcohol abuse and a violent act like an abduction (Gelles & Cornell, 1985). However, alcohol has been linked to family dysfunction (Kaufman, 1985). For these reasons, early childhood experiences were explored in this study.

22. Only limited support for the link between early childhood experiences and later abduction-related behavior was found among this sample of abducting parents. Given the more than 30-year age range of the sample, it is difficult to compare the incidence of such events with the general population of divorced adults. Six abductors spent some time in a single-parent family when young, a proportion slightly higher than the national average for the 1950s and 1960s, though not necessarily than that of the 1970s (U.S. Bureau of the Census, 1991). Six reported witnessing domestic violence that included hitting or more violent acts between their parents, a slightly higher proportion than that cited in Straus, Gelles, and Steinmetz' (1980) research where marital violence was reported to occur at some point in 28% of marriages (Gelles & Cornell, 1985). A similar number were physically or sexually abused during childhood (well above population estimates by Gelles and Conte [1990]), and five said at least one parent abused substances (one of every 11 Americans has been estimated to have a substance abuse problem [Kaufman, 1985]). A few experienced the death of a key family member while young. Only five of the 17 experienced none of these disruptive influences and events.

23. Courtship histories also did not seem to be predictive of later abductive behavior. They varied a great deal; some cohabited with their future spouses for years, while others married soon after they met. Four said that they married because of a pregnancy, and only a few said that they were ever happily married. Eight reported some domestic violence. Almost half felt that their marriages changed significantly for the worse or terminated with the birth of the first child. Some of these parents said they divorced because of unhappiness with the parenting style of the other parent or with that parent's lifestyle choices (drug abuse, overinvolvement with in-laws, neglectful behavior). As these marriages ended in divorce, it is not surprising that they were unhappy. It could be, however, that when poor parenting of children is responsible for divorce, there is a greater likelihood of abduction if later custody decisions are unsatisfactory.

24. Five of the nine fathers thought that their level of parenting involvement before abduction increased in reaction to their wives' withdrawal from parenting or because of maternal incompetence. The other four fathers viewed their involvement as being no greater than that of fathers in general.

25. The eight abducting mothers presented a less consistent picture, with two describing themselves as initially uninterested in parenting. Three mothers who were primary caretakers viewed their husbands' involvement as being typical of other fathers and competent. The final three mothers also viewed themselves as the primary caretakers and perceived their husbands as being typical in their level of involvement, but incompetent.

26. It was, thus, rare for the abductors, whether male or female, to describe themselves as notably uninvolved in child rearing. In addition, the abductors gave the impression of having a close relationship with their children. In some instances, interviews left the impression that emotional boundaries between them and their children were blurred to a dysfunctional extent and that the children, prior to the abduction, filled a gap in the abductor's life to an excess. For example, one father said that being a father "was the most important thing in life. It made up for many past mistakes and a failed marriage, so I took it seriously. It was a feeling and experience I had never known. I would die for her."

27. No clear psychological distress (depression, abnormal attachment to the ex-spouse, or anger) was noted following the administration of the Beck Depression Inventory (Short Form) (Gould, 1982), a measure that explores attachment between ex-spouses (Kitson, 1992), and the Trait Anger Scale (Spielburger, Jacobs, Russell, & Crane, 1983).

Reasons for Abduction

28. Although the complex fabric of parental interactions makes it difficult to discern the patterns that may promote abductions, there are common threads. Over two-thirds (12) of the abductors reported they had unsatisfactory contact with the court system or with professionals who were in a position to help them prior to the abduction. This experience was uniformly negative for these 12. One mother reported that during the time she and her husband were receiving divorce counseling through the courts, he beat her up and robbed her on the court steps. She complained, "Charges against him kept getting dropped, and the court wouldn't hold anything against him." Concerned about the environment her son was being exposed to when with his father, and unable to get any help with limiting visitation, she abducted. Another father, after watching his son being dragged out of school to attend a custody hearing, stated, "I felt I could not have survived [if I had not abducted] so I had to take some action. Things were stacked against me, and my lawyer was in cahoots with hers and filed papers late, and I kept on losing . . . My boy was miserable, and there was no evidence that any of this would ever get worked out."

29. In six of those 12 situations, the abductor reported that the child was being abused, neglected, or subjected to a psychologically unhealthy home environment when the child was with the other parent. These abductors (four men and two women) argued that they had to act to save their children. One father acted because, "They would come back after visitations with her, and I would see marks on their bodies that shouldn't have been there. I think they [the marks] were coming from some of the men she was hanging out with."

30. In another five of the 12 cases, the abductors believed that the court decision related to custody or visitation was unfair. In the 12th case, a mother with children from different marriages wanted to raise them together in Central America but had failed to win custody through the courts.

31. Sometimes multiple reasons were given for abduction. In six cases, the other parent reportedly had abducted or threatened to abduct first. Two fathers kidnapped out of anger at their ex-wives. A Caucasian American-born father who had married an African said, "I was deeply resentful and angry at her that she was no longer the compliant, obedient wife . . . In Africa, if there was a divorce and the children were over five, they would stay with the father." One woman was fleeing a battering relationship. Two fathers said their children begged them to take them, and two mothers stated that they abducted because they did not want their children to enter foster care.

32. From the interviews, it appears that early family history is not a reliable predictor of abduction-related behavior and that psychological profiles of abductors are difficult to draw from the data. Rather, contributing factors that lead a parent to abduct include a strong bond with the child, unsatisfactory interaction with the courts or child protective agencies coupled with concerns about the well-being of the child, the belief that the other parent may be incompetent, and a desire for revenge.

Current Relationship With Children

33. Since the abduction, what has been the long-term outcome of the abducting parents' attempts to secure custody and increased contact with their children? Of the nine fathers, three increased their contact after abduction by going from a situation where they had visitation to

where they had custody, two fathers' level of contact stayed essentially the same (i.e., visitation before the abduction and visitation after the abduction), and four fathers had reduced contact after abduction. Of the eight mothers, two had more contact with their children after the abduction, three had the same amount before and after the abduction, and three mothers had less contact after the abduction. An example of decreased contact would be an abductor who had liberal visitation before the abduction and ended with supervised visitation or with visitation being unsupported by the courts or unwanted by the children after the abduction.

34. The quality of the relationship between the abductor and child seemed to depend on the custody arrangements. All of the abductors who had custody after the abduction described the relationship positively, while the abductors with visitation were less satisfied. When the abductor gained custody after the abduction, it may have been because: (a) too much time had elapsed for the child to want to return to the searching parent, so the child's request was honored; (b) the abductor was always the custodial parent; or (c) the courts sided with the abductor in viewing the searching parent as being the less suitable parent. Some abductors without custody described strained relationships with the children, while others had no contact. In a few of the cases where there was no reported contact with the child, the searching parent had forbidden it or the courts had blocked it. In the others, the child reportedly did not want to see the abductor.

Discussion and Implications for Practice

35. The complex nature of these relationships suggests that parental abduction is not the result of one behavior or factor but of a confluence of factors. Because this is a sample of divorced parents, it is difficult to tease out why some divorced parents kidnap and others do not.

36. Almost half of the marriages were marked by domestic violence. Although the relationship between domestic violence and other behavior can only be suggested (Gelles & Maynard, 1987), research has found that the experience of being involved in a violent couple is related to aggression in other relationships (Gwartney-Gibbs, Stockard, & Bohmer, 1987). Clearly, a high-conflict couple that has resorted to violence in the past might be apt to consider precipitous action like abduction as a way of striking back or protecting a child.

37. Approximately half felt that their marriage changed significantly after the birth of the child. Research has shown that children may weaken a marriage by causing fatigue and reducing time for the adult relationship (Ventura,

1987) and by causing feelings of parental inadequacy (Wallace & Gotlib, 1990). Disagreements over parenting and disappointments in one's own parenting behavior or in the development of the child can shift the balance in a marriage. Withdrawal of one parent's attention from childrearing can foster an intense parent-child bond involving the other parent. Further, the birth of a child will not enhance those relationships that were unstable prior to the pregnancy (Wallace & Gotlib, 1990).

38. The reasons for abduction tend to revolve around fear for the child's safety, unhappiness with the court decision concerning custody and visitation, reaction to the other parent's abduction-related threats and actions, and anger. As has been recommended elsewhere (e.g. Johnston & Campbell, 1988), these factors indicate that court mediation may be helpful in high-conflict divorces. By addressing these problems early, prevention may be possible.

39. After the abduction was resolved, almost half of the abducting parents retained custody, perhaps illuminating the difficulty faced by the courts when one parent has been involved with a child for a long time to the exclusion of the other. Courts have a very difficult decision to make in deciding custody when the searching parent and recovered child do not know each other well (Greif & Hegar, 1993).

40. The findings point the practitioner in a number of directions related to prevention and mediation. Sound prevention can help relieve some of the abductors' feelings of unfairness and anxiety that lead to abduction. As recommended elsewhere (Greif & Hegar, 1993), mediation should be required in disputed custody cases, unless there is cause to believe that domestic violence or child abuse has occurred. Given the evidence from these 17 abductors' reports that current factors, rather than historical ones, weighed heavily on their decisions to act, many high-conflict custody battles could result in abduction. If those who appear at risk for abduction are informed of the potential legal punishment to the parent and psychological damage to the child that can flow from such an action, a few abductions may be averted. We wonder whether the abducting parents' concerns about abuse were taken seriously by the courts and by child protective services when they were voiced.

41. Continued pressure on lawmakers to more adequately fund court services in cases of disputes may have alleviated some of the misunderstandings that led to these precipitous actions (Greif & Hegar, 1991). For example, parents seeking protection orders in domestic violence cases, as well as those seeking temporary child custody in other situations, should have prompt and simplified access to the court system. Postdivorce custody mediation and counseling also should be available (Greif & Hegar, 1993). Practitioners can also support legislation that will guarantee greater cooperation between jurisdictions to resolve abductions quickly when they do occur.

42. An important focus of clinical work with abductors who are in hiding, or those who have resolved their situation, is to ascertain the abductor's perspective. These parents usually fiercely defend their actions and believe them to be justified. Taking a neutral stance on their actions until they have come to grips with the impact of those actions is recommended. After a period of time, the fierce defense will turn to ambivalence, even if abductors believe the abduction was warranted. Helping them to weigh the costs, and any benefits, of the abduction and to view their actions realistically can assist them in building future relationships among family members. Without achieving some sense of objectivity about their own actions, emotions are likely to affect future opportunities for cooperating.

43. Abductors also often see things in all-or-nothing terms. For example, they tend to demonize the legal system without considering some of the protections that the system offers. By taking an extreme position, they may miss a chance for reconciliation so that they can again start to parent the child in cooperation with the other parent. This is an important stage of development whether or not the abductor retains custody after the abduction is resolved.

44. It is not uncommon for practitioners to become involved with all the family members, with the initial contact being with the child, the searching parent, or the abductor. If the abductor has retained custody, visitation between the child and the searching parent may be required by the courts. The practitioner should be prepared to help with such arrangements. Sometimes a therapist who strongly aligns with children in therapy may have a negative emotional reaction to the abductor. The therapist needs to be aware of such tendencies and avoid siding with the parent who was previously searching. If the therapist unwittingly sides with that parent, the abductor may reexperience an earlier feeling of not being understood that may have led to the initial abduction.

45. One note of caution is in order concerning work with parents who may be abductors in hiding. The practitioner needs a thorough understanding of state child abuse reporting laws, state case law or statutes concerning duty to warn in cases where clients threaten others, and other civil or criminal liability issues. Most practitioners will want to seek legal counsel if unsure of their obligations.

Conclusion

46. Because this study is based on a self-selected sample with no control group, the findings must be viewed with caution. At the same time, the research provides an initial view of an understudied population. It appears that when enough risk factors accumulate, an abduction may occur. Among the parents interviewed, these factors included the perception that the child was being harmed, the belief that the courts were denying the abductor sufficient time with the child, and the feeling that the courts did not understand the abducting parent's position. When the other parent has also abducted, threatened to abduct, or been violent, the abductor may feel a particular sense of urgency. Future research using larger and more representative samples, as well as using comparison groups of parents from high-conflict divorces in which an abduction did not occur, can help clarify who is most at risk. The more information practitioners have about these volatile situations, the better the chances of preventing them from occurring and of treating them effectively when they do.

References

Agopian, M. W. (1980). Parental child stealing: Participants and the victimization process. *Victimology: An International Journal, 5*, 263-273.

Agopian, M. W. (1981). *Parental child stealing.* Lexington, MA: Lexington.

Browne, A. (1987). *When battered women kill.* New York: Free Press.

Finkelhor, D., Hotaling, G., & Sedlak, A. (1991). Children abducted by family members: A national household survey of incidence and episode characteristics. *Journal of Marriage and the Family, 53*, 805-817.

Gelles, R. J., & Conte, J. R. (1990). Domestic violence and sexual abuse of children. *Journal of Marriage and the Family, 52*, 1045-1058.

Gelles, R. J., & Cornell, C. P. (1985). *Intimate violence in families.* Beverly Hills: Sage.

Gelles, R. J., & Maynard, P. E. (1987). A structural family systems approach to intervention in cases of family violence. *Family Relations, 36*, 270-275.

Girdner, L. K., & Hoff, P. M. (1992). *Obstacles to recovery and return of parentally abducted children: Final report.* Washington, DC: Office of Juvenile Justice and Delinquency Prevention.

Gould, J. (1982). Psychometric investigation of the standard and short form of the Beck Depression Inventory. *Psychological Reports, 51*, 1167-1170.

Greif, G. L., & Hegar, R. L. (1991). Parents whose children are abducted by the other parent: Implications for treatment. *American Journal of Family Therapy, 19*, 215-225.

Greif, G. L., & Hegar, R. L. (1992). The impact of parental abduction on children: A review of the literature. *American Journal of Orthopsychiatry, 62*, 599-604.

Greif, G. L., & Hegar, R. L. (1993). *When parents kidnap: The families behind the headlines.* New York: Free Press.

Gwartney-Gibbs, P., Stockard, J., & Bohmer, S. (1987). Learning courtship aggression: The influence of parents, peers, and personal experiences. *Family Relations, 36*, 276-282.

Janvier, R. F., McCormick, K., & Donaldson, R. (1990). Parental kidnapping: A survey of left-behind parents. *Juvenile and Family Court Journal, 41*, 1-8.

Johnston, J. R., & Campbell, L. E. G. (1988). *Impasses of divorce.* New York: Free Press.

Johnston, J., Sagatun-Edwards, I., & Girdner, L. (1993). Risk factors for family abduction: Preliminary findings. In P. Hoff (Ed.), *Proceedings of the North American Symposium on International Child Abduction* (not paginated). Washington, DC: Office of Juvenile Justice and Delinquency Prevention.

Kaufman, E. (1985). *Substance abuse and family therapy.* Orlando: Grune & Stratton.

Kitson, G. (1992). *Portrait of divorce: Adjustment to marital breakdown.* New York: Guilford.

Long, N., Forehand, R., & Zogg, C. (1991). Preventing parental child abduction: Analysis of a national project. *Clinical Pediatrics, 30*, 549-554.

Office of Juvenile Justice and Delinquency Prevention. (1993). *Federal Register: Part VII* (Vol. 58, No. 86, pp. 27166-27183). Washington, DC: U.S. Government Printing Office.

Sagatun, I. J., & Barrett, L. (1990). Parental child abduction: The law, family dynamics, and legal system responses. *Journal of Criminal Justice, 18*, 433-442.

Saunders, D. G. (1994). Child custody decisions in families experiencing woman abuse. *Social Work, 39*, 51-59.

Spielburger, C. D., Jacobs, G., Russell, S., & Crane, R. S. (1983). Assessment of anger: The State-Trait Anger Scale. In J. N. Butcher & C. D. Spielburger (Eds.), *Advances in personality assessment: Vol. 2* (pp. 161-189). Hillsdale, NJ: Erlbaum.

Straus, M., Gelles, R., & Steinmetz, S. K. (1980). *Behind closed doors: Violence in the American family.* Garden City, NY: Anchor Press.

U.S. Bureau of the Census. (1991). *Marital status and living arrangements: March 1990.* (Series P-20, No. 450). Washington, DC: U.S. Government Printing Office.

Ventura, J. N. (1987). The stresses of parenthood reexamined. *Family Relations, 36*, 26-29.

Wallace, P. M., & Gotlib, I. H. (1990). Marital adjustment during the transition to parenthood: Stability and predictors of change. *Journal of Marriage and the Family, 52*, 21-29.

Factual Questions

1. According to the authors, is it easier to obtain samples of searching parents or samples of abductors?

2. What was the sample size?

3. How were most of the abductors located?

4. How long did the interviews last?

5. According to the authors, why must generalizing to other abducting parents (from the sample that was studied) be undertaken with great caution?

6. What reason is given for using qualitative interviews?

7. What was the average amount of time abducting parents spent in hiding?

8. How many of the subjects did not have disruptive early childhood experiences?

9. How many of the abductors reported unsatisfactory contact with the court system or with professionals in a position to help prior to abduction?

Questions for Discussion

10. Are there advantages and disadvantages of studying the motivations of abductors by getting reports from searching parents and abducted children? Explain. (See paragraphs 5, 8, and 11-13.)

11. Is it appropriate for the authors of the article to cite their own previous research in their review of the literature? Explain.

12. What is your opinion on paying respondents $50 for their participation?

13. In their presentation of the findings, the authors stress the results of the interviews instead of the results obtained by using the standardized scales. Do you think this was a good decision? Why?

14. Speculate on why the authors compared the incidence of early childhood experiences of the sample with population estimates of the same experiences. (See paragraph 22.)

15. Do the quotations of subjects' responses help you understand the findings? Would you like to see a larger or smaller number of quotations?

16. The authors report that the abductors seemed to have no clear psychological distress at the time of the interviews (see paragraph 27). Is it possible that they were distressed at the time of the abduction? Could this possibility be studied in future research? How?

17. The authors note that the lack of a control group is a weakness. In your opinion, is it an important weakness? Why?

18. Do you agree with the authors' decision to conduct a qualitative instead of a quantitative study of this topic? Why? Why not?

19. If you had major funding to do additional research on this topic, what changes, if any, would you make in the research methodology?

Quality Ratings

DIRECTIONS: Indicate your level of agreement with each of the following statements by circling a number from 5 for strongly agree (SA) to 1 for strongly disagree (SD). If you believe that an item is not applicable to this research article, leave it blank. Be prepared to explain your ratings.

A. The introduction establishes the importance of the research topic.
   SA   5   4   3   2   1   SD

B. The literature review establishes the context for the study.
   SA   5   4   3   2   1   SD

C. The research purpose, question, or hypothesis is clearly stated.
   SA   5   4   3   2   1   SD

D. The method of sampling is sound.
   SA   5   4   3   2   1   SD

E. Relevant demographics (for example, age, gender, and ethnicity) are described.
   SA   5   4   3   2   1   SD

F. Measurement procedures are adequate.
   SA   5   4   3   2   1   SD

G. The results are clearly described.
   SA   5   4   3   2   1   SD

H. The discussion/conclusion is appropriate.
   SA   5   4   3   2   1   SD

I. Despite any flaws noted above, the report is worthy of publication.
   SA   5   4   3   2   1   SD

ARTICLE 3

DROPPING OUT: ANOTHER SIDE OF THE STORY

Ted N. Okey

Philip A. Cusick

Dropping out of school is a national problem. Reducing the number of students who do so is a national goal. This study examines the school perspective of a set of families whose children dropped out. Working from audiotape-recorded interviews with 3 or more members of 12 families, the researchers describe a perspective that included a jaundiced view of education, a hostile view toward schooling, and a history of poor school performance at least two generations old. The families' children grew up fast, early on appropriating behaviors engaged in by older members. When they took these behaviors into school, they ran afoul of rules and regulations. For these families, school was a series of academic failures, conflicts with staff and peers, disciplinary hearings, suspensions, and expulsions. Dropping out was not a problem. It was a solution.

1.   The purpose of this study was to describe and explain the school perspective of a set of families whose children dropped out of school. The study was conducted with families of 12 adolescents who were all Caucasian, who had recently left school, and who had attended smaller school districts in the Midwest.

2.   With a substantial number of young people dropping out of school each year, the dropout issue is frequently cited as an example of education's malaise. The National Center for Educational Statistics (1993) reported that 14.8% of Americans aged 24-25 have not completed high school and are not currently enrolled (p. 252). Among Caucasians, the rate is 10.4%, among African Americans it is 14.1%, and among Hispanics it is 45.5%. Drop-out rates are also higher for students from low socioeconomic backgrounds, from single-parent families, and from families who migrated to the United States (p. 254). Several researchers — among them Gerics and Westheimer (1988) and Ekstrom, Goertz, Pollack, and Rock (1986) — have attempted to predict dropping out among students currently in school; to study the issue at midpoint rather than end point, as it were. Those researchers report that students who eventually leave school come from poorer and poorly educated parents, do less homework, are absent more, have lower grades and test scores,

and pose a greater share of the school's discipline problems.

3.   The issue is more than socioeconomic status (SES) and educational background. It is also family dynamics. Parsons (1955) argued that the family with its children is an institutionalized social system wherein the central focus of the process of socialization takes place. Furthermore, the family's socializing function holds even in a differentiated society, such as ours, where formal education has supplanted many family functions. Thus our initial argument is that dropouts may learn how to think about and behave in and toward school from their families. Several studies support that argument. Delgado-Gaitan (1988) studied the family context of 12 Hispanic students and found that the students who stayed in school had families who actively supported their school endeavors and who acted as advocates on their children's behalf. On the other hand, "Students without parents to advocate for them were frequently reduced [in school] to a shadow status that encouraged their failure" (p. 366). Cervantes (1965) concentrated on the "structure, dynamics and emotional climate of the family into which the teenage respondent was born" (p. 7) and reported family nurturing as the element most responsible for a student's good relation with school. Most interesting was Clark's (1983) study of African American children, some of whom succeeded in school, some of whom failed. Clark concluded that "it is the family members' beliefs, activities and overall cultural style, not the family unit's composition or social status, that produces the requisite mental structures of effective and desirable behavior during classroom lessons" (pp. 1-2). Further explicating the issue is the work of Rumberger, Ghatak, Poulos, and Ritter (1990), who studied the internal processes of dropouts' families. They reported that parents of dropouts were more permissive and that children in those families were more likely to make decisions on their own. Dropouts' parents were more likely to use negative sanctions against their children and were less involved in their children's school activities and performance than were parents of successful students. The connection between the family and dropping out was

further substantiated by Ekstrom et al. (1986). They reported that, compared with stayers, dropouts came from families who had less education, valued education less, expressed less concern with school progress, and had lower educational expectations for themselves and their children. A more general cultural connection between families and school performance was described by Willis (1977) and MacLeod (1987), whose deviant males described themselves as behaving in school the way their families had behaved in school and the way their families expected them to behave in school.

4.   Following Parsons (1955), who argues that the family is the child's major socializing system, and following researchers who cite strong relations between the family and poor school behavior, we reasoned that school is a serious matter and dropping out of school an equally serious matter, experienced not just by the dropout but by the entire family. Further, each family member has attended school, has views and experiences with school; and those views and experiences combine into a generalized perspective about school and education. We concluded that the event has a family history and we wanted to understand that history as well as the family's generalized perspective on school and education.

5.   Perspective is a useful construct for thinking about the meaning that individuals and groups give to events. It includes both events and the beliefs that underlie events. Shibutani (1967) defined perspective as

> an ordered view of one's world: what is taken for granted about the attributes of various objects, events and human nature. It is an order of things remembered and expected as well as actually perceived, an organized conception of what is plausible and what is possible. (p. 161)

6.   To elucidate the perspective, we centered the study on four general areas: (a) the family's background, (b) the educational experiences of

older family members, (c) the dropout's school experience and the family's views of that experience, and (d) the dropping out.

Method

Data Collection

7.   Our method was ethnographic: "What a proper ethnographer ought properly to be doing is going out to places, coming back with information about how people live there, and making that information available to the professional community in practical form" (Geertz, 1988, p. 1).

8.   What Geertz suggests is what we attempted. Our goal was to present the families' side of the dropouts' story to professionals who were trying to do something about the issue. We audiotape-recorded open-ended interviews with the dropouts and members of their families. Initial interviews with dropouts were conducted at their place of work or their home. One was conducted in the county jail to which the dropout had been remanded. After the dropouts had opened the way for us to talk to their families, interviews of 1 to 3 hours were conducted by one—sometimes both—researcher(s) in the family's home, usually the kitchen. In addition to parent(s) and stepparents, sometimes the dropout, other children, and other relatives attended. Questions were asked in chronological order, beginning with the family background, with the parents'—sometimes grandparents'—school experience, then the dropout's school experience, followed by the dropping out, its circumstances, and effects. Without exception, families were hospitable. The researchers were served lunch in one home, a specially baked cake in another, and were invited to "have a few beers" in another. One parent called in neighboring relatives to talk to "the man who's writing the book." Never did the interviewers feel that they were pushing a topic with people who did not care or did not want to talk. The families had strong feelings about school and the way in which they and their children had been treated. They had been waiting a long time to tell their side of the school story. Anonymity was guaranteed, not only to satisfy the dictates of courtesy and common sense but because many had harsh things to say about schools that their younger children were still attending. At times, we found ourselves being interviewed. The families, knowing who we were, would ask us our opinions of school events. Sometimes they asked questions about what school people could and could not do to their children. We respected the questions and answered them honestly, but sometimes we found that families wanted us to act as advocates for their children, a role we assiduously avoided.

9.   Interviewing allows a researcher to control the dialogue, to maintain flexibility, and to explore issues that suddenly emerge. One can later add one's own reflections on the settings and record nonverbal behaviors. There are, of course, problems with interviewing. Memories dim. There is a natural bias in self-reported data. Interviewees can easily distort controversial events and present hyperbole as fact. However, there are commonsense ways to guard against these dangers. First, a researcher can probe events and uncover details in a way that will discourage even intended distortions. Second, a researcher can interview the same person more than once and several people about the same event. Third, one may interview more than one person at the same time. According to Becker, Geer, and Hughes (1968), a researcher can attribute greater veracity to accounts given in the presence of others who also know the story. We found that during group interviews, one or another family member would occasionally correct another family member's account. Or one would give assent to one another's account, adding plausibility to the story as told.

10.   Protocols were typed, read, and reread. Validity and reliability were addressed as the researchers sifted through the protocols to see if the facts as presented were consistent and the emerging explanation sufficient and plausible. Stories were compared. Questions were rewritten and second and third interviews conducted to explore new avenues and to clear up confusing responses. Possible explanations were fashioned and refashioned, working hypotheses were formed, tested, pursued, and sometimes discarded. Facts were gleaned from the interviews and, when appropriate, presented in tables. The explanation was being drawn as the study continued. As new families were added, the emerging explanation was tested with them.

11.   Throughout this work there was the matter of what to call a "fact." We were interested in facts, of course. We were also interested in what the family regarded as facts, particularly in this study where we were hearing only the family's side. For example, that Ms. Roundtree's children were last to be picked up by the bus is a fact. That Ms. Roundtree regarded the sequence in which children were picked up as evidence of the school's bias against her and her children—she reasoned that the school did not like her because she was on welfare — is also a fact, and to the researchers, a more interesting fact. In another family, everyone could recite the story of the time "Mom hit the teacher." Perhaps Mom hit the teacher; perhaps Mom did not hit the teacher. We did not know. But we knew that an antischool story had attained the status of lore within that family; and

the presence of that piece of family lore was, to us, more interesting than whether Mom did or did not hit the teacher.

Sample

12.   The study required a sampling technique consistent with emerging theory.

> Theoretical sampling is the process of data collection for generating theory whereby the analyst jointly collects, codes, and analyzes his data and decides what data to collect next and where to find them in order to develop his theory as it emerges . . . the initial decisions for theoretical collection of data are based on a general sociological perspective and on a general subject or problem area. (Glaser & Strauss, 1970, p. 105)

We began with a simple definition of dropout, one adopted by the Michigan State Board of Education:

> A dropout from a regular K-12 school program is a student who has been enrolled in a district but leaves, for any reason other than death, the regular school program . . . before graduation and does not re-enroll in another regular K-12 school program.

13.   Because we wanted to study dropout families from smaller districts and because with few exceptions the population of such districts in our state is almost entirely Caucasian, so was our sample. The districts were K-12, each had fewer than 2,000 students and one high school, a situation duplicated in 70% of Michigan's 530 K-12 school districts. The district's expenditures per pupil were on a par with the state average and each school offered a comprehensive program in its high school and additional programs through intermediate districts and regional consortia.

14.   The initial task was to find a group of dropouts who would agree to talk about their dropping out and who would open the way for their families to talk to us. Administrators, counselors, and alternative-program teachers from area schools helped identify a pool of 70 students who had recently dropped out, and the list was narrowed to those that were still in the area. Following the advice of Glaser and Strauss (1970), we did not preselect the sample except to assure that each selectee was an instance of the case. An initial contact was made with a dropout; and after he and his family agreed to participate, we began the interviewing. At the same time, we contacted a second dropout, obtained her family's assent, and so on. We went on this way, talking to the members of one family while selecting the next, until we had completed the study with 12 families: 5 of female dropouts, 7 of male dropouts.

15.   Sample selection, data collection, and theory building went on at roughly the same time.

Table 1   *Demographics of families in the sample*

Family	Family Composition	Parents' Level of Education	Employment	Setting/Home Ownership
Roundtree/Walker (Tammy's family)	Divorced father, deceased; mother; one sibling	Both parents, dropouts	Mother: welfare, AFDC,[a] part-time cook	Dropout: rural and rents trailer; mother: rural and owns small house
Stanley (Jason's family)	Intact family: father, mother, one sibling	Father, high school graduate; mother, dropout	Father: unemployed; mother: civil service	Rural and owns small house
Menges (Tommy's family)	Divorced mother; three siblings	Both parents, dropouts	Mother: welfare, AFDC	Rural village and rents home
Clinton (Tom's family)	Intact family: father, mother, one sibling	Both parents, high school graduates	Father: computer technician; mother: sales clerk	Small town and owns small house
Vitale (Sonny's family)	Intact family: father, mother, four siblings	Father, dropout; mother, high school graduate	Father: retired factory worker; mother: shipping and stock clerk	Rural and owns a custom-built house
Small/Beauchamp (Bobbie Sue's family)	Stepparent family: stepfather; mother; one sibling, not at home	Both parents, dropouts; stepfather, high school graduate	Stepfather: factory worker; mother: homemaker	Small town and owns a trailer
Anderson/Workman (Wendy's family)	Stepparent family: father, deceased; stepfather, divorced; mother; seven siblings	Both parents, dropouts; stepfather, dropout	Mother: welfare, AFDC	Rural village and owns large house
Mandrick (Bob's family)	Intact family: father, mother, three siblings	Both parents, high school graduates	Father: factory worker; mother: homemaker, clerk	Rural and owns small house
Rogers (Susan's family)	Intact family: father, mother, five siblings	Father, dropout; mother, high school graduate	Father: construction worker; mother: homemaker	Small town and owns small house
Collins/Lamb (Mickey's family)	Stepparent family: stepfather, mother, one sibling	Both parents, dropouts; stepfather, high school graduate	Stepfather: city employee; mother: clerical	Rural village and owns modest house
Henry/Griggs (Ricky's family)	Stepparent family: stepfather, mother, no siblings	Father and stepfather, dropouts; mother, high school graduate	Stepfather: disabled; mother: waitress	Small town and owns small house
Walasek (Virginia's family)	Intact family: father, mother, two siblings	Father, dropout; mother, high school graduate	Father: construction worker; mother: homemaker	Rural and owns small house

[a]AFDC = Aid to Families with Dependent Children

As common themes and experiences were recorded, the explanation took shape. The study stopped when the school stories of 12 families had been collected. Why this number? Because, as we will demonstrate in the ensuing explanation, the same story kept coming up again and again. The categories that emerged with the 1st family — economic problems, risk factors, disinterest in academics, trouble with authorities — were, by the 12th family, fully saturated. No new categories arose. After 12 sets of interviews, we felt that the dictates of validity, reliability, and plausibility had been satisfied for families represented by the sample. Throughout, we remained aware of inherent problems in any attempt to portray one sort of life with the categories of another:

> The moral asymmetries across which ethnography works and the discursive complexity within which it works make any attempt to portray it as anything more than the representation of one sort of life in the categories of another impossible to defend. That may be enough. I myself think it is. (Geertz, 1988, p. 144)

The Road to Dropping Out

16. We will begin by describing the families' backgrounds, then move to the parents' school experiences, to the dropouts' school experience, to the parents' experiences with their child's schooling, and finally to the act of dropping out. In the following sections, the names accorded the families have been altered.

Family Background

17. Six of the 12 families contained both natural parents, and the remainder contained a stepparent or a mother raising children alone. Ten of the 12 families owned their own home. Two of the families were reasonably well off. In the remaining 10, someone worked, although among several families employment came and went, jobs were lost, regained, lost again; and drinking and dissolution took their toll. When a factory closed and a family member was laid off, he or she worked part-time, a spouse went to work, or the family lived on unemployment or welfare. Ten families reported that they were in the lower end of the economic scale. (See

Table 1 for a summary of the families' backgrounds.)

18. The researchers noted first the similarity between the way in which the parents approach work and the way in which they approach education. The parents surveyed work, their parents worked, and they expect their children to work. However, they do not associate work with long-term security, career success, or upward mobility. Nor do they speak of work in terms of self or social improvement. Similarly, the parents had gone to school and sent their children to school. But they do not speak of school in terms of social or academic advancement, nor of elevating grades to enter college. They agreed that one needed a diploma for an entry-level job and that one needed to go to school to obtain the diploma. But there was no talk of further education, nor of learning, nor of using school to obtain skills and competencies that they will use on jobs, nor of education as a means of upward mobility.

19. Educators and policymakers assume obvious connections between doing well in school,

Table 2 *Family experiences with risk factors*

Family	A	B	C	D	E	F	G	H	I	J	K	L	Total
Roundtree/Walker	X	X	X	X	X	X	X	X	X	X	X	0	11
Stanley	X	X	0	X	0	X	X	X	X	X	X	0	9
Menges	X	X	X	X	X	X	X	X	X	X	X	X	12
Clinton	0	X	X	0	0	X	X	X	X	X	0	X	8
Vitale	X	X	X	0	X	0	X	X	X	X	X	0	9
Small/Beauchamp	0	X	X	0	X	X	X	X	X	X	X	0	9
Anderson/Workman	X	X	0	X	0	0	X	X	X	X	X	0	8
Mandrick	X	X	0	0	0	0	X	X	X	0	0	X	6
Rogers	X	X	X	X	X	0	X	X	X	0	X	0	9
Collins/Lamb	X	X	X	0	0	0	0	0	0	X	X	X	6
Henry/Griggs	X	X	X	X	X	0	X	X	X	X	X	X	11
Walasek	0	X	X	0	0	X	X	0	X	X	0	0	6

Table key: A. Alcoholism/substance abuse in parents; B. Alcoholism/ substance abuse in dropouts; C. Physical, mental, or sexual abuse; D. Unemployment; E. Welfare/AFDC (Aid to Families with Dependent Children)/social security/disability; F. Frequent or traumatic moves; G. Termination of religious practice; H. Smoking/poor health in parents; I. Smoking/poor health in dropouts; J. Low social capital; K. Poor male role model; L. Criminal record for dropout; X. Risk factor present; 0. Risk factor absent.

doing well at work, and doing well financially and socially. The logic connecting these events was foreign to the families. They went to school because, according to the law, they had to and to enter the job market at the lowest level. They saw little connection between school and work and less connection between school and doing well financially and socially. One father connected success in school to success at showing up on time for work, but that was as close as anyone came to connecting what one did in school with what one did outside of school.

20. A second point about the families was that they reported multiple risk factors, for example, alcohol and substance abuse, poor health, and unemployment (see Table 2 for a full accounting of these factors). Children were not protected from these factors; indeed, they participated in them from their early years. For example, Tammy—a dropout—lives alone in a trailer supported by her deceased father's (who died drunk in a flaming car collision) social security. Her alcoholic mother lives on welfare. Tammy describes herself as a "recovering alcoholic and substance abuser." Tammy smokes heavily, as does almost everyone to whom we talked. Her sister Denise, who is losing her teeth, has two children and is pregnant a third time by a man whom she says she will marry "if he can keep his job at the ice cream company and not have any more affairs." Jason is currently unemployed. His father is a part-time auto mechanic and a self-described anarchist whose life ambition was "to go for a ride" on his motorcycle, which he does while his wife supports the family with her post office job. Lee, Jason's father, was unemployed and awaiting a hearing for his second charge of drunk driving. Moreover, he regularly smokes dope and gets drunk at home. Jason, described by his teachers as gifted, was recovering from a bad drug experience and was waiting for acceptance into the Coast Guard. He did not like school nor his classmates with whom he frequently fought. In his early school years, when both his parents left the house early, Jason would not go to school.

21. Tommy, a dropout, sells his blood for money and lives with his mother, a younger sister, a brother, and a cousin his mother is trying to adopt to increase her Aid to Families with Dependent Children (AFDC) payments. Tommy's father is an alcoholic and, according to Tommy's mother, $35,000 behind on his child support payments. Tommy is a heavy smoker and was expelled from school for dealing drugs. Sonny, whom the administrators encouraged to leave school after numerous disciplinary incidents, is enrolled in an alternative education program but admits to drinking heavily and neither attending classes nor working. His hard-working and reasonably well-off parents had both been heavy drinkers; and his father, when drunk, had often beaten Sonny with a belt or canoe paddle. Bobbie Sue lives with her mother and stepfather and does not like to talk about her father, whom she remembers as beating her and whom her sister remembers as carrying on affairs with his sister-in-law. Bobbie believes her father raped her sister. Mickey, who dropped out after his arrest for car theft and who admits to drug dealing, grew up with his mother and stepfather. His natural father had a long history of unemployment, part-time work, and welfare. Mickey's mother describes the natural father as "a real loser, and I'm not saying that because he's my ex-husband."

22. Wendy lives at home with her twice-divorced mother who supports the family with AFDC checks. There are seven older children in the family, one of whom is in prison for heroine addiction. Only one of the other seven graduated from high school; all are described by their mother as heavy drug users. Wendy smokes, drinks heavily, uses marijuana, and is involved with a man 10 years her senior. Ricky was introduced to drinking and drugs by his older cousins when he was 6 years old. He admitted to learning nothing in school and being given social promotions. Susan is the daughter of a sometimes-employed drywall man who drinks and smokes heavily and who is currently suffering from emphysema. Susan never did well in school and had trouble with classmates to a point that she would refuse to attend. She now lives on AFDC with a child fathered by a man who denies responsibility for the baby and deserted Susan. Susan's mother describes herself as a battered wife who lost two children in infancy.

23. Ricky's father is a truck driver whom Ricky's mother describes as an alcoholic and womanizer. He was taking Ricky to bars when the boy was 16. Ricky is currently in the county jail for breaking and entering, violating probation, and drunk driving. The man his mother lives with describes himself as an illiterate who was forced to resign from the armed service because he could not read. He has suffered a heart attack and is suing the former employer for disability. As soon as Virginia was 16, she left school to run with a hard-drinking, drug-using crowd. She now describes herself as a recovering alcoholic. Many of the parents, now in their 40s, are in ill health.

24. Drinking, drugs, divorce, desertion, and hard economic times are not limited to families of students who leave school without graduating. Thus the argument is not that risk factors occurred with greater or lesser frequency than they do in other families. The argument is that children in these families were exposed to the risk factors early on and participated in them early on. As did Rumberger et al. (1990), we found a high degree of permissive child rearing within the families. The extended and protected years of childhood common in the middle class did not occur in these families. By the time they were in junior high, these children had been given or had appropriated adult status and were engaging in the same behaviors their parents engaged in. We will return to this point when we describe the school behavior of these dropouts, because an important part of our explanation is that the behaviors exhibited by these students set them up for conflict with schools.

The Parents' Experience With Education

25.   Eight of the 40 grandparents about whom data were available, 4 of the 12 fathers, and 5 of the 12 mothers had graduated from high school. Even those who graduated described school in terms of boring classes, uncaring teachers, and abusive peers. (See Table 3 for complete tallies of family history with dropping out.)

26.   Parents described the diploma as a ticket to the workplace, nothing more. They stayed for extraneous reasons. For Gayle, the impetus to stay was her mother, who told her "get your diploma for me." Lee, who in his words wasn't "a big fan of education," described school as "a place to meet single girls." Diane stayed to please her parents but felt victimized by teachers: "They harass you. They're not pleasant with you. They're not eager to give you their time." Her husband graduated but bragged about making a game of school, of doing no more than he wanted to do. Sandy stayed for her prestigious friends: "I ran around with the big names back then." Sandy was rebellious:

> I didn't get along with authority real well, didn't get along with the teachers, didn't get along with the principal, didn't enjoy the classes . . . got lost somewhere . . . and I had this constant aggravation from the counselor, from the principal, from teachers who thought I was a troublemaker.

27.   Dan "personally hated school," skipped whenever he could, and had a tough time getting along with others: "I thought everyone disliked me. I didn't have any close friends. I really resented having to sit down and listen to a lecture . . . extremely boring. I hate arithmetic." Dan's jaded view supported his belief that there is little relation between what one does in school and what one does later on. The diploma was a ticket, a way to enter the job market, something one had to do, but it did not mean that one had learned anything: "If you take all the chemistry, all the math, all the English that they offer through high school, you still can't get a job as a chemist or a mathematician or a journalist."

28.   Injustice from classmates and teachers was a common theme among the dropouts' parents. As Diane explained,

> We were having a test and this little girl beside me kept copying off my paper, and I kept trying to hide it and she kept taking my shoulder and pulling it back and . . . I said, "Leave me alone." The teacher came up. She struck me across the hand with the ruler and I hit her . . . They suspended me for hitting a teacher and if she ever hit me again . . . I'd hit her again. I didn't learn anything.

29.   Donna Menges was picked on because of her obesity. "Kids are mean, nasty, when you're like that. They can be awful cruel and it hurts. That's the main reason I quit."

30.   Most parents described themselves as doing poorly in school. Fred "failed every grade right up to the 11th but liked art and sports, never learning to read." Their more pleasurable recollections were of resistance and opposition. Bobbie enjoyed telling the teacher what she "thought of MacBeth." Tom spoke of beating the system:

> I tried to get out of as much homework as possible. I disrupted class a lot . . . I joined the audiovisual group so I could come and go whenever I felt like it. The whole trick in high school was learning what your teacher wanted. I knew within 2 weeks of being in a classroom what that person expected of me or what kind of questions were going to show up.

31.   Gayle graduated from high school to please her mother. When asked if the diploma

meant that one was educated, she told of knowing four graduating classmates who could not read. To Lee, school was "where you learn to work for Henry Ford." Bob told of "always getting in some kind of trouble. I mean there ain't no getting around it. I've always been like that and still am. I never studied, I could carry C's and D's all through high school without studying."

32.   Childhood ended early in these families. Gus grew up in orphanages and had to go to work in his teens. Mary became pregnant in high school and was asked to leave. Martha fell in love and got married to an older man who had quit school to join the service. Arlene fell in love and quit. Others, expected by their mid-teens to support themselves and to help the family, had no more years to spend in school. No one regretted leaving. No one said he or she wished they had stayed, studied harder, or learned more. Their later experiences had not altered their jaundiced views, and they had no remorse about performing poorly.

33.   All disparaged the school's promised benefits. Fred, who could neither read nor write, explained, "I have a new house. I have a new car, a new truck. I've raised my family. I married Sandy. I don't see where not reading and writing has hurt me a bit." One parent said that she liked high school because it was an escape from home but she had to drop out when she became pregnant. At best, a few gave schooling grudging credit. As Donna said, "It's

Table 3   *Family history of dropping out*

Family	Paternal Grandfather	Maternal Grandfather	Paternal Grandmother	Maternal Grandmother	Father	Mother	Stepfather
Roundtree/Walker	X	0	0	X	0	0	NA
Stanley	X	NK	X	NK	0	(X)	NA
Menges	X	X	X	X	(X)	(X)	NA
Clinton	X	X	X	X	0	0	NA
Vitale	X	X	X	X	X	(X)	NA
Small/Beauchamp	NK	X	NK	X	(X)	X	0
Anderson/Workman	X	X	X	X	X	(X)	X
Mandrick	X	X	0	0	0	0	NA
Rogers	X	X	X	X	X	(X)	NA
Collins/Lamb	0	X	0	X	(X)	(X)	0
Henry/Griggs	X	0	X	0	X	0	X
Walasek	X	X	0	X	(X)	0	NA

Table key: X. Dropped out prior to high school graduation; (X). Dropped out of high school/earned diploma or general equivalency diploma (GED) later; 0. Graduated from high school/never dropped out; NK. Not known; NA. No answer.

the minimum for survival; without it you ain't getting nowhere."

34. Research cited earlier in this article suggests that children who do poorly and leave school early come from economically poorer families with a high number of risk factors. Although we did not select families on the basis of economic status or lifestyle, the families in the study were similar. Ten of the 12 were economically marginal. Smoking, drinking, drugs, and getting into trouble were common. Furthermore, the parents of the dropouts were themselves children of dropouts. They had entered school reluctantly, were unhappy there, were picked on by students, were bored by subjects, were disliked by teachers, and disliked teachers in return. They reported low effort, motivation, and interest; and they were often in trouble. According to their own recollections, they skipped school, fought, learned little or nothing, refused to comply, and dropped or were pushed out. They were indifferent to learning and the rewards it promised. Furthermore, within the family, the younger generation — among them the dropouts — had heard their parents' stories about school; the way in which their parents were treated; the injustices; and their parents' opposition, resistance, and defiance. "School as an all-around bad experience" was part of the family history and lore, passed from generation to generation.

The Dropouts' School Experience

35. Like their parents, the dropouts saw themselves as victims of unfeeling teachers, oppressive administrators, and bullying classmates. Suzi, Roger, and Bobbie Sue "always hated school." Some spoke of positive experiences in the earliest grades but had trouble and were retained by third or fourth grade and disliked school since. Sonny, who had trouble reading from the third grade on, was by the sixth grade regularly getting punished for his behavior: The principal "had this paddle and every time he would swat you, you had to write your name on it. He had to fill up two paddles with my name." Tammy, Jason, Tom, and Susan refused to do work they knew they could handle. Susan explained,

> I wouldn't do the work. I didn't like the teacher and I didn't like my mom and dad. So, even if I did my work, I wouldn't turn it in. I completed it. I just didn't want to turn it in. I was angry with my mom and dad because they were talking about moving out of state at the time.

36. Seven of the 12 dropouts had trouble reading and 5 were singled out for special assistance, which they did not like any better. Tammy refused for a whole year to speak to her speech therapist. As did their parents, the dropouts justified their animosity toward school with tales of unjust treatment. Sonny fought because he was picked on. Tommy dropped a pencil, bent over to pick it up, and "this teacher came by and pulled me by the hair and lifted me back into the seat." Later in high school, he was "slammed against the wall by a gym teacher." Tom's teacher threw the flowers he had brought her into the wastebasket and told him it was a more pleasant class without him.

37. Negative experiences started early on. Mickey skipped the first weeks of kindergarten by hiding in the bushes near the highway. Wendy recalled feeling "stupid and dumb" even in kindergarten. Ricky began beating up classmates in early elementary school, and Tom and Bob were getting beaten up by the first grade. Tom never made friends and Bobbie Sue and Virginia took as friends whoever accepted them. Sonny and Mickey, who reported being abused by their parents, were violent by middle school.

38. All the dropouts reported refusing to work and being rejected from any classes and activities that required effort. Even the few who were recognized or rewarded behaved no differently. Jason would do no work in his gifted class. Mickey and Ricky played football but took drugs before the games and got drunk after. Some talked about a teacher whom they liked, who seemed to care about them, and who made the class pleasant. But positive experiences had occurred only in early grades. And no dropout reported a carryover from a positive experience with a teacher to improving behavior or performance. By ninth grade, all were regularly defying the schools' minimal requirements that they show up and behave. They were drinking and taking drugs in school or on school time, skipping classes, and telling off teachers. They disliked school from the time they got on the bus. According to Tommy,

> The day begins riding a crowded bus. I don't like being crowded in like that. When you get to school, it's loud. You're half asleep. The halls are crowded and I'm tired. The first hour you walk in, it's English and there's a pop quiz. I see the words, but I can't understand it. Sometimes I have to read a question five or six times. Sometimes I put my name on the paper and turn it over so I don't have to look at it. I don't care if I pass or not. . . . I don't do any homework. If you don't have your homework, [the teachers] ignore you. So I ignore them. [Teachers] are arrogant. They have the answer book with all the answers written in it. How do you know they know anything you don't?

39. Five dropouts had been designated as "special." Nine were in the lowest tracks in the elementary school and four of those were retained in elementary school. All were in the lowest tracks by high school. Some reacted with embarrassment, some with anger. Others admitted that they learned nothing in their classes and said they were socially promoted. As Bobbie Sue said, "They would pass me just to get rid of me."

40. Several associated their academic status with their parents' social status. Mickey described himself as being with the in-crowd in early elementary but

> What changed? Material things. The in-crowd, things mattered to them that didn't matter to me. It not only didn't matter. It wasn't possible for me. . . . I guess we were pretty poor. My stepdad worked in construction and around third grade, I remember mom got fired.

41. Wendy's experience was similar: "The kids in my groups weren't as smart as everybody else. When you are in one of those groups, you are not one of the good kids." Tommy extended the notion:

> Unless you are rich, you are not going to do well in school. If they find out you are on AFDC, you are automatically one of the bad group. . . . You are going to get E's all the way.

42. Tommy's mother agreed: "They just look at the kids and they pick out the so-called low-class ones and they put them in special class, 'cause we're AFDC, we're low class." Tommy's mother also believed that the bus picked up her children last, not because of the location of her house but because she was on welfare.

43. The dropouts associated their social class with rejection by classmates. Bob was called "Bob the slob." Tom said, "Kids don't like me . . . I remember a kid asking me to stay after school. I don't remember exactly what happened but it ended up he turned the lights off and then he jumped me." Tammy was laughed at for her speech impediment; Jason's only friend, "a kid with bugs in his hair," was as unpopular and rejected as he was. Jason described his first day in the high school as follows:

> A kid pushed me to get out of the cafeteria, just decided he was going to push me and I turned around and pushed him back and we got into a scrap, right there on the first day in school.

44. By ninth grade, Mickey looked around and decided he "didn't have any friends." Bobbie Sue's solution to her general unpopularity was to hang out with the "burnouts": "That's what they called us. I figured I had my own way of being. If they were going to pick on me because I wasn't like they wanted me to be, I really didn't care." Susan blamed a girl [who] turned everyone against me. I was also fighting with another girl. It was the people I had problems with. You know when I came to school, everyone knew I was pregnant . . . and they screwed everything around about the story.

45. All dropouts reported extensive drug and alcohol abuse. Some indulged to escape, some for inclusion. The one drug dealer did it for profit and prestige. Substance abuse has its own behaviors and its own rewards. From fifth through eighth grade, Tammy refused to speak because other students mocked her speech impediment, but she began drinking in the sixth grade, and when she was drunk

> I just started talking. I became rowdy. I made fun of anything. . . . When I was drunk, I felt like I was in a playground. . . . You can laugh at things even if they aren't funny. It was okay if they left you alone. Then it was okay . . . and . . . if I was sent to the office, they would say, "Are you drunk?" And I would say, "What if I am?"

46. By high school she was drinking heavily, using marijuana, popping pills, and taking acid and cocaine. She was hospitalized on two occasions. In her sophomore year, Tammy quit. "School was an all-around disaster." Wendy smoked marijuana on the way to school, and at lunch she and Mickey "would go behind the school, smoke dope, and get wasted." Like the other dropouts, she found school difficult because, in part, she could not remember things when she was high. Tommy was "so stoned in typing class that he had to go to the nurse." Jason had flashbacks from his bad drug experience. Bobbie Sue and Virginia skipped classes to smoke and drink. Bob was suspended in eighth grade for selling drugs. He was later treated for alcoholism. Five of the dropouts had criminal records, and four of those five were convicted of drug- and alcohol-related crimes. They justified their drinking and drugs as a release:

> When you're high, you don't give a s—. On drugs or alcohol or whatever, it's like something happens to you. . . . When you get sober, you have to get high again. Your problems go away when you're stoned, but when you're back, they're there. You want a constant high so it doesn't matter.

47. Tommy was expelled for using and selling drugs. Jason was told by a substance abuse counselor, "You'll be dead before the year's over if you don't go to treatment." When told his son was on drugs, Sonny's father took him to be tested. According to the tests, Sonny was clean but the father admitted that alcohol, not drugs, was Sonny's problem.

The Parents' Experience With Their Child's Schools

48. As did Stevenson and Baker (1987), we inquired into the parents' involvement in their child's schooling. And like those researchers, we found that the parents of these dropouts did not advocate for their children with the school. But family-school relations were complicated by the parents' negative experiences in school and their continuing belief that school people were predisposed to dislike them and their children. Some of the mothers had tried to participate in their child's school in the early years. One made regular visits, attended school, and observed classes. Five more reported sporadic visits. One father made visits, and one stepfather joined a support group for parents of troubled students. But they did not like the way the school treated them:

> I never felt welcome. I didn't feel comfortable when I went to the parent conferences. I guess because Ricky wasn't all A's. You might have 10 minutes with a teacher. If they're talking to somebody that's got an all A student, then they're not going to take time out for me.

49. Parents felt that teachers thought, quite unjustifiably, that they (the teachers) were superior. Fred commented, "There's only one teacher up to that high school right now that I can walk in and talk to and he'll treat me just like anybody else and he'll do the same to my daughter." Bob commented that his son "had a couple of teachers making $15,000 to $18,000 a year and I'm making $30,000 to $35,000 and they were sticking their nose up in the air every time I talked to them. I'm looking at the bottom of their nostrils. It was the attitude." Lee, the self-described anarchist, was told by the school counselor that the family might not know how to handle their son, Jason, who had been judged gifted. Lee told the counselor: "That makes (Jason) the third smartest person in my house." Bob expressed another belief by several of the parents, that the school blamed the parents for problems that the school should handle:

> So they don't want any trouble with Bob, Jr. They wanted him to be able to walk through the door and do things their way, and when he presented problems, the answer was, "You fix it because that's not our job." How could we control him when they have him from 9 to 3? They wanted us to teach him everything he needed so they could just get by.

50. Initially, parents had sent the children into school disposed to learn. And in the elementary years, when the schools complained about the children, several parents had taken actions to improve their child's behavior. But by the students' middle years, the parents' patience with

what they see as uncaring teachers, unfair administrators, and cruel classmates had worn away. It was then that parents came to believe that the teachers, administrators, and students are picking on their children, just as they picked on the parents when they were in school. In the later years, the parents were called into suspension and expulsion hearings that their children's behavior fomented. So it is not that the parents were uninvolved or refused to advocate. They were defensively involved; and when they advocated, it was in defense of the children against the school.

Dropping Out

51. Tammy quit during her sophomore year, returned the next fall, and quit at the end of the first quarter. She recounted wanting to get away from school and school friends who wanted her to continue drinking and taking drugs. Jason, who at 19 had only sophomore status, was tired of hanging out with 15- and 16-year-olds: "I'd be 21 by the time I graduated. I wanted to get it over with. Just be done messing with it." Tommy was expelled for drug dealing, reenrolled in an alternative program, and quit soon after. Tom left after a string of discipline problems and an arrest. Sonny, who in his last year was suspended for 100 days, was one day brought home by the principal and vice principal, who told Sonny's father that Sonny—who was in special education—would be thrown out of school if he did not quit. They did not tell him that state laws forbid expelling special education students. His father took Sonny out of school.

52. Bobbie Sue, after being beaten by her father for skipping, ran away to live with her mother, joined the "burnout crowd," and quit. Wendy, tired of "being one of the dumb kids" and after an extended bout with drugs and alcohol, quit and enrolled in an alternative program. She was unable to tolerate even that program's modest constraints. Bob's father tried everything to make Bob attend school,

> from spanking to grounding. I mean truly. He would have spent his total life inside his room. Grounding didn't work. Taking things away didn't work. Nothing ever seemed to work. You don't know which way to go. You do everything you can. You're still wrong. You're not doing enough.

53. After an extended illness, Susan was unable to complete her work or catch up and was soon pregnant and so dropped out. After years of failure, no friends, and a series of run-ins with the law, Mickey quit. Ricky's school days, a series of failures and fights and suspensions, were cut short by his incarceration for drunk driving and "breaking and entering." Virginia, who "always hated school," quit on her 16th birthday: "Screw this," she told whoever was listening and walked out. Indeed, why not? For Virginia, like the other dropouts, school was a series of bad experiences from the beginning. School was not worth the trouble. And when the dropping out was done, the vice principal no longer calling, the source of embarrassment and conflict finished, the dropouts and their families were relieved. Having the child out of school was less trouble than having the child in.

Conclusion: The Families' Perspective

54. The purpose of the study was to describe and explain the perspective of a set of families whose children dropped out of school. For the families in this study, resistance to school is at least two generations old. Their antipathy toward education, schooling, academic learning, or any of the associated benefits is family and historically rooted. Parsons (1955) reminded us that "the conditions under which effective socialization can take place will include being placed in a social situation where the more powerful and responsible persons are themselves integrated into the cultural value system in question" (p. 58). But the powerful and responsible persons in those families, the parents, were only marginally integrated into the schools' cultural value system. Their ideas about achievement, economics, equality, deferred gratification, and authority are not those espoused and presented by the schools, and so they did not socialize their children into the school's version of society. They do not envision themselves as economically successful and therefore see no sense in succeeding academically. Nor do they believe that school is an equal-opportunity institution; it is rigged in someone else's favor. They reject polite middle-class values, regard school as obedience training, resent authority, and pass their jaded attitudes toward school on to their children, who take them into school and recreate the families' school experience.

55. More specifically, there are two elements in the perspective. First, within the families neither school nor what it promises was valued. School was to be tolerated as long as the law demands or as long as it takes to obtain a diploma for an entry-level job. However benign school people like to think of their efforts, what they are presenting is not valued by the families interviewed. Family members agreed that one needs a diploma only because employers ask for one, but a diploma does not signal a higher level of competence or ability and learning does not improve one nor does it hold intrinsic pleasure. Nor do family members believe that school will lead to economic and social improvement.

They did not see themselves as competing for society's preferred places, so they do not value school that claims to help one compete for preferred places. Those who felt a diploma — as opposed to an education — was desirable knew they could get one in evening school, in the military, or via the General Educational Development tests (GED). Regular school offers them little. Thus the first element in the perspective is the families' disdain for academic achievement.

56. The second element in the perspective is families' child-rearing practices. Most of the dropouts' parents were economically marginal. They had left school, gone to work, and had children early on. The protected years that middle- and upper-middle-class families enjoy and that allow young people in those families to continue school even to the early 20s were not for them nor for their children. That was not part of the families' history and families' resources did not allow it. Children from the dropouts' families grew up fast. The direct result of such child-rearing practices is that the families' children, having been given adult status at home, demand it from the school and long before the school will give it to them. Moreover, the behaviors they associate with adulthood are those their parents engage in: drinking, smoking, taking drugs, and running afoul of authority. Dropouts engage in those behaviors in school, just as did their parents when they were in school. The school reacts predictably and with the means at its disposal: parent conferences, special services, disciplinary procedures, truancy hearings, suspensions, and threats of expulsion. When that series of events has run its course and the children drop out, the parents do not try to make them go back. Indeed, what for? A different set of programs that carry the same assumptions about achievement, economics, and equality? Further denial of adulthood and further deferring of gratification? More trouble with peers, more academic failure, and more embarrassing conferences with the vice principal? No. For the dropout and his or her family, dropping out takes care of a bad situation.

57. In sum, there is a school perspective within the families that includes the families' educational history, beliefs about school and their experience in school, view of their place in society and the place of education in life, and child-rearing practices. From the families' perspectives, schools are unpleasant, oppressive, unfair, and biased; what they offer is of little social or economic value, and their rules and regulations are impossible. School stands as a public rebuke to everything they do and are. Dropping out makes sense.

What Is to Be Done?

58. We have tried to study this important issue and make "information available to the professional community in practical form" (Geertz, 1988, p. 1). From our small sample, we can make only limited inferences, but our findings are strengthened as they complement studies cited earlier in the article on family background and dropping out. Our conclusion is also strengthened as it reflects Parsons' (1955) notion of cultural value systems. The differences in "cultural value systems" are, according to our analysis, the sticking points between the schools that our dropouts attended and their families. Schools are founded on, and embody, a combination of values that is foreign to the families described.

59. Equally foreign to school people is the perspective of these families. School people constantly warn students of the competition for top- and middle-level jobs. But school people live in a middle-class world of reasonably steady incomes, opportunities for advancement, and employer-paid benefits. That was not true of the people to whom we talked. One was successfully self-employed. Three had blue-collar jobs and one had a post office job. The rest lived on the economy's third level with sometime and service jobs: part-time construction, part-time maintenance, part-time factory work, auto repair, truck driving, waitressing, and hair dressing. When hard times came, they resorted to welfare. Their parents got by. The dropouts had appraised the situation and decided that they too could get by, without a regular high school diploma. No more than any other educators do we wish to "blame the victim," but one cannot ignore the differences between the perspective from which families operate and the perspective from which the schools operate. Neither do we wish to blame the school for asking these students to honor majority values and refrain from emulating their elders while in school. Neither side is wrong; and dropping out is a tacit admission that, for the parties involved and for the situation as constructed, the conflict is impossible.

60. This is not an acceptable conclusion because it leaves the students and schools nowhere to go and it also denies students opportunities enjoyed by their peers and violates the school's commitment to equality and democracy. As Wehlage and Rutter (1986) said, "We have to think of another way to do it" (p. 388). Common are suggestions for large-scale redistribution of social resources (Fine, 1986, p. 407) or restructuring schools around work (Gerics & Westheimer, 1988). We do not see society redistributing its resources to favor families like we studied, nor do we see school restructuring as a solution. However schools are structured, or restructured, they will still embody the cultural values that our families found foreign. Nevertheless, we see some hope for the school capitalizing on the students' interest in work. Such capitalizing would not demand restructuring; it would ask only that the schools further specialize to attend to this particular group.

61. Thus, rather than suggesting a redistribution of social resources that we do not believe will happen or a restructuring of schools that might happen but that we do not think will address the problem, let us look for the soft spots in the conflict, openings that might be exploited and where some modest amelioration might be found. From the information presented in this study, we suggest three soft spots. First, the families love their children, want them to do well in school, and — at least initially — try to get them in line with school expectations. The school too cares about the children and wants them to do well. The common concern and interest by the parents and the school could be exploited more than it already is to increase understanding and communication on both sides. Elementary staffs already put considerable effort in this direction, and our study suggests that such efforts probably offer high payoffs and would benefit from expansion beyond the elementary school.

62. The second soft spot is the fact that the families we talk about are not to our knowledge welfare cheats or chronic criminals. Their crimes are not rape, murder, arson, or major drug dealing. They drive without valid licenses; get drunk in public; beat one another up; and fall behind on rent, alimony, and child support. African American, Caucasian, and Hispanic, they are the semirural underclass: they have been around forever; they live in every trailer park and down every dirt road in America; they are the people Carolyn Chute (1985) wrote about in *The Beans of Egypt, Maine;* they are self-righteous, they reject polite middle-class values; and they hate authority in whatever form it shows itself. Antipoverty programs, as Charles Murray (1984) pointed out, have not improved or much altered their situation. But they work, and they care about their work, and they reject chronic unemployment and permanent welfare. However, the labor market they inhabit is being squeezed as those with high school diplomas and training school experience are themselves squeezed and so move down the job chain ("Employing the young," 1994). They are aware that they are being squeezed and so may be more open than heretofore to school programs geared toward work and earlier access to those programs by their children. Their

concern for jobs as they define them can serve as an opening for the school to exploit. Efforts are already under way in several states where the legislature has revised its school code to open opportunities for students to remain students but leave school for job programs and job training.

63. Along with the families' love of their children and their desire and respect for work is a third possible soft spot: the school's need and openness to finding solutions to this expensive conflict. According to the analysis, the conflict is one of values, and although it is difficult for any group to alter its values, it may be easier for the school people to question their values than for the families to question theirs. We believe that schools are innately biased against the lower classes. If such a questioning of values by school people were combined with a greater appreciation of the dropouts' family situation as well as their concern for their children and their desire and respect for work, perhaps the conflict between these families and the school could be softened.

References

Becker, H. S., Geer, B., & Hughes, E. (1968). *Making the grade.* New York: Wiley.

Cervantes, L. F. (1965). *The dropout: Causes and cures.* Ann Arbor: University of Michigan Press.

Chute, C. (1985). *The Beans of Egypt, Maine.* New York: Warner.

Clark, R. M. (1983). *Family life and school achievement: Why poor Black children succeed or fail.* Chicago: University of Chicago Press.

Delgado-Gaitan, C. (1988). The value of conformity: Learning to stay in school. *Anthropology and Education Quarterly, 19,* 275.

Ekstrom, R., Goertz, M., Pollack, J., & Rock, D. (1986). Who drops out of high school and why? Findings from a national study. *Teachers College Record, 87,* 356-373.

Employing the young. (1994, March 19-25). *The Economist,* p. 27.

Fine, M. (1986). Why urban adolescents drop into and out of public high school. In G. Natriello (Ed.), *School dropouts.* New York: Teachers' College Press.

Geertz, C. (1988). *Works and lives.* Stanford, CA: Stanford University Press.

Gerics, J., & Westheimer, M. (1988). Dropout prevention: Trinkets and gimmicks or Deweyan reconstruction. *Teachers College Record, 90,* 41-60.

Glaser, B., & Strauss, A. (1970). Theoretical sampling. In N. Densin (Ed.), *Sociological methods* (pp. 105-106). Chicago: Aldine.

MacLeod, J. (1987). *Ain't no makin' it.* Boulder, CO: Westview.

Murray, C. (1984). *Losing ground.* New York: Free Press.

National Center for Educational Statistics. (1993). *The condition of education, 1993.* Washington, DC: U.S. Department of Education.

Parsons, T. (1955). *The structure of social action.* New York: Free Press.

Rumberger, R. W., Ghatak, R., Poulos, G., & Ritter, P. L. (1990). Family influences on dropout behavior in one California high school. *Sociology of Education, 63,* 283-299.

Shibutani, T. (1967). Reference groups as perspectives. In J. G. Manis & B. N. Meltzer (Eds.), *Symbolic interaction* (p. 161). Boston: Allyn & Bacon.

Stevenson, D. L., & Baker, D. P. (1987). The family-school relation and the child's school performance. *Child Development, 58,* 134-135.

Wehlage, G., & Rutter, R. (1986). Dropping out: How much do schools contribute to the problem? *Teachers College Record, 87,* 374-392.

Willis, P. (1977). *Learning to labor: How working class kids get working class jobs.* Hampshire, England: Gower.

Factual Questions

1. The authors state that they used what method of research?

2. Where were the initial interviews with the dropouts conducted?

3. Were the families hospitable to the researchers?

4. According to the authors, what are the advantages of interviewing (over other methods of data collection)?

5. Were the dropouts from large or small school districts?

6. Who helped identify the pool of recent dropouts?

7. Why did the researchers stop adding subjects after interviewing twelve families?

8. How many of the mothers graduated from high school (never dropped out)?

9. How many of the dropouts had trouble reading?

10. What do the researchers mean by "soft spots in the conflict"?

Questions for Discussion

11. What do you think the researchers mean by the term *open-ended interview*? (See paragraph 8.) Are there advantages and disadvantages to using this type of interview?

12. The family interviews with parents sometimes included other family members. Was this a good idea? Explain.

13. Might the subjects have been less than perfectly forthright despite being guaranteed anonymity?

14. In paragraph 9, the researchers note that interviewing more than one person at a time (about the same events) may yield more truthful information. Do you agree? Is it still possible for two family members to agree on an event and still be wrong?

15. The procedures described in paragraph 10 indicate that the researchers were "exploring" for explanations (as opposed to having a specific research hypothesis to test). Do you agree that this topic is appropriate for an exploratory study?

16. In the title of Table 1, the researchers use the term *demographics*. What does this term mean?

17. Examine the risk factors named in the key to Table 2 and in the discussion in paragraphs 20–24. Do some seem more important than others? Are there other risk factors that might have been examined? Explain.

18. The researchers note that 10 of the 12 families were economically marginal. Would it be of interest to compare dropouts from marginal families with dropouts from families that are not economically marginal? Explain.

19. Would you have been interested in seeing the results of a comparison with a control group of families (with similar demographics) whose children did not drop out? Explain.

20. The authors state that to the families "dropping out makes sense." In a sentence or two, explain what they mean by this.

21. Do you agree that only limited inferences can be made from this study? (See paragraph 58.)

22. If you were planning an additional study on this topic, would you plan a qualitative study (such as this one) or a quantitative study? Explain.

Quality Ratings

DIRECTIONS: Indicate your level of agreement with each of the following statements by circling a number from 5 for strongly agree (SA) to 1 for strongly disagree (SD). If you believe that an item is not applicable to this research article, leave it blank. Be prepared to explain your ratings.

A. The introduction establishes the importance of the research topic.
   SA   5   4   3   2   1   SD

B. The literature review establishes the context for the study.
   SA   5   4   3   2   1   SD

C. The research purpose, question, or hypothesis is clearly stated.
   SA   5   4   3   2   1   SD

D. The method of sampling is sound.
   SA   5   4   3   2   1   SD

E. Relevant demographics (for example, age, gender, and ethnicity) are described.
   SA   5   4   3   2   1   SD

F. Measurement procedures are adequate.
   SA   5   4   3   2   1   SD

G. The results are clearly described.
   SA   5   4   3   2   1   SD

H. The discussion/conclusion is appropriate.
   SA   5   4   3   2   1   SD

I. Despite any flaws noted above, the report is worthy of publication.
   SA   5   4   3   2   1   SD

TRANSITIONS FROM HETEROSEXUALITY TO LESBIANISM: THE DISCURSIVE PRODUCTION OF LESBIAN IDENTITIES

Celia Kitzinger *Loughborough University*
Sue Wilkinson *University of Hull*

This article explored the discursive production of a major disjuncture in sexual identity in adult life: women's accounts of transitions to lesbianism after a substantial period of heterosexuality. Eighty semistructured interviews with self-identified lesbians, all with at least 10 years prior heterosexual experience (plus additional materials drawn from published autobiographical sources), were analyzed within a social constructionist framework. The article examined the creation of contexts in which sexual identity transitions became possible, explored how such transitions are defined and marked, identified the consequences, and detailed the continuing development of lesbian identity posttransition. In conclusion, the article reflected on the status and salience of such data in supporting the social constructionist position, particularly in the face of the continuing popularity of essentialist theories of sexual identity development.

1. After more than two decades of social constructionist approaches to sexual identity (e.g., Gagnon & Simon, 1973; C. Kitzinger, 1987; McIntosh, 1968/1992; Plummer, 1981, 1992; Weeks, 1977), biological models of lesbianism and male homosexuality are becoming increasingly popular, both in the scientific literature (e.g., Ellis & Ames, 1987; LeVay, 1991) and in the media. Although biological and early socialization models may present homosexuality as either a natural variation or an unnatural deviation from the "norm" of heterosexuality, "caused" variously by brain structure or function, genetic or hormonal influences, or early childhood experiences, they invariably assume heterosexuality as a natural, unproblematic category (see, e.g., Money, 1988, p. 11). Such an analysis fails to recognize that the category *homosexual* can only exist in relation to the category *heterosexual* (part of the social constructionist argument) and is in direct contradiction to those radical feminist analyses of heterosexuality that present it as neither natural nor normal, but rather as a coercive patriarchal institution (e.g., Adams, Lenskyj, Masters, &

Randall, 1990; Rich, 1987; Wilkinson & Kitzinger, 1993).

2. There is now a large body of work on the assumption that lesbianism and male homosexuality are *essences* — core, fundamental ways of being that are determined prenatally or in early childhood. Key researchers in the field concur on this point: According to Bell, Weinberg, and Hammersmith (1981), adult homosexuality stems from homosexual feelings experienced during childhood and adolescence; according to Money (1988, p. 124), "the most important formative years for homosexuality, bisexuality, and heterosexuality are those of late infancy and prepubertal childhood." Within this framework, identifying oneself as homosexual (which is referred to by the lesbian and gay community as *coming out*) is merely a process of learning to recognize and accept what one was all along: Indeed, the very expression *coming out* suggests that the lesbian has always been inside, awaiting debut (Hollander & Haber, 1992).

3. This idea, that homosexuality and heterosexuality are fixed early on and persist relatively immutable to change, is reflected in the literature documenting the failure of conversion therapies (e.g., Halderman, 1991). It is frequently suggested that essentialism of such theories is a "straw man" erected by the social constructionists as a foil for their own perspective (cf. Stein, 1992, p. 326), but as has been argued elsewhere (C. Kitzinger, in press), such essentialist models of lesbianism and gay male identity development are, in fact, the norm, reflecting and perpetuating popular theories about homosexuality.

4. Essentialist arguments of this type fail to address the experience of many women. Recent research on heterosexuals who become lesbian (Golden, 1987) and on lesbians who become heterosexual (Bart, 1993) emphasizes the "fluctuating," "fluid," and "dynamic" nature of sexuality for "protean" women (pp. 246-247). Women's sexual fluidity has long been apparent in the psychological and sexological literature, but it is often submerged in the data rather than explicitly theorized. Drawing on data from

Kinsey, Pomeroy, Martin, and Gebhard (1953), McIntosh (1968/1992) pointed out that

> [I]t is interesting to notice that although at the age of 20 far more men than women have homosexual and bisexual patterns (27% as against 11%) by the age of 35 the figures are both the same (13%). Women seem to broaden their sexual experience as they get older, whereas more men become narrower and more specialized. (p. 154)

Most women who self-identify as lesbian do so only after an earlier period in their lives during which they identified as heterosexual. Researchers typically find that at least a quarter of their lesbian samples have been married (25%: Saghir & Robins, 1973; 35%: Bell & Weinberg, 1978), and estimates of the number of lesbians with heterosexual sexual experience range from 58% (Kenyon, 1968) to 84% (Bell & Weinberg, 1978).

5. Indeed, past heterosexual experience is taken for granted so much in lesbian circles that lesbians who have never been involved with men have complained of the oppressiveness of this assumption (Jo, Strega, & Ruston, 1990). Many self-identified lesbians report that they occasionally engage in heterosexual sex — 46% in one survey (Bright, 1992, p. 136), a third of these with gay or bisexual men (suggesting that, even for men, essentialist models of sexual

Kitzinger, C., & Wilkinson, S. (1995). Transitions from heterosexuality to lesbianism: The discursive production of lesbian identities. *Developmental Psychology, 31*, 95-104. Copyright © 1995 by the American Psychological Association. Reprinted with permission.

Celia Kitzinger, Social Sciences Department, Loughborough University, Loughborough, United Kingdom; Sue Wilkinson, Health Studies Research, Institute of Nursing Studies, University of Hull, Hull, United Kingdom.

We thank Corinna Petre (Institute of Nursing Studies) for her sterling secretarial support.

Correspondence concerning this article should be addressed to Sue Wilkinson, who is now at Social Sciences Department, Loughborough University, Loughborough, Leicestershire LE11 3TU, United Kingdom.

identity are seriously problematic)—while Kinsey et al. (1953) reported that 28% of all women in their U.S. sample have had sexual experience with another woman. The accounts such women (and men) present of their experience constitute inconvenient data from an essentialist perspective, which assumes an innate or fixed sexual identity and is, perhaps, why such data are undertheorized in the literature.

6. Our research aims to explore the psychological processes involved for women in making transitions from heterosexuality to lesbianism without resorting to essentialist models of sexuality, according to which such women would finally be discovering their "real" selves after a long period of repression or denial, or, conversely, adopting an inauthentic lifestyle in opposition to their real orientation. Very little research to date has addressed the processes by which such women negotiate transitions to lesbianism (although, see Cassingham & O'Neil, 1993; Charbonneau & Lander, 1991; French, 1992).

7. In seeking a theoretical model within which to conceptualize transitions to lesbianism after a substantial period of heterosexuality, we start from the assumption that adult women who make such transitions are no more driven by biology or subconscious urges than they are when, for instance, they change jobs; such choices could be viewed as influenced by a mixture of personal reevaluation, practical necessity, political values, chance, and opportunity. This might suggest that the transition process could then be conceptualized within the framework of the literatures on transitions as (a) stressful disjunctions in an individual's life or (b) markers of developmental stage or role change. However, the sexist and heterosexist assumptions underpinning the tradition of work on stressful life events (e.g., Fisher & Reason, 1988) would seem to render it largely unusable as a framework for examining transitions in sexual identity. Similarly, classic studies based on stage theories of life span development have been heavily criticized for their male bias and for cohort effects (e.g., Barnett & Baruch, 1978; Rossi, 1980). Moreover, in neither the life stress tradition nor the stage-role change tradition has the transition to lesbianism been addressed.[1]

8. Models of homosexual identity development have also been based on stage theories (e.g.. Coleman, 1981/1982; Troiden, 1979). Criticisms of these models have been directed against their male bias (with the notable exception of Cass [1979, 1984]), despite much

evidence of fundamental differences between lesbian and male homosexual experience (e.g., DeMontflores & Schultz, 1978; Hart & Richardson, 1981). Critics have also noted these models' reification of stages (Weinberg, 1984), their lack of acknowledgment or the situational determinants of identity (Omark, 1981, quoted in Troiden, 1984), and their insistence on a single linear developmental path in the face of the "dazzling idiosyncrasy" of sexual identity (Suppe, 1984, p. 17).

9. Such models are reviewed by Minton and McDonald (1984), whose own three-stage version is typical of the genre: The first (*egocentric*) stage typically occurs in childhood or adolescence and entails genital contact, emotional attachment, and fantasies about a member of one's own sex; in the second (*sociocentric*) stage, conventional assumptions about homosexuality as deviant, sick, or sinful are internalized, leading to secrecy, guilt, and isolation; and in the final (*universalistic*) stage, the individual realizes that societal norms can be critically evaluated, is able to accept and develop a positive homosexual identity, and is able to integrate this identity with all other aspects of self. Faderman (1985) pointed out that women who come to lesbianism through radical feminism appear to go through Minton and McDonald's stages in reverse order. This not only contributes to the critique of stage theories as rigidly sequential, but it is also a salient critique for the present study, given that such women constitute a subgroup of those who make transitions from heterosexuality to lesbianism.

10. The key criticism of such models, however, is their essentialism. They assume the existence of homosexuality as an innate, or early acquired, *sexual orientation*. The development of a homosexual identity, in this view, simply entails a gradually developing awareness and acceptance of one's real self. Sexual identity development is conceptualized either as a process of natural unfolding, albeit dependent on environmental interactions, much like any other process of development, or as a voyage of discovery. For example, Coleman (1981/1982) explicitly supported a biological basis for sexual preference, whereas Minton and McDonald (1984) stated that "the initial phase of homosexual identity formation appears to emerge in childhood or adolescence," although they left open the question of whether homosexuality "can be traced to early social learning or biological predisposition" (p. 97). Not surprisingly, then, the literature on homosexual identity development focuses almost exclu-

sively on adolescence (e.g., Gonsiorek & Rudolph, 1991).

11. This focus on adolescence is a consequence of an essentialism that assumes a dormant, true lesbian self waiting to be discovered or revealed at puberty or shortly thereafter. This kind of model has important implications for women who change their sexual identity from heterosexual to homosexual after a substantial period of heterosexuality. Such women tend to be conceptualized in one of two ways: Either (a) they were "really" lesbians all along but were repressing or denying it—this argument includes the concept of the *latent homosexual* (e.g., Socarides, 1965)—or (b) they are "not really" lesbians now—Bergler (1954), for example, identified 12 varieties of *spurious homosexuality*: The label *pseudo homosexual* is also used to discredit women who present their lesbianism in political terms and who are seen as distorting their natural sexual inclinations in the service of ideology (Defries, 1976).

12. The process of coming out in adulthood has been almost entirely neglected, and, Gonsiorek and Weinrich (1991) noted: "There is essentially no research on the longitudinal stability of sexual orientation over the adult life span" (p. 8; see also C. Kitzinger & Wilkinson, 1993a). The present study was designed to redress this dearth of information by focusing on disjunctures in sexual identity in adult life, specifically transitions to lesbianism after a substantial period of heterosexuality, and by seeking to explore the psychological processes entailed in such transitions.

13. The approach adopted here was a metalevel perspective regarding both biological and early socialization models as particular rhetorical constructions used for specific purposes. In so doing, we drew on the sociology of knowledge (e.g., Knorr-Cetina & Mulkay, 1983; Simons, 1989) and on a social constructionist perspective (e.g., Gergen, 1985; Stein, 1992), especially work on the construction of self and identity (e.g., Shotter & Gergen, 1989). For a detailed discussion of this approach to research on homosexuality, see C. Kitzinger (1987, chapters 1 and 2).

14. It must be emphasized that in social constructionist, discourse analytic research, the focus is on participants' accounts as primary data, rather than on the compilation of accurate and reliable facts about lesbian transitions. The aim is not to reveal the real histories, motives, and life events of the participants but to understand how they construct, negotiate, and interpret their experience. A more extended rationale for

---

[1] A single exception is Penelope (1993), who offered a tongue-in-cheek analysis of how the transition to lesbianism might occur at each state of the female life span.

eliciting and assessing lesbian accounts is given by C. Kitzinger (1987, chapter 3). An introduction to the principles and practice of discourse analysis is provided by Potter and Wetherell (1987).

Method

Participants

15. Criteria for inclusion in this study were that participants should report having a minimum of 10 years active heterosexual behavior, including coitus; no sense of uncertainty or doubt about being heterosexual during this period; and a current identity as unequivocally lesbian (with or without sexual experience with women).

16. Participants were recruited by using friendship pyramiding (Vetere, 1972). Twenty women were interviewed specifically about the psychological processes of transition from heterosexuality to lesbianism; 60 others who satisfied the criteria for inclusion were drawn from a larger project on lesbian identities of which transition processes were only one aspect (C. Kitzinger, 1987).

17. Because the focus of this study is on the development of lesbian identity, only women who, at the time of interview, identified as lesbian were included. The question as to why some women, with otherwise similar sexual and emotional profiles, instead identify as bisexual, heterosexual, or refuse any label is beyond the scope of the present project (but see Hutchins & Kaahumanu, 1991). Similarly, because the focus was on the development of lesbian *identities*, we decided not to exclude those without same-sex sexual experience, although in fact only one such woman volunteered for this study.

18. This study, then, is based on interviews with 80 lesbians, 68% of whom had been married. The average participant began to have heterosexual sexual relations at age 18, identified herself as lesbian at age 34, and took part in the interviews at age 36. All of the participants were White; the majority (87%) were in professional or skilled occupations, with only 20% identifying themselves as working class.[2] Because the aim of this study was to explore commonalties in accounts of transitions, it was not considered appropriate to subdivide and analyze our sample by demographic variables. In recognition of the fact that this study was limited mainly to a sample of White, middle-class lesbians, we also drew on published accounts by lesbians about their coming out experiences

that reflect a broad range of ethnic and class backgrounds. We used all such accounts available to us at the time of conducting the research.

Materials and Procedure

19. All of the participants were interviewed by C.K. in their own homes. With the exception of 3 women, who were available only for telephone interviews, all of the participants were interviewed face-to-face. Interviews lasted an average of 1.5 hr.

20. The interview schedule for the larger project on lesbian identities (60 interviews) was developed to elicit discourses of lesbian identity in an open-ended and flexible way. All 23 questions are quoted in full in C. Kitzinger (1987, pp. 74-75). For the purposes of the present research, the key questions were as follows (with probes in parentheses):

> Question 5: How did you first find out about lesbianism? (Feelings about it?)
> Question 6: When did you first begin to think that maybe that was what you were? (Was there something particular that happened that made you think you might be lesbian?)
> Question 7: What did you do about it? (Seek out other gay people? Seek out counselor? Information in books? Feelings about it?)
> Question 8: Had you had sex with men before you decided you were a lesbian? (Why or why not? Did you like it? Sex with men now, or in the future? Sexual feelings for men?)
> Question 9: Have you had sex with a woman? (Why not?) Tell me about your first lover. How did you meet her? How did you become sexually involved? How did you feel about it? What happened to that relationship?

21. All of the women included as participants in the specific project on the transition from heterosexuality to lesbianism (20 interviews) satisfied the criteria specified earlier (determined in a preinterview telephone screening check). The key question in this project was, "Tell me about the time when you first began to think of yourself as a lesbian." Subsidiary questions were, How old were you then? How did you feel about it? What did you do about it? Was sex an important part of your decision making? What things helped you during this time? What things made it harder for you during this time? Do you remember a specific

point at which you said "Yes, I am a lesbian"? How do you think your life is different because you have become a lesbian?

22. Additional material was collected from each participant concerning date of birth, place of birth, marital status, ethnicity, social class, and employment. All interviews were tape-recorded with the consent of participants and were transcribed and coded by C.K. The coded data were then subjected to a number of phases of discourse analysis, including the determination of patterns in the data (variability and consistency of discourse use) and examination of the functions and effects of specific discourses or types of discourse use. These procedures follow the 10 stages in the analysis of discourse outlined by Potter and Wetherell (1987, pp. 160-176).

Results and Discussion

23. Our presentation of women's accounts of transitions from heterosexuality to lesbianism is organized under three broad headings. First, the section *Getting There* examines accounts of the preparatory "work" that has to be done to create a context in which a transition in sexual identity is possible and looks at strategies used to avoid confronting the possibility of a lesbian identity. Second, the section *Making and Describing the Transition to Lesbian Identity* includes accounts of the transitions themselves: how they are defined and marked; how such experiences are described; and their consequences, costs, and benefits. Finally, the section *Going On* considers the accounts of the new lesbian after transition: the continuing development of her identity and her reflections on the past and future. In reporting the results, we follow the discourse analytic convention of illustrating our analytic categories with substantial extracts from the interview transcripts. Where appropriate, we give some indication of the frequency with which particular discursive strategies and accounts are used.[3]

Getting There: Barriers and Resistances to Identifying as Lesbian

24. *Compulsory heterosexuality.* In becoming lesbians, women are assuming an identity they were taught to avoid. Most women, as girls, are encouraged to conform to norms of femininity and heterosexuality (S. Kitzinger & Kitzinger, 1991, pp. 264-279). Lesbianism was described by the vast majority of participants as shrouded in silence and invisibility, or was rendered perverse and abnormal:

---

[2] This does not add up to 100% because several women in professional or skilled occupations identified themselves as working class.
[3] The frequencies given are based on the spontaneous emergence of themes in our participants' discourse. These are likely to be gross underestimates when compared with the percentages of women reporting such experiences in response to a survey questionnaire.

My concept of Lesbian — although I didn't really know the word until late adolescence — was formed by my unconsciously responding to the gaps, the silences and hesitations . . . Women related to men or ??? — *blank* — there was nothingness. Nothingness was loaded with dread, the fear of the unknown. (Anne, 1990, p. 38)

Acknowledging my lesbianism was a very slow process — partly because of not knowing other lesbians, partly because of the fear I felt. . . . People beat up lesbians. People exclude lesbians. People say we're not normal. My whole life was heterosexual and it felt like my whole life was under threat.[4]

Despite feminist analyses of heterosexuality as an institution that has to be "managed, organised, propagandised, and maintained by force" (Rich, 1987, p. 50), the assumption often remains that most women are either innately heterosexual or have "freely chosen" a heterosexual identity (C. Kitzinger & Wilkinson, 1993b). It is little wonder that women who violate this assumption by asserting a lesbian identity are subject to rejection, hostility, and violence (e.g., Herek & Berrill, 1992) and that most women express their awareness of this state of affairs.

25. *Multiple oppressions.* For women already oppressed for their ethnicity, age, social class, or disability, claiming a lesbian identity is at once exhilarating and threatening to self and society. Beck (1982) described the disbelief and veiled hostility she encountered on telling people she was working on a book about Jewish lesbians:

[M]y answer was met with startled laughter and unmasked surprise bordering on disbelief, "Are there *many*?"— as if the juxtaposition Jewish/lesbian were just too much. . . . [I]f you tried to claim both identities — publicly and politically — you were exceeding the limits of what was permitted to the marginal. You were in danger of being perceived as ridiculous — and threatening. (p. xiii)

Lesbians with disabilities, Black lesbians, and women who became lesbians in their 60s or 70s have all written of the obstacles put in their paths not just by antilesbianism but also by "ableism," racism, anti-Semitism, and ageism (Browne, Connors, & Stern, 1985; Macdonald & Rich, 1983; Smith, 1983). A substantial minority (*n* = 17) of lesbians in our sample reported other oppressions being used to negate their attempts to claim a lesbian identity:

Discovering I had MS [multiple sclerosis] at the same time that I fell in love with Sarah made everything much more complicated partly because of what it meant for us, of course, but also because Mike [husband] and Jim [marriage

counsellor] both came up with the idea I wasn't really a lesbian — I wanted to *be* Sarah, as someone younger and healthy.

Other — ageist — examples are given in the subsection, *"It's just a phase."*

26. *Blocking it out.* About a quarter (*n* = 19) of the participants who became lesbians after a substantial period of heterosexuality described how they had earlier in their lives refused to allow themselves even to address the question, "Am I a lesbian?" Asking oneself the question admits the possibility of the answer "yes"' and that answer often felt too dangerous. The following 2 women finally identified as lesbian in their 40s:

The first time I fell in love with a woman I was 25 and pregnant with my second child. I thought, "What's this? Are you bisexual or what?" And then I pushed it to the back of my mind. There was no way I could deal with it because I had these children, and a husband, and no way of supporting myself, so I just didn't think about it.

I had a growing feeling that I wanted . . . well, I didn't know what I did want . . . I blocked it out; I never finished that sentence even in my own mind. Looking back, it's obvious that I wanted to know women closely and, clearly, sexually, but I couldn't and didn't believe it. It seemed too extraordinary, too way out, too unlike my life, which was a secure middle-class life with a husband and two children. There wasn't any room for my fantasies — I tucked them away and hid them even from myself.

27. In refusing to address the question, in pushing it to the back of their minds or blocking it out, these women seemed to be buying time. On a smaller scale, some women on the verge of coming out as lesbian succeeded in postponing their moment of self-labeling until after some event in their lives that would be disrupted by their lesbianism: a much wanted exotic holiday with their husband ("I couldn't face the decision until after the holiday—I needed it so badly, I was so exhausted and run down") or their parents' golden wedding anniversary ("There was going to be this really big family party. How could I ruin it?"). Others bargained with themselves, saying that they will think about whether or not they might be lesbian "If I don't get pregnant in the next 6 months," "When the children start school," "When my husband gets a promotion," or "When the children are all married."

28. When women in this sample did finally address the question "Am I a lesbian?," they recalled having used various strategies, used to avoid the answer "yes":

29. *"We're just good friends."* One woman described how she was "in love with a woman and even though I did everything that is classic in the situation of being in love, I didn't think of it as being in love because you could only be in love with a man." Another told how she met another woman when they were students in 1954: Unable even to "notice" let alone express their love for each other, both married and lived hundreds of miles apart until, after 20 years of friendship expressed through frequent phone calls and letters, and infrequent visits, both became involved in feminism:

All that Corky and I never said began to unravel . . . We talked about our lives and the women we had become, and began to talk about the nature of a woman's love for other women. Corky reached for my hand and took it. We continued walking, holding on to one another. Later I wondered how it could have happened that we waited twenty years to clasp hands. (Poor, 1982)

30. Many lesbians' coming out stories (almost half of our sample: *n* = 38) reiterated this story of passionate feeling, never named as passion. Several (*n* = 9) acknowledged the role of the women's liberation movement as providing a catalyst for reexamination of such feelings and a context in which they could be named (Charbonneau & Lander, 1991).

31. *"It's just sex—I was only experimenting, and anyway I'm sexually attracted to men too."* The notion that no real lesbian ever feels any sexual attraction for men also prevented some women's self-identification. Some lesbians in our sample did report feeling sexually attracted to men. One woman told us: "I always enjoyed heterosexual sex — it was fine, an enjoyable sport, a means to an end, a way of achieving an orgasm." Another felt differently: "Sex with men was always a nightmare." Whether a woman has had or enjoyed sex with men was not a reliable guide to whether she became a lesbian. Some women did, however, report clinging to their sexual attraction for men as a way of avoiding the lesbian label:

After Judy and I made love for the first time I got very scared that this meant I was a lesbian. I withdrew right away. I said, "This doesn't mean I'm a lesbian. I just wanted to try it, and it was nice, but I don't want to do it again." And then I went out and got myself screwed by four or five men in order to *prove* I wasn't a lesbian.

32. In 61% of first same-sex sexual experiences, neither woman identifies herself as a lesbian (Vetere, 1972); furthermore, a heterosexual woman who has a sexual experience with a woman has only about a 50% chance of

---

[4]All otherwise unattributed quotations are taken from the interviews in this study.

developing a lesbian identity (DeMonteflores & Schultz, 1978).

33. *"It's just a phase."* In retrospect, this argument was often used by women in mid-life as a justification for not coming out when they were younger: "After I came out as lesbian at the age of 42, I remembered the passionate affair I'd had for 2 years with another girl at school. We told ourselves that it didn't mean anything; we were just practicing for the real thing"; or "I kept telling myself it was just a delayed adolescent phase. I was waiting to grow out of it." Looking at their current lives, they described their feelings as being caused by postnatal depression, empty-nest syndrome, or menopause. Others in their lives also used such developmental causes to dismiss their experience:

> My husband said it was the menopause. He actually got textbooks out of the library with cases of women who thought they were lesbian during the menopause and who subsequently turned out not to be, after they'd totally wrecked their lives.

34. *"I'm in love with a person who happens to be a woman."* This form of resistance to naming oneself as lesbian is well documented in lesbian coming out stories and psychological research alike (Cass, 1979; C. Kitzinger, 1987). Women have said, for example:

> We loved each other as "people who just happen to be female." . . . I was not a Lesbian. I just happened to be head over heels in love with another woman who was not a Lesbian either. (Dobkin, 1990, p. 3)

> I got involved in a sexual relationship with another woman and it was her first sexual relationship too, so that meant the transition to becoming lesbian was quite slow. I spent four or five months saying "I am in love with this woman," but not thinking that made me a lesbian.

An account of lesbianism in terms of romantic love enables the woman to present her supposedly deviant experience as conforming to the dominant heterosexual culture, and hence as morally unimpeachable. In one study of lesbian identity development, 45% of respondents did not see themselves as lesbian as a result of their first relationship (DeMonteflores & Schultz, 1978); this was also the case for over half (*n* = 49) of the women in our sample.

35. *"I can't be a lesbian because I . . . have children/enjoy cooking/have long hair/can't fix my own car."* Direct recourse to lesbian stereotypes was another very common strategy, reported by nearly three quarters (*n* = 57) of our sample:

I read *The Well of Loneliness* [Hall, 1928/1981] and some psychology textbooks. They told me that lesbians were aggressive, jealous, doomed, masculine, perverted, and sick. I was tremendously reassured. I knew that I couldn't possibly be one of those!

It seems hard to believe, but in the early part of our relationship we didn't use the word "lesbian" for the powerful feelings we were experiencing . . . After the first giddiness had passed, I began to try on the word lesbian: me? No! I would look funny in a crew cut. Certainly I could never learn to smoke cigars! My own stereotypes interfered with the unfolding of my new identity. Lesbians aren't mothers. I thought to myself, they probably don't like to cook or weave or do any of the things I like. (Spencer, 1989, p. 106)

36. *"She's the lesbian, not me."* Yet another way of avoiding claiming the lesbian label is to attribute it to the other. One researcher described how "two of the women in my sample were heterosexually married, but were involved in an intense affair with each other. Both maintained that they were heterosexuals. However, both attributed lesbianism to the *other*" (Ponse, 1978, p. 192). A lesbian in our sample remembered her first coming out in the following way:

> It was about five months into my relationship with Elaine and we were sitting talking and I actually sort of said, "you lesbians . . . ," and Elaine said, "What!?" You know, it was just too difficult to say "*us* lesbians." It was so hard to say, "Yes. I am a lesbian, a *lesbian*!" And Elaine said, "What are you then?," and I said, "I . . . am . . . a . . . lesbian." It was an extraordinary moment.

37. When someone challenges a woman's heterosexual identity, as Elaine challenged her lover in the extract above, she may still not accept the label *lesbian*. A quarter (*n* = 21) of the lesbians in our sample told painful stories about women lovers who fled from a lesbian identity: "She told me she was sexually attracted to me, and the next day she showed up with an engagement ring"; "she got married two months after we first slept together"; "we were involved for nearly two years. She kept saying she was going to leave her husband and she said she wasn't sleeping with him. As time went by it was obvious that she wasn't going to leave, and then she told me she was pregnant."

38. The fear and horror invested in the single word *lesbian* is such that women who are passionately involved with other women sometimes continue to construct accounts that maintain their heterosexual identity. Psychologists and psychiatrists collude with this process when they attempt to reassure women that they are probably "not lesbians really" or when they

construct rigid definitions of lesbianism such that the majority of lesbians are excluded (e.g., Defries, 1976; Shively, Jones, & DeCecco, 1984).

Making and Describing the Transition to Lesbian Identity

39. The woman who makes a transition to lesbianism, then, has already come a long way to reach the point in which claiming a lesbian identity is possible. How then does she make—and describe—the transition itself?

40. Over three quarters (*n* = 71) of the women in our sample described having sex with, or falling in love with, a woman as the marker of their transition to lesbianism:

> Within two days of meeting Barbara it became clear to me that I was a lesbian. I remember I was standing on a train platform and I came to the conclusion that *I must* be a lesbian, because I fancied her something rotten, and I couldn't *possibly* deny that, so I must be a lesbian, and please *please* God, could she feel the same way.

> Loving and making love with Ruth was the most amazing thing in my whole life ever. How could I *not* be a lesbian after that!

41. Insofar as sex with, or love for, other women is part of the commonsense definition of lesbianism, citing these important events in their own lives as moments of revelation is, for the women in our sample, to make sense of their personal histories in these terms. However, what is obscured in the telling of these stories is the ordinariness of the experiences described: Many women love other women or have sex with them, but this alone does not make them lesbians. To make a transition to lesbianism, it is necessary for a woman to acknowledge a passion for another woman, to claim a lesbian identity as one's own. This may entail piecing together fragmented experience and remembering and naming such fragments to form a coherent whole:

> I only started thinking that I was a lesbian last year. I did have a relationship with a woman about four years ago, after my marriage broke up, but I was convinced that I wasn't a lesbian at the time. I just *knew* I wasn't a lesbian. I was always so sure that I was a normal heterosexual woman, and the fact that I was in a sexual relationship with a woman didn't do anything to change my identity. . . . And then last year I joined a CR [consciousness raising] group and there were three lesbians in it, and I was quite fascinated by them. What did they *do*? I wondered what the difference between me and them was, these women who were so sure they were lesbians. And then, more recently, I was affected by the political lesbianism paper, the Leeds Revolutionary Feminist Paper,[5] and now I know

---

[5]This paper is reprinted in Onlywomen Press (1981).

I'm a lesbian and will never have a relationship with a man again. Nothing really happened except my consciousness getting raised.

42. It is certainly not the case that a woman has to experience sex with other women to identify as lesbian; she may even specifically decide not to do so:

> I decided I was a lesbian without sleeping with a woman. I didn't feel that my sense of identity was dependent on immediate sexual activity. I certainly don't think heterosexual women should have sex with lesbians as a way of deciding whether they're lesbians — because then some other poor woman has an experiment conducted on her.

43. For those who have already decided they are lesbians, sex may be no more than a confirmation, or simply a consequence, of that decision:

> It wasn't particularly significant the first time I slept with a woman. When it happened, I suddenly realized I'd done all the important stuff before that. Sex with a woman marked the end of the transition, not the beginning.

44. How do women describe the experience of transition to lesbianism? Poet Adrienne Rich first identified as lesbian at the age of 47, after marriage and three children:

> I have an indestructible memory of walking along a particular block in New York City, the hour after I had acknowledged to myself that I loved a woman, feeling invincible. For the first time in my life I experienced sexuality as clarifying my mind instead of hazing it over; that passion, once named, flung a long, imperative beam of light into my future. I knew my life was decisively and forever different. (Rich, 1979, p. 12)

45. This account has several typical features. There is often what one woman described as an "essential awakening," a moment of recognition, of first naming her lesbianism to herself:

> It was a really special moment. I was going out with this man and I was bored out of my head but I was lying to myself, trying to talk myself into liking him, into believing he was potentially quite a nice bloke. And my friend Karen said, "but Pauline, you don't even sound as if you *like* him." And we'd talked before about how maybe I could be a lesbian, and she just looked at me and said, "You *are*!" and I said "I *am*!" and we celebrated it, and I knew there was no going back.

A specific moment of naming oneself as lesbian was identified by a third (n = 26) of our sample.
46. A sense of self-discovery came through vividly in some women's accounts: They talked exuberantly of being reborn, of becoming alive or awake for the first time, of seeing the world anew. That moment of first naming was described as "an explosion of aliveness," "like

waking up having been half asleep all my life: like a conversion experience," and "like emerging from a chrysalis." One woman who became lesbian at the age of 52 said:

> It was as if, all those years before, I'd been starving for something and didn't even know it. And now I grabbed for it, rolled in it, sucked it in ravenously, devouring an essence of life I never even knew existed before. (Sally, in Lewis, 1979, p. 66)

47. Far from the liberal notion that becoming lesbian is an insignificant shift, such a transition was experienced by the majority of women in our sample as a very dramatic change: "a quantum leap," "it completely changed my life," and "my world was suddenly fundamentally and radically different." One woman (a psychologist) told us: "The moment I said I was lesbian, everything was both the same and utterly different: It was like the alternating cube, or the crone and the young girl drawing — something switches inside your head and the world never looks the same again." Seeking to articulate the enormity of the change they are experiencing, a substantial number of women described it in terms of altered perceptions: "It was like seeing everything in color after only having seen black and white all my life," "life suddenly became three-dimensional," and "the world swung into focus instead of being a confusing blur."
48. Few women, however, were able to face the first acknowledgement of their lesbianism without conflicting reactions. The split was generally described as being one between their relief, happiness, and sense of wholeness or rightness about their lesbianism and their fear of its implications in a society in which the predominant view of lesbianism is still a very negative one.

> I was looking at myself in the mirror, and I thought "that woman is a lesbian," and then I allowed myself to notice that it was me I was talking about. And when that happened, I felt whole for the first time, and also absolutely terrified.

> I had a dream one night, and I woke up after the dream and I remembered it immediately, and in the dream I was making love with Jillian, and it was lovely. It was a lovely, beautiful dream — one of the nicest I've had for years! And when I woke up, I had two thoughts simultaneously which were "Wow! How lovely!" and "Oh no, I'm *not* that."

49. Becoming a lesbian involves taking a leap into the unknown, claiming an outlaw identity. Material costs, particularly of leaving a marital relationship, can include the loss of insurance and pension benefits, possibly home and possessions, and perhaps even children or a job (Kirkpatrick, 1989/1993):

He made over the pension lump sum to his father, and asked [his Company] to take my name off the health insurance scheme. It even turned out that what I thought was 'my' car — I'd paid for it! — was registered in his name.

50. The move into a new world is accompanied by a move out of the old one. Social circles in which these women once moved freely and unquestioningly — to which heterosexuality provides an easy passport — were now seen as closed to them, and the women in our sample often described a painful sense of being outsiders to the world in which they once may have felt perfectly at home (see, e.g., Wilton, 1993). A substantial number of women in our sample talked about their sense of loss, of grieving for the old familiar world left behind — grief for the loss of relationships with a husband or boyfriend, grief for the pain caused to parents, and often the loss of those relationships too (Thompson, 1992). Despite this, only 2 or 3 of the women in our sample expressed major regrets about having made the transition to lesbianism. In a similar vein, Cassingham and O'Neil (1993) also reported that none of their sample of 36 previously married women regretted the decision to change her sexual identity.
51. Some women also described a sense of loss for the person they once knew themselves to be. One woman described how, 2 weeks after first saying to herself (and her husband of 15 years) "I am a lesbian," she sat for hours staring at the family photograph albums "trying to work out which one was me." Shortly after moving out of the matrimonial home, another woman described how she stood in the aisle of a supermarket with an empty trolley, staring at the shelves in total bafflement "because I was a lesbian now, and I didn't know what kind of groceries lesbians bought." These are vivid examples of common themes: dislocation from the past, the experience of autobiographical rupture, and an apparent need for total self-reconstruction.

Going On: Posttransition
52. Completing a transition from a heterosexual to a lesbian identity does not mean the achievement of a static identity — a sort of terminal lesbianism. Once a woman has said to herself "I am a lesbian," she continues to discover what being a lesbian will mean for her, how she wants to live her life as a lesbian, and what kind of lesbian she wants to be. In an important sense, she becomes lesbian, and then yet more lesbian. (Although none of our interviewees saw heterosexuality or bisexuality as possible future identities, these are, of course, posttransition possibilities, cf. Bart [1993]. Here, however, we focus on the continuing

posttransition construction of a lesbian identity.) Key aspects of developing and maintaining a lesbian self appear to be retrospective accounting ("How did I get to be here?") and future planning ("Where am I going now?").

53. The reconstruction of a past that offers a sense of continuity with the present meant that early experiences with women, probably shared by heterosexual and lesbian alike, often assumed an enormous importance for most (*n* = 66) women in our sample. Previously unrecognized feelings or forgotten experiences were brought to light. A 52-year-old woman, married for 22 years, described how she began to remember her lesbianism when she first became involved in feminist consciousness-raising groups:

> When that happened, I got in touch with my own background. And remembered that I had had these kinds of thoughts as a high-school kid, that I had crushes on women, that not only that, that I had had two small sexual experiences with women, and both were cases where I had touched their breasts. And that there was a period in my all-girls high school where I had worn men's shirts. (quoted in Ponse, 1978, p. 162)

One woman in our sample who came out as lesbian at the age of 27 said:

> In fact I did have a brief holiday relationship with a girl when I was 14, but I'd completely forgotten about it. I'd pushed it to the back of my mind as not being significant. In fact, it was very significant, but until recently that experience seemed very separate from my adult life.

54. It can seem, from stories like these, as though a woman's whole life was an unconscious acting-out of her lesbian destiny, only now apprehended as such. But same-sex erotic relationships are part of many women's experience (Bell & Weinberg, 1978). Many women who later identify themselves as heterosexual have learned to forget these feelings, to dismiss them as unimportant compared with their feelings for men, or to think of them as mere adolescent preparations for adult heterosexuality — and they are supported in this by the rigid definitions and misleading stereotypes of lesbianism identified earlier. For women in our sample, becoming a lesbian often meant reinterpreting these experiences within a different framework.

55. Almost all of the women in our sample (*n* = 72) reported that one of the first things they became aware of as new lesbians was the oppression to which they are likely to be subjected. Even though they may have had an intellectual understanding of antilesbianism, most said that they were unprepared for how it feels to be unable to touch lovers in public for

fear of assault, or to be unable to talk freely about weekend activities with colleagues at work for fear of reprisals. One woman said: "Now that I was excluded from them, I became acutely conscious of all the goodies you get by being heterosexual."

56. Creating a lesbian future involved, for many women in our sample, discovering and becoming involved in lesbian communities. New lesbians described becoming part of a world in which taken-for-granted truths are questioned and in which there is the possibility, in community with other lesbians, of developing a different culture and different values. However, some new lesbians (*n* = 11) described disillusionment when their idealistic expectations of warm acceptance into a utopian sisterhood came up against reality:

> Anyone who identified as a dyke I put up on a pedestal. I didn't know anything about what being a lesbian meant, and I allowed them to define it all for me. I used to think that all lesbians were wonderful. Now I think we all have the potential to be wonderful, but lots of us aren't.

57. The initial concerns of coming out as lesbian were described by most women in our sample as a mixed experience: of pain (and perhaps fear) as the old world offers rejection and oppression, but also of joy and excitement as a new world opens up and its possibilities are glimpsed:

> I had no idea how difficult it was going to be. Not just the mess surrounding leaving my husband, losing one of my children, financial insecurity, loss of privilege, safety, and status, but what it means and continues to mean to be a lesbian in this world — the weight and force of being "wrong," "bad," "wicked," "perverted," outside and ultimately apart from the codes and concepts of everyone else — vulnerable in the extreme. I had no idea how good it was going to be. Not only the warmth, the feeling of being on the same side, the sensuality, friendship, renewed energy, but the freedom to begin to think and act in new ways. (Mohin, 1981, pp. 59-60)

Conclusion

58. This study documents the existence of women who have made a transition to lesbianism after a substantial period of commitment to heterosexuality, and we have illustrated the discursive strategies and accounting mechanisms through which such an identity change is accomplished and sustained. This evidence of the discursive production of lesbian identities does not fit easily into an essentialist framework within which lesbianism is conceptualized as an innate or intrinsic characteristic of the individual, to be acknowledged or discovered or to be denied or repressed. The emphasis on the constitutive nature of discourse in enabling the

construction of identity accounts is characteristic of the social constructionist perspective; as such, our work contributes to the elucidation of processes involved in the construction of self and identity (cf. Shotter & Gergen, 1989).

59. When a woman makes a transition to lesbianism, the appropriate question (from a social constructionist perspective) is not: "Am I a lesbian?" — with concomitant attempts to match actual experience against some assumed template of "real" prototypical lesbian experience. The question is, rather, "Do I want to be a lesbian?," meaning "Do I want to construct my experience in that way?" From our perspective, there is no essential lesbian self, no set of uniquely lesbian experiences that can be discovered through introspection. What may feel like self-discovery — and that, not surprisingly (given the prominence of discovery accounting) was a frequently used discourse in our data and that of Charbonneau and Lander (1991) — is better considered as self-reconstruction:

> "True insight" is the application of socially derived intelligibility systems, conditions of "genuine self-knowledge" are a formalisation of our common rules for interpreting or describing social action. . . . Breakthroughs in self understanding are primarily breakthroughs in one's capacity to master an intelligibility system as it applies to one's own behaviour. Self-knowledge is not thereby increased; it is only reconstructed anew. (Gergen, 1977, p. 32)

60. Within such a social constructionist framework, we have offered an account of the ways in which women in transition construct and interpret their changing identities in relation to their constructions of the category *lesbian*. This has included the rootedness of such accounts in popular and scientific views of lesbianism, and the functions apparently served by particular types of accounting. Our account, of course, is also a construction based on the availability of a particular range of discourses, and our own assessments of these discourses.

61. Just as proponents of essentialism produce, as evidence for their theories, the stories of lesbians and gay men who "remember feeling different" or who are sexually attracted to the same sex from an early age, so we, as social constructionists, have produced the stories of women who reported constructing their lesbian identities.

62. It is not our intent, however, to use our participants' reported experience of transition from heterosexuality to lesbianism to support a social constructionist explanation of sexual identity in a manner paralleling the essentialists' use of the personal testimonies of those who "always knew they were gay." In part, this is because, just as social constructionists discount "born that way" (and similar) participant accounts as rooted in popular and scientific ways of explaining the world (rather than as transparent accounts revealing truths about experience), so essentialists, as mentioned earlier, can (and do) dismiss accounts using the language of choice as self-serving justifications and post hoc rationalizations for a predetermined sexual orientation only now revealed to conscious awareness.

63. At issue here is far more than a technical problem of interview methodology. Rather, in laying claim to the right to accept some participants' versions as true while discrediting others, social scientists are engaged in "a politics of experience" (C. Kitzinger & Perkins, 1993; Pollner, 1975, p. 427).

64. For one to take a radical social constructionist stance implies not only to regard personal accounts as constitutive, rather than reflective, of social "facts," but also to recognize that within this framework it is not possible to adjudicate between essentialism and social constructionism, because this debate itself is socially constructed. We have argued elsewhere (C. Kitzinger, in press) that the essentialist–social constructionist debate is not resolvable with reference to empirical fact, and it is not our intention (nor do we believe it possible) to prove essentialism wrong with our data here. Data cannot settle questions of epistemology. Rather, the contribution made by this article is to "up the stakes" for social scientists who want to maintain essentialist accounts of lesbian identity. It is not impossible to explain our findings with reference to essentialist theories, but they are inconvenient findings from an essentialist point of view — and far more difficult to incorporate into essentialist theories that assume a fixed sexual identity than are those accounts of lesbians and by men who speak of having been "born that way." By documenting these accounts of women's transitions from heterosexuality to lesbianism, we hope to force other researchers to defend themselves against our inconvenient data (and our interpretations of them) by refining and elaborating their own essentialisms, in response to our development of social constructionism. Only through such critical engagements, and through developments within *both* theoretical frameworks, can a vital and comprehensive psychology of lesbianism be developed.

References

Adams, M. L., Lenskyj, H., Masters, P., & Randall, M. (Eds.). (1990). Confronting heterosexuality [Special issue]. *Resources for Feminist Research/ Documentation sur la Recherché Feministe, 19*(3/4).

Anne, S. (1990). Opening the door. In J. Penelope & S. Valentine (Eds.), *Finding the lesbians: Personal accounts from around the world* (pp. 36-41). Freedom, CA: Crossing Press.

Barnett, R. C., & Baruch, G. K. (1978). Women in the middle years: A critique of research and theory. *Psychology of Women Quarterly, 3*, 187-197.

Bart, P. B. (1993). Protean woman: The liquidity of female sexuality and the tenaciousness of lesbian identity. In S. Wilkinson & C. Kitzinger (Eds.), *Heterosexuality: A Feminism & Psychology reader* (pp. 246-252). London: Sage.

Beck, E. T. (Ed.). (1982). *Nice Jewish girls: A lesbian anthology.* Watertown, MA: Persephone.

Bell, A. P., & Weinberg, M. S. (1978). *Homosexualities: A study of diversity among men and women.* London: Mitchell Beazley.

Bell, A. P., Weinberg, M. S., & Hammersmith, S. K. (1981). *Sexual preference: Its development in men and women.* Bloomington: Indiana University Press.

Bergler, E. (1954). Spurious homosexuality. *Psychiatric Quarterly Supplement, 28*, 68-77.

Bright, S. (1992). *Sexual reality: A virtual sex world reader.* San Francisco: Cleis Press.

Browne, S. E., Connors, D., & Stern, N. (Eds.). (1985). *With the power of each breath: A disabled women's anthology.* Pittsburgh: Cleis Press.

Cass, V. (1979). Homosexual identity formation: A theoretical model. *Journal of Homosexuality, 4*, 219-241.

Cass, V. (1984). Homosexual identity: A concept in need of definition. *Journal of Homosexuality, 9*, 105-126.

Cassingham, B. J., & O' Neil, S. M. (1993). *And then I met this woman: Previously married women's journeys into lesbian relationships.* Racine, WI: Mother Courage Press.

Charbonneau, C., & Lander, P. S. (1991). Redefining sexuality: Women becoming lesbian in midlife. In B. Sang, J. Winslow & A. J. Smith (Eds.), *Lesbians at midlife: The creative transition* (pp. 35-43). San Francisco: Spinsters Book.

Coleman, E. (1981/1982). Developmental stages of the coming out process. *Journal of Homosexuality, 7*, 31-43.

Defries, Z. (1976). Pseudohomosexuality in feminist students. *American Journal of Psychiatry, 133*, 400-404.

DeMonteflores, C., & Schultz, S. J. (1978). Coming out: Similarities and differences for lesbians and gay men. *Journal of Social Issues, 34*, 59-72.

Dobkin, A. (1990). Foreward: Finding the lesbians is good for us and good for women. In J. Penelope & S. Valentine (Eds.), *Finding the lesbians: Personal accounts from around the world* (pp. 3-17). Freedom, CA: Crossing Press.

Ellis, L., & Ames, M. A. (1987). Neurohormonal functioning and sexual orientation: A theory of homosexuality-heterosexuality. *Psychological Bulletin, 101*, 233-258.

Faderman, L. (1985). The "new gay" lesbians. *Journal of Homosexuality, 10*, 65-75.

Fisher, S., & Reason, J. (Eds.). (1988). *Handbook of life stress, cognition and health.* Chichester, England: Wiley.

French, M. (1992). Loves, sexualities and marriages: Strategies and adjustments. In K. Plummer (Ed.), *Modern homosexualities: Fragments of lesbian and gay experience* (pp. 87-97). London: Routledge.

Gagnon, J. H., & Simon, W. S. (1973). *Sexual conduct: The social sources of human sexuality.* Chicago: Aldine.

Gergen, K. J. (1977). The social construction of self-knowledge. In T. Mischel (Ed.), *The self: Psychological and philosophical issues* (pp. 28-56). Oxford, England: Blackwell.

Gergen, K. J. (1985). The social constructionist movement in modern psychology. *American Psychologist, 40*, 266-275.

Golden, C. (1987). Diversity and variability in women's sexual identities. In Boston Lesbian Psychologies Collective (Eds.), *Lesbian psychologies: Explorations and challenges* (pp. 19-34). Urbana-Champaign: University of Illinois Press.

Gonsiorek, J. C., & Rudolph, J. R. (1991). Homosexual identity: Coming out and other developmental events. In J. C. Gonsiorek & J. D. Weinrich (Eds.), *Homosexuality: Research implications for public policy* (pp. 161-176). Newbury Park, CA: Sage.

Gonsiorek, J. C., & Weinrich, J. D. (Eds.). (1991). *Homosexuality: Research implications for public policy.* Newbury Park, CA: Sage.

Halderman, D. C. (1991). Sexual orientation conversation therapy for gay men and lesbians: A scientific examination. In J. C. Gonsiorek & J. D. Weinrich (Eds.), *Homosexuality: Research implications for public policy* (pp. 149-160). Newbury Park, CA: Sage.

Hall, R. (1981). *The wellness of loneliness.* New York: Bard Avon Books. (Original work published 1928)

Hart, J., & Richardson, D. (Eds.). (1981). *The theory and practice of homosexuality.* London: Routledge & Kegan Paul.

Herek, G., & Berrill, K. (Eds.). (1992). *Hate crimes: Confronting violence against lesbians and gay men.* Newbury Park, CA: Sage.

Hollander, J., & Haber, L. (1992). Ecological transition: Using Bronfenbrenner's model to study sexual identity change. *Health Care for Women International, 13*, 121-129.

Hutchins, L., & Kaahumanu, L. (Eds.). (1991). *Bi any other name: Bisexual people speak out.* Boston: Alyson.

Jo, B., Strega, L., & Ruston. (1990). *Dykes-loving-dykes: Dyke separatist politics for lesbians only.* Oakland, CA: Jo, Strega & Ruston.

Kenyon, F. E. (1968). Studies in female homosexuality — Psychological test results. *Journal of Consulting and Clinical Psychology, 32*, 510-513.

Kinsey, A. C., Pomeroy, W. B., Martin, C. E., & Gebhard, P. H. (1953). *Sexual behavior in the human female.* Philadelphia: Saunders.

Kirkpatrick, M. (1993). Middle age and the lesbian experience. In M. L. Andersen and P. H. Collins (Eds.), *Race, class and gender: An anthology* (pp. 287-296). Belmont, CA: Wadsworth. (Original work published 1989 in *Women's Studies Quarterly, 17*, 87-96)

Kitzinger, C. (1987). *The social construction of lesbianism.* London: Sage.

Kitzinger, C. (in press). Social constructionism: Implications for lesbian and gay psychology. In A. D'Augelli & C. Patterson (Eds.), *Lesbian, gay and bisexual identities across the lifespan: Psychological perspectives on personal, relational and community processes*. New York: Oxford University Press.

Kitzinger, C., & Perkins, R. (1993). *Changing our minds: Lesbian feminism and psychology*. New York: New York University Press.

Kitzinger, C., & Wilkinson, S. (1993a). The precariousness of heterosexual feminist identities. In M. Kennedy, C. Lubelska, & V. Walsh (Eds.), *Making connections: Women's studies, women's movements, women's lives* (pp. 24-36). London: Taylor & Francis.

Kitzinger, C., & Wilkinson, S. (1993b). Theorizing heterosexuality. In S. Wilkinson and C. Kitzinger (Eds.), *Heterosexuality: A feminism & psychology reader* (pp. 1-32). London: Sage.

Kitzinger, S., & Kitzinger, C. (1991). *Tough questions: Talking straight with your kids about the real world*. Harvard, MA: Harvard Common Press.

Knorr-Cetina, K., & Mulkay, M. (Eds.). (1983). *Science observed*. London: Sage.

LeVay, S. (1991, August 30). A difference in hypothalamic structure between heterosexual and homosexual men. *Science, 253*, 1034-1037.

Lewis, S. G. (1979). *Sunday's women: A report on lesbian life today*. Boston: Beacon.

Macdonald, B., & Rich, C. (1983). *Look me in the eye: Old women, aging and ageism*. San Francisco: Spinsters, Ink.

McIntosh, M. (1992). The homosexual role. In E. Stein (Ed.), *Forms of desire: Sexual orientation and the social constructionist controversy* (pp. 152-164). New York: Routledge. (Original work published 1968 in *Social Problems, 16*, 182-192)

Minton, H. L., & McDonald, G. J. (1984). Homosexual identity formation as a developmental process. *Journal of Homosexuality, 9*, 91-104.

Mohin, L. (1981). Statement from [an] individual member of the collective. In *Love your enemy? The debate between heterosexual feminism and political lesbianism* (pp. 59-60). London: Onlywomen Press.

Money, J. (1988). *Gay, straight, and in-between: The sexology of erotic orientation*. Oxford, England: Oxford University Press.

Onlywomen Press. (1981). *Love your enemy? The debate between heterosexual feminism and political lesbianism*. London: Author.

Penelope, J. (1993). Heterosexual identity: Out of the closets. In S. Wilkinson and C. Kitzinger (Eds.), *Heterosexuality: A feminism & psychology reader* (pp. 261-265). London: Sage.

Plummer, K. (Ed.). (1981). *The making of the modern homosexual*. London: Hutchinson.

Plummer, K. (Ed.). (1992). *Modern homosexualities: Fragments of lesbian and gay experience*. London: Routledge.

Pollner, M. (1975). The very coinage of your brain: The anatomy of reality disjunctures. *Philosophy of the Social Sciences, 5*, 411-430.

Ponse, B. (1978). *Identities in the lesbian world: The social construction of self*. Westport, CT: Greenwood Press.

Poor, M. (1982). Older lesbians. In M. Cruikshank (Ed.), *Lesbian studies: Present and future* (pp. 57-69). New York: Feminist Press.

Potter, J., & Wetherell, M. (1987). *Discourse and social psychology: Beyond attitudes and behaviour*. London: Sage.

Rich, A. (1979). Foreword. In A. Rich, *On lies, secrets, silence: Selected prose 1966-1978* (pp. 9-18). London: Virago.

Rich, A. (1987). Compulsory heterosexuality and lesbian existence. In A. Rich, *Blood, bread and poetry: Selected prose 1979-1985* (pp. 23-75). London: Virago.

Rossi, A. S. (1980). Life-span theories and women's lives. *Signs, 6*, 4-32.

Saghir, M. T., & Robins, E. (1973). *Male and female homosexuality: A comprehensive investigation*. Baltimore: Williams & Wilkins.

Shively, M. G., Jones, C., & DeCecco, J. P. (1984). Research on sexual orientations: Definitions and methods. *Journal of Homosexuality, 9*, 127-136.

Shotter, J., & Gergen, K. J. (Eds.). (1989). *Texts of identity*. London: Sage.

Simons, H. W. (Ed.). (1989). *Rhetoric in the human sciences*. London: Sage.

Smith, B. (Ed.). (1983). *Home girls: A Black feminist anthology*. New York: Kitchen Table, Women of Color Press.

Socarides, C. W. (1965). Female homosexuality. In R. Slovenko (Ed.), *Sexual behavior and the law* (pp. 172-190). Springfield, IL: Charles C Thomas.

Spencer. (1989). Coming out. In J. Penelope & S. J. Wolfe (Eds.), *The original coming out stories* (pp. 105-119). Freedom, CA: Crossing Press.

Stein, E. (Ed.). (1992). *Forms of desire: Sexual orientation and the social constructionist controversy*. New York: Routledge.

Suppe, F. (1984). In defense of a multidimensional approach to sexual identity. *Journal of Homosexuality, 10*, 7-14.

Thompson, C. A. (1992). Lesbian grief and loss issues in the coming out process. *Women and Therapy, 12*, 175-185.

Troiden, R. R. (1979). Becoming homosexual: A model for gay identity acquisition. *Psychiatry, 42*, 362-373.

Troiden, R. R. (1984). Self, self-concept, identity and homosexual identity: Constructs in need of definition and differentiation. *Journal of Homosexuality, 10*, 97-109.

Vetere, V. A. (1972). The role of friendship in the development and maintenance of lesbian love relationships. *Journal of Homosexuality, 8*, 51-67.

Weeks, J. (1977). *Coming out: Homosexual politics in Britain from the nineteenth century to the present*. London: Quartet Books.

Weinberg, T. S. (1984). Biology, ideology and the reification of developmental stages in the study of homosexual identities. *Journal of Homosexuality, 10*, 77-84.

Wilkinson, S., & Kitzinger, C. (Eds.). (1993). *Heterosexuality: A feminism & psychology reader*. London: Sage.

Wilton, T. (1993). Sisterhood in the service of patriarchy: Heterosexual women's friendships and male power. In S. Wilkinson & C. Kitzinger (Eds.), *Heterosexuality: A feminism & pychology reader* (pp. 273-276). London: Sage.

Factual Questions

1. According to the researchers, what does it mean to say that lesbianism and homosexuality are "essences"?

2. Do the researchers start by assuming that transitions to lesbianism are highly driven by biology?

3. Are the researchers looking for the "real facts" or for the subjects' perceptions and understandings of their experiences?

4. In all, how many lesbians were interviewed by the researchers?

5. What percentage of the participants had been married?

6. At the time of the interviews, had the average participant held a lesbian identity for many years?

7. How long did the average interview last?

8. Which reference should you consult if you want to know more about the discourse analysis procedures used by the researchers?

9. Was the second quotation in paragraph 24 taken from a published source?

10. How many participants acknowledge the role of the women's liberation movement as providing a catalyst for reexamination of feelings of lesbianism?

Questions for Discussion

11. Which sentence in the introduction most clearly indicates the research purpose for this study?

12. Do the criteria for inclusion in this study seem reasonable in light of the researchers' purpose? (See paragraph 15.) Explain.

13. What do you think "friendship pyramiding" is? (See paragraph 16.)

14. What is your opinion on the researchers' decision not to subdivide and analyze by

demographic variables (such as comparing the transitions of working-class participants with those of professional participants)? (See paragraph 18.)

15. Sixty participants were asked somewhat different questions than the other 20. (See paragraphs 20-21). Is this a strength or weakness of the study? Explain.

16. Do you agree that the frequencies reported in the Results section may be gross under-estimates? (See footnote 3.)

17. To what extent do the quotations help you understand the results? Is the number of quotations about right, or would you like to see more or fewer quotations?

18. What is your opinion on the researchers' decision to include quotations from pub-lished autobiographical sources in the Results and Discussion section?

19. Do you agree with the researchers that the results they present do not fit easily into an essentialist framework? (See paragraph 58.)

20. Do you agree that the essentialist–social constructionist debate is not resolvable with reference to empirical fact? (See paragraph 64.)

21. If you were to conduct another study on this topic, would you use a qualitative approach (as was done here) or a quantitative ap-proach? Explain.

Quality Ratings

DIRECTIONS: Indicate your level of agree-ment with each of the following statements by circling a number from 5 for strongly agree (SA) to 1 for strongly disagree (SD). If you believe that an item is not applicable to this research article, leave it blank. Be prepared to explain your ratings.

A. The introduction establishes the importance of the research topic.
   SA   5   4   3   2   1   SD

B. The literature review establishes the context for the study.
   SA   5   4   3   2   1   SD

C. The research purpose, question, or hypothe-sis is clearly stated.
   SA   5   4   3   2   1   SD

D. The method of sampling is sound.
   SA   5   4   3   2   1   SD

E. Relevant demographics (for example, age, gender, and ethnicity) are described.
   SA   5   4   3   2   1   SD

F. Measurement procedures are adequate.
   SA   5   4   3   2   1   SD

G. The results are clearly described.
   SA   5   4   3   2   1   SD

H. The discussion/conclusion is appropriate.
   SA   5   4   3   2   1   SD

I. Despite any flaws noted above, the report is worthy of publication.
   SA   5   4   3   2   1   SD

MOTHERS' EXPECTATIONS FOR THEIR ADOLESCENT CHILDREN: A COMPARISON BETWEEN FAMILIES WITH DISABLED ADOLESCENTS AND THOSE WITH NON-LABELED ADOLESCENTS

Jean P. Lehmann *Colorado State University*
Cliff Baker *University of Northern Colorado*

Current federal mandates regarding the provision of transition services to students with disabilities have heightened the awareness of professionals regarding students' future outcomes. Families are an integral part of the transition planning process. Yet, little is known about parents' expectations for their adolescent children in the areas of future living arrangements, employment/education goals, and social relationships. The researchers also wanted to know if there were differences in the expectations of mothers of adolescents with severe disabilities and mothers of non-labeled adolescents. Forty mothers were interviewed and the data were analyzed using qualitative methodology. Findings show that both groups of mothers had similar expectations for their children, that is, independence. Mothers of adolescents with disabilities, however, did report the need of their children for support in order to achieve independence from their families. Implications and issues related to mothers' responses are discussed.

1. The current federal mandate regarding the provision of transition services to students with disabilities (i.e., Individuals With Disabilities Education Act P.L. 101-476) has heightened the awareness of professionals regarding the future needs of these students (Wehman, 1992). Current philosophy emphasizes that persons with disabilities have a right to obtain jobs and live in their communities like their non-labeled peers (Wehman, 1992). Further, it is generally understood that parents should be an integral part of the team that performs transition planning. The team's articulation of a desirable future for individual students provides a blueprint from which to develop educational curriculum (Rainforth, York, & McDonald, 1992). Early childhood specialists have long understood that the planning process requires an in-depth knowledge of the student and their family system (Dunst, Trivette, & Deal, 1988). Yet, little is known about parents' expectations for their adolescent children. Wehman and his colleagues (1988) report finding a paucity of research regarding parents' expectations for children labeled severely and profoundly disabled. More recently, Johnson and Rusch (1993) found only a few studies exploring families' perceptions about transition-related issues.

2. There is general agreement in the literature that independence is the primary expectation parents have for their children with disabilities (Birenbaum, 1971; Strom, Rees, Slaughter, & Wurster, 1981; Zetlin & Turner, 1985). Furthermore, Abramson and colleagues (1979) argue that all adolescents, those with disabilities and those never labeled, have similar social and emotional needs. These maturation issues, however, may be compromised by the cognitive limitations imposed by the disability (Zetlin & Turner, 1985). Davis, Anderson, Linkowski, Berger, and Feinstein (1985) conclude from their review of several studies that the achievement of some developmental stages is complicated by factors such as poor body image, rejection from peers, and overprotection by parents. Parents may, therefore, be in the awkward position of not knowing what normative expectations they should have for adolescents with disabilities (Zetlin & Turner, 1985).

3. The purpose of this study was to identify the expectations mothers have for their adolescent children in the areas of future living arrangements, employment/education goals, and social relationships. The researchers also wanted to know if mothers whose adolescents have severe disabilities differ in their expectations for their children from mothers of non-labeled adolescents. It was hoped that findings from this study would provide insights into mothers' perceptions regarding their children's futures.

Method

4. A primary qualitative research methodology was employed in this study because this type of research provides a greater understanding of how people see their world and act in it (Bogdan & Taylor, 1975; Miles & Huberman, 1984). The need for using qualitative research designs to study the complex variables surrounding the transition of students with disabilities into adult life situations (Blackorby & Edgar, 1992) and mothers' perspectives regarding childrearing (Attanucci, 1990) has been identified.

Participants

5. Mothers of students labeled by the schools as severely mentally retarded and who were nearing high school completion were identified as the target group. Persons with this label have IQs that measure 50 or less and are reported to need help taking care of themselves independently (Singer & Irvin, 1989). The focus on families of children with severe mental retardation reflected several considerations. First, given the magnitude of the disability, there was little ambiguity about the categorization of subjects into this subgroup. Second, these students were eligible for most community services available to adults with disabilities. It has been noted that many service agencies are overloaded with clients and may have waiting lists for their services. The limitations in the service system may, therefore, be a factor affecting parental expectations for children, as has been postulated by several researchers (e.g., Hill, Seyfarth, Banks, Wehman, & Orelove, 1987). It has also been argued that mothers of children

Lehmann, J. P., & Baker, C. (1995). Mothers' expectations for their adolescent children: A comparison between families with disabled adolescents and those with non-labeled adolescents. *Education and Training in Mental Retardation and Developmental Disabilities, 30,* 27-40. Copyright ©1995 by The Council on Exceptional Children. Reprinted by permission.

Correspondence concerning this manuscript should be addressed to Jean P. Lehmann, School of Education, Colorado State University, Fort Collins, CO 80523.

Received: 25 March 1994. Revision received: 15 September 1994. Initial acceptance: 8 November 1994. Final acceptance: 20 December 1994.

Table 1   *Demographic information*

	Mothers			
	of Non-Labeled Adolescents		of Adolescents with Disabilities	
	N	%	N	%
Marital status				
Married	16	80	16	80
Divorced	4	20	4	20
Education				
Some high school	2	10	0	0
Finished high school	6	30	6	30
Community college	8	40	7	35
Finished college	2	10	6	30
Other (graduate degree)	2	10	1	5
Employment status				
Full time	16	80	5	25
Part time	3	15	10	50
Unemployed	0	0	4	20
Retired	1	5	1	5
Family income*				
Under $10,000	0	0	1	5
$10,000–$19,999	3	15	3	15
$20,000–$29,999	1	5	1	5
$30,000–$39,999	8	40	6	30
$40,000 and over	8	40	8	40
Average age of respondents	41		44	
Range	(37–55)		(35–55)	

*Note. One mother did not disclose income information.

with severe disabilities have childrearing experiences that differ from the norm (Maccoby & Martin, 1983). Hence, their expectations about children's futures may reflect idiosyncratic parenting events. Mothers of non-labeled students nearing high school completion formed a comparison group.

Selection Procedure

6.   A nonprobability sampling method, purposive sampling, was used. The purpose of this sampling procedure is to discover in-depth information about particular individuals (Lincoln & Guba, 1985; McCracken, 1988). The intent of the researchers was to select informants whose differences in expectations for their children could not be easily dismissed as predictable when compared (e.g., college-bound students versus students with severe disabilities). Therefore, forty mothers were selected

whose children had similar profiles except in the area of cognitive functioning.

7.   The group of twenty mothers whose adolescent children had been labeled as severely mentally retarded was identified through a regional parent organization. The director of this organization contacted mothers whose children were between the ages of 16 and 20, involved in school programs designed for persons with severe mental retardation, but had not exhibited behavior problems. If mothers agreed to participate in the study, a time for an interview was scheduled. The comparison group consisted of mothers whose adolescents were similar to those with disabilities except in the area of cognitive functioning. The same procedure was used with this group except that a secondary vocational cooperative education teacher initially contacted potential study participants. The children of the mothers contacted by the

vocational teacher were in a cooperative education program in which they received high school credit for working and attending a job-related course. They had not been identified as requiring special education and were otherwise involved in academic classes. Both groups of adolescents received vocational training as part of the high school curriculum and were Caucasian.

8.   As shown in Table 1, in each group, 16 of the mothers were married and 4 were divorced or separated. The age range was 35 to 55 with a mean of 44.2 for mothers of children with disabilities and 41.2 for the mothers of non-labeled children. Mothers in both groups averaged three children each. Sixteen of the mothers of non-labeled children were employed full-time, compared to only five of the mothers of children with disabilities. Seven mothers of children with disabilities had received higher education degrees and only four mothers of non-labeled children had entered institutions of higher education. Differences in the areas of employment and education suggest that mothers are from different socio-economic statuses.

Data Collection and Analysis

9.   All of the families were interviewed by one of the authors. Each interview was audio tape-recorded and transcripts of the interviews served as the data for analysis. The interviewer also recorded notes in as much detail as possible during the interviews and immediately afterwards. These notes represented an attempt to document any observations, working hypothesis, or descriptions that were found important to the project.

10.   The Interview Guide was designed specifically for this study. The interview questions attempted to capture two types of information about mothers' expectations for their children. First, mothers were asked questions to elicit general information about their childrearing beliefs. These are overarching statements about their values and hopes. Mothers also responded to questions addressing the specific expectations they have for their children at the present time and in the near future. These answers reflected the reality of their children's futures in terms of where the children would be living, with whom they would be socializing, and whether they would be at school or working. The questions were adapted from the McGill Action Planning System (MAPS) (Forest & Lusthaus, 1987, in Vandercook & York, 1990). MAPS is one of several planning strategies that are used to elicit information from families, friends, service providers, and students about successful adult outcomes for persons with disabilities (Rainforth et al., 1992).

11. Data included descriptions of mothers' expectations for different types of children who are achieving adulthood. Data analysis involved assigning mothers' responses to preconceived categories, such as work, social relationships, and living arrangements. Frequencies of answers to inquiries and standardized probes were tabulated so that comparisons between participant groups could be made. Reliability was estimated by comparing categories generated from the data by one of the researchers to those of an independent researcher using a procedure described by Zetlin and Turner (1985) to establish the importance and accuracy of category designations. The reliability (percentage agreement with the researcher's codings) was 85.6 percent across ten percent of the transcribed material.

Results

12. Results for this study are reported in mothers' own words. Their responses to a series of questions about their perceptions regarding their children's future outcomes are presented in this section.

Living Arrangements

13. As shown in Table 2, both groups had relatively similar expectations regarding their adolescents' future living arrangements. The majority of mothers of the non-labeled children expected their children to remain at home after they graduated from high school or to move to an apartment not far from home. Hence, many responses were similar to this mother's: "Sam may stay at home for awhile, but I would expect Sam and his buddies to get a place somewhere in town soon after they graduate." Many of these mothers were unsure about with whom their child might potentially live and a type of residence in which their child might reside.

14. Similarly, mothers of adolescents with disabilities expected their children to leave home when they completed high school. There was general consensus that the children should live near parents so that the families might remain in regular contact. These mothers were more precise in their descriptions of the living arrangement they envisioned for their child. A major concern expressed about the children leaving home was the possibility of a child becoming socially isolated if no support was provided or if the child did not live close enough to family members. One mother explained:

I would like to see her live fairly close so that she can come over and visit when she wants to or if she needed help. She's going to have to have some support, I know that. There are lots of apartments close by that I think she can handle . . . and I would like to see her close enough so that we always have the constant, not constant, but we will always be there if she needs us. And

Table 2 *Living arrangements*

Non-Labeled Adolescents			Adolescents with Disabilities	
Frequency	%	*Location*	Frequency	%
6	30	at home	7	35
7	35	in the vicinity	11	55
5	25	in-state	1	5
2	10	out-of-state	1	5
		Roommate		
5	25	friend	6	30
4	20	alone	4	20
2	10	spouse	3	15
9	45	unsure	7	35
		Type of Residence		
12	60	apartment	7	35
2	10	house	2	10
		dorm	1	5
		trailer	1	5
		duplex	1	5
6	30	unsure	8	40

both Tim and I agree that that's something we will always do. We will be here. But, on the other hand, if we want to go away for a month, we'll know there are other people that can be called upon to give her the support she needs.

Employment/Education

15. Mothers were asked about their employment and educational expectations for their children. Mothers of non-labeled youth perceived their children as participating in one of three different environments upon high school graduation, the community college, employment, or the military (see Table 3). These mothers expressed hopes that their children would eventually enter into four-year university programs. The specific details of their children's futures, however, remained elusive to them. These mothers could not really predict in what career their children would eventually become involved.

16. A typical statement was, "I hope he is successful at anything he tries, not in terms of richness, but enough to be happy with himself." Mothers appeared to be expecting their children to make future decisions with little parental guidance. Mothers seemed more concerned that their children have an opportunity to achieve their personal dreams. For example, according to one respondent:

I would like her to go, not necessarily to college, if that is what she wants, fine, but into vocational school, some sort of vocation where she

can make a comfortable living, be secure, and take care of herself. But she has got to want to do it; we can't force it. We have to leave it up to her. We can't ride her all of the time. We tried that. It didn't work.

17. Mothers of adolescents labeled as severely mentally disabled described their children as immediately entering the workforce after they completed high school. As shown in Table 3, one-half of the mothers expected their children to enter in full-time employment, and the other half did not think their children could manage more than a part-time job. No mothers envisioned their child working less than 20 hours. Employment opportunities were described as requiring some type of support for their children. Generally, this group of mothers articulated more precisely the types of jobs their children might enter than the mothers of non-labeled youth. These mothers were aware of the type of jobs their children had experienced through school and summer programs and were evaluating work experiences in light of their children's perceived success. In the words of one mother:

What jobs do I see for her? Social jobs, I mean where there is interaction. To isolate her, she gets real unhappy. She likes the people orientation. With the different jobs she's done, the one that I've seen she liked the most was the one at a fabric store this year, and she liked that a lot. She worked at a department store and loved that.

Table 3 *School/work expectations*

Non-Labeled Adolescents*		Adolescents with Disabilities
Frequency	*Type*	Frequency
10	community college	1
4	military	
6	full-time work	10
6	part-time work	9

Note. Some mothers of non-labeled adolescents indicated the participation of their children in two settings. Generally, this was both community college and part-time work.

She's real people oriented. She was talking and able to interact.

18. Major issues expressed were that children be integrated into settings where other non-labeled persons were working and that the jobs offer opportunities for socialization. The desire for integrated employment settings was often justified in terms of children's abilities and personalities. For example, one mother expressed frustration about the types of jobs frequently offered to students with disabilities:

> I'm really against the idea that they put all special kids in either a janitorial job or a fast food restaurant. I think Lonny is capable of much better than that, and I want him to work for someone, a company that's large enough so that Lonny has benefits, and he has those kind of things. And he will have an opportunity to make more than minimum wage. He has job security. To begin with, he will need a job coach to learn his job, most likely.

Another mother felt her daughter should mingle with customers:

> Nat is not going to be happy making beds in a hotel, or she's not going to be happy stuck in a backroom doing dishes, but other than that, I think she can handle most anything. I can see Nat in an office working. She enjoys dressing up occasionally, and she'd be great at delivering papers or messages or refiling of papers and things like that. I think she would do fine in even like a fast food place if she could be kind of a greeter, clean off tables, whatever where she'd be around people. She likes animals; she worked at the Humane Society. She liked that, but it's so often it's stuck in the backroom cleaning cages, and I don't think she'd like that. She needs more contact with people.

19. Mothers who thought their children would only be working part-time gave two types of reasons for this choice. Some mothers thought their children would not be able to work more than that because of their attention span or due to physical limitations. For example, one mother stated that she expected her daughter to work part-time because "she has very tiny hands so doing a lot of physical chores is

always difficult. She tires fast." Mothers also mentioned that employers might not realistically hire their children for more than part-time work.

Social Relationships

20. Mothers of non-labeled adolescents responded to questions regarding their children's friends after high school graduation in terms of their children's current social situation or in terms of what they perceived as being usual for most people becoming adults. Table 4 lists the settings in which their children's current friendships developed.

21. Most friendships for these adolescents were made in the school system. Some of the adolescents had developed friendships at their jobs, and a few had friends from church. Only two mothers described their children as having many friends. More commonly mothers would respond as this mother did:

> He doesn't have that many friends, a few — maybe one or two good ones. But, it's hard for kids to fit in. So, it's kind of like you have the eggheads and you have your low ones. Kids are categorized too much these days.

22. The refrain that their children had had difficulty initiating and maintaining friendships in high school was repeated often as these mothers' expressed concerns illustrate:

> She got a little bit burnt out on them. She went through the prom scene with this group of kids and stuff, and then she had this argument. It was really terrible when she didn't make it on one of the [cheerleading] squads. Her best friend dropped her that same night. I was hoping she would get more involved in maybe something to meet people, but she just hasn't got a comfort level with enough people to get into something like that. 'Cause like photography, she really likes that, and the school has a photography course, but it is with the wrong kids. It's the nerdies, and if she wouldn't get labeled that, if people could see she had a real interest in it.

23. Once again these mothers seemed somewhat detached about their children. Many of them did not know with whom their children

were socializing. They also were not in contact with the parents of their children's friends. Mothers often joked about how they perceived their children treated them around high school friends. For example, one said:

> He's started to bring more friends around the house. Apparently, he's decided we're not as bad as we used to be because he brings them around more often. Maybe he thinks we've gotten smarter (laughs). He used to just slip them in the door—no real introductions, just take them right downstairs to his room.

24. Mothers spoke in positive terms about the friendships their children would enter into in the future. Mothers seemed to expect that their children's friendships would change once their children left high school and that this was "typical" for most adults. Mothers did not express any fears around the future of their children in terms of having friends. Mothers expected their children to find new friends. As one said, "Some friends I don't like, but I also know that she's growing up and going to have many types of friends."

25. Furthermore, none of these mothers worried about the prospect of no friends or "bad" friends. Similar to the mother quoted above, these mothers generally thought their children had outgrown this socialization phase in their lives. According to one mother, "I didn't care for her group of friends, but she has grown up and matured, and she chooses her friends a little differently now." All of the mothers in this group of participants thought their children would get married eventually.

26. The responses of mothers of adolescents with severe disabilities were much more complex. This topic was of great importance to the mothers as evidenced by the amount of time they spent reflecting on their children's friendships. The fear that their children might experience loneliness or be taken advantage of was mentioned by *every* mother. Central issues addressed during the interviews by mothers included the desire for their children to have friendships with non-labeled persons as well as with persons with disabilities.

27. As shown in Table 4, the source of these adolescents' friendships was varied. Most of the friendships had been developed from high school; friends had also been made from recreational activities or from the neighborhood:

> The two boys up here [in the neighborhood] are just good guys. Rich calls them a hundred times and wears them down and finally they'll stop and take him to pizza or something . . . Rich idolizes these boys. These boys are number one.

28. Twelve mothers indicated that their children's best friends were immediate or extended

Table 4 *Relationships*

Non-Labeled Adolescents		Adolescents with Disabilities
Frequency*	*Source of Current Friendships*	Frequency
20	school	20
	family	12
3	work	3
	recreation	3
	neighborhood	3
2	church	2
	paid professionals	2

Note. Mothers indicated more than one source of friendship.

family members. For example, according to one mother:

> My whole family lives here. I have sisters, and their families all live around here. My husband's family is the same way, and so Tom's very involved with the family a lot. And they have been so supportive, but I would like to see people outside of the family be his friends.

Another parent remarked that her sons remained close companions:

> John and Brent (brothers) were each other's playmate for many, many years, which is excellent for Brent because John was Brent's playmate when no one else would be. They are still close friends.

29. Other sources of friendships include church and work settings. In a few cases, friends seemed to result from more professional contacts. For instance, persons paid to work with their children in the capacity of job coaches or classroom aides sometimes became friends with the adolescent.

30. Several mothers specifically addressed the need for their children to have "normal" friends. Most of these mothers described the benefits of their children associating with people who were not acting or behaving in a strange manner. One mother related:

> He does not need to be overloaded with lots of friends, but if he could have one friend to do a few things with, that would be great. He needs a role model so he doesn't act retarded.

31. The need for children to have a variety of friends was also discussed. But some mothers indicated concerns about the fact that some friends were "social outcasts." Mothers were afraid these friends would take advantage of their children.

32. In terms of future friendships, most mothers indicated that they expected their children to remain in close contact with the friends made in high school. The reasons given for the lasting

friendships include the fact that these children were probably not moving far from home and that they would be participating in the same adult services as their high school peers. Another reason given was that no one else would be their friend as expressed by this mother:

> I think she'll stay with her same peer group from high school. Normal people, you know what I am saying by "normal," they are friendly to a handicapped person, but not so friendly necessarily that they would come up and say, "let's go to a movie" or whatever. It's not that they don't like them; it's just because of the difference. They don't fit into the crowd, so a lot of kids tend to stick around the same friends.

33. The topic of romantic relationships, marriage, and children brought tears to several mothers' eyes. Only two of the children were described as currently having boyfriends or girlfriends. Three mothers did mention that their children were interested in the opposite sex. Most mothers, however, did not expect their children to be involved in serious relationships for several years. A common refrain was that mothers did not think their children were ready yet. Many of the adolescents had attended dances and even gone to the prom but were not currently dating. The lack of dating was sometimes blamed on the attitudes of the opposite sex. This concern was most evident in the discussions about young women. One mother of an attractive adolescent daughter explained:

> Sexual pressure has really been much more prominent in high school. It's the way that guys look at the girls in special ed. They look at them differently than they do the "nice girls." If you're in special ed. you're not just a person; you're easy, and then they treat you as such. Nat doesn't date yet. It's not a comfort level that we have yet — someone that she's comfortable with, that I'm comfortable with, whose values are similar.

34. Mothers hoped their children would get married but were not sure this would be a

reality. Generally, mothers did not want their children to have children because they did not think their children could raise children themselves or because their child's disability was medically associated with fertility problems.

> I pray to God she never has children, but I can see her having a relationship and, at some point, maybe even being married because she is a sexual person, and I don't want to stifle that.

Discussion

35. The results show that mothers' expectations, whether their child is labeled as having a severe disability or not, are similar. Both groups of mothers expressed hope that their children would achieve independence from the family. Independence was defined differently by the two groups. Mothers of non-labeled youth may have already indicated the independence of their children by being less able to articulate the specifics of their children's futures, whereas mothers of adolescents with disabilities described a future that included support services. The authors realize that the two groups of mothers were from different socioeconomic statuses (SES), which could affect their expectations, rendering comparisons between their responses invalid. However, the purpose of the study was to compare expectations for adolescents enrolled in similar educational programs (i.e., vocational programming). Further, some insights into mothers' aspirations for their children with disabilities were gleaned and issues identified by attempting such a comparison. Importantly, one might assume that socioeconomic status is a major determinant in the formation of expectations. But, when examined in the context of this study, mothers were found to have similar expectations regardless of their socio-economic status.

Living Arrangements

36. Mothers' expectations contradicted some of the adolescent development research that portrays children as leaving home immediately after high school (Greene & Boxer, 1986). Many mothers of non-labeled youth expected that their children would remain at home following high school completion. They anticipated that their children would move away from home once the child was earning enough money to do so. These mothers did not expect their children to move far from the family's home. The delay in achieving independence is considered to be commonplace and to result almost entirely from economic factors (Vobejda, 1991).

37. Conversely, mothers of adolescents with disabilities expected their children to leave home as soon as possible following their

completion of high school. This finding may indicate mothers' fatigue resulting from the increased demands of raising a child with disabilities. The type of residence most of these mothers described included support from paid professionals for their children. They did not perceive that their children would be able to live without some form of assistance. This assistance was described to involve budgeting, cleaning, transportation needs, and perhaps, most importantly, support with identifying social and recreational opportunities. The responses of mothers of youth with disabilities confirm the results of the National Longitudinal Transition Study by Wagner and her colleagues (1991), who found that families of youth with disabilities expected their children to live away from home. However, the majority of the out-of-school youth with disabilities in their sample and in other research studies were still living with a parent or guardian in the first two years after high school (Tilson & Neubert, 1988; Wagner et al., 1991). Families may need to be forewarned that the possibility of their child leaving home immediately upon high school completion is limited and not even the norm for general populations (Vobejda, 1991). Community support services have long waiting lists (Davis, 1987). Families may therefore want to consider designing residential options outside of the service delivery system.

Employment/Education

38. Interestingly, both groups of adolescents seemed to be participating in similar types of jobs as part of their school programs. The jobs were described as entry-level, low-paying, menial jobs. According to Greenberger, Steinberg, and Ruggiero (1982), these are common descriptors for the jobs adolescents typically obtain. Perhaps because these jobs were viewed as being repetitive and as providing little possibility for career advancement, mothers of non-labeled adolescents did not expect their children to remain in these jobs for long. For the most part, the goal of the job was to acquire financial support and not to benefit their children's learning or future career opportunities. In fact, they hoped that their children would seek additional education in order to obtain better employment later. The employment situations appeared to have little or no relationship to the career aspirations mothers expressed for the future of their children except in the case of one adolescent who was working for a company that she planned to continue with in the future.

39. Generally, mothers of non-labeled children anticipated that their sons and daughters would continue in school, usually community college, and then pursue an education at a four-year college. Their expectations for their children's careers remained vague although some of these children were currently enrolled in community college programs. The lack of direction in career planning for people completing high school has also been documented by Rothstein (1980), who reported that most students during their first two years of college could not predict their later careers. Therefore, it is not unusual that these mothers were not able to clarify exactly what profession they anticipated their children entering. Their children had not yet made these decisions themselves.

40. The employment opportunities adolescents with disabilities had had in high school seemed to affect the perceptions of their mothers deeply. The jobs these adolescents had had were discussed as possibilities for future employment or analyzed in terms of components that were not satisfactory. Mothers' interest in their children's work experiences is reasonable given research findings. According to several studies, the participation of students with disabilities in employment situations during high school predicted post high school salaries and the number of hours they are hired to work (Cook, Roussel, & Skiba, 1987; Hasazi, Gordon, & Roe, 1985; Wagner, 1989). Unlike their non-labeled counterparts, employment also decreased their social isolation (Hasazi et al., 1985; Wagner et al., 1991).

41. Most mothers of youth with severe disabilities envisioned that their children would work full- or part-time and that this job status would not change over time. The types of jobs they considered for their children fit the definition of supported employment. Mothers described the need for some assistance on the job for their children in order for them to remain successfully employed. Only a few mothers mentioned sheltered employment as a potential job setting for their children. These mothers seemed to consider this type of segregated setting only grudgingly in the face of perceived limited options for the future of their children. This finding is in contrast to the study conducted by Hill et al. (1987), who found that parents felt workshop settings satisfied their children's vocational needs. The results of the current study may reflect the fact that supported work is becoming more common and is therefore an expected service for their children (cf. Tilson & Neubert, 1988). Many special education school programs and sheltered workshops have expanded their employment efforts to include mainstreaming adolescents with disabilities and adults into competitive employment settings with the support of paid assistants.

Social Relationships

42. Differences between the two groups of mothers were more pronounced in the area of social relationships. The majority of the friends with whom non-labeled adolescents interacted were from school. This finding is consistent with the Coleman Report that shows adolescent students regard the school as a primary social environment (Coleman, 1965). However, most mothers of non-labeled youth also reported their children were not involved in extracurricular activities. Further, mothers expressed concern that their children did not have many friends. Mothers perceived these worries to be temporary because they anticipated their children would identify more friends in the settings in which they engaged following high school.

43. The lack of social relationships and participation in extracurricular activities for these students may result from several factors. Mothers perceived their children's limited social achievements to be a product of the high school's tolerance for cliques of students that did not welcome all students, particularly their children. There is another possibility for this finding. According to a study by Steinberg, Greenberger, Garduque, Ruggiero, and Vaux (1982), students who are employed during high school are less involved with their schools, their families, and their peers. The demands of the workplace may limit students' opportunities to socialize (Steinberg et al., 1982). The adolescents with severe disabilities appeared to have a wider range of persons with whom they interacted, and they seemed to have a greater variety of friends than their counterparts. Mothers of youth with disabilities reported that their children participated in many more extracurricular and recreational activities than did mothers of non-labeled youth. These adolescents' exposures to a variety of social experiences may reflect the involvement of their mothers in arranging and promoting these events. The parental role of "social director" has been noted to be a key responsibility of parents during their children's adolescence (Turnbull, Summers, & Brotherson, 1986).

44. Paradoxically, although the adolescents were found to have a larger social network at the time of the study, their mothers described a bleak future in terms of their children's social relationships. Mothers may have dwelled on their anxieties about their children's social relationships for several reasons. For instance, mothers expressed concerns about the possibility that their children's rejection by "normal" peers would lead to placement of their children into segregated settings and create subsequent isolation. Therefore, mothers were actively seeking situations that facilitated the interaction of their children with many different individuals. Additionally, mothers were not satisfied with their children's current levels of social commitment because they perceived the interactions with non-labeled individuals as being superficial. They mentioned that their children would not, and perhaps could not, initiate friendships outside of the immediate family circle without assistance. The potential for loneliness in the future was mothers' greatest fear for their children. Unfortunately, according to a recent study conducted in Colorado, many adults with developmental disabilities do perceive themselves to be lonely (Colorado Division for Developmental Disabilities, 1993).

45.   The area of social relationships and friendships is recognized as being important to the success and well-being of students with disabilities (Rusch, Rusch, & O'Reilly, 1993; Wagner, 1989). According to Stainback and Stainback (1990), support networks between students with disabilities and their non-labeled peers must be encouraged if all students are going to be educated in the mainstream. Moreover, it is argued that integration into regular school programs increases the likelihood that students with disabilities will be socially accepted within the school (Wagner et al., 1991) and later on by the community, particularly employers (Brown et al., 1989). This study speaks to the need for increased efforts to build relationships between labeled and non-labeled individuals if mothers' concerns are to be addressed.

Summary

46.   Overall, both groups of mothers' expectations were typical of the normative stages presented in the literature (see Greene & Boxer, 1986). All mothers wanted a promising future for their children which involved leaving the family home, finding suitable employment, and having friends. Contrasts between the two sets of mothers were noted in the timeliness at which mothers expected their children to move away from home and designate their future careers. Mothers of non-labeled youth anticipated their children's leaving home and making career choices at a later time than the mothers of disabled adolescents. The later timetable may reflect financial considerations as well as their children's need to further explore the world of work. It may also indicate the desire of mothers of youth with disabilities to obtain respite from their intense caregiving activities.

47.   The domain of social relationships was of concern to all of the mothers interviewed, although for different reasons and to varying degrees. For example, mothers of non-labeled youth were generally not pleased with their

children's current social lives, though they predicted a much brighter future. Conversely, mothers of youth with disabilities were more concerned about the future than the present. Mothers of adolescents with disabilities seem to want their children to have access to typical living, work, and social situations. Service delivery models such as sheltered employment or group homes were rarely mentioned. Opportunities such as college were also not broached. The niche these mothers found for their expectations seems to resemble outcomes for persons from lower socio-economic backgrounds. This desire was best voiced by a mother who had just attended her own high school class reunion:

I attended my class reunion this year and was surprised. There was the valedictorian, with all those others sitting there that you thought would be really successful and doing really fantastic things. That's what the image is . . . you picture in your mind success, success, success, and yet 20 years later, well, it's really 23 years later, sitting there with this group of girls the other day and looking at their lives and looking at my life. I was kind of dreading going. I'm the only one with a special needs child and thinking, "Oh, Lord, what will they think?" And they all said, "Bring pictures of your children. Tell us what your children have been doing." And, I think, "God, mine is going to be so different." And yet getting there and talking with them, and finding out that the valedictorian didn't get married until five years ago. And she has had all kinds of odd jobs but nothing real substantial, and now her main thing is cooking for her husband and making a home for her husband. And she cleans her mother's house once a week for some spending money. It was just a total shock to me. And some of the gals, one went into the army, another one is a school teacher — it's just like that — the things that you would think they would do would be setting the world on fire; you know, the doctors, lawyers, the research people, the engineers. There wasn't one in the group, and these were the most popular girls in the high school — and then hearing about their children and some of them have gone on to college. Yeah, there's a couple that had kids and who are going to college. Others in high school have been somewhat successful. Gee, when I was explaining about Brent, you know, the 4-H projects that he has, working full-time in the summer on the farm. One of the girls finally turned to me about halfway through the afternoon. She said, "Liza, I thought he was handicapped." I said, "Well, he is, at least that's what he is labeled." And she just kind of laughed, and that really took me back. And I really had to stop myself and think, "Gee!" because he was doing the normal things that other people's kids were doing also — in a different way, but he is. It kind of woke me up again. It really kind of boosted me, you know. I was dreading going; and when I left that morning, I told my husband that I didn't want to go. I said, "I'll tell them I need to leave at 4:00 this

afternoon. I've got to get home, I've got another meeting or something." I found myself staying there until 6:30.

48.   The information procured in this study sheds light on mothers' perspectives. Previous research has given little attention to the perceptions of parents regarding their children's futures. This perspective may be essential in determining successful outcomes for individuals graduating from high school. Moreover, intelligent decisions regarding the provision and design of services can be made if mothers' expectations are better known and if the potential impact of these services on families is understood. This study, like many of those cited in the literature (cf. Kohler, Johnson, Rusch, & Rusch, 1993), presumes the ability of families to support their children in attaining suitable futures. Serious questions remain about the future of children whose families are not able to guide them.

References

Abramson, M., Ash, M. J., & Nash, W. R. (1979). Handicapped adolescents: A time for reflection. *Adolescence, 14,* 557-565.

Attanucci, J. (1990). Motherhood as experience and institution reconsidered: A review of Birn's and Hay's *The different faces of motherhood. Merrill-Palmer Quarterly, 36,* 425-429.

Birenbaum, A. B. (1971). The mentally retarded child in the home and the family cycle. *Journal of Health and Social Behavior, 21,* 55-65.

Blackorby, J., & Edgar, E. (1992). Longitudinal studies in the postschool-adjustment of students with disabilities. In F. R. Rusch, L. DeStefano, J. Chadsey-Rusch, L. A. Phelps, & E. Szymanski (Eds.). *Transition from school to work among persons with disabilities.* Sycamore, IL: Sycamore.

Bogdan, R., & Taylor, S. J. (1975). *Introduction to qualitative research methods: A phenomenological approach to the social sciences.* New York: John Wiley and Sons.

Brown, L., Long, E., Udavari-Solner, A., Davis, L., VanDeventer, P., Ahlgren, C., Johnson, F., Gruenewald, L., & Jorgensen, J. (1989). The home school: Why students with severe intellectual disabilities must attend the school of their brothers, sisters, friends, and neighbors. *The Journal of the Association for the Severely Handicapped, 14*(1), 1-7.

Coleman, J. S. (1965). *The adolescent and the schools.* New York: Basic Books.

Colorado Division for Developmental Disabilities. (1993, Fall). *Director's report.* Denver, CO: Author.

Cook, J. A., Roussel, A. E., & Skiba, P. J. (1987, April). *Transition into employment: Correlates of vocational achievement among severely mentally ill youth.* Paper presented at the Midwest Sociological Society Annual Meeting, Chicago.

Davis, S. (1987). *A national status report on waiting lists of people with mental retardation for community services.* Arlington, TX: Association for Retarded Citizens of the United States.

Davis, S. E., Anderson, C., Linkowski, D. C., Berger, K., & Feinstein, C. F. (1985). Developmental tasks and transitions of adolescents with chronic illnesses and disabilities. *Rehabilitation Counseling Bulletin, 29,* 69-80.

Dunst, C., Trivette, C., & Deal, A. (1988). *Enabling and empowering families: Principles and guidelines for practice.* Cambridge, MA: Brookline Books.

Forest, M., & Lusthaus, E. (1987). The kaleidoscope: Challenge to the cascade. In M. Forest (Ed.), *More education/integration,* (pp. 1-16). Downsview, Ontario: G. Allan Roeher Institute.

Greenberger, E., Steinberg, L., & Ruggiero, M. (1982). A job is a job is a job . . . or is it? *Work and Occupations, 9,* 79-96.

Greene, A. L., & Boxer, A. M. (1986). Daughters and sons as young adults: Reconstructing ties that bind. In N. Datan, A. L. Greene, & H. W. Reese (Eds.), *Life-span developmental psychology: Intergenerational relations* (pp. 125-150). Hillsdale, NJ: Lawrence Erlbaum Associates.

Hasazi, S. B., Gordon, L. R., & Roe, C. A. (1985). Factors associated with the employment status of handicapped youth exiting from high school from 1979 to 1983. *Exceptional Children, 54,* 9-23.

Hill, J. W., Seyfarth, J., Banks, P. D., Wehman, P., & Orelove, F. (1987). Parental attitudes about working conditions of their adult mentally retarded sons and daughters. *Exceptional Children, 54,* 9-23.

Johnson, J. R., & Rusch, F. R. (1993). Educational reform and special education: Foundations for a national research agenda focused upon secondary education. In P. D. Kohler, J. R. Johnson, J. Chadsey-Rusch, & F. R. Rusch (Eds.), *Transition from school to adult life: Foundations, best practices, and research directions,* (pp. 77-104). Transition Research Institute at Illinois, University of Illinois at Urbana-Champaign.

Kohler, P. D., Johnson, J. R., Chadsey-Rusch, J., Rusch, F. R. (1993). *Transition from school to adult life: Foundations, best practices, and research directions.* Transition Research Institute at Illinois, University of Illinois at Urbana-Champaign.

Lincoln, Y. S., & Guba, E. G. (1985). *Naturalistic inquiry.* Newbury Park, CA: Sage Publications.

Maccoby, E. E., & Martin, J. P. (1983). Socialization in the context of family: Parent-child interaction. In E. M. Hetherton (Ed.), P. H. Musen (Series Ed.), *Handbook of child psychology: Vol. 4, Socialization, personality, and social development* (pp. 1-101). New York: Wiley.

McCracken, G. (1988). *The long interview.* Newbury Park, CA: Sage Publications.

Miles, M. B., & Huberman, A. M. (1984). *Qualitative data analysis: A sourcebook for new methods.* Beverly Hills, CA: Sage Publications.

Rainforth, B., York, J., & McDonald, C. (1992). *Collaborative teams for students with disabilities.* Baltimore: Paul H. Brookes.

Rothstein, W. G. (1980). The significance of occupations in work careers: An empirical and theoretical review. *Journal of Vocational Behavior, 17,* 328-343.

Rusch, J., Rusch, F. R., & O'Reilly, M. F. (1993). Transition from school to integrated communities. In P. D. Kohler, J. R. Johnson, J. Chadsey-Rusch, & F. R. Rusch (Eds.), *Transition from school to adult life: Foundations, best practices, and research directions,* (pp. 1-30). Transition Research Institute at Illinois, University of Illinois at Urbana-Champaign.

Singer, G. H., & Irvin, L. K. (1989). Family caregiving, stress, and support. In G. H. Singer & L. K. Irvin (Eds.), *Support for caregiving families,* (pp. 3-25). Baltimore: Paul H. Brookes.

Stainback, W., & Stainback, S. (1990). *Support networks for inclusive schooling.* Baltimore: Paul H. Brookes.

Steinberg, L. D., Greenberger, E., Garduque, L., Ruggiero, M., & Vaux, A. (1982). Effects of working on adolescent development. *Developmental Psychology, 18,* 385-395.

Strom, R., Rees, R., Slaughter, H., & Wurster, S. (1981). Child-rearing expectations of families with atypical children. *American Journal of Orthopsychiatry, 51,* 285-296.

Tilson, Jr., G. P., & Neubert, D. A. (1988). School-to-work transition of mildly disabled young adults. *Journal for Vocational Special Needs Education, 11*(1), 33-37.

Turnbull, A. P., Summers, J. A., & Brotherson, M. J. (1986). Family life cycle. In J. J. Gallagher & P.M. Vietze (Eds.), *Families of handicapped persons,* (pp. 45-65). Baltimore: Paul H. Brookes.

Vandercook, T., & York, J. (1990). A team approach to program development and support. In W. Stainback & S. Stainback (Eds.), *Support networks for inclusive schooling,* (pp. 95-122). Baltimore: Paul H. Brookes.

Vobejda, B. (1991, September). Declarations of dependence: It's taking longer to become an adult. *The Washington Post National Weekly Edition,* p. 9.

Wagner, M. (1989). *Youth with disabilities during transition: An overview of descriptive findings from the National Longitudinal Transition Study.* Stanford, CA: SRI International.

Wagner, M., Newman, L., D'Amico, R., Jay, E. D., Butler-Nalin, P., Marder, C., & Cox, R. (1991, February). *Youth with disabilities: How are they doing?* (Contract No. 300-87-00540). Washington, D. C.: The Office of Special Education Programs, U.S. Department of Education.

Wehman, P. (1992). *Life beyond the classroom: Transition strategies for young people with disabilities.* Baltimore: Paul H. Brookes.

Wehman, P., Moon, M. S., Everson, J., Wood, W., & Barcus, J. M. (1988). *Transition from school to work.* Baltimore: Paul H. Brookes.

Zetlin, A. G., & Turner, J. L. (1985). Transition from adolescence to adulthood: Perspectives of mentally retarded individuals and their families. *American Journal of Mental Deficiency, 89,* 570-579.

Factual Questions

1. In which paragraph is the purpose of the study first stated?

2. What reasons did the researchers give for using a qualitative approach?

3. What method of sampling was used?

4. Why did the researchers *not* use mothers of college-bound students as the comparison group?

5. How were the mothers of labeled adolescents identified?

6. What was the age of the youngest mother of a non-labeled adolescent?

7. Why were notes taken during the interview?

8. How was reliability estimated?

9. How many more mothers of non-labeled adolescents than mothers of adolescents with disabilities expected their children to go to community college?

Questions for Discussion

10. Does the sample size seem adequate for a qualitative study?

11. Are the mothers of non-labeled adolescents and the mothers of adolescents with disabilities reasonably similar in terms of demographics (i.e., background characteristics)? Explain.

12. Are there advantages and disadvantages to tape-recording research interviews, as was done in this study?

13. To what extent do the quotations in the Results section help you understand the results?

14. Based on Table 4, are the two groups reasonably similar in their sources of current friends? Explain.

15. Do you agree with the authors' view on the possible effects of the difference in socio-economic status between the two groups of mothers? (See paragraph 35.)

16. If you were to conduct another qualitative study on the same topic, what changes, if any, would you make in the research methodology?

17. In your opinion, have the authors achieved their research purpose, which is stated in paragraph 3?

18. In your opinion, would it be of value to also conduct a quantitative study on this topic? Explain.

Quality Ratings

DIRECTIONS: Indicate your level of agreement with each of the following statements by circling a number from 5 for strongly agree (SA) to 1 for strongly disagree (SD). If you believe that an item is not applicable to this research article, leave it blank. Be prepared to explain your ratings.

A. The introduction establishes the importance of the research topic.
   SA   5   4   3   2   1   SD

B. The literature review establishes the context for the study.
   SA   5   4   3   2   1   SD

C. The research purpose, question, or hypothesis is clearly stated.
   SA   5   4   3   2   1   SD

D. The method of sampling is sound.
   SA   5   4   3   2   1   SD

E. Relevant demographics (for example, age, gender, and ethnicity) are described.
   SA   5   4   3   2   1   SD

F. Measurement procedures are adequate.
   SA   5   4   3   2   1   SD

G. The results are clearly described.
   SA   5   4   3   2   1   SD

H. The discussion/conclusion is appropriate.
   SA   5   4   3   2   1   SD

I. Despite any flaws noted above, the report is worthy of publication.
   SA   5   4   3   2   1   SD

ARTICLE 6

PARENTS' THINKING ABOUT STANDARDIZED TESTS AND PERFORMANCE ASSESSMENTS

Lorrie A. Shepard

Carribeth L. Bliem

examples & its importance

FC

1. In Palo Alto recently, a group of high-tech parents organized to oppose the new "fuzzy math" curriculum introduced by the California Mathematics Framework. The group wants to restore the teaching of "math basics" and computational skills instead of what one parent called "no-correct-answer math." In Littleton, Colorado, new school board members elected on a "back-to-basics" antireform platform promised to eliminate performance-based high-school proficiency requirements. Opposition to the newly instituted reform reflected a variety of concerns: too much emphasis on self-esteem, too little attention to skills in whole-language instruction, fear that students would be ill prepared for the SAT, and one board member's worry that school-developed performance assessments lacked sufficient reliability and validity evidence to make high-stakes graduation decisions.

2. Instances such as these are part of a backlash against standards-based reform and new forms of assessment that have arisen nationally, in most cases before reform efforts have gotten off the ground. On the surface, the controversy seems perplexing. Who could be against the rhetoric of the reform — setting high academic standards for all students, developing challenging assessments to reflect the standards, creating the conditions necessary to ensure student learning? Indeed, each side in this many-sided debate claims to be working to ensure academic excellence.

3. The effort to set standards raises fundamental questions, however, about what students should know, about the nature of subject matter, how best to support learning, and how to measure what has been learned. Most reformers envision a curriculum that fosters thinking and depth of understanding, where the "big ideas" in a discipline are emphasized and skills are learned and applied in authentic contexts. Nonetheless, some standards efforts have produced exhaustive lists of content that could not possibly be taught within the constraints of a normal school year. Some business leaders see the need to broaden school curricula to develop students' communication skills, their abilities to

work in groups, to use technology, and so forth. In contrast, many parents and other citizen groups see teaching practices that diverge from their own school experiences as an abandonment of academic rigor. Their fears are sometimes exacerbated by poorly implemented versions of reform. Some groups see the emphasis on thinking per se to be a threat to authority and to a basic-skills definition of achievement. These themes are familiar, but how the lines of dispute are drawn may vary from one community to the next.

Interest in Parents' Thinking About Assessment

study begins

4. Three years ago, a team of researchers from the University of Colorado at Boulder began working with third-grade teachers in three schools to develop classroom-based performance assessments in reading and mathematics. From the beginning of the project, we were interested — along with district leaders — in parents' views about performance assessments, particularly in contrast to their views regarding more familiar standardized tests. Our concern about parent acceptance and support of new forms of assessment had both classroom- and district-level implications. At the classroom level, we had often heard teachers refer to parents' expectations as the justification for classroom-assessment practices. For example, teachers might give timed tests on math facts because "parents expect it" or might use chapter pre- and posttests to be able "to defend" grades to parents. Therefore, teachers' willingness to try new forms of assessment in their classrooms could very likely be influenced by anticipated and real parent reactions. At the district level, curriculum specialists were developing their own performance assessments to be used along with standardized tests. Although there was not the same dissension that arose the next year in neighboring Littleton, enough questions had been raised about curriculum changes to make district leaders wary that controversy might suddenly erupt if assessment changes were perceived as radical. For example, sympathetic members of the district accountability com-

mittee asked that we stop using the term *alternative* assessment because it connoted lack of standards and rigor. We agreed thereafter to refer to the assessments we were developing as *performance assessments.*

The Study

5. In the context of our work with teachers we used the terms *performance assessments, authentic assessments,* and *direct assessments* interchangeably, the idea being to judge what students can do in terms of the actual tasks and end performances that are the goals of instruction. In reading, this meant evaluating fluency during oral reading and measuring comprehension by having students talk and write about what they had read. In mathematics, newly adopted district frameworks emphasizing problem solving and communicating mathematically, and introducing new topics such as geometry and probability, implied a shift in content as well as in the mode of assessment.

6. In planning a collateral study to collect data from parents, our purpose was to examine systematically the attitudes and thinking about testing sometimes ascribed to parents. Is it the case, for example, that parents disdain the use of performance assessments as less rigorous or objective? We especially wanted to focus parent attention on the content and form of these two types of measures by showing them examples of questions from each measure. By means of both questionnaire surveys and extended interviews, we wanted to learn specifically how parents evaluate the usefulness of standardized tests compared to less formal types of information such as report cards, talking to the teacher, or seeing samples of their child's work. Do parents value different types of information when judging the quality of the school instead of learning about their own child's progress? We

Shepard, L. A., & Bliem, C. L. (1995). Parents' thinking about standardized tests and performance assessments. *Educational Researcher, 24*(8), 25-32. Copyright © 1995 by the American Educational Research Association. Reprinted by permission of the publisher.

various views (3)

also wanted to analyze interview data in sufficient detail to understand the reasons behind parent preferences for standardized tests or performance assessments and to see if their preferences vary depending on whether the purpose of testing is for classroom instruction or district accountability purposes.

7.   Interview and questionnaire data were collected in the fall and spring of the first project year using non-overlapping random samples. A total of 60 interviews were conducted with individual parents or parent dyads following regularly scheduled parent-teacher conferences. Questionnaires were also administered in control schools. Detailed analyses of results are provided in technical papers by Shepard and Bliem (1993, 1994). In this article we focus on the most important insights gained from talking to parents that might be applicable to other settings where assessment reforms are contemplated. Fall data are emphasized because this was the time when parents were least familiar with the assessment project; therefore, their reactions were more analogous to what first-time encounters with performance assessments might be like in other districts.

What Parents Want to Know About Their Child's Progress in School

8.   We wanted to ask parents questions about testing and assessment in the context of other sources of information used to follow their child's progress or to judge the quality of their child's school. An example of one question set from the questionnaire is shown in Table 1 with data from the fall. Overwhelmingly, parents indicated that they learn the most about their child's progress by talking with the teacher; 77% rated this source of information as very useful. Results were highly consistent, across project schools and control schools, and between survey and interview responses— except that interview data collected just after parent conferences showed an even more "euphoric" endorsement of the value of talking to their child's teacher.

9.   Given our prior, framing set of issues regarding the need for external and objective measures, we were surprised that parents rated informal sources of information — talking to the teacher and seeing graded samples of their child's work — as more useful than standardized tests for learning about their "child's progress in school" and even for judging the "quality of education provided at their child's school." Note that we do not promote these findings as an all-time plebiscite for or against traditional standardized tests. A sample of third-grade parents is not likely to respond in the same way as high-school parents; and we

Table 1   *Parent questionnaire ratings of the usefulness of different types of information for learning about their child's progress in school (n = 105)*

| | How useful | | | | | |
Type of information	Not at all 1	2	3	4	Very 5	Blank/ missing
Report cards	2%	2%	20%	33%	43%	
My child's teacher talking about his/her progress	0%	2%	4%	17%	77%	
Standardized tests	6%	15%	41%	22%	14%	2%
Seeing graded samples of my child's work	0%	0%	10%	30%	60%	

confirmed, based on Gallup Poll questions embedded in the survey, that our sample was less favorably disposed toward standardized tests than the national sample. Nonetheless, the pattern of preferences reported here was true even for the subsample who strongly endorsed standardized tests on the Gallup questions. Therefore, what is most important for us to understand is the reasoning behind parents' valuing of informal sources of information.

10.   In support of their ratings parents offered comments that emphasized the value of receiving specific information about their child's strengths and weaknesses.

> Talking with my child's teacher is most helpful because I learn first-hand what progress is being made in class, where the shortcomings are, and how I can best help at home.

> This way I can see the actual work, the teacher's response, and evaluate what I understand the child's level of learning to be.

11.   When the questions were changed to focus on information used to "evaluate the quality of education provided at your child's school," the percentage of parents who considered standardized tests to be useful increased (from 36% to 45% in the corresponding fall questionnaire sample). Approximately one third of the interview sample elaborated that it was the normative or comparative information provided by such tests that made them useful for this second purpose.

> That is one of the reasons I like the standardized tests, because to me if you have a national standard test for third graders, it shows you where your kid is against national standards. Which doesn't necessarily say anything about your kid, but it might point out there is a problem here . . . [at this school]

12.   Even for the purpose of evaluating the school, however, parents found talking to the teacher and seeing graded samples of work to be more useful than standardized tests. More-

over, in follow-up comments parents gave justifications that showed they understood the accountability purpose of this second set of questions. Parents explained that these informal sources help them learn about the quality of education by giving them first-hand information about the school curriculum, what expectations were being set, and how caring the teacher is with students. In particular, parents said that seeing the actual work that students brought home let them judge whether what was being taught was worthwhile.

> I can see what kind of work the teacher is handing out. The teacher is the one that's in there quarterbacking the classroom. You know, if she's handing out pretty basic stuff to the kids to work on, then that's pretty boring, you know, 'get-me-through-the-school-day' type of activities as far as I'm concerned. But if she's handing out stuff that will keep their interest and get their initiative going as far as keeping them active in school, and wanting to learn, that pretty much sets the tone for the school year and gives me an indication of what kind of quality teachers there are, and what kind of quality programs are here at this school.

13.   Given the arguments for external, accountability testing, two things surprised us about parent responses to this series of questions. First, parents seemed consistently to trust teachers and to have confidence in teachers' professional judgment.

> She's the trained professional, she knows what to look for if something should come up that we should be aware of. . . To be able to talk with somebody who can see their development and be there at all times is very important.

Parents' reported trust in teachers' first-hand knowledge and ability to judge their child's progress was especially striking given teachers' worries throughout our project that they needed to justify and objectify their evaluations to satisfy parents. Second, many parents expressed a need for what we would call normative data but felt that this need was met if teachers could tell them how their child was doing in relation to grade-level expectations. This suggests that parents would value even locally developed benchmarks or performance standards. As an example in our own project, teachers developed a grade-level continuum with benchmark examples to evaluate the text difficulty of chapter books being used in their classrooms. This helped parents see not only whether their child was reading with understanding but also whether he or she could handle grade-level material.

Parents' Evaluations of Standardized Tests and Performance Assessments

14. On the questionnaire, parents were provided with displays showing multiple-choice questions in reading and mathematics like those on the standardized test used by the district and a sample of more open-ended questions used in performance assessments. Parents were asked to rate their approval or disapproval of each type of measure but were not forced to choose one type of measure over the other. Although the majority of parents approved of both types of measures, performance assessments had higher approval ratings than did standardized tests. For example, in mathematics 18% strongly approved of standardized tests, whereas 31% strongly approved of the use of performance assessments.

15. Although the quantitative questionnaire data give a systematic summary of parent reactions from both participating and control schools, interview data provided a much richer and elaborated account of parent responses to the two types of measures. Interviews were conducted with sample assessments and test questions on the table as prompts. Figures 1 and 2 show some of the examples provided in mathematics for multiple-choice and performance-assessment questions, respectively. In reading, the standardized test examples included vocabulary items, a reading passage, and comprehension questions. The performance assessment in reading included a 15-page booklet with a complete story and attractive line drawings; open-ended questions with multiple formats were used where students completed a chart, drew a picture, and wrote about why things happened in the story. Parents were asked to indicate whether they approved or disapproved of each type of measure and then to say what they thought were "the advantages and disadvantages of using tests (or performance assessments) with questions like these." After parents discussed both types of measures in both reading and mathematics, they were then asked one final pair of questions about

Computation		Concepts and Applications
Add.		**1.** What is 763 rounded to the nearest hundred?
1. 3842 + 4104	○ 7946 ○ 7746 ○ 7906 ○ 7942 ○ None of these	○ 700 ○ 750 ○ 760 ○ 800
Subtract.		**2.** How much change will you get if you have $6.55 and spend $4.32?
2. 82 - 3 =	○ 89 ○ 79 ○ 81 ○ 52 ○ None of these	○ $2.23 ○ $2.43 ○ $3.23 ○ $10.87
Multiply.		**3.** What is the perimeter of this shape?
3. 6 x 9	○ 63 ○ 48 ○ 54 ○ 69 ○ None of these	
Divide.		○ 20 ft
4. 8⟌16	○ 2 ○ 24 ○ 20 ○ 8 ○ None of these	○ 21 ft ○ 22 ft ○ 23 ft

Figure 1 *Examples of questions on third-grade standardized achievement tests in mathematics*

which they would prefer to see used in classrooms for instructional purposes.

16. Apart from insights gained from the data, conducting these interviews was a valuable learning experience for the team of 10 faculty and graduate students. Whereas beforehand we had been mindful of not taking too much of parents' time, it was our impression that almost all parents were intrigued by the opportunity to have a close look at both standardized test questions and performance assessments for third graders. Despite being presented with these examples near the end of the interview, most parents took time to look through the materials carefully. They "got into it." They worked through the problems, asked questions about how they were administered typically, and occasionally asked how to do a particular problem (such as the "dot" problem).

17. The sample interview segment in Figure 3 gives the flavor of how parents talked as they looked through the examples and gave their reactions, often pointing to specific items. We created a notational system to make it clear which structured question had just been asked and how each measure was rated. For example, the transcript segment in Figure 3 begins in response to the question about approval or disapproval of performance assessments in reading. The respondent previously indicated approval of standardized tests in reading (STreading+) and strongly approved of performance assessments in reading (PAreading++). The parenthetical notations (ST) and (PA) are used whenever parents pointed to one of the examples in front of them.

18. Qualitative analysis was used to develop categories representing different positions. Entire transcript segments from this portion of the interview were read and sorted into categories resulting in the final categorization scheme shown in Table 2. The counts in Table 2 are for the fall interviews. Only 3 of the 33 fall parents or parent dyads preferred the use of

1. Bus Ride -- A friend of yours, who just moved to the United States, must ride the bus to and from school each day. The bus ride costs 50 cents. Your friend must have exact change and must use only nickels, dimes, and quarters. Your friend has a problem because she does not yet understand our money, and she does not know how to count our money.

Help your friend find the right coins to give to the bus driver. Draw and write something on a whole sheet of paper that can help her. She needs a sheet of paper that can show which combinations of coins can be used to pay for the 50-cent bus ride.

Sample Student Answer 1

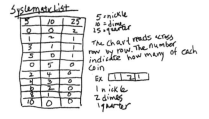

Sample Student Answer 2

2. For the figure at left, show 1/2 in as many ways as you can. You may draw more figures, if necessary. For each way you find, explain how you know you have 1/2.

3. Suppose you couldn't remember what 8 x 7 is. How could you figure it out?

4. Our class of 26 students is going to the Denver Art Museum. How many cars do we need if 4 students can go in each car? How many do we need if only 3 students can go in each car?

5. Adam says that 4 + 52 is 452. Is he right or wrong? What would you tell Adam?

6. Put 4 different one-digit numbers in the boxes to make the largest possible answer.

☐☐
+ ☐☐

How did you know what to choose?

Figure 2 *Examples of third-grade performance assessment questions in mathematics*

Note: The first two examples are reproduced with permission from Pandey, T. (1991). *A sampler of mathematics assessment.* Sacramento, CA: California Department of Education.

standardized tests for both district and instructional purposes. Respondents in this category saw standardized tests as more cut and dried, more aligned to instruction, easier, and providing more support (because having the answers there made it clear what was expected). Figure 4 provides an excerpt representative of responses in this category.

19. By far the majority of respondents preferred performance assessments. Twelve interview segments were placed in the category "Prefers performance assessments (likes both)" and another 11 responses were in the "Strongly prefers performance assessments" category illustrated by the interview segment in Figure 5. Although the "Prefers PA (likes both)" category was heterogeneous, the dominant response was to approve of both kinds of measures being used for district purposes but to prefer that performance assessments be used for classroom instruction. Across responses in all categories the most frequently mentioned feature of performance assessments is that they make children think.

> I like the idea that they read the story, and they really have to get into it, and have to answer some questions and think about it a little harder than the standardized one. I think it would make them comprehend it a little more.

> Strongly approve. I mean they make the child think. They have to think about what they read. They have to think about what they're going to write. It helps with their work on their writing skills even. This (ST) is just coloring in a box, you know.

> F: Again I think it gives them a broader understanding of what they're doing, rather than just A + B = C. . . . It's like, well how did you get it? Use logic rather than just being told this is the answer. Use your logic, use your mind, picture. . . . M: It's not just memorization. . . . F: Yeah exactly, there you go. Be able to work it out instead of just memorizing.

> I think in order to learn any kind of subject you have to have concepts down, and I think number 2 (PA) is going to show how to develop the concepts better. . . . You need to get those basics. . . But I do think this (PA) is going to make them think more.

Even respondents who preferred standardized tests for other reasons often noted that performance assessments would stimulate children's imagination or make them have to think.

20. Beyond their overall evaluations of the two types of measures, parents demonstrated remarkable sophistication in their analysis of the strengths and weaknesses of standardized tests and performance assessments, in many cases anticipating issues of concern to measurement experts. We developed a "key features" coding

(STreading+)(PAreading++) . . . Actually I'd like to see them have this type of test but you have to start really young with them, showing them how to communicate and how to really write that out, bring it out of themselves . . . I would go with this one (PA). I would strongly approve of this type. I want my son to learn how to write more, communicate better . . . This seems the faster way (ST) as far as a test time goes, but this (PA) looks like they've really worked out the problem. They've had to sit there and think about it and take the time to do it.

(STmath+) I'm comfortable with these still, so I approve of them.

(PAmath+) This would be interesting. I'd like to see them start working some of these into the program.

(Instruction?) I would like to see them use these (PA), because as I'm looking at this, you're reading it and it's asking you, and it's almost as though you're talking to the teacher one on one. As you're looking at this (ST), you say 4 times 8, what is that? Well, this one (PA) is giving you a little bit more challenge. It's kind of almost speaking, you say OK, now you figure this out. "Suppose you couldn't remember what 8 x 7 is. How could you figure it out?" It seems like this is better communicated this way.

Figure 3   *Sample interview segment illustrating the "Prefers performance assessments (likes both)" category*

Note: Notations in parentheses indicate approval ratings of standardized tests (ST) and performance assessments (PA) from strong approval (+ +) to strong disapproval (– –). Notations help keep track of the question being responded to in these shortened excerpts; ST and PA abbreviations are also used when respondents point to a test or assessment sample.

system to represent issues as they arose in the data. The codes are shown in Table 3 along with response frequencies for the fall interviews. Parents tended to agree on these characterizations regardless of which type of measure they preferred. For example, parents at both ends of the preference continuum noted that standardized tests have clear-cut right or wrong answers (the Yes/No code) and are more objective. They also seemed easier to a number of parents than performance assessments. Less frequently, parents commented that standardized tests are important because they give you normative information. Only parents who preferred standardized tests commented that they measure what you really need to know in real life, especially math skills. In contrast, a number of parents noted that standardized tests allow students to get the right answer by guessing, but this characterization was made by parents who preferred performance assessments.

21. As stated previously, making kids "think" was the most frequently cited feature of performance assessments. In addition nearly half of the parents also explained that performance assessments could be used "diagnostically" by teachers because the way children answered would reveal their thought process.

> The other tests (PAmath) kind of makes them tell you the concept, not just the right answer. I like the "explain your choice," or "what would you tell Adam type" questions. . . . This would give a teacher more information to think about, especially on the concepts that they haven't quite grasped yet.

Parents commented that performance assessments allow students to use their "imagination" and be creative. Performance assessments appear to be harder, prompting several parents to ask if this was really third-grade work, and they were perceived by a number of parents to be potentially "unfair" particularly to the low kids

in the class or for kids who have trouble writing. Although reading level and writing demand were mentioned as problems to be resolved, for the most part they did not appear to affect parents' enthusiasm for using performance assessments in instruction. For some parents in the "Prefers PA (likes both)" category, however, these features were cited specifically as the reason that both types of tests should be used at least for district purposes. "Different children learn in different ways." Some children, especially those who "are not good with words," would be helped by having the answers there so they could show that they understood.

22. Nine of 33 parents or parent dyads commented on the issue of instructional "alignment" (our term, not theirs) for performance assessments. They insisted that it would not be fair to test children with these kinds of assessments unless teachers also taught using the same kinds of problems.

> I'm assuming that if they were going to be testing this way they would be doing, of course, more papers this way in the first place to get them ready for it.

Parents recognized that performance assessments are more "subjective" and therefore more difficult to score, but some said that this was how good teachers should spend their time. Less frequently (but in greater numbers than for standardized tests) parents said things like "performance assessments would really tell what students 'know' " and "this kind of problem is what kids need to know in 'real life.' "

Parents' Conceptions of Subject Matter

23. For some parents, attitudes toward performance assessments and standardized tests appeared to be related to beliefs about subject matter. A distinct subgroup of parents preferred standardized tests for mathematics instruction because "in math there is only one right answer." We noted in the questionnaire responses that the proportion of parents favoring the use of performance assessments in reading was much larger than in math. In reading, 58% favored performance assessments compared to 21% preferring standardized tests; in mathematics the margin was much narrower, with 44% favoring performance assessments versus 31% favoring standardized tests. The same pattern emerged in interview ratings but with collateral parent talk explaining or revealing reasons behind their preferences. As shown in Table 2, a category was created for 4 of 33 parent interviews who favored standardized tests for math and performance assessments for reading. We think this category warrants interpretation not only because the same preference occurred

Table 2   *Parent interview categories: Preferences for standardized tests or performance assessments (n = 33 parents or parent dyads)*

Preference category	n
Strongly prefers standardized tests	2
Prefers standardized tests (likes both)	1
Standardized tests math/performance assessments reading	4
Standardized tests reading/performance assessments math	1
Both: likes both, wants both in instruction	2
Prefers performance assessments (likes both)	12
Strongly prefers performance assessments	11

(STreading++) Well, I think it's really clear cut what is expected of these kids. It's easy for them to understand, it's easy for them to answer it.

(PAreading–) Well, the disadvantages of it are that there are too many right or wrong answers. I think that is kind of hard for kids that age to comprehend all this. Maybe the advantage of it would be they are more able to use their imagination.

(PAmath–) For one thing, the child might understand how to do something like this but they don't know how to explain it. They have trouble with words . . . Just that a test like this might be useful again to get an idea of how they are comprehending different things but it wouldn't really be fair to grade their learning on this.

(Instruction?) Oh. Standardized. Because I feel that that is easier to teach and easier for the kids to learn and easier to grade them on it.

Figure 4 *Sample interview segment illustrating the "Strongly prefers standardized tests" category*

Note: Notations in parentheses indicate approval ratings of standardized tests (ST) and performance assessments (PA) from strong approval (+ +) to strong disapproval (– –). Notations help keep track of the question being responded to in these shortened excerpts; ST and PA abbreviations are also used when respondents point to a test or assessment sample.

(STreading–) M: . . . It doesn't really force you to think, I mean, the answers are right there . . . F: It makes you have one of their choices instead of one of your own choices.

(PAreading+) M: . . . This one has you also explain. Like right here (ST) you don't really have to think too much about it, and this one (PA) you really have to kind of pull it all together and reason it out . . . The only problem I see with this is if they were at a lower level of third grade reading, you know, they probably couldn't grasp some of this.

(STmath–) (PAmath ++) F: If I had the option, something like this (PA) would be a little bit better. . . . M: Yeah. I think this would make them, if they were to teach, obviously they'd have to teach this to take these tests. We'd probably get better quality in teaching. Things would probably stick with them a little bit more. . . . I think you can probably guess more on (ST). On these (PA) you can't really guess, you kind of have to think about it. F: Plus, I think this (PA) makes it a little bit more interesting for the kids. This (ST) is pretty cut and dried.

(Instruction?) F: Well, like we said, this one (PA). This one, I think. The kids could relate to this . . . M: It's more practical. You can apply it; it stresses more of life skills.

Figure 5 *Sample interview segment illustrating the "Strongly prefers performance assessments" category*

Note: Notations in parentheses indicate approval ratings of standardized tests (ST) and performance assessments (PA) from strong approval (+ +) to strong disapproval (– –). Notations help keep track of the question being responded to in these shortened excerpts; ST and PA abbreviations are also used when respondents point to a test or assessment sample. The abbreviations F and M stand for father and mother, respectively.

several times but also because the reasoning expressed was highly similar and recurred again in spring cases.

24. For this subgroup of parents, the difference in preference for the two types of measures was associated with differences in their views about the nature of reading and the nature of mathematics or how mathematics is taught in school. Doing well in reading (and writing) allows for individual expression, whereas for mathematics, it is important to know the one correct way:

(Instruction?)(PAreading+) In mathematics, I think this type (ST) is probably the best . . . because math is pretty basic as far as having the right answer, and you have to have the right answer. With this (PAreading) they can use their imagination and they can tell you a story the way they see it rather than, you know, it doesn't always have to be one way.

(Instruction?) I'd say the performance assessments (in reading) because it still does give him a chance to tell his part. (In math?) I would have to say I prefer the standardized because that's not an option, there's only one answer, you know.

This same type of response occurred again in spring interviews, but interestingly some of the parents who commented "math is black and white" were willing in the spring to suggest using both types of measures rather than only standardized tests for mathematics. Unfortunately, numbers are too small to claim that this change was reliable, but it is possible that

parents were more accepting of open-ended math problems after seeing them used in their child's classroom during the school year.

Conclusions

25. The purpose of the study was to examine parent opinions about standardized tests and new performance assessments in greater depth than can be understood from national survey data. The classic Gallup Poll question showing a high percentage of citizens and public school parents in favor of standardized national tests (Elam, Rose, & Gallup, 1992) is often interpreted as a mandate for external, machine-scorable, accountability measures. What was discovered in this study is that parents' favorable ratings of standardized national tests do not imply a preference for such measures over other less formal sources of information for monitoring their child's academic progress or for judging the quality of education provided at their local school. Approval of standardized tests likewise does not imply disapproval of performance assessments.

26. In this study, third-grade parents considered report cards, hearing from the teacher, and seeing graded samples of student work to be much more useful in learning about their child's progress than standardized tests. Though in interview data parents often mentioned the need for comparative information to know how to interpret their own child's progress, they trust the teacher to tell them how their child is doing in relation to grade-level expectations or to other children in the class. These parents of early elementary school children rarely mentioned the need for comparison to external or national norms. Even for accountability purposes, the usefulness ratings for standardized tests increased but did not equal parents' high ratings for talking to the teacher and seeing student work. According to parents, seeing graded samples of student work is an important indicator of school quality because it shows them what is being taught and what expectations are set by the classroom teacher.

27. When parents were provided with specific examples of the types of questions used on standardized tests and on performance assessments, the majority of parents approved of both types of measures, giving stronger approval ratings to performance assessments. Recurring themes in parent interviews were that performance assessment problems "make children think" and that they are likely to give teachers better insights about what children are understanding and where they are struggling. Parents commented frequently about the desirability of having children explain their answers in mathematics and being encouraged to express

Table 3   *Key features of standardized tests and performance assessments mentioned by parents in interview responses (n = 33)*

Standardized tests		Performance assessments	
Code	*n*	Code	*n*
Guess	16	Think	24
Yes/No	15	Imagination	18
Easy	8	Diagnostic	16
Objective	8	Hard	10
Support	6	Unfair	10
Know	4	Know	10
Real life	3	Aligned	9
Norm	3	Subjective	8
		Real life	6

themselves in response to stories they read. Standardized tests were seen as easier and more supportive by some parents because having answer choices communicates what's expected and allows children who aren't very verbal to show what they know; at the same time, parents complained frequently that multiple-choice questions allow children to guess the right answer "25% of the time."

28. In the context of controversy surrounding educational reform and the development of new forms of assessment, our surveys of parent opinions and extended interviews were remarkably noncontroversial. We do not think it was because this lower- and middle-class district has such an unusual population of parents; for example, the religious right is well represented and has been vocal on curricular matters; in our project some parents asked for and took advantage of the opportunity to review "secure" assessments used as end-of-project outcome measures because they wanted to be sure there was no objectionable content.

29. We attribute the generally favorable response and the absence of any angry or disruptive reactions to two factors that may be replicable and useful elsewhere. First, the changes being proposed were not radical, wholesale changes. It was the climate of the district, and the tone of our questions, such that use of performance assessments did not imply throwing out standardized tests. Second, parents were able to look closely at performance assessment problems, the "stuff" of the reform, before it had been characterized pejoratively in the local media. When given the chance, parents seemed intrigued with the opportunity to examine in detail questions from both standardized tests and performance assessments. Although nearly all indicated that what they saw on the performance assessments was different from their own test-taking experiences, most were satisfied that the material was challenging and worth learning.

30. Parents are essential to any educational reform effort. Individually they support their children's learning, and collectively they can unseat professionally developed, research-based curriculum and assessment changes, as has been demonstrated in several states and local districts. It is important to understand parent perspectives on academic standards and what they think is important for students to learn, not so that past curricular practices will always dictate future curriculum but so that points of agreement can be identified. For example, many parents fear the abandonment of basic skills. Our experience suggests that parents are more likely to be reassured if they see problems like "If you couldn't remember what 8 x 7 is, how could you figure it out?" or "How would you pick four digits to make the largest sum?" than if reformers lead with calculator use in the early grades. Even considering all the contending views of what it means to achieve academic excellence, there is a large common ground on which to build support for reform.

References

Elam, S. M., Rose, L. C., & Gallup, A. M. (1992). The 24th annual Gallup-Phi Delta Kappan Poll of the public's attitudes toward the public schools. *Phi Delta Kappan, 74,* 41-53.

Pandey, T. (1991). *A sampler of mathematics assessment.* Sacramento, CA: California Department of Education.

Shepard, L. A., & Bliem, C. L. (1993, April). *Parent opinions about standardized tests, teacher's information, and performance assessments.* Paper presented at the Annual Meeting of the American Educational Research Association, Atlanta.

Shepard, L. A., & Bliem, C. L. (1994). *An analysis of parent opinions and changes in opinions regarding standardized tests, teacher's information, and performance assessments* (Tech. Rep.). Los Angeles: Center for Research on Evaluation, Standards, and Student Testing.

Factual Questions

1. What was the problem with the term *alternative assessment*?

2. What is the stated purpose of the research?

3. What method of sampling was used to select the parents?

4. According to the data in Table 1, what is the *second* most useful type of information for learning about children's progress in school?

5. How did the authors determine that their sample was *not* representative of a national sample?

6. Did parents rush through the testing materials or did they take their time?

7. What does "STreading+" mean?

8. What does "PAmath–" mean?

9. What was the most frequently mentioned feature of performance assessments in the interviews?

Questions for Discussion

10. Apparently, only parents who attended parent-teacher conferences were included in the sample. (See paragraph 7.) Is this a strength or weakness of the study? Explain.

11. Parents were shown *samples* of standardized test items and performance assessments. Is it important to know whether the samples were representative? Why? Why not?

12. How important are the quotations in Figures 3, 4, and 5 in helping you understand the results of the study?

13. Based on the data in Table 3, how would you characterize parents' reactions to performance assessments? Would you expect

their support of PA to be unanimous at a school board meeting?

14. Are there ways this study could be improved without significantly increasing the cost of conducting it? Explain.

15. If you wished to replicate this study in another school district, but only had the resources to conduct either a quantitative or qualitative study, which would you choose? Why?

Quality Ratings

DIRECTIONS: Indicate your level of agreement with each of the following statements by circling a number from 5 for strongly agree (SA) to 1 for strongly disagree (SD). If you believe that an item is not applicable to this research article, leave it blank. Be prepared to explain your ratings.

A. The introduction establishes the importance of the research topic.

SA   5   4   3   2   1   SD

B. The literature review establishes the context for the study.

SA   5   4   3   2   1   SD

C. The research purpose, question, or hypothesis is clearly stated.

SA   5   4   3   2   1   SD

D. The method of sampling is sound.

SA   5   4   3   2   1   SD

E. Relevant demographics (for example, age, gender, and ethnicity) are described.

SA   5   4   3   2   1   SD

F. Measurement procedures are adequate.

SA   5   4   3   2   1   SD

G. The results are clearly described.

SA   5   4   3   2   1   SD

H. The discussion/conclusion is appropriate.

SA   5   4   3   2   1   SD

I. Despite any flaws noted above, the report is worthy of publication.

SA   5   4   3   2   1   SD

ARTICLE 7

A COMPARISON OF HOW TEXTBOOKS TEACH
MATHEMATICAL PROBLEM SOLVING IN JAPAN AND THE UNITED STATES

Richard E. Mayer   *University of California, Santa Barbara*
Valerie Sims   *University of California, Santa Barbara*
Hidetsugu Tajika   *Aichi University of Education, Japan*

This brief report compared the lesson on addition and subtraction of signed whole numbers in three seventh-grade Japanese mathematics textbooks with the corresponding lesson in four U.S. mathematics textbooks. The results indicated that Japanese books contained many more worked-out examples and relevant illustrations than did the U.S. books, whereas the U.S. books contained roughly as many exercises and many more irrelevant illustrations than did the Japanese books. The Japanese books devoted 81% of their space to explaining the solution procedure for worked-out examples compared to 36% in U.S. books; in contrast, the U.S. books devoted more space to unsolved exercises (45%) and interest-grabbing illustrations that are irrelevant to the lesson (19%) than did the Japanese books (19% and 0%, respectively). Finally, one of the U.S. books and all three Japanese books used meaningful instructional methods emphasizing (a) multiple representations of how to solve worked-out examples using words, symbols, and pictures and (b) inductive organization of material beginning with familiar situations and ending with formal statements of the solution rule. The results are consistent with classroom observations showing that Japanese mathematics instruction tends to emphasize the process of problem solving more effectively than does U.S. mathematics instruction (Stevenson and Stigler, 1992).

1. National and international assessments of mathematics achievement have consistently revealed that students in the United States perform more poorly than their cohorts in other industrialized nations, particularly students from Asian nations such as Japan (Robitaille & Garden, 1989; Stevenson, Lee, Chen, Stigler, Hsu, & Kitamura, 1990; Stevenson & Stigler, 1992; Stigler, Lee, & Stevenson, 1990). The relatively poor performance of U.S. students occurs not only on tests of basic computational skills but also on tests of mathematical problem solving.

2. Converging evidence suggests that an explanation for cross-national differences can be found in the *exposure hypothesis*: cross-national differences in mathematics achievement are related to differences in the quantity and quality of mathematics instruction (Mayer, Tajika, & Stanley, 1991; McKnight et al., 1987; Stevenson & Stigler, 1992). Stevenson, Stigler, Lee, Kitamura, Kimura, and Kato (1986) point out that Japanese students spend approximately twice as many hours per week on mathematics as U.S. students spend. Perhaps even more importantly, Stevenson and Stigler (1992) provide evidence that Japanese schools tend to emphasize the process of problem solving whereas U.S. schools tend to emphasize the mastery of facts and procedures for computing the correct answer. For example, compared to U.S. elementary school mathematics teachers, Japanese teachers provide more verbal explanations, engage students in more reflective discussion, are more likely to use concrete manipulatives to represent abstract concepts, are more likely to include a real-world problem in a lesson, present more coherent lessons, ask questions that require longer answers, provide more critical feedback, and focus on fewer problems in more depth (Stevenson & Stigler, 1992).

3. The present study compared how mathematical problem solving is taught in mathematics textbooks used in Japan and in the United States. In particular, we examined the hypothesis that a typical Japanese textbook is more oriented toward teaching conceptual understanding and problem-solving skills whereas typical U.S. textbooks are more oriented toward teaching isolated facts and rote computation. This study extends earlier research comparing how mathematical problem solving is taught in Japanese and U.S. classrooms (Stevenson & Stigler, 1992) and contributes to an emerging research base on cross-national comparisons of textbooks (Chambliss & Calfee, 1989; Okamoto, 1989; Stevenson & Bartsch, 1991).

4. Cross-national comparisons of mathematics textbooks are important in light of evidence that U.S. textbooks constitute a sort of de facto national curriculum. For example, Armbruster and Ostertag (1993, p. 69) assert that "the powerful role of textbooks in the American curriculum is by now well established." Garner (1992, p. 53) notes that "textbooks serve as critical vehicles for knowledge acquisition in school" and can "replace teacher talk as the primary source of information." Glynn, Andre, and Britton, (1986, p. 245) propose that across many disciplines students experience "a heavy reliance on textual materials for a great deal of their knowledge." It follows that examining the content and teaching methods used in American and Japanese mathematics textbooks provides a partial account of how mathematics is taught in the two nations.

Method

Materials

5. The data source consisted of lessons on addition and subtraction of signed whole numbers taken from three Japanese textbooks (Fukumori et al., 1992, pp. 19-25; Kodaira, 1992, pp. 27-32; Fujita & Maehara, 1992, pp. 17-25) and four U.S. textbooks (Bolster, Crown, Hamada, et al., 1988, pp. 354-359; Fennell, Reys, Reys, & Webb, 1988, pp. 428-431; Rucker, Dilley,

Mayer, R. E., Sims, V., & Tajika, H. (1995). A comparison of how textbooks teach mathematical problem solving in Japan and the United States. *American Educational Research Journal, 32,* 443-460. Copyright © 1995 by the American Educational Research Association. Reprinted with permission.

Richard E. Mayer is a Professor of Psychology and Education, Department of Psychology, University of California, Santa Barbara, CA 93106. His specializations are educational and cognitive psychology. Valerie Sims is a Ph.D. Candidate, Department of Psychology, University of California, Santa Barbara, CA 93106. Her specializations are cognitive and developmental psychology. Hidetsugu Tajika is an Associate Professor, Department of Psychology, Aichi University of Education, Kariya, Aichi 448 Japan. His specializations are memory and cognitive processes.

Lowry, & Ockenga, 1988, pp. 332-335; Willoughby, Bereiter, Hilton, & Rubinstein, 1991, pp. 260-265) commonly used to teach seventh-grade mathematics. The number of pages for the lesson in the Japanese books ranged from 7 to 9 based on an average page size of 5.5 x 7.5 inches, and from 4 to 6 in the U.S. books based on a page size averaging 7 x 9.5 inches. The Japanese books were approved by the Japanese Ministry of Education and were highly similar to one another because they conformed to detailed governmental specifications; the U.S. books were from publishers' series that were approved for adoption by the California State Department of Education. The books were selected as typical based on consultations with teachers and school administrators in Japan and the United States. The lesson in all books described how to add and subtract positive and negative whole numbers, such as $3 + 8 = $ __ , $-3 + 8 = $ __ , $3 + -8 = $ __ , $-3 + -8 = $ __ , $3 - 8 = $ __ , $-3 - 8 = $ __ , $3 - -8 = $ __ , and $-3 - -8 = $ __ . In each of the Japanese books, the material was contained in the lesson entitled, "Addition and Subtraction," taken from the chapter entitled, "Positive and Negative Numbers" (Fujita & Maehara, 1992; Fukumori et al., 1992; Kodaira, 1992). In the U.S. books, the material was contained in lessons entitled, "Adding and Subtracting Signed Numbers" (Willoughby, Bereiter, Hilton, & Rubinstein, 1991); "Adding Integers" and "Subtracting Integers" (Fennell, Reys, Reys, & Webb, 1988; Rucker, Dilley, Lowry, & Ockenga, 1988); or "Adding Integers: Same Sign," "Adding Integers: Different Signs," and "Subtracting Integers" (Bolster, Crown, Hamada, et al., 1988). We also included the exercises involving addition and subtraction of signed integers in the end-of-the-chapter test. We did not include sections on addition and subtraction of signed fractions, signed decimals, or three or more signed numbers, because this material was not covered in all books. In short, the data source consisted of seven lessons on addition and subtraction of signed integers, ranging from 4 to 9 pages in length.

Procedure

6.   To conduct a quantitative analysis of the instructional methods used for teaching students how to solve signed arithmetic problems, two independent raters broke each lesson into four parts — exercises, irrelevant illustrations, relevant illustrations, and explanation — and resolved conflicts by consensus. First, the raters circled the exercise portions of each lesson using a colored marker. We defined an exercise as a symbol-based problem involving addition or subtraction of two signed integers for which no answer or explanation was provided, such as -8

$+ 3 = $ __ . In the Japanese books, the exercises were labeled as "Problem" or "Exercise"; contained the instructions, "Calculate the following"; and were numbered consecutively. In the U.S. books, the exercises were presented under labels such as "Exercise" or "Practice"; contained instructions such as, "Give each sum," "Give each difference," "Add," or "Subtract"; and were numbered consecutively. The raters counted the number of exercise problems involving addition or subtraction of two signed numbers in each lesson, including exercise problems given at the end of the chapter. We did not include exercises involving fractions, decimals, or more than two numbers. There were no unresolved disagreements between the raters.

7.   Second, the raters circled the irrelevant illustrations in each lesson using a colored marker and circled the relevant illustrations using a different colored marker. We defined an illustration as any line drawing, chart, picture, or photograph. Furthermore, we defined a relevant illustration as any line drawing or chart that represented the steps in the solution of a signed arithmetic problem and an irrelevant illustration as a picture or photograph that did not correspond to the steps in the solution of a signed arithmetic problem. To ensure consistency, the raters maintained a list of illustrations that were classified as relevant and a list of illustrations that were classified as irrelevant. Relevant illustrations included line drawings showing changes in the water level of a water storage tank, changes in position on a number line, or changes in mixtures of negative and positive ions in a beaker; irrelevant illustrations included a picture of a tape measure, a drawing of a ski village, a drawing of a mad scientist, a drawing of a submarine, a mural from an ancient Egyptian pyramid, a photo of a woman swinging a golf club, and a photo of hockey players skating on ice. A series of line drawings about the same problem presented together on a page was counted as one illustration. The raters counted the number of relevant and irrelevant illustrations in each lesson. There were no unresolved disagreements.

8.   Third, the remaining portions of the lesson constituted the explanation and were circled with a colored marker designating explanation. Each rater counted the number of worked-out examples in the explanation portion of the lesson. A worked-out example was defined as a signed arithmetic problem in which the answer and verbal description of how it was generated were given. In most cases, the worked-out examples were presented under the heading, "Example." Each rater also counted the number of words in the explanation section of the

lesson; words in headings and in relevant illustrations were included. A word was defined as any letter or letter group found in a dictionary. We did not include mathematical symbols such as numerals, +, −, or =. There were no unresolved disagreements between the raters.

9.   One of the raters used a ruler to measure the space (in square inches) occupied by exercises, irrelevant illustrations, relevant illustrations, and explanation for each lesson. In measuring the areas, margin space was not included. Given the objective nature of these measurements, a second rater was not needed.

10.   In sum, the quantitative data for each lesson included the number of exercises, the number of irrelevant illustrations, the number of relevant illustrations, the number of worked-out examples, the number of words, the area occupied by exercises, the area occupied by irrelevant illustrations, the area occupied by relevant illustrations, and the area occupied by explanation.

Results and Discussion

11.   *The instructional lesson is much longer in Japan than in the U.S., but the exercise set is about the same length in both nations.* Research on instructional methods has emphasized the role of meaningful explanation rather than unguided hands-on symbol manipulating activities in promoting problem-solving competence (Mayer, 1987). The instructional part of the lesson — that is, the part of the lesson that did not contain to-be-solved exercises — was more than four times longer in the Japanese books than in the U.S. books: The mean number of words in the U.S. books was 208 compared to 925 in the Japanese books. However, the exercise part of the lesson, which emphasizes unguided symbol manipulation, was about the same in the two nations: The Japanese books contained an average of 63 exercises on addition and subtraction of signed numbers, whereas the U.S. books averaged 51 exercises. In both nations, additional worksheets and workbooks are available to supplement the textbook exercises. Overall, these data show a difference in the relative emphasis of Japanese and U.S. books: There were 14.7 words of instruction per exercise in the Japanese books compared to an average of 3.9 words of instruction per exercise in the U.S. books.

12.   *Worked-out examples and concrete analogies are more common in Japan than in the U.S.* Research on multiple representations, case-based reasoning, and analogical reasoning has demonstrated the important role of worked-out examples and concrete analogies in helping students to improve their problem-solving skills (Mayer, 1987). Worked-out examples serve to

model appropriate problem-solving processes, and concrete analogies provide a means for connecting procedures to familiar experience. On average, worked-out examples were three times more common in the Japanese textbooks than in the U.S. textbooks: U.S. books averaged approximately 4 worked-out examples compared to 15 in the Japanese lessons.

13. The Japanese books employed the same concrete analogy throughout the lesson on addition and subtraction of signed numbers. For example, one book presented a tank for storing water in which a rise in the water level is expressed by a positive number and a fall in the water level is expressed by a negative number. According to this analogy, addition of signed numbers occurs when the water level is changed twice — for example, a first change in the water level plus a second change in the water level produces a total change in the water level; subtraction of signed numbers occurs when one knows the total change and the second change but wants to find the first change. The analogy was represented in multiframe illustrations 9 times, indicating changes that corresponded to arithmetic operations. Another book used the analogy of walking east or west along a path, which was portrayed as arrows along a number line. The book contained 7 multiframe illustrations showing the process of taking two trips along the number line. For example, the problem $(+8) + (-3) = \_\_$ was represented as two parts of a trip: an arrow from 0 to 8 (labeled as +8) and an arrow from 8 to 5 (labeled as −3). Below this figure, the solution was represented as an arrow from 0 to 5 (labeled as +8 − 3). A third book represented addition and subtraction of signed numbers as movement along a number line, including 6 sets of illustrations of number lines.

14. In contrast, the U.S. books used concrete analogies such as changes in temperature on a thermometer, keeping score in golf or hockey, matter and antimatter annihilation, and beakers containing positive and negative ions. However, in three out of four cases, the analogy used to represent addition was different from the analogy used to represent subtraction, and none of the analogies was represented in a multiframe illustration depicting changes that correspond to addition or subtraction. In the U.S. books, analogies used to describe addition of signed numbers were insufficient to describe subtraction of signed numbers. For example, in the matter/antimatter analogy, combining 5 bricks and 2 antibricks yielded 3 bricks (analogous to $5 + -2 = 3$). However, this analogy breaks down for situations in which a negative number is subtracted from another number (such as $5 - -2 = 7$), so the textbook used a

different analogy, temperatures on a thermometer, to represent subtraction of signed numbers.

15. *Relevant illustrations were more common in Japanese books than in U.S. books, but irrelevant illustrations were more common in U.S. books than in Japanese books.* Research on illustrations reveals that some kinds of illustrations have more instructional value than others (Levin & Mayer, 1993; Mayer, 1993). Illustrations that simply decorate the page are instructionally irrelevant, whereas illustrations that explain the process of signed arithmetic are instructionally relevant. Other than the first page of the chapter, the Japanese books contained more relevant and fewer irrelevant illustrations than U.S. books: The Japanese books contained an average of 0 irrelevant and 11 relevant illustrations compared to an average of 2 irrelevant and 4 relevant illustrations in the U.S. books. The irrelevant illustrations in U.S. textbooks may be intended to make the material more interesting, but recent research on seductive details reveals that the addition of highly interesting and vivid material to a text often diminishes students' recall of the important information (Garner, Brown, Sanders, & Menke, 1992; Wade, 1992).

16. In summary, the foregoing analyses indicate that the Japanese books contain far more worked-out examples and relevant illustrations than the U.S. books, whereas U.S. books contain roughly as many exercises and more irrelevant illustrations than Japanese books. Another way to examine these kinds of differences is to compare the allocation of page space in Japanese and U.S. lessons, which is done in the next section.

17. *Japanese books excel in devoting page space to explanation of problem-solving procedures, whereas U.S. books excel in devoting page space to unsolved exercises and interest-grabbing illustrations.* The allocation of space in Japanese and U.S. textbooks represents the values of the cultures that produced them. An emphasis on understanding the process of problem solving is reflected in the use of worked-out examples which model the problem-solving process in words, symbols, and illustrations. Research on the teaching of problem-solving processes indicates that successful programs rely on the use of cognitive modeling techniques—such as detailed descriptions of worked-out examples (Mayer, 1992). On average, 81% of the page space in Japanese books was devoted to explanation of problem-solving procedures (63% emphasizing worked-out examples and 18% for corresponding illustrations) compared to 36% in U.S. books (25% emphasizing worked-out examples and 11% for corresponding illustrations).

18. In contrast, an emphasis on the product of problem solving is reflected in the presentation of lists of to-be-solved exercise problems. On average, 45% of the page space in U.S. books was devoted to presenting lists of exercise problems compared to 19% in Japanese books. Perhaps to compensate for what might be considered the boring task of having to solve exercise problems without guidance, authors of U.S. books added interest-grabbing illustrations that were irrelevant to the problem-solving procedures. On average, U.S. books devoted 19% of their space to irrelevant illustrations compared to 0% in Japanese books. Figure 1 summarizes these differences in the use of space in Japanese and U.S. textbooks.

19. *Meaningful instructional methods emphasizing the coordination of multiple representations were more common in Japanese books than in U.S. books.* Research in mathematics education emphasizes the importance of helping students build connections among multiple representations of a problem and of helping students induce solution rules based on experience with familiar examples (Grouws, 1992; Hiebert, 1986). To analyze these aspects of meaningful instruction and to supplement the foregoing quantitative analyses, we analyzed the ways that the textbooks explained one type of signed arithmetic—namely, adding two numbers with different signs, such as $(+ 3) + (-8) = -5$ or $(-4) + (+3) = -1$. To assess the use of multiple representations in each lesson, we examined whether the lesson presented complete symbolic, verbal, and pictorial representations of a problem-solving procedure for addition of integers with different signs. In particular, we evaluated whether or not the lesson included symbolic, verbal, and visual representations for the first step (i.e., determining the value of the first number), the second step (i.e., adding the value of the second number), and the third step (i.e., using the resulting number as the final answer). To assess the use of an inductive method in each lesson, we determined whether or not the lesson progressed from familiar examples to a formal statement of the rule for addition of integers with different signs.

20. All three of the Japanese books systematically built connections among symbolic, verbal, and pictorial representations for each of three steps in solving the problem. In explaining how to add two numbers with different signs, one Japanese book (Kodaira, 1992) began by describing a water tank analogy in words. The book (p. 27) stated that "when the water level changes twice in succession, we can express the changes, starting with the first change as: (the first change) + (the second change)." In relating this analogy to addition of two numbers with

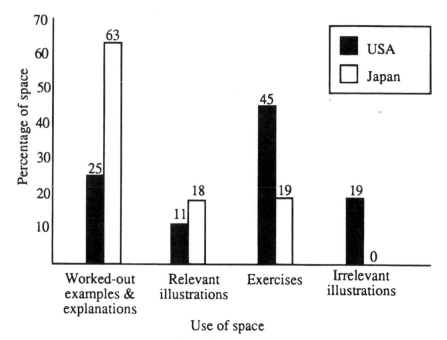

Figure 1. **Proportion of page space devoted to explanations, relevant illustrations, exercises, and irrelevant illustrations in Japan and the United States**

different signs, the book (p. 28) described the situation in words: "If the first change is –3 cm and the second change is +8 cm, then the total change is (–3) + (+8), and this is +5 cm." Then the book presented the problem in symbolic form as "(–3) + (+8) = +5." Next to this was a pictorial representation of the problem consisting of three labeled frames, as shown in Figure 2a. Each step in the problem was represented, starting with negative 3, adding positive 8, and ending with positive 5. At the end of a series of examples, the book presented a rule for addition of numbers with different signs (p. 30):

> In seeking the sum of two numbers with different signs, consider only their absolute values and subtract the smaller absolute value from the larger. Then assign to the sum the sign of the number with the larger absolute value. If the absolute values are equal, then the sum is 0.

Thus, the lesson was organized inductively, beginning with a familiar analogy and ending with a formal statement of the solution rule.

21. A second Japanese book (Fujita & Maehara, 1992) began its discussion of addition of different-signed integers by describing a walk along a road (p. 17):

> Imagine that you are walking a road which runs east and west in a straight line . . . You first walk 3 meters to the east and then walk 5 meters to the west. Moving to the east will be used as the positive numbers and moving to the west will be used as the negative numbers.

Then, the book describes the computation in words and symbols (p. 17): "Two movements and their results will be expressed as follows, when positive and negative numbers are used.... The first movement is +3 m, the second movement is –5 m, the result is –2 m." On the right, the book presented a number line with an arrow from 0 to 3 corresponding to the first movement, from 3 to –2 corresponding to the second movement, and from 0 to –2 corresponding to the answer. This illustration is summarized in Figure 2b. Next, the example was expressed in symbolic form (p. 18):

> When moving twice in succession, the results. . . are expressed as follows by adding two numbers: (the first movement) + (the second movement). When the results are expressed like this, the calculation for the example is as follows: (+3) + (–5). The answer is –2, and so the computation is expressed as follows: (+3) + (–5) = –2.

Finally, after presenting several examples in verbal, visual, and symbolic forms, the section ended with a statement of the general principle (p. 20): "The sum of numbers with different signs: You can subtract the smaller absolute value from the larger one and assign to the sum the sign of the number with the larger absolute value. When the absolute values are equal the sum is 0." As in the other Japanese book, this lesson was organized inductively — beginning with a familiar situation of walking east and west along a road and ending with a formal

statement of the procedure for addition of numbers with different signs.

22. The third book (Fukumori et al., 1992, pp. 18-19) also used verbal, visual, and symbolic representations to explain what to do "when you add a positive and negative number." The book connected symbols, words, and pictures as follows: "(–7) + 5 means to get a number that is 5 larger than –7. A number 5 larger than –7 is the number –2, which is 2 smaller than 0, as you can see on the number line below." Directly below was an illustration of a number line with an arrow from –7 to –2, and below that was the symbolic form of the problem, "(–7) + 5 = –2." After presenting several other examples of the same form in the same way, the section ended with a statement of general principle: "Addition of a negative and positive number means subtraction of the negative number from the positive number . . . 3 + (–5) = 3 – 5 = –2." Again, as in the other Japanese books, instruction moved from the familiar statement of a problem in words and pictures to a formal statement of the solution procedure as a rule.

23. In contrast, only one of the four U.S. books contained symbolic, verbal, and pictorial representations of example problems involving addition of integers with different signs. For example, one U.S. textbook (Willoughby, Bereiter, Hilton, & Rubinstein, 1991) began by presenting word problems about familiar analogies such as a thermometer: "The temperature is –4C. If it goes up 3C, what will it be?" For each word problem, the book stated the problem in symbolic form but did not give an answer, such as "–4 + 3 = ?" Thus, the book presented only the first two steps in the problem—namely, starting at negative 4 and adding positive 3; it failed to describe the third step—namely, ending at negative 1. The book also failed to connect the verbal and symbolic representation of the problem to a pictorial representation. In the next section of the chapter, entitled "Adding and Subtracting Signed Numbers," the book (p. 263) listed rules such as: "To add 2 signed numbers, if the signs are different, subtract the smaller absolute value from the larger and use the sign of the one with the larger absolute value." Then, the book provided exercises such as "(–8) + (+7) = n" along with instructions to use the above rule. This is a deductive approach because it begins with stating a rule and then tells the learner to apply the rule to exercise problems.

24. In another U.S. textbook (Rucker, Dilley, Lowry, & Ockenga, 1988), the section on "Integers" began by representing positive and negative integers as beakers containing positive and negative charges. Then, in the section on "Adding Integers," the book presented several

2a. Excerpt from Japanese textbook that includes verbal, visual, and symbolic representations for each of three problem-solving steps.

We have a tank for storing water. If we put in or take out water, the water level in the tank goes up or down. If we express a change which raises the water level with a positive number, then we can express a change which lowers the water level with a negative number. If the water level rises 5 cm, the change in the water level is +5 cm. If the water level decreases 3 cm, the change in the water level is -3 cm...When the water level changes twice in succession we can express the change as:...

If the first change is:	-3 cm
and the second change is:	+8 cm
then the total change is:	(-3) + (+8)
and this is +5 cm.	(-3) + (+8) = +5

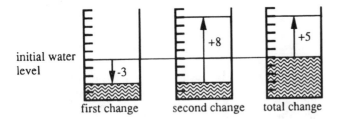

2b. Excerpt from Japanese textbook that includes verbal, visual, and symbolic representations for each of three problem-solving steps.

When you walk from A...you first walk 3 m to the east and then 5 m to the west. The two movements...will be expressed using positive and negative numbers. The first movement is +3 m, the second movement is -5 m, the result is -2 m... The calculation is expressed as follows: (+3) + (-5) = -2.

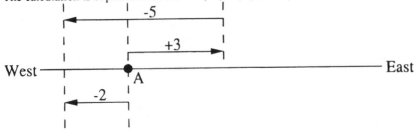

Figure 2. **Representations used in Japanese textbooks to teach addition of numbers with different signs.**

Note. 2a is adapted from Kodaira (1992); 2b is adapted from Fujita and Maehara (1992).

examples. For each, there was a picture of one beaker containing positive or negative charges being poured into another beaker containing positive or negative charges and the resulting beaker; below the picture was a symbolic representation of the problem. For example, Figure 3a shows a beaker containing one positive charge being poured into a beaker containing 5 negative charges, and the result is a beaker containing 4 free negative charges. Directly under

this picture was the equation, "-5 + +1 = -4." This lesson used symbols and pictures to present all three steps in the procedure — starting with negative 5, adding positive 1, and ending with negative 4—but failed to connect them to words. There was no verbal description other than the general statement, "To understand how to add integers, you can think about putting charges together." The book then moved di-

rectly to exercises without ever presenting the solution rule.

25. Another book (Fennell, Reys, Reys, & Webb, 1988) used a creative analogy about annihilation of matter and antimatter to explain addition of signed integers (p. 428):

> In a galaxy totally different from our own, a scientist named Dr. Zarkov discovered antimatter. When he puts antimatter together with antimatter nothing happens. For example, if he puts 4 cups of antiwater together with 3 cups of antiwater, he gets 7 cups of antimatter. Strange as it may seem, however, when he puts equal amounts of matter and antimatter together, they both disappear. For example, if he puts 2 telephones and 2 antitelephones together, he is left with nothing. In his latest experiment, Dr. Zarkov added 2 antibricks to a box containing 5 bricks. There was a blinding flash of light. When the smoke cleared, he was left with 3 bricks.

There was no illustration for the bricks example, although there was an illustration depicting 2 light and 2 dark telephones being placed together, and then disappearing in a "poof." Later in the section, the bricks example was represented symbolically as, "2 antibricks + 5 bricks = 3 bricks," and as, "-2 + 5 = 3." In this case, the book described the three steps in the addition of signed integers within the context of an interesting situation and related them to a symbolic representation but failed to relate them to a pictorial representation. In addition, the book failed to state the solution rule in a formal way, but it asked the students to do so as an exercise (p. 429): "State rules for adding a positive integer and a negative integer."

26. Finally, the fourth U.S. book (Bolster et al., 1988) used a hockey analogy to explain addition of signed integers in a section entitled "Adding Integers: Different Signs." The section (p. 356) started by describing a hockey scoring procedure: "Angelo's hockey coach uses a plus/minus system to rate the performance of the players. If a player is on the ice when his team scores, he gets 1. If he is on the ice when the other team scores, he gets -1. For his first 10 games, Angelo's plus rating was 4, and his minus rating was -7. What was his overall rating?" Next the book stated the problem symbolically: "Find 4 + (-7)." Finally, the book used a captioned number line illustration as shown in Figure 3b to represent the three steps in solving the problem. The caption described the steps: "Starting at zero, move 4 units to the right. From there, move 7 units to the left. His overall rating was -3." Although very short, this lesson makes connections among symbolic, verbal, and visual representations of all three steps in the example problem. Unlike the Japanese book which included many complete

3a. Excerpt from U.S. textbook that includes visual and symbolic representations for some of three problem-solving steps.

Example. -5 + +1 = ?

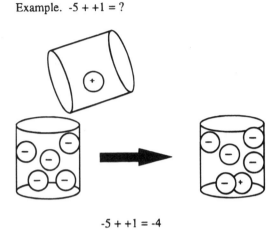

-5 + +1 = -4

3b. Excerpt from U.S. textbook that includes verbal, visual, and symbolic representations for each of three problem-solving steps.

Find 4 + (-7)

Starting at zero, move 4 units to the right.
From there, move 7 units to the left.

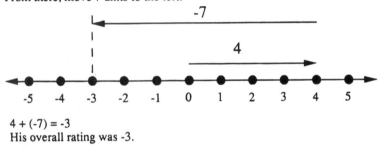

4 + (-7) = -3
His overall rating was -3.

Figure 3. **Representations used in the U.S. textbooks to teach addition of numbers with different signs.**
Note. 3a is adapted from Rucker, Dilley, Lowry, and Ockenga (1988); 3b is adapted from Bolster et al. (1988).

examples, however, this book presented only one complete example. Finally, the lesson ended with a statement of the solution rule (p. 357): "To add two integers with different signs, consider the distance each integer is from zero. Subtract the shorter distance from the longer distance. In your answer, use the sign of the number farther from zero." Like the Japanese book, this textbook used an inductive approach, moving from familiar examples to a formal statement of the rule.

27. In summary, the books differed in their use of multiple representations to explain how to add a negative and positive integer and in their inclusion of a statement of the solution rule. The Japanese books presented complete explanations of at least two examples of addition of a positive and negative integer; in these examples, all three steps in the procedure were presented symbolically, verbally, and pictorially, and the solution rule was clearly stated at the end of the explanation. In contrast, one U.S. textbook presented a complete explanation of

one example and a statement of the rule, one presented an explanation that lacked a pictorial representation and a statement of the rule, one presented an explanation that lacked a verbal representation and a statement of the rule, and one presented an explanation that lacked a pictorial representation and lacked portions of the symbolic and verbal representations. Overall, all of the Japanese books presented multiple representations of example problems and presented material in inductive order, whereas most of the U.S. books did not employ these meaningful instructional methods.

28. *The lesson was better integrated into the Japanese books than into the U.S. books, and the U.S. books were much longer than the Japanese books.* Research on text structure has highlighted the importance of organizing topics in a simple and coherent structure (Britton, Woodward, & Binkley, 1993; Jonassen, Beissner, & Yacci, 1993). The Japanese books, averaging less than 200 pages in length, contained an average of 7 chapters with each one divided into two or three coherent sections, whereas the U.S. textbooks, averaging 475 pages in length, contained an average of 12 chapters with each including approximately a dozen loosely related topics. For example, each of the Japanese books contained an entire chapter, entitled "Positive and Negative Numbers," devoted exclusively to signed numbers. The chapter consisted of three related sections involving an introduction to signed numbers, addition/subtraction of signed numbers, and multiplication/division of signed numbers. In contrast, lessons on addition and subtraction of signed numbers were presented as short fragments within more diverse chapters throughout most of the U.S. books. In three U.S. books, material on addition and subtraction of signed numbers was in the same chapter as solving equations and coordinate graphing of equations; in another, it was taught in a chapter that included units of measure, mixed numbers, and improper fractions. Overall, compared to the U.S. textbooks, the Japanese textbooks were more compact, presented a clearer structure, and covered fewer topics in more depth.

Conclusion

29. If textbooks serve as a sort of national curriculum, then international comparisons of textbook lessons can provide a partial picture of not only what is taught but also how it is taught across nations. Two competing methods for teaching students how to solve mathematics problems are drill and practice—in which page space is devoted to unexplained exercises involving symbol manipulation — and cognitive modeling — in which page space is devoted to

presenting and connecting multiple representations of step-by-step problem-solving processes through worked-out examples. The drill-and-practice approach follows from a view of learning as knowledge acquisition that emphasizes the *product of problem solving*—that is, getting the right answer; in contrast, the cognitive modeling approach follows from a view of learning as knowledge construction, which emphasizes the *process of problem solving*—that is, how to get the right answer (Mayer, 1989).

30. In this study, we are concerned with how much space in Japanese and U.S. mathematics textbooks is devoted to unexplained exercises consisting of symbol manipulation and how much space is devoted to building and connecting multiple representations for problem solving through worked-out example problems. Building on the exposure hypothesis, which originally focused on the allocation of instructional time (Mayer, Tajika, & Stanley, 1991; Stevenson & Stigler, 1992), the amount of space in mathematics textbooks that is devoted to meaningful explanation of problem-solving strategies may be an important determinant of students' mathematical problem-solving competence.

31. If textbook page space is viewed as a limited resource, then the allocation of that space reflects the priorities of the cultures that produced them. In Japan, the major use of page space is to explain mathematical procedures and concepts in words, symbols, and graphics, with an emphasis on worked-out examples and concrete analogies. In U.S. books, where the use of page space for explanation is minimized relative to Japanese books, the major use of page space is to present unexplained exercises in symbolic form for the students to solve on their own. These lessons are supplemented with attention-grabbing graphics that, unlike those in the Japanese books, are interesting but irrelevant. Japanese textbooks devote over 80% of their space, and U.S. books devote less than 40% of their space to instruction in the process of problem-solving (i.e., words, pictures, and symbols that explain how to add and subtract signed numbers), whereas U.S. books devote over 60% of their space, and Japanese books devote less than 20% of their space to hands-on exercises without guidance and interesting-but-irrelevant illustrations. A further analysis of lessons provides converging evidence: All three of the Japanese books and only one of the four U.S. books presented worked-out examples that explained how to solve problems in words, symbols, and pictures.

32. In Japan, the textbooks provide worked-out examples that model successful problem-solving strategies for students; in the U.S.,

textbooks are more likely to provide lots of exercises for students to solve on their own without much guidance. In Japan, the textbooks provide concrete analogies that help the student relate the concepts of addition and subtraction of signed numbers to a familiar situation; in the U.S., textbooks may give rules without much explanation. In Japan, the textbooks devote space to explaining mathematical ideas in words, whereas U.S. textbooks devote relatively more space to manipulating symbols.

33. The picture that emerges from our study of mathematics textbooks is that cognitive modeling of problem-solving processes is emphasized more in Japan than in the United States, whereas drill and practice on the product of problem solving is emphasized more in the United States than in Japan. Japanese textbooks seem to assume the learner is a cognitively active problem solver who seeks to understand the step-by-step process for solving a class of problems. In contrast, U.S. textbooks seem to assume the learner is a behaviorally active knowledge acquisition machine who learns best from hands-on activity in solving problems with minimal guidance and who needs to be stimulated by interesting decorative illustrations.

34. Our study is limited and should be interpreted as part of a converging set of research results. First, our data source involves only three Japanese and four U.S. books. Although we chose books that are widely used, we did not exhaustively review other books and supplemental materials, such as workbooks. Second, we examined only one lesson—amounting to a few pages in each of the books in our sample. Although the material is a typical component of the mathematics curriculum in both nations, we did not review other lessons. Furthermore, our subsequent analysis was even more restrictive, examining only addition of signed numbers with different signs. Finally, we focused on properties of the lessons that are related to problem-solving instruction, rather than on other aspects of the text such as its readability.

35. Ultimately, the practical goal of this study is to provide suggestions for the improvement of textbooks aimed at mathematical problem solving. The following suggestions need to be subjected to research study: (a) present a few basic topics in depth, organized into coherent lessons, rather than a huge collection of fragments; (b) embed the lesson within a familiar situational context so that verbal, visual, and symbolic representations are interconnected; (c) use worked-out examples to emphasize the process of problem solving; (d) present a verbal statement of the solution rule after presenting familiar worked-out examples. Finally, it

should be noted that additional research is needed to determine not only how to design effective textbooks but also how to use them successfully in classrooms (Driscoll, Moallem, Dick, & Kirby, 1994).

Note

This project was supported by a grant from the Pacific Rim Research Program. Hidetsugu Tajika translated two of the Japanese textbook lessons into English.

References

Armbruster, B., & Ostertag, J. (1993). Questions in elementary science and social studies textbooks. In B. K. Britton, A. Woodward, & M. Binkley (Eds.), *Learning from textbooks: Theory and practice* (pp. 69-94). Hillsdale, NJ: Erlbaum.

Bolster, L. C., Crown, W., Hamada, R., Hansen, V., Lindquist, M. M., McNerney, C., et al. (1988). *Invitation to mathematics* (7th grade). Glenview, IL: Scott, Foresman & Co.

Britton, B. K., Woodward, A., & Binkley, M. (Eds.). (1993). *Learning from textbooks: Theory and practice.* Hillsdale, NJ: Erlbaum.

Chambliss, M. J., & Calfee, R. C. (1989). Designing science textbooks to enhance student understanding. *Educational Psychologist, 24,* 307-322.

Driscoll, M. P., Moallem, M., Dick, W., & Kirby, E. (1994). How does the textbook contribute to learning in a middle school science class? *Contemporary Educational Psychology, 19,* 79-100.

Fennell, F., Reys, B. J., Reys, R. E., & Webb, A. W. (1988). *Mathematics unlimited* (7th grade). New York: Holt, Rinehart & Winston.

Fujita, H., & Maehara, S. (Eds.). (1992). *New math* (in Japanese). Tokyo: Shoseki.

Fukumori, N., Kikuchi, H., Miwa, T., Iijima, Y., Igarashi, K., Iwai, S., et al. (1992). *Math 1* (in Japanese). Osaka, Japan: Keirinkan.

Garner, R. (1992). Learning from school texts. *Educational Psychologist, 27,* 53-63.

Garner, R., Brown, R., Sanders, S., & Menke, D. J. (1992). "Seductive details" and learning from text. In K. A. Renninger, S. Hidi, & A. Krapp (Eds.), *The role of interest in learning and development* (pp. 239-254). Hillsdale, NJ: Erlbaum.

Glynn, S. M., Andre, T., & Britton, B. K. (1986). The design of instructional text. *Educational Psychologist, 21,* 245-251.

Grouws, D. A. (1992). (Ed.). *Handbook of research on mathematics teaching and learning.* New York: Macmillan.

Hiebert, J. (1986). (Ed.). *Conceptual antiprocedural knowledge: The case of mathematics.* Hillsdale, NJ: Erlbaum.

Jonassen, D. H., Beissner, K., & Yacci, M. (1993). *Structural knowledge.* Hillsdale, NJ: Erlbaum.

Kodaira, K. (Ed.). (1992). *Japanese grade 7 mathematics* (H. Nagata, Trans.). Chicago: University of Chicago. (Original work published 1984)

Levin, J. R., & Mayer, R. E. (1993). Understanding illustrations in text. In B. Britton, A. Woodward, & M. Binkley (Eds.), *Learning from textbooks: Theory and practice* (pp. 95-113). Hillsdale, NJ: Erlbaum.

Mayer, R. E. (1987). *Educational psychology: A cognitive approach.* New York: Harper Collins.

Mayer, R. E. (1989). Cognition and instruction in mathematics. *Journal of Educational Psychology, 81,* 452-456.

Mayer, R. E. (1992). *Thinking, problem solving, cognition* (2nd ed.). New York: Freeman.

Mayer, R. E. (1993). Illustrations that instruct. In R. Glaser (Ed.), *Advances in instructional psychology* (Vol. 4, pp. 253-284). Hillsdale, NJ: Erlbaum.

Mayer, R. E., Tajika, H., & Stanley, C. (1991). Mathematical problem solving in Japan and the United States: A controlled comparison. *Journal of Educational Psychology, 83,* 69-72.

McKnight, C. C., Crosswhite, F. J., Dossey, J. A., Kifer, E., Swafford, J. O., Trayers, K. J., & Cooney, T. J. (1987). *The underachieving curriculum: Assessing U.S. school mathematics from an international perspective.* Champaign, IL: Stipes.

Okamoto, Y. (1989, April). *An analysis of addition and subtraction word problems in textbooks: An across national comparison.* Paper presented at the Annual Meeting of the American Educational Research Association, San Francisco.

Robitaille, D. F., & Garden, R. A. (1989). *The IEA study of mathematics II: Contexts and outcomes of school mathematics.* Oxford, England: Pergamon.

Rucker, W. E., Dilley, C. A., Lowry, D. W., & Ockenga, E. G. (1988). *Heath mathematics* (7th grade). Lexington, MA: D. C. Heath.

Stevenson, H. W., & Bartsch, K. (1991). An analysis of Japanese and American textbooks in mathematics. In R. Leetsma & H. Walberg (Eds.), *Japanese educational productivity.* Ann Arbor: Center for Japanese Studies.

Stevenson, H. W., Lee, S-Y., Chen, C., Stigler, J. W., Hsu, C-C., & Kitamura, S. (1990). Contexts of achievement: A study of American, Chinese, and Japanese children. *Monographs of the Society for Research in Child Development, 55,*(1-2, Serial No. 221).

Stevenson, H. W., & Stigler, J. W. (1992). *The learning gap.* New York: Summit.

Stevenson, H. W., Stigler, J. W., Lee, S-Y., Kitamura, S., Kimura, S., & Kato, T. (1986). Achievement in mathematics. In H. Stevenson, H. Azuma, & K. Hakuta (Eds.), *Child development and education in Japan* (pp. 201-216). New York: Freeman.

Stigler, J. W., Lee, S-Y., & Stevenson, H. W. (1990). *Mathematical knowledge of Japanese, Chinese, and American elementary school children.* Reston, VA: National Council of Teachers of Mathematics.

Wade, S. E. (1992). How interest affects learning from text. In K. A. Renninger, S. Hidi, & A. Krapp (Eds.), *The role of interest in learning and development* (pp. 254-277). Hillsdale, NJ: Erlbaum.

Willoughby, S. S., Bereiter, C., Hilton, P., & Rubinstein, J. H. (1991). *Real math* (7th grade). La Salle, IL: Open Court.

Factual Questions

1. What hypothesis was examined in this study?

2. How did the researchers determine that the books in this study were typical?

3. How much longer is the instructional part of the lesson in the Japanese books than in the U.S. books?

4. What percentage of the space in the U.S. books is devoted to irrelevant illustrations?

5. How do the authors define "inductive" instruction?

6. According to the authors, why is their study "limited"?

Questions for Discussion

7. To what extent do you agree with the assumption stated in the last sentence of paragraph 4?

8. Is the procedure (see paragraphs 6 through 10) adequately described?

9. Speculate on why the researchers used two raters instead of just one. (See paragraphs 6 through 8.)

10. Would it be of interest to know the qualifications of the raters? Explain.

11. Do you believe that the researchers have presented sufficient data to support their conclusion stated in the last sentence of paragraph 27? Explain.

12. In paragraph 29, the authors state that international comparisons of textbooks can provide a partial picture of how mathematics is taught across nations. In addition to examining textbooks, how else could such a picture be obtained? Are there advantages and disadvantages to other methods you mention?

13. If you were to conduct a similar content analysis of textbooks, what changes, if any, would you make in the methodology?

14. Has this study convinced you that there are important differences between Japanese and U.S. textbooks? Explain.

15. To what extent do the data support the researchers' hypothesis?

16. This study is an example of content analysis (also known as documentary analysis) in which the contents of documents are analyzed. In general, what is your opinion of content analysis as a method for acquiring information important to psychology and education? Has this study contributed important information?

Quality Ratings

DIRECTIONS: Indicate your level of agreement with each of the following statements by circling a number from 5 for strongly agree (SA) to 1 for strongly disagree (SD). If you believe that an item is not applicable to this research article, leave it blank. Be prepared to explain your ratings.

A. The introduction establishes the importance of the research topic.
SA   5   4   3   2   1   SD

B. The literature review establishes the context for the study.
SA   5   4   3   2   1   SD

C. The research purpose, question, or hypothesis is clearly stated.
SA   5   4   3   2   1   SD

D. The method of sampling is sound.
SA   5   4   3   2   1   SD

E. Relevant demographics (for example, age, gender, and ethnicity) are described.
SA   5   4   3   2   1   SD

F. Measurement procedures are adequate.
SA   5   4   3   2   1   SD

G. The results are clearly described.
SA   5   4   3   2   1   SD

H. The discussion/conclusion is appropriate.
SA   5   4   3   2   1   SD

I. Despite any flaws noted above, the report is worthy of publication.
SA   5   4   3   2   1   SD

DEATH AS PORTRAYED TO ADOLESCENTS THROUGH TOP 40 ROCK AND ROLL MUSIC

Bruce L. Plopper   *University of Arkansas at Little Rock*
M. Ernest Ness   *University of Central Arkansas*

Rock and roll music, an important influential communication source, provides adolescents with messages about death in our society. The first 37 years of Top 40 rock songs (1955-1991) were examined, and songs that included a past death or an impending death were identified. The popularity of the songs, cause of death, gender of the deceased, and relationships among characters were determined. Analysis of song content was conducted, with specific emphasis on attitudes toward and means of coping with death. Results indicate that death songs comprise a disproportionately popular subset of Top 40 music, males dominate the obituaries, and grieving responses are restricted. Findings are discussed from a sociocultural perspective, with attention to their significance for adolescents.

Introduction

1. The influence of popular media in American culture has been widely studied (e.g., Wartella & Reeves, 1985). In particular, rock and roll music is one of the many elements of popular media to be analyzed as an integral part of society (e.g., Curtis, 1987), and it also has been acknowledged as an important channel for the communication and expression of adolescent values, conflicts, attitudes, and emotions (Leger, 1980; Santiago, 1969; Davis, 1985; Wells & Hakanen, 1991). More specifically, Fulton and Owen (1987-88) suggested that media proliferation has altered the ways death is portrayed in society, and that it is within this context that adolescents express their fears and frustrations about it.

2. Thrush and Paulus (1979) published the first structured analysis of death concerns in popular music and concluded that ". . . the vast majority of the songs address themselves to death and dying in a manner acceptable to 'median taste'" (p. 227). Teenage "coffin songs" (those ending with the death of one or both teenage lovers) also have been analyzed from the conceptual framework of death as a form of adolescent rebellion (Denisoff, 1983). Attig (1986) provided the most recent and

thorough review of death themes in rock and roll lyrics, and he suggested the necessity to "record the evolution of adolescent music, with particular emphasis on the presence of death and death-related themes, as it moves from its classic period into and through the 1980s" (p. 53).

3. A comprehensive analysis of death themes in rock music requires a methodology more precise than those employed in previous studies. First, a broad segment of the rock era should be reviewed. Second, there must be a clear and consistent definition of "death song." Third, some of the central features of death songs need to be uniformly coded.

4. The current investigation, using a rigorous methodology, addressed four questions: (1) How prominent has death been in rock and roll music? (2) How has death been depicted in selected demographic terms, e.g., who dies, how do they die, and what relationships are depicted? (3) What death-related attitudes and behaviors are portrayed in the lyrics of rock and roll death songs? (4) Have there been any trends in the prominence and content of death songs?

Method

5. Two steps were taken to operationally define popular rock and roll death songs. One step was to designate Top 40 "singles" as the record domain because they receive a greater amount of airplay than do album tracks. Another reason for using this set of songs was that the Recording Industry Association of America (1989) has indicated that adolescents and young adults make up the largest segment of the Top 40 record-buying public. *The Billboard Book of Top 40 Hits* (Whitburn, 1992) was selected as the definitive source for the chart history of the 9,311 singles that reached the pop music charts from January 1, 1955 to July 31, 1991.

6. The second step was to identify "death songs," using the following three-part definition: (1) one or more persons in the song clearly had to have died or the death(s) had to be imminent (going to occur within a few days); (2) the

deceased (or soon to be deceased) had to (a) be identified either by name or as a member of a small, identifiable group, (b) be the singer, (c) be in a clearly defined relationship with the singer, or (d) be essential to the meaning of the song, i.e., without mention of the deceased, the song's story line would significantly change; and (3) the deceased could not be a ghost or an apparition.

7. This strict definition excluded songs that (a) focused on reflections about death or other existential concerns, (b) deathbed fantasies or dreams about people who were not actually dead, or (c) predicted global holocaust. Instrumental versions of various songs also were excluded.

8. Three broad classifications for death songs also were identified: (a) songs about everyday, common people who either were fictitious or unknown to the general public; (b) songs about celebrities or public figures; and (c) novelty songs, which were defined as those which tended to be humorous or treated death lightly.

9. Each author independently reviewed all song titles in *The Billboard Book* and selected those songs that met the predetermined criteria of a death song. When both authors were uncertain about a song's lyrics, others who knew the song were consulted or the lyrics were obtained and analyzed.

10. Five facts about each record were collected during the review process. One, related to song popularity, was the highest position a record reached on the chart. A second, related to death-song chronology, was the date each

Plopper, B. L., & Ness, M. E. (1993). Death as portrayed to adolescents through top 40 rock and roll music. *Adolescence, 28*, 793-807. Copyright © 1993 by Libra Publishers. Reprinted with permission.

M. Ernest Ness, Director, Counseling Center, University of Central Arkansas.

Reprint requests to Bruce L. Plopper, Ph.D., Associate Professor, Department of Journalism, University of Arkansas at Little Rock, 2801 S. University Ave., Little Rock, Arkansas 72204-1099.

record entered the chart. The remaining facts focused directly on song content, and included cause of death, gender of the deceased, and relationships described by the lyrics.

11. The authors constructed an 11-category descriptive code for cause of death and a 10-item descriptive code for relationships (to classify story line interactions). To prevent group deaths from skewing the analysis, single-instance causes that killed single-gender groups were counted only once in either category, e.g., a shipwreck killing 29 men was counted once as a cause of death and once as a male death.

12. Song titles and lyrics also were analyzed to identify attitudes toward death, responses to death, and references to the tangible realities of death. Subcategories within each of these topic areas were developed during this analysis.

13. Inevitably, a number of songs containing death-related elements were excluded because they clearly did not meet the operational definition used in this study (e.g., "And When I Die" by Blood, Sweat and Tears). Also, several songs were excluded because listeners would require information in addition to the lyrics to know that they were death songs (e.g., "Everything I Own" by Bread and "Knockin' on Heaven's Door" by Bob Dylan).

Results

14. A total of 90 different death-related songs was identified. There were 69 songs dealing with the deaths of common people, 13 songs about the deaths of celebrities or public figures, and eight novelty songs containing death-related themes. In addition to the 90 songs used for the majority of the analyses, 12 other versions of these songs, recorded by other than the original artists, were included only in the calculations relating to song popularity. All songs used in this study are listed in the Appendix.

15. The analysis of chart history showed that death-related songs were substantially more popular than other songs reaching the Top 40. While 25.5% of death-related songs reached the No. 1 spot, only 8.6% of other songs reached that position. Additionally, while 57.8% of death-related songs reached the Top 10, only 36.2% of other songs made it that high on the charts.

Death songs about common people
16. This type of song was introduced late in the 1950s (seven songs), peaked in the 1960s (35 songs), declined slightly in the 1970s (26 songs), and experienced a precipitous drop-off in the 1980s and early 1990s (eight songs). Chronologically, 96% of the songs reaching the No. 1 position and 81% of the songs reaching the Top 10 did so prior to 1975.

17. Various causes of death were noted. Murder accounted for 24% of the deaths identified, other violent ends such as executions and shooting of criminals accounted for 24%, accidents caused 16%, and suicides caused 9%. War, illness, and disasters were infrequently cited, but natural causes were mentioned the least. Cause of death was unspecified in 23% of the songs, but in many of these songs, natural causes were implied.

18. Violence of one kind or another was the leading cause of death in each decade through the 1980s. The only other dominant cause of death/decade was accidents, which accounted for 29% of the deaths in songs from the 1960s. Where gender of the deceased could be determined, 70% were males, a percentage that was fairly consistent over time.

19. Analysis of the relationships described by the lyrics indicated that peer-romance was present in 30% of the songs, although nearly one-third of these songs were about individuals murdering their lovers. Family relationships were described in 22% of the songs, with husband-wife ties present one-third of the time and parent-child ties present two-thirds of the time.

20. In 16% of the songs, no relationship was discernible, but in nearly two-thirds of these songs, random murder was evident. Another type of relationship, friendship, appeared in 12% of the songs. Additionally, adversarial situations in the Old West were described in 7% of the songs, and pending executions were described in another 6%. Finally, coworkers were portrayed in 3% of the songs, people's lives were chronicled in 3% of the songs, and teenage rivalry between strangers was depicted in 1% of the songs.

21. Most songs reflected some attitude toward death. A fairly even distribution of 10-12 songs sent single messages that either life is cheap, death can be deserved, death can be a calculated risk, or death is not final. In some cases, one song sent two or more such messages. Nine songs reflected the attitude that death is a part of life, but only three explicitly wove death into a narrative which generally traced long periods in one person's life. By far, the attitudes least embraced were that life is dear and death is undeserved.

22. Although most types of identifiable attitudes were distributed quite evenly over time, prior to 1962 and after 1975 there seemed to be a disproportionate concentration of the attitudes that life is cheap (e.g., "Mack the Knife" and "18 and Life") and/or death is a calculated risk (e.g., "Don't Take Your Guns to Town" and "Renegade"). Many of the songs exhibiting

these attitudes described random violence or premeditated murder.

23. Behavioral, emotional, and cognitive responses to death also were evident in some of the songs. Behavioral responses were most prevalent. They included praying, committing suicide, trying to be good, being lethargic, writing a song, getting drunk, leaving town/staying away from home, and in the case of one cowboy song, hanging up the gunbelt.

24. Few emotional responses were mentioned, and some of them were tied to behavioral responses. They included crying and/or feeling lonely, sad, blue, hurt, empty, angry, or helpless.

25. Cognitive responses were quite narrow in nature, being limited primarily to thinking about the deceased, remembering words the deceased had spoken, and asking questions about the deceased. Other cognitive responses included not wanting to die, doubting God, wanting to quit school, missing the deceased, and longing to see the deceased again.

26. The final aspect of the analysis involved an examination of the ways song titles and lyrics referred to death. Only four titles contained a direct reference to death through use of some form of the words *dead* or *dying*. Also, one song title used the word *killing*, and two titles employed a form of the word *angel*.

27. Song lyrics, however, freely referred to death, both directly and euphemistically. Nearly one-third contained some form of the words *die* or *dead*. The others mentioned the deceased as having gone, passing away, meeting his fate, cashing it in, being shot down, floating face down, going to the happy hunting ground, going to heaven, being taken, or having his life ended.

28. References to what could be called the tangible realities of death were limited. Some lyrics, however, alluded to bodies, pine boxes, grave markers, preachers, and epitaphs, but relatives were infrequently mentioned.

Death songs about celebrities or public figures
29. Songs devoted to celebrities or public figures have been a relatively minor but constant contributor to the Top 40 rock and roll charts. For the most part, they remember entertainers, with just a few mentioning other public figures. All but one celebrity or public figure died tragically and prematurely.

30. Of the five songs that appeared in the 1950s, four were different versions of "The Ballad of Davy Crockett." Of the six that appeared in the 1960s, three were different versions of "Abraham, Martin, and John," one was about the notorious criminals Bonnie and Clyde, and one was about country music performers ("I Dreamed of a Hillbilly Heaven"). Three that made the charts in the 1970s were dedicated to singers or musicians, and one was about an artist ("Vincent"). Similarly, two from the 1980s concerned singers, and one was about an actress ("Candle in the Wind"). No celebrity death songs reached the Top 40 through the first 19 months of the 1990s.

31. In terms of popularity, three celebrity songs reached No. 1, and 10 reached the Top 10. While two of the three No. 1 songs reached that position in the 1970s, the distribution of Top 10 songs was fairly constant across decades.

32. Only four female celebrities were named among the 32 individuals referred to in the 13 different songs. Generally, the singer seemed to be an admirer of the deceased. Accidents, murder, and suicide accounted for the vast majority of these deaths.

33. Attitudes toward death and responses to death were nearly nonexistent in these songs. The most prevalent was the belief that death is not final, although this concept arose in only five of the songs.

34. There was no mention of death in any of the song titles in this category, although *heaven* was mentioned twice and *angel* was mentioned once. Some form of the word *die* was mentioned in the lyrics of a few songs, but direct and euphemistic references to death were much scarcer in these songs than in the songs about common people.

Novelty death songs

35. The smallest number of death-related songs fell into the novelty category, with one charting in the 1950s and seven charting in the 1960s. The last one to reach the Top 40 did so in 1967. Two novelty death songs reached No. 1, and four made the Top 10.

36. Male deaths dominated this category, too, by a 3-1 ratio. Three songs involved war-related casualties, two songs involved accidents, one song involved a romantic relationship, one involved friendship, and one involved an Old West murder.

37. Attitudes toward death and responses to death were generally not included in these novelty songs. The word "death" appeared in one title, and the lyrics to five of the songs mentioned some form of the word "die," but emotions were scarce. Responses included not wanting to die and tanning the deceased person's hide.

Discussion

Popularity

38. Rock and roll death songs constitute a disproportionately popular subset of Top 40 music, despite the fact that they account for only a small percentage of the songs reaching the charts since 1955. Additionally, as defined by average number of death songs/year, this prominence appears to be cyclical.

39. To some extent, these findings may be explained both in terms of adolescent interests and the cultural environment. From the late 1950s to the early 1960s, songs about adolescent romance ending in death were abundant. This was an age of social innocence in the United States, when an adolescent subculture, with a distinct identity, was emerging. Other death songs during this era included "Dead Man's Curve," a song about drag racing (another adolescent pastime), and a variety of hits by country artists singing about death in a frontier setting. Popularity of the latter type of song paralleled popularity of the television western.

40. Deaths of common people were portrayed in this period primarily as either the result of romantic tragedy (often through suicide and accidents) or the natural end to cowboy conflict (generally a gunfight), although a scattering of other causes also was evident. In reality, accidents were, and still are, a major cause of teenage death.

41. From the mid-1960s through the 1970s, death songs continued to be popular, but their content began to reflect a harsher reality. It was an era when teenagers were being drafted, when racial and economic strife was a staple of daily news reports, and when illegal drugs were more openly used and discussed. Top 40 death songs began to incorporate these concerns, including war casualties, violence in the ghetto, violence involving war protests, drug overdoses, and random violence on the streets.

42. From 1980-1984, only one death song reached the Top 40, and several factors may account for this. First, the Reagan presidency promoted the attitude that "everything was okay" and that the United States could feel good about itself. Perhaps death had no place in a feel-good scenario.

43. Additionally, as a result of the social upheaval of the 1960s, avenues other than recorded music offered ways to explore and reflect upon death. Books, call-in talk shows, and classes exploded into the culture as alternative sources of exposure. Talking openly about death became more acceptable in the late 1960s and early 1970s, so by the 1980s rock and roll was no longer one of few channels through which adolescents could express their attitudes and values.

44. Only three death songs appeared on the Top 40 chart from 1985-1988, but a resurgence occurred in 1989-1990, when seven death songs charted. These songs portrayed death primarily as an unhappy or violent end, with little attention to death as the natural end to a long life. Similar stresses characterized the social milieu during this period, in which the war against illegal drugs was stepped up, worldwide military intervention in Kuwait occurred, and more public awareness of other social ills such as homelessness and AIDS was evident.

Gender

45. Concerning sex of the deceased, males dominated the obituary columns throughout the period under investigation. This finding is in keeping with the stereotypic image of men as reckless and aggressive, although several songs from the early 1970s to the late 1980s portrayed women as committing murder when relationship conflicts arose. Culturally, men still dominate most aspects of society, so it would not be unexpected to find them as primary players in adolescent music.

Relationships

46. Over time, some noteworthy changes in relationships occurred; one was the decline of boy-girl relationships. Prior to 1970, nearly one-half of the death songs referred to some form of intimate relationship involving boyfriends and girlfriends, while after 1970, just over one-fourth of the songs described such a relationship.

47. This phenomenon is an extension of the portrayal of young love as romantic tragedy, which for centuries has captured public attention. A partial explanation for the decline of this story line in Top 40 rock and roll may be that as women have become more liberated, they have become less absorbed with dating relationships in general and more interested in a broader scope of interpersonal issues.

48. Another change concerning relationships was that after 1979, no songs in which the narrator(s) died reached the chart. Thus for a long time, death has been portrayed to adolescents as something that happens to someone else. Also, death has been pictured primarily as an individual event that rarely receives community attention. In fact, death appears to affect only one survivor.

49. Regarding other relationships, few songs concerned husbands and wives, but this is not surprising, given that most adolescents have not been married. Overall, husband-wife death songs, and parent-child death songs after 1965, incorporated family references that did not center around rebellion and defiance. This tells adolescents that when relationships are more stable, death is less likely to be violent.

Attitudes

50. While there is not one predominant attitude displayed toward death in rock music, approximately half of the songs about common people portrayed death as an abrupt end to a reckless, aggressive, or evil life. Through such lyrics, adolescents are told that death is the ultimate price one pays for taking risks and living dangerously, and this mimics traditional news media content about the deaths of common people.

51. Concomitantly, there is almost as much interest shown in the punishment of evildoers as there is interest in their victims. The earliest of the songs, "Tom Dooley," implores the murderer to "Hang down your head and cry" because "Poor boy, you're bound to die."

52. In contrast, deaths of the elderly are generally neglected in Top 40 songs, and rarely is death integrated into story lines as a part of the life cycle. Where such themes are found, the stability within a lifetime also is emphasized, as in "The Three Bells" and "Eleanor Rigby."

53. The attitude linked to death by suicide is that it is a way to deal with pain and loss. This is true for songs about a variety of relationships, including those of romance, friendship, and family. The most recently introduced reason for suicide is that of frustration with "the system," as in the song "Something to Believe In," which deals with the suicide of a disillusioned Viet Nam veteran. In this song, the singer wonders "why so many lose and so few win."

54. Although death is not often glorified, it is sometimes portrayed as heroic. For example, in "Big Bad John," the main character is killed in the act of saving lives. In "Ballad of the Green Berets," the theme of pride in dying for one's country is portrayed.

55. While celebrities are not generally depicted as heroic, death songs devoted to them illustrate that cultural idols do die, although in all but one case, they have died tragically and prematurely. "Abraham, Martin, and John" even focuses on the perception that "it seems the good die young." The message seems to be that death from natural causes does not deserve much attention.

Responses

56. When responses to death are evaluated, it is clear that the primary focus in rock and roll death songs is on the act (how the person died), and not upon the less exciting effects of death. Other characters in the songs can then be detached observers, personally removed from the death experience, who can avoid having to cope with loss. These songs offer few models for adolescents to emulate in terms of appropriate behavioral responses to death, and how survivors are supposed to think and feel about death.

57. In terms of behavioral responses, the models provided in rock and roll death songs indicate that escape and avoidance are most appropriate. Leaving town, joining the deceased in death, or engaging in some other diversionary behavior are the most frequently cited acts.

58. Emotionally, mourning is portrayed as an abbreviated process, with little sustained attention given to grief and grieving. This may reflect the belief that adolescents have not learned to grieve over their losses, except in cases of parental death. In those cases, lyrics show a greater depth of feeling and sentimentality beyond the moment. "Alone Again, Naturally" contains the foremost example of such emotion, as the son says, "I remember I cried when my father died, never wishing to hide the tears."

59. Sadness, though, often is ignored or at best implied. In "Honey," the husband laments, "I miss you and I'm feeling blue," but few songs approach even that old level of emotional expression. Instead, adolescent listeners are given the impression that intimate and personal responses to death are unusual.

60. On a cognitive level, little conscious attention is given to the meaning of death or trying to understand it; this tells adolescents that death is incomprehensible. The music does, however, suggest it is possible to have regrets about things not said to a loved one during life. For example, in "The Living Years," the son says, "I wasn't there that morning, when my father passed away. I didn't get to tell him all the things I had to say."

Other death references

61. The tangible realities of death, the visible reminders, are markedly absent. The deceased, both figuratively and literally, is seldom laid to rest. Thus adolescents are shown that the finality of death is not something to be confronted. In fact, songs about common people and celebrities support the illusion that the deceased is not gone, so the memory of the deceased is allowed to live on. Unpleasant thoughts and images are avoided, with ceremonies and rituals occurring at some later time.

62. In another sense, references to a spiritual afterlife are sometimes evident through various allusions to heaven. For example, in "Rock and Roll Heaven," the singers proclaim, "If you believe in forever, then life is just a one-night stand," and in "Fly to the Angels," the boyfriend says, "Heaven awaits your heart." Such references reflect the traditional belief in an afterlife, and they are common ways of denying the finality of death. The belief that immortality is assured provides adolescents an answer to the question, "What happens after we die?"

63. Finally, the analysis of novelty songs showed that humor in death is no longer part of Top 40 music. The last novelty death song appeared in 1967, and this reflects the loss of childhood innocence adolescents experienced in the 1960s. Perhaps humor in death is outdated, for as society became more harsh, adolescents matured earlier, both emotionally and cognitively. In modern society, death is a somber event.

Conclusion

64. A variety of death songs appeared during the first 37 years of rock and roll Top 40, but there were distinct changes in their content and popularity as the adolescent environment changed from an era of innocence to one of social awareness. Some of the changes also reflected social evolution toward openness about death and interest in contemporary social concerns.

65. This study identified specific communication trends in the way death is portrayed to adolescents and linked them to sociocultural developments, but the world continues to change.

66. As national and international events alter the environment, review of future death-song incarnations could determine if their ties to socio-political events are strengthened or diminished.

67. Ultimately, the culture surrounding the fourth decade of rock and roll death songs already has brought with it many promises and threats, thus making continued analysis desirable. This, coupled with the effects of worldwide political events, should make the subsequent period of rock and roll history valuable for further research.

APPENDIX
TOP 40 DEATH SONGS
(* denotes remake of an original)

Chart Debut	Title	Artist	Chart Debut	Title	Artist
Songs About Common People			2/74	Last Kiss*	Wednesday
10/58	Tom Dooley	The Kingston Trio	2/74	Seasons in the Sun	Terry Jacks
2/59	Don't Take Your Guns to Town	Johnny Cash	5/74	Billy, Don't Be a Hero	Bo Donaldson and the Heywoods
8/59	The Three Bells	The Browns			
9/59	Mack the Knife	Bobby Darin	8/74	I Shot the Sheriff	Eric Clapton
9/59	The Three Bells*	Dick Flood	3/75	Emma	Hot Chocolate
11/59	El Paso	Marty Robbins	8/75	Rocky	Austin Roberts
12/59	Running Bear	Johnny Preston	8/75	Run Joey Run	David Geddes
1/60	Teen Angel	Mark Dinning	11/75	The Last Game of the Season (A Blind Man in the Bleachers)	David Geddes
5/60	Mack the Knife*	Ella Fitzgerald			
6/60	Tell Laura I Love Her	Ray Peterson	1/76	Hurricane	Bob Dylan
2/61	Ebony Eyes	The Everly Brothers	2/76	Bohemian Rhapsody	Queen
5/61	Moody River	Pat Boone	9/76	The Wreck of the Edmund Fitzgerald	Gordon Lightfoot
9/61	Frankie and Johnny	Brook Benton	7/77	The Killing of Georgie	Rod Stewart
10/61	Big Bad John	Jimmy Dean	7/78	Copacabana	Barry Manilow
4/62	Old Rivers	Walter Brennan	4/79	Renegade	Styx
5/62	Liberty Valance	Gene Pitney	12/83	Think of Laura	Christopher Cross
9/62	Patches	Dickey Lee	9/85	Spanish Eddie	Laura Brannigan
8/63	Frankie and Johnny*	Sam Cooke	1/89	The Living Years	Mike and the Mechanics
9/63	Last Kiss	J. Frank Wilson	7/89	18 and Life	Skid Row
3/64	Dead Man's Curve	Jan and Dean	10/89	Don't Close Your Eyes	Kix
3/64	Miller's Cave	Bobby Bare	12/89	Janie's Got a Gun	Aerosmith
10/64	Leader of the Pack	The Shangri-Las	9/90	Fly to the Angels	Slaughter
11/64	Ringo	Lorne Greene	10/90	Something to Believe In	Poison
6/65	Give Us Your Blessings	The Shangri-Las			
8/65	One Dyin' and A-Burying	Roger Miller	**Songs About Celebrities or Public Figures**		
11/65	I Can Never Go Home Anymore	The Shangri-Las	2/55	The Ballad of Davy Crockett	Bill Hayes
2/66	Ballad of the Green Berets	Sgt. Barry Sadler	3/55	The Ballad of Davy Crockett*	Fess Parker
4/66	Frankie and Johnny*	Elvis Presley	3/55	The Ballad of Davy Crockett*	"Tennessee" Ernie Ford
6/66	Hey Joe	The Leaves	4/55	The Ballad of Davy Crockett*	The Voices of Walter Schumann
7/66	Billy and Sue	B. J. Thomas			
9/66	Eleanor Rigby	The Beatles	4/59	The Three Stars	Tommy Dee
1/67	Green Green Grass of Home	Tom Jones	12/60	Ballad of the Alamo	Marty Robbins
8/67	Ode to Billy Joe	Bobby Gentry	8/61	I Dreamed of a Hillbilly Heaven	Tex Ritter
3/68	Honey	Bobby Goldsboro	3/68	The Ballad of Bonnie and Clyde	Georgie Fame
4/68	Delilah	Tom Jones	11/68	Abraham, Martin, and John	Dion
6/68	Folsom Prison Blues	Johnny Cash	7/69	Abraham, Martin, and John*	Moms Mabley
7/68	Eleanor Rigby*	Ray Charles	7/69	Abraham, Martin, and John*	The Miracles
9/68	I've Gotta Get a Message to You	The Bee Gees	7/71	American Pie	Don McLean
1/69	I Started a Joke	The Bee Gees	12/72	Vincent	Don McLean
5/69	In the Ghetto	Elvis Presley	6/74	Rock and Roll Heaven	The Righteous Brothers
10/69	Reuben James	Kenny Rogers & the First Edition	4/77	Sir Duke	Stevie Wonder
			3/85	Night Shift	The Commodores
11/69	Eleanor Rigby*	Aretha Franklin	11/87	Candle in the Wind	Elton John
7/70	Ohio	Crosby, Stills, Nash, & Young	1/89	Angel of Harlem	U2
			Novelty Death Songs		
8/70	Patches*	Clarence Carter	5/59	The Battle of New Orleans	Johnny Horton
9/70	Fire and Rain	James Taylor	8/60	Bad Man's Blunder	The Kingston Trio
2/71	D.O.A.	Bloodrock	9/60	Mr. Custer	Larry Verne
4/71	Timothy	Buoys	6/63	Tie Me Kangaroo Down, Sport	Rolf Harris
7/72	Alone Again, Naturally	Gilbert O'Sullivan	12/64	Leader of the Laundromat	The Detergents
9/72	Freddie's Dead	Curtis Mayfield	5/66	The Ballad of Irving	Frank Gallop
10/72	Papa Was a Rolling Stone	The Temptations	12/66	Snoopy vs. the Red Baron	The Royal Guardsmen
3/73	Daisy a Day	Jud Strunk	6/67	Ding Dong! The Witch Is Dead	The Fifth Estate
3/73	The Night the Lights Went Out in Georgia	Vicki Lawrence			
6/73	Daddy Could Swear, I Declare	Gladys Knight and the Pips			
2/74	Dark Lady	Cher			

References

Attig, T. (1986). Death themes in adolescent music: The classic years. In C. A. Coor & J. N. McNeil (Eds.), *Adolescence and death,* (pp. 32-56). New York: Springer Publishing Company.

Curtis, J. (1987). *Rock eras: Interpretations of music and society, 1954–1984.* Bowling Green, Ohio: Bowling Green State University Popular Press.

Davis, S. (1985). Pop lyrics: A mirror and a molder of society. *Et cetera, 42,* 167-169.

Denisoff, R. S. (1983). Teen angel: Resistance, rebellion, and death—revisited. *Journal of Popular Culture, 16,* 116-122.

Fulton, R., & Owen, G. (1987-88). Death and society in twentieth century America. *Omega, 18,* 379-395.

Leger, R. E. (1980). Where have all the flowers gone? A sociological analysis of the origins and content of youth values of the seventies. *Adolescence, 15,* 283-300.

Recording Industry Association of America. (1989). *Inside the recording industry: A statistical overview.* Washington, DC: Author.

Santiago, L. (1969). The lyrical expression of adolescent conflict in the Beatles songs. *Adolescence, 4,* 199-210.

Thrush, J. C., & Paulus, S. (1979). The concept of death in popular music: A social psychological perspective. *Popular Music and Society, 6,* 219-228.

Wartella, E. & Reeves, B. (1985). Historical trends in research on children and the media: 1900–1960. *Journal of Communication, 35,* 118-133.

Wells, A., & Hakanen, E. (1991). The emotional use of popular music by adolescents. *Journalism Quarterly, 68,* 445-454.

Whitburn, J. (1992). *The Billboard book of top 40 hits* (5th ed.). New York: Billboard Publications, Inc.

Factual Questions

1. In which paragraph are the research questions for this study first stated?

2. How were novelty songs defined in this study?

3. For this study, did the researchers examine the lyrics of all 9,311 songs? Explain.

4. How many death-related songs were identified for this study?

5. Were death-related songs more or less popular than other songs reaching the Top 40?

6. Were behavioral or emotional responses to death more prevalent in the songs?

7. Would examination of only the titles of the songs be a good way to identify death-related songs?

Questions for Discussion

8. In general, what does the term "operational definition" mean? Is the definition of "popular rock and roll death songs" fully operationalized? (See paragraphs 5 and 6.)

9. In your opinion, does this study deal exclusively with adolescents? Explain.

10. What is your opinion of the researchers' decision to count the death of a single-gender group by a single cause (such as a shipwreck) as a single death?

11. What is your opinion of the researchers' explanation of the popularity of death-related songs in terms of adolescent interests and the cultural environment? (See paragraphs 38–44.)

12. Throughout the discussion, the researchers note that death-related songs provide messages (for example, see paragraph 50). Is there evidence that these messages influence adolescents? Are you willing to assume that they are an important influence?

13. The researchers do not discuss the interrater reliability of their data. Is this a flaw? Explain.

14. Do you agree with the researchers' suggestion that continued analysis of death-related songs in the future is desirable? Explain.

15. This study is an example of "content analysis," a type of study in which the contents of documents (in this case, lyrics) are examined to generate data. Are there other types of documents to which adolescents are exposed that might be a valuable source of data? Explain.

16. In general, what is your opinion on content analysis as a research method? In comparison to other methods, are there advantages and disadvantages to this method?

17. If you were to conduct this study again, what changes, if any, would you make in the research methodology?

Quality Ratings

DIRECTIONS: Indicate your level of agreement with each of the following statements by circling a number from 5 for strongly agree (SA) to 1 for strongly disagree (SD). If you believe that an item is not applicable to this research article, leave it blank. Be prepared to explain your ratings.

A. The introduction establishes the importance of the research topic.
   SA   5   4   3   2   1   SD

B. The literature review establishes the context for the study.
   SA   5   4   3   2   1   SD

C. The research purpose, question, or hypothesis is clearly stated.
   SA   5   4   3   2   1   SD

D. The method of sampling is sound.
   SA   5   4   3   2   1   SD

E. Relevant demographics (for example, age, gender, and ethnicity) are described.
   SA   5   4   3   2   1   SD

F. Measurement procedures are adequate.
   SA   5   4   3   2   1   SD

G. The results are clearly described.
   SA   5   4   3   2   1   SD

H. The discussion/conclusion is appropriate.
   SA   5   4   3   2   1   SD

I. Despite any flaws noted above, the report is worthy of publication.
   SA   5   4   3   2   1   SD

ARTICLE 9

HAS PUBLIC INTEREST IN ANIMAL RIGHTS PEAKED?

Harold A. Herzog, Jr. *Western Carolina University*

1. The animal rights movement has emerged over the past 20 years as a highly visible and effective social movement. The growth of public interest in issues associated with the treatment of animals, and especially with their use in behavioral and biomedical research, has been spectacular. The use of animals in psychological research has come under particularly heavy criticism from animal activists. For example, Rollin (1981) has referred to experimental psychology as "the field most consistently guilty of mindless activity that results in great suffering" (p. 124). Although psychologists who work with nonhuman species have mounted a counterattack (e.g., Miller, 1985), the negative image of behavioral research with animals persists among many segments of the public. Domjan and Purdy (1995) have recently argued that even the authors of introductory textbooks seldom acknowledge the contributions of animal studies to advances in psychology.

2. Although it is commonly believed that the rise of widespread animal protectionism is a recent phenomenon, this is not the case. An organized antivivisection movement emerged in England and the United States in the latter half of the 19th century. Victorian animal activists, like their modern counterparts, were particularly critical of psychological research with animals (Dewsbury, 1990). However, public interest in social issues rises and falls (Hilgartner & Bosk, 1988). For example, the high point of Victorian antivivisectionism was reached in the years preceding World War I. By 1920, interest in animal protectionism had largely declined, only to reemerge several generations later. In this comment, I report evidence that a similar decline in the public visibility of this issue may now be taking place in the United States.

3. Concern with a social problem is reflected by the degree of media attention it receives. The number of magazine and newspaper articles devoted to a social problem can serve as a gauge of public interest. For example, Phillips and Sechzer (1989) examined awareness of ethical issues associated with the use of animals within the scientific community by analyzing the coverage of the topic in scientific books and journals. They found an explosive rise in the number of articles appearing in the scientific literature during the period 1965-1985. I have surveyed recent trends in the coverage of topics related to the animal rights movement and the treatment of animals in popular periodicals and in major newspapers. The results of my analysis suggest that the visibility of the animal rights movement has leveled off and may be declining.

4. I manually searched *The Reader's Guide to Periodical Literature* and conducted a computer search of *Newspaper Abstracts* to examine changes in the coverage of the animal rights movement over the past 20 years. The *Reader's Guide* is a bibliographic index that surveys 250 popular and semipopular periodicals. I began the *Reader's Guide* search with articles published in 1975 (Volume 35), the year of publication of Peter Singer's influential book *Animal Liberation,* often referred to as the bible of the animal rights movement. I ended the search with Volume 54 (December 1994). All articles related to animal welfare issues and the animal rights movement were included in the tabulation. The key words and phrases used to access the articles varied from year to year as the movement developed. They included *animal experimentation, animal treatment, animal rights movement,* and *animal liberation.* Articles dealing with a wide variety of topics, such as the treatment of particular species, the search for alternatives to the use of animals in consumer product testing, the campaign against furs, and articles about animal protection organizations (e.g., People for the Ethical Treatment of Animals, the Humane Society of the United States, and the Animal Liberation Front) were included in the tally. Articles related to wildlife management, hunting, trapping, and the smuggling of animal products were not counted unless they were directly referenced under a topic such as animal treatment.

5. The bound edition of the *Reader's Guide* does not include newspaper articles. I searched *Newspaper Abstracts* through First Search, an online information service. *Newspaper Abstracts* is a bibliographic database that covers 25 major newspapers published in the United States. (It also includes one foreign newspaper, the *Manchester Guardian.* Articles from the *Guardian* were not included in this tally.) *Newspaper Abstracts* is more limited than the *Reader's Guide* in that it only covers issues of newspapers published since January 1, 1989. The computer search was conducted using the key word phrase *animal rights or animal treatment.*

6. The *Reader's Guide* results are shown in Figure 1. Throughout the 1980s, there was a general increase in articles devoted to animal welfare and the animal rights movement. But the number of articles peaked in 1990 and has shown a significant decline since then. The same trend was evident in the number of articles appearing in American newspapers. The number of articles listed in *Newspaper Abstracts* doubled between 1989 and 1990, from 163 articles to 338 articles. Since 1990, however, there has been a steady downward trend (245 articles in 1991, 208 in 1992, 191 in 1993, and 142 in 1994).

7. Mutual fund brochures routinely caution readers that past performance is no guarantee of future behavior. The same proviso applies here. In the long run, the decline in coverage of the animal rights movement in newspapers and periodicals may reflect merely a transient downturn in public interest. On the other hand, it is possible that, like Victorian antivivisectionism, the contemporary animal rights movement is running out of steam.

8. There are other signs that suggest that interest in animal protectionism may have peaked. In recent years, contributions to animal rights organizations have not followed the pattern of dramatic growth seen in the 1980s. Trends in the consumption of products in the United States offer other examples. Animal activists sometimes take credit for the fact that fur sales declined 40% between 1987 and 1991. However, sales of fur coats have increased 20% over the past two years. The consumption of meat by Americans has followed a similar pattern; the number of beef cattle raised annually declined steadily between 1984 and 1988, but has increased since 1990.

Figure 1   *Number of articles pertaining to the treatment of animals and the animal rights movement referenced in the Reader's Guide to Periodical Literature*

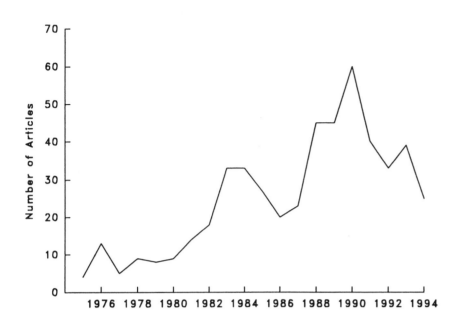

Hilgartner, S., & Bosk, C. L. (1988). The rise and fall of social problems: A public arena model. *American Journal of Sociology, 94,* 53-78.

Miller, N. E. (1985). The value of behavioral research on animals. *American Psychologist, 40,* 423-440.

Orlans, F. B. (1993). *In the name of science: Issues in responsible animal experimentation.* New York: Oxford University Press.

Phillips, M. R., & Sechzer, J. A. (1989). *Animal research and ethical conflict: An analysis of the scientific literature: 1966-1968.* New York: Springer-Verlag.

Rollin, B. E. (1981). *Animal rights and human morality.* Buffalo, NY: Prometheus.

Singer, P. (1975). *Animal liberation.* New York: New York Review of Books.

U.S. Department of Justice. (1993). *Report to Congress on the extent and effects of domestic and international terrorism on animal enterprises.* Washington, DC: Author.

Factual Questions

1. When did the first organized animal rights movement emerge?

2. Did the author read articles in periodicals and newspapers to obtain the data?

3. How did the author identify articles of interest?

4. The only increase in the number of newspaper articles on animal rights or animal treatment in this study occurred between what two years?

5. In 1990, what percentage of Americans agreed that animals have rights and that the way they are used should be limited?

Questions for Discussion

6. The first two sentences in paragraph 3 state key assumptions underlying this research. To what extent do you agree with the assumptions? Explain.

7. What are the advantages and disadvantages of using "key words" (see paragraphs 4 and 5) instead of actually reading the articles in a study of this type?

8. The data for periodicals are presented in a graph (i.e., statistical figure) while the data for newspapers are presented in the text. Which approach do you favor? Why?

9. Several factors might explain the decline in media coverage of the animal rights movement. First, legislative reforms such as 1985 amendments to the Animal Welfare Act have led to enhanced oversight of research and may have taken some of the wind out of the sails of animal activists. Second, some animal protection organizations have shifted strategies away from the barricades and toward courtrooms and statehouses. A report by the United States Department of Justice on terrorist activities by animal activists indicated that the frequency of incidents such as the theft of laboratory animals and harassment of researchers increased steadily between 1976 and 1988, but it has subsequently shown a consistent decline (U.S. Department of Justice, 1993). Clearly, fire bombings are more likely to attract media attention than subcommittee hearings.

10. Finally, as evidenced by the 1994 elections, the mood of the public has become decidedly more conservative. The contemporary animal liberation movement is the direct descendant of the civil rights and women's movements (Singer, 1975). It is no surprise that animal protectionism, like older social causes based on liberal political principles (in a broad sense), may have a harder time attracting attention and public sympathy in the Gingrich era.

11. There is no doubt that the animal protection movement has had a major and possibly permanent impact on how people perceive other species and our moral obligation to them. A 1990 survey of Americans found that 80% of the public agreed with a statement indicating that animals have rights that should limit the way they are used (Orlans, 1993). And the movement continues to generate controversy and significant, albeit reduced, media coverage. Increasingly, the battle for the "hearts and minds," particularly with regard to the use of animals in research, is being played out in educational settings, as partisans on both sides attempt to sway the opinions of young people (Blum, 1994), and the long-term effect of the debate over the moral status of animals remains to be seen. Recent trends in media coverage, however, suggest that animal rights activism may be following the cyclical pattern that is characteristic of other social movements.

References

Blum, D. (1994). *The monkey wars.* New York: Oxford University Press.

Dewsbury, D. (1990). Early interactions between animal psychologists and animal activists and the founding of the APA Committee on Precautions in Animal Experimentation. *American Psychologist, 45,* 315-327.

Domjan, M. & Purdy, J. E. (1995). Animal research in psychology: More than meets the eye of the general psychology student. *American Psychologist, 50,* 496-503.

9. In the second and third sentences of paragraph 6, the author interprets the data in Figure 1. Do you agree with his interpretation? Explain.

10. In addition to conducting a content analysis of newspaper and magazine articles, how else could data on this topic be gathered? Are there advantages and disadvantages to other methods? Explain.

11. Briefly describe another research problem for which it might be appropriate to conduct a content analysis of documents other than newspaper and magazine articles.

Quality Ratings

DIRECTIONS: Indicate your level of agreement with each of the following statements by circling a number from 5 for strongly agree (SA) to 1 for strongly disagree (SD). If you believe that an item is not applicable to this research article, leave it blank. Be prepared to explain your ratings.

A. The introduction establishes the importance of the research topic.
   SA   5   4   3   2   1   SD

B. The literature review establishes the context for the study.
   SA   5   4   3   2   1   SD

C. The research purpose, question, or hypothesis is clearly stated.
   SA   5   4   3   2   1   SD

D. The method of sampling is sound.
   SA   5   4   3   2   1   SD

E. Relevant demographics (for example, age, gender, and ethnicity) are described.
   SA   5   4   3   2   1   SD

F. Measurement procedures are adequate.
   SA   5   4   3   2   1   SD

G. The results are clearly described.
   SA   5   4   3   2   1   SD

H. The discussion/conclusion is appropriate.
   SA   5   4   3   2   1   SD

I. Despite any flaws noted above, the report is worthy of publication.
   SA   5   4   3   2   1   SD

ARTICLE 10

GENDER DIFFERENCES OF REPORTED SAFER SEX
BEHAVIORS WITHIN A RANDOM SAMPLE OF COLLEGE STUDENTS

Michele J. Hawkins *The Catholic University of America*
Cathleen Gray *The Catholic University of America*
Wesley E. Hawkins *National Institute of Drug Abuse, Baltimore, Maryland*

This study investigated the frequency of safer sex behaviors with a random sample of sexually active college students (N = 315) at a university in the Northwest. The most frequent safer sex behaviors were discussion of contraceptives (58.6%), being more selective (46.5%), and reducing the number of sexual partners (43.6%). The least frequent safer sex behaviors included discussion of partner's sexual health prior to sexual behavior (26.1%), using condoms or dental dams (24.4%), one sexual partner (22.6%), and abstaining from sex as a safer sex practice (12.3%). The only two behaviors which indicated gender differences were (a) if they were being more selective as a safer sex practice and (b) reducing number of sexual partners as a safer sex practice. Women were more likely to state that they were "almost always" more selective than their male peers. Findings from this study indicated that a substantial number of students reported "at risk" sexual practices. These findings indicated a need for HIV-prevention efforts.

1. The Centers for Disease Control reported that 441,528 people in the USA have been diagnosed with AIDS (Centers for Disease Control and Prevention, December, 1994). In 1989, AIDS became the sixth leading cause of death for youth between 15 and 24 years of age (National Center for Health Statistics, 1992). Currently, there are 1,965 reported cases of HIV in youth between 13 and 19 years of age and 16,575 persons in the 20–24 yr. age group (Centers for Disease Control and Prevention, December, 1994).

2. In 1992, HIV/AIDS became the second leading cause of death among persons ages 25 to 44 years. For males of this age, HIV/AIDS is the leading cause of death. Due to the long incubation period of HIV/AIDS, many of the infected persons were probably infected during their teens or early twenties. Although there is no known cure for the deadly virus, safer sexual behaviors have been suggested as the appropriate prevention against the disease. These behaviors include (a) abstinence, (b) discussion of

partner's sexual health prior to sexual behaviors, (c) being more selective, (d) decreasing number of sexual partners (preferably monogamy), and (e) using condoms and/or dental dams.

3. While safer sex behaviors have been recommended, adolescents continue to engage in behaviors which put them at risk for HIV as well as other sexually transmitted diseases. In a recent study of sexually active college students a majority of the respondents stated that they continue to engage in unprotected sexual relations (Simkins, 1994). Similarly, in a study of high school students reported in the CDC *Morbidity and Mortality Weekly Report* (1992), 19% of the students reported having had four or more partners during their lifetimes and 44.9% stated that they or their partners had used a condom at their last intercourse. Past research with college students (American Medical Association, 1990) indicated only one-fourth of sexually active female students reported their partners used a condom, whereas 57% of the men reported using condoms. Baldwin and Baldwin (1988) found that only 34% of sexually active students reported using condoms during sexual intercourse. Similarly, men have reported being more comfortable discussing the subject of condom use with potential partners (men 56.6% vs. women 44.2%), becoming more selective in their choice of partners, and having fewer partners than women during the past year (Carroll, 1990). Although estimates vary on the extent of safer sex practices, these findings are quite alarming given estimates that three-quarters of the college population are sexually active (DeLamater & MacCorquodale, 1979).

4. Although these studies have indicated that students are not engaging in safer sex practices, few studies have used random sampling techniques and included undergraduate and graduate students. Therefore, the primary purpose of this study was to examine frequency by gender of safer sex practices with a random sample of undergraduate and graduate college students.

Method

5. The sampling frame (entire college campus) consisted of 16,593 students attending a university in the northwestern part of the United States. Names were randomly generated by the Office of Student Affairs. Instrument packages were mailed to each randomly selected student through the U.S. Postal System. Instrument packages contained an introductory covering letter, a survey, an optical scan sheet, and a return envelope. Of 1,200 students sampled, the 531 students responding constituted a 44% return rate. The demographic distribution of the sample approximated the total population of the student body. Women represented 51% of the sample while men represented 49%. Most respondents were Caucasian (81%) with the remainder being Asian/Pacific Islander (13%), African American (1.5%), Latino/Mexican-American (1.5%), other (1.9%), and those not reporting ethnicity (1.9%). Class standing of respondents were 17.1% graduate, 28.8% senior, 16.9% junior, 21.1% sophomore, and 14.3% freshmen. Finally, most respondents lived off campus (44%); one-third lived in residence halls (33%). Eleven percent lived with their parents, 8% in Greek housing, and 2% in cooperative housing. Of the total respondents, more than 73% stated that they were sexually active. Only the data from those students stating they were sexually active during the past year were analyzed (*N* = 315).

Results

6. The survey contained questions regarding safer sex behaviors related to HIV/AIDS

Hawkins, M. J., Gray, C., & Hawkins, W. E. (1995). Gender differences of reported safer sex behaviors within a random sample of college students. *Psychological Reports*, 77, 963-968. Copyright © Psychological Reports, 1995.

Address inquiries to Michele J. Hawkins, Ph.D., The Catholic University of America, National Catholic School of Social Service, Washington, DC 20064.

Table 1 *Number and percent* of sexual partners of sexually active single college students*

No. of Sexual Partners in Past 5 Years	Women		Men		Total	
	f	%	f	%	f	%
1	49	24.6	22	19.0	71	22.6
2–4	91	45.7	55	47.4	146	46.3
5–10	47	23.6	25	21.6	72	22.9
11 or more	12	6.0	14	12.1	26	8.3
Total	199	63.2	116	36.8	315	100.0

*May not add up to 100% due to rounding.

(Tables 1 and 2). For the use of program planning, one question regarding use of birth control was included. The first question pertained to the number of partners with whom the students had sex in the past five years. Twenty-two percent stated that they had one partner, 46.3% had two to four partners, with 31.2% having five or more (see Table 1). There were no gender differences.

7.   Next, questions pertaining to respondents' specific safer sex practices were asked (see Table 2). The least frequent sexual behavior respondents stated they had been engaged in was "abstaining from sex as a safer sex practice" (12.3%). Further, only 24.4% of the students stated that they "almost always" used condoms or dental dams as a safer sex practice, with 55.5% stating that they rarely or never used

Table 2 *Safer sexual practices of sexually active single respondents*

Practice	Gender	Almost Always		Often		Rarely		Never		N/A		Total		χ^2
		f	%	f	%	f	%	f	%	f	%	f	%	
Abstaining from sex as a safer sex practice	F	26	13.3	50	25.5	47	24.0	58	29.6	15	7.7	196	63.2	
	M	12	10.5	24	21.1	34	29.8	31	27.2	13	11.4	114	36.8	3.25
	T	38	12.3	74	23.9	81	26.1	89	28.7	28	9.0	310	100.0	
Using condoms or dental dams	F	43	21.6	29	14.6	44	22.1	72	36.2	11	5.5	199	63.2	
	M	34	29.3	17	14.7	31	26.7	28	24.1	6	5.2	116	36.6	5.79
	T	77	24.4	46	14.6	75	23.8	100	31.7	17	5.4	315	100.0	
Discuss partner's sexual health prior to sexual behavior	F	60	30.2	35	17.6	36	18.1	48	24.1	20	10.1	199	63.4	
	M	22	19.1	19	16.5	29	25.2	35	30.4	10	8.7	115	36.6	6.46
	T	82	26.1	54	17.2	65	20.7	83	26.4	30	9.6	314	100.0	
Reducing number of sexual partners as safer sex practice	F	99	50.0	25	12.6	11	5.6	8	4.0	55	27.8	198	63.1	
	M	38	32.8	25	21.6	10	8.6	12	10.3	31	26.7	116	36.9	14.26†
	T	137	43.6	50	15.9	21	6.7	20	6.4	86	27.4	314	100.0	
Being more selective as a safer sex practice	F	108	54.5	35	17.7	8	4.0	9	4.5	38	19.2	198	63.1	
	M	38	32.8	42	36.2	6	5.2	4	3.4	26	22.4	116	36.9	18.50 ‡
	T	146	46.5	77	24.5	14	4.5	13	4.1	64	20.4	314	100.0	
Discuss contraception prior to sexual behavior	F	121	61.1	29	14.6	19	9.6	7	3.5	22	11.1	198	63.1	
	M	63	54.3	24	20.7	19	16.4	4	3.4	6	5.2	116	36.9	7.83
	T	184	58.6	53	16.9	38	12.1	11	3.5	28	8.9	314	100.0	

†$p < .01$, ‡$p < .001$

condoms or dental dams. Respondents were asked if they discussed their partners' sexual health prior to engaging in sexual behavior. Of those stating that such a discussion was applicable, 43.3% said that they always or often had such a discussion, and 47.1% said they rarely or never did. Forty-three percent of the students stated that they reduced their number of sexual partners as a safer sex practice, but 13% stated that they rarely or never reduced their number of sexual partners. Of those stating that a discussion of contraception was applicable, 75.5% almost always or often discussed contraception before sexual relations while 15.6% rarely or never discussed the topic (see Table 2).

8. Finally, gender differences were noted for two safer sex behaviors. The first was with "being more selective as a safer sex practice," with women reporting more selectivity than men (54.5% vs. 32.8%). Similarly, women reported reducing the number of their sexual partners more often than did men (50.0% vs. 32.8%, respectively).

Discussion

9. Several important findings emerged from this study. First, as in previous studies, approximately 75% of the responding students reported being sexually active. For the purpose of this study, only responses from students engaging in sexual behaviors during the past year were examined. These results indicated that many students were engaging in behaviors that put them at risk of contracting sexually transmitted diseases.

10. Of particular concern were the number of persons (31%) having five or more sexual partners. Traditionally, it has been thought that women have fewer sexual partners than their male peers; however, this was not found in this study. Although there were no gender differences in number of sexual partners, women were more likely than men to report that they were more selective and more likely to reduce their number of sexual partners as safer sex practices.

11. Although many college students reported having multiple partners, this did not increase "safe sex" behaviors such as using condoms. Over half of the students surveyed stated that they rarely or never used condoms or dental dams. Almost half of the respondents (47%) stated that they rarely or never discussed their partners' sexual health prior to sexual activities.

12. Students were asked if they used contraception during sexual activities. Most of the students did discuss contraception with their partner (75%). Within the scope of this study, it was not ascertained as to the type of contraception discussed. For instance, if condoms are

being used for contraception, this would assist in safer sex. Apparently, the majority of these students were more comfortable discussing contraception than they were in discussing their partners' sexual health and sexual behaviors prior to sexual relations. More in-depth research needs to be conducted to assess whether comfort is higher for discussions of contraception than for sexual health. There may be factors that influence students' comfort in such discussions. These factors may include fear of insulting a partner, fear of appearing promiscuous, or simply less comfort discussing previous intimate relations with other partners. Finally, students may have been exposed to more discussions regarding contraception than sexual health with parents, peers, and educators. Research examining cultural acceptability of contraception versus sexual health discussions may prove to be useful. Further, researchers could also examine personality characteristics of students who do or do not discuss safer sex prior to sexual relations. These personality characteristics may predispose some students to initiating conversations regarding condom use and history of previous sex partners, and may also affect their specific sexual practices.

13. In conclusion, the results of this study indicated that many students at this university campus in the Pacific northwest put themselves at risk of contracting sexually transmitted diseases. Although there have been attempts to increase college students' awareness of the importance of safer sex practices, students continue to engage in risky sexual behaviors. It should be noted that this college campus has sponsored such events as "Condom Day," health fairs, and required a personal health course, in which the necessity of using a condom during the HIV epidemic was stressed. Although these programs were not formally evaluated for effectiveness, disseminating knowledge may not be enough to change students' risky sexual behaviors. In recent studies knowledge about HIV/AIDS has not been predictive of using safer sex practices (Ajdukovic & Ajdukovic, 1991; Hays & Hays, 1992; Simkins, 1994). This indicates that traditional programs that are educational only may not be sufficient for increasing safer sex behaviors. Researchers should examine behavioral change in-depth using interventions directed toward actual change of college students' sexual behaviors.

References

Ajdukovic, D., & Ajdukovic, M. (1991). University students and AIDS: Knowledge, attitudes, and behavioral adjustment. *Psychological Reports, 69,* 203-210.

American Medical Association. (1990). *Healthy youth 2000.* (Excerpted from the U.S. Public Health Service's "Healthy People 2000: National Health Promotion and Disease Prevention Objectives"). American Medical Association, Department of Adolescent Health, 515 N. State Street, Chicago, IL 60610.

Baldwin, J. D., & Baldwin, J. I. (1988). Factors affecting AIDS-related sexual risk-taking behavior among college students. *The Journal of Sex Research, 25,* 181-196.

Carroll, L. (1990). Gender, knowledge about AIDS, reported behavior change and the sexual behavior of college students. *Journal of American College Health, 40,* 51-52.

Centers for Disease Control and Prevention. (1994). *HIV/AIDS Surveillance Report, 6*(2), 15.

DeLamater, J., & MacCorquodale, P. (1979). *Premarital sexuality: Attitudes, relationships, behavior.* Madison, WI: University of Wisconsin Press.

Hays, H., & Hays, R. (1992). Students' knowledge of AIDS and sexual risk behavior. *Psychological Reports, 71,* 649-650.

National Center for Health Statistics. (1992). *Advance report of final mortality statistics 1989.* Hyattsville, MD: U.S. Department of Health and Human Services. Public Health Services, CDC (*Monthly vital statistics report, 40,* 3 suppl.).

Selected behaviors that increase risk of HIV infection among high school students. *Morbidity and Mortality Weekly Report* (April 10, 1992), *41*(14), 237-240.

Simkins, L. (1994). Update on AIDS and sexual behavior of college students: Seven years later. *Psychological Reports, 74,* 208-210.

Factual Questions

1. According to the authors, what have few previous studies done?

2. How many students were selected at random?

3. How were the students contacted?

4. What percentage of the respondents reported being sexually active?

5. What percentage of the men reported having 5–10 sexual partners in the past five years?

6. Was the difference between men and women on "abstaining from sex as a safer sex practice" statistically significant?

7. The differences between men and women on "being more selective as a safer sex practice" were statistically significant at what probability level?

8. What is the name of the test of statistical significance used in this study?

Questions for Discussion

9. Speculate on why the authors did not name the specific university where the research was done.

10. In your opinion, is a 44% return rate adequate? Why? Why not?

11. When you have received questionnaires in the mail, what are some factors that have led you to either return or discard them? Would you probably have responded to the questionnaire in this study? Why? Why not?

12. What is your opinion on the researchers' decision to analyze data only for those who were sexually active during the past year?

13. In paragraphs 6 and 10, the authors note that in this study there were "no gender differences" in the number of sexual partners. However, Table 1 clearly shows observed differences. Speculate on the reason for this apparent discrepancy.

14. Do the results of this study indicate that the health programs on this campus were ineffective? Could it be that the rates of risky behaviors are higher on campuses without such programs?

15. The authors note that traditional educational programs may not increase safer sex behaviors. What else might be tried?

16. To what population(s), if any, would you be willing to generalize the results of this study?

17. If you were to conduct this study on another campus, what changes in research methodology, if any, would you make?

Quality Ratings

DIRECTIONS: Indicate your level of agreement with each of the following statements by circling a number from 5 for strongly agree (SA) to 1 for strongly disagree (SD). If you believe that an item is not applicable to this research article, leave it blank. Be prepared to explain your ratings.

A. The introduction establishes the importance of the research topic.
   SA   5   4   3   2   1   SD

B. The literature review establishes the context for the study.
   SA   5   4   3   2   1   SD

C. The research purpose, question, or hypothesis is clearly stated.
   SA   5   4   3   2   1   SD

D. The method of sampling is sound.
   SA   5   4   3   2   1   SD

E. Relevant demographics (for example, age, gender, and ethnicity) are described.
   SA   5   4   3   2   1   SD

F. Measurement procedures are adequate.
   SA   5   4   3   2   1   SD

G. The results are clearly described.
   SA   5   4   3   2   1   SD

H. The discussion/conclusion is appropriate.
   SA   5   4   3   2   1   SD

I. Despite any flaws noted above, the report is worthy of publication.
   SA   5   4   3   2   1   SD

ARTICLE 11

AMERICANS TODAY ARE DUBIOUS ABOUT
AFFIRMATIVE ACTION

David W. Moore

Editor's Note: "A Note to Our Readers" below appears at the beginning of each issue of *The Gallup Poll Monthly* and the section titled "Design of the Sample" appears at the end of each issue. These should be referred to when interpreting "The Report on Affirmative Action," presented below.

A Note to Our Readers

The Sample

1. The sampling, data collection and data processing procedures followed by the Gallup Poll are designed to provide representative samples of the adult civilian population living in telephone households in the continental U.S. Data are collected by telephone interviews unless otherwise indicated on data tables. In cases for which telephone interviewing is not the mode of data collection, a description of sampling and data collection methods will be provided. National survey results presented in *The Gallup Poll Monthly* are based on interviews with 1000 or more adults, unless otherwise noted.

Sampling Tolerances

2. Readers are cautioned that all sample surveys are subject to the potential effects of sampling error, a divergence between the survey results based on a selected sample and the results that would be obtained by interviewing the entire population in the same way. The risk of this kind of divergence is necessary if probability sampling is used, and probability sampling is the basis for confidence in the representativeness of sample survey results.

3. The chance that sampling error will affect a percentage based on survey results is mainly dependent upon the number of interviews on which the percentage is based. In ninety-five out of 100 cases, results based on national samples of 1000 interviews can be expected to vary by no more than 4 percentage points (plus or minus the figure obtained) from the results that would be obtained if all qualified adults were interviewed in the same way. For results based on smaller national samples or on sub-samples (such as men or persons over the age of fifty), the chance of sampling error is greater and therefore larger margins of sampling error are necessary in order to be equally confident of survey conclusions.

4. Each table shows the number of inter-interviews in each sub-sample to enable readers to determine the appropriate margin of sampling error, or "sampling tolerance" for percentages based on that sub-sample. Further information on sampling tolerances appears at the end of this report.

5. In addition to sampling error, readers should bear in mind that question wording and practical difficulties encountered in conducting surveys can introduce additional systematic error or "bias" into the results of opinion polls. Unlike sampling error, it is not possible to estimate the risk of this kind of error in a direct way, but survey organizations can protect against the effects of bias on survey conclusions by focusing careful attention on sampling, questionnaire construction, and data collection procedures and by allowing adequate time for the completion of data collection.

Design of the Sample

6. The Gallup Poll gathers information both in personal interviews and in interviews conducted by telephone. Although the method for selecting households in which to conduct interviews is different, the goal is the same: to provide representative samples of adults living in the United States. In either case, the standard size for Gallup Polls is 1000 interviews. More interviews are conducted in specific instances where greater survey accuracy is desired.

Design of the Sample for Personal Surveys

7. The design of the sample for personal (face-to-face) surveys is that of a replicated area probability sample down to the block level in the case of urban areas and to segments of townships in the case of rural areas.

8. After stratifying the nation geographically and by size of community according to information derived from the most recent census, over 350 different sampling locations are selected on a mathematically random basis from within cities, towns and counties that have in turn been selected on a mathematically random basis.

9. The interviewers are given no leeway in selecting the areas in which they are to conduct their interviews. Each interviewer is given a map on which a specific starting point is marked, and is instructed to contact households according to a predetermined travel pattern. At each occupied dwelling unit, the interviewer selects respondents by following a systematic procedure. This procedure is repeated until the assigned number of interviews has been completed.

Design of the Sample for Telephone Surveys

10. The samples of telephone numbers used in telephone interview surveys are based on a random digit stratified probability design. The sampling procedure involves selecting listed "seed" numbers, deleting the last two digits, and randomly generating two digits to replace them. This procedure provides telephone samples that are geographically representative. The random digit aspect, since it allows for the inclusion of unlisted and unpublished numbers, protects the samples from "listing bias"— the unrepresentativeness of telephone samples that can occur if the distinctive households whose telephone numbers are unlisted and unpublished numbers are excluded from the sample.

Weighting Procedures

11. After the survey data have been collected and processed, each respondent is assigned a weight so that the demographic characteristics of the total weighted sample of respondents matches the latest estimates of the demographic characteristics of the adult population available from the U.S. Census Bureau. Telephone surveys are weighted to match the characteristics of the adult population living in households with access to a telephone. The weighting of personal interview data includes a factor to improve the representation of the kinds of people who are less likely to be found at home.

12. The procedures described above are designed to produce samples approximating the

Moore, D. W. (1995). Americans today are dubious about affirmative action. *The Gallup Poll Monthly*, (No. 354), March 1995, 36-38. Copyright © 1995 by The Gallup Poll. Reprinted by permission.

adult civilian population (18 and older) living in private households (that is, excluding those in prisons, hospitals, hotels, religious and educational institutions and those living on reservations or military bases) — and in the case of telephone surveys, households with access to a telephone. Survey percentages may be applied to census estimates of the size of these populations to project percentages into numbers of people. The manner in which the sample is drawn also produces a sample which approximates the distribution of private households in the United States; therefore, survey results can also be projected to numbers of households.

Sampling Tolerances

13. In interpreting survey results, it should be borne in mind that all sample surveys are subject to sampling error, that is, the extent to which the results may differ from what would be obtained if the whole population surveyed had been interviewed. The size of such sample errors depends largely on the number of interviews.

14. The following tables may be used in estimating the sampling error of any percentage in this report. The computed allowances have taken into account the effect of the sample design upon sampling error. They may be interpreted as indicating the range (plus or minus the figure shown) within which the results of repeated sampling in the same time period could be expected to vary, 95 percent of the time, assuming the same sampling procedure, the same interviewers and the same questionnaire.

15. Table A shows how much allowance should be made for the sampling error of a percentage.

16. The table would be used in the following manner: Let us say a reported percentage is

thirty-three for a group that included 1000 respondents. First we go to the row headed "percentages near thirty" and go across to the column headed "1000". The number at this point is four, which means that the 33 percent obtained in the sample is subject to a sampling error of plus or minus four points. Another way of saying it is that very probably (ninety-five chances out of 100) the average of repeated samplings would be somewhere between twenty-nine and thirty-seven, with the most likely figure the thirty-three obtained.

17. In comparing survey results in two samples, such as, for example, men and women, the question arises as to how large must a difference between them be before one can be reasonably sure that it reflects a real difference. In the following tables, the number of points that must be allowed for in such comparisons is indicated.

18. Two tables are provided. Table B is for percentages near twenty or eighty; Table C for percentages near fifty. For percentages in between, the error to be allowed for is between those shown on the two tables.

19. Here is an example of how the tables would be used: Let us say that 50 percent of men respond a certain way and 40 percent of women respond that way also, for a difference of ten percentage points between them. Can we say with any assurance that the ten-point difference reflects a real difference between men and women on the question? The sample contains approximately 600 men and 600 women.

20. Since the percentages are near fifty, we consult Table C, and since the two samples are about 600 persons each, we look for the number in the column headed "600" that is also in the row designated "600". We find the number

Table B   *Recommended allowance for sampling error of the difference; In percentage points (at 95 in 100 confidence level)**

For percentages near 20 or percentages near 80

Size of sample	750	600	400	200
750	5			
600	5	6		
400	6	6	7	
200	8	8	8	10

*The chances are 95 in 100 that the sampling error is not larger than the figures shown.

Table C   *Recommended allowance for sampling error of the difference; In percentage points (at 95 in 100 confidence level)**

For percentages near 50

Size of sample	750	600	400	200
750	6			
600	7	7		
400	7	8	8	
200	10	10	10	12

*The chances are 95 in 100 that the sampling error is not larger than the figures shown.

seven here. This means that the allowance for error should be seven points, and that in concluding that the percentage among men is somewhere between three and seventeen points higher than the percentage among women we should be wrong only about 5 percent of the time. In other words, we can conclude with considerable confidence that a difference exists in the direction observed and that it amounts to at least three percentage points.

21. If, in another case, men's responses amount to 22 percent, say, and women's 24 percent, we consult Table B because these percentages are near twenty. We look in the column headed "600" that is also in the row headed "600" and see that the number is six. Obviously, then, the two-point difference is inconclusive.

The Report on Affirmative Action

22. Americans are somewhat more supportive of affirmative action for women than for minorities, although they are equally likely to say that such preferential treatment to overcome discrimination is no longer needed by either group. While the public is divided on giving

Table A   *Recommended allowance for sampling error of a percentage; In percentage points (at 95 in 100 confidence level)**

	Sample size					
	1000	750	600	400	200	100
Percentages near 10	2	3	3	4	5	7
Percentages near 20	3	4	4	5	7	9
Percentages near 30	4	4	4	6	8	10
Percentages near 40	4	4	5	6	8	11
Percentages near 50	4	4	5	6	8	11
Percentages near 60	4	4	5	6	8	11
Percentages near 70	4	4	4	6	8	10
Percentages near 80	3	4	4	5	7	9
Percentages near 90	2	3	3	4	5	7

*The chances are 95 in 100 that the sampling error is not larger than the figures shown.

special treatment to women, it is generally opposed to giving such treatment to minorities.

23. According to a recent Gallup poll, 50 percent approve and 45 percent disapprove of affirmative action for women, while 40 percent approve and 56 percent disapprove of affirmative action for racial minorities. But when it comes to assessing whether the program is needed for each group, the views are virtually identical: by a margin of 57 percent to 41 percent, Americans say it is not needed for women; and by 56 percent to 41 percent say it is not needed for racial minorities.

24. It is somewhat paradoxical that more people support affirmative action for women than feel the program is needed, while about the same number of people who support affirmative action for racial minorities say the program is needed. This difference suggests that giving special treatment to women to overcome past discrimination has greater legitimacy among the public than the same efforts for racial minorities. Furthermore, this seeming incongruity is found among both men and women, and among white and non-white respondents.

Programs Were Needed When First Introduced

25. In the poll, half the respondents were asked about affirmative action for women and the other half were asked about the program for racial minorities. Overall, Americans strongly agree (by 86 percent to 12 percent for each group) that when affirmative action was initiated some thirty years ago, it was needed by both women and racial minorities to overcome discrimination. And for the most part Americans believe the program has been successful. Three quarters of the public believes that the programs have helped women (76 percent) rather than hurt them (12 percent), while only 9 percent believe the effort has had no effect. Similarly, most people (70 percent) believe affirmative action has helped racial minorities rather than hurt them (11 percent), although 16 percent believe the effort has had no effect.

Programs Are Partisan, Racial and Gender Issues

26. Affirmative action, whether for women or racial minorities, receives somewhat more support from women than men, and much more support from racial minorities than from whites. Just over half (55 percent) of women support the program for women, compared with 45 percent of men. And 43 percent of women support the program for racial minorities, compared with 37 percent of men. The differences between racial groups are much greater: 46 percent of whites express support for affirmative action for women, compared with 78 percent of non-whites. On affirmative action for racial

As you know, some affirmative action programs are designed to give preferential treatment to (women/racial minorities) in such areas as getting jobs and promotions, obtaining contracts, and being admitted to schools. Do you generally approve or disapprove of such affirmative action programs?

Do you approve of affirmative action programs that use quotas — by requiring specific numbers of (women/racial minorities) to be given jobs or admitted to schools — or do you approve of affirmative action programs only if they do not use quotas?**

Affirmative Action Programs

	For women	For racial minorities
Approve	**50%**	**40%**
with quotas	10	13
no quotas	40	27
Disapprove	**45**	**56**
No opinion	**5**	**4**
	100%	**100%**

**Sample A (women): 506 respondents, +/–5%; Sample B (racial minorities): 497, +/–5%.

Approval by Sub-groups: for Women

	Approve, with quotas	Approve, no quotas	Disapprove	No opinion
Sex				
Men	7%	38%	51%	4%
Women	12	43	40	5
Race				
White	8	38	49	5
Non-white	23	55	16	6
Politics				
Republican	9	30	55	6
Independent	5	50	38	7
Democrat	17	40	42	1

Approval by Sub-groups: for Racial Minorities

	Approve, with quotas	Approve, no quotas	Disapprove	No opinion
Sex				
Men	11%	26%	61%	2%
Women	14	29	52	5
Race				
White	9	27	61	3
Non-white	33	33	30	4
Politics				
Republican	7	26	65	2
Independent	10	25	60	5
Democrat	22	33	42	3

Today do you think affirmative action programs are needed to help (women/racial minorities) overcome discrimination, or are they not needed today?

Programs Still Needed?

	For women	For racial minorities
Needed	41%	41%
Not needed	57	56
No opinion	2	3
	100%	100%

When affirmative action programs were first adopted almost thirty years ago, do you think they were needed to help (women/racial minorities) overcome discrimination, or were they not needed thirty years ago?

Were They Needed?

	For women	For racial minorities
Needed	86%	86%
Not needed	12	12
No opinion	2	2
	100%	100%

Overall, do you think affirmative action programs for the past thirty years have helped (women/racial minorities), hurt them, or had no effect one way or the other?

Have They Worked?

	For women	For racial minorities
Helped	76%	70%
Hurt	12	11
No effect	9	16
No opinion	3	3
	100%	100%

minorities, 36 percent of whites support it, compared with 66 percent of non-whites.

27. Republicans are strongly opposed to affirmative action for either group (by 55 percent to 39 percent for women, and by 65 percent to 33 percent for racial minorities), while Democrats express support for the program for both groups (57 percent to 42 percent for women, and 55 percent to 42 percent for racial

minorities). Independents, on the other hand, support the program for women by 55 percent to 38 percent, while they oppose it for racial minorities by 60 percent to 35 percent.

White Men
28. Affirmative action programs were designed to overcome the advantage that white men enjoy in American society, and not surprisingly they are the group most opposed to those efforts. By a margin of 58 percent to 39 percent, they currently oppose such programs for women and by 65 percent to 33 percent oppose such programs for racial minorities.
29. Nowhere is the contrast between white men and white women greater than among those with a college education: By 68 percent to 32 percent, these women support affirmative action for women, but the men oppose it, 70 percent to 28 percent. Among those with high school education or less, however, white men and women express similar views: men support affirmative action for women by 51 percent to 45 percent; women by 50 percent to 41 percent.
30. There is not the same schism between white men and women on affirmative action for minorities, with strong majorities of each sex opposed.

Methodology

31. This poll included telephone interviews with a randomly selected national sample of 1,003 adults, conducted February 24-26, 1995. About half the sample (506) was asked questions about women, the other half (497) about racial minorities. For results based on each half-sample, one can say with 95 percent confidence that the error attributable to sampling and other random effects could be plus or minus five percentage points. In addition to sampling error, question wording and practical difficulties in conducting surveys can introduce error or bias into the findings of public opinion polls.

Factual Questions

1. What is the definition of the population for the telephone surveys reported in *The Gallup Poll Monthly*?

2. How is "sampling error" defined?

3. Is it possible to directly estimate the effects of bias?

4. Are interviewers allowed to select the areas in which they conduct interviews?

5. Why are random digits used in telephone interviewing?

6. Suppose that 50% of a sample of 1,000 approve of a government program. Using Table A, we can say that very probably (95 chances out of 100), the average of repeated samplings would be somewhere between what two percentages?

7. Suppose that 80% of a sample of 200 women and 86% of a sample of 400 men approve of a government program. Should the six-point difference be regarded as conclusive?

8. What percentage of the subjects in this study thinks that affirmative action programs were needed for racial minorities 30 years ago?

9. Which group is most opposed to affirmative action programs?

10. Forty percent of the total sample approve of affirmative action programs for racial minorities. Using the information in paragraph 31, calculate the percentages between which we can have 95% confidence that the true percentage lies.

Questions for Discussion

11. Briefly describe in your own words the purpose of the weighting procedure.

12. Is the sample for face-to-face interviews or the sample for telephone interviews likely to be more representative of the entire adult civilian population? Explain.

13. Consider Tables A, B, and C. In them, the recommended allowances for sampling error are larger for smaller samples than for larger samples. Does this make sense? Why? Why not?

14. The report does not directly address the issue of nonrespondents (people who are selected as subjects but refuse to participate in a survey). Is this an important issue? Why? Why not?

15. What is your interpretation of the finding that 50% approve of affirmative action programs for women but only 41% say the programs are needed to help women overcome discrimination?

16. Would it be helpful to know how the terms "white" and "non-white" were defined and measured in this survey? Explain.

17. Would it be interesting to know how many Republicans, Independents, and Democrats were included in the survey? Why? Why not?

18. In paragraph 31, the author notes that question wording can introduce error or bias. What is your opinion on the wording of the questions for this survey?

19. Are there other questions about affirmative action that you would like to see included in future surveys on this topic? Explain.

Quality Ratings

DIRECTIONS: Indicate your level of agreement with each of the following statements by circling a number from 5 for strongly agree (SA) to 1 for strongly disagree (SD). If you believe that an item is not applicable to this research article, leave it blank. Be prepared to explain your ratings.

A. The introduction establishes the importance of the research topic.
   SA   5   4   3   2   1   SD

B. The literature review establishes the context for the study.
   SA   5   4   3   2   1   SD

C. The research purpose, question, or hypothesis is clearly stated.
   SA   5   4   3   2   1   SD

D. The method of sampling is sound.
   SA   5   4   3   2   1   SD

E. Relevant demographics (for example, age, gender, and ethnicity) are described.
   SA   5   4   3   2   1   SD

F. Measurement procedures are adequate.
   SA   5   4   3   2   1   SD

G. The results are clearly described.
   SA   5   4   3   2   1   SD

H. The discussion/conclusion is appropriate.
   SA   5   4   3   2   1   SD

I. Despite any flaws noted above, the report is worthy of publication.
   SA   5   4   3   2   1   SD

ARTICLE 12

ADOLESCENT PERCEPTIONS OF BODY WEIGHT AND WEIGHT SATISFACTION

Randy M. Page *University of Idaho*
Ola Allen *University of Mississippi*

Analysis of perception of body weight and weight satisfaction among 1,915 adolescents showed that a perception of being too fat was particularly dissatisfying for girls while a perception of being much too thin was most dissatisfying for boys.

1. Perhaps no other age group is more preoccupied with body image and appearance than adolescents. In fact, adolescents report concern about physical appearance to be their most worrisome problem (Eme, Maisak, & Goodale, 1979). Researchers have found high dissatisfaction with body weight among adolescents, particularly adolescent girls (Davies & Furnham, 1986; Paxton, Wertheim, Gibbons, Szmukler, Hillier, & Petrovich, 1991).

2. The present purpose was to assess the extent of the association between perceived body weight and satisfaction with weight in a sample of 1,915 9th to 12th graders. For students of seven high schools in one central Mississippi county, perceived body weight and weight satisfaction were assessed using a written questionnaire. Subjects were grouped into five categories by perceived weight based on whether the students rated their current weight as much too thin, a little too thin, just right, a little too fat, or much too fat. Satisfaction with weight was assessed by asking subjects to rate their satisfaction with current weight on a 5-point scale which ranged from completely dissatisfied (1) to completely satisfied (5). One-way analysis of variance tests were computed to examine whether perceived weight groups differed on weight satisfaction.

3. There was a significant effect by perceived-weight group on satisfaction with weight for both boys ($F_{4,903} = 66.4$, $p < .0001$) and girls ($F_{4,951} = 143.7$, $p < .0001$). Table 1 lists the mean scores on satisfaction with weight for boys and girls by their perceived-weight category. From these data, it appears that the perception of being much too fat ($M = 1.5$) is the most dissatisfying perception of weight for girls. Conversely, the most dissatisfying perception of weight for boys is being much too thin ($M = 2.2$). Having a perception of being a little too thin or much too thin was more dissatisfying for boys than girls, whereas the perception of being just right, a little too fat, or much too fat was more dissatisfying for girls than boys. These data confirm that perceived fatness is distressful for girls because the ideal female body image is typified by thinness. On the other hand, the perception of being too thin is contrary to the muscular ideal of a male body image.

References

Davies, E., & Furnham, A. (1986). Body satisfaction in adolescent girls. *British Journal of Medical Psychology*, *59*, 279-287.

Eme, R., Maisak, R., & Goodale, W. (1979). Seriousness of adolescent problems. *Adolescence*, *14*, 93-99.

Paxton, S. J., Wertheim, E. H., Gibbons, K., Szmukler, G. I., Hillier, L., & Petrovich, J. L. (1991). Body image satisfaction, dieting beliefs, and weight loss behaviors in adolescent girls and boys. *Journal of Youth and Adolescence*, *20*, 361-379.

Factual Questions

1. Subjects were drawn from how many high schools?

2. For both boys and girls, the average satisfaction was highest for which weight perception group?

3. Girls in which weight perception group were least satisfied?

4. Were girls in the "much too thin" or the "a little too thin" group more satisfied with their weight?

5. What inferential statistical test was used?

6. For boys, the differences among the means were statistically significant at what probability level?

Questions for Discussion

7. Would you be interested in knowing how many students were in each body weight perception group (for example, how many boys reported being much too thin)? Why? Why not?

8. Does it surprise you that the average student who said that he or she was "just right" was less than perfectly satisfied? (Note: A mean of less than 5.0 indicates less than perfect satisfaction for the average respondent.)

Table 1 *Satisfaction with weight: Mean scores by perception of body weight category (N = 1,915)*

Perception of Body Weight	Boys		Girls	
	M	*SD*	*M*	*SD*
Much too thin	2.2	1.3	2.5	1.3
A little too thin	2.8	0.9	3.2	0.9
Just right	3.7	0.8	3.5	0.9
A little too fat	2.8	0.8	2.2	0.8
Much too fat	2.7	1.8	1.5	1.1

Page, R. M., & Allen, O. (1995). Adolescent perceptions of body weight and weight satisfaction. *Perceptual and Motor Skills, 81*, 81-82. Copyright © 1995 Perceptual and Motor Skills. Reproduced with permission of authors and publisher.

Address requests for reprints to Randy M. Page, Ph.D., Division of Health, Physical Education, Recreation, and Dance, University of Idaho, Moscow, ID 83844-2401.

9. *SD* stands for what? (See Table 1.) What type of information does this statistic provide?

10. In this study, the researchers measured "perceived weight" rather than measuring weight objectively by actually weighing them. Which type of measure is more appropriate in light of the purpose of this study? Explain.

11. What are the practical implications, if any, of this study?

12. To what populations, if any, would you be willing to generalize the results of this study? Explain.

13. In a future study on this topic, what changes, if any, would you make in the research methodology?

Quality Ratings

DIRECTIONS: Indicate your level of agreement with each of the following statements by circling a number from 5 for strongly agree (SA) to 1 for strongly disagree (SD). If you believe that an item is not applicable to this research article, leave it blank. Be prepared to explain your ratings.

A. The introduction establishes the importance of the research topic.
   SA   5   4   3   2   1   SD

B. The literature review establishes the context for the study.
   SA   5   4   3   2   1   SD

C. The research purpose, question, or hypothesis is clearly stated.
   SA   5   4   3   2   1   SD

D. The method of sampling is sound.
   SA   5   4   3   2   1   SD

E. Relevant demographics (for example, age, gender, and ethnicity) are described.
   SA   5   4   3   2   1   SD

F. Measurement procedures are adequate.
   SA   5   4   3   2   1   SD

G. The results are clearly described.
   SA   5   4   3   2   1   SD

H. The discussion/conclusion is appropriate.
   SA   5   4   3   2   1   SD

I. Despite any flaws noted above, the report is worthy of publication.
   SA   5   4   3   2   1   SD

ARTICLE 13

VARIANCE IN SUBSTANCE USE BETWEEN RURAL BLACK AND WHITE MISSISSIPPI HIGH SCHOOL STUDENTS

Ola Allen *University of Mississippi*
Randy M. Page *University of Idaho*

The purpose of this study was to determine the extent to which the use of substances varies between black and white students in a sample of primarily rural Mississippi adolescents. It was found that black adolescent males were significantly less likely than white adolescent males to drink alcohol, get drunk, smoke cigarettes, use smokeless tobacco, hallucinogens, and sedatives. Black adolescent females were significantly less likely than white adolescent females to drink alcohol, get drunk, smoke cigarettes, and use marijuana. Differences in proportions of black and white females were more pronounced than differences between black and white males. Possible reasons for these differences are explored.

1. Alcohol and other drug use usually begins between the ages of 12 and 20 (DuPont, 1991). Patterns of use, which are established in youth, often persist into adulthood and contribute substantially to chronic disease (e.g., lung cancer, heart disease, chronic obstructive lung disease), motor-vehicle accidents, low educational achievement, unemployment, AIDS, and other serious consequences (Centers for Disease Control, 1991; Hawkins, Catalano, & Miller, 1992). National health objectives have been set to substantially reduce the use of alcohol and other drugs among both youth and adults in order to curb these consequences (U.S. Dept. of Health & Human Services, 1991).

2. The purpose of the present study was to determine the extent to which the use of substances varies between black and white students in a sample of primarily rural Mississippi adolescents.

Method

Subjects

3. The subjects for this study were 1,915 adolescents from seven high schools in Mississippi. These schools represent a mix of students: low, middle, and upper socioeconomic status; black and white students; and public and private schools in a primarily rural Mississippi school district. Male students comprised 48.8% of the sample and females 51.2%. Freshmen accounted for 15.2%, sophomores 36.9%, juniors 29.5%, and seniors 18.4%. About three-fourths (73.1%) of the subjects were white and one-fourth (24.9%) were black. Two percent of sample members identified themselves as either Native American, Hispanic, Asian, or other.

Procedure

4. Data were collected via a drug frequency questionnaire in regularly scheduled classes.

Students were informed that their participation was voluntary and were instructed not to place their name upon the questionnaire. They were asked to indicate whether they drink alcohol during the average month; get drunk during an average month; smoke cigarettes during an average day; use smokeless tobacco during an average day; and used cocaine, marijuana, hallucinogens, amphetamines, or sedatives during the past month. The percentages of black males and females and white males and females using various substances are shown in Table 1. Chi-square tests were calculated to determine differences in substance use categories between black and white males as well as for black and white females. These are noted in the table.

Results

5. Black males were significantly less likely than white males to drink alcohol, get drunk, smoke cigarettes, use smokeless tobacco, hallucinogens, and sedatives. They also reported using cocaine and amphetamines less than did white males although these differences were not statistically significant. Black females were significantly less likely than white females to drink alcohol, get drunk, smoke cigarettes, and use marijuana. Black females were also less likely to use smokeless tobacco, hallucinogens, amphetamines, and sedatives than were white females; however, these differences were not statistically significant.

6. Differences between black and white females were more pronounced than those between black and white males. The proportion of white females using alcohol (white = 54.7%, black = 23.5%) and hallucinogens (white =

Allen, O., & Page, R. M. (1994). Variance in substance use between rural Black and White Mississippi high school students. *Adolescence, 29,* 401-404. Copyright © 1994 by Libra Publishers. Reprinted with permission.

Ola Allen is with the University of Mississippi, School of Nursing, 2500 North State, Jackson, MS 39216. Reprint requests to Randy M. Page, Ph.D., University of Idaho, Division of H.P.E.R.D., Moscow, ID 83843.

Table 1 *Percentages of students using various substances*

	Black males	White males	Black females	White females
Drink alcohol during the average month	50.0	58.5[a]	23.5	54.7[b]
Get drunk during the average month	33.2	46.4[a]	9.7	32.7[b]
Daily cigarette smoker	13.3	21.3[a]	1.3	20.7[b]
Used cocaine in the past month	6.4	7.7	1.3	1.2
Used marijuana in the past month	10.8	15.6	2.1	6.4[b]
Daily user of smokeless tobacco	7.0	25.3[a]	0.0	0.3
Used hallucinogens in the past month	4.4	9.6[a]	0.8	2.0
Used amphetamines in the past month	3.4	6.7	0.8	2.6
Used sedatives in the past month	3.0	6.7[a]	0.8	2.6

[a]Black males differed significantly ($p < .05$) from white males
[b]Black females differed significantly ($p < .05$) from white females

2.0%, black = 0.8%) was more than double that of black females. More than three times as many white females as black females get drunk (32.7%, 9.7%), use marijuana (6.4%, 2.1%), amphetamines (2.6%, 0.8%), and sedatives (2.6%, 0.8%). Nearly 16 times as many white females (20.7%) as compared to black females (1.3%) were daily cigarette smokers.

Discussion

7. The results of the current study are in agreement with other studies comparing alcohol and drug use in black and white youth (Bachman, Wallace, O'Malley, Johnston, Kurth, & Neighbors, 1991; Hartford, 1986; Mensch & Kandel, 1988) reporting lower use among black youth. This lower use is in contrast with the fact that blacks are overrepresented in public drug treatment programs, hospital admissions for drug problems, drug-related mortality, and arrests with drug-positive urine samples (Edmonds, 1990). Mensch and Kandel (1988) point out that members of minority groups may be more inclined to provide socially desirable responses to survey questions about drug use than are white (majority) youth. Black youth may feel more threatened by the perceived consequences of their acknowledgment of drug use. Further, they may have less trust in researchers.

8. On the other hand, Bachman et al. (1991) conclude that black-white differences in self-reports are largely the result of genuine differences in substance use rates between the two subgroups. To support this claim, they cite that black youth are less likely to have friends who smoke, drink alcohol, and get drunk. Further, black youth are more disapproving of drug use and more likely to perceive the high risks involved.

9. More research is needed to determine why drug use rates are lower in black youth. Watts and Wright (1986/87) suggest that the conservative Protestant upbringing of many blacks is a possible reason. Differences in community, peer, and family norms and attitudes regarding the use of drugs may provide other explanations (Bachman et al., 1991).

10. Drug use rates by blacks do not appear to exceed those of whites until middle adulthood, at which point rates are often higher (Bachman et al., 1991). This could explain higher rates of drug-related morbidity and mortality among black adults as compared to whites.

References

Bachman, J. G., Wallace, J. M., O'Malley, P. M., Johnston, L. D., Kurth, C. L., & Neighbors, H. W. (1991). Racial/ethnic differences in smoking, drinking, and illicit drug use among American high school seniors, 1976-89. *American Journal of Public Health, 81,* 372-377.

Centers for Disease Control. (1991). Current tobacco, alcohol, marijuana, and cocaine use among high school students — United States, 1990. *Morbidity and Mortality Weekly Report, 40,* 659-663.

DuPont, R. L. (1991). *Crack cocaine: Challenge for prevention. OSAP Monograph-9* DHHS Publication No. (ADM) 91-1806. Rockville, MD: Office for Substance Abuse Prevention.

Edmonds, J. T. (1990). Reaching black inner-city youth. In E. B. Arkin, & J. E. Funkhouse (Eds.). *Communicating about alcohol and other drugs: Strategies for reaching populations at risk, OSAP Monograph-5* DHHS Publication No. (ADM) 90-1655 (pp. 121-170). Rockville, MD: Office for Substance Abuse Prevention.

Hartford, T. C. (1986). Drinking patterns among black and nonblack adolescents: Results of a national survey. *Annals of the New York Academy of Science, 472,* 130-141.

Hawkins, J. D., Catalano, R. F., & Miller, J. Y. (1992). Risk and protective factors for alcohol and other drug problems in adolescence and early adulthood: Implications for substance abuse prevention. *Psychological Bulletin, 112*(1), 64-105.

Mensch, B. S., & Kandel, D. B. (1988). Underreporting of substance use in a national longitudinal youth cohort. *Public Opinion Quarterly, 52,* 100-124.

U.S. Department of Health and Human Services. (1991). *Healthy people 2000: National health promotion and disease prevention objectives* (Publication No. PHS 91-50213). Washington, DC; U.S. Government Printing Office.

Watts, T. D., & Wright, R. (1986/87). Prevention of alcohol abuse among black Americans. *Alcohol Health and Research World, 2* (Winter), 40-41.

Factual Questions

1. What percentage of the subjects were seniors?

2. What test was used to determine the significance of the differences?

3. Was the difference between black and white males for cocaine use statistically significant?

4. At what probability level was the difference between black and white females for smoking cigarettes daily significant?

Questions for Discussion

5. Would it be interesting to know how many students did not volunteer to answer the questionnaire? Why? Why not?

6. Would it be helpful to know whether the black and white students were comparable in terms of socioeconomic status? Why? Why not?

7. Speculate on why the students were instructed not to place their name on the questionnaire.

8. What is your opinion on the possibility that members of minority groups may be more inclined to provide socially desirable responses on drug use than majority youth?

9. The authors tested for the significance of the differences between blacks and whites. Would you also be interested in the significance of the differences between males and females? Why? Why not?

Quality Ratings

DIRECTIONS: Indicate your level of agreement with each of the following statements by circling a number from 5 for strongly agree (SA) to 1 for strongly disagree (SD). If you believe that an item is not applicable to this research article, leave it blank. Be prepared to explain your ratings.

A. The introduction establishes the importance of the research topic.
SA   5   4   3   2   1   SD

B. The literature review establishes the context for the study.
SA   5   4   3   2   1   SD

C. The research purpose, question, or hypothesis is clearly stated.
SA   5   4   3   2   1   SD

D. The method of sampling is sound.
SA   5   4   3   2   1   SD

E. Relevant demographics (for example, age, gender, and ethnicity) are described.
SA   5   4   3   2   1   SD

F. Measurement procedures are adequate.
SA   5   4   3   2   1   SD

G. The results are clearly described.
SA   5   4   3   2   1   SD

H. The discussion/conclusion is appropriate.
SA   5   4   3   2   1   SD

I. Despite any flaws noted above, the report is worthy of publication.
SA   5   4   3   2   1   SD

RISK FACTORS FOR SEXUAL VICTIMIZATION IN DATING: A LONGITUDINAL STUDY OF COLLEGE WOMEN

Melissa J. Himelein *University of North Carolina at Asheville*

In this longitudinal study of college women, nine risk characteristics assessed prior to the start of college were examined in the effort to identify predictors of sexual victimization in college dating. A total of 100 women were followed for 32 months, with information about personal history, behaviors, and attitudes collected at Time 1 and information about subsequent sexual victimization collected at Time 2. Although four risk factors were significantly associated with victimization, a logistic regression analysis revealed that the best prediction model contained only two variables: Precollege sexual victimization in dating was positively correlated with college victimization, and sexual conservatism was negatively correlated with college victimization. Discussion focused on the needs for improved sex education for teenagers, prevention programs aimed at the precollege level, and increased research and clinical attention to the phenomenon of revictimization.

1. Despite significant attention from the national media, rape and other forms of sexual aggression continue to occur frequently on college campuses. Most sexual violence in this setting is perpetrated by acquaintances, with the majority of acquaintances described by victims as "dates" (Gavey, 1991; Koss, Dinero, Seibel, & Cox, 1988).

2. Craig's (1990) situational model of coercive sexual behavior in dating suggests that sexually aggressive men do not choose their victims arbitrarily. Both dating partners and circumstances are thought to be selected for potential vulnerability to sexual coercion. Consistent with this perspective, prior research has attempted to identify female experiences, behaviors, traits, attitudes, and situations associated with greater risk of victimization (e.g., Amick & Calhoun, 1987; Himelein, Vogel, & Wachowiak, 1994; Koss & Dinero, 1989; Muehlenhard & Linton, 1987); the most predictive risk profile appears to comprise a combination of factors rather than any one variable alone (Koss & Dinero, 1989). The goal of the present study was to test the validity of previous findings using a more rigorous, longitudinal research design. This research attempted to predict sexual victimization during college on the basis of nine attributes assessed prior to the start of college: three personal history experiences (child sexual abuse, precollege dating victimization, and consensual sexual experience), two behaviors (alcohol use on dates and assertiveness), and four attitudinal characteristics.

3. It is critical to emphasize that investigation of risk characteristics for sexual victimization in no way mitigates a sexually aggressive man's responsibility for his behavior. The immediate cause of any crime is the criminal; most prevention efforts correctly begin with this guiding principle. Risk research offers an ancillary approach to crime prevention, one that aims to situationally reduce the opportunity for crime through "target hardening," that is, making the objects of crime less vulnerable (see Clarke, 1983). Sexual aggression that occurs in the context of dating may be less random and more preventable than stranger rape. The primary objective of this research was to uncover information about vulnerability that could facilitate prevention efforts aimed at both aggressors and their targets.

Personal History Characteristics

4. Several previous investigations have demonstrated a link between child sexual abuse (CSA) and sexual victimization in adulthood. Survivors of CSA are significantly more likely to be victimized by rape or attempted rape as adults than are women with no CSA history (Russell, 1986), and women who are sexually victimized as adults report CSA experiences at a rate two to three times greater than nonvictimized women (Himelein et al., 1994; Koss & Dinero, 1989; Wyatt, Guthrie, & Notgrass, 1992). One recent study, distinguished by its unique adoption of a prospective research design, confirmed the impact of both CSA and adolescent victimization on likelihood of subsequent victimization (Gidycz, Coble, Latham, & Layman, 1993). Several long-term effects of CSA may heighten a woman's vulnerability to victimization in adulthood, including low self-esteem, depression, substance abuse, and interpersonal difficulties (for reviews, see Beitchman et al., 1992; Browne & Finkelhor, 1986). Gidycz et al. suggested that cognitive correlates of unresolved sexual trauma such as powerlessness and unworthiness may have a clear and direct impact on likelihood of victimization. Perhaps even more damaging is the impact of CSA in the sexual domain. Survivors may display age-inappropriate sexual knowledge and interest, have difficulty setting sexual limits, or be prone to use sexual behavior as a means of gaining attention (Lundberg-Love & Geffner, 1989; Russell, 1986), characteristics likely to be misinterpreted in adolescent dating situations.

5. This study distinguishes between CSA and a second type of sexual victimization: victimization in early, precollege dating experiences. Although popular press and research reports have tended to focus attention on sexual aggression in the college population, both dating and aggression in dating likely begin long before the college years (Himelein et al., 1994). Women whose initial dating partners prove to be coercive may never learn that they have the right to reject sexual advances, much less how to do so. Because traditional dating scripts tend to place women in the role of gatekeeper, women who struggle with this role are at particular risk of victimization.

6. Consensual sexual experience is the third historical characteristic that appears to be

Himelein, M. J. (1995). Risk factors for sexual victimization in dating: A longitudinal study of college women. *Psychology of Women Quarterly, 19,* 31–48. Copyright © 1995 by Cambridge University Press. Reprinted with the permission of Cambridge University Press.

This research was supported in part by the Division of Student Affairs at the University of North Carolina at Charlotte. I thank Nancy Schoeps for assistance in statistical analysis, Ron Vogel for help in Time 1 survey design and data collection, and Dale Wachowiak, Jacquelyn White, and two anonymous reviewers for comments on earlier versions of this manuscript.

Address correspondence and reprint requests to: Melissa J. Himelein, Department of Psychology, UNC-Asheville, Asheville, NC 28804.

related to victimization risk. Women who engage in sexual intercourse at an earlier age and report a greater number of sexual partners are more likely to be sexually victimized (Himelein et al., 1994; Koss, 1985; Koss & Dinero, 1989), an association that may reflect sheer statistical opportunity (Koss, 1985). Because one precursor of heightened sexual activity appears to be CSA history (Browne & Finkelhor, 1986; Himelein et al., 1994; Russell, 1986), this relationship might also be explained by the pre-existing presence of CSA. For example, the experience of CSA may leave a woman ill-equipped to conduct nonsexual relationships with men. Consensual sexual experience may thus mediate the relationship between CSA and sexual victimization in adulthood.

Behaviors

7. Behavioral correlates of victimization have been explored in several investigations. Heavy use of alcohol has been consistently associated with greater risk of sexual victimization (Koss & Dinero, 1989; Miller & Marshall, 1987; Muehlenhard & Linton, 1987; Myers, Templer, & Brown, 1984; Vogel & Himelein, 1990). A coercive male may view his date's intoxication as evidence of her willingness to engage in sex (Koss & Dinero, 1989) and consequently may feel less inhibited about using force to obtain it. Norris and Cubbins (1992) demonstrated that college students tend to assume that a date involving mutual drinking is likely to be followed by sexual activity. Alcohol may also serve to impair a woman's ability to decode cues signaling danger (Richardson & Hammock, 1991) and to physically resist attack (Muehlenhard & Linton, 1987).

8. In contrast to drinking behavior, assertive behavior is believed to reduce a woman's risk of victimization. Coercive men may view assertive women as unlikely targets, or assertiveness may empower a woman to forcefully refuse sexual demands before they become aggressive. However, evidence for a relationship between assertiveness and vulnerability is mixed. The Rathus Assertiveness Schedule (Rathus, 1973) was positively associated with nonvictimization in two studies (Myers et al., 1984; Vogel & Himelein, 1990), but failed to discriminate attempted from completed victimization in a third (Amick & Calhoun, 1987). Similarly, measures of dominance and social presence, two personality characteristics related to assertiveness, have predicted nonvictimization both successfully (Amick & Calhoun, 1987; Myers et al., 1984; Selkin, 1978) and unsuccessfully (Koss, 1985). Such contradictory findings are not surprising in that these investigations encompass a wide variety of target populations (clinical vs.

nonclinical), definitions of victimization (rape only vs. a continuum of sexual aggression; aggression in dating only vs. aggression by strangers or acquaintances), measurement methods (self-ratings vs. ratings of others), and goals (prediction of resistance to aggression vs. prediction of victimization). The one clear commonality among previous studies is their dependence on retrospective assessment. This methodology is particularly problematic in the case of assertiveness, where an observed deficit might well be a consequence rather than cause of victimization.

Attitudinal Characteristics

9. The relationship between attitudinal measures and sexual victimization risk is similarly unclear. Attention has focused primarily on attitudes and beliefs thought to be supportive of rape, including the acceptance of interpersonal violence, sexual conservatism, adversarial sex beliefs, and rape myth acceptance (see Burt, 1980). The social control model of rape vulnerability (Koss, 1985; Koss & Dinero, 1989) posits that women who subscribe to such attitudes are more at risk because they may respond to men passively, feel unjustified in stopping unwanted sexual advances, or even expect some degree of aggression in relationships.

10. Limited support for the social control perspective is provided by the findings of two studies focused specifically on sexual aggression in dating. In contrast to nonvictimized women, victimized women were found to be more accepting of violence against women (Muehlenhard & Linton, 1987) and to view relationships as more adversarial (Muehlenhard & Linton, 1987; Vogel & Himelein, 1990). However, studies of aggression occurring in any context (i.e., perpetrated by dates, acquaintances, or strangers) have revealed no reliable attitudinal differences between victims and nonvictims (Koss, 1985; Koss & Dinero, 1989) or between successful and unsuccessful victimization resisters (Amick & Calhoun, 1987). Again, prospective methodology is necessary to clarify whether attitudinal differences, if present, heighten the risk of attack or merely develop as the result of attack.

Current Study

11. Despite the considerable research literature on risk factors, the findings of previous studies are clearly weakened by their reliance on retrospective data. Most critically, retrospective methodology precludes the establishment of cause and effect relationships; observed differences between victims and nonvictims may be either the antecedents or the consequences of victimization. Even in the case of the time-

specific variable of CSA, simultaneous recall of both child and adult victimization experiences suggests at least two different interpretations of their association: (a) CSA may underlie adulthood victimization, or (b) women victimized as adults may be more prone to recollect earlier abuse experiences. In the only investigation to date to employ a prospective research design (Gidycz et al., 1993), participants were assessed at two time periods just 9 weeks apart.

12. The present study adopted a longitudinal design to test the findings of previous victimization risk research. This investigation spanned 32 months, with a nonclinical population of female college students surveyed on two occasions: prior to the start of their first academic year and at the close of their third academic year. Risk factor information was collected at the first assessment session, and college victimization was assessed at the follow-up.

Method

Procedure

13. *Time 1.* The initial (Time 1) sample consisted of 330 women entering their first year of college at a large, southeastern, public university. Men were also assessed at this time period, but the present analysis is restricted to female respondents.

14. Students were surveyed during the university's precollege orientation sessions, 2-day programs presented by the Division of Student Affairs in which incoming students are introduced to both academic and social aspects of college life. Students choose to attend one of eight sessions offered at various times prior to the start of the academic year.[1] Participants for the study were solicited from four of the eight sessions, preselected on the basis of pre-enrollment figures. The Time I investigators attended each of the four sessions and made a brief presentation to all students about the research. Students were informed that the purpose of the study was to gather information regarding sexual aggression in the context of dating, that participation was voluntary, and that their responses would be confidential. These points were repeated in an informed consent form attached to the questionnaire.

15. In the largest orientation session, questionnaires were completed by participants immediately following the investigators' presentation, during a 30-minute time period scheduled by the orientation program coordinator. In the remaining three sessions, questionnaires were administered by orientation counselors later in the day, in small groups of 15–25 students. These counselors, advanced students who were hired by the orientation coordinator to help with all aspects of the orientation program, attended a

81

training session on date rape offered by one investigator prior to the start of the project. A total of 415 women were invited to take part in the study, with 85% ($n = 352$) electing to participate. Surveys in which 20% or more of the items were not completed were eliminated ($n = 22$).[2]

16. *Time 2.* Prior to their participation at Time 1, students were informed that another purpose of the study was to follow dating behavior over time. They were asked to include their social security numbers (but not names) on their answer sheets if they would be willing to be recontacted at a later date regarding participation in a follow-up investigation. Confidentiality of responses was again stressed.

17. Time 2 data were collected approximately 32 months after Time 1. The Time 2 questionnaire was mailed to all Time 1 participants who provided social security numbers and for whom current address information could be obtained. A cover letter describing both the initial and follow-up studies accompanied the questionnaire. Surveys were coded prior to the mailing so that anonymity of responses could be preserved. Approximately 1 to 2 weeks after mailing, the investigator attempted to telephone all participants residing locally in order to verbally request participation. Time 2 surveys were estimated to require approximately 10 minutes for completion.

Participants

18. *Time 1.* The mean age of the initial sample of 330 women was 18.4 years, and most participants (99%) were single. Seventy-three percent of the women were White, 24% were Black, and 4% were from other minority backgrounds. The predominant religion was Protestant (78%), with 10% Roman Catholic and 12% other or none. These data are consistent with the overall demographic profile of first-year female students at the university during the year these data were collected. Among a total of 937 incoming first-year female students with a mean age of 18.1 years, 72% were White, 26% were Black, 3% were from other minority backgrounds, and 99% were single. Analyses of the survey responses of the Time 1 sample are presented elsewhere (Himelein et al., 1994; Vogel & Himelein, 1990).[3]

19. Approximately 65% of the Time 1 sample ($n = 215$) provided social security numbers on their questionnaires, indicating their willingness to participate in the follow-up study. Chi-square and *t* tests revealed that follow-up volunteers did not significantly differ from nonvolunteers in age, race, or religion, or on any of the risk variables.

20. *Time 2.* University records indicated that 139 of the 215 follow-up volunteers (65%) were still enrolled, and 76 (35%) had left the university at Time 2. Of 209 women (97%) for whom addresses were available, 100 (48%) completed and returned their Time 2 surveys; this number included both current students (79%) and women who had left the university (21%). Women who returned the Time 2 questionnaire did not differ from women who failed to return the questionnaire (52%; $n = 109$) on either the demographic or risk variables. However, women who were enrolled at the university returned the questionnaire at a higher rate than women who were no longer enrolled (57% vs. 30%; χ^2 [1, $n = 209$] = 13.43, $p < .001$).

21. The final Time 2 sample of 100 women had a mean age of 21.0 years. Other demographic characteristics are as follows: 89% were single, 5% married, 5% cohabiting, and 1% divorced; 78% were White, 19% Black, and 3% other minorities; and 75% were Protestant, 12% Roman Catholic, and 13% other or no religion. Of the 21% who were no longer enrolled at the university, 12 had transferred to other 4-year universities or to community colleges, 6 were working full time, 1 was taking time off due to marriage, and 2 provided no reasons for their departures.

Measures

22. Nine risk, or predictor, variables were measured via the 120-item Time 1 questionnaire: child sexual abuse (CSA), sexual victimization in dating occurring prior to college, consensual sexual experience, alcohol use in dating, assertiveness, and four attitudinal scales. Demographic information was also collected at Time 1. Sexual victimization in dating that occurred subsequent to Time 1, the criterion variable, was assessed through the 45-item Time 2 questionnaire. Both questionnaires were largely composed of adaptations of existing measures.

23. *Child sexual abuse (CSA).* An adaptation of Finkelhor's (1979) instrument was employed to assess CSA occurrence. Participants were asked if they had ever been the unwilling victim of any of seven sexual experiences *in other than dating relationships* prior to the age of 16. Consequently, sexual victimization by a dating partner, at any age, was not considered CSA in this research. Responses were classified according to the most invasive level of abuse experienced: 1 = no CSA, 2 = noncontact CSA (being showed or showing sex organs), 3 = fondling (being fondled in a sexual manner or having sex organs touched), 4 = attempted rape (intercourse attempted but did not occur), and 5 = rape (oral, anal, or vaginal intercourse). Although this rank ordering is based on evidence

of a relation between the degree of invasiveness of abuse and trauma (e.g., Beitchman et al., 1992; Browne & Finkelhor, 1986), many other factors obviously contribute to a victim's perception of the severity of CSA.

24. *Precollege sexual victimization in dating.* The 10-item Sexual Experiences Survey (SES; Koss & Gidycz, 1985; Koss & Oros, 1982) was adapted to measure sexual victimization in dating that occurred prior to the start of college. Consisting of behaviorally specific questions assessing varying levels of victimization, Koss and Gidycz (1985) reported an internal consistency reliability of .74, 1-week test-retest agreement of 93%, and a validity coefficient (comparisons between SES self-report and responses to an interviewer's questions) of .73.

25. This study's focus on victimization specific to dating was accomplished by adding the phrase "on a date with a man" to each item of the SES. All references to an explicit time frame of occurrence (e.g., "since the age of 14") were deleted, and a dichotomous yes–no response format was adopted. For example, a question assessing rape was altered as follows (changes italicized): "Have you ever had sexual intercourse *on a date with a man* when you didn't want to because *your date* threatened or used some degree of physical force (twisting your arm, holding you down, etc.)?" An operational definition of dating that included nontraditional dating experiences during which an opportunity for sexual aggression might be present was provided at the beginning of the questionnaire: " 'Dating' refers to a mutually planned or spontaneous social activity with someone of the opposite sex . . . attending a movie, going for a walk, leaving a party with someone, meeting someone in a bar, playing tennis with someone, or going 'parking' to name just a few."

26. Four categories of victimization can be derived from the SES. In order of SES presentation, these include: (a) sexual contact, defined as unwanted sex play (kissing, fondling, petting) obtained through a man's verbal pressure, position of authority, threat of force, or force; (b) attempted rape, incidents of unwanted sexual intercourse attempted, but not completed, through a man's threat of force, force, or administration of alcohol or drugs; (c) sexual coercion, unwanted sexual intercourse obtained through verbal pressure or a position of authority; and (d) rape, unwanted sexual, anal, or oral intercourse obtained through threat of force, force, or administration of alcohol or drugs. As with CSA scoring, participants were classified according to the most invasive level of victimization they reported, although it is likely that factors other than invasiveness also influence the perceived severity of sexual assault. The categories of attempted rape and sexual coercion were combined because no a priori rationale for ranking one as more invasive than the other was apparent. Consequently, levels of victimization in dating were ordered as follows: 1 = no victimization in dating; 2 = low victimization in dating (sexual contact); 3 = moderate victimization in dating (attempted rape or sexual coercion); and 4 = severe victimization in dating (rape).

27. *Consensual sexual experience.* An index of consensual sexual experience was constructed from participants' responses to two questions: age of first consensual experience of sexual intercourse (1 = no prior consensual experience; 2 = 17 or older; 3 = 15 or 16; 4 = 14 or younger) and total number of consensual sexual partners (1 = no prior consensual experience; 2 = 1 partner; 3 = 2-5 partners; 4 = 6-10 partners; 5 = more than 10 partners). Responses to each question were then added together, resulting in an index with a theoretical range of 2 (no prior consensual experience) to 9 (first consensual experience at age 14 or younger and more than 10 partners).

28. *Alcohol use in dating.* Three questions were derived from the protocol of Koss and Dinero (1989) to measure alcohol use: frequency of use of alcohol, amount usually drunk, and perceived degree of intoxication. Questions were edited to refer specifically to alcohol use in dating situations (e.g., "When drinking on a date, how much do you usually drink?"), and responses were rated on 5-point scales (e.g., 0 = none at all; 4 = usually more than six cans of beer or five or more glasses of wine or mixed drinks). Responses to each of the three questions were added together to form one overall index of alcohol use with a theoretical minimum of 0 (no drinking on dates) and maximum of 16 (drink on all dates, drink more than six cans of beer or its equivalent, and affected by drinking very much).

29. *Assertiveness.* The 30-item Rathus Assertiveness Schedule (RAS; Rathus, 1973) was adopted as the measure of assertiveness or social boldness. Rathus reported a split-half internal consistency of .77, 2-month test-retest reliability of .78, and validity coefficients ranging from .33 to .62 (comparisons between RAS self-report and others' ratings of related traits).

30. *Attitude scales.* Four attitude scales were selected from Burt's (1980) research on rape-supportive beliefs. The 9-item Adversarial Sexual Beliefs Scale (Cronbach's alpha = .80) measures the expectation that sexual relationships are basically exploitative and sexual partners manipulative and untrustworthy (e.g.,

"Women are usually sweet until they've caught a man, but then they let their true self show"). The 10-item Sexual Conservatism Scale (Cronbach's alpha = .81) assesses traditional, restrictive beliefs about sexual motivations and behaviors (e.g., "People should not have oral sex"). The 6-item Acceptance of Interpersonal Violence Scale (Cronbach's alpha = .59) measures the perspective that violence against women has a legitimate place in a heterosexual relationship (e.g., "Sometimes the only way a man can get a cold woman turned on is to use force").

31. Burt's Rape Myth Acceptance Scale, which assesses adherence to cultural rape myths, was abbreviated from 19 to 12 items. Because pilot testing of the instrument revealed infrequent endorsement of many items, some statements were modified to reflect modern word choice (e.g., "In the majority of rapes, the victim is promiscuous or has a bad reputation" was changed to "In the majority of rapes, the victim is promiscuous") or a more moderate position (e.g., "A woman who is stuck-up and thinks she is too good to talk to guys on the street deserves to be taught a lesson" was changed to "The victims of rape are usually a little to blame for the crime"). Burt reported a Cronbach's alpha of .88; the modified scale had a Cronbach's alpha of .79.

32. *Sexual victimization in dating during college.* The SES, adapted as previously described, was administered to participants a second time via the Time 2 questionnaire. Instructions preceding the Time 2 SES informed students that the questions pertained "*only* to experiences you have had in the course of dating since you began college at (name of college) in (month, year)." Participants who had not been engaged in heterosexual dating since that time were advised to skip these questions; 4 students (4%) did not complete the SES at Time 2.

Results

Prevalence of Sexual Victimization in Dating

33. Examination of the Time 1 Sexual Experiences Survey (SES) revealed that 38% of participants had been sexually victimized in dating situations prior to entering college. Classified according to the most severe level of victimization experienced, 15% reported low victimization (sexual contact), 17% reported moderate victimization (sexual coercion or attempted rape), and 6% reported severe victimization (rape).

34. Time 2 SES data revealed that 29% of students had been sexually victimized in dating since entering college. Low, moderate, and severe levels of victimization were experienced by 8%, 13%, and 8% of women, respectively.

Women who were enrolled at the university were victimized at approximately the same rate (19%) as women who had left the university (25%; χ^2 [1, $N = 96$] = .42, ns).[4]

35. The percentage of women experiencing sexual victimization in dating across both time periods (precollege and during college) was also calculated. A total of 52% of the sample had experienced some type of sexual victimization in dating during their lifetimes; 19% reported low victimization, 22% reported moderate victimization, and 11% reported severe victimization. In their national survey of similarly aged (21.4 years) college students, Koss, Gidycz and Wisniewski (1987) reported that 53.7% of women had experienced some type of sexual victimization in their lifetimes (14.4% low, 24% moderate, and 15.4% high victimization). Although the same instrument was used to measure victimization in both studies, Koss et al. surveyed both stranger and acquaintance sexual victimization experiences in contrast to the present focus on victimization in dating.

Data Analyses

36. In order to explore the relationships among the variables of interest, zero-order correlations were computed for all possible pairs of variables. The three categories of sexual victimization (low, moderate, and severe) were combined, creating a single, dichotomous criterion variable: no type of victimization in dating during college versus some type of victimization in dating during college. The decision to convert victimization to an all-or-none index was based in part on the pragmatic constraint of low sample size across categories. In addition, because any type of victimization is likely to result in significant trauma, predicting victimization in general seemed a more fundamental goal than predicting a specific type of victimization. The complete correlation matrix is presented in Table 1.

37. Significant correlates of sexual victimization during college included precollege sexual victimization, consensual sexual experience, alcohol use, and sexual conservatism. Thus, women were more likely to be victimized in college dating situations if prior to attending college they had experienced some type of victimization in dating, had engaged in higher levels of consensual sex, reported greater use of alcohol in dating situations, or held less conservative attitudes about sexual behavior. The three personal history risk variables (child sexual abuse, precollege sexual victimization in dating, and consensual sexual experience) were significantly associated with one another, with intercorrelations ranging from .20 to .27. The four attitude risk measures were also

Table 1 *Intercorrelations between risk variables and sexual victimization during college*

Variables	1	2	3	4	5	6	7	8	9	10
1. Child sexual abuse	—	.26**	.27**	.06	-.02	.26**	.10	.12	.04	.10
2. Precollege sexual victimization		—	.20*	.26**	-.09	.14	-.01	.13	.04	.34***
3. Consensual sexual experience			—	.31**	.21*	.28**	-.24*	.19	.21*	.24*
4. Alcohol use in dating				—	.09	.08	-.18	-.03	-.11	.22*
5. Assertiveness					—	-.19	-.24*	-.10	-.10	-.02
6. Adversarial sexual beliefs						—	.28**	.36***	.44***	-.13
7. Sexual conservatism							—	.15	.20*	-.27**
8. Acceptance of interpersonal violence								—	.60***	-.01
9. Rape myth acceptance									—	-.13
10. Sexual victimization during college										—

$*p < .05$, $**p < .01$, $***p < .001$

predominantly intercorrelated; five of six correlations were significant, ranging from .20 to .60.

38. In order to examine the unique contributions of the risk factors in predicting victimization during college, a stepwise logistic regression analysis was conducted. This procedure regresses a dichotomous response variable on a set of independent (predictor) variables by the method of maximum likelihood (see Bieber, 1988; Hosmer & Lemeshow, 1989). The SAS program for logistic regression was adopted, and all nine risk factors were included in the analysis. The first variable selected, sexual victimization in dating prior to college, yielded a model, $\chi^2 (1, N = 93)$ of 10.640, $p = .001$, indicating that this risk factor significantly improved upon the constant in predicting sexual victimization during college. Only one other risk factor, sexual conservatism, was able to further improve the model, $\chi^2 (2, N = 93) = 17.52, p < .001$.

39. An examination of descriptive data revealed that 57% of college victims had also been victimized in dating before entering college, with 46% experiencing moderate or severe levels of prior victimization. In contrast, 31% of college nonvictims had been previously victimized, with 15% experiencing moderate or severe levels of prior victimization, $\chi^2 (3, N = 95) = 13.49, p < .01$. On the Sexual Conservatism Scale, college victims scored .6 of a standard deviation below college nonvictims ($M = 16.0$ vs. 19.3, respectively); $t (94) = 2.82, p < .01$.

40. To aid in evaluating the practical value of these findings, classification results reveal an overall rate of correct classification of 73%, based on a model with two predictors (sexual victimization in dating prior to college and sexual conservatism). Although 91% of nonvictims

were accurately classified, only 32% of victims were accurately classified, indicating that the model erred primarily in predicting nonvictimization for women who were in fact victimized.

Discussion

41. The present study attempted to predict sexual victimization in college dating based on nine risk factors assessed prior to the start of college. Although correlational analyses indicated that four risk variables were significantly associated with sexual victimization in college, only sexual victimization in dating prior to college and sexual conservatism made unique contributions to the logistic regression model. However, the information provided by these two risk factors alone resulted in the accurate identification of the majority of nonvictims and approximately one third of victims.

42. Prior victimization in dating emerged as the strongest predictor of college dating victimization, supporting the findings of another recent study of sexual victimization in college women (Gidycz et al., 1993). Gidycz et al. demonstrated that even before a subsequent victimization, women victimized in adolescence were more depressed and anxious than women who had not been previously victimized. This difference suggests that the psychological consequences of initial victimization may account in part for future vulnerability.

43. Turning attention specifically to victimization in dating, the focus of the present study, both emotional and cognitive factors are important in understanding how the consequences of an initial sexual trauma serve to increase the likelihood of a second. Consider the findings of research on *normal* female adolescence: In comparison to adolescent boys, adolescent girls tend to experience greater declines in self-

esteem, self-image, and self-confidence, have lower expectations of their abilities, and engage in more internal attributions for failures and more external attributions for success (e.g., American Association of University Women, 1991; Bush & Simmons, 1987; Dweck, 1986; Erkut, 1983; Stipek, 1984). Add to this depiction an experience in which a young girl's explicit nonconsent is ignored. A tendency to internalize blame suggests that victimization would exacerbate existing self-doubts, making future attempts at assertion in sexual situations more difficult. Likewise, a failure to externalize blame might prevent aggressive males from receiving feedback that their conduct is inappropriate. Perceptions of heterosexual dating are likely to be profoundly altered; females may view males as sexually uncontrollable and themselves, at least in the sexual arena, as powerless to control.

44. Bush and Simmons (1987) attributed the loss of self-esteem observed among junior high girls involved in dating to "boys' attempts to be dominant in a dating relationship" (p. 199). Yet, relationships are an important source of female adolescent self-esteem, with popularity valued over competence and independence (Bush, Simmons, Hutchinson, & Blyth, 1978); motivation to preserve them may be strong. For some teen victims of sexual aggression, the "solution" may lie in adopting an externalized attitude toward sex that enables both dating and coercion to continue, as in, "I don't like it, but I can't do anything about it."

45. The correlates rather than the consequences of prior victimization may also contribute to the risk of revictimization. In this study, greater use of alcohol in dating and higher levels of consensual sex were associated with dating victimization at both time periods. As has been suggested previously (Koss & Dinero, 1989; Muehlenhard & Linton, 1987), sexually coercive men may prey on women with these characteristics because they believe them to be more likely sexual partners and "safer" victims.

46. Child sexual abuse (CSA) did not predict college victimization in the present investigation, although CSA was related to precollege victimization. In other words, CSA was a better short-term than long-term predictor of revictimization. In Gidycz et al.'s study, adolescent victimization was also more strongly related to college victimization than was CSA, though both correlations were statistically significant. However, Gidycz et al.'s sample at follow-up was younger than the present study's sample, exposed to the risk of college victimization for just 9 weeks (versus 32 months). Perhaps the effect of CSA on risk is time-limited; the more time that elapses from CSA without further incident of victimization, the less CSA contributes to overall vulnerability. In the present research, 40% of contact CSA survivors who were revictimized in precollege dating were also victimized in college, whereas 25% of contact CSA survivors who were not victimized in precollege dating were victimized in college. Just as risk of cancer relapse diminishes with every symptom-free year, revictimization risk for CSA survivors may be reduced with every aggression-free dating relationship. Such resilience may occur spontaneously through normal growth and change, or for some survivors, through formal sources of assistance such as counseling or support groups. Finally, the psychological impact of CSA is related to a multitude of factors, and consequently, is highly variable. More profoundly, affected CSA survivors may experience a heightened risk of revictimization for a longer period of time; yet, given the relationship between CSA and school/learning problems (see Kendall-Tackett, Williams, & Finkelhor, 1993), it is likely that these women less frequently enter a college population.

47. One attitudinal measure emerged as an important risk factor: More sexually conservative women were *less* likely to be victimized in college. This result is interesting in that this measure has not been found to correlate with victimization in previous studies employing retrospective methodology (Koss & Dinero, 1989; Vogel & Himelein, 1990). However, Koss and Dinero did find a relationship between victimization risk and more liberal sexual attitudes, defined by greater approval and enjoyment of sexual activity. More sexually conservative women in the current study also tended to possess less consensual sexual experience, less assertiveness, more adversarial sexual beliefs,

and greater acceptance of rape myths. Taken together, these data suggest that traditional attitudes may reduce a woman's risk of sexual victimization insofar as they increase her mistrust of dating and decrease her involvement in sex.

48. In addition, so-called "sexual liberation," when defined by an attitude in which sex is a frequent but often meaningless act, may in fact contribute to victimization. In her exploration of the dynamics of coercive sex, Gavey (1989) noted that women who adopt a discourse, or schema, of permissive sexuality are devoid of a rationale for refusing sex. Although such women would not consider unpleasant sexual encounters to be nonconsensual (i.e., rape or attempted rape), such experiences might well fit the present study's definition of sexual coercion, included in the category of moderate victimization.

49. In all, only two of six behavioral and attitudinal risk characteristics were significantly associated with victimization. As the only longitudinal study to date to assess the impact of these variables, these data argue against existing notions that assertiveness or rape-supportive attitudes (i.e., acceptance of interpersonal violence, adversarial sexual beliefs, and rape myth acceptance) increase victimization risk. However, one problem with existing behavioral and attitudinal indices may be their overly generalized focus. To be effective predictors, such measures may need to focus more narrowly on the criterion behavior of interest, in this case, sexual aggression in dating. For example, alcohol use, which emerged as a useful predictor in this research, was operationalized as alcohol use *in dating* rather than overall alcohol use. Other measures might benefit from the same precision: Assertiveness *in sexual situations* rather than a broad measure of assertiveness, or acceptance of interpersonal violence *in heterosexual dating situations* rather than general acceptance of interpersonal violence, might prove to be more sensitive indices.

50. What are the implications of these findings for prevention efforts to deter sexual aggression? First, this research highlights the need for more sophisticated and thorough sexual education for teenagers. The pressure and confusion experienced by adolescents making their initial foray into the sexual arena is considerable. Yet, by twelfth grade, 66.6% of females and 76.3% of males are sexually active (Centers for Disease Control, 1992). Formal opportunities for open discussion of anxieties and uncertainties are needed; accurate information about consensual sex can empower both women and men to reduce victimization risk.

51. Sex education can also serve to promote egalitarian sexual values, striving to strip away the traditional sexual scripts that make men initiators and women defenders. Such antiquated notions place the burden of sexual decision-making on teenage girls who may be ill-equipped for refusal. However, the promotion of egalitarian sexual values should not be confused with the promotion of sexual activity. It is certainly possible to teach about sexual ethics and mutual respect while encouraging responsibility, caution, and assertiveness in sexual matters. Although the present data indicate that sexual conservatism may be one safeguard against victimization, it is unlikely that advocating avoidance of sex will be an effective preventive for a significant proportion of the adolescent population.

52. Second, these data, along with those from related studies (Gidycz et al., 1993; Himelein et al., 1994), point to a dramatic need for prevention programs aimed specifically at the precollege level. Contrary to the media images of date rape as a university phenomenon, sexual aggression in dating appears to be widespread from its roots in early adolescence. Further, the present study suggests that prevention of precollege victimization may be the best means of preventing college victimization.

53. Third, both research and applied clinical work must begin to focus more explicitly on the prevention of revictimization. Future research might attempt to follow sexual abuse victims longitudinally in the effort to gain insight into the processes through which vulnerability to revictimization is initiated. In clinical work with victimized women, therapists must push beyond the emotional impact of early victimization experiences to the exploration of cognitive and interpersonal ramifications that contribute to future risk. Without specific focus on sexual rights and assertiveness as well as "safe" dating behaviors, a previously victimized woman may never develop a sense of sexual control.

54. Finally, although this research successfully identified four correlates of victimization risk, the magnitude of the relationships was relatively small, with two thirds of victims unable to be distinguished from nonvictims. This finding suggests that much victimization has little to do with the history, behaviors, or attitudes of victims. Such numbers remind us that large scale prevention must begin with the true cause of sexual aggression: the aggressor.

Notes

1. Although this university does not *require* students to participate in its new student orientation program, 98-99% of entering first-year students attend orientation each year. One factor likely accounting

for such a high rate of participation is that new student registration for first-semester classes takes place during each of the eight orientation sessions.

2. Although exact figures by gender are not available, combined participation and completion rates for both genders were much greater when questionnaires were administered by the investigators immediately following the presentation (96.1%) than when questionnaires were administered by orientation counselors at a later point (63.5%).

3. Previous analyses of the Time 1 sample revealed that 38.5% of women had experienced at least one form of sexual victimization in dating prior to attending college and that precollege victimization was associated with both childhood sexual abuse and consensual sexual experience (Himelein, Vogel, & Wachowiak, 1994). Discriminant function analysis of these initial data indicated that five risk variables contributed to a model that correctly classified 44.3% of cases into five categories of precollege victimization, ranging from no victimization to rape: childhood sexual abuse, adversarial sexual beliefs, frequency of alcohol use on dates, quantity of alcohol use on dates, and assertiveness (Vogel & Himelein, 1990).

4. Because victimization reported at Time 2 could have occurred at any time during the previous 32 months, it cannot be assumed that victimization among women who had left the university occurred *prior* to their departure. The precise timing of Time 2 victimization for any Time 2 participants could not be established on the basis of existing data.

References

American Association of University Women. (1991). *Shortchanging girls, shortchanging America.* Washington, DC: Greenberg-Lake Analysis Group.

Amick, A. E., & Calhoun, K. S. (1987). Resistance to sexual aggression: Personality, attitudinal, and situational factors. *Archives of Sexual Behavior, 16,* 153-163.

Beitchman, J. H., Zucker, K. J., Hood, J. E., daCosta, G. A., Akman, D., & Cassavia, E. (1992). A review of the long-term effects of child sexual abuse. *Child Abuse & Neglect, 16,* 101-118.

Bieber, S. L. (1988). Multiple regression and its alternatives. *The Social Science Journal, 25,* 1-19.

Browne, A., & Finkelhor, D. (1986). Impact of child sexual abuse: A review of the research. *Psychological Bulletin, 99,* 66-77.

Burt, M. R. (1980). Cultural myths and supports for rape. *Journal of Personality and Social Psychology, 38,* 217-230.

Bush, D. M., & Simmons, R. B. (1987). Gender and coping with the entry into early adolescence. In R. C. Barnett, L. Biener, & G. K. Baruch (Eds.), *Gender and stress* (pp. 186-217). New York: Macmillan.

Bush, D. M., Simmons, R. G., Hutchinson, B., & Blyth, D. A. (1978). Adolescent perception of sex roles in 1968 and 1975. *Public Opinion Quarterly, 41,* 459-474.

Centers for Disease Control. (1992, January). Sexual behavior among high school students: U.S. 1990. *Morbidity and Mortality Weekly, 40,* 885-888.

Clarke, R. V. (1983). Situational crime prevention: Its theoretical basis and practical scope. In M. Tonry & N. Morris (Eds.), *Crime and justice: An annual review of research* (pp. 225-256). Chicago: University of Chicago Press.

Craig, M. E. (1990). Coercive sexuality in dating relationships: A situational model. *Clinical Psychology Review, 10,* 395-423.

Dweck, C. S. (1986). Motivational processes affecting learning. *American Psychologist, 41,* 1040-1048.

Erkut, S. (1983). Exploring sex differences in expectancy, attribution, and academic achievement. *Sex Roles, 9,* 217-231.

Finkelhor, D. (1979). *Sexually victimized children.* New York: Free Press.

Gavey, N. (1989). Feminist poststructuralism and discourse analysis: Contributions to a feminist psychology. *Psychology of Women Quarterly, 13,* 459-475.

Gavey, N. (1991). Sexual victimization prevalence among New Zealand university students. *Journal of Consulting and Clinical Psychology, 59,* 464-466.

Gidycz, C. A., Coble, C. N., Latham, L., & Layman, M. J. (1993). Sexual assault experience in adulthood and prior victimization experiences. *Psychology of Women Quarterly, 17,* 151-168.

Himelein, M. J., Vogel, R. E., & Wachowiak, D. G. (1994). Nonconsensual sexual experiences in precollege women: Prevalence and risk factors. *Journal of Counseling and Development, 72,* 411-415.

Hosmer, D. W., & Lemeshow, S. (1989). *Applied logistic regression.* New York: Wiley.

Kendall-Tackett, K. A., Williams, L. M., & Finkelhor, D. (1993). Impact of sexual abuse on children: A review and synthesis of recent empirical studies. *Psychological Bulletin, 113,* 164-180.

Koss, M. P. (1985). The hidden rape victim: Personality, attitudinal, and situational characteristics. *Psychology of Women Quarterly, 9,* 193-212.

Koss, M. P., & Dinero, T. E. (1989). Discriminant analysis of risk factors for sexual victimization among a national sample of college women. *Journal of Consulting and Clinical Psychology, 57,* 242-250.

Koss, M. P., Dinero, T. E., Seibel, C. A., & Cox S. L. (1988). Stranger and acquaintance rape: Are there differences in the victim's experience? *Psychology of Women Quarterly, 12,* 1-24.

Koss, M. P., & Gidycz, C. A. (1985). Sexual experiences survey: Reliability and validity. *Journal of Consulting and Clinical Psychology, 53,* 422-423.

Koss, M. P., Gidycz, C. A., & Wisniewski, N. (1987). The scope of rape: Incidence and prevalence of sexual aggression and victimization in a national sample of higher education students. *Journal of Consulting and Clinical Psychology, 55,* 162-170.

Koss, M. P., & Oros, C. J. (1982). Sexual experiences survey: A research instrument investigating sexual aggression and victimization. *Journal of Consulting and Clinical Psychology, 50,* 455-457.

Lundberg-Love, P., & Geffner, R. (1989). Date rape: Prevalence, risk factors, and a proposed model. In M. A. Pirog-Good & J. E. Stets (Eds.), *Violence in dating relationships: Emerging social issues* (pp. 169-184). New York: Praeger.

Miller, B., & Marshall, J. C. (1987). Coercive sex on the university campus. *Journal of College Student Personnel, 28,* 38-47.

Muehlenhard, C. L., & Linton, M. A. (1987). Date rape and sexual aggression in dating situations: Incidence and risk factors. *Journal of Counseling Psychology, 34,* 186-196.

Myers, M. B., Templer, D. I., & Brown, R. (1984). Coping ability of women who become victims of rape. *Journal of Consulting and Clinical Psychology, 52,* 73-78.

Norris, J., & Cubbins, L. A. (1992). Dating, drinking, and rape: Effects of victim's and assailant's alcohol consumption on judgments of their behavior and traits. *Psychology of Women Quarterly, 16,* 179-191.

Rathus, S. A. (1973). A 30-item schedule for assessing assertive behavior. *Behavior Therapy, 4,* 398-406.

Richardson, D. R., & Hammock, G. S. (1991). Alcohol and acquaintance rape. In A. Parrot & L. Bechofer (Eds.), *Acquaintance rape: The hidden crime* (pp. 83-95). New York: Wiley.

Russell, D. E. H. (1986). *The secret trauma: Incest in the lives of girls and women.* New York: Basic Books.

Selkin, J. (1978). Protecting personal space: Victim and resister reactions of assaultive rape. *Journal of Community Psychology, 6,* 263-268.

Stipek, D. J. (1984). Sex differences in children's attributions for success and failure on math and spelling tests. *Sex Roles, 11,* 969-981.

Vogel, R. E., & Himelein, M. J. (1990, March). *Discriminant function analysis of date rape: Preliminary findings regarding risk factors.* Paper presented at the meeting of the Academy of Criminal Justice Sciences, Denver, CO.

Wyatt, G. E., Guthrie, D., & Notgrass, C. M. (1992). Differential effects of women's child sexual abuse and subsequent sexual revictimization. *Journal of Consulting and Clinical Psychology, 60,* 167-173.

Factual Questions

1. How many predictors were examined in this study?

2. The acronym *CSA* stands for what words?

3. On what basis were four of the eight orientation sessions selected?

4. Of the 415 women who were invited to take part in the study, what percentage elected to participate?

big names n CSA

5. What percentage of the Time 1 sample provided social security numbers, permitting contact at Time 2?

6. What was the average age of the Time 2 sample?

7. Which correlation coefficient in Table 1 indicates the strongest relationship?

8. The relationship between sexual conservatism and sexual victimization in dating during college was statistically significant at what probability level?

9. What is the value of the correlation coefficient for the relationship between child sexual abuse and sexual conservatism?

10. Which two variables emerged from the regression analysis as being important?

11. The author suggests that for attitudinal indices to be more effective predictors, they may need to focus more narrowly on what?

Questions for Discussion

12. Explain in your own words the methodological problem with conducting retrospective studies on the role of assertiveness in victimization. (See paragraph 8.)

13. Describe the difference between a retrospective study and a prospective study. (See paragraphs 8-11.)

14. What is an "informed consent form"? (See paragraph 14.)

15. Why is it important to know that those who provided social security numbers and those who did not provide them were not significantly different on demographic or risk variables? (See paragraph 19.)

16. Of the 330 initial subjects at Time 1, data were available on only 100 at Time 2. Speculate on measures that might be taken to lessen this attrition rate in future studies.

17. In paragraph 25, the author uses the term "operational definition." What does this mean?

18. In paragraph 29, the author states that the Rathus Assertiveness Schedule has a "2-month test-retest reliability of .78." What does this mean?

19. What does "*ns*" in paragraph 34 mean?

20. Table 1 shows a significant correlation coefficient of −.24 between variable 3 (consensual sexual experience) and variable 7 (sexual conservatism). Briefly interpret this finding with attention to the fact that the coefficient is negative.

21. The author states four implications. (See paragraphs 50-54.) Do you agree with them? Explain.

22. To what population(s) would you be willing to generalize the results of this study?

23. In your opinion, has this study made an important contribution to our understanding of risk factors for sexual victimization in dating? Explain.

Quality Ratings

DIRECTIONS: Indicate your level of agreement with each of the following statements by circling a number from 5 for strongly agree (SA) to 1 for strongly disagree (SD). If you believe that an item is not applicable to this research article, leave it blank. Be prepared to explain your ratings.

A. The introduction establishes the importance of the research topic.
   SA   5   4   3   2   1   SD

B. The literature review establishes the context for the study.
   SA   5   4   3   2   1   SD

C. The research purpose, question, or hypothesis is clearly stated.
   SA   5   4   3   2   1   SD

D. The method of sampling is sound.
   SA   5   4   3   2   1   SD

E. Relevant demographics (for example, age, gender, and ethnicity) are described.
   SA   5   4   3   2   1   SD

F. Measurement procedures are adequate.
   SA   5   4   3   2   1   SD

G. The results are clearly described.
   SA   5   4   3   2   1   SD

H. The discussion/conclusion is appropriate.
   SA   5   4   3   2   1   SD

I. Despite any flaws noted above, the report is worthy of publication.
   SA   5   4   3   2   1   SD

ARTICLE 15

QUALITY OF THE LITERACY ENVIRONMENT IN DAY CARE AND CHILDREN'S DEVELOPMENT

Loraine Dunn *University of Oklahoma*
Sara Ann Beach *University of Oklahoma*
Susan Kontos *Purdue University*

Although traditional assessments of day care environments have been linked to children's development, understanding of the specific characteristics of the environment that enhance language, literacy, and cognitive development is sketchy. The purpose of this study was to explore the environment for literacy in day care centers, its relationship with traditional measures of day care quality and its influence on children's cognitive and language development. Observation of the environments in the 30 community-based day care classrooms sampled revealed relatively impoverished environments. Correlation and multiple regression analyses indicated that settings of higher day care quality also had higher quality environments. In separate hierarchical regression analyses, controlling for variance due to family factors, both day care quality and the environment predicted a significant portion of the variance in children's language development but not in children's cognitive development.

1. Theory and research clearly point to the importance of the environment in facilitating young children's development of language, literacy and cognition. Bronfenbrenner's (1979) social-ecological theory argues that the specific contexts or environments that children experience influence their concurrent behaviors as well as their subsequent development. Similarly, Vygotsky's (1978) socio-cultural theory contends that the specific society and culture in which children are raised plays an important role in their development. Research linking children's developmental outcomes and the environments they experience supports these theoretical notions. Stimulating home environments have been shown to positively predict children's performance on measures of language and cognitive development (Bradley & Caldwell, 1984; Elardo, Bradley, & Caldwell, 1977). High quality day care environments also have a positive influence on children's language and cognitive development (Howes, 1988; McCartney, 1984). Taken together, these theoretical notions and the research supporting them suggests that for many preschool-age children, the quality of the environment in day care settings should play as important a role in their development as the quality of the home environment.

2. While work is available describing day care environments and their influence on children's development, missing from our knowledge base is information on the environment for literacy typically available to young children in community-based day care programs. It seems logical that a high quality day care environment would be rich in reading and writing artifacts and experiences and that this environment would influence children's development.

3. In fact, the quality of the home environment for literacy has been documented as having a significant effect on children's language development (Beach, 1991; Chomsky, 1972; Heath, 1983). Children from homes where parents provide materials and activities that promote literacy are often those children who become successful readers and writers at an early age, in many cases before formal school instruction has begun. Characteristics of these homes have included an availability of both reading and writing materials for children's use, adult models of language use within a wide range of social spheres, and interaction between children and adults around meaningful reading and writing activities (Durkin, 1966; Leichter, 1984; Taylor, 1983).

4. Having materials available to children (Cochran-Smith, 1984; Ferreiro & Teberosky, 1982; Morrow, 1990), displaying functional and environmental print (McGee, Lomax, & Head, 1988; Schickendanz & Sullivan, 1984), engaging in interactive storybook reading (Beach, Kincade, & Asundi, 1992; Mason, 1990; Morrow & Weinstein, 1986), and including materials that promote literacy in play settings (Neuman & Roskos, 1990, 1993; Pellegrini, 1985; Schrader, 1990) have also been shown to enhance the development of literacy and language.

5. Scholars studying the environment stress that in order to understand how environments influence children's development the environment must be measured directly rather than through proxy or social address variables (e.g., Bronfenbrenner, 1986; Wachs, 1983). Direct or specific measures of environments allow scholars to pinpoint those characteristics of the environment most salient to specific domains of development. For example, the availability of stimulating toys and materials in homes and in day care centers has been positively related to children's cognitive development (Bradley & Caldwell, 1984; Clarke-Stewart & Gruber, 1984; Wachs & Gruen, 1982). Similarly, the quality of children's interactions with teachers in day care centers has been positively related to their language development (McCartney, 1984). Research on other specific features of the environment may also provide valuable information on children's developmental potential. One likely candidate for investigation is the quality of the environment to promote literacy in day care programs. For the remainder of the article, references to the environment imply an environment to promote literacy, unless otherwise stated.

6. As with other specific measures of the day care environment, examination of the environment to promote literacy is most likely to be

Dunn, L., Beach, S. A., & Kontos, S. (1994). Quality of the literacy environment in day care and children's development. *Journal of Research in Childhood Education, 9,* 24-34. Reprinted by permission of the author and the Association for Childhood Education International, 11501 Georgia Avenue, Suite 315, Wheaton, MD. Copyright © 1994 by the Association.

Thanks to Linda Hestenes, Lora Andrada and Terri Underwood for assistance with data collection and coding. This study was partially funded by a David Ross grant from the Purdue University Research Foundation to the first and third authors. This paper was presented at the 1993 American Educational Research Association Annual Conference, Atlanta.

useful when examined in the context of other measures of day care quality (i.e., structural and global quality assessments). In terms of structural quality, variables such as teacher-child ratio, group size and teacher training are often addressed. Global quality is typically assessed with the Early Childhood Environment Rating Scale (ECERS, Harms & Clifford, 1980), an observational instrument which rates both static and process features of day care programs through items on a variety of subscales related to the physical and educational environment.

7. Ample evidence is available linking these traditional assessments of the day care environment to children's development. Low teacher-child ratios (few children per adult) have been associated with children's language development (McCartney, 1984; Phillips, Scarr, & McCartney, 1987). Lower group sizes have been associated with children's achievement and language development (Ruopp et al., 1979). Teachers' child-related training has been associated with children's achievement (Ruopp et al., 1979) and children's cognitive functioning (Clarke-Stewart & Gruber, 1984). Children in higher global quality centers (ECERS total score) have been found to have more advanced language development (Phillips et al., 1987).

8. Within a given structural or global quality level, what specific characteristics of the environment contribute to children's development? Current understanding of this issue is relatively sketchy. Children in programs with low adult-child ratios are more likely to experience higher levels of global quality in the form of developmentally appropriate care giving. And children in programs with lower group sizes are more likely to experience higher global quality in the form of developmentally appropriate activities (Howes, Phillips, & Whitebook, 1992). Children are more likely to experience a variety of play materials and caregiver stimulation of cognitive development in programs with higher global quality ratings (ECERS total score) and larger group sizes (Dunn, 1993).

9. Are environments that stimulate literacy more likely to occur in day care settings scoring high on measures of structural and global quality? Do these environments have an impact on children's development? This study was designed to provide preliminary answers to these questions by (a) describing the environment available in typical day care classrooms, (b) determining the relationship between day care quality and the quality of the environment and (c) exploring the influence of the day care environment on children's cognitive and language development. Because of the theoretical linkages between literacy and children's cognitive and language development (Vygotsky, 1978,

1986) the focus was on these two forms of children's development. It was hypothesized that programs scoring high on traditional measures of day care quality would also score high on assessments of the environment and that children in day care programs with rich environments would display more advanced cognitive and language development.

Method

Sample

10. *Centers.* The sample, taken from a larger study of day care quality and children's development, consisted of 30 classrooms in 24 licensed community day care centers in an 8-county region of a midwestern state. In order to obtain classrooms representing the widest range of day care quality possible all licensed centers in the geographic area were invited to participate. Fifty-two percent of the eligible centers agreed to participate in the study. Refusals to participate typically related to undesirable timing, policies against observation by outsiders or reluctance to be observed. No more than two classrooms from any one center were included. Eight of the participating centers were nonprofit, 16 were for profit. Both private for-profit and for-profit franchises were represented. Information obtained from directors during recruitment were compared using χ^2 and t tests. There were no differences between participating and nonparticipating centers in terms of auspice, center size, number of teachers employed, training of staff or staff turnover.

Centers participating in the study employed fewer aides, t (40) = 2.29, $p < .05$, than nonparticipating centers. Average annual staff turnover rates for participating centers was 42% for teachers, 48% for aides and 8% for directors. Average group size and teacher-child ratio in the participating classrooms are reported in Table 1.

11. *Teachers.* The teachers were 30 females with an average age of 31.67 years, $SD = 7.09$. The majority of teachers were white (3 African-Americans). As seen in Table 1, their mean level of education was similar to that in other studies (see Whitebook, Howes, & Phillips, 1989). Nineteen of the teachers reported some education beyond high school and 15 reported college level work in a child-related major. Only 6 of the 15 teachers reported majoring in early childhood education or child development. When asked if they had any training specifically related to child care, early childhood education or child development, the average teacher response was Junior College/Technical School training or an Associate's degree. A little less than half (43%) of the teachers had some kind of teacher certification (5 early childhood, 5 elementary, 1 CDA credential, 1 other). As reported in Table 1, teachers' mean level of experience in the field of day care was high and the range of experience was quite broad. Teachers' mean level of experience in the present centers was somewhat lower.

12. *Children.* One male and one female child was randomly selected from each participating

Table 1 *Descriptive statistics of the sample*

Variables	Mean	Mean Item Score	SD	Range
Group size	21.47		6.67	12–40
Ratio	1:12.82		2.77	1:9–1:20
Teachers				
Education (yrs)	14.57		2.17	12–18
Experience in field (yrs)	6.27		5.26	.33–24
Experience in centers (yrs)	2.98		2.66	.25–11
Quality				
Language/reasoning	16.47	4.12	4.57	7–25
Dev. approp. activity	36.66	3.67	10.13	15–57
Variety	4.90		1.88	1–8
Literacy activities	.93		.73	0–2
Literacy quality	30.57	3.05	5.98	19–39
Children				
Verbal intelligence	33.47		7.29	19–49
Achievement	45.10		8.98	24–61

classroom. Eligibility requirements for children focused on normal development, age (between 36 and 60 months) and day care history. The goal was to obtain children who attended day care full-time (at least 25 hours per week) and who had been enrolled in the target centers at least six months. In the few cases where it was not possible to recruit one child of each gender, due to a lack of eligible children, two children of one gender were randomly selected. This sampling procedure resulted in 34 (57%) females and 26 (43%) males with a mean age of 51.85 months, $SD = 6.71$. The majority of the children were white (6 African-Americans). Mean length of time the children had been enrolled in the centers was 1.25 years, $SD = .89$. Children's mean age of entry into day care was 17.43 months, $SD = 15.59$.

13. *Family characteristics.* Because family background characteristics are known to interact with day care quality and children's development (Howes & Stewart, 1987), family background information was requested from each child's mother. Family information was obtained from 57 of the 60 families (95%). The majority of the mothers (77.2%) were living with a spouse or partner. Mean age for mothers and fathers was 30.68, $SD = 4.5$, and 34.19, $SD = 4.71$, years respectively. Educational attainment averaged 13.4, $SD = 1.97$, years for mothers and 13.87, $SD = 2.57$, years for fathers. The average family income ranged between $29,000 and $34,999. Mean socioeconomic status level for the sample fell in category IV of the Hollingshead (1976) four factor index: medium business, minor professional and technical workers.

Measures

14. *Center and teacher characteristics.* During the recruitment interview directors were asked to provide information about the size and auspice (profit/nonprofit) of each center. Information on the teachers was obtained from questionnaires. Each teacher provided information on her age, educational level, training, teacher certification status and experience.

15. *Day care quality.* Structural day care quality variables included teachers' education, training, certification, and experience, as well as teacher-child ratio and group size. An onsite teacher interview and observation was used to obtain information on group size and teacher-child ratio. Teacher-child ratio was calculated by dividing the number of adults present in the classroom by the number of children in the group. Global day care quality was obtained with the Early Childhood Environment Rating Scale (ECERS; Harms & Clifford, 1980). The ECERS is a 37-item scale designed to assess

multiple aspects of day care environments through subscales on personal care, creative activities, language and reasoning activities, furnishings/display, fine/gross motor activities, social development and adult facilities/opportunities. The authors of the scale report good interrater reliability, .93, and internal consistency, .83 (Cronbach's alpha), for the instrument. For this study an interrater reliability of 94% was established prior to data collection. Reliability checks conducted for three classrooms at 10 observation intervals indicated interrater reliability averaged 92%.

16. Each classroom was observed for two hours and then each of the 37 ECERS items were rated on a 7-point Likert scale. Two scores were derived from the ECERS for this study. First, a score for the quality of the language and reasoning environment based on the subscale of the same name. This subscale describes classroom activities and materials related to the development of concepts and language. Internal consistency for the subscale was .90 (Cronbach's alpha). The second ECERS score was the developmentally appropriate activities factor identified by the National Child Care Staffing Study (Whitebook et al., 1989). This factor describes the physical environment of the classroom and the availability of learning activities which invite exploration and experimentation but does not include any items from the language and reasoning subscale. Internal consistency for the factor in this sample was .92 (Cronbach's alpha). The language/reasoning subscale and the appropriate activities factor were chosen because they represent features of the day care environment most likely to be related to the quality of the literate environment and to children's cognitive and language development. ECERS scores (see Table 1) indicate the classrooms represented moderate quality (i.e., better than average but less than good quality).

17. A specific quality assessment of the day care environment was obtained by evaluating the variety of play materials available in the environment. An evaluation scheme developed by Kritchevsky (1967) was used for this purpose. During play time an observer identified all possible play units available. Play units were defined as materials or equipment available for play. Examples include a table with puzzles or manipulatives, a block area, a book/library area or a water table. Each play unit was coded for the primary type of activity it invited such as climbing, looking at books, pretending or building. To create the variety score the number of different types of activities available were summed. Interrater reliability for variety coding was established at 93% before data collection

was begun. Reliability checks conducted for three classrooms at ten observation intervals indicated interrater reliability averaged 98%. A moderate variety of activities were available in the classrooms (see Table 1).

18. *Environments to promote literacy.* Two variables describing the environment were included as specific quality measures. The first variable was created by determining the number of literacy-related activities available to children from the play units identified for the variety score. Literacy-related activities were defined as play units containing reading and writing artifacts such as a table with paper and pencil or a chalk board, a library corner, or a housekeeping center with environmental print. The data were examined and coded by two judges: one an expert in early literacy and the other an expert in early childhood education. Disagreements in coding were discussed and resolved. The total number of literacy-related activities in each classroom was recorded.

19. The second specific quality variable was an assessment of the quality of the reading and writing environment. This score was obtained from an observation based rating scale: the Observational Rating Scale for Language Development and Literacy Programs in Preschools (Hyson, Van Trieste, & Rauch, 1989). The scale, based on the National Association for the Education of Young Children's guidelines for developmentally appropriate practices, contains 10 items which are rated on a 5-point Likert scale ranging from "not at all like this classroom" to "very much like this classroom." The items refer to the presence of functional print in the environment (i.e., classroom charts) and children's access to books, writing materials, drawing materials and story dictation activities in both structured and unstructured situations. Examples of items include "students have the opportunity to dictate stories" and "children have the opportunity daily to use crayons, chalk, markers, paper and other materials in ways of their own choosing."

20. Observation for the environment occurred in conjunction with the two-hour ECERS classroom observation. Interrater reliability of 90% was established before data collection was begun. Reliability checks conducted for three classrooms at 10 observation intervals indicated interrater reliability remained at 90%. Item scores were summed to create a total score. Internal consistency for the scale with this sample was .81 (Cronbach's alpha).

21. *Children's development.* Children's language development was assessed with a teacher rating scale, the verbal intelligence subscale of the Classroom Behavior Inventory (Schaefer & Edgerton, 1978). The subscale contains 10 items which are rated on a 1, *not at all like*, to 5, *very much like*, scale. The scale authors report an internal consistency of .95 for the subscale. Internal consistency for the verbal intelligence subscale with this sample was .90 (Cronbach's alpha).

22. Children's cognitive development was assessed with the Preschool Inventory—Revised Edition (PSI, Caldwell, 1970), an individually administered achievement test. The PSI contains 64 items and requires about 20 minutes to administer. The author reports split-half reliability as .92 (Spearman-Brown corrected) and .91 (Kuder-Richardson 20). The instrument assesses children's knowledge of common objects and situations through questions such as "If you wanted to buy some gas where would you go?" and "Put three cars in the big box." As can be inferred from this description, the PSI does not focus specifically on literacy skills but rather on common knowledge. The total number of correct responses were tallied and used as the achievement score. Percentile scores based on age norms are available but were not used because percentile scores do not represent interval level data (Popham & Sirotnik, 1973). Instead, this study used the PSI raw scores (number of correct responses). Children's mean scores for the verbal intelligence rating and the PSI are reported in Table 1.

Procedure

23. An initial phone call was made to each center to interview the director regarding the characteristics of the center. Each classroom was visited at least three times. During the first visit an observer rated the classroom using the ECERS and literacy instruments. The observer also recorded the number of children and adults present in the classroom, interviewed the teacher regarding structural quality variables and distributed questionnaires to the teachers. During the second visit another observer blind to the ECERS and literacy ratings observed the classroom during playtime to record the play units present. The teacher questionnaires were also retrieved during this visit. During the third visit an experimenter blind to the ECERS, literacy and play unit ratings administered the PSI to the children.

Results

Environment

24. The environments observed in the day care classrooms sampled were less than optimal. As seen in Table 1 very few free play activities were literacy-related. Nine classrooms had books or book areas, nine had blank paper and writing materials, one had a bookmaking activity, two had chalk and chalkboards for writing

Table 2   *Correlations between day care quality and literacy environment (n = 30)*

Day Care Quality	Literacy Quality	Literacy Activities
Lang./reasoning	.73***	.12
Approp. activity	.86***	.39*
Variety	.33	.32

*p < .05, ***p < .001

and/or drawing, two had computers, and two had letter cards. Seven classrooms had two literacy-related activities. The maximum number of literacy-related play units in any classroom was two. Nine classrooms (30%) had no literacy-related play units. The two-hour observation of the environment indicated the literacy quality of the classrooms was moderate. Although some literacy-related activities were available throughout the day, the lack of emphasis on literacy-related activities during free play periods suggests literacy-related activities were not a prime focus in these classrooms.

Day Care Quality and Literacy Quality

25. Pearson product moment correlations were computed to determine the relationships between day care quality and the environment and between the two environment variables. There were no relationships between structural forms of quality and the number of literacy-related activities available. Only one structural quality variable correlated with the quality of the environment: teacher certification, *r* = .37, *p* < .05. Those teachers who held some form of teacher certification provided classrooms that were rated higher on the literacy quality scale. Because of the small number of certified teachers (*n* = 12), additional analyses to determine possible differences in the environment as a function of certificate type were not performed. The quality of the environment was highly correlated with the number of literacy-related activities available, *r* = .52, *p* < .01.

26. As seen in Table 2, global day care quality (ECERS scores), but not specific day care quality (variety), was related to the quality of the literate environment and to the number of literacy-related activities available. Classrooms that were rated higher on the language/reasoning subscale scored higher on the literacy quality measure. Classrooms scoring higher on the appropriate activities factor had more literacy-related activities available for children and were rated higher on the literacy quality measure. Regression analyses confirmed these findings regarding the quality of the environment (see Table 3). Three regression models were tested. A single independent variable was regressed on the dependent variable, literacy quality, in each of the three equations: language/reasoning, appropriate activities, and variety. The developmentally appropriate activities factor and the language/reasoning subscale both predicted substantial portions of the variance in literacy quality. A fourth equation simultaneously regressed the appropriate activities factor and the language/reasoning score on literacy quality (see Table 3). Together the two ECERS scores predicted a large portion of the variance in literacy quality. These findings provide support for a hypothesis articulating a relationship between traditional measures of day care quality and the quality of the environment.

Children's Development

27. *Child and family characteristics.* Children's cognitive and language development were related to several family and child characteristics. Specifically, language development was more advanced when maternal, *r* = .28, *p* < .05, and paternal education, *r* = .29, *p* < .05, levels were higher and when family socioeconomic status was higher, *r* = .39, *p* < .01. Language development was not related to children's age, gender, age at entry into day care, maternal or paternal age, parents' marital status or income. As reported elsewhere (Dunn, 1993), children's cognitive development in the form of achievement scores was very highly correlated with their age, *r* = .63, *p* < .001.

Table 3   *Regressions of literacy quality from predictors of day care quality*

Models	beta	R^2	F	df
Language/reasoning	.95***	.53	31.96***	1,28
Approp. activity	.51***	.74	81.35***	1,28
Variety	1.05	.11	3.43	1,28
Language/reasoning	.26	.76	3.43	2,27
Approp. activity	.42***			

***p < .001

Table 4 *Hierarchical regression analyses of socioeconomic status, appropriate activities, language/reasoning and literacy quality on language development*

Language		B	R^2	R^2 Change	Intercept
Step 1	SES	.27**	.15**	.15**	
Step 2	Approp. Act.	.24**	.24**	.09*	13.87*
Step 1	SES	.31**	.15**	.15**	
Step 2	Lang. Reas.	.63**	.28**	.13**	10.68
Step 1	SES	.27**	.15**	.15**	
Step 2	Literacy	.35*	.22**	.07**	11.85

*$p < .05$, **$p < .01$

Therefore, children's age was partialed out of all analyses involving achievement scores. Again as reported in the larger study, children's cognitive development was correlated with their race, age of entry into day care, their mothers' age and education, their fathers' age and education, family income and socioeconomic status. Children's PSI scores were not related to their gender or parents' marital status.

28. *Day care quality.* Children's achievement scores were not related to any form of day care quality. The teacher ratings of children's language development were related to the developmentally appropriate activities factor, $r = .34$, $p < .01$, and the language/reasoning subscale, $r = .36$, $p < .01$, indicating children in higher quality environments had more advanced language development.

29. Hierarchical regression analyses were conducted to determine if the relationships between children's language development and day care quality were still significant after controlling for family factors. Because children's language development was related to multiple family characteristics a stepwise regression analysis was performed to identify the best predictor. Age was not included because it did not correlate with the language outcome measure. Family socioeconomic status emerged as the best predictor of children's language development, $R^2 = .17$, $F(1,42) = 8.89$, $p < .01$.[1] The hierarchical regression analyses indicated that day care quality as measured by the appropriate activities factor and the language/reasoning subscale did account for a significant portion of the variance in children's language development after controlling for variance due to family socioeconomic status (see Table 4).

30. *Literacy.* Limited support was found for the hypothesized relationship between the environment and children's development. Children's language development was positively related to the quality of the environment, $r = .32$, $p < .05$, but not to the number of literacy-related activities available. When age was controlled, children's achievement scores on the PSI were not related to either the quality of the environment or the number of literacy-related activities available. Thus, the environment did not influence children's cognitive development as assessed here.

31. An hierarchical regression analysis was performed to determine the influence of the literacy environment on children's language development after accounting for the influence of family characteristics. Family socioeconomic status, identified in the stepwise regression analysis above, was used as the family variable in step one of the hierarchical regression equation. As seen in Table 4, literacy quality, entered in step 2, predicted a significant portion of the variance in children's language development.

Discussion

Environment to Support Literacy

32. The data reported here describe day care environments that were quite impoverished in terms of literacy quality. The low incidence of reading and writing activities observed is a particular cause for concern. Almost one-third of the classrooms observed offered no literacy-related activities or materials to children during play time. The activities and materials that were available were quite conventional (books and writing materials). Noticeably absent were play materials containing functional and environmental print such as groceries in the housekeeping area or labels on pieces of play equipment. These data suggest that the typical free play environment provided for children in day care centers is unlikely to facilitate children's development of symbolic understanding (i.e., language and literacy) as well as it potentially could. Enrichment of play settings with print-related artifacts has resulted in children using more reading and writing behaviors in their play, using written language for a variety of purposes, incorporating familiar literacy activities in their play, collaborating with one another in learning about literacy through conversations during play, and engaging in numerous interactions with environmental and functional print, leading to increased ability to read environmental print and label functional items (Morrow, 1990; Neuman & Roskos, 1991, 1993; Schrader, 1989, 1990). The environments observed here are unlikely to produce these types of behaviors in the young children who experience them.

33. Because the assessment of literacy-related activities occurred during the free play period of a single day, the scores reported here may not well represent the cumulative total of literacy-related activities that typically occur in day care classrooms. Indeed the assessment of literacy quality painted a more positive picture of the day care environments observed than did the measure of literacy-related activities. Examining the scores on both the literacy quality and literacy activity variables suggests that although opportunities for enhancing literacy development were present during free play and other parts of the classroom day, relatively few opportunities were made available to the children during free play. The range of literacy quality scores observed indicates some classrooms were providing few or no opportunities for learning about literacy while other classrooms were providing many opportunities. Additional data are needed to describe the type of events that occur in day care settings that might support literacy throughout the classroom day. In the meantime, it appears that teacher training on the importance of a print-rich environment for preschool age children and how such an environment can be provided in a day care setting is sorely needed.

Day Care Quality

34. The supposition that classrooms higher on traditional measures of day care quality would also be higher in literacy quality was supported. The global quality variables were more efficacious in illuminating this link than the structural quality variables. The only structural quality variable correlated with the environment was teacher certification status. Although this lone

---

[1]Editor's note: The R^2 of .17 in this paragraph refers to a stepwise regression model. The R^2 of .15 in Table 4 refers to a series of hierarchical regressions. Because the same variables were not in the stepwise model that were in the hierarchical model, it is not surprising that the R^2s are different.

association could be spurious, it is noteworthy because structural quality variables are more easily regulated than other forms of quality assessment. The relationship between teacher certification status and literacy quality suggests that more optimal environments in day care are provided by teachers who have received some type of formal teacher training and whose work with children has been observed by experts and found acceptable. Perhaps teachers without formal teacher preparation do not share the knowledge base of those with formal teacher preparation. Important components of this knowledge base may be the theoretical linkages between language, literacy and cognition, the emergent literacy paradigm and the potentially powerful influence of the environment on children's cognitive and language development. Note, however, that this study provided no information on teachers' knowledge of children's development of language, literacy or cognition. Regardless of teachers' knowledge base, the quality of the environments observed in this study had considerable room for improvement.

35. The correlation and regression analyses indicated literacy quality and the two ECERS scores share substantial variance. Good environments tend to occur in higher quality settings. Consequently, the environment can be considered as an important component of specific day care quality. Investigations describing how the environment influences or interacts with other features and processes of day care environments might further explain the potential impact of this quality feature on children and families.

Children's Development

36. Congruent with previous research (Howes, 1988; McCartney, 1984), this study indicated that the quality of the day care environment plays a role in children's development. In this study though, this role was limited to the enhancement of children's language development. Children's cognitive development was not affected by any form of day care quality including the specific quality assessments of the environment to support literacy. This finding may be due to the relatively inadequate nature of the environments observed, particularly literacy-related activities, and the restricted variability of both literacy measures. The fact that both global day care quality and literacy quality were able to predict children's language development after family characteristics had been controlled indicates that the impact of children's experiences in day care should not be underestimated.

37. Given the known empirical and theoretical linkages between the quality of the environment

in settings other than day care and children's symbolic development (Bronfenbrenner, 1979; Evans & Carr, 1985; Neuman & Roskos, 1993; Taylor, Blum, & Logsdon, 1986; Vygotsky, 1986) efforts to enhance the quality of environments available to children in day care should be worthwhile. Because many young children now spend large portions of the day in day care programs with relatively poor environments rather than in their homes, which may have rich environments, the potential impact of day care environments is an important and timely issue. To further advance the knowledge base in this area research is needed that specifically examines relationships between children's literacy development, the literacy-related events they experience and the quality of the environments to support literacy found in day care programs.

References

Beach, S. A. (1991). *Toward a model of the development of reader resources in the emergence and acquisition of literacy skill.* Unpublished doctoral dissertation, University of California, Riverside, CA.

Beach, S. A., Kincade, K., & Asundi, M. (1992, December). *The effects of structured literacy experiences on prekindergartners' perceptions of themselves as readers and writers.* Paper presented at the annual meeting of the National Reading Conference, San Antonio, TX.

Bradley, R. H., & Caldwell, B. M. (1984). The relation of infants' home environments to achievement test performance in first grade: A follow-up study. *Child Development, 55,* 803-809.

Bronfenbrenner, U. (1979). *The ecology of human development.* Cambridge, MA: Harvard University Press.

Bronfenbrenner, U. (1986). Ecology of the family as a context for human development: Research perspectives. *Developmental Psychology, 22,* 723-742.

Caldwell, B. (1970). *Cooperative preschool inventory* (revised edition). Monterey, CA: Educational Testing Service.

Chomsky, C. (1972). Stages in language development and reading exposure. *Harvard Educational Review, 42,* 1-33.

Clarke-Stewart, A., & Gruber, C. (1984). Daycare forms and features. In R. C. Ainslie (Ed.), *Quality variations in daycare* (pp. 35-62). New York: Praeger.

Cochran-Smith, M. (1984). *The making of a reader.* Norwood, NJ: Ablex.

Dunn, L. (1993). Proximal and distal features of day care quality and children's development. *Early Childhood Research Quarterly, 8,* 167-192.

Durkin, D. (1966). *Children who read early.* New York: Teachers College Press.

Elardo, R., Bradley, R., & Caldwell, B. (1977). A longitudinal study of the relation of infants' home environments to language development at age three. *Child Development, 46,* 71-76.

Evans, M. A., & Carr, T. H. (1985). Cognitive abilities, conditions of learning, and the early development of reading skills. *Reading Research Quarterly, 22,* 327-350.

Ferreiro, E., & Teberosky, A. (1982). *Literacy before schooling.* Exeter, NH: Heinemann.

Harms, T., & Clifford, R. (1980). *Early childhood environment rating scale.* New York: Teachers College Press.

Heath, S. B. (1983). *Ways with words: Language, life, and work in communities and classrooms.* New York: Cambridge University Press.

Hollingshead, A. B. (1976). *Four factor index of social status.* Unpublished manuscript, New Haven, CT. Yale University.

Howes, C. (1988). Relations between early child care and schooling. *Developmental Psychology, 24,* 53-57.

Howes, C., Phillips, D. A., & Whitebook, M. (1992). Thresholds of quality and implications for the social development of children in center based child care. *Child Development, 63,* 449-460.

Hyson, M., Van Trieste, K., & Rauch, V. (1989, November). *What is the relationship between developmentally appropriate practices and preschool and kindergarten children's attitudes towards school?* Presented at the annual meeting of the National Association for the Education of Young Children, Atlanta.

Kritchevsky, S. (1967). Physical settings in day care centers: teachers, program and space. In E. Prescott & E. Jones (Eds.), *Group day care as a child-rearing environment: An observational study of day care program* (pp. 258-336). Washington, DC: Children's Bureau, Social Security Administration, U.S. Department of Health, Education and Welfare.

Leichter, H. (1984). Families as environments for literacy. In H. Goelman, A. Oberg, & F. Smith (Eds.), *Awakening to literacy* (pp. 38-50). Exeter, NH: Heinemann.

Mason, J. M. (1990). *Reading stories to preliterate children: A proposed connection to reading.* University of Illinois, Champaign: Center for the study of Reading, Technical Report No. 510.

McCartney, K. (1984). The effect of quality of day care environment upon children's language development. *Development Psychology, 20,* 244-260.

McGee, L. M., Lomax, R. G., & Head, M. H. (1988). Young children's written language knowledge: What environmental and functional print reading reveals. *Journal of Reading Behavior, 20,* 99-118.

Morrow, L. M. (1990). Preparing the classroom environment to promote literacy during play. *Early Childhood Research Quarterly, 5,* 537-554.

Morrow, L., & Weinstein, C. S. (1986). Encouraging voluntary reading: The impact of literature program on children's use of library corners. *Reading Research Quarterly, 21,* 330-346.

Neuman, S. B., & Roskos, K. (1990). Play, print, and purpose: Enriching play environments for literacy development. *The Reading Teacher, 44,* 214-221.

Neuman, S. B., & Roskos, K. (1991). Peers as literacy informants: A description of young children's literacy conversations in play. *Early Childhood Research Quarterly, 6,* 233-248.

Neuman, S. B., & Roskos, K. (1993). Access to print for children of poverty: Differential effects of adult mediation and literacy-enriched play settings on environmental and functional print tasks. *American Educational Research Journal, 30*, 95-122.

Pellegrini, A. (1985). The relationship between symbolic play and literate behavior: A review and critique of the empirical literature. *Review of Educational Research, 55*, 207-221.

Phillips, D., Scarr, S., & McCartney, K. (1987). Dimensions and effects of child care quality: The Bermuda study. In D. Phillips (Ed.), *Quality in child care: What does the research tell us?* (pp. 43-56). Washington, DC: National Association for the Education of Young Children.

Popham, W. J., & Sirotnik, K. A. (1973). *Educational statistics: Use and interpretation.* 2nd Edition. New York: Harper & Row.

Ruopp, R., Travers, J., Glantz, F., & Coelen, C. (1979). *Children at the center: Final results of the National Day Care Study.* Cambridge, MA: Abt Associates.

Schickendanz, J., & Sullivan, M. (1984). Mom, what does U-F-F spell? *Language Arts, 61*, 7-17.

Schrader, C. T. (1989). Written language use within the context of young children's symbolic play. *Early Childhood Research Quarterly, 4*, 225-244.

Schrader, C. T. (1990). Symbolic play as a curricular tool for early literacy development. *Early Childhood Research Quarterly, 5*, 79-103.

Taylor, D. (1983). *Family literacy: Young children learning to read and write.* Exeter, NH: Heinemann.

Taylor, N. E., Blum, I. H., & Logsdon, D. M. (1986). The development of written language awareness: Environmental aspects and program characteristics. *Reading Research Quarterly, 21*, 132-149.

Vygotsky, L. S. (1978). *Mind in society: The development of higher psychological processes* (Michael Cole, Trans.). Cambridge, MA: Harvard University Press.

Vygotsky, L. S. (1986). *Thought and language.* Cambridge, MA: MIT Press.

Wachs, T. (1983). The use and abuse of environment in behavior-genetic research. *Child Development, 54*, 396-407.

Wachs, T., & Gruen, G. (1982). *Early experience and human development.* New York: Plenum.

Whitebook, M., Howes, C., & Phillips, D. (1989). *Who cares? Child care teachers and the quality of care in America: Final Report, National Child Care Staffing Study.* Oakland, CA: Child Care Employee Project.

Factual Questions

1. What is the hypothesis?

2. Why did some centers refuse to participate?

3. What was the average group size?

4. Family information was obtained for what percentage of the 60 families?

5. In this study, what does the term "auspice" refer to?

6. What is the value of the Pearson product moment correlation coefficient for the relationship between quality of the environment and teacher certification?

7. The correlation between family socioeconomic status and language development was statistically significant at what probability level?

Questions for Discussion

8. Is it important to know how participating and nonparticipating centers differ? (See paragraph 10.) Why? Why not?

9. Was the selection of the children from the participating centers biased or unbiased? Explain.

10. Was the interrater reliability of the Early Childhood Environment Rating Scale adequate? Explain.

11. What is a Likert scale? (See paragraphs 16 and 19.)

12. In paragraph 25, the researchers interpret a correlation of .52 as indicating a high degree of correlation. Do you agree with this interpretation? Explain.

13. In paragraph 27, the researchers report a correlation coefficient of .28 for the relationship between language development and maternal education. Is this a strong relationship? Explain.

14. The researchers state in paragraph 27 that children's age was "partialed out" of all analyses involving achievement scores. What does "partialed out" mean?

15. In the first sentence of paragraph 33, the researchers note a potential limitation of their study. In your opinion, is this an important limitation? Could it be overcome in future studies? Explain.

16. If you were to conduct a study on the same topic, what changes in research methodology, if any, would you make?

17. Would it be possible to conduct a true experiment (that is, where children are assigned at random to different treatments) on this topic? Explain.

18. To what populations, if any, would you be willing to generalize the results of this study?

19. Does this study have practical implications? If yes, what are they?

Quality Ratings

DIRECTIONS: Indicate your level of agreement with each of the following statements by circling a number from 5 for strongly agree (SA) to 1 for strongly disagree (SD). If you believe that an item is not applicable to this research article, leave it blank. Be prepared to explain your ratings.

A. The introduction establishes the importance of the research topic.
SA   5   4   3   2   1   SD

B. The literature review establishes the context for the study.
SA   5   4   3   2   1   SD

C. The research purpose, question, or hypothesis is clearly stated.
SA   5   4   3   2   1   SD

D. The method of sampling is sound.
SA   5   4   3   2   1   SD

E. Relevant demographics (for example, age, gender, and ethnicity) are described.
SA   5   4   3   2   1   SD

F. Measurement procedures are adequate.
SA   5   4   3   2   1   SD

G. The results are clearly described.
SA   5   4   3   2   1   SD

H. The discussion/conclusion is appropriate.
SA   5   4   3   2   1   SD

I. Despite any flaws noted above, the report is worthy of publication.
SA   5   4   3   2   1   SD

INFORMATION SEARCH STRATEGIES IN
LOOSELY STRUCTURED SETTINGS

Ching-Kuch Chang *National Changhua University of Education*
Ernest D. McDaniel *Purdue University*

This study was designed to reveal search strategies in a loosely structured information environment and to examine cognitive and motivational correlates of particular search strategies. Subjects browsed freely through a hypercard program containing 105 topics on the Vietnam War. Search strategies were evaluated on a continuum ranging from random search to planned, investigative searches. The findings show search strategies to be significantly related to cognitive complexity, academic ability, and need for cognition. More investigative search strategies were also associated with more complex summaries of the information viewed. The search strategies observed are consistent with other studies of search behavior and learning orientations, and tend to validate the role of ability, cognitive complexity and need for cognition as predisposing variables influencing behavior in loosely structured information settings.

1. Cognitive strategies have been an important research area since the late 1950s [1]. In the last few decades, research on cognitive strategies has made notable progress in the areas of problem solving, comprehension, and memory in such domains as reading, writing, mathematics, and science [2]. In these studies, subjects are generally provided with well-structured information and a set of well-defined questions or problems to solve. Researchers then identify subjects' cognitive strategies [1] or compare strategies used by experts and novices [3]. Very little research has been done to reveal the strategies used by subjects working with ill-defined questions in loosely structured information environments.

2. Galotti points out that well-defined questions are appropriate for studying logical thinking, but ill-defined questions may be more typical of thinking in everyday situations [4]. Moreover, thinking processes in well-structured environments may differ from processes employed in loosely structured environments [5, 6].

3. Individuals encountering loosely structured information environments make sense of such environments by selecting [7], connecting [8], organizing, integrating [9], elaborating [10, 11], and interpreting [12, 13] information.

4. The present study was designed to reveal the search strategies that individuals use in a loosely structured yet information-rich environment where no clear questions were provided to give direction to the search. We hypothesized that subjects would exhibit a variety of search behaviors ranging from relatively random to highly directed. In addition, we expected positive relationships between search strategies (with directed search scored high) and measures of academic ability, cognitive complexity, need for cognition, and orientation toward learning. We further expected highly directed search behaviors to be positively related to the complexity of summaries written after completion of the exercise. Finally, we expected that the complexity of the summaries would also be correlated with the cognitive and affective measures collected on the subjects.

Method

5. Subjects browsed freely through a hypercard program containing 105 topics on the Vietnam War. As subjects moved from topic to topic, they were queried by the investigator to determine reasons behind each choice of topic.

6. We anticipated that some students would browse the material in a relatively random manner while others would exhibit planning and investigative themes. In tracing the routes constructed through the material by the subjects, our primary interest was observing the emergence, or absence, of planned, investigative uses of the information.

7. Selected cognitive and affective tests were administered to the subjects in an effort to relate search behaviors to cognitive and affective variables: scholastic aptitude, need for cognition, learning orientations and cognitive complexity.

8. Finally, subjects wrote brief summary paragraphs following their search of the information.

Subjects

9. Thirty-two students enrolled in Introductory Psychology at Purdue University served as subjects. Twenty-two of the subjects were males and ten females. The students were mostly sophomores and juniors and tended to be nineteen to twenty years old. Modal responses on a pretest questionnaire indicated that the students had "average" knowledge about the Vietnam War and "moderate" interest in it.

Materials

The Vietnam War: A Hypercard History Book [14]
10. The Vietnam War is a hypercard software program consisting of 105 topics divided into six categories: chronological topics, general topics, personalities, maps, charts, and movie reviews and interviews. The program allows the user to search through the topics in a number of different ways reflecting various search strategies. From the menu, the user can go directly to any of the 105 topics listed. Within a large category, the user may proceed sequentially from one topic to the next. Additionally, the user can move from one topic to a related topic by "clicking" the mouse on a key word printed in capitals within the text.

The Scholastic Aptitude Test

11. The Scholastic Aptitude Test (SAT) is a widely recognized measure of general academic ability. The SAT consists of two subtests: Verbal (SAT-V) and Numerical (SAT-N). The internal reliability of these two subtests is typically about .90. Numerous studies have shown that college performance is predicted by the combined SAT V and N at $r = \sim .42$.

Chang, C.-K. & McDaniel, E. D. (1995). Information search strategies in loosely structured settings. *Journal of Educational Computing Research, 12,* 95-107. Copyright © 1995 by Baywood Publishing Company, Inc. Reprinted by permission.

Direct reprint requests to Dr. Ernest D. McDaniel, Purdue University School of Education, 1446 Liberal Arts & Education Building, Room 5108, West Lafayette, IN 47907-1446.

The Need for Cognition Scale [15]

12. The eighteen-item version of the original forty-five-item scale is claimed by Cacioppo and Petty to indicate a tendency to engage in and enjoy thinking. People with a high need for cognition are likely to organize, elaborate, and evaluate information. The test-retest reliability of the Need for Cognition Scale is reported to be .72. Studies of the validity of the Need for Cognition Scale are provided by Petty and Cacioppo [10].

The Inventory of Learning Processes [11]

13. This inventory consists of sixty-two true-false, self-report items and provides four sub-scores describing various learning styles. Two of the scales were used in this study.

14. The Deep Processing scale (18 items) measures the extent to which subjects critically evaluate, conceptually organize, and compare and contrast the information they study. The internal consistency of this subscale is .82.

15. The Elaborative Processing subscale measures the extent to which subjects translate new information into their own terminology, generate concrete examples from their own experience, apply new information to their own lives, and use visual imagery to encode new ideas. The internal consistency of this subscale is .74 [11].

16. Schmeck suggests that scores on these two scales might be combined to ". . . assess a continuum with 'deep-elaborative learners' (those who 'think' while they study on one end) and 'shallow-reiterative learners' (those who rely on sheer repetition) on the other end" [16, p. 271].

17. For this study, the Deep Processing and the Elaborative Processing scores were combined and named Learning Orientation. High scores on this scale indicate a tendency to organize, evaluate and apply information.

The Bomb Factories Exercise [12].

18. This exercise was designed as a measure of cognitive complexity. It consists of a fourteen-minute segment of an ABC videotape describing nuclear weapons production and the associated problems with plant safety and environmental pollution. After viewing the tape, subjects write their analyses and interpretations of the situation. The written responses are evaluated using an explicit scoring rationale and assigned a score from one to five indicating the level of cognitive complexity reflected in the analysis. The levels of cognitive complexity are summarized below:

Level 1: Unilateral Descriptions — Simplifies the situation, makes unsupported good-bad assertions, and simply paraphrases or restates information.

Level 2: Simplistic Alternative — Identifies obvious conflicts, but does not pursue or analyze them; develops a position by dismissing or ignoring one alternative.

Level 3: Emergent Complexity — Identifies more than one perspective or explanation; establishes and preserves complexity.

Level 4: Broad Interpretations — Uses broad ideas to help define and interpret the situation; manipulates ideas within the perspective established.

Level 5: Integrated Analysis — Restructures or reconceptualizes the situation and approaches the problem from a new point of view; constructs a network of cause-and-effect relationships.

19. The interrater reliability of the Bomb Factories exercise is reported as .80 for independent scoring of responses of thirty-nine high school students. Validity of the exercise is supported by relatively high correlations with other exercises designed to measure thinking processes [12].

Procedure

20. The experiment was conducted in two sessions. During the first session, the group was administered a brief questionnaire pertaining to knowledge about and interest in the Vietnam War, the Need for Cognition Scale, the Deep-Elaborative Processing scales, and the Bomb Factories Exercise.

21. During the second session, subjects were tested individually. Subjects were seated at a Macintosh computer and told that the experiment concerned the way individuals use a software program about the Vietnam War. They were also told that they would be writing a brief summary of their ideas about the war after their exploration of the program was finished. Following an orientation demonstration, the subjects spent approximately thirty minutes searching through the information contained in the program.

22. During the information search period, the subjects were instructed to "think aloud," verbalizing thoughts and reasons associated with decisions to select particular topics. If no reasons were offered after moving to a new topic, the experimenter queried, "Why did you choose that topic?" A videotape record of the subject's on-screen search responses was obtained for all subjects.

23. After the search period, subjects wrote one or two paragraphs describing their ideas about the Vietnam War. Subjects were then briefly interviewed concerning their search strategies.

Evaluating Search Strategies

24. After all subjects had completed the second session, transcripts were made of the video tapes of the searches. The transcripts of each subject were evaluated independently by the first author and an advanced graduate student in psychology and assigned a rating of one to four based on the following criteria.[1]

Search Strategies

Level 1 — Search was random and exploratory with no detectable goals, few questions, and no evidence of direction or planning.

Level 2 — Search was driven by interest or a desire to obtain concrete facts (who? what? where? and when?); little involvement in larger issues or questions.

Level 3 — Search was motivated by limited issues or questions with little attempt to integrate the results into broader understandings.

Level 4 — Search was directed at broad understandings and explanatory themes with evidence of logical connections and an investigative strategy.

25. The interrater reliability was .89. Differences between raters were resolved by discussion and the adjudicated rating used for subsequent data analysis.

Evaluating the Vietnam War Summaries

26. The Vietnam War summaries written by students after the information search were rated independently by the first author and an advanced graduate student in psychology. The summaries were assigned a rating of one to five using the cognitive complexity scoring rationale described earlier. The interrater reliability for these ratings was .75. Again, differences between raters were adjudicated prior to data analysis.

Analysis and Results

Further Elaboration of "Search Strategies" and Frequency of Students in Each Category

27. As the individual search protocols were studied and rated, a more elaborate picture of the construct, search strategies, emerged. Based on the kinds of topics chosen, the relationships among these topics, and the reasons advanced

---

[1]Appreciation is expressed to Kurt Frey for rating the search protocols and the Vietnam War summaries.

at each choice point, we developed the following categories corresponding to levels one through four of the rating scheme.

The Aimless Wanderer

28. The search is random and exploratory, with no detectable goals or purposes. The searcher seems curious about the contents of a particular topic, but has few, if any, questions and there is no evidence of direction or planning in moves from one topic to the next. The search is characterized by aimless wandering through isolated topics, or by simply reading through topics in the order they are presented. Twelve students fell in this category.

The Fact Retriever

29. The search is driven by interests and isolated questions. The search is directed by a desire to obtain concrete facts within topics of interest. Topic choices are not connected by investigative themes or conceptual relationships. Fifteen students fell in this category.

The Casual Investigator

30. The search is motivated by a series of limited issue-relevant questions. There is, however, little or no attempt to integrate the results of the limited investigation into broader understandings or to construct explanatory themes. Two students fell in this category.

The Integrative Analyst

31. The search is characterized by attempts to arrive at broad understandings and explanatory themes. The searcher deliberately integrates background factors and other information that elucidates the overall situation. There is evidence of logical connections among topic choices and evidence that current information determines subsequent choices. Moreover, there is evidence of an investigative strategy and efforts to integrate information as the search progresses. Three students fell in this category.

32. These four patterns of search behavior were sufficient to classify the full range of search behaviors observed in this study and we believe that they are sufficiently general to be of use in other studies of information search behavior. Complete transcripts of the search protocols for the thirty-two subjects are provided by Chang [16].

The Influence of Knowledge and Interest

33. It was assumed that knowledge about and interest in the Vietnam War would have a marked influence on the subjects' information search strategies, but we found no significant correlations among the self-reported indications of interest and knowledge from the preliminary questionnaire and the levels of search strategy.

The Influence of Ability and Motivation on Search Strategies

34. A correlation matrix was generated from the scores for the SAT (V and N combined), Need for Cognition, Learning Orientation, Bomb Factories Exercise, Search Strategy, and Vietnam War Summaries. This matrix is presented below.

35. From Table 1, it may be observed that significant correlations were obtained between the search strategies and three of the four cognitive variables with the highest correlation, .45 *(p < .01)*, occurring between cognitive complexity (Bomb Factories) and Search Strategies. This suggests that, among the cognitive variables studied, the most important single characteristic in determining whether a student will search randomly or with some investigative direction is cognitive complexity, i.e., the tendency to preserve complexity in situations, to seek organizing structures and to build cause and effect networks. The other cognitive variables which were significantly associated with search patterns are the total score of the SAT, .32 *(p < .01)* and Need for Cognition, .29 *(p < .05)*. We did an exploratory stepwise regression to see how the other cognitive variables might contribute to a multiple correlation coefficient with search strategies, but only cognitive complexity entered the equation.

36. Summarizing the findings to this point, we have suggested that four distinct types of search strategies are discernible in the search protocols of students browsing the 105 topics of the Vietnam War. We have further noted that cognitive complexity, scholastic ability and the need for cognition are all separately related to the levels of search strategy, but that the single variable, cognitive complexity, accounts for a major portion of the variance in a multiple regression analysis.

Relationship among Search Strategies and Summaries

37. In asking subjects to write a summary of their search results, we phrased the request in such a way that the students would have maximum freedom to select, organize and interpret the information they had browsed during their search. We did not ask the subjects to review, analyze, or interpret; simply to "write a summary of your ideas after reading about the Vietnam War."

38. The same scoring rationale was applied to these summaries as was used in evaluating the Bomb Factories responses. That is, scores of one to five were assigned reflecting, at the low end, descriptive content and simplistic conclusions and, at the high end, interpretive and analytic responses. The following distribution of ratings was obtained for the Vietnam War summaries:

Level 1: 12
Level 2: 9
Level 3: 5
Level 4: 2
Level 5: 4

39. The last column of Table 1 presents the correlation coefficients among the Vietnam War Summaries and Bomb Factories, Scholastic Aptitude Tests, Need for Cognition, Learning Orientation and Search Strategies.

40. As expected, a significant correlation, .55 *(p < .01)*, was obtained between Search Strategies and the cognitive complexity of the Vietnam War Summaries. It is also evident that an even higher correlation was obtained between the cognitive complexity of the summaries and the SAT scores, .70 *(p < .01)*. In addition, the complexity of the summaries was significantly correlated with the Bomb Factories, .47 *(p < .01)*; Learning Orientation, .34 *(p < .01)*; and Need for Cognition, .30 *(p < .05)*.

41. As earlier, we performed an exploratory multiple regression analysis to see if a particular pattern of cognitive variables would be related to the complexity of the Vietnam War summaries. This analysis yielded a Multiple *R* of .78 with SAT (Beta = .58) and Search

Table 1   *Correlations among Bomb Factories Exercise, SAT, Need for Cognition, Learning Orientation, Search Strategies and Vietnam War Summaries (N = 32)*

	BF	SAT	NC	LO	SEARCH	VWS
BF	—	26	36**	−02	45**	47**
SAT		—	31**	44**	32**	70**
NC			—	62**	29*	30*
LO				—	17	34**
SEARCH					—	55**
						—

Note: Decimals omitted. *p < .05, **p < .01, one-tailed test.

Strategies (Beta = .36) entering into the equation. This finding suggests that the academic ability of the student plays a major role in the complexity of the summaries with the search strategies playing an important, but secondary, role.

Summary of Results

42. The results reveal a great deal of variation in the way college students browse a loosely structured information environment. A large number of students appeared to wander aimlessly through the program moving from one interesting topic to another guided mostly by curiosity or personal associations with the topic. A much smaller number of students appeared to develop strands of connected interests and to develop investigative themes as they moved through the program.

43. Cognitive complexity, as measured by the Bomb Factory Exercise, turned out to be the major cognitive component associated with search strategies. Students who interpreted a videotape about the production of nuclear weapons and the hazards to workers and the environment with a high level of complexity exhibit more connectedness between topic choices in the Vietnam War program and more investigative themes.

44. On the other hand, the SAT scores exhibit the highest correlation with complexity of the Vietnam War Summaries, but significant improvement in predicting the complexity of the summaries is obtained by adding the information search strategies ratings.

45. Taken together, these findings suggest that search strategies in an unconstrained task may be largely a function of the individual's cognitive complexity, i.e., the tendency to perceive situations as complex clusters of events, to construct cause and effect relationships and to use broad concepts and world knowledge in interpreting situations. Search strategies which reflect planning and investigative themes coupled with high academic aptitude are associated with information summaries which are well integrated, complex and reflect cause-effect relationships.

46. Cognitive complexity may translate to an intention to understand, to avoid premature closure, to consider alternative viewpoints, and to arrive at reasonable conclusions. Indeed, a striking feature of the search behaviors observed was the emergence of profiles which suggest marked differences in intentionality of the searchers. These intentions were not a consequence of interest in or knowledge about the Vietnam War but did reflect cognitive complexity, general scholastic ability and need for cognition.

Discussion

47. The four search strategies described above bear a resemblance to the learning strategies described by Pask [17] cited by Schmeck [18]. Pask observed two general learning styles among college students. *Holistic* learners attempt to build up the big picture and determine where the details fit. This learning style appears to be closely related to our "Integrative Analysts."

48. Pask's contrasting learning style is *serialistic* and such "operational learners" tend to proceed linearly through a topic building up details. Serialistic learners appears to be related to our "Casual Investigators" who tend to proceed from one topic to the other without unifying the particular investigations. According to Pask, the pathology associated with serialistic learning is *improvidence.* Such learners fail to build up overall maps thus seeing the trees but missing the forests. These "improvident learners" bear a marked resemblance to our "Fact Retrievers" who also do not organize information beyond the isolated topic at hand. If, in fact, learners carry within them relatively fixed habits and cognitive structures which facilitate or inhibit meaningful organization of new information, then such predispositions may override external attempts to assist analysis and interpretation of information.

49. Thornburg and Pea investigated the effects of two software programs designed to assist students' reasoning abilities [19]. Students accessed and organized information through the aid of two software programs, *IDEA* and *Notecards,* and used the information to write essays. The major findings showed improved essays associated with use of the programs, but no carryover to a transfer task. This finding seems to support our supposition that internal characteristics of the learner may override external assistance.

50. The minor findings of Thornburg and Pea are also interesting and relevant to the present study:

> Two general profiles emerged as we reviewed the data: those students that tended to explore more structural aspects of the *IDEA* and *Notecards* . . . also tended to review and revise their work more and write essays with a more elaborated "nested" organization — both before and after the project; and those students who interacted less with the two technologies, rarely reviewed or revised work, and wrote essays of a more general, "linear" argumentation structure [19, pp. 153-154].

51. The first group, those making most use of the programs, also used more information, more counterarguments, and, after the project wrote more detailed essays than before the project. The second group used less information, used the literal text in their writing, and referred to the advice cards more frequently than the other group.

52. Thornburg and Pea go on to say that none of the information known about the students (achievement in social studies or English, experience with computers, gender or cultural background) differentiated the two groups.

53. It seems reasonable to suggest that the introduction of a highly focused task may have essentially eliminated the search strategies of the "aimless wanderer" and the "fact collector." The two profiles noted by Thornburg and Pea may represent contrasts between groups which we called the "casual investigator" and the "integrative analyst." The findings of our study suggest that measures of cognitive complexity, need for cognition and general academic ability might have differentiated between Thornburg and Pea's two groups. Indeed, our findings support the claims of both McDaniel and Lawrence [12] and Petty and Cacioppo [10] that cognitive complexity and need for cognition predispose subjects toward more complex and complete assembly and analysis of information in situations which are open to interpretation.

54. Salomon, Perkins, and Globerson have recently noted that the outcomes of computer searches greatly depend on the "mindful engagement" of the searcher. In their words,

> The very idea of working with an intelligent tool is based on the assumption that users explore, design, probe, write, or test hypotheses in ways that couple the tool's intelligence with theirs in mindful engagement with the task. It thus follows that only when learners function mindfully will the upgrading of performance while working with a computer tool take place [20, p. 4].

55. Some fairly direct questions are suggested by this work. What instructional arrangements might facilitate student growth from "fact collectors" to "integrative analysts"? Shiang and McDaniel found no effect from inserting high level questions or even giving students opportunities to ask their own questions when students searched a computer program offering information about what happened at Pearl Harbor [21]. We know very little about how to set the switches which start the student to transforming the material into the learner's own cognitive structures. The present study does, however, suggest a method for further study of the way information is selected and used. By observing the selection of information, choice by choice, and by noting how each new choice constrains and directs the next choice, we have a minute by minute record of the transformation of information into constructed insights and larger patterns of meaning. As this methodology for observing and classifying search strategies becomes more refined, researchers will have a useful tool for examining the way information is utilized in building larger cognitive schema.

References

1. R. S. Siegler and E. Jenkins, *How Children Discover New Strategies*, Lawrence Erlbaum Associates, Hillsdale, New Jersey, 1989.
2. C. B. McCormick, G. E. Miller, and M. Pressley (eds.), *Cognitive Strategy Research: From Basic Research to Educational Applications*, Springer-Verlag, New York, 1989.
3. W. D. Rohwer and J. W. Thomas, Domain-specific Knowledge, Metacognition, and the Promise of Instructional Reform, in *Cognitive Strategy Research: From Basic Research to Educational Applications*, C. B. McCormick, G. E. Miller, and M. Pressley (eds.), Springer-Verlag, New York, pp. 104-132, 1989.
4. K. M. Galotti, Approaches to Studying Formal and Everyday Reasoning, *Psychological Bulletin*, *105*:3, pp. 331-351, 1989.
5. R. J. Spiro, Cognitive Flexibility Theory: Advanced Knowledge Acquisition in Ill-structured Domains, *Tenth Annual Conference of the Cognitive Science Society*, Erlbaum, Hillsdale, New Jersey, 1988.
6. R. A. Jones, To "Crisscross" in Every Direction; or Why Hypermedia Works, *Academic Computing*, *4*:4, pp. 20-21, 30, 1990.
7. J. St. B. T. Evans, *Bias in Human Reasoning: Causes and Consequences*, Lawrence Erlbaum, New York, 1989.
8. M. Minsky, *The Society of Mind*, Simon and Schuster, New York, 1986.
9. N. Anderson, Integrated Theory Applied to Cognitive Responses and Attitudes, in *Cognitive Responses in Persuasion*, R. Petty, T. Ostrom, and T. Brock (eds.), Erlbaum, Hillsdale, New Jersey, 1981.
10. R. E. Petty and J. T. Cacioppo, *Communication and Persuasion: Central and Peripheral Routes to Attitude Change*, Springer-Verlag, New York, 1986.
11. R. R. Schmeck, F. D. Ribich, and N. Ramanaiah, Development of a Self Report Inventory for Assessing Individual Differences in Learning Processes, *Applied Psychological Measurement*, *1*:3, pp. 413-431, 1977.
12. E. McDaniel and C. Lawrence, *Levels of Cognitive Complexity: An Approach to the Measurement of Thinking*, Springer-Verlag, New York, 1990.
13. E. A. Peel, *The Nature of Adolescent Judgment*, Wiley-Interscience, New York, 1971.
14. P. Gabel, *The Vietnam War: A Hypercard History Book* (2.0.1 ver.), Paul Gabel Regeneration Software, Scotts Valley, California, 1989.
15. J. T. Cacioppo and R. E. Petty, The Need for Cognition, *Journal of Personality and Social Psychology*, *42*:1, pp. 116-131, 1982.
16. C. K. Chang, The Effects of Cognitive Complexity, Need for Cognition, and Orientation toward Learning on Information Search Strategies, unpublished doctoral dissertation, Purdue University, West Lafayette, Indiana, 1991.
17. G. Pask, Styles and Strategies of Learning, *British Journal of Educational Psychology*, *46*, pp. 128-148, 1976.
18. R. R. Schmeck, Learning Styles of College Students, in *Individual Differences in Cognition: Volume 1*, R. F. Dillon and R. R. Schmeck (eds.), Academic Press, New York, pp. 233-279, 1983.
19. D. G. Thornburg and R. D. Pea, Synthesizing Instructional Technologies and Educational Culture: Exploring Cognition and Metacognition in Social Studies, *Journal of Educational Computing Research*, *7*:2, pp. 121-164, 1991.
20. G. Salomon, D. N. Perkins, and T. Globerson, Partners in Cognition: Extending Human Intelligence with Intelligent Technologies, *Educational Research*, *20*:3, pp. 2-9, 1991.
21. C. P. Shiang and E. McDaniel, Examining the Effects of Questioning on Thinking Processes with a Computer-based Simulation to Measure Thinking, *Journal of Educational Computing Research*, *7*:2, pp. 203-218, 1991.

Factual Questions

1. In the introduction, how do the researchers define "loosely structured environments"?

2. How many subjects were used?

3. The Bomb Factories Exercise was designed to measure what psychological construct?

4. How many students were classified as "aimless wanderers"?

5. Was there a significant relationship between the subjects' interest in the Vietnam War and their levels of search strategies?

6. According to Table 1, the strongest relationship is between which two variables?

7. Is the negative correlation coefficient in Table 1 statistically significant?

8. Where can you find complete transcripts of the search protocols for the 32 subjects?

Questions for Discussion

9. What is a "modal response"? (See paragraph 9.)

10. What do "internal reliability" and "internal consistency" mean? (See paragraphs 11, 14, and 15.)

11. What does "test-retest reliability" mean? (See paragraph 12.)

12. What does "interrater reliability" mean? (See paragraphs 19, 25, and 26.)

13. Is the discussion of the validity of the instruments in paragraphs 11–19 adequate? Explain.

14. The researchers refer to this study as an "experiment." (See paragraphs 20–21.) Is this study a traditional experiment? Explain.

15. What are the advantages of having a videotape record of the subjects' on-screen search behavior? (See paragraphs 22 and 24.)

16. What is an "adjudicated rating"? (See paragraphs 25 and 26.)

17. The footnote to Table 1 indicates that decimals are omitted. If they were included, where would they be placed?

18. The researchers note that in the past, research on cognitive strategies has emphasized strategies used when subjects are given well-structured information and well-defined questions or problems to solve. (See paragraph 1.) In light of this article, do you think it is equally important to study strategies in loosely structured settings?

19. Do you think that this study supports the supposition that internal characteristics of learners may override external attempts to foster higher levels of cognitive functioning? (See paragraphs 47–48.) Explain.

20. To what population(s), if any, would you be willing to generalize the results of this study? Explain.

21. If you were to conduct a study on the same topic, what changes in research methodology, if any, would you make?

Quality Ratings

DIRECTIONS: Indicate your level of agreement with each of the following statements by circling a number from 5 for strongly agree

(SA) to 1 for strongly disagree (SD). If you believe that an item is not applicable to this research article, leave it blank. Be prepared to explain your ratings.

A. The introduction establishes the importance of the research topic.

    SA   5   4   3   2   1   SD

B. The literature review establishes the context for the study.

    SA   5   4   3   2   1   SD

C. The research purpose, question, or hypothesis is clearly stated.

    SA   5   4   3   2   1   SD

D. The method of sampling is sound.

    SA   5   4   3   2   1   SD

E. Relevant demographics (for example, age, gender, and ethnicity) are described.

    SA   5   4   3   2   1   SD

F. Measurement procedures are adequate.

    SA   5   4   3   2   1   SD

G. The results are clearly described.

    SA   5   4   3   2   1   SD

H. The discussion/conclusion is appropriate.

    SA   5   4   3   2   1   SD

I. Despite any flaws noted above, the report is worthy of publication.

    SA   5   4   3   2   1   SD

ARTICLE 17

FURTHER VALIDATION OF THE
SELF-DEFEATING PERSONALITY SCALE

Lynn E. McCutcheon   *Florida Southern College*

In a sample of 51 women and 35 men, those who scored higher on the Self-defeating Personality Scale reported having "dropped out" of useful activities more often and scored as less assertive on the Assertiveness Self-report Inventory. Women were more likely than men to report having experienced at least one self-defeating relationship. Attempts to replicate gender differences reported earlier were partially successful. The results provide additional validation for the Self-defeating Personality Scale.

1. The Self-defeating Personality Scale (Schill, 1990) was developed to aid in identifying persons showing clusters of such behaviors. Since eight criteria are used to diagnose self-defeating personality (American Psychiatric Association, 1987), validation studies should tap all eight. Thus far the scale has been validated by correlations with various adjectives from the Adjective Checklist (Gough & Heilbrun, 1980) which describe such personalities (Schill, 1990). The scale has also been shown to correlate .44 with a measure of depression, a finding that makes sense inasmuch as pessimism, guilt, and self-criticism play major roles in self-defeating behavior (Schill & Kramer, 1991). Schill (1991) noted college students' (*M* age = 19 years) Self-defeating Personality Scale scores correlated negatively with scores on the Dating and Assertion Questionnaire (Levenson & Gottman, 1978).

2. In this same study, subjects were asked: "Sometimes people get into relationships in which they are taken advantage of, treated unfairly, and end up suffering. Such relationships are clearly self-defeating. Have you ever been in such a relationship? Please indicate the number of times." Subjects selected "none" (scored as 1), "one or two" (scored 2), "three or four" (scored 3), or "more than four" (scored 4); and "We sometimes stay in such relationships even after we realize we are being taken advantage of. For the situation you remember best, how long did you stay in the relationship after you realized you were being taken advantage of? How many weeks?" Subjects were asked to choose either "less than one" (scored as 1),

"one or two" (scored 2), "three or four" (scored 3), "five to eight" (scored 4), or "more than eight weeks" (scored 5).

3. Women were more likely than men (47% and 18%, respectively) to report at least one self-defeating relationship, and women who scored higher on the scale reported more self-defeating relationships and reported staying in them longer (Schill, 1991). For men there was no relationship between scores on the Self-defeating Personality Scale and number of self-defeating relationships reported. Further, men with high scores tended to report leaving self-defeating relationships *sooner* rather than later. Schill questioned the reliability of this unexpected finding, given that only nine men reported having any self-defeating relationships (1991). He also suggested that "it may be socially desirable and less threatening for college men to fail to define prior relationships as self-defeating" (p. 130).

4. The present study was designed to provide additional validation for the Self-defeating Personality Scale. Specifically, scores on the scale were correlated with a general measure of assertion and an index of dropping out of worthwhile programs. The present study also was designed to replicate the gender differences cited above.

Method

5. Ten students from an introductory psychology class participated in a discussion of self-defeating personality and assertiveness. Evolving from this discussion was a set of five questions designed to explore Criterion 6, "fails to accomplish tasks crucial to his personal objectives despite demonstrated ability to do so" (Schill, 1990, p. 1343). The questions were "Have you ever dropped out of high school or trade school?", "Ever dropped out of college for reasons other than financial?", "Ever dropped out of a smoking treatment program?", "Ever dropped out of an exercise program?", and "Ever changed jobs for one that was worse than the one you had?" Each "yes" answer was scored one point on a "dropout index." This index was included on a covering page designated "Personality Research," along with the

two questions about self-defeating relationships and the request for name, age, and gender. The covering page was stapled to the Self-defeating Personality Scale and a 25-item Assertiveness Self-report Inventory (Herzberger, Chan, & Katz, 1984). The order of the two scales was alternated to minimize the possibility of an order effect.

6. The ten students recruited 90 adult subjects (9 each) from the Orlando area, most of whom were friends or acquaintances of the students. Consent forms were not used but those who expressed concern were assured that all results would be confidential. "Personality Research" was administered individually or in groups of two or three to 51 women (*M* age = 38 yr., *SD* = 11) and 35 men (*M* age = 39 yr., *SD* = 12). Data from four subjects were discarded for omissions. Subjects were not told about the measures or the specific purpose of the study until completion of the measures. Analyses are based on two-tailed tests.

Results

7. For the present sample coefficient alpha was .81. This compares favorably with the value (.68) reported by Schill (1990).

8. Fifty-one percent of the men (*n* = 18) and 76% of the women (*n* = 38) reported having had at least one self-defeating relationship. These percentages paralleled those given by Schill (1991) but were higher, perhaps because these subjects were older and had experienced a larger number of relationships. Among those women who reported at least one self-defeating relationship, the number of these relationships correlated .25 (*ns*) and the length of them correlated .41 (*p* < .05) with scores on the Self-defeating Personality Scale (*M* = 17.8, *SD* =

McCutcheon, L. E. (1995). Further validation of the Self-defeating Personality Scale. *Psychological Reports*, 76, 1135-1138. Copyright © by Psychological Reports, 1995.

The author is grateful for the enthusiastic assistance in collecting data shown by this introductory psychology class. Request reprints of L. McCutcheon, Florida Southern College, 8578 Avenue C, Orlando, FL 32827.

5.5). These Pearson correlation coefficients are identical in direction and similar in magnitude to those reported by Schill (1991). Among men who reported at least one self-defeating relationship the number of relationships correlated .54 ($p < .05$) and their length correlated .26 (ns) with scores on the Self-defeating Personality Scale ($M = 16.1$, $SD = 4.1$). These two results are different from the findings for men in the Schill study (1991), suggesting that age or college experience may be important variables.

9. Scores on the Self-defeating Personality Scale (women's $M = 16.8$, $SD = 5.7$; men's $M = 17.0$, $SD = 4.8$) correlated inversely with assertiveness as measured by the Assertiveness Self-report Inventory for both men ($r = -.68$, $p < .001$) and women ($r = -.57$, $p < .001$). Since Schill (1991) used a different measure of assertion, this finding increases the confidence with which one could state that scores on the Self-defeating Personality Scale are inversely related to the assertiveness construct.

10. Dropout index scores were significantly correlated with Self-defeating Personality Scale scores for women ($r = .34$, $p < .05$) and for the sample as a whole ($r = .32$, $p < .01$). Dropping out could be defined as the failure to complete an important task which one has the ability to complete. Since this failure is one of the components of the self-defeating personality, these significant correlations provide additional validation for the scale. Although not definitive, they represent a step in clarifying the functional properties of Schill's new scale and their similarity to those of other measures.

11. One limitation of the present study is the low power stemming from the small sample collected by students relatively inexperienced in the conduct of research. Another is that both the predictor and outcome variables were self-reports and so potentially subject to the same response-style bias.

References

American Psychiatric Association. (1987). *Diagnostic and statistical manual of mental disorders*. (3rd ed., Rev.) Washington, DC: Author.

Gough, H., & Heilbrun, A. B. (1980). *The Adjective Checklist manual*. Palo Alto, CA: Consulting Psychology Press.

Herzberger, S. D., Chan, E., & Katz, J. (1984). The development of an Assertiveness Self-report Inventory. *Journal of Personality Assessment, 48*, 317-323.

Levenson, R. W., & Gottman, J. M. (1978). Toward the assessment of social competence. *Journal of Consulting and Clinical Psychology, 46*, 453-462.

Schill, T. (1990). A measure of self-defeating personality. *Psychological Reports, 66*, 1343-1346.

Schill, T. (1991). Self-defeating personality and problems with dating, assertion, and relationships. *Psychological Reports, 68*, 128-130.

Schill, T., & Kramer, J. (1991). Self-defeating personality, self-reinforcement, and depression. *Psychological Reports, 68*, 137-138.

Factual Questions

1. In the study cited in the introduction, did a larger percentage of men or women report at least one self-defeating relationship?

2. Who participated in the discussion that led to the development of a measure of Criterion 6?

3. What was the average age of the 35 men in this study?

4. In this study, how many women reported having had at least one self-defeating relationship?

5. For women with at least one self-defeating relationship, was the correlation between the number of these relationships and scores on the Self-defeating Personality Scale statistically significant?

6. According to the information in paragraph 9, were the scores of women or the scores of men more variable?

7. The two correlation coefficients reported in paragraph 9 are each statistically significant at what probability level?

Questions for Discussion

8. In your opinion, how useful is the correlation between scores on the Self-defeating Personality Scale and scores on a measure of depression for understanding the validity of the instrument? (See paragraph 1.)

9. Schill has suggested that there may be gender differences in the social desirability of reporting self-defeating relationships. (See paragraph 3.) Do you agree? Explain.

10. Comment on the adequacy of the "dropout index." What changes, if any, would you make in the questions?

11. What is your opinion on not telling the subjects the specific purpose of the study? Does this pose ethical problems? (See paragraph 6.)

12. The author mentions an "order effect" in paragraph 5. What is this?

13. What is "coefficient alpha"? What does it tell us?

14. Would you characterize the correlation coefficient of .41 reported in paragraph 8 as indicating a strong relationship? Explain.

15. In your opinion, how important is the second limitation mentioned by the author?

16. If you were to conduct another study on the same topic, what changes, if any, would you make in the research methodology?

Quality Ratings

DIRECTIONS: Indicate your level of agreement with each of the following statements by circling a number from 5 for strongly agree (SA) to 1 for strongly disagree (SD). If you believe that an item is not applicable to this research article, leave it blank. Be prepared to explain your ratings.

A. The introduction establishes the importance of the research topic.
SA   5   4   3   2   1   SD

B. The literature review establishes the context for the study.
SA   5   4   3   2   1   SD

C. The research purpose, question, or hypothesis is clearly stated.
SA   5   4   3   2   1   SD

D. The method of sampling is sound.
SA   5   4   3   2   1   SD

E. Relevant demographics (for example, age, gender, and ethnicity) are described.
SA   5   4   3   2   1   SD

F. Measurement procedures are adequate.
SA   5   4   3   2   1   SD

G. The results are clearly described.
SA   5   4   3   2   1   SD

H. The discussion/conclusion is appropriate.
SA   5   4   3   2   1   SD

I. Despite any flaws noted above, the report is worthy of publication.
SA   5   4   3   2   1   SD

Psychometric Properties of the Life Role Salience Scales: Some Construct Validation Evidence From a Sample of Nonprofessional Women

Kathleen M. Campbell *National University of Singapore*
Donald J. Campbell *National University of Singapore*

For work-family research programs to progress satisfactorily, investigators need questionnaire instruments that possess adequate construct validity. The Life Role Salience Scales (LRSS) displayed promising psychometric characteristics in the initial normative samples of college students and professional employees. This study provides additional construct validation evidence for the LRSS within a sample of 94 nonprofessional working women. Three kinds of information are examined: (a) comparisons with the original sample in terms of means, intercorrelations, and reliabilities; (b) effects of actual role status on the various life role scales; and (c) evidence of scale convergence and divergence with a selected set of appropriate variables. Overall, with the exception of this study's inability to reproduce the "value" and "commitment" distinctions found in the original analyses, the results of this examination offer reasonable evidence supporting the scales' construct validity and provide another normative base against which future research can be compared.

1. In light of the increasingly larger proportion of women in the workforce (Bureau of National Affairs, 1986) and the rapid proliferation of research on the work-family interface (e.g., Anderson-Kulman & Paluti, 1986; Frone & Rice, 1987; Frone, Russell, & Cooper, 1992; Greenhaus, Parasuraman, Granrose, Rabinowitz, & Beutell, 1989; Higgins, Duxbury, & Irving, 1992; Menaghan & Parcel, 1990; Pleck, 1985; Tiedje et al., 1990; Voydanoff, 1988), the availability of standardized and psychometrically sound measures of the constructs central to this research area is crucial. Without such measures, researchers are often forced to rely on ad hoc operationalizations (e.g., Bielby & Bielby, 1989; Orthner & Pittman, 1986) that have unknown psychometric properties. Although such measures may be entirely adequate and appropriate for the purposes of the original investigation, their unknown (or undocumented) psychometric characteristics prevent reliable cross-study comparisons and analysis. These measurement difficulties have been recognized as one factor hindering the field's theoretical growth, with some reviewers (e.g., Oliveri, 1990) urging researchers to stop developing ad hoc scales and to use standardized instruments already available.

2. In this regard, the work of Amatea and her colleagues (Amatea, Cross, Clark, & Bobby, 1986) is noteworthy. To help researchers avoid some of the conceptual and psychometric limitations of prior measures, these individuals developed the Life Role Salience Scales. These scales were designed to assess an individual's attitude toward four life roles: (a) occupational, (b) marital, (c) parental, and (d) home care. Meant to be applicable to both men and women, each scale gauges the perceived *value* of the specific role to the individual and the level of *commitment* the person has to that role.

3. The original report on the LRSS showed the scales to possess favorable psychometric properties, including both appropriate factor analytic support and high coefficient alpha reliability. However, as recognized by the authors themselves, these encouraging initial results represent only the beginning of the construct validation process. As Amatea et al. (1986) have suggested, the LRSS still need to be examined for their ability to discriminate and converge with other appropriate variables, to correlate with relevant behavioral indicators such as actual role status, and to predict within samples different from the college and professional groups on which the LRSS were originally developed.

4. Researchers have already begun to adopt the instruments (e.g., Aryee & Tan, 1992), and these scales have been included in a volume of measurement tools recommended for use by family investigators (e.g., Touliarous, Perlmutter, & Straus, 1990). To further foster the use of psychometrically sound instrumentation, the present study provides additional documentation of the construct validity of the LRSS. Specifically, the research investigated the characteristics of the LRSS using a sample of women holding nonprofessional jobs. These individuals are different from the managerial and professional women comprising the original sample and are more representative of the typical working woman. Additionally, information on the convergent and discriminant ability of several of the scales is provided. Scores on the Parental Scale for subgroups of parents and nonparents are examined, and scores on the Occupational Scale for subgroups of high and low job performers are compared, and so on.

Method

Subjects

5. Research data were collected from 94 of 150 frontline tellers, receptionists, and secretaries employed in various branches of a large American financial institution, for a response rate of 62%. All participants were White females between the ages of 18 and 65, with most (78%) being 35 years of age or younger. The majority (78%) were married and 60% had children. All respondents but one had a high school diploma, and 43% had addition education. Seven respondents had college degrees. In terms of work experience, the majority (65%) had been in the workforce for less than 13 years and 67% had been with the current firm 6 years or less.

Campbell, K. M., & Campbell, D. J. (1995). *Educational and Psychological Measurement, 55*(2), 317-328. Copyright © 1995 by Sage Publications, Inc. Reprinted with permission of Sage Publications, Inc.

This research is based on data collected by D. Kennard for an MBA paper supervised by D. Campbell at Bowling Green State University, Bowling Green, OH. Correspondence should be addressed to Kathleen M. Campbell, Department of Organizational Behavior, National University of Singapore, 10 Kent Ridge Crescent, Singapore, 0511, Republic of Singapore.

Procedure

6. A member of the research team distributed to each potential participant a survey packet containing an explanatory cover letter and the various questionnaire instruments. The cover letter assured participants that they did not have to participate and that the individual responses of those who did participate would be kept confidential. A stamped, addressed envelope was enclosed with the survey materials, allowing respondents to send the completed questionnaire directly to the investigators.

Measures

7. Three kinds of information were collected within the questionnaires: family demographic data, attitudinal measures such as the LRSS, and actual job performance as appraised by the respondent's manager.

Family Demographic Data

8. This section included such items as the individual's (a) age, (b) marital status, (c) the number and ages of each of her children, (d) individual and family income levels, (e) number of years in the workforce, and (f) number of years with the current organization.

Attitudinal Orientation

9. This section contained five scales for gauging an individual's family and work attitudes, including the four scales of the LRSS developed by Amatea et al. (1986) and the Organizational Commitment Questionnaire (OCQ) developed by Mowday, Steers, and Porter (1979).

10. The LRSS consist of four 10-item scales. As noted earlier, each focuses on a particular life role (i.e., the occupational, marital, parental, and home-care roles), and each measures both the value of the particular role to the individual (five items) and his or her commitment to it (five items). Thus each scale is composed of two subscales. Amatea et al. (1986) have shown that the four scales appear to possess satisfactory psychometric properties.

11. Scale items have a 5-point agree-disagree response format. Sample items include "Having work/a career that is interesting and exciting to me is my most important life goal" (Occupational); "I expect to be very involved in the day-to-day matters of rearing children of my own" (Parental); "My life would seem empty if I never married" (Marital); and "It is important to me to have a home of which I can be proud" (Home-Care).

12. To complement the Occupational Scale of the LRSS, the research questionnaire also included the standard 15 items of the OCQ (Mowday et al., 1979). The OCQ has documented and satisfactory psychometric

properties and has been used extensively in organizational research. This instrument uses a 7-point agree-disagree response format. A typical item reads, "For me this is the best of all possible organizations for which to work."

Job Performance

13. To obtain measures of work performance, all office managers within the firm were asked to review recent annual performance evaluations to provide a global appraisal (ranging from 1 = *poor performance* through 5 = *best performance*) for each employee in his or her work unit. These ratings, identified only by social security number, were then passed on to the university investigators.

14. Although the research questionnaire did not identify participants by name, one item requested the individual's social security number. Most respondents (94%) provided this information.

15. To verify the accuracy of the global evaluations, the researchers requested a random sample of past performance appraisals. The firm provided copies of actual performance appraisal forms (again with only social security numbers as identification) for about 25% of the study's respondents. These evaluations

consisted of seven work-related dimensions (e.g., knowledge and ability), each rated on a 5-point scale. A mean score was computed for each participant that was correlated with the global rating provided earlier. As anticipated, this correlation was highly significant, $r(23) = .92$, $p < .001$, indicating that the manager's global evaluations accurately reflected the respondents' job performance as contained in official organizational records.

Results and Discussion

Original Sample Comparisons

16. For the final version of the LRSS, Amatea et al. (1986) provided scale means, Cronbach's alphas, and intercorrelations for all eight subscales. Table 1 contains the equivalent means and Cronbach's alphas for this sample, with the Amatea et al. (1986) values in parentheses. As Table 1 shows, subscale means for both samples were similar. In general, relative to the original sample, the current sample had slightly lower means scores on the Occupational and Marital subscales, slightly higher values on the Home-Care subscales, and higher Parental Role Commitment but lower Parent Role Value scores.

Table 1 *Means, standard deviations, and coefficient alphas for the eight subscales of the LRSS*

Scale dimension	Mean	SD	Alpha coefficient
Occupational Role Value	17.65	3.57	.69
	(18.40)	(NR)	(.86)
Occupational Role Commitment	15.01	4.27	.85
	(16.90)	(NR)	(.83)
Parental Role Value	22.42	3.61	.80
	(23.70)	(NR)	(.84)
Parental Role Commitment	21.67	3.24	.70
	(20.10)	(NR)	(.80)
Marital Role Value	20.75	4.13	.87
	(21.30)	(NR)	(.94)
Marital Role Commitment	21.44	3.00	.72
	(22.60)	(NR)	(.81)
Home-Care Role Value	21.89	2.49	.79
	(20.60)	(NR)	(.82)
Home-Care Role Commitment	21.46	2.42	.67
	(19.10)	(NR)	(.79)

Note. $N = 89$ due to listwise deletion of missing data. Values in parentheses were reported by Amatea, Cross, Clark, & Bobby (1986). (NR) = not reported.

Table 2 *Intercorrelations of the eight subscales of the LRSS*

	ORV	ORC	PRV	PRC	MRV	MRC	HRV
ORV							
ORC	.68*						
	(.39)						
PRV	−.22	−.17					
	(−.20)	(.04)					
PRC	−.13	−.16	.64*				
	(−.21)	(−.04)	(.38)				
MRV	−.12	−.15	.39*	.38*			
	(−.11)	(.01)	(.40)	(.03)			
MRC	−.10	−.10	.36*	.53*	.71*		
	(.06)	(.04)	(.33)	(.37)	(.40)		
HRV	.08	−.02	.11	.16	.39*	.38*	
	(.07)	(−.08)	(.24)	(.26)	(.17)	(.19)	
HRC	.03	−.07	.16	.34*	.22	.29*	.55*
	(−.02)	(−.07)	(.20)	(.21)	(.19)	(.21)	(.59)

Note. N = 89 due to listwise deletion of missing data. Values in parentheses are reported by Amatea et al. (1986). *p < .01.

17. In terms of Cronbach's alpha, Table 1 indicates that the Amatea et al. (1986) sample typically displayed higher reliabilities. On two of the subscales (Occupational Role Value and Home-Care Role Commitment), alpha fell slightly below .70 in the current sample, representing drops in reliability of .17 and .12, relative to Amatea et al. (1986). Although these differences may simply reflect random error variance, two other interpretations are possible. First, the declines could reflect differences in *readability* of the items for high school-educated respondents; second, they might reflect differences in *applicability* of the items for nonprofessional workers relative to college-educated professional employees. The current study cannot tease these possibilities apart.

18. Table 2 contains the intercorrelations of the eight subscales, with the results of the Amatea et al. (1986) sample again in parentheses. An examination of this table suggests that the pattern of intercorrelations is generally similar within the two samples. However, among the subscales that are significantly correlated, the magnitude of the correlations is substantially higher in the current sample. This is especially the case for the diagonal entries, which contain the correlations between the value and commitment subscales for each of the life roles. In the original sample, the highest of these four correlations equaled .59, for the Home-Care Role. In the current sample, the correlation for this role equaled .55, but this

was the *lowest* of the four. The Marital Role value and commitment correlation equaled .71 (versus .40), whereas the Occupational Role and Parental Role correlations equaled .68 (versus .39) and .64 (versus .38), respectively. These results indicate that the value and commitment subscales overlapped substantially.

19. This finding may reflect the "true" state of affairs for this group of nonprofessional women. However, it could also indicate that the value/commitment distinction is simply too fine for the scales to separate reliably, at least when used with individuals who may be less sensitive to subtle nuances in language.

Role Status Effects

20. Amatea et al. (1986) indicated that they wanted to develop scales that could serve two distinct populations: those individuals currently engaged in the specific life role and those individuals *anticipating* engagement in that role. However, the investigators did not note any anticipated differences between these two groups in terms of their responses to the scales, nor did they suggest how to interpret any differences if such were found. Presumably, these questions were seen as empirical issues warranting additional research.

21. Because participants in the current study held different roles, an analysis of their responses (broken down by role) can address several of these matters. Specifically, responses of married women to the Marital Role scales can

be compared to the responses of unmarried women, and responses of mothers to the Parental Role scales can be compared to nonmothers. Of course, such comparisons are limited in that they can address only the most basic adequacy of the instrument. Nevertheless, even these limited comparisons are helpful because a *failure* to discriminate at this fundamental level suggests a potential problem.

Married Versus Unmarried

22. Table 3 contains the means and standard deviations for married and unmarried women on all eight subscales of the LRSS as well as the combined score for each scale. As the table shows, married women scored slightly higher on the Marital, Parental, and Home-Care Roles, and noticeably lower on the Occupational Role.

23. A series of *t* tests were computed to determine if any of the differences were significant. Only responses to the Occupational Role Commitment scale were significantly different, with married women (*M* = 14.14, *SD* = 4.43) expressing lower commitment than unmarried women (*M* = 17.24, *SD* = 3.91), *t*(92) = −2.90, *p* < .01. This difference remained significant when the two subscales were combined (*M* = 31.49, *SD* = 7.16 vs. *M* = 35.95, *SD* = 7.37), *t*(91) = −2.50, *p* = .01.

24. In summary, these data suggest that marital status has no effect on a woman's attitudes toward marriage, parenting, and home care, but it appears to dampen her commitment to having a career or holding a job.

25. On a more basic level, these results also highlight an important conceptual issue regarding the LRSS. Specifically, the issue is whether the general lack of differences between married and unmarried women on the family-oriented scales is problematical. On one hand, Amatea et al. (1986) deliberately wanted to create an instrument that could tap the role expectations of individuals both anticipating the role and already engaged in the role. Thus similarity between the role expectations of married and unmarried women may be highly appropriate if such similarity simply reflects broad-based anticipatory socialization.

26. On the other hand, conventional wisdom suggests that individuals already engaged in a role, both because of self-selection and because of their intimate knowledge of what the role actually entails, should react to the role differently from those not holding the role. If so, then the findings reported above may represent a weakness in the Marital Scale. It is possible that a portion of the unmarried women who responded to the survey were living with a significant other. If so, this could account for the lack of differences. At this point, it is not clear

Table 3 *Means and standard deviations for married and unmarried women and for mothers and nonmothers on the LRSS*

Scale	Married[a] M	SD	Unmarried[b] M	SD	Mothers[c] M	SD	Nonmothers[d] M	SD
Marital Role	42.77[e]	5.89	40.57	8.44	41.87[g]	6.67	42.78[h]	6.55
Role Value	21.13[e]	3.82	19.76	4.97	20.47[g]	4.36	21.33[h]	3.80
Role Commitment	21.73[e]	2.70	20.81	3.73	21.46	2.80	21.51	3.25
Parental Role	44.55[e]	6.04	42.00	6.58	45.87[g]	3.75	41.08[h]	8.04
Role Value	22.68[e]	3.56	21.19	3.75	23.53[g]	2.29	20.58[h]	4.56
Role Commitment	21.87[e]	3.14	20.81	3.40	22.35[g]	2.21	20.50[h]	4.14
Home-Care Role	43.44[f]	4.34	43.19	4.55	43.38[g]	4.22	43.38	4.68
Role Value	21.92[f]	2.50	21.71	2.51	21.87[g]	2.52	21.89	2.51
Role Commitment	21.58[f]	2.49	21.48	2.44	21.57	2.41	21.49	2.60
Occupational Role	31.49[f]	7.16	35.95	7.37	30.25[g]	7.38	35.78	6.30
Role Value	17.32[f]	3.43	18.71	3.95	16.87[g]	3.57	18.78	3.38
Role Commitment	14.14	4.43	17.24	3.91	13.36	4.61	17.00	3.37

a. $n = 73$, b. $n = 21$, c. $n = 56$, d. $n = 37$, e. $n = 71$ due to missing data, f. $n = 72$ due to missing data, g. $n = 55$ due to missing data, h. $n = 36$ due to missing data.

whether this failure points to a methodological issue, a psychometric flaw, an empirical limitation, or some combination thereof.

Parent Versus Nonparent

27. Table 3 also contains the means and standard deviations for mothers and nonmothers on all eight subscales of the LRSS. As the table shows, the Parental Role scales of the LRSS were sensitive to a participant's parental status. As might be expected, individuals who were mothers valued the parental role ($M = 23.53$, $SD = 2.29$) significantly more than nonmothers ($M = 20.58$, $SD = 4.56$), $t(47) = 3.59$, $p = .001$, and were also significantly more committed to it ($M = 22.35$ vs. 20.50), $t(48) = 2.45$, $p = .02$). These differences remained significant after the scales were combined ($M = 45.87$ vs. 41.08), $t(45) = 3.34$, $p = .002$.

28. In addition, parental status had an effect on individuals' responses to the Occupational Role scales of the LRSS. As the table indicates, mothers valued the occupational role ($M = 16.87$, $SD = 3.57$) significantly less than nonmothers ($M = 18.78$, $SD = 3.38$), $t(90) = -2.58$, $p = .02$, and were significantly less committed to it ($M = 13.36$ vs. 17.00), $t(90) = -4.40$, $p < .001$. The two groups were, of course, significantly different on the combined scale ($M = 30.25$, $SD = 7.38$ vs. $M = 35.78$, $SD = 6.30$), $t(90) = -3.73$, $p < .001$. Parental status had no effect on responses to the Marital or Home-Care scales of the LRSS.

Occupational Attitudes and Job Performance

29. Because the Occupational Role scales were designed to gauge the strength of an individual's orientation toward work, it seemed useful to examine these scores in light of the person's actual job performance. The expectation was that individuals who placed a high value on working and who were highly committed to having a job would outperform individuals less oriented toward work. If such a relationship was uncovered, it would provide additional evidence of the scales' construct validity by demonstrating a connection between scale scores and actual behavior.

30. Therefore, respondents were divided into two groups based on their combined Occupational Role score. Those individuals scoring above the mean on the combined scale ($n = 43$) were classified as having a strong orientation toward work, and those scoring below the mean ($n = 38$) were classified as having a weak orientation. (Smaller sample size reflects missing data, generally on the performance variable.) A t test was then used to analyze job performance ratings.

31. The results did *not* confirm a relationship between a person's work orientation and her job performance. Women who had a strong work orientation were rated no differently on job performance than women having a weak orientation ($M = 4.14$, $SD = .71$ vs. $M = 4.16$, $SD = .68$), $t(79) < 1.00$, $p = $ n.s.

32. Although these findings do *not* provide support for the construct validity of the Occupational Role scale, the lack of a performance relationship should be interpreted cautiously. It may be inappropriate to assume that individuals can directly translate positive occupational attitudes into positive performance behaviors on the job. Individual competence and job difficulty, for example, may simply be stronger determinants of performance than occupational attitudes. Additional evidence is needed here.

Table 4 *Correlations of the LRSS with age, education, work experience, income, and commitment*

	Age	Education	Years in Work Force	Income	Organizational Commitment
Occupational Role	−.17*	−.06	−.13	.04	.22*
Role Value	−.15	−.15	−.05	.05	.18*
Role Commitment	−.20*	.03	−.18*	.02	.23*
Parental Role	.03	.08	−.06	.03	.06
Role Value	.03	.11	−.03	.03	−.02
Role Commitment	.02	.03	−.08	.01	.14
Marital Role	−.10	−.04	−.12	−.06	.09
Role Value	−.11	−.09	−.12	−.10	.10
Role Commitment	−.11	.04	−.13	.01	.03
Home-Care Role	−.07	−.01	.05	−.10	.01
Role Value	−.01	.08	.10	−.10	.08
Role Commitment	−.09	−.10	.01	−.09	−.05

Note: $N = $ from 88 to 94 due to missing data. *$p < .05$, one-tailed.

Experience, Income, Commitment

33. Table 4 summarizes the relationship between the eight subscales of the LRSS and several other variables: (a) age, (b) educational levels, (c) years in the workforce, (d) personal incomes, and (e) organizational commitment, as measured by the OCQ (Mowday et al., 1979). These variables were examined to test the ability of the LRSS to discriminate and to converge appropriately.

34. With the exception of an expected relationship between the Occupational Role scales and the OCQ, no other relationships were hypothesized. Based on the stated intentions of Amatea et al. (1986), we did not expect the LRSS to be sensitive to differences in age, education, work experience, or income.

35. As Table 4 indicates, the LRSS demonstrated the general pattern of anticipated relationships. As expected, the Occupation Role scales were weakly related to scores on the OCQ, $r(88) \geq .18$, $p < .05$. Given that the OCQ measures a person's commitment to a specific organization, whereas the Occupational Role scales measure commitment to work and a career, the magnitude of the correlations appears reasonable.

36. Table 4 also provides some weak evidence that the Occupational Role scales may be sensitive to an individual's age and work experience. As the table shows, Occupational Role Commitment declined with increases in a woman's age, $r(93) = -.20$, $p < .05$, and work experience, $r(93) = -.18$, $p < .05$. These findings appear consistent with similar declines found in the job satisfaction literature.

37. In terms of divergence, Table 4 shows that the family-oriented scales of the LRSS showed no significant relationships with any of the five variables examined. Because no theoretical or conceptual reason exists for expecting such links, the lack of significant findings is appropriate.

Summary

38. Overall, the findings reported here provide additional psychometric evidence reasonably supportive of the LRSS.[1] Validation efforts clearly should continue. Data from samples of men only, particularly men in nonprofessional jobs, would be especially interesting. Research into the within-couple scores of employed husbands and wives also would be helpful. The end result of these efforts will be the existence of a detailed normative base against which future work-family results can be examined.

Note

1. Additionally, several factor analyses were also conducted. Because of the small item-subject ratio, these analyses are not reported in this article.

However, the analyses did produce interpretable and generally anticipated factor patterns. Tabular results are available from the first author.

References

Amatea, E., Cross, E., Clark, J., & Bobby, C. (1986). Assessing the work and family role expectations of career-oriented men and women: The Life Role Salience Scales. *Journal of Marriage and the Family. 48*, 831-838.

Anderson-Kulman, E., & Paluti, M. (1986). Working women and the family context, *Journal of Vocational Behavior, 28*, 241-253.

Aryee, S., & Tan, K. (1992). Antecedents and outcomes of career commitment. *Journal of Vocational Behavior, 40*, 288-305.

Bielby, W., & Bielby, D. (1989). Family ties: Balancing commitment to work and family in dual-earner households. *American Sociological Review, 54*, 776-789.

Bureau of National Affairs. (1986). *Work and family: A changing dynamic* (Product Code No. 45 LD SR-37). Washington, DC: Bureau of National Affairs.

Frone, M., & Rice, W. (1987). Work-family conflict: The effect of job and family involvement. *Journal of Occupational Behavior, 8*, 45-53.

Frone, M., Russell, M., & Cooper, M. (1992). Antecedents and outcomes of work-family conflicts: Testing a model of the work-family interface. *Journal of Applied Psychology, 77*, 65-78.

Greenhaus, J., Parasuraman, S., Granrose, C., Rabinowitz, S., & Beutell, N. (1989). Sources of work-family conflict among two-career couples. *Journal of Vocational Behavior, 35*, 133-153.

Higgins, C., Duxbury, L., & Irving, R. (1992). Work-family conflict in the dual-earner family. *Organizational Behavior and Human Decision Processes, 51*, 51-75.

Menaghan, E., & Parcel, T. (1990). Parental employment and family life: Research in the 1980s. *Journal of Marriage and the Family, 52*, 1079-1098.

Mowday, R., Steers, R., & Porter, L. (1979). The measurement of organizational commitment. *Journal of Vocational Behavior, 14*, 224-247.

Oliveri, M. E. (1990). Book review of *Handbook of Family Measurement Techniques. Journal of Marriage and the Family, 52*, 799-800.

Orthner, D., & Pittman, J. (1986). Family contributions to work commitment. *Journal of Marriage and the Family, 49*, 573-581.

Pleck, J. (1985). *Working wives/working husbands.* Beverly Hills, CA: Sage.

Tiedje, L., Wortman, C., Downey, G., Emmons, C., Biernat, M., & Lang, E. (1990). Women with multiple roles: Role compatibility, perceptions, satisfaction and mental health. *Journal of Marriage and the Family, 52*, 63-72.

Touliarous, J., Perlmutter, B., & Straus, M. (Eds.). (1990). *Handbook of family measurement techniques.* Newbury Park, CA: Sage.

Voydanoff, P. (1988). Work role characteristics, family structure demands and work-family conflict. *Journal of Marriage and the Family, 50*, 749-761.

Factual Questions

1. What was the response rate?

2. What is the response format of the LRSS?

3. What did the researchers do to maintain the confidentiality of the job performance evaluations?

4. In the present study, the highest average was obtained on which LRSS scale dimension?

5. According to Table 2, the strongest correlation for the present study is between which two variables?

6. The married and unmarried women were significantly different on the Occupational Role Commitment scale at what probability level?

7. What inferential test was used to determine the significance of the differences between parents and nonparents?

8. Is the relationship between occupational role commitment and age direct or inverse?

Questions for Discussion

9. Speculate on why the subjects were allowed to mail the completed questionnaires directly to the investigators.

10. Compare the sample occupational item in paragraph 11 with the sample OCQ item in paragraph 12. Based on the two items, do the two instruments appear to measure the same variable? Explain.

11. In your opinion, does the failure of the family-oriented scales of the LRSS to discriminate between married and unmarried women argue against the validity of these scales?

12. What inferences, if any, are you willing to draw about the validity of the LRSS based on the comparisons between parents and nonparents?

13. Do you agree with the authors' overall evaluation of the LRSS stated in the first sentence of paragraph 38?

14. If you were to conduct an additional validity study of the LRSS, how would your
study be different from the current one?

15. If you were to conduct another study on the
same topic, what changes in the research
methodology, if any, would you make?

Quality Ratings

DIRECTIONS: Indicate your level of agreement with each of the following statements by
circling a number from 5 for strongly agree
(SA) to 1 for strongly disagree (SD). If you
believe that an item is not applicable to this
research article, leave it blank. Be prepared to
explain your ratings.

A. The introduction establishes the importance
of the research topic.
SA   5   4   3   2   1   SD

B. The literature review establishes the context
for the study.
SA   5   4   3   2   1   SD

C. The research purpose, question, or hypothesis is clearly stated.
SA   5   4   3   2   1   SD

D. The method of sampling is sound.
SA   5   4   3   2   1   SD

E. Relevant demographics (for example, age,
gender, and ethnicity) are described.
SA   5   4   3   2   1   SD

F. Measurement procedures are adequate.
SA   5   4   3   2   1   SD

G. The results are clearly described.
SA   5   4   3   2   1   SD

H. The discussion/conclusion is appropriate.
SA   5   4   3   2   1   SD

I. Despite any flaws noted above, the report is
worthy of publication.
SA   5   4   3   2   1   SD

SCREENING CHILDREN AT RISK FOR SCHOOL
MALADJUSTMENT: FURTHER EVIDENCE FOR THE VALUE OF THE AML

Janet F. Gillespie *SUNY College at Brockport*
Joseph A. Durlak *Loyola University Chicago*

This paper reports the results of two screening studies using the AML, a brief teacher rating scale, to detect school maladjustment in primary grade children. Identical experimental procedures were used in each study. Teachers in grades 1-3 in two public schools rated children using the AML. The classroom behavior of children identified by the AML as having school adjustment problems was then independently assessed. Data from well-adjusting peers were used to determine the range of normal behavior in each classroom. In Study 1 the AML successfully identified children whose classroom behavior was beyond normal limits. These findings were replicated in Study 2. Across both studies, the AML had a true-positive hit rate of 93% and a false-positive rate of only 7% in identifying school maladjustment.

1. Research in secondary prevention and early intervention for children in the school setting requires effective methods to detect early behavior problems. Moreover, to be suitable for wide-scale application, the methods used for identifying such problems must be economical, user friendly, and ecologically valid. The measure that has received the most attention in school programs has been the AML (Cowen et al., 1973). The AML is a brief classroom rating scale that asks teachers to describe children's acting-out and shy-withdrawn behaviors and also to estimate incipient learning difficulties.

2. Several lines of evidence support the AML's ability to identify maladapting schoolchildren (Cowen, Dorr, & Orgel, 1971; Cowen et al., 1973; Dorr, Stephens, Pozner, & Klodt, 1980; Durlak, Stein, & Mannarino, 1980; Lorion & Cowen, 1978). In most of these investigations, however, AML scores have been compared to additional teacher ratings, clinical judgments, or other test or program data. The need to assess the behavioral differences that emerge between maladapting and adapting schoolchildren as reflected by AML ratings is suggested by Durlak et al.'s (1980) findings. Durlak et al. conducted independent classroom observations of children receiving different AML ratings. They reported statistically signif-

icant correlations between several indices of classroom behavior and AML scores, but, at the same time, noted considerable overlap in observer-rated classroom behavior and AML ratings.

3. Teachers using the AML may be able to judge certain types of problems more accurately than others. For instance, more data exist to support the validity of teacher reports in reference to externalizing rather than internalizing symptomatology (Green, Beck, Forehand, & Vosk, 1980). Lambert, Theisinger, Overly, and Knight (1990) have pointed to a lessened opportunity on the part of teachers to observe overcontrolled problem behaviors such as depression and shyness. Allen, Chinsky, Larcen, Lochman, and Selinger (1976) examined the accuracy of teachers' referrals of 52 children identified as "socially isolated." Independent behavioral observations of the referred children found nearly one third actually to be highly interactive with peers. Finally, Green et at. (1980) found that behavioral data did not confirm teachers' perceptions of which children in their class were shy and withdrawn.

4. The present article reports the results of two studies using the AML as a quick screening device to detect school maladjustment in primary grade children. Identical experimental procedures were used in the second study in an attempt to replicate the positive findings achieved in Study 1. The primary research question is how well the AML discriminates behaviorally between individual maladapting schoolchildren and their classroom peers. Data from well-adjusting peers were used to determine the range of normal behavior in each classroom. It was hypothesized that the AML would successfully identify children whose inappropriate classroom behavior is beyond normal limits.

Method

5. Two studies were conducted over successive school years. Because the setting and experimental procedures were identical in both studies, they are described together.

Setting

6. Data were collected in two K-3 public elementary schools located in a small college town in the rural Midwest. The schools were comparable in physical structure, number and experience of teaching staff, and average class size and served children from economically and racially diverse families.

Participants

7. Participants included 172 six- to eight-year-old children from grades 1-3. These children consisted of those who were assumed to be displaying signs of early school maladjustment based on their AML ratings (target children, total $N = 58$), and children who did not receive high AML ratings and were viewed as adjusting satisfactorily to school (peers, total $N = 114$). Target children and peers were comparable in terms of proportionate distribution by race (70% were Caucasian) and gender (80% were male).

Measures

8. *AML.* The AML is an 11-item, three-factor mass screening teacher rating scale designed to detect early school maladjustment (Cowen et al., 1973). Teachers rate children's classroom behavior using 5-point frequency scales (1 = "never," 5 = "most or all of the time"). The AML yields a total score and subscale scores reflecting three general behavior domains of acting-out (five items, e.g., "disrupts discipline"), moody-shy-withdrawn behavior (five items, e.g., "is unhappy or depressed"), and

Gillespie, J. F., & Durlak, J. A. (1995). Screening children at risk for school maladjustment: Further evidence for the value of the AML. *Journal of Community Psychology, 23,* 18-27. Copyright © 1995 by Clinical Psychology Publishing Co., Inc. Reprinted by permission of Clinical Psychology Publishing Co., Inc.

This work was conducted while both authors were at Southern Illinois University. The authors wish to thank the Carbondale, Illinois, public schools for their cooperation. Address correspondence to Janet F. Gillespie, Department of Psychology, SUNY Brockport, 350 New Campus Drive, Brockport, NY 14420-2977.

learning difficulties (one item, "has difficulty learning"). The 11-item AML has been revised into a 12-item instrument that retains the same three factors (Primary Mental Health Project, 1989). Only the total scores on the acting-out and shy-withdrawn subscales were used for screening in this study; on each scale higher scores reflect more serious problems.

9. *Behavioral observations.* The classroom behavior of target children and peers was evaluated using a behavioral coding system developed by Gillespie, Durlak, and Sherman (1982), based on the observational procedures of Solomon and Wahler (1973). This time-sampling coding system permits recording of a range of classroom social and academic behaviors exhibited by children plus the teacher's positive or aversive response to the child's behavior. In the current study, only data involving children's behaviors are presented. Behavioral codes yielded summary scores reflecting the percentage of the child's total behavior that was appropriate or inappropriate. Because the AML is a measure of school maladjustment, the percentage of inappropriate behavior served as the unit of analysis. Inappropriate behaviors included such dimensions as rule violation, noncompliance, complaint, off-task, lack of eye contact during conversations, inattentiveness to peers during social activities, and social noninteraction. These behaviors paralleled the acting-out and shy-withdrawn dimensions of the AML.

10. *Observers and training.* Thirty-four advanced undergraduates who received academic credit for their participation were trained as behavioral observers over a 15-hour period. Training included: (1) didactic instructions regarding each behavior code; (2) presentation of training videotapes; (3) role plays to practice observation and coding; and (4) practice field observations at a university day care facility. Observers were required to attain 80% agreement with trainer-established scoring criteria on a final test videotape before they were allowed into the schools.

Criterion for Screening Efficacy

11. Peer behavior within each classroom served as the standard for assessing the AML's efficacy in detecting school maladjustment. Given the many differences that exist across classrooms based on teaching styles, classroom organization and routine, and peer influences upon behavior, each classroom seemed to be the best ecological niche for assessing behavior. Moreover, previous findings suggest that teacher AML ratings are best viewed in a relative rather than absolute sense. For example, if AML ratings are interpreted literally, children with scores in the top of the distribution are

supposedly engaging in inappropriate behavior "most or all the time." Behavioral data indicate that this is not the case (Durlak et al., 1980). Instead, it appears that teachers rate children in relative terms; children with higher scores thus engage in relatively more inappropriate behavior than their classroom peers. If this is so, then peer data could be used to establish the range of normal behavior within the classroom.

12. Once the mean percentage of inappropriate classroom behavior was computed for both target children and peers, the following equation was used:

$$\frac{\text{Target child's behavior} - \text{Peers' behavior}}{\text{Standard deviation obtained from peer behavior}}$$

13. A cutoff score of greater than or equal to 1.00 was the criterion used to assess the screening efficacy of the AML. Cutoff scores ≥ 1.00 indicated that the target child's inappropriate behavior was beyond normal limits. Cutoff scores less than 1.00 indicated that AML was identifying a child whose inappropriate behavior was within normal limits for that classroom. Others (Kendall & Zupan, 1981; Trull, Nietzel, & Main, 1988) have used the criterion of one standard deviation to define the range of normal behavior. For example, suppose that in Classroom A the mean percentage of inappropriate behavior for peers was 10.00 with a standard deviation of 5.00, and two target children observed in this class displayed mean levels of inappropriate behavior of 14 and 25. The difference scores of 0.80 (i.e., 14 minus 10 then divided by 5) and 3.00 (25 minus 10 then divided by 5) would indicate that the former target child's behavior was within normal limits whereas the latter child's was not.

Procedure

14. *Teacher ratings.* In each school year all children in grades one through three were rated by teachers using the AML during the first 2 weeks in October. Given available treatment resources, children receiving total acting-out or shy-withdrawn subscale ratings in the top 15% of the distribution at each school were targeted for intervention in a secondary prevention school-based program. Teachers completed the AMLs without knowledge of their specific use in the intervention program. The final decision to include a child in the intervention depended on subsequent information collected via classroom observations (described here), the use of another teacher rating scale, an interview with the teacher, and, of course, gaining permission from the child's parent for participation. There were no refusals from parents.

15. *Behavioral observations.* Within each classroom, behavioral observations were conducted on each target child and a randomly selected group of peers. A different number of peers was observed in each classroom (range = 4-8, mean = 5.43) due to the requirement that all peers had to be engaged in the same classroom activity as the target child. A 10-second observe, 10-second record, time sampling technique was used. For 85% of the observations, one observer recorded the behavior of a target child while a second observer simultaneously recorded the behaviors of peers. A different peer was observed in successive intervals until each peer selected for observation in that class was observed once; then the cycle of peer observations was repeated. To synchronize target and peer observations, observers wore earphones attached to the same tape recorder that signaled observation and recording intervals.

16. When only one observer was available, procedures described by Walker and Hops (1978) were used. A target child was observed during the first observational interval, a peer during the next observational interval, the same target child during the third interval, a different peer in the fourth interval, and so on until the daily observational period ended.

17. Target children and peers were observed over a 2-week period for an average of five, 10-minute daily sessions (range 4-7). Observations were not always completed on consecutive school days due to child absences from school or the unavailability of observers.

18. Observers entered the classroom when children were with their homeroom teachers, with daily observations scheduled for different times during the school day to gain a representative sample of the children's total classroom behavior. Although teachers indicated that visitors frequently entered classrooms, the first daily observations in each classroom were not included in data analyses in order to reduce any reactivity due to the observers' presence. Observers were kept blind to the purposes of the classroom observations and had no knowledge of the AML administration.

Reliability of Observations

19. The reliability of observations was assessed by having a pair of observers independently code the same children's classroom behavior for 5 minutes. A total of 130 reliability estimations was calculated (approximately half on target children and half on peers) including 12 unannounced reliability checks conducted by the trainers. Pairs of observers were systematically altered during observations and reliability checks to help control for criterion drift (O'Leary & Kent, 1973). Using

Table 1 *Mean percentage of inappropriate behavior of target children and classroom peers and cutoff scores in Study 1*

School A	Mean	SD	Cutoff Score
Classroom # 1 (Grade 1)			
Target child # 1	27.50	21.49	2.33
Target child # 2	43.59	20.77	4.97
Peers (N = 6)	13.33	6.09	
Classroom # 2 (Grade 2)			
Target child # 3	13.33	14.40	2.89
Target child # 4	20.60	34.85	6.68
Peers (N = 4)	7.78	1.92	
Classroom # 3 (Grade 2)			
Target child # 5	27.78	13.24	1.57
Target child # 6	41.66	22.48	3.17
Target child # 7	29.17	6.63	1.73
Peers (N = 8)	14.17	8.67	
Classroom # 4 (Grade 3)			
Target child # 8	30.83	14.14	4.88
Peers (N = 4)	8.80	4.51	
Classroom # 5 (Grade 3)			
Target child # 9	25.34	16.59	4.42
Target child # 10	67.20	11.98	19.81
Target child # 11	29.17	20.97	5.82
Peers (N = 8)	13.33	2.72	
School B			
Classroom # 6 (Grade 1)			
Target child # 12	39.17	26.01	21.59
Target child # 13	26.67	32.83	10.81
Target child # 14	16.70	19.43	2.22
Target child # 15	26.70	11.86	10.84
Peers (N = 8)	14.13	1.16	
Classroom # 7 (Grade 1)			
Target child # 16	9.63	12.18	2.05
Target child # 17	9.50	9.86	2.01
Target child # 18	6.66	6.65	1.16
Target child # 19	21.65	7.75	5.65
Peers (N = 4)	2.79	3.34	
Classroom # 8 (Grade 1)			
Target child # 20	8.90	3.10	1.25
Target child # 21	10.80	5.05	1.86
Peers (N = 5)	5.00	3.12	
Classroom # 9 (Grade 1)			
Target child # 22	22.70	6.70	2.19
Target child # 23	37.50	21.66	4.39
Peers (N = 5)	7.54	6.93	

Table 1 *Continued*

School B	Mean	SD	Cutoff Score
Classroom # 10 (Grade 3)			
Target child # 24	41.40	10.61	2.65
Peers (N = 6)	24.33	6.45	
Classroom # 11 (Grade 3)			
Target child # 25	55.00	12.41	5.21
Target child # 26	41.90	8.64	3.57
Target child # 27	56.83	25.22	5.44
Peers (N = 6)	13.40	7.99	

kappa, mean interobserver agreement for the inappropriate behavior category was 85% (range of 78% to 95% across observers).

Results

Study 1

20.   Twenty-seven target children from eleven classrooms received AML total scores in the top 15% of the distribution in Study 1. The mean rates of inappropriate classroom behavior for each target child and for 64 classroom peers are presented in Table 1, along with the cutoff score for each target child. The cutoff scores for all 27 target children were greater than 1.00.

Study 2

21.   Thirty-one children from ten classrooms at the two schools received AML total scores in the top 15% of the distribution in Study 2. The classroom behaviors of these 31 target children and 50 peers were compared the second year using the same procedure. The cutoff scores for 27 of 31 target children were greater than 1.00. Table 2 summarizes these data.

22.   In summary, in Study 1 the AML successfully identified children whose classroom behavior was beyond normal limits, and these findings were replicated in Study 2. Across both program years, substantial behavioral differences appeared between 93% of target children (54 of 58) and peers.

Supplementary Analyses

23.   To provide further information on school maladjustment, we categorized children in each study according to their presenting problems by comparing their AML ratings to available norms (Primary Mental Health Project, 1971). The distributions of AML scores obtained in Study 1 and 2 were comparable to these normative data. For each study we had selected children in the highest 15% of the distribution of AML scores. Therefore, children were classified as acting-out, shy-withdrawn, or mixed

problem types if their AML ratings were in the top 15% of the normative distribution for the acting-out subscale, the shy-withdrawn subscale, or for both scales, respectively. Others (Lorion, Cowen, & Caldwell, 1974) have used a similar typology to classify young children's school problems. Although children were not selected for the presence of learning problems, we also noted if they fell into the top 15% of the normative distribution for this problem area as well.

24.   In Study 1, 30% of the children were classified as having primarily acting-out problems, 15% had primarily shy-withdrawn problems, 37% had mixed symptomatology, and 18% did not fit into any problem category. The corresponding percentages for Study 2 were 26%, 13%, 35%, and 26%, respectively. For each study, a comparable percentage of children (17% and 20%) also had learning problems in addition to their behavioral difficulties at school.

25.   As noted above, all of the children in Study 1 with high AML ratings differed behaviorally from their classroom peers, but in Study 2, four did not. Three of these children were classified as shy-withdrawn problem types and one was mixed.

Discussion

26.   The AML appears very successful as a screening instrument to identify young maladapting schoolchildren. Specifically, two studies conducted over successive school years yielded a 93% true-positive hit rate for the AML (54 of 58 children), and only 7% false positives. Moreover, the criterion used in this study to assess screening efficacy required that the AML detect a clinically significant or meaningful difference rather than merely a statistical difference in behavior between identified and nonidentified children. The mean rate of inappropriate classroom behavior for the 58 target children with the highest AML ratings was almost four standard deviations ($M = 3.98$) higher than those of their peers. This is a substantial difference in terms of classroom behavior norms. Results of the current study thus add further evidence for the usefulness of the AML as a screening measure to detect early signs of school maladjustment.

27.   There are some limitations to the current study that should be mentioned. Unfortunately, the AML's hit rate for identifying true or false negatives could not be determined by this study's design. Surveys indicate that up to 30% of children have at least mild adjustment problems at some point in their school career (Glidewell & Swallow, 1969). It is likely that maladapting schoolchildren not detected by the

Table 2 *Mean percentage of inappropriate behavior of target children and classroom peers and cutoff scores in Study 2*

School A	Mean	SD	Cutoff Score
Classroom # 1 (Grade 1)			
Target child # 1	17.75	15.20	2.90
Target child # 2	25.75	11.17	4.73
Peers (N = 4)	5.00	4.39	
Classroom # 2 (Grade 1)			
Target child # 3	14.20	8.41	1.59
Target child # 4	25.25	14.12	3.51
Target child # 5	17.00	10.20	2.08
Target child # 6	29.75	16.58	4.29
Target child # 7	18.25	9.81	2.30
Target child # 8	41.50	20.68	6.33
Peers (N = 8)	5.00	5.77	
Classroom # 3 (Grade 3)			
Target child # 9	42.25	15.63	5.86
Target child # 10	34.25	18.37	4.30
Target child # 11	36.50	14.97	4.74
Peers (N = 4)	12.25	5.12	
Classroom # 4 (Grade 3)			
Target child # 12	47.00	11.50	3.60
Target child # 13	40.75	18.55	2.89
Target child # 14	41.50	14.83	2.97
Peers (N = 4)	15.25	8.83	
School B			
Classroom # 5 (Grade 1)			
Target child # 15	32.25	8.41	3.88
Target child # 16	32.25	8.41	3.88
Target child # 17	18.25	7.83	1.62
Peers (N = 6)	8.25	6.18	
Classroom # 6 (Grade 1)			
Target child # 18	1.01	5.00	-1.21
Target child # 19	15.25	10.34	1.02
Peers (N = 4)	8.75	6.39	
Classroom # 7 (Grade 1)			
Target child # 20	29.75	9.36	2.22
Target child # 21	29.60	10.36	2.20
Target child # 22	51.50	24.36	4.94
Target child # 23	14.00	10.14	0.25
Peers (N = 6)	12.00	8.00	

Table 2 *Continued*

School B	Mean	SD	Cutoff Score
Classroom # 8 (Grade 2)			
Target child # 24	27.75	17.72	1.87
Target child # 25	23.25	11.29	1.35
Target child # 26	14.00	10.16	0.29
Peers (N = 6)	11.50	8.69	
Classroom # 9 (Grade 3)			
Target child # 27	24.50	12.76	2.50
Target child # 28	36.00	15.12	4.32
Peers (N = 4)	8.75	6.30	
Classroom # 10 (Grade 3)			
Target child # 29	24.25	8.46	2.58
Target child # 30	11.50	12.40	0.67
Target child # 31	43.50	17.82	5.46
Peers (N = 4)	7.00	6.68	

AML might be discovered using other screening measures such as peer sociometrics or playground or lunchroom observations.

28. Behavioral observational data were combined to yield a global measure of inappropriate classroom behavior. It is not known, however, which specific behaviors are most critically related to school adjustment. Moreover, although the classroom is the most natural ecological context in which to evaluate schoolchildren's behavior, the data from Tables 1 and 2 indicate the relativity of such behavior. Rates of inappropriate behavior for supposedly well-adjusting peers ranged from 2.79% to 24.33% across classrooms (Classrooms 7 and 10 in Study 1, respectively). Understanding the factors that influence these behavioral rates is an important issue for those studying school adjustment.

29. Our choice to target children in the top 15% of the distribution of AML total scores was based on resources available to treat identified children. Other cutoff points for identifying school dysfunction might easily identify a group of children with different behavioral characteristics.

30. Finally, results of this study should not be construed as suggesting that the AML be used as the sole criterion for identifying school maladjustment. The authors of the AML (Cowen et al., 1973; Primary Mental Health Project, 1989) stress its utility as a screening instrument only. For the purposes of both good research and good clinical practice, information from the AML should be combined with data from addi-

tional sources such as other rating scales, teacher interviews, and child assessments.

31. For example, in Study 2, three of the four children who were not distinguished from their peers based on behavioral criteria were classified as having primarily shy-withdrawn difficulties. Although the numbers are small, these data confirm earlier findings (Green et al., 1980) that teachers may be more effective in identifying children with externalizing rather than internalizing problems. At the same time, behavioral observations are not ideal in detecting internalizing symptomatology. Some researchers (e.g., Reynolds, 1992) emphasize that internalizing disorders are best evaluated by direct self-report and clinical interviews.

References

Allen, G. J., Chinsky, J. M., Larcen, S. W., Lochman, J. E., & Selinger, H. V. (1976). *Community psychology and the schools: A behaviorally-oriented multilevel preventive approach.* Hillsdale, NJ: Lawrence Erlbaum.

Cowen, E. L., Dorr, D., Clarfield, S., Kreling, B., McWilliams, S. A., Pokracki, F., Pratt, D. M., Terrell, D., & Wilson, A. (1973). The AML: A quick-screening device for early identification of school maladaptation. *American Journal of Community Psychology, 1,* 12-35.

Cowen, E. L., Dorr, D., & Orgel, A. R. (1971). Interrelationships among screening measures for early detection of school dysfunction. *Psychology in the Schools, 8,* 135-139.

Dorr, D., Stephens, J., Pozner, R., & Klodt, W. (1980). Use of AML scale to identify adjustment problems in fourth-, fifth-, and sixth-grade children. *American Journal of Community Psychology, 8,* 341-352.

Durlak, J. A., Stein, M. A., & Mannarino, A. P. (1980). Behavioral validity of a brief teacher rating scale (the AML) in identifying high-risk acting-out school children. *American Journal of Community Psychology, 8,* 101-115.

Gillespie, J. F., Durlak, J. A., & Sherman, D. (1982). Relationship between kindergarten children's interpersonal problem-solving skills and other indices of school adjustment: A cautionary note. *American Journal of Community Psychology, 10,* 149-153.

Glidewell, J. C., & Swallow, C. S. (1969). *The prevalence of maladjustment in elementary schools.* (Report prepared for the Joint Commission on Mental Health of Children). Chicago: University of Chicago Press.

Green, K. D., Beck, S. J., Forehand, R., & Vosk, V. (1980). Validity of teacher nominations of child behavior problems. *Journal of Abnormal Child Psychology, 8,* 397-404.

Kendall, P. C., & Zupan, B. A. (1981). Individual versus group application of cognitive-behavioral self-control procedures with children. *Behavior Therapy, 12,* 344-359.

Lambert, M. C., Theisinger, C., Overly, K., & Knight, F. (1990). Teacher and parent ratings of behavior problems in Jamaican children and adolescents: Convergence and divergence of views. *International Journal of Intercultural Relations, 14,* 177-191.

Lorion, R. P., & Cowen, E. L. (1978). Referral to a school mental health project: A screening note. *American Journal of Community Psychology, 6,* 247-251.

Lorion, R. P., Cowen, E. L., & Caldwell, R. A. (1974). Problem types of children referred to a school-based mental health program: Identification and outcome. *Journal of Consulting and Clinical Psychology, 42,* 491-496.

O'Leary, K. D., & Kent, R. N. (1973). Behavior modification for social action: Research tactics and problems. In L. A. Hamerlynck, L. C. Handy, & E. J. Mash (Eds.), *Behavior change: Methodology, concepts, and practice* (pp. 69-96). Champaign, IL: Research Press.

Primary Mental Health Project. (1971). *Special Bulletin. AML Norms: 1971.* Rochester, NY: Author.

Primary Mental Health Project. (1989). *PMHP Evaluation instruments and forms.* Rochester, NY: Author.

Reynolds, W. M. (1992). *Internalizing disorders in children and adolescents.* New York: Wiley.

Solomon, R. W., & Wahler, R. G. (1973). Peer reinforcement control of classroom problem behavior. *Journal of Applied Behavior Analysis, 6,* 49-55.

Trull, T. J., Nietzel, M. T., & Main, A. (1988). The use of meta-analysis to assess the clinical significance of behavior therapy for agoraphobia. *Behavior Therapy, 19,* 527-538.

Walker, H. M., & Hops, H. (1978). Social validity: The case for subjective measurement or how applied behavior analysis is finding its heart. *Journal of Applied Behavior Analysis, 11,* 203-214.

Factual Questions

1. What is the hypothesis?

2. The AML measures what three general behavior domains?

3. How long was the training period for the observers?

4. If the mean percentage of inappropriate behavior for peers was 15.00 with a standard deviation of 5.00, what is the cutoff score for a target child with a mean level of inappropriate behavior of 20.00?

5. How were peers selected within each classroom?

6. How many of the 58 target children had cutoff scores greater than 1.00?

7. The highest average percentage of inappropriate behavior by peers in Study 2 was observed in which classroom?

8. In Study 2, which child was the largest number of standard deviations above his/her peers?

9. Calculate the cutoff score for Target Child # 1 in Table 2 using the means and standard deviation given there. Is the reported cutoff score of 2.90 for this child correct?

Questions for Discussion

10. In several places, the researchers refer to their "experimental procedures." Do these procedures make this study an "experiment," as it is usually defined?

11. In paragraph 7, the researchers note that target children and peers were comparable in terms of race and gender. Is this important? Why? Why not?

12. Is the description of the behavioral observations in paragraphs 9 and 10 adequate? Explain.

13. In paragraphs 11–13, the researchers describe a method for identifying children with behavior outside normal limits *relative to the behavior of peers in the same classroom.* Thus, a child who is within limits in his or her classroom might be outside the limits relative to the mean of another classroom. What is your opinion on this relative method?

14. Why do you think the researchers used "time sampling"? (See paragraph 15.)

15. What do you think the researchers mean by "reactivity"? (See paragraph 18.)

16. In your opinion, were the observations sufficiently reliable? (See paragraph 19.)

17. Was the use of many classrooms (and teachers) an important strength of this study? Why? Why not?

18. Based on the data reported in this study, what is your opinion on the validity of the AML as a screening instrument? Would it be desirable to conduct additional studies on its validity? Explain.

19. Is this study an example of a criterion-related validity study? If yes, what was the criterion? If no, why not?

20. In paragraphs 27 through 31, the authors discuss limitations of their study. Are there other limitations they did not discuss? Explain.

Quality Ratings

DIRECTIONS: Indicate your level of agreement with each of the following statements by circling a number from 5 for strongly agree (SA) to 1 for strongly disagree (SD). If you believe that an item is not applicable to this research article, leave it blank. Be prepared to explain your ratings.

A. The introduction establishes the importance of the research topic.
   SA   5   4   3   2   1   SD

B. The literature review establishes the context for the study.
   SA   5   4   3   2   1   SD

C. The research purpose, question, or hypothesis is clearly stated.
   SA   5   4   3   2   1   SD

D. The method of sampling is sound.
   SA   5   4   3   2   1   SD

E. Relevant demographics (for example, age, gender, and ethnicity) are described.
   SA   5   4   3   2   1   SD

F. Measurement procedures are adequate.
   SA   5   4   3   2   1   SD

G. The results are clearly described.
   SA   5   4   3   2   1   SD

H. The discussion/conclusion is appropriate.
   SA   5   4   3   2   1   SD

I. Despite any flaws noted above, the report is worthy of publication.
   SA   5   4   3   2   1   SD

ARTICLE 20

SEXUAL ORIENTATION OF ADULT SONS OF GAY FATHERS

J. Michael Bailey *Northwestern University*
David Bobrow *Northwestern University*
Marilyn Wolfe *Northwestern University*
Sarah Mikach *Northwestern University*

The sexual development of children of gay and lesbian parents is interesting for both scientific and social reasons. The present study is the largest to date to focus on the sexual orientation of adult sons of gay men. From advertisements in gay publications, 55 gay or bisexual men were recruited who reported on 82 sons at least 17 years of age. More than 90% of sons whose sexual orientations could be rated were heterosexual. Furthermore, gay and heterosexual sons did not differ on potentially relevant variables such as the length of time they had lived with their fathers. Results suggest that any environmental influence of gay fathers on their sons' orientation is not large.

1. An appreciable minority of both gay men and lesbians have children (Bell & Weinberg, 1978), and although difficult to document, it seems likely that increasing numbers of openly gay and lesbian people are forming families. Development of children of gay and lesbian parents has begun receiving the attention of researchers (e.g., Patterson, 1992) for both scientific and social reasons. A primary scientific question is whether children of gay and lesbian parents are especially likely to become gay or lesbian themselves, and if so, why. The primary social question, whether gay and lesbian parents are as desirable as heterosexual parents, has arisen most vividly in child custody cases. The scientific and social issues are closely related, because a primary focus of expert testimony in custody cases has been the impact of being reared by a gay or lesbian parent on children's sexual orientations (Falk, 1989; Harvard Law Review, 1989).

Sexual Development of Children of Gay and Lesbian Parents

2. Children of gay and lesbian parents might be expected to have elevated rates of homosexuality because they receive both environmental and genetic input from their parents. At least three environmental transmission routes are conceivable. The most obvious possibility is that children may acquire their sexual orientations in part by imitating their parents. By this model (discussed generally by, e.g., Sears, Rau, & Alpert, 1965), a child identifies with his same-sex parent and thereby adopts the kind of love object preferred by that parent. An immediate problem with this model is that most gay men and lesbians have heterosexual parents and thus develop opposite to the model's prediction. Psychoanalytic theorists (e.g., Bieber, 1962) have attempted to resolve this paradox by hypothesizing that, as children, homosexual individuals identified with their opposite-sex parents. In men, such atypical identification supposedly results from an unusually close mother-son relationship coupled with a distant father-son relationship. In women, according to psychoanalytic theory, an especially antagonistic relationship with the mother impedes identification. Consistent with the theory, gay men tend to recall their fathers as having been emotionally distant and lesbians tend to report poorer relationships with their mothers (Bell, Weinberg, & Hammersmith, 1981; Van den Aardweg, 1984). However, the effect size compared with heterosexual individuals is weak, and causal interpretation of the findings is problematic (Bell et al., 1981; Freund & Blanchard, 1983). Although, to our knowledge, psychoanalytic writers have not extended this theory to the development of children of gay and lesbian parents, it would be consistent with an increased rate of homosexuality among the same-sex children of such parents, provided their relationship was not distant (which would impede identification).

3. Socialization is a second possible route by which children of gay and lesbian parents may have an increased likelihood of developing homosexually. Gay and lesbian parents might conceivably either reinforce behavior that increases the probability of a homosexual outcome or else fail to discourage such behavior in their children. For example, many gay men and lesbians were atypical children with respect to their sex-typed behavior (Bailey & Zucker, 1995). If, because of their own experiences, they are more tolerant of such behavior in their children, and cross-gendered behavior is caus-ally antecedent to homosexuality (as suggested by Green, 1987, p. 382), their children would exhibit higher rates of homosexuality. Patterson's (1992) review found little evidence that children of gay and lesbian parents were atypical with respect to either gender identity or sex-typed behavior, although available studies were insufficiently large to generate much statistical power. Alternatively, gay fathers and lesbian mothers may reinforce (or fail to discourage) other causally relevant behavior unrelated to gender identity or sex-typed behavior, but it is at present unclear what behavior might be relevant.

4. A third potential environmental route has been debated primarily in journals of opinion rather than in academic journals. Some writers (e.g., Arkes et al., 1994; Krauthammer, 1993; Pattullo, 1992) have suggested that destigmatizing homosexuality makes it easier for those who are so predisposed to become homosexual, and thus increases the rate of homosexuality in those cultures or subcultures in which it is destigmatized. It is at least plausible that being reared by a gay or lesbian parent has the effect of making homosexuality a more acceptable alternative. People who have gay or lesbian acquaintances are relatively tolerant of homosexuality (Herek & Glunt, 1993; Schmalz, 1993).

5. No existing theory of parent-to-child environmental transmission of sexual orientation has received unambiguous empirical support.

Bailey, J. M. et al. (1995). Sexual orientation of adult sons of gay fathers. *Developmental Psychology, 31*, 124-129. Copyright © 1995 by the American Psychological Association. Reprinted with permission.

J. Michael Bailey, Marilyn Wolfe, and Sarah Mikach, Department of Psychology, Northwestern University; David Bobrow, Department of Psychiatry, Northwestern University. We gratefully acknowledge the suggestions of David Uttall. Correspondence concerning this article should be addressed to J. Michael Bailey, Department of Psychology, Northwestern University, 2029 Sheridan Road, Evanston, Illinois 60208-2710.

Studies have clearly demonstrated the importance of environmental determinants of sexual orientation (Bailey & Pillard, 1991; Bailey, Pillard, Neale, & Agyei, 1993), but contrary to parent-to-child transmission, these determinants appear primarily to operate within families to make siblings differ from each other (i.e., they are within-family environmental effects; Plomin & Daniels, 1987). Parent-to-child environmental transmission cannot presently be rejected, however, because of methodological limitations of existing studies, and because analyses from relevant epidemiological studies (performed from the framework of quantitative genetics) do not sensitively gauge the importance of relatively rare factors such as having a gay or lesbian parent. (This is because the magnitudes of effects due to particular environments or genes are weighted by their frequency; thus, rare environments or genes will contribute less to the heritability or environmentality estimates.)

6. Aside from environmental transmission, children of gay and lesbian parents would be more likely to develop homosexually if there were additive genetic variation for sexual orientation. Additive genetic variation is the portion of genotypic variance that causes parent-child resemblance (Falconer, 1981; in contrast, nonadditive variation, such as dominance or epistatic effects, decreases parent-child resemblance). Although there is empirical support for partial genetic transmission of both male (Bailey & Pillard, 1991) and female (Bailey et al., 1993) sexual orientation, the existence of additive genetic variation for male or female sexual orientation remains uncertain because of methodological limitations of studies to date (especially ascertainment problems; see Bailey & Pillard [1991] and Bailey et al. [1993] for extended discussions) and the inefficiency of twin studies in distinguishing additive and nonadditive genetic variation (Grayson, 1989). Furthermore, evolutionary considerations argue against the likelihood of substantial additive genetic variation for traits related to fertility (Falconer, 1981), as sexual orientation seems to be. Although many gay and lesbian people reproduce, their fertility is markedly lower than that of heterosexual people (Bell & Weinberg, 1978).

7. Neither environmental nor additive genetic transmission has yet been established for either male or female sexual orientation. Indeed, it remains unclear if children of gay and lesbian parents have elevated rates of homosexuality. Patterson (1992) reviewed studies of children of gay and lesbian parents, including their adjustment, sexual orientation, gender identity, and sex-typed behavior, and concluded that evidence suggested little difference between such children and those of heterosexual parents. However, available studies were both few and modestly sized. For example, the largest study (Miller, 1979) concerning offspring sexual orientation consisted of 27 adult daughters and 21 adult sons of gay men.

8. It is important to note that at this stage of research, sons and daughters should be considered separately, because it is plausible that they are affected differently. For example, sexual orientation may be differentially malleable for the two sexes: if so, offspring of the more malleable sex could be especially influenced by parents' sexual orientation. Similarly, a child may be differently affected according to whether the father or mother is homosexual, and thus offspring of gay fathers should be considered separately from offspring of lesbian mothers. Moreover, some explanations, such as identification, depend on whether the child is the same or the opposite sex as the homosexual parent. Thus, to provide a complete answer, researchers must eventually fill the four cells of a Parent (gay father vs. lesbian mother) x Offspring (son vs. daughter) table-of-outcome data.

Social Implications

9. Few rights are as fundamental as the right of parents to raise their own children. Yet some courts have viewed the prospect of lesbians and gay men raising children so negatively that they have denied custody to such parents solely on the basis of their sexual orientation. Those opposed to granting custody to gay and lesbian parents have cited several concerns, including the possibilities that such parents are less mentally healthy, that they will molest their children, and that such children will be stigmatized by their peers (for reviews of these arguments, see Falk, 1989; Harvard Law Review, 1989; Kleber, Howell, & Tibbits-Kleber, 1986). Perhaps the most frequently noted concern, and the one most relevant to this article, is that children raised by gay or lesbian parents are especially likely to become gay or lesbian themselves (Falk, 1989).

10. Even if children of gay and lesbian parents were more likely to become homosexual, we do not believe that this would be a problem, much less that it would justify forfeiture of custody. Nevertheless, a substantial proportion of Americans appear to disagree (Schmalz, 1993). If Patterson (1992) is correct that children of gay men and lesbians are no more likely than children of heterosexual people to become homosexual, then it is unnecessary to reach consensus on the desirability of heterosexual versus homosexual outcomes, at least in the context of child custody. It is of course impossible to prove the null hypothesis, but it should be possible to determine whether being reared by a homosexual parent makes an appreciable difference in a child's sexual orientation.

Overview

11. This article reports the largest study to date of adult sons of gay fathers. We focused on one cell of the table of outcomes to maximize sample size, and sons of gay fathers were most relevant to other research we were pursuing when we began this project (Bailey & Pillard, 1991). We interviewed gay fathers and a majority of their adult sons, and we focused particularly on the sons' sexual orientations. Finally, we examined potential predictors of sons' homosexuality.

Method

12. The methodology of this study closely followed that of several prior studies (Bailey & Benishay, 1993; Bailey & Pillard, 1991; Bailey et al., 1993). They can be consulted for additional details regarding our procedure.

13. We recruited gay and bisexual fathers by means of advertisements in homophile publications in Chicago, St. Louis, Milwaukee, Dallas, San Antonio, Austin, and Houston. The advertisements stated that we sought to study gay or bisexual men with sons at least 17 years old and gave the phone number of our laboratory. Subjects who met inclusion criteria were scheduled for a 1-hr interview. We interviewed 55 biological fathers. All of the interviews were conducted with informed consent. The interview included questions concerning the fathers' marital histories: the quality of current relationships with both the sons and the sons' mothers, the length of time fathers lived with sons, and the frequency of contact between fathers and sons. In addition, we asked about both fathers' and sons' sexual orientations.

14. Fathers reported on 82 sons. At the conclusion of their interviews, we asked fathers for permission to contact sons through a questionnaire, which fathers examined before making their decisions. The premise of the questionnaire and accompanying cover letter was that we were studying the degree to which unspecified traits ran in families. The letter did not mention our interest in sexual orientation. The questionnaire included a variety of questions about social attitudes, personality, and family relationships, in addition to five questions regarding sexual orientation. If a son did not respond to our initial mailing within approximately 1 month, we sent him an additional questionnaire. We halted our efforts only if at least two mailings of the questionnaire were unsuccessful and (a) no telephone number was available for the son, (b) repeated telephone calls were unsuccessful, or (c) the son declined to participate. Fifty-seven fathers allowed their sons to be contacted, of whom 41 responded by questionnaire. An additional 2 sons agreed to a short phone interview in lieu of filling out questionnaires. Thus, complete data were available for 43 (52%) of the 82 sons.

15. We assessed sons' sexual orientations in two ways. First, we asked fathers whether they believed their sons' sexual orientation to be heterosexual, homosexual, or bisexual. In addition, each father also rated his confidence regarding each son's sexual orientation using a 4-point scale, ranging from 1 = *completely certain,* indicating that the son had told him outright; to 2 = *virtually certain,* indicating that he had a high degree of certainty based on the son's behavior alone; to 3 = *moderately certain* and 4 = *uncertain,* both of which represented lower levels of confidence. Second, questionnaires sent to sons asked them to rate themselves as heterosexual, bisexual, or homosexual. Sons completing questionnaires also gave ratings of their attraction to men and women, as well as separate Kinsey ratings for adult fantasy and behavior (Kinsey, Pomeroy, & Martin, 1948). Kinsey scores range from 0 (*completely heterosexual in fantasies and behavior*) to 6 (*completely homosexual in fantasies and behavior*).

16. Sons' self-ratings of sexual orientation were used when available. However, these data were lacking for a large percentage of sons. Previous research has found that gay and lesbian probands are quite accurate at predicting siblings' self-ratings of sexual orientation, when they do so with confidence (Bailey & Benishay, 1993; Bailey & Pillard, 1991; Bailey et al., 1993; Pillard & Weinrich, 1986). The accuracy of gay fathers in rating their sons is, of course, a separate though related empirical question, which we address herein.

Results

17. Table 1 presents some descriptive information about the fathers. The large majority of fathers (89%) currently identified themselves as gay rather than bisexual. Although all of the

Table 1   *Characteristics of 55 gay fathers*

Item	%	M	SD
Age (years)		35.5	9.0
Marital status			
Currently married	5		
Widowed	4		
Separated or divorced	91		
Sexual orientation			
Homosexual	89		
Bisexual	11		
Age when family became aware of homosexuality, if ever (years)		35.3	12.5

fathers had been married, the large majority (91%) were separated or divorced.

18. Table 2 contains the results of fathers' ratings, and sons' self-ratings, of sons' sexual orientation (heterosexual vs. nonheterosexual). In the 41 cases in which fathers were at least "virtually certain" about their sons' orientation and sons provided data as well, fathers were incorrect only once, kappa = .88, p < .001. The lone mistake occurred when a father rated his son as heterosexual and the son rated himself bisexual. Because of the high degree of accuracy of fathers' ratings, we used them when sons' self-ratings of sexual orientation were unavailable, provided fathers' ratings were made with at least "virtual certainty." Prior research (Pillard & Weinrich, 1986) has suggested that when participants are less certain, their accuracy diminishes appreciably, and more specifically, they tend to overassess homosexuality. Thus, we omitted sons for whom self-ratings were unavailable if fathers were only moderately certain or uncertain. Of 7 sons omitted for this reason, 4 were believed by their fathers to be heterosexual, 2 were believed to be nonheterosexual, and 1 son was given no rating by his father. Table 3 contains the frequency of heterosexuality and nonheterosexuality among the sons. Of sons whose sexual orientation could be rated with confidence, 9% (7/75) were

nonheterosexual, and 91% (68/75) were heterosexual.

19. Table 3 also provides some descriptive data concerning some variables potentially relevant to environmental hypotheses of father-son resemblance. For example, there is a wide range of values for the number of years sons lived with fathers, from 1 to 28 years. An environmental theory of father-son resemblance for sexual orientation would probably predict that sons who lived the longest with their fathers would most likely also be gay. This was not true in the present sample, however. In fact, gay sons had lived for a somewhat shorter time with their fathers, 6.4 years versus 11.2 years for heterosexual sons, though this difference was not significant, t(72) = 1.5, p = .15. Nor was sons' sexual orientation related to the frequency of contact with their fathers during the previous year, t(70) = 0.1, p = .90. Sons' sexual orientation was also unrelated to the degree that sons presently accepted their fathers' sexual orientation, t(53) = 0.1, p > .70, and to the quality of the present father-son relationship, t(69) = −.30, p > .75. (Degrees of freedom varied because some participants did not answer all questions.)

20. We repeated these analyses using four alternative indicators of sons' sexual orientation: combined behavior and fantasy Kinsey rating for adolescence, combined Kinsey rating for

Table 2   *Sexual orientation ratings of 82 sons of gay fathers by sons and their 55 fathers*

	Self-rating by son		
Rating of son by father	Heterosexual	Nonheterosexual	Could not contact
Father at least "virtually certain" of son's orientation			
Heterosexual	36	1	31
Nonheterosexual	0	4	1
Father less confident of son's orientation	1	1	7

Table 3   *Characteristics of 82 adult sons of gay fathers*

Item	Range	M	SD	n
Age (years)	17-43	25.3	6.2	
Years lived with father	1-28	10.9	8.1	
Quality of father-son relationship[a]	1-4	1.6	0.9	
Knowledge of father's homosexuality[b]	1-4	3.5	1.0	
Acceptance of father's homosexuality[c]	1-4	3.7	0.7	
Frequency of contact (no. of days, last year)	0-365	89.7	112.0	
Sexual orientation				
Heterosexual				68
Nonheterosexual				7
Unable to rate with confidence				7

[a]From 1 = *very good* to 4 = *poor*. [b]From 1 = *none* to 4 = *definitely knows*. [c]From 1 = *very rejecting* to 4 = *accepting*.

adulthood, sexual interest in men, and sexual interest in women. These variables made finer distinctions than *heterosexual-homosexual* and, in that respect, provided potentially more powerful tests. On the other hand, these data were available only for sons who participated, and thus sample sizes for these analyses were somewhat smaller, ranging from 33 to 40. The correlations between these indicators of sexual orientation and quality of the father-son relationship, son's acceptance of father's homosexuality, and the length of time fathers and sons lived together were uniformly low (r < .15) and nonsignificant (p > .35).

Discussion

21. Results of this study are consistent with corresponding figures in Patterson's (1992) review, suggesting that approximately 10% of sons of gay or bisexual men also become nonheterosexual. Relevant studies included fewer than 50 sons of gay fathers; thus, this study substantially enlarges the available database. Before examining the scientific and social implications of our findings, we address the study's methodological limitations.

Methodological Issues

22. Two limitations of this study should be acknowledged in any discussion of its implications. The more serious limitation concerns the recruitment of gay fathers by means of advertisements. This recruitment strategy cannot guarantee a representative sample of either gay fathers or sons of gay fathers. The most important potential bias is that fathers' decisions to participate might depend, in part, on their sons' sexual orientations, a kind of bias that Kendler and Eaves (1989) called *concordance-dependent ascertainment bias* in the context of twin

research. We suspect that if this kind of bias occurred, it worked to inflate the rate of homosexuality among the sons in our sample. For example, fathers with gay sons may have been more inclined to volunteer for a study of gay fathers because they believed that we would find them especially interesting, or because they had less concern about potential friction with their sons over their involvement in such a study. However, the existence and direction of concordance-dependent bias are not ultimately resolvable with data from this study.

23. The second limitation concerns the absence of a control group. Typically in studies concerned with familial aggregation, probands with and without the trait of interest are recruited and their relatives compared. This design allows the comparison of participants recruited by use of identical strategies and assessed with identical instruments. No control group of heterosexual fathers was recruited for the present study. However, at least two general bodies of available data can be used to derive rates for comparison: recent population surveys of homosexual behavior and family-genetic studies of homosexuality using other kinds of relatives.

24. Several recent large population-based surveys have provided generally consistent estimates for the frequency of male homosexual behavior in contemporary western societies (ACSF Investigators, 1992; Billy, Tanfer, Grady, & Klepinger, 1993; Johnson, Wadsworth, Wellings, Bradshaw, & Field, 1992). The estimates varied with respect to the stringency of the criterion, from 1% to 2% (for exclusive homosexuality over a several-year period) to nearly 5% (for any lifetime homosexual experience). Our criterion, homosexual or bisexual identification, is probably relatively stringent, and thus the percentage of men

meeting it was nearer the lower figure. If so, it could be argued, the rate of homosexuality in the sons (9%) is several times higher than that suggested by the population-based surveys and is consistent with a degree of father-to-son transmission. The 95% confidence interval of the sons' rate of homosexuality, 3% to 16%, exceeds the smallest population-based estimate (Billy et al., 1993).

25. Comparison of our rates with those of the population-based surveys may be inappropriate, however. We have noted that our methodology probably inflated the rate of homosexuality among sons. In contrast, the population surveys may have underestimated the population rate of homosexuality, as a result of noncooperation or underreporting of gay and bisexual men (Fay, Turner, Klassen, & Gagnon, 1989). In another study (Bailey & Pillard, 1991), we examined rates of homosexuality in relatives of gay and bisexual men recruited similarly to the gay fathers of the present study, and those results may yield more appropriate comparisons. In that study, we recruited gay men with a twin or adoptive brother. The rate of homosexuality among sons (9%) was comparable with the rate we obtained for adoptive brothers (11%) and was significantly lower than what we obtained for dizygotic (DZ) twins (22%), chi square (1, N = 129) = 4.2, p < .05. Thus, the rate of homosexuality in sons of gay fathers in the present study was lower than that obtained for another kind of first-degree relatives (DZ twins) of comparably recruited participants in a prior study. There are at least three possible explanations. First, concordance-dependent ascertainment bias may have been greater in the previous study, creating a spurious difference. Second, DZ twins may share environmental influences not shared by fathers and sons. The third possible explanation is genetic. Siblings share one fourth of nonadditive genetic variation, but parents and offspring share none. Thus, nonadditive genetic effects would cause greater resemblance between brothers than between fathers and sons. This pattern could also be attributable to X-linkage, a possibility supported by a recent report (Hamer, Hu, Magnuson, Hu, & Pattatucci, 1993).

Implications

26. The present study cannot definitively answer the basic question of whether sons of gay fathers have elevated rates of homosexuality. It does, however, support one conclusion that, although quite general, may also be important: The large majority of sons of gay fathers are heterosexual. It is difficult to imagine that any methodological limitation of this study biased results to such an extent that a future, more careful study would contradict this conclusion. If male sexual orientation is somewhat heritable, as we have argued elsewhere (Bailey & Pillard, 1991), an elevation in the sons' rate of homosexuality consistent with present results could be explained genetically. Consistent with a genetic hypothesis, the rate for sons was much lower than what we obtained for monozygotic (MZ) twins (52%), chi square (1, $N = 132$) = 29.0, $p < .001$. Studies that use more careful sampling techniques will be necessary to test for a modest elevation in the rate of homosexuality among the offspring of gay and lesbian parents and to determine whether any such elevation is genetic or environmental or both.

27. Inconsistent with environmental transmission, sexual orientation was not positively correlated with the amount of time that sons lived with their fathers. However, because there were only 7 nonheterosexual sons, this was not a statistically powerful test. If replicated in a larger sample, this finding would provide strong evidence against an environmental influence of gay fathers on their sons' sexual orientations. Although our results do not absolutely exclude the possibility of father-to-son environmental transmission, they suggest that any such influence is not large. As we already noted, conclusions from the present study may not apply to daughters of gay men or to children of lesbians.

28. The available evidence, including this study, fails to provide empirical grounds for denying child custody to gay or lesbian parents because of concern about their children's sexual orientation. The fact that sons' sexual orientation was unrelated to the time lived with fathers is especially relevant, because that analysis represented a relatively direct test of the assumption that custody decisions affect children's sexual orientation. Although we reemphasize

the need to replicate the finding by using larger samples, our study suggests that allowing gay men to retain custody of their sons does not substantially increase the likelihood that the sons will become gay adults.

29. At least two kinds of future studies may provide valuable information about the sexual development of offspring of gay men and lesbians. Investigations of adult children will be most useful if they explore specific hypotheses rather than merely focus on the rate of homosexuality among the children. Exploring which, if any, variables distinguish children who became heterosexual from those who became homosexual could support or falsify specific developmental theories. Moreover, these analyses may be less sensitive to methodological difficulties such as potentially biasing self-selection. At least two variables are especially relevant: the degree of exposure of a child to a gay or lesbian parent, and the degree of genetic relatedness between parent and child. Exploring the importance of the former allows tests of environmental hypotheses. Exploring the importance of the latter, for example, by comparing natural children and stepchildren of gay and lesbian parents, allows an examination of the importance of genetic influences.

30. An alternative strategy is to recruit gay and lesbian parents whose children are too young to have established sexual orientations, then to follow them prospectively. Although this design would be more expensive and onerous, it will help minimize concordance-dependent ascertainment bias and allow more confidence in frequency estimates. Another advantage to this approach is that specific hypotheses could be tested prospectively rather than retrospectively. The ultimate goal of studies in this area should be to illuminate the mechanism, as well as the fact, of any environmental or genetic transmission of sexual orientation.

References

ACSF Investigators. (1992). AIDS and sexual behavior in France. *Nature, 360,* 407-409.

Arkes, H., Berke, M., Bradley, G., Dalin, D., Fortin, E., Garcia, J., Gellman, M., George, R., Haffenreffer, H., Hittinger, J., Hittinger, R., Jenson, R., Meilaender, G., Muller, J., Neuhaus, R. J., Novak, D., Nuechterlein, J., Stackhouse, M., Turner, P., Weigel, G., & Wilken, R. (February 24, 1994). Morality and homosexuality. *Wall Street Journal,* p. A-18.

Bailey, J. M., & Benishay, D. S. (1993). Familial aggregation of female sexual orientation. *American Journal of Psychiatry, 150,* 272-277.

Bailey, J. M., & Pillard, R. C. (1991). A genetic study of male sexual orientation. *Archives of General Psychiatry, 48,* 1089-1096.

Bailey, J. M., Pillard, R. C., Neale, M. C., & Agyei, Y. (1993). Heritable factors influence sexual

orientation in women. *Archives of General Psychiatry, 31,* 217-223.

Bailey, J. M., & Zucker, K. J. (1995). Childhood sex-typed behavior, and sexual orientation: A conceptual analysis and quantitative review. *Developmental Psychology, 31,* 43-55.

Bell, A. P., & Weinberg, M. S. (1978). *Homosexualities: A study of diversity among men and women.* New York: Simon & Schuster.

Bell, A. P., Weinberg, M. S., & Hammersmith, S. K. (1981). *Sexual preference: Its development in men and women.* Bloomington: Indiana University Press.

Bieber, I. (1962). *Homosexuality: A psychoanalytic study.* New York: Basic Books.

Billy, J. O. G., Tanfer, K., Grady, W. R., & Klepinger, D. H. (1993). The sexual behavior of men in the United States. *Family Planning Perspectives, 25,* 52-60.

Falconer, D. S. (1981). *Introduction to quantitative genetics* (2nd ed.). London: Longman.

Falk, P. J. (1989). Lesbian mothers: Psychosocial assumptions in family law. *American Psychologist, 44,* 941-947.

Fay, R. E., Turner, C. F., Klassen, A. D., & Gagnon, J. H. (1989). Prevalence and patterns of same-gender sexual contact among men. *Science, 243,* 338-348.

Freund, K., & Blanchard, R. (1983). Is the distant relationship of fathers and homosexual sons related to the son's erotic preference for male partners or to the son's atypical gender identity, or both? In M. W. Ross (Ed.), *Homosexuality and social sex roles* (pp. 7-25). New York: Haworth.

Grayson, D. A. (1989). Twins reared together: Minimizing shared environmental effects. *Behavior Genetics, 19,* 593-604.

Green, R. (1987). *The "sissy boy syndrome" and the development of homosexuality.* New Haven, CT: Yale University Press.

Hamer, D. H., Hu, S., Magnuson, V. L., Hu, N., & Pattatucci, A. M. L. (1993). A linkage between DNA markers on the X chromosome and male sexual orientation. *Science, 261,* 321-327.

Harvard Law Review. (1989). *Sexual orientation and the law.* Cambridge, MA: Harvard University Press.

Herek, G. M., & Glunt, E. K. (1993). Interpersonal contact and heterosexuals' attitudes toward gay men: Results from a national survey. *Journal of Sex Research, 30,* 239-244.

Johnson, A., Wadsworth, J., Wellings, K., Bradshaw, S., & Field, J. (1992). Sexual lifestyles and HIV risk, *Nature, 360,* 410-412.

Kendler, K. S., & Eaves, L. J. (1989). The estimation of probandwise concordance in twins: The effect of unequal ascertainment. *Acta Geneticae et Medicae Gemellologiae, 38,* 253-270.

Kinsey, A. C., Pomeroy, W. B., & Martin, C. E. (1948). *Sexual behavior in the human male.* Philadelphia: W. B. Saunders.

Kleber, D. J., Howell, R. J., & Tibbits-Kleber, A. L. (1986). The impact of parental homosexuality in child custody cases: A review of the literature. *Bulletin of the American Academy of Psychiatry and the Law, 14,* 81-87.

Krauthammer, C. (May 2, 1993). Gays and the demand for legitimation. *Chicago Tribune*, p. 3.

Miller, B. (1979). Gay fathers and their children. *Family Coordinator, 28*, 544-552.

Patterson, C. J. (1992). Children of lesbian and gay parents. *Child Development, 63*, 1025-1042.

Pattullo, E. L. (December, 1992). Straight talk about gays. *Commentary, 94*, 21-24.

Pillard, R. C., & Weinrich, J. D. (1986). Evidence of familial nature of male homosexuality. *Archives of General Psychiatry, 43*, 808-812.

Plomin, R., & Daniels, D. (1987). Why are children in the same family so different from one another? *Behavioral and Brain Sciences, 10*, 1-60.

Schmalz, J. (1993, March 5). Poll finds an even split on homosexuality's cause. *New York Times*, p. 11.

Sears, R. R., Rau, L., & Alpert, R. (1965). *Identification and child rearing*. Stanford, CA: Stanford University Press.

Van den Aardweg, G. J. M. (1984). Parents of homosexuals — not guilty? Interpretation of childhood psychological data. *American Journal of Psychotherapy, 38*, 180-189.

Received December 31, 1993, Revision received March 25, 1994, Accepted March 28, 1994

Factual Questions

1. According to the authors, what is a primary scientific question regarding the development of children of gay and lesbian parents?

2. How were the fathers recruited?

3. Complete data were available for what percentage of the sons?

4. Had heterosexual sons or homosexual sons lived longer with their fathers?

5. What two limitations of the study are discussed by the researchers?

6. Was the rate of homosexuality in this study higher or lower than the estimate for the general population of dizygotic twins?

7. What was the rate of homosexuality for monozygotic twins?

Questions for Discussion

8. What is your opinion on the way the fathers were recruited? Are there other ways to recruit them? Explain.

9. The letter sent to the sons did not mention the researchers' special interest in sexual orientation (see paragraph 14). Speculate on why the authors did not do this. Does this pose ethical problems?

10. In paragraph 22, the authors speculate that fathers of gay sons may have been more inclined to volunteer for this study than fathers of heterosexual sons. Do you agree? Why?

11. Would the inclusion of a control group have significantly improved the quality of this study? Explain.

12. Speculate on why gay and bisexual men might underreport or fail to report their sexual orientation in national surveys (see paragraph 25). In your opinion, is this study also subject to this potential problem?

13. If you were to conduct a study on the same topic, what changes, if any, would you make in the research methodology?

14. In your opinion, are the implications stated by the authors supported by the data they present? Explain.

15. Does this study make a significant contribution to understanding the origins of homosexual orientation? If yes, how? If not, why?

Quality Ratings

DIRECTIONS: Indicate your level of agreement with each of the following statements by circling a number from 5 for strongly agree (SA) to 1 for strongly disagree (SD). If you believe that an item is not applicable to this research article, leave it blank. Be prepared to explain your ratings.

A. The introduction establishes the importance of the research topic.
SA   5   4   3   2   1   SD

B. The literature review establishes the context for the study.
SA   5   4   3   2   1   SD

C. The research purpose, question, or hypothesis is clearly stated.
SA   5   4   3   2   1   SD

D. The method of sampling is sound.
SA   5   4   3   2   1   SD

E. Relevant demographics (for example, age, gender, and ethnicity) are described.
SA   5   4   3   2   1   SD

F. Measurement procedures are adequate.
SA   5   4   3   2   1   SD

G. The results are clearly described.
SA   5   4   3   2   1   SD

H. The discussion/conclusion is appropriate.
SA   5   4   3   2   1   SD

I. Despite any flaws noted above, the report is worthy of publication.
SA   5   4   3   2   1   SD

ARTICLE 21

PSYCHOLOGICAL CHARACTERISTICS OF ADOLESCENT STEROID USERS

Kent F. Burnett *University of Miami*
Mark E. Kleiman *University of Miami*

The Millon Adolescent Personality Inventory and the Profile of Mood States were used to assess a broad range of psychological characteristics in 24 adolescent athletes who reported steroid use. In addition, a steroid knowledge questionnaire was administered and an evaluation of physical symptoms of steroid use was conducted. Corresponding data were obtained from 24 adolescent athletes who did not use steroids, and 24 nonathletic adolescents. Although some personality variables differentiated between athletes and nonathletes, no personality variables significantly differentiated between athletes who used steroids and athletes who did not use steroids. Steroid users, however, had significantly higher levels of muscular density and hardness, bloating, gynecomastia, and acne than did athletes who did not use steroids; steroid users who were currently on a steroid use cycle had significantly more depression, anger, vigor, and total mood disturbance than those who were not on a cycle. Prospective longitudinal studies are needed to develop our understanding of psychological issues related to adolescent steroid use.

1. While anabolic-androgenic steroids have been used since the early 1950s to enhance athletic performance, the incidence of use appears to have increased considerably in recent years (Buckley et al., 1988; Duda, 1988; Johnson, Jay, Shoup, & Rickert, 1989; Nightingale, 1986; Office of the Inspector General (OIG), 1990; Tierney & McLain, 1990; Windsor & Dumitru, 1989; Yesalis et al., 1989). Particularly disturbing is the increased frequency of their use among adolescents.

2. Although there are no definitive national statistics, the estimated incidence of use by adolescents in the United States ranges from 6.6% of male 12th grade students (Buckley et al., 1988; Johnson et al., 1989; OIG, 1990) to 11.1% of male 11th grade students (Johnson, 1990). It has been estimated that at least 700,000 high school students use anabolic steroids (Tierney & McLain, 1990) and that at least two thirds begin use by 16 years of age (Johnson, 1990; OIG, 1990; Yesalis et al., 1989).

Among both adults and adolescent steroid users, the majority increase the dosages, variety, and length of time drugs are taken while on a steroid use cycle (Neff, 1990; OIG, 1990). Many users also engage in a practice known as "stacking"; that is, using several steroids at once (Bohigian et al., 1988; Donohoe, Blackwell, & Johnson, 1986; Pope & Katz, 1988).

3. There have been reports of addictive behavior and habituation among both adult and adolescent steroid users (Brower, Blow, Beresford, & Fuelling, 1989; Scott et al., 1990; OIG, 1990; Taylor, 1985; Yesalis et al., 1989), as well as reports of affective and psychotic symptoms, often characterized by impulsive, aggressive, and violent behavior (Lubell, 1989; Pope & Katz, 1988; Pope & Katz, 1990).

4. Adolescent steroid users appear to be at special risk for many of the adverse psychological and physical consequences of steroid use (Nideffer, 1989; OIG, 1990). Recent literature clearly shows that adolescent users believe that steroids produce the physical effects they desire, and approximately 86% of those cited in the 1990 study of the OIG have no plans to stop using steroids. Nearly all the adolescent users interviewed in the OIG report (93%) stated that starting steroid use was a good decision (1990). Recent studies also indicate that many adolescent users are either unaware or unconvinced of negative physical and psychological effects of steroids (Dunsky, 1990).

5. The growing evidence of habituation among adolescent steroid users, and the powerfully reinforcing properties of the drugs, have created a pressing need for more information about the psychosocial characteristics of the adolescents who use these drugs. Such information would serve an important role in the development of effective intervention and prevention programs. Thus, the goals of the present study were to systematically assess a wide variety of psychosocial characteristics in both steroid-using and nonsteroid-using adolescents and to determine if any of these characteristics might prove useful in differentiating between these groups.

Method

Subjects

6. Participants in this study consisted of 72 male adolescents ranging in age from 16-19. Of these, 24 were self-identified as serious weight trainers or bodybuilders who reported using steroids and were currently either on a steroid use cycle or between cycles. Another 24 consisted of adolescents who identified themselves as serious weight trainers who reported no use of anabolic steroids. Serious weight training was defined as participating three or more times per week. The third group of 24 adolescents consisted of nonathletic, nonweight trainers who did not participate in competitive, organized sports. Only male subjects were chosen to control for the possible confounding effects of gender.

7. Both the athletic steroid user and nonuser samples were secured through the junior author's personal contacts with operators of various gyms in the South Florida area, through contacts with athletes at those gyms, and through contacts with athletes at body building events. The nonathlete, nonweight training sample was obtained through health education classes at a senior high school located in the same geographic area.

8. All subjects from the steroid user and weight training nonuser groups were paid 10

Burnett, K. F., & Kleiman, M. E. (1994). Psychological characteristics of adolescent steroid users. *Adolescence, 29*, 81-89. Copyright © 1994 by Libra Publishers. Reprinted with permission.

This research was based in part on a doctoral dissertation conducted by the junior author. The authors would like to express appreciation to Joseph F. Brownholtz, Carolyn S. Garwood, Phillip M. McCabe, and Rick S. Zimmerman, whose scholarly counsel greatly enhanced the quality of this research.

Mark Kleiman, Ph.D., Counseling Psychology Program, School of Education, University of Miami, Coral Gables, Florida 33124.

Reprint requests to Kent F. Burnett, Ph.D., Counseling Psychology Program, School of Education, 312 Merrick Building, University of Miami, Coral Gables, FL 33124.

dollars for their participation in the study. The nonathlete nonusers were paid 5 dollars for their participation. All subjects were offered feedback regarding the results and findings of the research.

Instrumentation and Materials

9. The Millon Adolescent Personality Inventory (MAPI) is a measure devised by Theodore Millon, based on his comprehensive theory of personality (Millon, Green, & Meagher, 1982). It is designed to measure personality styles salient to the teenage years and is geared to the sixth-grade reading level. The inventory consists of 150 items, which are completed by most subjects in approximately 20 minutes.

10. The MAPI yields scores on eight personality variables: introversive, inhibited, sociable, confident, forceful, respectful, and sensitive. Eight additional scales measure clinical issues: self-concept, personal esteem, body comfort, sexual acceptance, peer security, social tolerance, family rapport, and academic confidence. The final four scales of the MAPI measure behavioral correlates such as school-related attendance, school achievement, social conformity, and impulse control.

11. The Profile of Mood States (POMS) (McNair, Lorr, & Droppleman, 1981) is designed to measure transient, fluctuating mood states. It consists of 65 adjective rating scales. Subjects were asked to describe how they have been feeling during the past week. Subjects take approximately four minutes to complete the instrument. The POMS has been used extensively in studying mood variability in competitive athletes, including adult athletes who use steroids (Humbert, 1990).

12. The POMS measures six identifiable mood states: Tension–Anxiety (T); Depression–Dejection (D); Anger–Hostility (A); Vigor–Activity (V); Fatigue–Inertia (F); and Confusion–Bewilderment (C).

13. The POMS was used to assess the level of transient mood disturbance among adolescents who were using anabolic steroids. It was expected that the user group that was currently between steroid use cycles would display less elevation in POMS scores than would the user group currently on a use cycle.

Procedure

14. All interviews and ratings were conducted on an individual basis. The strong assurances of anonymity that were provided were critical to obtaining valid data, since the adolescent steroid user is engaging in an illegal activity which is currently listed under the Federal Controlled Substances Act (BonDurant, 1991).

15. Participants from each group were administered a brief personal background questionnaire, the MAPI, the POMS, and a structured interview, including a steroid knowledge test and questions about physical health symptoms reportedly associated with steroid use (e.g., sleep problems, gynecomastia, shrunken testicles). While participants in the steroid user group and the athletic nonuser group completed these materials, the junior author rated each participant on physical characteristics commonly associated with steroid use (e.g., acne, muscular density, muscular hardness). These ratings, as well as the steroid knowledge assessment, were made in an attempt to corroborate participants' self-reported use or nonuse of steroids.

16. The assessments were identical for all groups, except that no ratings of physical characteristics were made for nonathletes nor were any questions asked about personal steroid use. The nonathletes were questioned, however, concerning general knowledge about steroids.

Research Design

17. Data were collected on three groups: athletic steroid users, athletic nonsteroid users, and nonathletic nonusers. The three groups were treated as an independent variable. Dependent variables consisted of each of the scale level scores on the MAPI and the POMS, as well as individual item scores on the steroid knowledge test, item level scores on the physical characteristics and symptoms of steroid use test. A series of univariate one-way analyses of variance were used to examine between-group differences on each of the dependent variables. Due to the exploratory nature of the study, and the small sample size ($n = 24$ per group), the .10 probability level was adopted.

Results

Overview

18. The results are presented in the following order: demographic information; personality characteristics; steroid use patterns; steroid users: on-and-off cycle; secondary hypotheses: steroid knowledge and physical characteristics.

Demographic Information

19. The mean age for the user group was 18.6, for the athletic nonuser group 17.9, and for the nonathletic nonweight training group, 15.8. The nonweight training group was significantly younger than the other groups ($F = 39.27$, $p < .0001$). The younger age of the nonathletic group was due to the composition of the health classes from which this group was selected, and was a limitation of the study.

20. The subjects were 63% Hispanic, 1% black, 26% Caucasian, and 10% for other ethnic groups. Except for the percentage of blacks (7%), these totals are representative of the demographics of the metropolitan area within which the study was conducted (Dade County Public Schools, 1990, p. 540). The user group contained the highest percentage of Hispanics, 75%, with the nonathletic group the lowest at 54%.

Personality Characteristics

21. Based on the anecdotal reports and the scant research literature, it was predicted that adolescent steroid users would score significantly higher on the following measures: (1) confidence, (2) forcefulness, (3) body image, (4) self-esteem, (5) short-term mood disturbance. To examine these hypotheses, a series of one-way analyses of variance were conducted.

22. On these a priori hypotheses, a between-group difference was found only on forcefulness ($F(2,68) = 3.083$, $p < .08$), which was significantly higher for steroid users than nonathletes (Fisher Least Significant Difference = 12.905, $p < .05$). The mean score on forcefulness for the athletic nonusers was between that of the steroid users and the nonathletes. Although a strong trend was evident, differences in scores between the athletic users and nonusers were not statistically significant.

23. One-way analysis of variance was used to explore between-group differences on all of the remaining personality and mood variables. Significant between-group differences were found on the following MAPI personality style measures: sexual acceptance ($F(2,68) = 3.083$, $p < .08$), impulsivity ($F(2,68) = 3.248$, $p < .05$), and cooperativeness ($F(2,68) = 2.678$, $p < .08$).

24. For both impulsivity and cooperativeness, comparison of individual group means showed significant differences between steroid users and nonathletes, with steroid users having higher levels of impulsivity (Fisher LSD = 13.687, $p < .05$) and lower levels of cooperativeness (Fisher LSD = 13.552, $p < .05$) than nonathletes. As with forcefulness, the means for impulsivity and cooperativeness for the athletic nonusers were between those of the steroid users and the nonathletes. Although strong trends were evident on both of these variables, the differences between the athletic users and nonusers were not statistically significant.

25. Comparison of individual group means showed that compared to the nonathletes, the athletic nonusers possessed significantly higher levels of personal satisfaction with their sexuality and with their heterosexual relationships than did nonathletes (Fisher LSD = 10.689, $p < .05$).

Steroid Use Patterns

26. Of the 24 users in the sample, 21% ($n = 5$) reported that they were currently on a cycle, 79% ($n = 19$) reported that they were not on a cycle, and 75% of the user group reported that they were either currently stacking or had stacked steroids during previous cycles. Of the five users currently on a cycle, all reported stacking on the current cycle. The mean amount of time for steroid use among the sample was 16.5 months, with a range from 2 to 48 months. The mean amount of time between cycles among steroid users was 4.2 months, with a range from zero to 18 months. Sixty-four percent of the users' steroid dosages were at what has been defined as moderate levels, and 18 percent were at both the low and high levels (Duchaine, 1989; Phillips, 1991). Of the five steroid users who were on a cycle at the time of the study, one was at a low dosage level, three were on a moderate level, and one was at a high level.

27. A total of 16 different steroids were used by the sample. In addition, one diuretic was used in conjunction with one subject's pre-contest preparation. The most commonly used injectable steroid was testosterone cypionate, with 16 subjects either current or past users. The most commonly used oral steroid was Anadrol, with six subjects either current or past users.

Steroid Users: On-Off Cycle

28. A series of two-tailed t tests were conducted to examine differences between users currently on a steroid use cycle and those not currently on a cycle. Users currently on a cycle reported significantly higher levels of depression, anger, and vigor as compared to those not on a cycle ($p < .05$ for all). In addition, total mood disturbance was significantly higher in users currently on a cycle ($p < .10$).

Steroid Knowledge

29. There were significant between-group differences, determined by using one-way analysis of variance, in levels of knowledge about anabolic steroids ($F(2,68) = 69.887$, $p < .0001$), with the steroid users demonstrating significantly higher levels of knowledge about anabolic steroids than did either of the other groups.

Physical Characteristics

30. A series of group mean comparisons were performed to examine differences between steroid users and athletic nonusers. The steroid users had higher levels of bloating, gynecomastia, muscular density and hardness, shrunken testicles, and acne about the face, neck, shoulders, and back ($p < .05$ for all).

Discussion

31. The assessment of personality characteristics revealed that adolescent steroid users had significantly higher levels of forcefulness and impulsiveness and lower levels of cooperativeness than did nonathletes. On each of these measures, the athletes who did not use steroids (i.e., nonusers) scored between the steroid users and the nonathletes. Although strong trends were evident on each of these measures, the differences between the athletes who used steroids and the athletes who did not use steroids were not statistically significant. Thus, based on the present data, adolescent athletes who adopt steroid use appear to be relatively similar to other athletic adolescents in terms of personality. Given the strong trends that were evident, this conclusion merits further investigation with a larger sample.

32. Assessment of mood states revealed that steroid users who were currently on a steroid use cycle had significantly higher levels of depression, anger, vigor, and total mood disturbance than did steroid users who were not currently on a steroid use cycle. These data are consistent with Humbert's (1990) findings, obtained with an adult sample, of greater mood disturbance in steroid users while on a steroid use cycle. These findings have important clinical implications, since many adolescents can be expected to have significant difficulty in coping with such mood states.

33. The measures used to assess knowledge about anabolic steroids clearly differentiated between the three groups, with the user group displaying significantly higher levels of knowledge than did either the athletic nonusers or the nonathletes. Evaluation of the physical symptoms of steroid use also clearly distinguished between steroid users and nonusers. In addition to having higher levels of muscular density and hardness than the nonusers, the steroid users also had significantly higher levels of bloating, gynecomastia, and acne about the face, neck, shoulders, and back. These findings are consistent with previous literature indicating that it is possible for an experienced observer to accurately identify athletes who are steroid users, particularly those who are currently on a steroid use cycle.

34. An important limitation of the current study is that no cause-and-effect conclusions are possible regarding psychological characteristics. Given the cross-sectional nature of the present research, one can only hypothesize as to whether a particular psychological characteristic (e.g., personality style or mood state) predisposes an adolescent athlete to adopt steroid use, whether this characteristic develops only as a result of steroid use, or whether it is merely correlated with another unidentified variable. Cause-and-effect hypotheses regarding psycho-

logical characteristics can be more adequately addressed in prospective, longitudinal research.
35. In the case of adolescent steroid use, this would involve intensively tracking adolescents prior to, during, and after their decision to begin (or refrain from) steroid use. For the research to be generalizable, large numbers of male and female subjects from diverse ethnic and cultural subgroups would need to be studied. In addition to the obvious high costs of such research, long-term tracking of adolescents who are engaging in an illegal behavior will involve surmounting numerous ethical and legal constraints. Although fraught with significant difficulties, prospective longitudinal investigations are clearly needed in order to increase our understanding of this complex phenomenon.

36. In summary, the data did not identify any unique personality characteristics that differentiate athletic adolescents who use steroids from athletic adolescents who do not use steroids. Although steroid use does produce physical effects that are desired by many athletes (e.g., increased muscular hardness and density), the data clearly show many negative physical side effects. Further, while no cause-and-effect conclusions can be drawn, the mood disturbance data indicate that there are some potentially serious negative psychological effects during steroid use cycles.

References

Bohigian, G. M., Estes, E. H., Friedlander, I. R., Kennedy, W. R., Moxley, J. H., Salva, P. H., Scott, W. C., Skom, J. H., Steinhilber, R. M., Strong, J. P., Wagner, H. M., Hendee, W. R., McGivney, W. T., & Proudifit, C. M. (1988). Drug abuse in athletes: Anabolic steroids and human growth hormone. *Journal of the American Medical Association, 259*, 1703-1705.

BonDurant, M. (1991, March). The natural bodybuilder. *Florida Muscle News*, p. 63.

Brower, J. B., Blow, F. C., Beresford, T. P., & Fuelling, C. (1989). Anabolic-androgenic steroid dependence. *Journal of Clinical Psychiatry, 5*, 31-33.

Buckley, W. E., Yesalis, C. E., Friedl, K. E., Anderson, W. A., Streit, A. L., & Wright, J. E. (1988). Estimated prevalence of anabolic steroid use among male high school seniors. *Journal of the American Medical Association, 260*, 3441-3445.

Dade County Public Schools (1990). *County-wide school demographic statistics* (Dade County Public Schools). Miami, FL: Office of Information Services.

Donohoe, T., Blackwell, B., & Johnson, N. (1986). Anabolic steroids. In T. Donohoe & B. Blackwell, (Eds.), *Foul play: Drug abuse in sports* (pp. 38-65). Oxford, U. K.

Duchaine, D. (1989). *Underground steroid handbook*. Venice, CA: HLR Technical Books.

Duda, M. (1988). Gauging steroid use in high school kids. *The Physician and Sports Medicine, 16,* 16-17.

Dunsky, L. (1990, September). Coming clean: Part IV: "Dear Johnny . . ." *Ironman,* pp. 111-112.

Humbert, M. (1990). *Psychological effects of self-administered anabolic steroids on male athletes: Hostility, depression, vigor, fatigue, anxiety and confusion.* Unpublished doctoral dissertation, United States International University, San Diego.

Johnson, N. P., Jay, S., Shoup, B., & Rickert, V. I. (1989). Anabolic steroid use by male adolescents. *Pediatrics, 83,* 921-924.

Johnson, N. P. (1990, March). Steroids: Just the facts. *CAM Magazine,* pp. 27-29.

Lubell, A. (1989). Does steroid abuse cause or excuse violence? *The Physician and Sports Medicine, 17,* 176-185.

McNair, D. M., Lorr, M., & Droppleman, L. F. (1981). *Edits Manual: Profile of Mood States.* San Diego: Educational and Industrial Testing Service.

Millon, T., Green, C. J., & Meagher, R. B. (1982). *Millon Adolescent Personality Inventory.* Minneapolis: National Computer Systems (NCS).

Neff, C. (Ed.). (1990, September). Hooked. *Sports Illustrated,* p. 27.

New law to start. (1991, March). *Miami Herald,* p. 8.

Nideffer, R. M. (1989). Factors contributing to the use of steroids in sports. *Sports Medicine Update, 4,* 15-19.

Nightingale, S. (1986). Illegal marketing of anabolic steroids to enhance performance charged: Letter from the Food and Drug Administration. *Journal of the American Medical Association, 256,* 1851.

Office of the Inspector General (1990). *Adolescent steroid use: A user's perspective* (Draft). Washington, DC: U.S. Government Printing Office.

Pope, H. G., & Katz, D. L. (1988). Affective and psychotic symptoms associated with anabolic steroid use. *American Journal of Psychiatry, 145,* 487-490.

Pope, H. G., & Katz, D. L. (1990). Homicide and near homicide by anabolic steroid users. *Journal of Clinical Psychiatry, 51,* 28-31.

Scott, W. C., Bernstein, S. L., Coble, Y. D., Eisenbrey, A. B., Estes, E. H., Karlan, M. S., Kennedy, W. R., Numann, P. J., Skom, J. H., Steinhilber, R. M., Strong, J. P., Wagner, H. N., Hendee, W. R., McGivney, W. T., & Robertson, J. J. (1990). Medical and nonmedical uses of anabolic-androgenic steroids. *Journal of the American Medical Association, 262,* 2923-2927.

Taylor, W. N. (1985). *Hormonal manipulation: A new era of monstrous athletes.* Jefferson, NC: McFarland and Company.

Tierney, R., McLain, L. G. (1990). The use of anabolic steroids in high school students. *American Journal of the Diseases of Children, 144,* 99-103.

Windsor, R., Dumitru, D. (1989). Prevalence of anabolic steroid use by male and female adolescents. *Medicine and Science in Sports and Exercise, 21,* 494-497.

Yesalis, C. E., Streit, A. L., Vicary, J. R., Friedl, K. E., Brannon, D., & Buckley, W. E. (1989). Anabolic steroid use: Indications of habituation among adolescents. *Journal of Drug Education, 19,* 103-115.

Factual Questions

1. About how many high school students are estimated to use anabolic steroids?

2. What is the definition of *stacking*?

3. The MAPI is geared to what reading level?

4. What is the name of the instrument used to measure transient, fluctuating mood states such as depression-dejection?

5. What is the independent variable?

6. In the Results section, what "limitation" is mentioned by the authors?

7. There was a significant difference on cooperativeness between which two groups?

8. What test of statistical significance was used to test for differences in steroid knowledge?

9. The difference in bloating between steroid users and athletic nonusers was statistically significant at what probability level?

Questions for Discussion

10. In which paragraph is the research purpose most clearly stated?

11. In paragraph 6, the authors state that "Only male subjects were chosen to control for the possible confounding effects of gender." What does the term *confounding* mean in research?

12. Speculate on whether the subjects, especially those using steroids, were honest in their responses.

13. In paragraph 17, the authors identify the *independent* and *dependent* variables. In general, what do these terms mean?

14. What is a *structured interview*? (See paragraph 15.) How is it different from a *semistructured* or *unstructured interview*? What are the advantages and disadvantages of each type?

15. The authors selected the .10 probability level as the level at which they would reject the null hypothesis. (See paragraph 17.)

Based on your reading of other research articles, is this a commonly used level?

16. Why is it desirable for the three groups to be similar in their demographics?

17. Of the 24 steroid users, 5 were on a cycle. Would it be desirable to study a larger sample of those on a cycle? Explain.

18. Because there were three groups, three types of differences were examined in the Results section: differences between (1) athletic steroid users and athletic nonusers, (2) athletic steroid users and nonathletic nonusers, and (3) athletic nonusers and nonathletic nonusers. In your opinion, which of the three types is most important for understanding steroid use?

19. Do you agree with the authors that no cause-and-effect conclusions are possible based on this study? (See paragraph 34.) Explain.

20. Would it be possible to conduct a true experiment on the effects of steroid use? Explain. (Note: In a true experiment, subjects are assigned at random to experimental treatment and control conditions.)

21. If you had major funding to conduct a similar study, what changes, if any, would you make in the research methodology?

Quality Ratings

DIRECTIONS: Indicate your level of agreement with each of the following statements by circling a number from 5 for strongly agree (SA) to 1 for strongly disagree (SD). If you believe that an item is not applicable to this research article, leave it blank. Be prepared to explain your ratings.

A. The introduction establishes the importance of the research topic.

SA   5   4   3   2   1   SD

B. The literature review establishes the context for the study.

SA   5   4   3   2   1   SD

C. The research purpose, question, or hypothesis is clearly stated.

SA   5   4   3   2   1   SD

D. The method of sampling is sound.

SA   5   4   3   2   1   SD

E. Relevant demographics (for example, age, gender, and ethnicity) are described.

    SA   5   4   3   2   1   SD

F. Measurement procedures are adequate.

    SA   5   4   3   2   1   SD

G. The results are clearly described.

    SA   5   4   3   2   1   SD

H. The discussion/conclusion is appropriate.

    SA   5   4   3   2   1   SD

I. Despite any flaws noted above, the report is worthy of publication.

    SA   5   4   3   2   1   SD

ARTICLE 22

THE INFLUENCE OF MISOGYNOUS RAP MUSIC ON SEXUAL AGGRESSION AGAINST WOMEN

Christy Barongan *Kent State University*
Gordon C. Nagayama Hall *Kent State University*

The purpose of this study was to determine the effects of cognitive distortions concerning women on sexually aggressive behavior in the laboratory. Twenty-seven men listened to misogynous rap music and 27 men listened to neutral rap music. Participants then viewed neutral, sexual-violent, and assaultive film vignettes and chose one of the vignettes to show to a female confederate. Among the participants in the misogynous music condition, 30% showed the assaultive vignette and 70% showed the neutral vignette. In the neutral condition, 7% showed the sexual-violent or assaultive vignette and 93% showed the neutral vignette. Participants who showed the sexual-violent or assaultive stimuli reported that the confederate was more upset and uncomfortable in viewing these stimuli than did participants who showed the neutral vignette. These findings suggest that misogynous music facilitates sexually aggressive behavior and support the relationship between cognitive distortions and sexual aggression.

1. Misogynous messages are common in the media. Such messages are particularly common in pornography, which may contribute to negative attitudes and behaviors toward women (Brownmiller, 1975). Pornography has been defined in numerous ways, ranging from sexually explicit materials to any materials that encourage sexually abusive and degrading treatment of women (Mayerson & Taylor, 1987). The subject of such pornographic materials often involves the domination and objectification of women. Often women are depicted as being useful solely for the purpose of men's sexual gratification, which can involve both rape and violence. Pornography often portrays violence against women as being justified, positive, and sexually liberating (Linz, 1989).

2. Pornographic and other misogynous media depictions may lead some men to believe that their own sexual aggression against women is justified (Hall & Hirschman, 1991). Because the media often portray rape as being enjoyable to the victim, some men may not view their sexually aggressive behavior as offensive or harmful to the victim. Moreover, because misogynous media depictions are relatively common, some men may infer that sexually aggressive behavior is sanctioned by society and is not deviant (Hall & Hirschman, 1991). Such cognitive distortions concerning sexually aggressive behavior are particularly relevant in situations of acquaintance rape, which often occurs in college populations and may be the most common form of sexual aggression (Koss, 1985; Yegidis, 1986; Koss, Gidycz, & Wisniewski, 1987).

3. Russell (1993) offers a causal model that describes the way in which pornography can induce men to rape women. According to this theory, pornography can (a) make some men who may not have initially wished to do so want to rape women, as well as intensify a predisposition to rape women; (b) undermine some men's internal inhibitions against actually raping a woman, and (c) undermine some men's external or social inhibitions against actually raping a woman (p. 126).

4. Empirical research suggests that pornography can have a negative impact on men's attitudes and behavior toward women. Sommers and Check (1987) found that partners of battered women read or viewed more pornographic materials than did partners of nonabused women. Also, a significantly greater percentage of battered women than nonabused women reported that their partner had upset them in the past by trying to get them to do what their partners had seen in pornographic pictures, movies, or books. Marshall (1988) found that rapists and nonincestual child molesters used sexually explicit materials (magazines, films, videotapes) more often than did incest offenders or nonoffender controls. Rapists and child molesters also reported using these materials frequently while preparing to commit an offense. However, both of these studies were correlational and do not demonstrate that pornography causes aggression.

5. Pornography has been found to lead to negative attitudes toward women in studies in which exposure to pornographic materials was manipulated. Men who are exposed to films portraying positive effects of sexual aggression show an increased acceptance of interpersonal violence against women, such as sexual aggression and wife battering (Malamuth & Briere, 1986). Even when participants are exposed to nonviolent pornography, they report less support for the women's movement and more sexual callousness toward women than those who are not exposed to nonviolent pornography (Zillmann & Bryant, 1982).

6. Exposure to pornography has also been related to beliefs in rape myths. Malamuth and Check (1985) found that men who read sexually explicit magazines were also more likely to believe that women enjoy forced sex than men who did not read such magazines. Depictions that suggest that rape results in the victim's arousal made this rape myth more believable, especially to men with higher inclinations to aggress against women. Thus, some men may be more affected by pornography than others, particularly those who are predisposed to aggression.

7. Although extensive research has been conducted on pornographic materials, such as movies and magazines, limited research has been conducted on music that may qualify as pornographic. Some musical lyrics express negative and sexist attitudes about women that are very similar to the messages found in pornographic movies and magazines, including the idea that coercive sexual activity is enjoyable for women. Although albums that contain such lyrics may display a warning that some of the

Barongan, C., & Hall, G. C. N. (1995). The influence of misogynous rap music on sexual aggression against women. *Psychology of Women Quarterly, 19*, 195-207. Copyright © 1995 by Cambridge University Press. Reprinted with permission of Cambridge University Press.

This work is based on a master's thesis conducted by Christy Barongan under the direction of Gordon C. Nagayama Hall. We thank Mike Foster for helping conduct the experiment.

Address correspondence and reprint requests to: Gordon C. Nagayama Hall, Department of Psychology, Kent State University, Kent, OH 44242-0001.

lyrics may be offensive, these albums are commercially available to anyone. Pornographic movies and magazines, on the other hand, can only be purchased or viewed by those who are at least 18 years of age. The difference in the availability of these types of materials suggests that pornographic music is not considered detrimental in fostering negative attitudes and behavior toward women.

8.   There is some evidence to suggest that viewing rock videos has the same effect as viewing pornography in that men who were shown violent rock videos expressed more calloused and antagonistic attitudes toward women than did men who were shown nonviolent rock videos (Peterson & Pfost, 1989). Lawrence and Joyner (1991) found that exposure to heavy-metal rock music, irrespective of lyrical content, increased men's sex-role stereotyping and negative attitudes toward women. However, one limitation of this study is that the lyrics in the heavy-metal rock music were difficult to discern.

9.   To our knowledge, there have been no previous studies of the lyrical content of rap music, although this type of music is gaining considerable popularity. Unlike heavy-metal or rock music in which the lyrics may not be emphasized, rap music is unique in that the lyrics are the focus of attention. Thus, it is possible that the content of rap music may play a more important role in influencing its listeners than other forms of contemporary music. Men and women alike may begin to accept the negative messages these songs present concerning women's lack of worth.

10.   The previously reviewed studies on pornography have relied on self-report measures. However, self-report of past or potential sexually aggressive behavior is not necessarily predictive of an individual's behavior in any particular context, and self-report does not allow the direct observation of aggressive behavior (Hall & Hirschman, 1993). Laboratory paradigms are an alternative method of assessment that allow direct observation of aggressive behavior.

11.   Laboratory paradigms of physical aggression have been adapted for the study of sexual aggression by examining men's willingness to aggress against women. Aggression in the form of laboratory shock against a woman modeled by a male confederate has been shown to increase men's administration of shock against a female confederate (Donnerstein & Hallam, 1978). Attitudinal acceptance of violence toward women has been consistently associated with men's laboratory punishment of women (Malamuth, 1983, 1988; Malamuth & Ceniti, 1986). Sexist attitudes in general (e.g., women

should be subservient to men) were associated with laboratory aggression against women in one study (Malamuth, 1988), but not in another (Donnerstein & Hallam, 1978). Exposure to sexually explicit films also has not generally affected laboratory aggression against women (Donnerstein & Hallam, 1978; Malamuth & Ceniti, 1986). Sexually explicit films, however, do appear to facilitate more laboratory aggression against women when angered participants are provided with repeated opportunities to be aggressive (Donnerstein & Hallam, 1978) or when women are depicted as enjoying pornography (Leonard & Taylor, 1983). Violent pornography, however, appears to facilitate laboratory aggression against women even when men are not angered (Donnerstein, 1980; Donnerstein & Berkowitz, 1981). Although the delivery of shock or another aversive stimulus to a subject may constitute an analog of physical aggression, it may not be analogous to sexual aggression (Hall & Hirschman, 1993; Hall & Hirschman, 1994; Hall, Hirschman, & Oliver, 1994).

12.   This study attempts to determine whether or not listening to misogynous rap music has negative consequences for women by using the laboratory analog of sexual aggression developed by Hall and Hirschman (1993). Because most forms of sexual aggression involve acts in which the men are the perpetrators and the women are the victims, this study focuses solely on the effects of misogynous rap music on men. The definition of sexual aggression used in this study is similar to the definition used by Hall and Hirschman (1993). In their definition, sexual aggression is defined broadly, ranging from sexually impositional acts such as telling a sexually oriented joke to someone who finds such jokes offensive to extreme forms of sexual aggression like rape. Although the sexual aggression that one would expect in the current study would fall at the mild range of the continuum, it is nevertheless an important aspect of sexual aggression because of its negative impact on women. In this study, it is predicted that men who are exposed to misogynous rap music will be more likely to show a woman a misogynous vignette that involves either physical aggression or rape than men who are exposed to neutral rap music. The act of showing such a misogynous vignette is considered to be an act of sexual imposition, both because of the content of the stimulus and because participants who show such misogynous vignettes perceive the women as being upset and uncomfortable with the vignettes (Hall & Hirschman, 1994).

Method

Participants

13.   Fifty-four college men volunteered to participate in this experiment as part of a course requirement for general psychology. Recruitment of participants was based on a voluntary sign-up sheet that contained a brief description of the study. Participants who chose to participate were randomly assigned to control or misogynous music conditions. Twenty-seven participants in the control condition were exposed to neutral rap music and 27 participants were exposed to misogynous rap music. Of the 54 participants, 6 were African American, and 2 were Asian American.

Procedure

14.   A female graduate student was the experimenter for 34 participants. Eighteen participants were in the misogynous music condition, and 16 participants were in the neutral music condition. A male graduate student was the experimenter for 20 participants. Nine participants were in the misogynous music condition and 11 participants were in the control condition. The use of the male and female experimenters was not counterbalanced with the experimental conditions. Participants were told that the purpose of the experiment was to determine their attitudes toward themes in the media and that the experiment involved listening to music and watching video clips. They were informed that they would be viewing materials that contained sexually explicit and violent subject matter that might be arousing or upsetting. Participants were assured of anonymity and given an opportunity to withdraw from the experiment at any time without penalty. All participants agreed to participate.

15.   Participants first listened to four rap songs that they rated on a 5-point Likert Scale (1 = *strongly dislike*, 2 = *dislike*, 3 = *neutral*, 4 = *like*, 5 = *strongly like*). The ratings served to ensure that participants listened to each song. In the control condition the four songs were: (a) "Brothers Gonna Work It Out" — Public Enemy; (b) "The Nation's Anthem" — Poor Righteous Teachers; (c) "Pure Poverty" — Poor Righteous Teachers; and (d) "Nighttrain" — Public Enemy. The rap songs in this group contained no references to sex or violence and were primarily concerned with the problems of social injustice facing African Americans in America. Examples of lyrics from these songs are: "Each and every day . . . I'm gonna show and prove and teach the righteous way. The knowledge is the foundation, the wisdom is the way." The total time for the neutral rap songs was 17:02 min.

16. In the misogynous condition, participants listened to four rap songs that contained frequent references to both sex and violence. These songs often referred to women as "bitches" and "hoes" and suggested that women enjoy coercive sex. The songs in this group were: (a) "Mo' Pussy"—DJ Quik; (b) "Just Ain't Me"—2nd II None; (c) "One Less Bitch"—NWA; and (d) "She Swallowed It"—NWA. Examples of lyrics from these songs are: "I can't take no for an answer baby, it just ain't me," " . . . ho's like you, you only come a dime a dozen," and "the bitch tried to gank me so I had to kill her . . . loaded up the .44 . . . and smoked the ho." The total time for the misogynous rap songs was 16:30 min.

17. After listening to the rap music, participants were shown three 2 min vignettes from the film *I Spit On Your Grave.* The neutral vignette involved a neutral conversation between a man and a woman (neutral stimulus). The sexual-violent vignette consisted of a man who rips off a woman's clothes and rapes the woman with the help of several other men (sexual-violent stimulus). The assaultive vignette consists of a man physically aggressing against a seminude woman (e.g., hitting, shoving, throwing furniture at her) and calling her names (e.g., bitch) while other men watch (assaultive stimulus).

18. After they viewed all three vignettes, participants chose one of the vignettes that they would like to show to one of two undergraduate women who volunteered to serve as confederates. Participants were told that the confederate was another female student participating in the experiment. The confederate then entered the room, and the participants showed her their chosen film vignette. Participants were required to show the vignette to the confederate in order to examine their actual film-showing behavior rather than their self-report of what they would do in this situation.

19. The confederates had been instructed not to react to the film vignettes shown to them. Before participating in the study, confederates were given the opportunity to view the vignettes before deciding whether or not they wanted to participate in the experiment. Repeated efforts were also made by the authors to ensure that the confederates felt comfortable viewing the vignettes by asking them if they were comfortable playing the role of the confederate and by giving them the opportunity to discontinue the study if they were not comfortable. No confederate chose to withdraw from the experiment.

20. This measure of sexual aggression has been demonstrated to have internal validity in that men who showed the sexual-violent or assaultive vignette believed that the woman who viewed the vignette was more upset and uncomfortable with their selection (Hall & Hirschman, 1994). This finding supports the idea that showing a woman one of the sexually aggressive vignettes is a sexually impositional or sexually aggressive act. Also, men who admitted to "real life" sexually aggressive acts were more likely to show either the sexual-violent or the assaultive vignette than men who denied being sexually coercive, which is evidence of external validity for this film-showing procedure (Hall & Hirschman, 1994).

21. After participants had shown the film vignette, the experimenter reentered the room and had participants complete questionnaires on the music and video clips that they had watched. The music questionnaire consisted of a 5-point Likert scale that assessed how discomforting the music was (1 = *very uncomfortable* to 5 = *very comfortable*), open-ended questions regarding how often participants had listened to similar music in the past and the theme of the music to determine the subjects' comprehension of the lyrics. The video questionnaire consisted of a 5-point Likert scale that assessed how participants perceived the other student's (confederate's) reaction to the clip they chose (1 = *extremely upset* to 5 = *extremely happy*) and how comfortable they thought the other student was (1 = *extremely uncomfortable* to 5 = *extremely comfortable*) in viewing the clip they selected. Participants also described in writing why they chose a particular film clip.

22. At the end of the study, the experimenter gave participants a copy of the Check and Malamuth (1984) debriefing statement, which has had an educational impact upon participants' attitudes toward rape in studies employing pornographic rape depictions (Check & Malamuth, 1984). Participants were also asked to attend a delayed debriefing at the end of the semester, at which time they would be told that the other student was a confederate working for the experimenter. Participants were not told, however, that showing the sexual-violent and assaultive vignettes was considered a sexually impositional act because such an explanation would have implied that those who chose one of those vignettes were engaging in a socially undesirable behavior.

Results

23. A chi-square analysis revealed no significant differences in film showing between the participants who had the female experimenter versus the male experimenter, chi square (l) = .26, (p = .61). This finding indicates that the gender of the experimenter did not contribute significantly to which vignette participants chose to show to the confederate.

24. There was no significant difference in liking of the music between participants who chose to show the misogynous (*M* = 2.70, *SD* = 1.34) versus the neutral vignette (*M* = 2.77, *SD* = 1.11), *t*(51) = .17, *p* = .87. This finding indicates that how much participants liked the music did not significantly contribute to which vignette they showed to the confederate.

25. Of the participants in the misogynous music condition, 23 indicated that the music contained references to sex, and 4 indicated the music contained references to both sex and violence. Of the participants in the neutral music

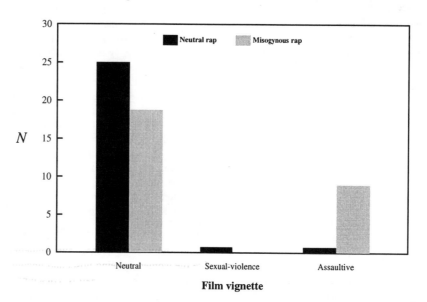

Figure 1 *Film vignette showing as a function of music condition.*

condition, 23 of the 27 correctly identified the theme of the music. The remaining 4 participants identified the neutral music as having references to sex and/or violence.

26. Overall, 19% of all men showed a sexual-violent or assaultive film vignette to a woman. The frequency of film vignette showing as a function of music condition is presented in Figure 1. The percentage of participants in the misogynous music condition who showed the assaultive vignette (30%) was significantly greater than the percentage of participants in the neutral music condition who showed either the sexual-violent or assaultive vignettes (7%), chi square (1) = 4.42, (p < .05). Of the four participants who thought the misogynous music contained both sex and violence, two showed the neutral vignette and two showed the assaultive vignette. The four participants who misidentified the neutral music as having references to sex and/or violence all showed the neutral vignette.

27. The participants who showed the sexual-violent or assaultive vignettes reported that the confederate was significantly more upset by the vignette (M = 2.10, SD = 0.74) than did those participants who showed the neutral vignette (M = 3.27, SD = 0.45), t(52) = 6.54, p < .0005. Participants who showed the sexual-violent or assaultive vignettes also reported that the confederate was significantly less comfortable in viewing the vignette (M = 2.20, SD = 0.92) than did participants who showed the neutral vignette (M = 3.82, SD = 1.04), t(52) = 4.53, p < .0005.

28. Among the participants who showed the sexual-violent or assaultive vignettes, four chose the vignette because it contained sex and/or violence, three stated that the first vignette was too boring and the second vignette was too upsetting to show, and one chose the vignette because he wanted to see the other subject's reaction. One subject in the neutral music condition and one subject in the misogynous music condition stated that they chose the assaultive vignette because it was the only one in which the woman had a chance to fight back.

Discussion

29. As hypothesized, a significantly greater proportion of men showed a sexually aggressive film vignette to a woman after hearing misogynous rap music than did men who heard neutral rap music. This finding suggests that misogynous music facilitates sexually aggressive behavior in the laboratory and lends support to the relationship between cognitive distortions and sexually aggressive behavior (Hall & Hirschman, 1991).

30. Despite the confederates not reacting to either of the film vignettes, participants perceived the confederates who viewed either the assaultive or sexual-violent vignettes as more upset and uncomfortable than the confederates who viewed the neutral vignette. This finding is consistent with that of Hall and Hirschman (1994) and suggests that the assaultive and sexual-violent vignettes are considered by participants as harmful to the confederate. Thus, to the extent that the presentation of sexual-violent or assaultive material is perceived as harmful to the confederate, presentation of such material constitutes a sexually aggressive act. Participants offered various reasons for showing the sexual-violent or assaultive vignettes to the confederate that were not necessarily aggressive (e.g., personal preference, to see the confederate's reaction, the woman in the vignette had a chance to fight back), but by showing the vignettes, these participants disregarded their own perceptions that the sexual-violent and assaultive vignettes were harmful to the confederate.

31. One interpretation rivaling the previous one is that the confederates did actually appear more upset and uncomfortable viewing the sexual-violent and assaultive vignettes, and consequently, the participants were rating the response of the confederate correctly. Although this possibility cannot be ruled out completely because the responses of the confederates were not taped and rated independently, confederates were given explicit instructions not to respond to any of the videos, and experimenters observed the confederate and participant through a one-way mirror.

32. Another rival interpretation is that participants who showed a sexual-violent or assaultive vignette may not have intended to upset the confederate, even though they believed afterwards that their choice was upsetting to the confederate. Hall and Hirschman (1993) argued, however, that the negative consequences of the behavior to the recipient is what makes showing such a vignette a sexually imposing act rather than the intention of the participant per se. They also pointed out that perpetrators of sexual aggression often claim an innocent intent (e.g., raping a woman will be good for her) or believe that their behavior is a function of extrinsic factors (e.g., most people are not offended by a sexually oriented joke; Hall & Hirschman, 1994).

33. This study is an improvement over previous research because the content of the lyrics was discernible. Only a minority of the participants misidentified the theme of the music in the neutral music condition, and all participants correctly identified the theme of the music in the misogynous music condition. The fact that

all the participants did not correctly identify the theme of the music still remains a problem, however. Those participants who misidentified the neutral rap music as involving either sex or violence may have not been listening to the lyrics, may not have understood the lyrics, and/or may have assumed that all rap music involves references to either sex or violence. Nevertheless, most of the participants could understand the lyrics; thus, it appears that the difference in sexually aggressive behavior between music conditions was a function of the content of the lyrics.

34. The current results suggest that misogynous rap music had a priming effect on the participants' film-showing behavior, perhaps because the assaultive film was an audiovisual representation of the misogynous rap lyrics. It appears that the presentation of misogynous rap music conveyed the cognitive distortion that violence toward women is acceptable in that it is being portrayed as acceptable in the media. Moreover, because misogynous rap music is not restricted as other pornographic materials are, it is more readily available to a wider audience, and the availability of rap music may make the cognitive distortions conveyed in the lyrics more acceptable to its listeners. It does not appear that general arousal created by rap music was a major instigator of sexually aggressive behavior, in that only 2 of the 27 participants who listened to neutral rap music presented a sexual-violent or assaultive vignette to the confederate. Although it is possible that the misogynous music evoked anger toward women, it is unlikely that participants highly susceptible to anger provocation would be represented in a college population in which self-control and conformity are highly valued (Hall & Hirschman, 1991; Sears, 1986). Another possible motivational mechanism could be sexual arousal elicited by the misogynous rap music. However, high levels of sexual arousal in response to violence toward women is uncommon among college students (Malamuth, 1986) and even among many convicted rapists (Hall, 1989). Nevertheless, the motivational mechanisms in the influence of misogynous rap music on laboratory sexual aggression toward women warrant additional investigation.

35. An unexpected finding in this study was that all the participants in the misogynous music condition who showed a sexually aggressive vignette chose the assaultive vignette. One possible explanation is that the participants believed that choosing the assaultive vignette was more socially desirable than choosing the sexual-violent vignette because media portrayals of violence are more common than portrayals of rape. Hall and Hirschman (1994) found

that 50% of the participants who showed the assaultive vignette did so because they believed that this vignette was less upsetting or offensive than the sexual-violent vignette. However, only one third of the current participants who chose to show the assaultive vignette considered the sexual-violent vignette too upsetting to show. Another possible explanation is that participants who listened to the misogynous music may have perceived it to be more degrading toward women than sexually violent. Therefore, the misogynous music may have aroused more aggressive motives in these men than sexually aggressive motives per se, and the assaultive vignette was chosen because it corresponded more closely to the misogynous music than did the sexual-violent vignette.

36. A potential criticism of this study is its use of a college sample. However, a college sample is appropriate because the most common forms of sexual aggression occur in college populations (Koss et al., 1987), and college students may be particularly susceptible to cognitive distortions concerning sexually aggressive behavior (Hall & Hirschman, 1991). Nevertheless, a larger sample of younger, less educated participants may be of interest because the content of the lyrics may be even more influential for these persons. Adolescent participants may be of particular interest because they are more likely to perceive rap artists as role models, and consequently, they may be more likely to believe the artists' messages concerning women. Russell (1993) argued that children may be more susceptible to imitating the acts suggested in pornography than are adults, which lends further support to the importance of examining the effects of misogynous rap music on a younger population.

37. Another limitation of this study is that it only examined the negative consequences of misogynous rap music on men. It is also likely that there are negative consequences for women. Perhaps women who are exposed to misogynous rap music are more likely to have a lower self-image or lower self-esteem than women who are not exposed to such music. Russell (1993) argued that one of the negative consequences of pornography is that it makes women more vulnerable to sexual assault because women exposed to such materials are more likely to believe that such acts are normative and are more likely to feel obligated to perform such acts.

38. Another potential criticism is that sexually aggressive vignette showing could be explained by an overrepresentation in the misogynous music condition of men who were predisposed to aggressive behavior. However, participants in this study were randomly assigned to music

conditions. In a study in which men were pre-selected for sexually aggressive behavior, Hall and Hirschman (1994) found that 52% of highly sexually coercive men showed a sexually aggressive vignette, whereas only 7.7 % of men who were not sexually coercive showed a sexually aggressive vignette. In the current study, the percentage of men who showed a sexually aggressive vignette lies between these two figures (19%), which suggests that the current results were not a function of sampling error.

39. It is unknown if the sexually aggressive behavior investigated in the current experiment is predictive of sexually aggressive behavior outside the laboratory context. In a sample of men selected for extreme levels of sexually coercive and noncoercive behavior in "real-life" settings, 90% of the men who showed the sexual-violent or assaultive vignettes had been sexually aggressive in real-life settings (Hall & Hirschman, 1994). The predictive validity of this laboratory paradigm remains to be investigated. However, the purpose of the current study was to investigate basic motivational processes in sexually aggressive behavior, and the current results suggest that cognitive distortions concerning women facilitate men's sexual aggression toward women. These results also suggest that the potential detrimental effect that musical lyrics can have on men's behavior toward women needs to be taken more seriously than in the past.

40. Although this study contributes significantly to our understanding of the way in which misogynous rap music can affect men's behavior, many questions remain unanswered. Other variables such as the frequency of exposure to misogynous rap music, predisposition to be aggressive, and attitudes concerning violence against women may play an important role in contributing to the negative effects of misogynous rap music. Furthermore, more research on the validity of the laboratory analog to sexual aggression used in this study is needed. For example, would men be equally likely to show an assaultive or sexual-violent vignette to another man? If so, would they believe that showing such a vignette would be equally upsetting to a male confederate? Also, would participants rate other offensive scenes that are not necessarily sexual or aggressive as being upsetting to the confederate? Studies that examine these questions could potentially lend greater support to the idea that this laboratory analog is, indeed, analogous to sexual aggression.

First draft received: April 25, 1994
Final draft received: November 4, 1994

References

Brownmiller, S. (1975). *Against our will: Men, women, and rape.* New York: Simon & Schuster.

Check, J. V. P., & Malamuth, N. M. (1984). Can there be positive effects of participation in pornography experiments? *Journal of Sex Research, 20,* 14-31.

Donnerstein, E. (1980). Aggressive erotica and violence against women. *Journal of Personality and Social Psychology, 39,* 269-277.

Donnerstein, E., & Berkowitz, L. (1981). Victim reactions in aggressive erotic films as a factor in violence against women. *Journal of Personality and Social Psychology, 41,* 710-724.

Donnerstein, E., & Hallam, J. (1978). Facilitating effects of erotica on aggression against women. *Journal of Personality and Social Psychology, 36,* 1270-1277.

Hall, G. C. N. (1989). Sexual arousal and arousability in a sexual offender population. *Journal of Abnormal Psychology, 98,* 145-149.

Hall, G. C. N., & Hirschman, R. (1991). Toward a theory of sexual aggression: A quadripartite model. *Journal of Consulting and Clinical Psychology, 59,* 662-669.

Hall, G. C. N., & Hirschman, R. (1993). Use of a new laboratory methodology to conceptualize sexual aggression. In G. C. N. Hall, R. Hirschman, J. R. Graham, & M. S. Zaragoza (Eds.), *Sexual aggression: Issues in etiology, assessment, and treatment* (pp. 115-132). Washington, DC: Taylor & Francis.

Hall, G. C. N., & Hirschman, R. (1994). The relationship between men's sexual aggression inside and outside the laboratory. *Journal of Consulting and Clinical Psychology, 62,* 375-380.

Hall, G. C. N., Hirschman, R., & Oliver, L. L. (1994). Ignoring a woman's dislike of sexual material: Sexually impositional behavior in the laboratory. *Journal of Sex Research, 31,* 3-10.

Koss, M. P. (1985). The hidden rape victim: Personality attitudes and situational characteristics. *Psychology of Women Quarterly, 9,* 193-212.

Koss, M. P., Gidycz, C. A., & Wisniewski, N. (1987). The scope of rape: Incidence and prevalence of sexual aggression and victimization in a national sample of higher education students. *Journal of Consulting and Clinical Psychology, 55,* 162-170.

Lawrence, J. S. S., & Joyner, D. J. (1991) . The effects of sexually violent rock music on males' acceptance of violence against women. *Psychology of Women Quarterly, 15,* 49-63.

Leonard, K. E., & Taylor, S. P. (1983). Exposure to pornography, permissive and nonpermissive cues, and male aggression toward females. *Motivation and Emotion, 7,* 291-299.

Linz, D. G. (1989). Exposure to sexually explicit materials and attitudes toward rape: A comparison of study results. *Journal of Sex Research, 26,* 50-84.

Malamuth, N. M. (1983). Factors associated with rape as predictors of laboratory aggression against women. *Journal of Personality and Social Psychology, 45,* 432-442.

Malamuth, N. M. (1986). Predictors of naturalistic sexual aggression. *Journal of Personality and Social Psychology, 50,* 953-962.

Malamuth, N. M. (1988). Predicting laboratory aggression against female and male targets: Implications for sexual aggression. *Journal of Research in Personality, 22,* 474-495.

Malamuth, N. M., & Briere, J. (1986). Sexual violence in the media: Indirect effects on aggression against women. *Journal of Social Issues, 42,* 75-92.

Malamuth, N. M., & Ceniti, J. (1986). Repeated exposure to violent and nonviolent pornography: Likelihood of raping ratings and laboratory aggression against women. *Aggressive Behavior, 12,* 129-137.

Malamuth, N. M., & Check, J. V. P. (1985). The effects of aggressive pornography on beliefs in rape myths: Individual differences. *Journal of Research in Personality, 19,* 299-320.

Marshall, W. L. (1988). The use of sexually explicit stimuli by rapists, child molesters, and nonoffenders. *Journal of Sex Research, 25,* 267-288.

Mayerson, S. E., & Taylor, D. A. (1987). The effects of rape myth pornography on women's attitudes and the mediating role of sex role stereotyping. *Sex Roles, 17,* 321-338.

Peterson, D. L., & Pfost, K. S. (1989). Influence of rock videos on attitudes of violence against women. *Psychological Reports, 64,* 319-322.

Russell, D. E. H. (1993). Pornography and rape: A causal model. In D. E. H. Russell (Ed.), *Making violence sexy: Feminist views on pornography* (pp. 120-150). New York: Teachers College Press.

Sears, D. O. (1986). College sophomores in the laboratory: Influences of a narrow data base on social psychology's views of human nature. *Journal of Personality and Social Psychology, 51,* 515-530.

Sommers, E. K., & Check, J. V. (1987). An empirical investigation of the role of pornography in the verbal and physical abuse of women. *Violence and Victims, 2,* 189-209.

Yegidis, B. L. (1986). Date rape and other forced sexual encounters among college students. *Journal of Sex Education and Therapy, 12,* 51-54.

Zillmann, D., & Bryant, J. (1982). Pornography, sexual callousness, and the trivialization of rape. *Journal of Communication, 32,* 10-21.

Factual Questions

1. According to the researchers, why do the studies cited in paragraph 4 fail to demonstrate that pornography causes aggression?

2. What is the researchers' criticism of self-report measures used in previous studies?

3. How were the subjects recruited?

4. On what basis were the volunteers assigned to experimental and control conditions?

5. Why did the researchers ask the participants to describe the theme of the music they listened to?

6. What is the name of the significance test used in paragraph 23?

7. What is the name of the significance test used in paragraph 24?

8. Is the probability yielded by the significance test in paragraph 24 greater than or less than .05?

9. How did the researchers gather evidence on whether the confederates did not actually appear more upset when viewing the sexual-violent and assaultive vignettes than when viewing the neutral ones?

Questions for Discussion

10. In your opinion, is the "prediction" in paragraph 12 a research hypothesis?

11. The title indicates that the dependent variable is sexual aggression. In paragraph 12 it is operationalized (that is, cast into physical, behavioral terms) as a man showing "a woman a misogynous vignette that involves either physical aggression or rape." The operationalization is also discussed in paragraph 30. What is your opinion on how it was operationalized?

12. Was it a good idea to allow participants to withdraw from the study at any time without penalty? Explain.

13. Are the treatments described in sufficient detail? (See paragraphs 14 through 19.) Explain.

14. In light of the context in paragraphs 18 and 19, what do the researchers mean by the term "confederate"?

15. Do you agree with the researchers' decision not to tell the participants during debriefing that showing the sexual-violent and assaultive vignettes was considered a sexual imposition? Explain.

16. What is your opinion on the use of a college sample for a study of this type? (See paragraph 36.)

17. The authors frequently mention that the study was conducted in a laboratory setting. For example, see paragraph 39. Are there advantages and disadvantages to conducting this study in a laboratory? Explain.

18. Are any of the unanswered questions in paragraph 40 especially interesting to you? Explain.

Quality Ratings

DIRECTIONS: Indicate your level of agreement with each of the following statements by circling a number from 5 for strongly agree (SA) to 1 for strongly disagree (SD). If you believe that an item is not applicable to this research article, leave it blank. Be prepared to explain your ratings.

A. The introduction establishes the importance of the research topic.
   SA   5   4   3   2   1   SD

B. The literature review establishes the context for the study.
   SA   5   4   3   2   1   SD

C. The research purpose, question, or hypothesis is clearly stated.
   SA   5   4   3   2   1   SD

D. The method of sampling is sound.
   SA   5   4   3   2   1   SD

E. Relevant demographics (for example, age, gender, and ethnicity) are described.
   SA   5   4   3   2   1   SD

F. Measurement procedures are adequate.
   SA   5   4   3   2   1   SD

G. The results are clearly described.
   SA   5   4   3   2   1   SD

H. The discussion/conclusion is appropriate.
   SA   5   4   3   2   1   SD

I. Despite any flaws noted above, the report is worthy of publication.
   SA   5   4   3   2   1   SD

THE EFFECT OF RAPE TYPE AND INFORMATION ADMISSIBILITY ON PERCEPTIONS OF RAPE VICTIMS

James D. Johnson *University of North Carolina at Wilmington*

An experiment was conducted to assess whether the judgmental effects of inadmissible evidence would vary as a function of type of rape. Subjects (predominantly Caucasian) read rape scenarios that depicted either an acquaintance rape or a stranger rape, which contained information implying that the victim had a promiscuous serial history. In one condition, subjects were instructed to disregard this information (inadmissible condition), while in the other condition, subjects received no such instructions (admissible condition). The results indicated that (1) males perceived that there was a higher probability of victim enjoyment than females, (2) perceptions of those in the admissible condition were less favorable than those in the inadmissible condition, and (3) perceptions of those in the acquaintance rape conditions were less favorable than those in the stranger rape condition. The results also indicated that perceptions of the probability of victim enjoyment did not vary as a function of type of rape when the information was admissible. On the other hand, when the information was inadmissible, perceptions of the probability of victim enjoyment in the acquaintance rape conditions were higher than those in the stranger rape condition. The possible bases of these findings are discussed.

1. Social scientists have focused extensively on factors which affect juror decision making (Hans & Vidmar, 1986; Hastie, Penrod, & Pennington, 1983; Pfeifer & Ogloff, 1991; Wiener, Habert, Shkodriani, & Staebler, 1991). One line of research in this area involves the effects of exposure to inadmissible information on judicial judgments. In earlier research, Sue, Smith, and Caldwell (1973) demonstrated that evidence ruled inadmissible did affect final judgments of the jurors, especially when other evidence was weak. Subsequently, research by Wolf and Montgomery (1977) indicated that strong admonishment by a judge in his instructions to disregard certain information actually tended to increase the use of such information. They accounted for these counterintuitive, albeit interesting findings with a reactance explanation. Additionally, research has indicated that

judicial decisions are also affected by inadmissible information that originated outside of the courtroom situation. To amplify, Green and Russel (1988) showed that exposure to newspaper articles focusing on court cases similar to the relevant case tended to affect subjects' judgments.

2. One shortcoming of the research presented above involves the fact that it only assesses the judgmental consequences of exposure to inadmissible evidence regarding the defendant. Indeed, there are situations in which the jurors are exposed to inadmissible evidence regarding the victim. Rape victim advocates have often expressed concern over the possibility of detrimental information involving the accuser's sexual past being "slipped in" by rape defendant attorneys. Furthermore, jurors may be exposed to information regarding the victim's sexual past due to factors such as pretrial publicity, which has been clearly shown to have a profound effect on juror decision making (Moran & Cutler, 1991). For example, Warshaw (1988) reports that an acquaintance rape victim kept a diary that documented various aspects of her physical and mental health (including sexual activity). Although the judge ruled that the only parts of the diary that were admissible involved the reports of her physical and mental states around the time of the rape, the story that leaked to the public suggested there was a "sex diary." In addition, the defendant's attorney constantly "slipped in" questions about the sexual activity reported in the journal. Clearly, due to various exclusionary rules the judge would advise that sexual history information that is slipped in by an attorney or reported by the media should be disregarded and not used in making final judgments. The relevant question here is whether exposure to such information affects perceptions of the rape victim, even though it is inadmissible. Despite the importance of this issue for justice in rape trials, it has received minimal empirical attention. *Thus, one purpose of the present study is to assess whether exposure to inadmissible evidence affects perceptions of a rape victim.*

3. As cited above, there are a number of factors that might moderate any potential effect of

inadmissible evidence. For example, inadmissible evidence is more likely to affect judgments when the other evidence is weak (Sue, Smith, & Caldwell, 1973) and when the judge issues an admonishment to the jury (Wolf & Montgomery, 1977). Additionally, it has been shown that there is a differential effect of inadmissible evidence as a function of the nature of this evidence. Thompson, Fong, and Rosenhan (1981) demonstrated that judgments were more likely to be affected by proacquittal inadmissible evidence than proconviction inadmissible evidence. One potential moderating factor of inadmissible evidence in rape cases is the type of rape. There is evidence that suggests perceptions of rape cases vary as a function of whether the defendant is an acquaintance or a stranger. Although it has been estimated that over half of all rapes involve an acquaintance (Harney & Muehlenhard, 1990; Koss, 1992), the common perception that acquaintance rape is not as "real" as stranger rape persists (Lafree, 1980. Empirical evidence indicates that this misperception has an effect on judgments. For example, Johnson and Russ (1989) showed that acquaintance rape victims were perceived as receiving more enjoyment from and being more responsible for a rape than a stranger rape victim. Similarly, other research consistently demonstrates that perceptions of acquaintance rape victims tend to be less favorable than those of stranger rape victims (Kanekar, Shaherwalla, & Franco, 1991; Bridges, 1991).

4. Will the effect of inadmissible evidence regarding the victim be moderated by the type of rape? Prior research clearly indicates that type of rape does tend to moderate the effect of various other factors. For example, Johnson and Russ (1989) demonstrated that the effects of accessibility to various constructs that sensitized subjects to women's issues and women's rights tend to vary as a function of type of rape. Specifically, they showed that when subjects read a

Johnson, J. D. (1994). The effect of rape type and information admissibility on perceptions of rape victims. *Sex Roles, 30,* 781-792. Copyright © 1994 by Plenum Publishing Corporation. Reprinted with permission.

stranger rape scenario, judgments of a rape victim did not vary as a function of accessibility to the consciousness-raising information on women's rights. The victim was not held responsible, regardless of the accessibility to such information. On the other hand, when subjects read an acquaintance rape scenario, perceptions of those in the accessible condition were more favorable towards the victim than those in the nonaccessible condition. Although the research above suggests that the effect of inadmissible evidence will be moderated by type of rape, this issue has not been empirically investigated. *Thus, the second purpose of the present research is to assess whether the effect of inadmissible evidence will vary as a function of type of rape.*

5.   The relevant hypotheses are as follows:

Hypothesis 1 (Subject Gender)

6.   Compared to females, males would attribute more responsibility for rape to the victim and perceive a higher probability of victim enjoyment. This finding was expected because a number of researchers have demonstrated that males tend to be more critical of a rape victim and more lenient toward a rape defendant than females (Blumberg & Lester, 1991; Kanekar et al., 1991; Schult & Schneider, 1991). In addition, males tend to have a stronger belief in stereotypical rape myths such as the victim "asking for it," "being responsible for it," and "enjoying it" than females (Brady, Chrisler, Holsdale, & Osowiecki, 1991; Johnson & Russ, 1989; Lottes, 1991).

Hypothesis 2 (Information Admissibility and Type of Rape)

7.   Given the promiscuous nature of the victims' sexual history information, it was expected that judgments would not vary as a function of type of rape when subjects were allowed to use such information in making judgments (admissible condition). More specifically, it was expected that when subjects were not told to ignore this information that characterized the victim as extremely promiscuous, judgments of the stranger rape and acquaintance rape victims would be equally unfavorable. This particular finding was expected because there is extensive evidence suggesting that any factor that minimizes the general credibility of a victim tends to lead to less favorable responses toward her (Lafree et al., 1985; Sanders, 1980). Clearly, implications of a promiscuous sexual history would tend to minimize her credibility. On the other hand, when subjects were told to disregard the sexual history information (inadmissible condition), it was expected that victim perceptions of those in the acquaintance rape conditions would be less

favorable than victim perceptions of those in the stranger rape scenario. This finding was expected because of the possibility that information that is to be disregarded is not necessarily "erased" from memory. It is very possible that such inadmissible information may still be accessible to subjects and affect subsequent judgments. Researchers have shown that any type of cognitive bias, such as racism (Ugwegbu, 1979) or, more germane to the present study, accessible information (Johnson, Jackson, & Smith, 1989), tends to be more likely to affect judgments in situations that involve some degree of ambiguity. Therefore, we expected that inadmissible information would be more likely to lead to negative victim perceptions in the acquaintance rape condition vs. the stranger rape condition, given that there tends to be more ambiguity in the former.

Method

Subjects

8.   Thirty-five male and 49 female (predominantly Caucasian) introductory psychology students participated in the experiment to fulfill a course requirement. The subjects were primarily first-year students and were randomly assigned to conditions.

Procedure

9.   In order to reduce the probability of demand bias, subjects were told that they would be participating in research that focused on factors involved in impression formation. The subjects were informed they would be reading three passages and would be asked to answer various questions that assessed their perceptions of those passages. The subjects read two irrelevant passages that (1) gave the record of a young man who was attempting to enter graduate school, and (2) gave the record of a young woman attempting to secure an accountancy position. Subjects answered questions that assessed the probability of future success for the individual, etc.

10.   In the third passage (experimental passage), subjects read a passage that described a rape incident. The subjects in one condition read about a female student who left work late and was followed, forced into her car, and raped by a complete stranger *(stranger rape condition)*. The rapist was a maintenance man who was a substitute for the regular maintenance person. The victim did admit speaking to the man as she was leaving the building. The subjects in the second condition read about a female student who went out on a date and was forced to have intercourse when she invited the young man into her apartment to talk *(acquaintance rape condition)*. After the rape incident

was described in the experimental passage, there was some information regarding the reactions of classmates to the alleged rape. The classmates reported that, given the victim's history, they did not believe an actual rape had occurred. They implied the victim had a clear history of being extremely promiscuous and a propensity to be involved in meaningless sexual affairs. In fact, a number of the young men reported that they had engaged in casual sex with the victim, at one time or another, prior to the alleged incident. In one condition, subjects were given explicit instructions that due to various exclusionary rules, any information regarding the plaintiff's sexual history is not relevant to the present case and should be completely disregarded and not used in making final judgments *(inadmissible condition)*. The other subjects received no such instructions and were allowed to use the sexual history information in making final judgments *(admissible condition)*.

11.   After the subjects completed the reading of the information, they were instructed to answer questions that assessed their perceptions. These questions, which served as the dependent variables, were chosen because they represent common rape myths. Additionally, it is clear that in rape cases, juror decision making is based heavily on their perceptions of the victim's responsibility and behavior (Lafree et al., 1985; Sanders, 1980; Warshaw, 1988). The exact questions, which were answered on nine-point scales, were as follows: (1) What is the probability that the young woman received any enjoyment from the act? (1: extremely improbable; 9: extremely probable). (2) How responsible is the young lady for the incident which occurred? (1: totally unresponsible; 9: totally responsible). After completing the questionnaires, subjects were debriefed and released. Probability of victim enjoyment and attribution of responsibility were analyzed separately with a 2 (information admissibility—admissible, inadmissible) x 2 (type of rape—acquaintance, stranger) x 2 (gender—male, female) analysis of variance.

Results

Subject Gender

12.   The results give partial support to Hypothesis 1. There was a significant effect of gender on the enjoyment dependent variable that illustrated that males perceived a higher probability of victim enjoyment than females, $F(1, 75) = 5.7, p < .05$. The effect on attribution of responsibility did not reach significance, $F(1, 75) = .2, p > .05$.

Table 1   *Perception means by gender, information admissibility, and type of rape with F values for univariate effects[a]*

Effect	(n)	Enjoyment of Rape		Attribution of Responsibility	
		Mean	F	Mean	F
Gender			5.7[b]		.2
Male	35	3.7		3.5	
Female	49	2.9		3.4	
Information			9.8[c]		15.1[d]
Admissible	42	3.9		4.2	
Inadmissible	42	2.5		2.5	
Rape type			14.1[d]		30.3[d]
Acquaintance	42	3.9		4.4	
Stranger	42	2.6		2.2	

[a]Higher numbers indicate higher probability of victim enjoyment and greater attributions of victim responsibility. [b]$p < .05$, [c]$p < .01$, [d]$p < .001$.

Information Admissibility

13. As Table 1 indicates, subjects in the admissible condition perceived a higher probability of victim enjoyment than those in the inadmissible condition, $F(1, 75) = 9.8$, $p < .01$. Similarly, subjects in the admissible condition attributed more responsibility to the victim than those in the inadmissible condition, $F(1, 75) = 15.1$, $p < .001$.

Type of Rape

14. As Table 1 indicates, subjects in the acquaintance rape condition perceived a higher probability of victim enjoyment than those in the stranger rape condition, $F(1, 75) = 14.1$, $p < .001$. Similarly, subjects attributed more responsibility in the acquaintance rape condition than the stranger rape condition, $F(1, 75) = 30.3$, $p < .001$.

Information Admissibility and Type of Rape

15. The results give partial support to Hypothesis 2. For the probability of enjoyment dependent variable, the interaction of information admissibility and type of rape was significant $F(1, 75) = 8.4$, $p < :05$. As Table 2 indicates, when subjects were allowed to use the sexual history information (admissible condition), perceptions of the probability of victim enjoyment did not vary as a function of type of rape. On the other hand, when the information was inadmissible, subjects in the acquaintance rape condition perceived a higher probability of victim enjoyment than those in the stranger rape condition. A planned comparison indicated that the perceptions of the victim did not differ as a

function of rape type when the information was admissible, $t(40) = 1.1$, $p > .05$. On the other hand, when the information was inadmissible, the perceptions of those in the acquaintance rape condition were less favorable than those in the stranger rape condition, $t(40) = 7.2$, $p < .001$. The interactive effect did not reach significance on the attribution of responsibility dependent variable, $F(1, 75) = 2.7$, $p = .10$.

Discussion

16. The present study yielded a number of interesting and relevant findings regarding factors that affect processes involved in simulated jury decision making. More specifically, the results indicated that males tend to perceive a higher probability of victim enjoyment than females. This finding is consistent with other research that focused on factors that affect perceptions of

sexual victimization (Blumberg & Lester, 1991; Schult & Schneider, 1991). It should also be noted that the gender effect did not reach significance on the attribution of responsibility dependent variable. These results are consistent with other rape perception studies that have found gender differences on some variables but not others (Krahe, 1988; Malamuth & Check, 1980; Malamuth, Haber, & Feshback, 1980; Malamuth, Heim, & Feshback, 1980). This inconsistency of gender effects in the present study and previous research suggests that male perceptions of rape might be more complex than previously believed. The results indicating that perceptions of an acquaintance rape victim tend to be less favorable than those of a stranger rape victim are also consistent with previous research (Check & Malamuth, 1983; Johnson & Russ, 1989). The most important finding indicates that the effect of inadmissible information does tend to be moderated by the type of rape. The perceptions of the probability of victim enjoyment did not vary as a function of type of rape when the sexual history information was admissible. On the other hand, when the sexual history information was inadmissible, those in the acquaintance rape condition perceived a higher probability of victim enjoyment than those in the stranger rape condition.

17. One relevant issue here involves why the perceptions of the probability of victim enjoyment did not vary as a function of type of rape when the information was admissible. One possible explanation for this finding might involve the tendency for judgments toward rape victims to be less favorable when there is any factor present that might minimize her credibility. Warshaw (1988) suggested that juries are extremely reluctant to convict a rapist if there is any hint of victim "misconduct." Similarly, Lafree et al. (1985) noted that jurors tended to be more lenient toward a defendant if the victim drank, used drugs or alcohol, had premarital

Table 2   *Perception means by type of rape information admissibility[a]*

	Perception of Enjoyment	
	Admissible mean (n)	Inadmissible mean (n)
Stranger	3.8 (20)	1.6 (22)
Acquaintance	4.0 (22)	3.7 (20)
	Attribution of Responsibility	
	Admissible mean (n)	Inadmissible mean (n)
Stranger	3.5 (20)	1.6 (22)
Acquaintance	4.8 (22)	3.9 (20)

[a]Higher numbers indicate higher probability of enjoyment and greater attributions of responsibility.

sex, or knew the defendant. Finally, Sanders (1980) found that in many cases victims, law enforcement officials, and jurors made a distinction between a "true" victim and a "bad" victim. More specifically, any victim who had a pronounced sexual history or questionable moral character was categorized as "bad" and an indictment or prosecution of a defendant in such a case was considered unlikely. Thus in the present study, it is not surprising that when subjects were allowed to use the sexual history information, their perceptions of the probability of the victim enjoyment was relatively high across rape conditions.

18. Why did perceptions of victim enjoyment vary as a function of type of rape when the information that alleged victim promiscuity was inadmissible? More specifically, it is not clear why exposure to such information would lead to less favorable victim perceptions in an acquaintance rape situation when compared to a stranger rape situation. Subjects may make a conscious effort not to use inadmissible information, but there is not evidence to suggest that subjects can magically "erase" such information. Such information may still be very accessible to subjects, and thus under certain conditions affect their perceptions. Under what conditions would such information tend to have an effect on judgments? Previous research clearly indicates that any type of cognitive bias, such as accessible information, tends to have a strong effect on information that has a certain degree of ambiguity (Duncan, 1976; Johnson, Jackson, & Smith, 1989). Clearly, there is more ambiguity in an acquaintance rape incident than a stranger rape incident, especially on issues such as victim consent to intercourse. This ambiguity may be due to a number of factors that tend to be common in an acquaintance rape situation such as the plaintiff being with the victim willingly, the plaintiff consuming alcohol, or the plaintiff willingly engaging in certain acts (e.g., kissing, petting, etc.) before the alleged rape occurs. The present findings that indicate stronger effects (i.e., less favorable victim perceptions) of accessible information in the acquaintance rape situation are consistent with research by Johnson et al. (1989). They demonstrated that exposure to consciousness-raising information (for women's issues) had a greater effect on perceptions of an acquaintance rape scenario than a stranger rape scenario.

19. It is not entirely clear why the interaction and the effect of gender failed to reach significance for the attribution of responsibility dependent variable. The term "responsibility" may have been too nebulous and ambiguous, thus increasing the possibility of multiple interpretations and inconsistent findings. It is

possible that certain subjects thought that the man should have been held responsible for his aggressiveness or some may have thought that she could have been held responsible for inviting him back to her apartment. On the other hand, the consistent effects of perception of the probability of victim enjoyment suggest that it was a less ambiguous concept. Additionally, previous research suggests that it may be more relevant in decision making involving rape trials than attributions of responsibility. Specifically, perceptions of victim enjoyment seem to suggest that victim resistance was minimal. This is relevant because research indicates that, in order for a rape victim to have credibility, she must "clearly resist her attacker" (Clark & Lewis, 1977) and this resistance must occur "from the inception to the close of the sexual interaction" (Cobb & Shaver, 1971). Check and Malamuth (1983) suggest that any ambiguity associated with such resistance will lead to less favorable perceptions of the rape victim.

20. In summary, the present findings do seem to have interesting legal implications. First, they support the contention that regardless of the type of rape involved, allowing subjects to use information indicating that the victim has a promiscuous sexual history will tend to elicit more negative perceptions of her. Second, they suggest that even if the negative sexual history information is declared inadmissible, it is likely to have an effect on perceptions of victim enjoyment (especially in an acquaintance rape situation). Interestingly enough, the findings might be relevant to the much publicized William Kennedy Smith acquaintance rape case. More specifically, the news media made numerous references to Mr. Smith's sexual past and there was extensive concern that the jurors may have been exposed to and biased by such pretrial publicity ("Case No. 91-5482," 1991; "The case," 1991). Unfortunately for the plaintiff, there seemed to be less concern about the references made in the media regarding her sexual past. The present findings suggest that such information, although inadmissible, may have played a role in the acquittal of Mr. Smith.

21. The major purpose of the present study was to assess the effects of various factors on perceptions of rape victims. Even though it is clear that in rape cases such perceptions, especially perceptions of the probability of victim enjoyment, tend to be predominant factors in final decision making (Lafree et al., 1985; Sanders, 1980; Warshaw, 1988), there are a number of ways that future research can extend the present findings to more directly simulate an actual criminal trial. First, subjects could be allowed to deliberate in groups of six or twelve. This would be interesting because there is

extensive evidence suggesting that such a deliberation process tends to increase leniency toward the defendant (see MacCoun & Kerr, 1988, for a review). In the present study, there seemed to be only one condition in which subjects did not show leniency toward the defendant (stranger-inadmissible condition). It is possible that a deliberation process may increase the probability that a defendant could receive leniency in that condition. Second, a "no sexual history information group" could help clarify assessment of the influence of inadmissible/admissible sexual history information. Third, the effects of exposure to inadmissible victim sexual information on judgments of the defendant (defendant guilt, appropriate sentencing, etc.) could be assessed. Finally, the study could be repeated in the general adult population who will more likely be actual jurors than first-year psychology students. Although the present study does not directly simulate an actual trial situation, the findings still clearly suggest that those in the legal community should be concerned about the effects of inadmissible information regarding a victim and how these effects might interact with other factors to possibly modify judicial outcomes. Hopefully, future research can shed further light on the various processes that might underlie the present findings.

References

Blumberg, M., & Lester, D. (1991). High school and college students' attitudes towards rape. *Adolescence, 26,* 727-729.

Brady, E., Chrisler, J., Holsdale, D., & Osowiecki, D. (1991). Date rape: Expectations, avoidance strategy and attitudes towards the victim. *Journal of Social Psychology, 131,* 417-429.

Bridges, J. (1991). Perceptions of date and stranger rape: A difference in sex role expectation and rape supportive beliefs. *Sex Roles, 24,* 291-307.

Check, J., & Malamuth, D. (1983). Sex role stereotyping and depictions of stranger versus acquaintance rape. *Journal of Personality and Social Psychology, 45,* 344-356.

Clark, L., & Lewis, D. (1977). *The price of coercive sexuality.* Toronto: The Women's Press.

Cobb, K., & Shaver, N. (1971). Michigan Criminal Assault Law. In D. Chappel, R. Geis, & G. Geis (Eds.), *Forcible rape: The crime, the victim, & the offender.* New York: Columbia University Press.

Duncan, B. (1976). Differential social perception and attribution of intergroup bias: Testing the lower limits of stereotyping blacks. *Journal of Personality and Social Psychology, 34,* 590-598.

Green, E., & Russel, W. (1988). Pretrial publicity and juror decision making. *Applied Cognitive Psychology, 2,* 123-135.

Hans, V., & Vidmar, N. (1986). *Judging the jury.* New York: Plenum.

Harney, P., & Muehlenhard, C. (1990). Rape. In E. Graverholz & M. Kurlewski (Eds.), *Sexual coercion*. Lexington, MA: Lexington Books.

Hastie, R., Penrod, S. P., & Pennington, N. (1983). *Inside the jury*. Cambridge, MA: Harvard University Press.

Johnson, J., Jackson, L. A., & Smith, G. (1989). The role of ambiguity and gender in mediating the effects of salient cognitions. *Personality and Social Psychology Bulletin, 15*, 52-60.

Johnson, J., & Russ, I. (1989). Effects of salience of consciousness-raising information on the perception of acquaintance versus stranger rape. *Journal of Applied Social Psychology, 19*, 182-197.

Kanekar, S., Shaherwalla, P., & Franco, B. (1991). The acquaintance predicament of a rape victim. *Journal of Applied Social Psychology, 21*, 1524-1544.

Koss, M. (1992). The underdetection of rape: Methodological choices influence incidence estimates. *Journal of Social Issues, 48*, 61-75.

Lafree, G. (1980). Variables affecting guilty pleas and convictions in rape cases. *Social Forces, 58*, 833-850.

Lafree, G., Reskin, B., & Visher, C. (1985). Juror responses to victim behavior and legal issues in sexual assault trials. *Social Problems, 32*, 398-407.

Lottes, I. (1991). Belief systems: Sexuality and rape. *Journal of Psychology and Human Sexuality, 4*, 37-59.

MacCoun, R., & Kerr, N. (1988). Asymmetric influence in mock jury deliberation: Jurors bias for leniency. *Journal of Personality and Social Psychology, 54*, 21-33.

Malamuth, J., & Check, N. (1980). Sexual arousal to rape and consenting depictions: The importance of the woman's arousal. *Journal of Abnormal Psychology, 10*, 528-547.

Malamuth, J., Haber, S., & Feshback, S. (1980). Testing hypothesis regarding rape: Exposure to sexual violence, sex differences, and the "normality" of rapists. *Journal of Research in Personality, 14*, 121-137.

Malamuth, J., Heim, M., & Feshback, S. (1980). Sexual responsiveness of college students to rape depictions: Inhibitory and disinhibitory effects. *Journal of Personality and Social Psychology, 38*, 399-408.

Moran, G., & Cutler, B. (1991). The prejudicial impact of pretrial publicity. *Journal of Applied Social Psychology, 21*, 345-367.

Newsweek. (1991). Case no. 91-5482 comes to court. *118*, p. 25.

Pfeifer, J., & Ogloff, J. (1991). Ambiguity and guilt determinations: A modern racism perspective. *Journal of Applied Social Psychology, 21*, 1713-1725.

Sanders, W. (1980). *Rape and woman's identity*. Beverly Hills, CA: Sage Publications.

Schult, D., & Schneider, L. (1991). The role of sexual provocationness, rape history and observer gender in perception of blame in sexual assault. *Journal of Interpersonality Violence, 6*, 94-101.

Sue, S., Smith, R., & Caldwell, C. (1973). Effects of inadmissible evidence on the decisions of simulated jurors: A moral dilemma. *Journal of Applied Social Psychology, 3*, 345-353.

Thompson, W., Fong, G., & Rosenhan, D. (1981). Inadmissible evidence and juror verdicts. *Journal of Personality and Social Psychology, 40*, 453-463.

Time. (1991) The case that was not heard. *138*, p. 38.

Ugwegbu, D. C. (1979). Racial and evidential factors in juror attribution of legal responsibility. *Journal of Experimental Social Psychology, 15*, 133-146.

Warshaw, R. (1988). *I never called it rape*. New York: Harper & Row.

Wiener, R., Habert, K., Shkodriani, G., & Staebler, C. (1991). The social psychology of jury nullification: Predicting when jurors disobey the law. *Journal of Applied Social Psychology, 21*, 1379-1401.

Wolf, D., & Montgomery, D. (1977). Effects of inadmissible evidence and judicial admonishment. *Journal of Applied Social Psychology, 53*, 14-29.

Factual Questions

1. According to the first hypothesis, compared to females, males would do what two things?

2. According to the second hypothesis, when subjects were told to disregard sexual history information, what was expected?

3. Who were the subjects?

4. What were the dependent variables in this study?

5. What is the size of the difference between males and females on the enjoyment of rape variable?

6. Table 1 reports on the results of six significance tests. Which one was *not* statistically significant?

7. According to the means in Table 2, under what pair of conditions was the perception of enjoyment the lowest?

Questions for Discussion

8. Were any of the findings reported in the review of the literature especially interesting or surprising to you? Explain.

9. How important is it to know that the subjects were randomly assigned to conditions? (See paragraph 8.)

10. Speculate on why the subjects were first given two irrelevant passages to read.

11. The *dependent* variables are explicitly identified in paragraph 11. What are the *independent* variable(s)?

12. The author says he *debriefed* the subjects. What does this mean?

13. This study is an example of a laboratory experiment because it was not conducted with real jurors under actual courtroom conditions. What are the advantages and disadvantages of a laboratory study for this research topic?

14. What is your opinion on the four suggestions for future research in the discussion? If you could follow only one of them in a future study, which one would you choose?

Quality Ratings

DIRECTIONS: Indicate your level of agreement with each of the following statements by circling a number from 5 for strongly agree (SA) to 1 for strongly disagree (SD). If you believe that an item is not applicable to this research article, leave it blank. Be prepared to explain your ratings.

A. The introduction establishes the importance of the research topic.
   SA   5   4   3   2   1   SD

B. The literature review establishes the context for the study.
   SA   5   4   3   2   1   SD

C. The research purpose, question, or hypothesis is clearly stated.
   SA   5   4   3   2   1   SD

D. The method of sampling is sound.
   SA   5   4   3   2   1   SD

E. Relevant demographics (for example, age, gender, and ethnicity) are described.
   SA   5   4   3   2   1   SD

F. Measurement procedures are adequate.
   SA   5   4   3   2   1   SD

G. The results are clearly described.
   SA   5   4   3   2   1   SD

H. The discussion/conclusion is appropriate.
   SA   5   4   3   2   1   SD

I. Despite any flaws noted above, the report is worthy of publication.
   SA   5   4   3   2   1   SD

FACILITATING CHANGES IN EXERCISE BEHAVIOR:
EFFECT OF STRUCTURED STATEMENTS OF INTENTION ON PERCEIVED BARRIERS TO ACTION

D. Craig Huddy *Appalachian State University*
Jaimie L. Hebert *Appalachian State University*
Gerald C. Hyner *Purdue University*
Robert L. Johnson *Appalachian State University*

Two groups of worksite employees (58 in a control, 53 in an experimental group) underwent three 90-min. educational sessions designed to increase participation in exercise. At the end of the third session, experimental subjects were asked to complete a structured statement of exercise intention which addressed the major barrier to exercise. Two weeks following the program, chi-square analysis showed that the two groups were proportionately different in changes in frequency and intensity of exercise such that the experimental group in both cases showed greater changes than the control. Experimental subjects showed a twofold increase in frequency and intensity of exercise over the control group. Pearson r indicated a statistically significant association between the completeness of structured statements of intention and an increase in frequency of exercise. We conclude that structured statements of intention are useful for distinguishing between contrived barriers to exercise (excuses) and actual barriers that require practical solutions.

1. Among the myriad challenges to practitioners of health promotion, none is more formidable than the requisite to modify life-threatening behaviors responsible for the major chronic illnesses. With most authorities agreeing that over half of all premature death is directly attributable to cigarette smoking, sedentary lifestyle, and high-fat/low-fiber diets (Centers for Disease Control, 1986), the search continues for behavioral paradigms which provide strategies for fostering salubrious behaviors.

2. Behavioral models have focused on readiness to change (Prochaska & DiClemente, 1983; Prochaska, DiClemente, Velicer, Ginpil, & Norcross, 1985; Prochaska & DiClemente, 1986), barriers to action (Janz & Becker, 1984), perceived control (Wallston & Wallston, 1978), intention to change (Fishbein & Ajzen, 1975, pp. 335-383; Fishbein, 1980; Carter, 1990),

self-efficacy (Bandura, 1977; Bandura & Adams, 1982), and attribution (Lewis & Daltroy, 1990). Most models such as the Health Belief Model emphasize one or more salient dimensions, e.g., perceptions of barriers to action versus anticipated benefits of a protective behavior, as the rationale for predicting the likelihood of undertaking a recommended preventive health behavior (Janz & Becker, 1984). A few models have integrated salient dimensions of other paradigms into eclectic explanations, e.g., a theory of planned behavior, which is an amalgamation of reasoned action and self-efficacy theories (Ajzen, 1985, 1991; Ajzen & Madden, 1986).

3. This study drew from two major theoretical frameworks, the Health Belief Model and the theory of reasoned action as a basis for investigating facilitation of changes in self-reported exercise behavior (frequency, duration, and intensity) among participants in a worksite setting. In addition, behavioral contracting, a technique employed by behavior modification, was also employed.

4. Studies employing the Health Belief Model have indicated that perceptions of barriers to action is the single best predictor of preventive health behavior (Janz & Becker, 1984). Presumably, the fewer the barriers or the less threatening the barriers, the more likely a person is to undertake a recommended health behavior. For practitioners, the implication is that clients require assistance to find ways of circumventing identified barriers. Part of this process involves the realization that many identified barriers may be imagined or contrived, i.e., rationalizations or excuses, and others real, i.e., actual impediments to a healthy lifestyle requiring well-conceived strategies for management.

5. The theory of reasoned action stipulates that a person's stated intention corresponds well with probability of behavior when certain

criteria are satisfied. The more complete the intention, i.e., the more fulfilled the criteria, the more likely is a corresponding behavior (Fishbein, 1980). When the criteria are vague or incomplete, the likelihood of the behavior diminishes. The utility of these intentional criteria for practitioners is that clients may be helped to clarify their thinking and move away from vague commitments toward stronger, less ambiguous intentions.

6. Behavior modification is based on principles of conditioning (Weiten, 1989). In this approach, changing undesirable behaviors involves contracting either with another person or with oneself. The contract usually specifies what behavior is expected, when, under what conditions, and so on (Martin & Pear, 1988, pp. 353-376). One principal utility of the contract is the cognitive processing required to spell out details involved in the change which might have been overlooked in less well thought-out attempts to curtail unhealthy behavior (or to initiate healthy behavior).

7. This study focused on two hypotheses. The first hypothesis was that the employees who completed a statement of exercise intention (experimental group) would show proportionately more changes in exercise behaviors than those employees who did not complete such a statement (control group). The second hypothesis was that there would be proportionately more changes in exercise behavior within the experimental group for those employees

Huddy, D. C. et al. (1995). Facilitating changes in exercise behavior: Effect of structured statements of intention on perceived barriers to action. *Psychological Reports, 76,* 867-875. Copyright © Psychological Reports 1995.

Address correspondence to D. Craig Huddy, Ph.D., C.H.E.S., Department of Health, Leisure, and Exercise Science, Appalachian State University, Boone, NC 28608.

who had the most complete statements of intention.

Method

Subjects

8. Subjects (*N* = 111) were volunteers recruited from employees of a major law firm (58, control group) and from a national insurance company (53, experimental group). Subjects' characteristics are depicted in Table 1. In general, the subjects were middle-aged, predominantly white, married, and well-educated.

Research Design and Protocol

9. A pre-post design, employing a random assignment of subjects to a control or experimental group, was selected. The investigation took place at the worksite during regularly scheduled working hours. Following the assignment of subjects, the study proceeded to three 90-min. educational sessions, one session per day over a three-day period. At the beginning of each session, participants were required to complete questionnaires pertaining to the following day's session.

10. The first session, "Orthobiosis," consisted of general information which emphasized the importance of personal behavior and the acceptance of personal responsibility for one's health. This session was also designed to familiarize the participants with the leading causes of death and the relationship of faulty diets, sedentary living, cigarette smoking, and obesity to major chronic diseases. At the beginning of the session, participants completed the Carter Center for Emory University Health Risk Appraisal.

11. Session 2, "Health Benefits of Exercise," addressed the importance of regular aerobic activity as an effective means of lowering the risk of cardiovascular diseases, especially coronary artery disease, and controlling weight. The subject of obesity was also discussed in terms of the risk posed for coronary heart disease, hypertension, and cancer. At the beginning of this session, participants completed a questionnaire on exercise behavior and were provided personalized printouts summarizing responses to the appraisal completed previously.

12. Session 3, "Barrier Identification," concerned participants' barriers to implementing specific suggestions for behavioral change made during Sessions 1 and 2. Participants completed a measure of barriers to exercise and were encouraged to share their feelings about their personally identified barriers to regular exercise. Strategies for circumventing identified barriers were discussed extensively and practical suggestions for implementing these strategies emphasized. Participants in the experimental group were then asked to complete a structured statement of intention to exercise.

Follow-up

13. Two weeks later, participants were asked to complete the questionnaire on exercise behavior. Comparisons were made between scores obtained pre- and postcompletion of the statement to ascertain changes in self-reports for exercise behaviors.

The Structured Statement of Intention to Exercise

14. The theory of reasoned action refers to "intentions" as the precursors of behaviors (Fishbein, 1980). Intentions which meet the specific criteria alluded to earlier have a good probability of becoming acts. The criteria are "target" (the specific reason for undertaking a particular behavior), "action" (the specific behavior), "time" (when the behavior will be executed), and "context" (where the behavior will take place). For this study, an instrument was developed to incorporate these criteria into a "statement of intention" (a form of personal contracting used in self-directed behavioral change) which addressed specific identified "barriers" to action. In this way, the statement incorporated the criteria for an intention plus the dimension of the Health Belief Model shown to be most predictive of preventive health behaviors. "Structured" implies that the statement was formulated by the participant in terms of the personally identified major barrier to participation in exercise.

Scoring the Structured Statement of Intention to Exercise

15. The procedure for awarding points on the statement of intention was as follows: For "identifying the major barrier," 1 point; for expressing an intent to "do something about this barrier," 1 point; for expressing "a specific reason for engaging in a behavior" (target), 1 point; for stipulating a "specific behavior" (action), 1 point; for stating "when the behavior would take place" (time), 1 point; and for stating "where the behavior would occur" (context), 1 point. An intention statement with all criteria satisfied earned 6 points; scores less than 6 points indicated vagueness or omission of intent. Fig. 1 is an example of a completed statement with all criteria satisfied and the maximum of 6 points awarded. Fig. 2 depicts a completed statement with missing criteria due to vagueness and 3 points awarded.

16. Since the scoring of the statements relied heavily on expert judgment, rater's reliability was deemed essential to minimize error of

Table 1   *Subjects' characteristics: Means, standard deviations, percents*

Measure	Control Group		Experimental Group	
	M	*SD*	*M*	*SD*
Age, yr.	35	10	38	10
Height, cm	172	10	173	10
Weight, kg	70	13	75	16
Race, % White	97		94	
Gender, %				
Male	47		58	
Female	53		42	
Years of Education, %				
12	22		19	
> 12 but < 16	16		11	
> 16	62		70	
Occupation, %				
Professional	72		93	
Clerical	28		7	
Marital Status, %				
Single	17		17	
Married	74		76	
Divorced	9		7	

The MAJOR reason (barrier) I have for <u>not</u> exercising is:

  Can't seem to find enough time.

Do you intend to do something about this reason that is currently preventing you from exercising?

  Yes   X _____   No _____   Undecided _____

(1) What is your MAJOR REASON for starting or improving your exercise program?

  I need to lose about 10 pounds.

(2) WHAT KIND(S) of exercise(s) are you going to do?

  Jog

(3) WHEN do you intend to begin?   January (during first week)

(4) WHERE do you intend to do your exercise(s)?   Neighborhood streets

<u>POINTS AWARDED</u>:

BARRIER IDENTIFIED	Lack of time	1 pt.
INTENT TO ACT	Yes	1 pt.
TARGET	Lose weight	1 pt.
ACTION	Jogging	1 pt.
TIME	First week of January	1 pt.
CONTEXT	Neighborhood streets	1 pt.
SCORE: 1 + 1 + 1 + 1 + 1 + 1 = 6 Pts.		

Figure 1   *Completed statement of exercise intention with all criteria satisfied: Actual participant's response and scoring*

---

judgment. To estimate reliability, a second rater scored the statements. Differences noted between the ratings were statistically nonsignificant.

Analysis

17. All statistical procedures were performed with SAS, Version 6 (SAS Institute, Inc., 1989). Means and standard deviations were computed for all variables; chi-square was used to test between-groups differences (pre- and poststatement) on frequency, duration, and intensity of exercise. Pearson r was the estimate of the association of scores on the structured statement of intention to exercise and changes in frequency, duration, and intensity of exercise within the experimental group. A p value of .05 was chosen.

Results and Discussion

18. Supporting the first hypothesis, chi-square analysis showed that the two groups were proportionately different on self-reported changes in frequency of exercise (Table 2) and intensity of exercise (Table 3). The experimental group on both measures showed greater changes than the control group. Twenty-five percent of both groups combined showed an increase in frequency of exercise, but the experimental group had a 34% increase in frequency while the control had only a 17% increase; 15% of the groups combined showed an increase in intensity of exercise, but the experimental group had a 21% increase while the control group had only a 10% increase.

19. In support of the second hypothesis, Pearson r indicated a statistically significant association between scores on intent and the reported frequency of exercise ($r = .31$, $p < .05$) but not between scores on intent and duration or intensity of exercise. The more complete the statement of intention, the more likely was there an increase in reported frequency of exercise.

20. This study was successful in showing the utility of structured statements of intention to exercise in a worksite health-promotion program designed to assist employees in the identification and management of barriers to exercise. Participants who were more specific (less vague) in their intentions were more likely to increase their frequency of exercise.

21. Research on the identification of barriers to exercise has not included descriptions of how barriers influence participation in exercise (Godin, Desharnais, Valois, Lepage, Jobin, & Bradet, 1994). Steinhardt and Dishman (1989) have said that a major problem with such research has to do with standards of uniform measurement. According to their research, effort, time, and health problems were major impediments to habitual exercise. Tappe, Duda,

Table 2   *Number of persons reporting changes in exercise frequency (days per week): Chi-square*

Change	Control Group		Experimental Group		Total
	f_o	f_e	f_o	f_e	
Increase	10	14.6	18	13.4	28
No Change	43	36.6	27	33.4	70
Decrease	5	6.8	8	6.2	13
Total	58		53		111

$\chi^2 = 6.42$, $p = .04$

The MAJOR reason (barrier) I have for <u>not</u> exercising is:

Too much going on at work right now

Do you intend to do something about this reason that is currently preventing you from exercising?

Yes _____ No _____ Undecided (probably) _____

(1) What is your MAJOR REASON for starting or improving your exercise program?

Improve my health

(2) WHAT KIND(S) of exercise(s) are you going to do?

Walk (maybe do some hiking)

(3) WHEN do you intend to begin? | Sometime after the holidays

(4) WHERE do you intend to do your exercise(s)? | Probably around the neighborhood or in the nearby park.

POINTS AWARDED:

BARRIER IDENTIFIED	Job demands	1 pt.
INTENT TO ACT	Undecided	0 pt.
TARGET	Health reasons	0 pt.
ACTION	Walking	1 pt.
TIME	After holidays	0 pt.
CONTEXT	Neighborhood	1 pt.

<u>SCORE</u>: 1 + 0 + 0 + 1 + 0 + 1 = 3 Pts.

Figure 2 *Completed statement of exercise intention with missing criteria: Actual participant's response and scoring*

and Ehrnwald (1989) suggested that barriers may differ depending upon age and sex; Slenker, Price, Roberts, and Jurs (1986) found among joggers versus nonjoggers that almost 40% of the variance in exercise behavior could be explained by perceived barriers, with "lack of time" most frequently cited as the major obstacle. Dishman, Sallis, and Orenstein (1985), Yoshida, Allison, and Osborn (1988), and Godin, Shepard, and Colantonio (1986) all reported "lack of time" as the major self-reported barrier to exercise. In our analysis, we found lack of time, work schedules, and family responsibilities, respectively, were mentioned as frequent problems in regular participation in exercise. We also observed in this study that employees' perceived barriers became less threatening and viewed as more manageable as strategies for circumventing them were explored in the discussion session. It was not uncommon for participants to acknowledge that what was at first perceived to be an insurmountable barrier was, after discussion, more of an unintentionally contrived barrier, i.e., an excuse.

22. The real utility of the process of identification of barriers and the subsequent application of structured statements of intention to exercise lies in the recognition of contrived barriers (excuses) and the discovery of actual barriers that require solutions. The implication is that practitioners need to engage clients in identification of barriers (resulting in the establishment of priorities) before stated intentions to act become bona fide intentions.

References

Ajzen, I. (1985). From intentions to actions: A theory of planned action. In J. Kuhl & J. Bechman (Eds.), *Action control: From cognitions to behavior.* New York: Springer. Pp. 11-39.

Ajzen, I. (1991). The theory of planned behavior. *Organizational Behavior and Human Decision Processes, 50,* 179-211.

Ajzen, I., & Madden, T. (1986). Predictions of goal-directed behavior: Attitudes, intentions, and perceived behavioral control. *Journal of Experimental Social Psychology, 22,* 453-474.

Bandura, A. (1977). Toward a unifying theory of behavior change. *Psychological Review, 84,* 191-215.

Bandura, A., & Adams, N. (1982). Analysis of self-efficacy theory of behavioral change. *Cognitive Therapy and Research, 1,* 287-310.

Carter, W. B. (1990). Health behavior as a rational process: Theory of reasoned action and multiattribute utility theory. In K. Glanz, F. M. Lewis, & B. K. Rimer (Eds.), *Health behavior and health education.* San Francisco, CA: Jossey-Bass. Pp. 63-91.

Centers for Disease Control. (1986). Premature mortality in the United States: Public health issues in the use of years of potential life lost. *Morbidity and Mortality Weekly Report,* No. 35.

Table 3 *Number of persons reporting changes in exercise intensity (perceived exertion): Chi-square*

Change	Control Group		Experimental Group		Total
	f_o	f_e	f_o	f_e	
Increase	6	8.8	11	8.1	17
No Change	45	39.2	30	35.8	75
Decrease	7	9.9	12	9.1	19
Total	58		53		111

$\chi^2 = 6.43, p = .04$

Dishman, R., Sallis, J., & Orenstein, D. (1985). The determinants of physical activity and exercise. *Public Health Reports, 100,* 158-171.

Fishbein, M. (1980). Factors influencing health behaviors: A theory of reasoned action. In M. Fishbein, *Understanding attitudes and predicting social behavior.* Englewood Cliffs, NJ: Prentice-Hall. Pp. 223-260.

Fishbein, M., & Ajzen, I. (1975). *Beliefs, attitudes, intentions and behavior: An introduction to theory and research.* Reading, MA: Addison-Wesley.

Godin, G., Desharnais, R., Valois, P., Lepage, L., Jobin, J., & Bradet, R. (1994). Differences in perceived barriers to exercise between high and low intenders: Observations among different populations. *American Journal of Health Promotion, 8,* 279-285.

Godin, G., Shepard, R., & Colantonio, A. (1986). The cognitive profile of those who intend to exercise but do not. *Public Health Reports, 101,* 521-526.

Janz, N., & Becker, M. (1984). The health belief model: A decade later. *Health Education Quarterly, 11,* 1-47.

Lewis, F., & Daltroy, L. (1990). How causal explanations influence health behavior: Attribution theory. In K. Glanz, F. M. Lewis, & B. K. Rimer (Eds.), *Health behavior and health education.* San Francisco, CA: Jossey-Bass. Pp. 92-114.

Martin, G., & Pear, J. (1988). *Behavior modification: What it is and how to do it.* (3rd ed.) Englewood Cliffs, NJ: Prentice-Hall.

Prochaska, J., & DiClemente, C. (1983). Stages and processes of self-change of smoking: Toward an integrated model of change. *Journal of Consulting and Clinical Psychology, 51,* 390-395.

Prochaska, J., & DiClemente, C. (1986). Toward a comprehensive model of change. In W. Miller & N. Heather (Eds.), *Treating addictive behaviors.* New York: Plenum. Pp. 3-27.

Prochaska, J., DiClemente, C., Velicer, W., Ginpil, S., & Norcross, J. (1985). Predicting change in smoking status for self-changes. *Addictive Behavior, 10,* 395-406.

SAS Institute, Inc. (1989). *SAS user's guide: Statistics. Version 6.* Cary, NC: Author.

Slenker, S., Price, J., Roberts, S., & Jurs, S. (1986). Joggers versus nonexercisers: An analysis of knowledge, attitudes and beliefs about jogging. *Research Quarterly for Exercise and Sport, 55,* 371-378.

Steinhardt, M., & Dishman, R. (1989). Reliability and validity of expected outcomes and barriers for habitual physical activity. *Journal of Occupational Medicine, 31,* 536-546.

Tappe, M., Duda, J., & Ehrnwald, P. (1989). Perceived barriers to exercise among adolescents. *Journal of School Health, 59,* 153-155.

Wallston, B., & Wallston, K. (1978). Locus of control and health: A review of the literature. *Health Education Monographs, 6,* 107-117.

Weiten, W. (1989). Learning through conditioning. In W. Weiten, *Psychological themes and variations.* Pacific Grove, CA: Brooks/Cole. Pp. 189-227.

Yoshida, K., Allison, K., & Osborn, R. (1988). Social factors influencing perceived barriers to physical exercise among women. *Canadian Journal of Public Health, 79,* 104-108.

Factual Questions

1. What are the names of the two major theoretical frameworks used by the authors?

2. How many hypotheses are explicitly stated by the authors?

3. How did the researchers measure exercise behavior?

4. What evidence is given that indicates the reliability of the scoring of the statements of exercise intention?

5. What is the name of the significance test applied to the data in Tables 2 and 3?

6. The differences in Table 3 are statistically significant at what probability level?

7. Is the Pearson r in paragraph 19 based on data for both the experimental and control groups? Explain.

8. What barriers to exercise were frequently mentioned by subjects in this study?

Questions for Discussion

9. Based on the data in Table 1, do you believe that the experimental and control groups are reasonably similar in their background characteristics?

10. Based on paragraphs 8 and 9, do you think that (1) individuals were assigned at random to treatments regardless of their place of employment or (2) the law firm group was randomly assigned to one condition and the insurance group to the other? Is this important? Explain.

11. In your opinion, are the treatments (independent variable) adequately described? Explain.

12. The researchers used self-reported changes in exercise behavior to measure the outcome (dependent variable). Are there advantages and disadvantages to using self-reports to measure exercise behavior? Explain.

13. Results of previous studies are cited in the Results and Discussion section (see paragraph 21). Do you believe that it would have been better to cite them in the introduction? Why? Why not?

14. To what population(s) would it be appropriate to generalize the results of this study?

15. If you were to conduct a study on this topic, what changes, if any, would you make in the research methodology?

Quality Ratings

DIRECTIONS: Indicate your level of agreement with each of the following statements by circling a number from 5 for strongly agree (SA) to 1 for strongly disagree (SD). If you believe that an item is not applicable to this research article, leave it blank. Be prepared to explain your ratings.

A. The introduction establishes the importance of the research topic.
SA   5   4   3   2   1   SD

B. The literature review establishes the context for the study.
SA   5   4   3   2   1   SD

C. The research purpose, question, or hypothesis is clearly stated.
SA   5   4   3   2   1   SD

D. The method of sampling is sound.
SA   5   4   3   2   1   SD

E. Relevant demographics (for example, age, gender, and ethnicity) are described.
SA   5   4   3   2   1   SD

F. Measurement procedures are adequate.
SA   5   4   3   2   1   SD

G. The results are clearly described.
SA   5   4   3   2   1   SD

H. The discussion/conclusion is appropriate.
SA   5   4   3   2   1   SD

I. Despite any flaws noted above, the report is worthy of publication.
SA   5   4   3   2   1   SD

ARTICLE 25

INCREASING DESIGNATED DRIVING WITH A
PROGRAM OF PROMPTS AND INCENTIVES

Thomas A. Brigham   *Washington State University*
Steven M. Meier   *University of Idaho*
Viki Goodner   *Washington State University–Vancouver*

Designated driving (DD) is a potentially viable but underutilized component of efforts to reduce driving while intoxicated. A reversal design was used to evaluate the effects of prompts and incentives in a bar on the frequency of DD. The results showed an approximate doubling of the number of designated drivers during the two intervention periods.

DESCRIPTORS: *alcohol-impaired driving, designated driving, prompts, incentives*

1. Considerable evidence indicates that driving while intoxicated (DWI) remains a serious social and public health problem. For example, it is estimated that 40% of all persons in the United States will be involved in an alcohol-related traffic accident ("Alcohol-Related Traffic Fatalities," 1990). Although suppression efforts using increased legal sanctions and enhanced enforcement programs have affected these problems (National Highway Traffic Safety Administration, 1990), the young adult group continues to display high rates of DWI, with drivers 21 to 24 years of age having the highest proportion of intoxicated drivers among all age groups (Washington Traffic Safety Commission, 1994).

2. Over the past decade, a variety of federal, state, and private agencies have advocated the use of designated driver (DD) programs to reduce DWIs and alcohol-related accidents (Wagenaar, 1992). Designated drivers act as chauffeurs for groups of drinkers, and do not consume alcohol themselves on these occasions. In this manner, sober individuals are available to safely drive the possibly intoxicated group, reducing the risk to themselves and others. Despite its intuitive appeal and the considerable attention it has received, very little is known about DD, and the idea remains somewhat controversial. For instance, Dejong and Wallack (1992), in a critique of the concept of designated driving, argued that these programs have the potential to produce such negative side effects as encouraging excessive drinking by the driver's companions and distracting attention from other public health issues related to alcohol use. To date, however, there have been few studies of the actual frequency of DD or the variables that affect such behavior (Wagenaar, 1992). Because an informal survey of local drinking establishments revealed that few people were participating in existing DD programs, we designed an experiment to test the effects of prompts and incentives on the frequency of DD at a local bar.

Method

3. A local bar, patronized primarily by college students and other young adults who drive to the premises, agreed to participate in a study of DD. The establishment is divided into a "sports" bar area and a separate restaurant. After 9 p.m. on the weekends, the restaurant is closed and becomes a dance area with a video jockey, and the entire establishment functions as a single bar. This bar had a long-established program in which designated drivers were given free soft drinks or coffee. To participate, a person simply identified himself or herself to a server or the bartender. The number of people identifying themselves as designated drivers was the primary dependent variable for this experiment.

4. Teams of four undergraduates, supervised by a graduate student, observed in the bar from 8:30 p.m. until 1:00 a.m. on Friday and Saturday nights. They were stationed near the bar so that when the bartender received a designated driver drink order, he signaled the observers. Two observers then followed the server and noted who received the drink. The observers had to agree on the identification for the person to be counted as a designated driver. This person was periodically observed during the evening and was followed when the group left the bar in order to determine if the individual was in fact a designated driver. In addition, once every half hour the observers made a rough count of patrons to insure that variations in the number of designated drivers did not simply reflect how busy the bar happened to be.

5. An ABAB reversal design was used to evaluate the effects of a new DD program. First, a stable baseline was established for the number of designated drivers observed with the bar's standard program of free soft drinks and coffee. The subsequent intervention consisted of two components. Three framed posters (50 cm by 70 cm) were mounted strategically around the bar and 10 placards (12 cm by 16 cm) were placed on tables. The announcements were multicolored and presented the following text: "Designated drivers, tell your server who you are, your drinks are on us! Free O'Doul's, Cutter, Sharp's or other non-alcoholic beers & wines, mixed drinks & coffees." We hypothesized that the combination of prominent announcements and instructions and the availability of more desirable alternative beverages would increase the number of people volunteering to be designated drivers. All other procedures remained the same. These conditions were in effect until the frequency of designated drivers stabilized. Next, the signs and observers were withdrawn, and the standard designated driver program was reinstated for 6 weeks. This period corresponded to the university's semester break and the first 3 weeks of the new term. The observers then returned to the bar, and a second baseline was established, followed by the reintroduction of the signs and alternative

Brigham, T. A., Meier, S. M., & Goodner, V. (1995). Increasing designated driving with a program of prompts and incentives. *Journal of Applied Behavior Analysis, 28*, 83-84. Copyright © 1995 by the Society for the Experimental Analysis of Behavior, Inc. Reprinted by permission.

This investigation was supported by funds provided for medical and biological research by the State of Washington Initiative Measure 171. We are grateful for the cooperation and support of the owners of Pete's Bar and Grill, M. Bryne and F. Maryott and their staff. Requests for reprints should be sent to T. A. Brigham, Department of Psychology, Washington State University, Pullman, Washington 99164-4820. Received February 2, 1994; final acceptance June 21, 1994; Action Editor, Richard Winett.

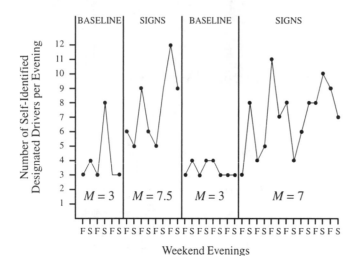

Weekend Evenings

beverages. Because the research began early in the spring term, it was possible to run the second intervention considerably longer than the first.

Results and Discussion

6.   The observers were able to locate 194 (93%) of the 209 designated drivers identified to the bartender and to follow 175 of those individuals into the parking lot. All of the identified designated drivers except two actually drove their group from the establishment. Of the 194 designated drivers, 101 were white males, 6 were African American males, and 87 were white females. This pattern generally reflects the distribution of patrons frequenting the bar. Attendance per night was also very consistent over the course of the study (respective means were on Fridays: Baseline 1 = 157, Intervention 1 = 160, Baseline 2 = 158, Intervention 2 = 152; on Saturdays: Baseline 1 = 74, Intervention 1 = 74, Baseline 2 = 73, Intervention 2 = 71); thus, the data should represent a reliable picture of DD.

7.   The main results of the experiment are presented in the figure, which shows that the prompts, incentives, and rewards had a clear and substantial effect on the numbers of self-identified designated drivers at this bar. The median number of designated drivers per night in each baseline condition was 3; the median increased to 7.5 for the first intervention period and was 7 during the replication. In contrast to earlier failures of programs based in Greek houses or residence halls to increase DD (e.g., Shore, Gregory, & Tatiock, 1991), the present results are encouraging and suggest that it is possible to increase DD in a college bar with a relatively simple intervention. Because of this simplicity, the bar has maintained the program and continues to be pleased with it. The generality and social significance of the results remain open to question. It is beyond the scope of

this paper to discuss all of the variables that affect alcohol-related accidents and how increased DD might interact with them. Nevertheless, the issue of whether having a designated driver sanctions increased or abusive drinking by the rest of the group needs to be addressed. In the present study, it was not possible to determine with confidence whether or not increased drinking occurred, but over the course of the study no group with a designated driver ever became disruptive. Moreover, a recently completed survey of 400 individuals who reported being a designated driver in the past found that less than 5% of respondents reported that DD was used as a procedure for everybody else to get excessively intoxicated (Meier, Brigham, Sanford, Warren, & Richmond, 1994).

8.   Thus, it appears the potential dangers of designated driving have been overstated, but it also seems unlikely that increasing DD will be the single solution to the problems of alcohol-impaired driving. Rather, DD can play an important role as a model of positive social behavior for young adults while contributing to efforts to reduce alcohol-related accidents.

References

Alcohol-related traffic fatalities among youth and young adults—United States, 1982-1989. (1990). *Morbidity and Mortality Weekly Report, 40*, 187-198.

DeJong, W., & Wallack, L. (1992). The role of designated driver programs in the prevention of alcohol-impaired driving: A critical reassessment. *Health Education Quarterly, 19*, 429-442.

Meier, S., Brigham, T. A., Sanford, A., Warren, L., & Richmond, E. (1994). *Designated driving behavior: A survey of attitudes, opinions, and behavior in three communities.* Manuscript under review.

National Highway Traffic Safety Administration. (1990). *Fatal accident reporting system (FARS 90).* Washington, DC: U.S. Government Printing Office.

Shore, E. R., Gregory, T., & Tatlock, L. (1991). College students' reactions to a designated driver program: An exploratory study. *Journal of Alcohol and Drug Education, 37*, 1-6.

Wagenaar, A. (1992). Designated driver programs: A commentary on the DeJong and Wallack article. *Health Education Quarterly, 19*, 443-445.

Washington Traffic Safety Commission. (1994). *1993 fatal collisions in Washington.* Olympia, WA: Washington Department of Transportation.

Factual Questions

1. The letters "DD" stand for what words?

2. What is the primary dependent variable?

3. The observers were able to locate what percentage of the 209 designated drivers identified to the bartender?

4. How many of the 175 identified designated drivers who were followed into the parking lot actually drove their group?

5. On the average, how many designated drivers per night were identified during the first intervention period?

Questions for Discussion

6. Have the researchers described the bar in sufficient detail?

7. Speculate on why the researchers had designated drivers identified by two observers instead of only one.

8. In general terms, what is an "ABAB reversal design"? (See paragraph 5.)

9. In general terms, what is a "baseline"?

10. What was the independent variable?

11. Why is it important to know that "attendance per night was very consistent over the course of the study"? (See paragraph 6).

12. The researchers report the "median" number of designated drivers per night. What is the definition of the "median"?

13. Is the "replication" of the study (that is, establishing a second baseline and introducing the intervention a second time) an important feature of this research project? Explain.

14. Might the behavior of the designated drivers be affected if they became aware that they were being followed by observers into the parking lot? Explain.

15. To what population(s), if any, would you be willing to generalize the results of this study?

16. How difficult would it be to collect data on "the issue of whether having a designated driver sanctions increased or abusive drinking by the rest of the group"? (See paragraph 7.) How might you collect such data in a future study?

17. Why is this study classified as a type of "experiment" in this book? (See the table of contents of this book.) In other words, what feature(s) of this study make it an experiment?

Quality Ratings

DIRECTIONS: Indicate your level of agreement with each of the following statements by circling a number from 5 for strongly agree (SA) to 1 for strongly disagree (SD). If you believe that an item is not applicable to this research article, leave it blank. Be prepared to explain your ratings.

A. The introduction establishes the importance of the research topic.
SA   5   4   3   2   1   SD

B. The literature review establishes the context for the study.
SA   5   4   3   2   1   SD

C. The research purpose, question, or hypothesis is clearly stated.
SA   5   4   3   2   1   SD

D. The method of sampling is sound.
SA   5   4   3   2   1   SD

E. Relevant demographics (for example, age, gender, and ethnicity) are described.
SA   5   4   3   2   1   SD

F. Measurement procedures are adequate.
SA   5   4   3   2   1   SD

G. The results are clearly described.
SA   5   4   3   2   1   SD

H. The discussion/conclusion is appropriate.
SA   5   4   3   2   1   SD

I. Despite any flaws noted above, the report is worthy of publication.
SA   5   4   3   2   1   SD

ARTICLE 26

EFFECTS OF COLLABORATIVE PEER TUTORING
ON URBAN SEVENTH GRADERS

Glenn M. Roswal *Jacksonville State University*

Aquilla A. Mims *Jacksonville State University*

Michael D. Evans *F. C. Hammond Junior High School, Virginia*

Brenda Smith *F. C. Hammond Junior High School, Virginia*

Mary Young *F. C. Hammond Junior High School, Virginia*

Michael Burch *F. C. Hammond Junior High School, Virginia*

Ronald Croce *University of New Hampshire*

Michael A. Horvat *University of Georgia*

Martin Block *University of Virginia*

The effects of a collaborative peer tutor teaching program on the self-concept and school-based attitudes of seventh-grade students at a large urban junior high school were explored. Many of the students in the sample had been previously identified to be at risk by traditional school identification strategies. The study consisted of the 282 subjects enrolled in the seventh grade at F. C. Hammond Junior High School in Alexandria, Virginia. The Piers-Harris Self-Concept Scale was used to measure self-concept in subjects. The Demos D (Drop-out) Scale was used to measure student tendency to drop out of school. Data were collected at two points during the 16-week period (immediately before program onset and immediately after program completion). A post hoc analysis revealed that students in the collaborative peer tutor teaching program demonstrated significant improvement in dropout scores compared with students in both the traditional class using group learning activities and the traditional class using individual learning activities. There were no significant differences between the traditional class groups. The results of this study indicate that a collaborative peer tutor teaching program can be effective in eliciting improvements in self-concept and attitudes toward school in seventh-grade urban students.

1. Instructional strategies to enhance the learning environment in schools serving urban adolescents have become prevalent in the recent literature. Cooperative learning, peer/cross-age grouping, peer tutoring, teacher training, and school-community support have been discussed as viable strategies (Franklin, 1992; Prater, 1992). Cooperative teaching (Self, Benning, Marston, & Magnusson, 1991), the collaborative team (Greer, 1991), and peer collaboration (Johnson & Pugach, 1991) have been used successfully with "at-risk" students. Other studies have been conducted with students in urban areas and from lower socioeconomic backgrounds. In the early 1980s, several studies revealed significant differences in the academic engagement of high- and low-socioeconomic status students (Greenwood, 1991), and collaborative teams were recommended as effective in the educational process of lower socioeconomic students (Harry, 1992). Other literature identified the junior or middle school years as critical to enhancing appropriate learning skills and attitudes as a predictor of school-based achievement and subsequent school dropout. Large percentages of students who dropped out during the middle school years were linked with nonintact families and were identified as at risk (Kortering, Haring, & Klockars, 1992). Research has indicated that students may fail and drop out because of low self-concept; thus, enhancing self-concept and self-esteem to combat the problem is recommended (Obiakor, 1992).

2. In particular, strategies using a collaborative teaching approach and peer tutoring have shown promise for decreasing school drop-out rates and increasing academic achievement. Interpersonal collaboration has been defined in the literature as "a style for direct interaction between at least two coequal parties voluntarily engaged in shared decision making as they work toward a common goal" (Friend & Cook, 1992, p. 5), and collaboration has been presented as an important concept at all levels of education (Stevens, Slaton, & Bunney, 1992). Collaboration has been recommended between general and special education teachers (Graden, 1989; Pugach & Johnson, 1989) to enhance achievement and provide a more appropriate education for students. Presently, students identified with specific learning difficulties have the highest drop-out rate among all students; 47% leave school early (Education of the Handicapped, 1988). A collaborative approach has been used as a means to confront this and other problems (Graden, 1989; Pugach & Johnson, 1989).

3. Peer tutoring is an effective strategy in fostering academic achievement of students. Stainback, Stainback, and Wilkinson (1992) recommended peer supports for achievement, and MacArthur, Schwartz, and Graham (1991) reported significant achievement using the peer tutoring strategy to help improve composition skills.

4. Our purpose in this project was to ascertain if a collaborative peer tutor teaching program could improve the self-concept and school-based attitudes of seventh-grade

Roswal, G. M. et al. (1995). Effects of collaborative peer tutoring on urban seventh graders. *Journal of Educational Research, 88,* 275-279. Reprinted with permission of the Helen Dwight Reid Educational Foundation. Published by Heldref Publications, 1319 Eighteenth St., N.W., Washington, DC 20036-1802. Copyright © 1995.

Address correspondence to Glenn M. Roswal, Jacksonville State University, Department of Health, Physical Education, & Recreation, 700 Pelham Road N., Jacksonville, AL 36265-9982.

The authors gratefully acknowledge the assistance of the Alexandria Public Schools and Robinette Banks-Williams and Don McDonough in conducting the project.

students at F. C. Hammond Junior High School. We hypothesized that a class based on a collaborative peer tutor teaching program would elicit greater positive changes in subjects than would classes based on traditional group learning activities or traditional individual learning activities. Specifically, participants were compared on measures of self-concept and school-based attitudes.

Method

Participants

5.   Our participants consisted of 282 seventh-grade students enrolled at F. C. Hammond Junior High School in Alexandria, Virginia. Hammond Junior High School is a part of the 10,000-student Alexandria Public School System located just outside Washington, DC. The age range of the students was 12 through 14 years, with a mean age of 13.6 years. Our sample included all students enrolled in the seventh grade at Hammond Junior High School who completed the project. Students were assigned to one of three groups, based on class assignment. The 101 students (48 boys and 53 girls) assigned to Group 1 participated in a class based on a collaborative peer tutor teaching program. The 95 students (47 boys and 48 girls) assigned to Group 2 participated in a traditional class based on group learning activities. The 86 students (45 boys and 41 girls) assigned to Group 3 participated in a traditional class based on individual learning activities. The groups' members were similar regarding primary language and race. English was the primary language for 97% of the students in Group 1 and Group 3 and for 96% of the students in Group 2. In Group 1, 80% of the students were African American; 15%, Caucasian; 3%, Hispanic; and 2%, other races. In Group 2, 78% were African American; 14%, Caucasian; 4%, Hispanic; and 4%, other races. In Group 3, 80% were African American; 14%, Caucasian; 3%, Hispanic; and 3%, other races.

Instrumentation

6.   We used the Piers-Harris Self-Concept Scale (Piers & Harris, 1969) to measure self-concept. The Piers-Harris scale is a self-report inventory consisting of 80 first-person declarative statements to which the subject responds yes or no. It is intended for use with students in Grades 4 through 12 and can be administered individually or in a group setting. Reading ability is estimated at the third-grade level. The scale produces an overall score in self-concept or a profile of six cluster scores in anxiety, popularity, happiness, satisfaction, physical appearance and attributes, behavior, and intellectual and school status. Reliability of the test is

reported by the authors with coefficients of .78 to .93 on the Kuder-Richardson formula, .90 and .97 in the Spearman-Brown odd-even formula, and .71 to .72 on test-retest reliability coefficients. Validity was ascertained through positive correlations with other self-concept scales.

7.   We used the Demos D (Dropout) Scale (Demos, 1970) to measure student tendency to drop out of school. The Demos D Scale consists of 29 statements for which the student indicates degree of agreement by choosing one of five response statements (*nearly always, most of the time, sometimes, very few times, or nearly never*). The scale was designed for students in Grades 7 through 12 and has applicability for students with fifth-grade reading ability. The scale may be administered individually or in a group setting. The Demos D manual reports adequate validity and reliability for use with the project sample. Specifically, face validity and content validity were determined by 69 psychological experts, used as judges, serving as one operational criterion. The judges screened all of the attitude scales and eliminated all elements of item irrelevance and ambiguity prior to final scale development. Reliability was reported with retest reliability coefficients of correlation ranging from .50 to .86. In addition, mean total score differences and individual scale differences between dropout and nondropout groups indicated adequate validity and reliability (Demos, 1970).

8.   We also ascertained participant attitude toward school by comparing school attendance for the 4 weeks before the intervention program with attendance for the final 4 weeks of the program.

Data Collection

9.   Pretest data collection was conducted 1 day before the initiation of the intervention program in January. Posttest data collection occurred 1 day after the completion of the intervention program in May. All data collection occurred during regularly scheduled class sessions.

Intervention Program

10.   The student participants were assigned to one of three groups depending on their class assignment. The intervention program was conducted over 16 weeks during January through May 1993. All the participants received instruction in English, mathematics, science, and social studies according to the regularly scheduled seventh-grade curriculum at Hammond Junior High School. Academic instruction for subjects assigned to Group 1 was through a 16-week collaborative peer tutor teaching program. Instruction was based on strategies

prevalent in the literature regarding the retention of at-risk students. However, the program also included elements from successful competitive programs in athletics (sports competition) and academics (scholar bowls). The inherent incentives of competition and the discipline necessary to achieve success in competitive programs have been shown to be effective in retaining students in school. This incentive may be especially true for students with little incentive to remain in school.

11.   Subjects assigned to Group 1 were divided into four teams of 25 subjects each. Teams were stratified to consist of approximately equal distributions of (a) high-achieving and low-achieving academic students, (b) heterogeneous academic levels, (c) multicultural social and economic backgrounds, (d) language differences, and (e) male and female students. Most important, each team consisted of low achievers (students most at risk to leave school early), moderate achievers (undermotivated students), and high achievers (motivated students). The four seventh-grade teachers conducting the collaborative peer tutor program assigned the students to teams. Teams were further subdivided into working groups of 5 participants each to facilitate student collaborative learning and peer tutoring. The teachers assigned the participants to teams based on their subjective analysis of the students' class achievement, classroom behavior, school effort, and daily attendance. Under the teachers' guidance, teams worked on a series of sequentially more difficult academic tasks 25 min. each day. The 25-min. period allowed teams to review materials, practice skills, and design questions under the direct guidance of higher achieving students and seventh-grade teachers.

12.   The team learning environment was structured to provide for a high degree of interaction between teachers and teams and a high degree of collaboration among team members, thus facilitating peer tutoring in an integrated setting. In particular, principles of curricula in collaborative teaching and peer tutoring framed the learning milieu. Each day, each team studied as a group and participated in group activities to facilitate learning in all of the curriculum areas. Thus, the students were involved in the collaborative peer tutor teaching program daily over the 16-week program (a total of 80 program days). As part of the daily instructional process, the teams designed and submitted four academic questions (with answers) in each of the four academic areas (English, mathematics, science, social studies) to the teachers. Questions were based on material learned during regular class periods. The teachers reviewed and compiled a pool of questions. Also, each day there

was an academic competition among four of the subteams with questions from the question pool. The competition took the form of a scholar bowl competition; teams responded to questions from a moderator in a panel format. Teams answered questions to accumulate points. Additional team points were awarded for appropriate student behavior during the week. Team success was based on the efforts of all the students on the team. Therefore, to be successful, all members of the team had to work together and support one another to ensure team success.

13. Throughout the program, the team of four seventh-grade teachers conducting the collaborative peer tutor program met to review program objectives, discuss student progress, and monitor each other's teams to ensure compliance with the intervention program model. In addition, one teacher, designated as the team leader, communicated with the teachers of Group 2 and Group 3 to ensure the overall integrity of the program.

14. The participants assigned to Group 2 and Group 3 also received instruction in English, mathematics, science, and social studies according to the regular seventh-grade academic program at Hammond Junior High School. Students in Group 2 and Group 3 participated in more traditional classroom settings with instruction based on traditional learning practices common in most academic settings — skill instruction through classroom lecture, academic skills and practice, audiovisual presentations, and homework. Group 2 focused on methods based on a traditional class using group learning activities. Group 3 concentrated on a traditional class setting using individual learning activities.

Results and Discussion

15. We analyzed the data using analysis of variance (ANOVA) procedures in a 3 x 2 (Group x Test) design, with group at three levels (collaborative peer tutor group, traditional class using group learning activities, traditional class using individual teaming activities) and test at two levels (pretest, posttest) for each dependent variable (Piers-Harris Self-Concept Scale scores and Demos D Scale scores). ANOVA procedures demonstrated a significant main effect for self-concept scores, $F(2, 279) =$ 21.39, $p < .0001$. A Fisher's protected LSD revealed that Group 1, the collaborative peer tutor teaching program, demonstrated a significant improvement in self-concept scores over both Group 2, the traditional class using group learning activities program ($p < .001$), and Group 3, the traditional class using individual learning activities program ($p < .05$). There was no

significant difference between Group 2 and Group 3. The group means and standard deviations for self-concept are reported in Table 1.

16. ANOVA procedures also demonstrated a significant main effect for Demos D (Dropout) Scale scores, $F(2, 279) = 9.76$, $p < .0001$. A Fisher's protected LSD revealed that Group 1, the collaborative peer tutor teaching program, demonstrated a significant improvement in dropout scores, compared with both Group 2 and Group 3. There was no significant difference between Group 2 and Group 3. The group means and standard deviations for dropout scale scores are reported in Table 2.

17. The data indicate that students participating in the collaborative peer tutor teaching program demonstrated a significant improvement over both traditional classroom groups in both self-concept and attitudes toward school as demonstrated by the dropout scale. As expected, self-concept scores increased for students participating in the collaborative peer tutor teaching program. It appeared that as students began to understand that the success of the team was dependent upon the success of each member of the team, self-concept was enhanced. Teacher anecdotal information indicated that this was true for both low achievers (those most at risk to leave school early) and high achievers.

18. The self-concept scores remained relatively stable for students who participated in the traditional classes and were not exposed to the

collaborative peer tutor program. Also, data relating to school-based attitudes, as measured by the Demos D Scale, indicated increased motivation to be in school, better attitudes toward school and teachers, and an enhanced awareness of the value of school attendance for those students involved in the collaborative peer tutor teaching program. Scores remained relatively stable in the two traditional classes.

19. It is important to note that objective data were also supported by anecdotal data collected by the teachers indicating that the students participating in the collaborative peer tutor teaching program enjoyed working together on their academic teams, turned in homework more frequently, exhibited more tolerant behaviors of their classmates, and demonstrated greater motivation to attend school to participate in the academic competitions. Teachers also used a teacher-made subjective checklist to chart discipline problems. Teachers reported that, in general, student referrals for discipline problems dramatically decreased for students in the collaborative peer tutor teaching group. There did not appear to be a substantial difference in student discipline problems in the other groups.

20. A visual inspection of attendance data indicated a meaningful increase in student attendance in the collaborative peer tutor group. During the 4 weeks preceding the intervention program, the students in Group 1 missed a total of 161 days of school, those in Group 2 missed a total of 168 days, and those in Group 3

Table 1 *Means and standard deviations for Piers-Harris Self-Concept Scale scores*

	Pretest		Posttest	
	M	SD	M	SD
Group 1 (n = 101) Collaborative program	56.90	16.54	63.26	12.28
Group 2 (n = 95) Group activities	56.16	16.46	53.76	16.87
Group 3 (n = 86) Individual activities	48.65	23.25	53.20	20.85

Table 2 *Means and standard deviations for Demos D (Dropout) Scale scores*

	Pretest		Posttest	
	M	SD	M	SD
Group 1 (n = 101) Collaborative program	64.06	37.41	54.00	10.55
Group 2 (n = 95) Group activities	65.38	16.57	71.20	19.69
Group 3 (n = 86) Individual activities	68.78	21.79	69.91	24.59

missed 93 days of school. During the final 4 weeks of the intervention program, student attendance increased in Group 1 (74 total days of school missed), increased slightly in Group 2 (120 total days of school missed), and remained basically unchanged in Group 3 (96 total days of school missed). The student attendance data conformed with subjective observations from the teachers that the students in Group 1 appeared to be more motivated about coming to school and staying in school. Subjective student comments indicated that school had become a more exciting place for the students in Group 1.

21. This study focused on the effect of the collaborative peer tutor teaching program on self-concept and school-based attitudes in seventh-grade students. There was no attempt to ascertain the effects on student achievement or student academic performance. Further study should investigate the effect on performance as measured by standardized tests, curricular grades, and intelligence test scores. Also, it might be appropriate to investigate the long-term effects of the program on student progress with all three teaching methods used in this study.

22. The results of this study indicate that a collaborative peer tutor teaching program can be effective in eliciting improvements in self-concept and attitudes toward school in seventh-grade urban students. Further, it appears that introducing a novel student-oriented program can result in improved attendance among students.

References

Demos, G. D. (1970). *The Demos D Scale*. Los Angeles: Western Psychological Services.

Education of the Handicapped. (1988). *Legislation News Service, 14*(5), 1, 5, 6.

Franklin, M. E. (1992). Culturally sensitive instructional practices for African-American learners with disabilities. *Exceptional Children, 59*(2), 115-122.

Friend, M., & Cook, L. (1992). *Interactions: Collaboration skills for school professionals*. New York: Longman.

Graden, J. L. (1989). Redefining prereferral intervention as intervention assistance: Collaboration between general and special education. *Exceptional Children, 56*(3), 227-231.

Greenwood, C. R. (1991). Longitudinal analysis of time, engagement, and achievement in at-risk versus non-risk students. *Exceptional Children, 57*(6), 521-535.

Greer, J. V. (1991). At-risk students in the fast lanes: Let them through. *Exceptional Children, 57*(5), 390-391.

Harry, B. (1992). Making sense of disability: Low-income, Puerto Rican parents' theories of the problem. *Exceptional Children, 59*(1), 27-40.

Johnson, L. J., & Pugach, M. C. (1991). Peer collaboration: Accommodating students with mild learning and behavior problems. *Exceptional Children, 57*(5), 454-461.

Kortering, L., Haring, N., & Klockars, A. (1992). The identification of high-school dropouts identified as learning disabled: Evaluating the utility of a discriminant analysis function. *Exceptional Children, 58*(5), 422-435.

MacArthur, C. A., Schwartz, S. S., & Graham, S. (1991). Effects of a reciprocal peer revision strategy in special education classrooms. *Learning Disabilities Research and Practice, 6*(4), 201-210.

Obiakor, F. E. (1992). Self-concept of African-American students: An operational model for special education. *Exceptional Children, 59*(2), 160-167.

Piers, E. V., & Harris, D. B. (1969). *Piers-Harris Self-Concept Scale*. Nashville: Counselor Recordings and Tests.

Prater, L. P. (1992). Early pregnancy and academic achievement of African-American youth. *Exceptional Children, 59*(2), 141-149.

Pugach, M. C., & Johnson, L. J. (1989). The challenge of implementing collaboration between general and special education. *Exceptional Children, 56*(3), 232-235.

Self, H., Benning, A., Marston, D., & Magnusson, D. (1991). Cooperative teaching project: A model for students at risk. *Exceptional Children, 58*(1), 26-34.

Stainback, W., Stainback, S., & Wilkinson, A. (1992). Encouraging peer supports and friendships. *Teaching Exceptional Children, 24*(2), 6-11.

Stevens, K. B., Slaton, D. B., & Bunney, S. (1992). A collaborative research effort between public schools and university faculty members. *Teacher Education and Special Education, 15*(1), 1-8.

Factual Questions

1. In which paragraph is the research hypothesis explicitly stated?

2. Are the data in this study based on all students enrolled in the seventh grade at Hammond Junior High School? Explain.

3. How was the validity of the Piers-Harris scale determined?

4. What was the average pretest score for Group 3 on the Piers-Harris Self-Concept Scale?

5. The self-concept scores on the pretest were most variable in which group?

6. The difference between Groups 1 and 2 on self-concept was statistically significant at what probability level?

7. How were discipline problems measured in this study?

8. What was the *average* number of days absent in Group 1 during the four weeks preceding the intervention? (Divide the number of absences by the number of students in the group.)

9. Which of the three groups received the collaborative peer tutoring intervention?

Questions for Discussion

10. The title of the article does not mention the major dependent variables (self-concept and dropping out). Should it? (Keep in mind that titles should be concise.)

11. The authors cite literature on collaboration between general and special education teachers in their literature review. What is your opinion on this?

12. What was the basis for assigning students to one of the three groups? For the purposes of experimentation, is it a good way to assign students to treatments? Explain.

13. Is it important to know that the three groups of students were similar in terms of primary language and race? (See paragraph 5.) Would you also be interested in knowing whether they were similar on other variables? Explain.

14. Is the test-retest reliability of the Piers-Harris Self-Concept Scale adequate? (See paragraph 6.)

15. Would you like to know more about the validity of the Demos D Scale? Why? Why not?

16. Is the intervention program described in sufficient detail to permit replication? (See paragraphs 10 through 13.) Explain.

17. Would you be interested in knowing more about the teachers who conducted the three types of instruction? Why? Why not?

18. In your opinion, are the anecdotal data important? (See paragraph 19.) Would you like to know more about them? Explain.

19. Do you think the authors should have conducted significance tests on the attendance data? Explain.

20. In paragraph 21, the authors note that they did not attempt to determine the effects on student achievement or academic performance. Would this be an important topic for future research? Explain.

21. Why is it important to have a control group (in this case, Groups 2 and 3) in a study of this type?

22. In this book, this study is classified as a "quasi-experiment." (See the table of contents for the classifications.) Is this the appropriate classification? Why? Why not?

23. If you could make just one change in the research methodology in a future study on this topic, what would it be?

24. To what population(s), if any, would you be willing to generalize the results of this study?

25. Has this article convinced you that your local junior high school should consider using collaborative peer tutoring? Why? Why not?

Quality Ratings

DIRECTIONS: Indicate your level of agreement with each of the following statements by circling a number from 5 for strongly agree (SA) to 1 for strongly disagree (SD). If you believe that an item is not applicable to this research article, leave it blank. Be prepared to explain your ratings.

A. The introduction establishes the importance of the research topic.
   SA   5   4   3   2   1   SD

B. The literature review establishes the context for the study.
   SA   5   4   3   2   1   SD

C. The research purpose, question, or hypothesis is clearly stated.
   SA   5   4   3   2   1   SD

D. The method of sampling is sound.
   SA   5   4   3   2   1   SD

E. Relevant demographics (for example, age, gender, and ethnicity) are described.
   SA   5   4   3   2   1   SD

F. Measurement procedures are adequate.
   SA   5   4   3   2   1   SD

G. The results are clearly described.
   SA   5   4   3   2   1   SD

H. The discussion/conclusion is appropriate.
   SA   5   4   3   2   1   SD

I. Despite any flaws noted above, the report is worthy of publication.
   SA   5   4   3   2   1   SD

USING RELAXATION TECHNIQUES AND POSITIVE SELF-ESTEEM TO IMPROVE ACADEMIC ACHIEVEMENT OF COLLEGE STUDENTS

Elliott H. Schreiber *Rowan College of New Jersey*
Karen N. Schreiber *University of Delaware*

This study examined whether after 20 sessions over 10 weeks of Jacobson's muscle relaxation accompanied by encouragement of positive self-esteem academic examination scores of 22 undergraduate college students would improve by comparison with those of a control group of 30 students. The relaxation group had significantly higher examination grades than the control group, but there was no significant mean difference between the groups on the Cattell and Scheier Anxiety Scale or a two-item measure of self-esteem.

1. Previous work (e.g., 2, 4, 5, 6) indicated relaxation techniques can improve achievement scores and skills. In this study, undergraduate students' anxiety, self-esteem, and examination scores in educational psychology before and after practice with muscle relaxation techniques were examined.

Method

2. A sample of 52 students between 19 and 40 years of age ($M = 23$ yr.) volunteered to participate. They were predominantly Caucasian and of middle socioeconomic status. In the relaxation group were six men and 16 women whose average SAT score was 970; in the control group, there were 13 men and 17 women whose average SAT score was 980. Scores were taken with permission from cumulative college records. Both groups had an over-all college grade average of C+ and were nonpsychology majors. Classes, randomly selected from 11 sections of educational psychology, were taught by a colleague.

3. During the first week of the semester, one group was told that beginning at Week 5 during the last 15 min. of class, twice a week for 10 weeks, they would be instructed in muscle relaxation which would help them in their course work. The control group was told that they would be given guidance to help them to do superior work in class. Both classes were told that their names would be kept confidential and were asked not to discuss the class with other students.

4. Jacobson muscle relaxation techniques (2) were used to build concentration skills and recall of coursework. The students were taught how to contract muscle groups of the body to produce tension and then to relax these muscle groups. Also, Rogers' (3) positive self-concept with emphasis on personal worth and self-actualization was used with the relaxation group. The control class was given 15-min. review sessions. Both groups were told to attend all classes; data of those students who missed two sessions were not analyzed.

5. The two groups were examined on self-esteem and anxiety using the Cattell and Scheier Anxiety Scale (1). Self-esteem was evaluated on the basis of response to two questions about feelings. At the beginning of the semester and prior to the final examination, students were asked to write how they felt, either positively or negatively, about themselves in the course and how they felt about their success in the course.

Results

6. The groups were given midterm examinations in Week 9 and final examinations in Week 15. Differences between means on these tests were assessed by *t* tests. On the midterm examination, means of the two classes were significantly different ($t_{50} = 2.13$, $p < .03$) on a one-tailed test, with higher grades by the relaxation group. Final examination mean scores were also significantly different ($t_{50} = 1.90$, $p < .05$) on a one-tailed test, with higher scores for the relaxation group. (See Table 1.)

Table 1 *Grades on midterm and final examinations by two groups*

Group	n	Midterm Examination M	SD	Range	Final Examination M	SD	Range
Relaxation	22	79.0	10.1	40–98	75.0	9.7	57–90
Control	30	73.0	10.2	40–92	70.0	8.8	47–89

Table 2 *Mean scores and standard deviations on Cattell and Scheier Anxiety Scale by sex and class*

Group	Sex	n	Pretest Scores M	SD	Range	Posttest Scores M	SD	Range
Relaxation	Men	6	34	5	31–44	32	2	29–35
	Women	16	30	11	2–53	26	11	2–40
Control	Men	13	29	5	16–37	31	9	14–44
	Women	17	31	11	17–52	30	12	12–60

Schreiber, E. H., & Schreiber, K. N. (1995). Using relaxation techniques and positive self-esteem to improve academic achievement of college students. *Psychological Reports*, 76, 929-930. Copyright © Psychological Reports 1995.

Address correspondence to Elliott H. Schreiber, Ed.D., Psychology Department, Rowan College of New Jersey, 201 Mullica Hill Road, Glassboro, NJ 08028.

7. Scores on the Cattell and Scheier Anxiety Scale for the two groups are shown in Table 2. There were no significant differences between groups. Also, on both items of self-esteem six students of the relaxation group and eight students of the control group expressed positive feelings at pretest; prior to the final examination, 18 of 22 and 15 of 30 students, respectively, expressed positive feelings. These results indicate research with larger and more heterogeneous samples of college students and high school students is advisable.

References

1. Cattell, R. B., & Scheier, I. H. *The meaning and measurement of neuroticism and anxiety*. New York: Ronald, 1961.
2. Jacobson, E. *Progressive relaxation*. Chicago, IL: Univer. of Chicago Press, 1938.
3. Rogers, C. R. *Client centered therapy*. Boston, MA: Houghton Mifflin, 1951.
4. Schreiber, E. H. Using hypnosis to improve performance of college basketball players. *Perceptual and Motor Skills*, 1991, *72*, 536-538.
5. Schreiber, E. H. A study of hypnosis in improving academic achievement of college students. *Psychological Reports*, 1992, *71*, 1161-1162.
6. Wolpe, J. *The practice of behavior therapy*. New York: Pergamon, 1969.

Factual Questions

1. What was the total number of students in the relaxation group?

2. What was the relaxation group told during the first week of the semester?

3. Did the treatments begin before or after the midterm examination was administered?

4. On the midterm examination, the average student in the relaxation group was how many points higher than the average student in the control group?

5. What inferential statistic was used to test for significance?

6. Were the differences between the means on the Cattell and Scheier Anxiety Scale statistically significant?

7. Eighteen of 22 relaxation group students expressed positive feelings on the two self-concept items prior to the final examination. This is 81.8% of the group. (Note: 18 divided by 22 times 100 yields 81.8.) What is the corresponding percentage for the control group?

Questions for Discussion

8. Is it important to know that the two groups were similar in average SAT scores? Why? Why not?

9. Were individual subjects assigned at random to the relaxation and control groups? Is this important to know when evaluating the design of the study? Why? Why not?

10. Name the independent variable(s). Are they described in sufficient detail?

11. Name the dependent variable(s). Are they described in sufficient detail?

12. On the basis of the information in this report, do you believe that the difference between the two means on the final examination was caused by the treatments?

13. Would you classify the design used in this study as true-experimental, quasi-experimental, or pre-experimental? Explain.

14. To what population(s), if any, would you be willing to generalize the results of this study?

15. If you were conducting another study on the same topic, what changes, if any, would you make in the research methodology?

16. What is your opinion on the researchers' suggestion for future research in this area?

Quality Ratings

DIRECTIONS: Indicate your level of agreement with each of the following statements by circling a number from 5 for strongly agree (SA) to 1 for strongly disagree (SD). If you believe that an item is not applicable to this research article, leave it blank. Be prepared to explain your ratings.

A. The introduction establishes the importance of the research topic.
SA   5   4   3   2   1   SD

B. The literature review establishes the context for the study.
SA   5   4   3   2   1   SD

C. The research purpose, question, or hypothesis is clearly stated.
SA   5   4   3   2   1   SD

D. The method of sampling is sound.
SA   5   4   3   2   1   SD

E. Relevant demographics (for example, age, gender, and ethnicity) are described.
SA   5   4   3   2   1   SD

F. Measurement procedures are adequate.
SA   5   4   3   2   1   SD

G. The results are clearly described.
SA   5   4   3   2   1   SD

H. The discussion/conclusion is appropriate.
SA   5   4   3   2   1   SD

I. Despite any flaws noted above, the report is worthy of publication.
SA   5   4   3   2   1   SD

ISOLATING THE EFFECTS OF ACTIVE RESPONDING IN COMPUTER-BASED INSTRUCTION

Roger M. Tudor *Westfield State College*

This experiment evaluated the effects of requiring overt answer construction in computer-based programmed instruction using an alternating treatments design. Four college students worked through an instructional program that alternated between presenting frames with blanks requiring overt responses and complete frames without blanks. All students produced a higher percentage of correct posttest answers corresponding to program segments that required overt answer construction.

DESCRIPTORS: academic behavior, programmed instruction. computer-based instruction, instructional design, alternating treatment design

1. The increased use of computers in education has created a resurgence of interest in programmed instruction as a method for establishing new repertoires. In well-designed programmed instruction, the student is required to respond actively. Tudor and Bostow (1991) found that students who overtly constructed and typed their responses to computer-presented frame blanks answered more posttest questions correctly, on average, than those who simply read through frames without blanks. Because this was a between-groups study, averaging across subjects within groups made it more difficult to identify functional relationships and limits the generality of the results. The present experiment replicates and extends the results of Tudor and Bostow by using an alternating treatments design to isolate more carefully the effects of active responding in programmed instruction. By alternating the presentation of frames with blanks requiring an overt response and complete frames without blanks to each student, the independent contribution of these two presentation formats was evaluated.

Method

2. Four undergraduates worked through a computer program that presented operant conditioning and instructional design principles. From a 315-frame program originally used by Tudor and Bostow (1991), 189 frames were selected. All instructional stimuli were presented on IBM® PS2, Model 30 computers that included color monitors, disk drives, and keyboards.

3. The present analysis used an alternating treatments design similar to one described by Sindelar, Rosenberg, and Wilson (1985). The program was divided into four equal segments, each with an independent (nonoverlapping content) set of instructional frames. The segments alternated between having students type responses to frame blanks and read complete frames without blanks. When responses were typed the computer presented the words "correct" or "incorrect," followed by the next frame with the correct answer. These conditions are directly comparable to stimuli previously presented to subjects of Groups 1 and 5 by Tudor and Bostow (1991).

4. Two students were randomly assigned to work through program segments in the following order: (a) overt responding to blanks, (b) reading frames without blanks, (c) overt responding to blanks, and (d) reading frames without blanks (OROR). To control for the effects of sequence and any possible changes in program difficulty, 2 additional students were assigned to work through the same program in the opposite order: (a) reading frames without blanks, (b) overt responding to blanks, (c) reading frames without blanks, and (d) overt responding to blanks (RORO).

5. One day before the experiment, students supplied written answers to a 60-item fill-in-the-blank pretest. These questions corresponded to important program-presented concepts and principles. As students subsequently worked through overt response segments, the number of correct and incorrect responses was recorded, as was the time to complete each segment. Synonyms were not accepted as correct responses. Immediately after finishing the program, each student completed a posttest that was identical to the pretest.

Results and Discussion

6. Each student's responses on the pretest and posttest were evaluated and then partitioned into one of four program segments. The numbers of posttest questions corresponding to these program segments were 13, 16, 15, and 16, respectively. As shown in the figure, all students produced a higher percentage of correct posttest answers when they overtly constructed answers to frame blanks compared to reading frames without blanks. The added contribution of overt answer construction above that of simply reading completed frames was (from left to right for each student in the figure) 26.5%, 28%, 12%, and 23.5%, an overall average difference of 22.5%. The benefits of overt answer construction did not appear to vary with the presentation order of program segments. The results of a paired t test showed overt answer construction to be superior to reading completed frames, $t(3) = 2.37$, $p = .05$. The effect size corresponding to this t value is .65. When working through program segments that required overt answer construction, students averaged 66.9% correct in typing responses. Typing responses into the computer increased the length of time needed to complete these program segments by an average of 10 min. Prolonged exposure to these instructional stimuli may have contributed to higher posttest scores. In addition, the effects of the pretest in each student's immediate history may have also influenced these results in unknown ways.

7. These results replicate and extend those of Tudor and Bostow (1991). First, the instructional effects of overt answer construction were reproduced in all students. Active responding appears to be functionally related to greater achievement. Second, the counterbalanced design permitted the isolation of the effects of active responding. Other single-subject research designs are not as easily adapted to evaluate the

Tudor, R. M. (1995). Isolating the effects of active responding in computer-based instruction. *Journal of Applied Behavior Analysis*, 28, 343-344. Copyright © 1995 by the Society for the Experimental Analysis of Behavior, Inc. Reprinted by permission.

Address correspondence and reprint requests to Roger M. Tudor, Department of Psychology, Westfield State College, Westfield, Massachusetts 01086. Received November 21, 1994; final acceptance May 28, 1995; Action Editor, Donald Hantula.

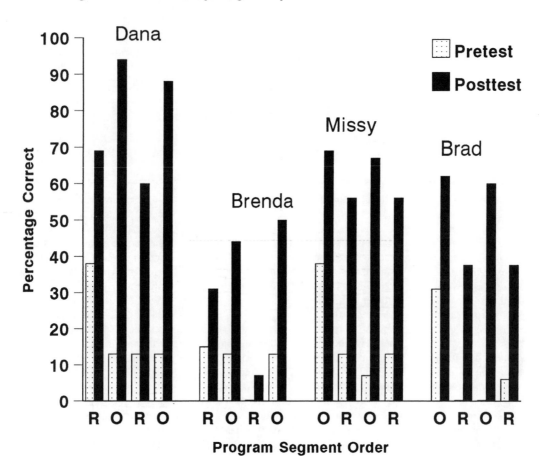

cumulative response-strengthening effects of programmed instruction. A number of variables related to the effectiveness of instructional programs and computer-based instruction can now be reexamined with increased resolving power.

8. Additional problems do remain to be solved, however. For example, answers to test questions may not adequately summarize all that is learned in programmed instruction. They are a superficial and rare form of verbal behavior in which responses are evoked out of order and topography is overemphasized. Tudor and Bostow (1991) have previously reported that students could better apply their "knowledge" (as measured by a subsequent application task) after completing an interactive program. Unfortunately, the present research did not evaluate generalization, because separate application tasks could not be designed for individual program segments. Evaluating the effects of generalization will remain a challenge for future research.

References

Sindelar, P. T., Rosenberg, M. S., & Wilson, R. J. (1985). An adapted alternating treatments design for instructional research. *Education & Treatment of Children, 8,* 67-76.

Tudor, R. M., & Bostow, D. E. (1991). Computer-programmed instruction: The relation of required interaction to practical application. *Journal of Applied Behavior Analysis, 24,* 361-368.

Factual Questions

1. What does the researcher mean by "independent" set of instructional frames?

2. In "OROR," what does "O" stand for?

3. In "OROR," what does "R" stand for?

4. How many students were assigned to the RORO condition?

5. According to the figure, were there gains from pretest to posttest in the R (reading without blanks) condition?

6. According to the figure, did the R or O condition produce higher posttest scores?

7. What test of statistical significance was used?

8. The difference between the two conditions (O and R) was statistically significant at what probability level?

9. On the average, how much longer did it take the students to complete the program segments when responding overtly?

Questions for Discussion

10. Would it be helpful to know the content (subject matter) covered by the program? Explain.

11. If all four students had been assigned to work through the program in the OROR order, would the design of the study be stronger or weaker?

12. The researcher states that "synonyms were not accepted as correct responses." What is your opinion on this decision?

13. Do you agree with the researcher's statement that "Prolonged exposure to these instructional stimuli may have contributed

to higher posttest scores"? (See paragraph 6.) Explain.

14. In paragraph 7, the author uses the term "counterbalanced design." What does this mean?

15. In your opinion, how important is the problem discussed in paragraph 8?

16. To what population(s), if any, would you be willing to generalize the results of this study?

17. If you were conducting another study on this topic, what changes in research methodology, if any, would you make?

Quality Ratings

DIRECTIONS: Indicate your level of agreement with each of the following statements by circling a number from 5 for strongly agree (SA) to 1 for strongly disagree (SD). If you believe that an item is not applicable to this research article, leave it blank. Be prepared to explain your ratings.

A. The introduction establishes the importance of the research topic.
   SA   5   4   3   2   1   SD

B. The literature review establishes the context for the study.
   SA   5   4   3   2   1   SD

C. The research purpose, question, or hypothesis is clearly stated.
   SA   5   4   3   2   1   SD

D. The method of sampling is sound.
   SA   5   4   3   2   1   SD

E. Relevant demographics (for example, age, gender, and ethnicity) are described.
   SA   5   4   3   2   1   SD

F. Measurement procedures are adequate.
   SA   5   4   3   2   1   SD

G. The results are clearly described.
   SA   5   4   3   2   1   SD

H. The discussion/conclusion is appropriate.
   SA   5   4   3   2   1   SD

I. Despite any flaws noted above, the report is worthy of publication.
   SA   5   4   3   2   1   SD

ARTICLE 29

AN EXERCISE FOR INCREASING STUDENTS' UNDERSTANDING OF LIFE-SPAN DEVELOPMENTAL PSYCHOLOGY

F. Richard Ferraro *University of North Dakota*

During the first week of a class in developmental psychology, students listed 5 to 7 characteristics they believed represent life-span developmental characteristics for the categories of infants, young children, adolescents, middle-aged adults, and older adults. Students retained their lists, which were referred to during discussion throughout the course. Students reported this activity increased their understanding of topics central to life-span developmental psychology.

1. Students from many varied disciplines, e.g., psychology, nursing, occupational therapy, physical therapy, and sociology, enroll in developmental psychology courses. To take advantage of this variation, an exercise during the first week of class can identify students' perceptions and thoughts concerning developmental psychology. This exercise (a) allows students to elaborate on their conceptions of developmental psychology, (b) allows for an educational experience which can be referenced at any point during the course, and (c) increases students' understanding of various components of developmental psychology.

2. In particular, this exercise illustrates the subtle biases and stereotypes people hold, especially about elderly persons, e.g., ageism. For instance, one point made immediately after students turn in their lists of characteristics is how closely the characteristics of infants and older adults match, i.e., dependent, helpless, and fragile. As the semester progresses, we discuss what ageism is and how it develops (Atchley, 1983; Butler, 1969). Students are reminded of the characteristics they listed earlier for older adults. We then discuss how the students formed their particular views of elderly persons.

3. During the first week of class (enrollment averages 165 students per semester), students write down the following five category headings: infants, young children, adolescents, middle-aged adults, and older adults. Next, they are instructed to list five to seven characteristics which typify each of these categories. This exercise requires approximately 5 to 10 min. to complete. When finished, students hand in their responses for discussion. Having tallied their replies, the next scheduled class period students' responses are returned for later reference with a summary of type and frequency of responses from the various categories. Responses are quite varied, as illustrated in Table 1 by data of two randomly chosen students.

4. I have used this activity for three years and plan to continue doing so. I also use this technique in an advanced developmental psychology class (open to upper-division undergraduates and graduate students), which is typically a much smaller class. In both classes, students fill out standard course evaluations required by the department and the university. In addition to standard multiple-choice questions, the evaluation form allows written comments. Students list three good and three bad aspects of the course in this space. The majority of students always indicate participating in this exercise is informative, especially when their responses are reviewed during class.

5. In summary, this exercise has several benefits. First, it increases students' understanding of issues relating to developmental psychology. Second, it provides an adequate context from which to begin a discussion at any point during the semester. Third, it works well in small and large classes, thereby personalizing the discussions that often result, i.e., more students participate and become involved in classroom discussions, even in the large groups. Finally, students can compare their (often biased) expectations against the empirical literature. Students indicate in participation and on evaluation forms that they enjoy this exercise.

References

Atchley, R. C. (1983). *Aging: Continuity and change.* Belmont, CA: Wadsworth.

Butler, R. (1969). Ageism: Another form of bigotry. *Gerontologist, 9,* 243.

Table 1 *Sample response patterns of developmental psychology characteristics by category*

Subject	Category				
	Infants	Young Children	Adolescents	Middle Age	Old Age
1	dependent	energetic	choices	loving	frail
	small	selfish	moody	open	dependent
	helpless	school	acceptance	family	helpless
	fragile	active	wild	mature	wise
	tiny	fun	innocent	work	senile
	need help	struggle	plans	achieve	slow
2	fussy	eager	rude	happy	unhappy
	needs care	carefree	rebel	family	disease
	annoying	bold	cool	hopeful	sickly
	tired	partying	literate	home	retired
	diapers	curious	energetic	sure	diapers
	unsure	playful	sociable	kind	slow

Ferraro, F. R. (1995). An exercise for increasing students' understanding of life-span developmental psychology. *Psychological Reports, 76,* 1209-1210. Copyright © Psychological Reports 1995.

Address correspondence to F. Richard Ferraro, Department of Psychology, Box 8380, University of North Dakota, Grand Forks, ND 58202-8380; e-mail: FERRARO@NDSUMV1.BITNET.

Factual Questions

1. The students in this study were enrolled in what type of course?

2. What point is made immediately after students turn in their lists?

3. In which paragraph is the treatment described?

4. How does the author know that the majority of students find the treatment informative?

Questions for Discussion

5. The study is an example of an informal experiment conducted in the classroom. Briefly describe how you might do a rigorous study on the effects of the treatment described in this report.

6. Are there advantages and disadvantages to using comments on course evaluations as a way of measuring student reactions to the treatment? Are there other ways to measure it? Explain.

7. Do you think this report will convince professors of developmental psychology to try the exercise described in this article?

8. In general, do you think that it is appropriate for academic journals to devote space to reports of informal classroom research?

Quality Ratings

DIRECTIONS: Indicate your level of agreement with each of the following statements by circling a number from 5 for strongly agree (SA) to 1 for strongly disagree (SD). If you believe that an item is not applicable to this research article, leave it blank. Be prepared to explain your ratings.

A. The introduction establishes the importance of the research topic.
SA   5   4   3   2   1   SD

B. The literature review establishes the context for the study.
SA   5   4   3   2   1   SD

C. The research purpose, question, or hypothesis is clearly stated.
SA   5   4   3   2   1   SD

D. The method of sampling is sound.
SA   5   4   3   2   1   SD

E. Relevant demographics (for example, age, gender, and ethnicity) are described.
SA   5   4   3   2   1   SD

F. Measurement procedures are adequate.
SA   5   4   3   2   1   SD

G. The results are clearly described.
SA   5   4   3   2   1   SD

H. The discussion/conclusion is appropriate.
SA   5   4   3   2   1   SD

I. Despite any flaws noted above, the report is worthy of publication.
SA   5   4   3   2   1   SD

ARTICLE 30

SELF-ESTEEM OF LOW ACHIEVING FIRST GRADE READERS FOLLOWING INSTRUCTIONAL INTERVENTION

Elaine Traynelis-Yurek *University of Richmond*

T. Stevenson Hansell *Wright State University*

Neuroanatomical perspectives on self-esteem as a feedback system that creates awareness of effective or ineffective processing support educational research and practice. First grade students who have been identified as performing in the lowest twenty percent of their class on reading tasks, received instructional intervention through Reading Recovery. A self-esteem questionnaire was then administered individually to the students. Seventy-eight to ninety-six percent of the students responded positively to each statement. Overall, responses indicated positive self-esteem, but the variability of the responses suggests the students were discriminating among the items.

1. Self-esteem is a term that has been associated with reading achievement at various times. It is ordinarily thought that low reading achievement and low self-esteem are connected as well as good self-esteem and growth in reading achievement. A search of the literature indicated that most studies involving low self-esteem and low reading achievement showed high correlations in older children; however, below the age of eight the data was conflicting (Hansford and Hattie, 1982).

2. Neuroanatomical explanations of self-esteem describe it as a feedback system that registers the efficiency of the central nervous system (Westman, 1990). Harris (1986) suggests that self-esteem is possibly mediated by the non-dominant, medial, frontal lobe. He further explains that this self-esteem mechanism allows one to experience the effectiveness or the ineffectiveness of the central nervous system processing. From this perspective, self-esteem is not a mechanism which can be injured or exercise value judgment, but rather a mechanism which has the capability to affect the feeling of oneself (Westman, 1990). In addition to giving feedback to oneself, the system is sensitive to interpersonal relations and emotional states of those around us. Explicit or tacit approval or disapproval provides information about goodness of processing. Westman quotes Briggs (1975) when he describes an optimal level of self-esteem as a feeling of "being at home in one's body, a sense of self-confidence, and an assuredness of recognition and acceptance by those who count in one's life." An interruption to the flow of positive self-esteem is described as experiences of helplessness accompanied by emotions of shame and humiliation. The primary goal of individuals in this situation is not creativity but safety in order to escape the painful feelings of inadequacy.

3. The term self-concept is also associated with reading achievement. Self-concept is reported by Westman (1990) as different than self-esteem in that self-concept consists of knowledge about oneself which comes through information processing. Self-concept is dependent on the level of cognitive development which allows one to see oneself as both subject and object (e.g., I have big ears). Children below the age of eight who may not have developed strong self-concepts about themselves due to metacognitive abilities not yet well developed are probably receiving feedback from their self-esteem regulating systems. Educational research on self-esteem may be interpreted to support Westman's theory. Young children described in educational research often reflect the pain of feeling inadequate by acting out or refusing to attempt tasks. It is possible that the relationship between low self-esteem and reading failure is long term and has its beginning in early and consistent reading failure. Lerner (1988) states that self-esteem is attained through successful achievement that gains the respect of peers and fosters feelings of self-confidence. The low relationships found in the literature between reading ability and self-esteem in primary grade students may be due to the fact that researchers are assessing self-concept rather than self-esteem. Another reason why there may be low relationships between reading ability and self-esteem in primary grades in that researchers have not assessed self-esteem as directly related to reading. This paper describes the responses to a measure of self-esteem by first grade students. These students had been in the lowest 20 percent of their class in reading achievement. After they had received intensive individual instruction designed to help them read as well as the average of their class, they responded to a questionnaire.

Method

Subjects

4. <u>One hundred and seventy-three first grade students were the subjects in this study.</u> All subjects had completed a full year of kindergarten experience before first grade. The students ranged in age from 6 years, 10 months to 7 years, 9 months. Students selected for this program met three or four criteria. First, each student had to be identified by the classroom teacher as performing in the lowest 20 percent of the class. Second, each student had to have been considered eligible by having one of the ten lowest scores on a series of diagnostic tests. Third, if the teacher was funded through Chapter I funds, each student had to have been eligible for Chapter I services according to district criteria. Finally, each student had to be attending first grade for the first time. First grade repeaters were not eligible for the program. Subjects came from the states of Ohio and Virginia. Fifty-six (56) students attended schools in urban areas. Sixty-six (66) students were in

Traynelis-Yurek, E., & Hansell, T. S. (1993). Self-esteem of low achieving first grade readers following instructional intervention. *Reading Improvement*, 30, 140-146. Copyright © 1993 by Project Innovation of Mobile. Reprinted by permission.

Elaine Traynelis-Yurek is an Associate Professor at the University of Richmond and has been with the Education Department since 1980. Her teaching responsibilities include both undergraduate and graduate courses in specific learning disabilities and reading specialization. At the present time, Dr. Traynelis-Yurek is the Graduate Coordinator in Education. Requests for reprints should be sent to Elaine Traynelis-Yurek at the Department of Education, University of Richmond, Richmond, VA 23173.

T. Stevenson Hansell is a Professor at Wright State University in Dayton, Ohio. He teaches undergraduate and graduate courses in reading education. Dr. Hansell is a teacher-leader in the Reading Recovery network and has helped low achieving first graders learn to read on a daily basis since 1985.

an upper-middle-class suburban district, thirty-two (32) students attended small town schools, and nineteen (19) students attended rural schools.

Procedure

5. The 173 first grade students who were subjects in this study were participants in a Reading Recovery intervention (Clay, 1985). These students received their instruction from 23 teachers who were completing a year-long in-service in Reading Recovery. These students receive 1:1 instruction for 30 minutes daily. The goal of the program is to help the identified students learn to read as well as the average of their class so they can fully benefit from classroom instruction. Classroom teacher judgment about student performance is the basis for deciding that each student has reached the goal. Instruction follows a general emphasis on reading little books; writing messages by the student; and working on word analysis within the context of understanding a particular book or writing a specific word. While general procedures and the emphasis on early reading strategies (such as monitoring one's own reading and/or working to correct oral reading errors which influence comprehension) are standard, each child reads and rereads different books, composes a text of his own and is introduced to one new book each day. Text difficulty is gradually increased from simple 10 to 16 word texts that label pictures to complex 300 word texts such as *Little Bear* (Minarik, 1957). Teachers introduce more difficult books as the child learns to use key strategies to make sense of more complete text. One aspect of the instructional program is that teachers comment positively about partially successful as well as fully successful reading work. Students were individually presented with the questionnaire in early May. By this time, each student had worked with the teacher extensively (from 20 to 100 lessons).

6. The teacher explained the procedure and read each statement to the student. The teacher then waited until the student had made one of the three responses. As a result the highest number of omissions per item on the questionnaire was 2.

7. In addition, questionnaires about the effectiveness of the instruction were filled out by principals, parents, and teachers. While these questionnaires were not designed to provide information about self-esteem, spontaneous comments provided additional information to validate the results of the student questionnaire.

Apparatus

8. The questionnaire (Table I) was developed to assess change in self-esteem in regard to reading. Subjects anonymously filled out the questionnaire and no attempt was made to note sex or exact age. This questionnaire was designed to assess three different areas that are indicators of the student's self-esteem. These areas are: how the *students* feel about their reading ability, how the students perceive others feel about their reading ability, and how the students feel about the reading program. Fourteen questions elicited this information. The response choices were: *yes, sometimes,* and *no.* Based on the work of Osgood, Succi, and Tannenbaum (1971), the response options closely resemble the Semantic Differential. Bipolarity assessed with a semantic differential correlates highly with results obtained with the Thurstone Scales (Osgood et al., 1971). The response option *sometimes* was interjected because of the attribute of this age group to be concrete. It is difficult for children to intellectualize oppositional meanings with no neutral ground. Faces represented the choices with a smile for *yes,* a straight mouth for *sometimes,* and a down-turned mouth for *no.* An assumption for choosing a nonverbal representation for the choice is that verbal fluency and vocabulary are a function of age and intelligence. Often at this age

level, the students identify with the image (Locklin, 1961).

Results

9. The results are overwhelmingly positive. However, the variability of the responses suggests the students were discriminating among the items. On only two items (7 & 12) did less than 135 of the 173 students answer *yes.* On the other hand, students appeared to understand the differences addressed in the questions. Items 2, 3, and 5 asked the student to reflect on his or her views of the teacher, of the student him/herself, and of the tutor's views of his/her reading improvement. Students responded *yes* 144 times when asked if their classroom teacher thought they were reading better, 153 times when asked if they themselves thought they were reading better, and 166 times when asked if they thought the tutor thought they were reading better. Similarly, students seemed able to discriminate between their reading ability and their interest in reading. While 151 students said they were reading better in their classrooms (item 1) and 150 students said they like to read better (item 4), the remaining 19 students responded *sometimes* to item 1 while there were 18 *sometimes* and 5 *no* responses to item 4.

10. The items which received the highest positive responses dealt with tutor perspective

Table I   *Number and percent of student responses by item*

Item	Yes	Sometimes	No
1. You are reading better in your classroom.	151(87%)	19(11%)	2(1%)
2. Your teacher thinks you are reading better in class.	144(83%)	25(14%)	4(2%)
3. You know you are reading better.	153(88%)	13(8%)	7(4%)
4. You like to read better than before you worked with your tutor.	150(87%)	18(10%)	5(3%)
5. Your tutor thinks that you are reading better.	166(96%)	7(4%)	0
6. Working with your tutor helps you read better.	162(94%)	10(6%)	0
7. You write better than before you worked with your tutor.	134(78%)	30(18%)	7(4%)
8. You are glad you were in the program.	162(94%)	8(5%)	2(1%)
9. You would do this again.	138(80%)	20(12%)	14(8%)
10. You would tell your friends to do this if they need help in reading.	152(89%)	11(6%)	9(5%)
11. You are glad that you are doing all your work in class now.	148(87%)	18(11%)	5(2%)
12. You read more at home now than before.	134(78%)	27(16%)	11(6%)
13. You are a good student.	158(92%)	13(7%)	2(1%)
14. You are happy to read in school now.	151(88%)	15(9%)	6(3%)

Table II *Representative unsolicited comments about self-esteem and self-concept*

From Parents:

1. The program not only helped Ericka's reading, but it gave her the encouragement and confidence to know she can achieve reading and other subjects.
2. Not only has this program helped Mary Leigh's reading, it has given her a new confidence in herself and has shown her that extra effort pays off.
3. It is an important, positive opportunity for any child having difficulties, and to take advantage of it. It also helps build self-esteem and a strong interest in reading and comprehension.
4. It is an excellent opportunity to capture your child's imagination and self-esteem.
5. It has made school more enjoyable because he is learning faster. This makes him proud of himself.
6. Adam has gone from "I don't want to go to school" to "Mom, guess what I did I couldn't do before, but today I did it all by myself." He's willing to try new things because he's gained confidence and an interest in reading.
7. It builds individual skills that help to strengthen a child's abilities to be able to perform at acceptable levels at school and it helps build self-esteem.

From Classroom Teachers:

1. The self-confidence exhibited by the students is overwhelming and much appreciated.
2. The children can attack words and figure unknown words out better. Often, their self-esteem improves because they are having success.
3. More confidence in their ability and a willingness to try! Their reading level has improved. Their self-confidence has improved and they are eager to learn.
4. They are willing to try now—and have more confidence which has carried over into other subjects.
5. It has given many children the additional boost needed to be good readers. It has given them self-confidence and built good self-esteem.
6. Higher self-esteem, increased confidence, increased knowledge, positive attitude toward school.
7. Better motivated, self-confidence and self-esteem have both improved tremendously.
8. One child had developed much confidence in his reading. He has good self-esteem. He is keeping up well in reading.

From Administrators:

1. Parents with whom I have spoken have mentioned the improved self-confidence and more wholesome self-image they have seen in their children. They are very appreciative of the efforts of our teacher, Mrs. R, in helping their children find early success here at our school.
2. Positive results. This is an effective program. Students are testing out and observed feeling extremely good about themselves.
3. The program has enhanced their self-esteem as it has improved their reading skills. It has given them the tools and methodology to learn how to read.

(item 5); tutor value (item 6); if the student was glad to receive tutoring (item 8); and, most importantly, if subjects considered themselves a good student (item 13).

11. Two items tied for the fewest positive responses. Item 7 asked if the students write better than before and item 12 asked if students read more at home now. However, these items also had the most *sometimes* responses, 30 and 27 respectively. So, another question (item 9) had the most negative responses. Item 9 asked if students would do this again.

Discussion and Conclusions

12. The negative response to item 9 suggests two possible interpretations. Perhaps students interpreted the statement literally to say they would be asked to begin instruction again immediately. A second interpretation, that students prefer to remain in the classroom rather than in a pullout program, suggests the instruction was not beneficial to self-esteem. But the highly positive responses to item 6, Working with a tutor helps you read better, and item 8, You are glad you were in the program, suggest that this second interpretation is invalid. The overall positive response to every item suggests that students who were the lowest achievers in their classrooms before their tutoring, had strong feelings of self-worth at the end of the school year. Therefore, we reject the second interpretation that students prefer to remain in a classroom and conclude that students interpreted the question to mean that they would begin instruction again. Items 7 and 12, which tied for fewest positive responses, reflected transfer of instruction to other settings. Although students were asked to write a sentence or two each day, we assume they write outside of the intervention program as well. The *sometimes* responses could reflect that they write better when they work at it. For item 12, 134 students say they do read more at home, twenty-seven (27) sometimes read more at home, and eleven (11) students do not read more at home as a result of this intervention. Students who have completed instruction were included in the results. Those students may have less access to books and less encouragement to read at home. Therefore, we expect these students are in fact reading less at home.

13. It is interesting to note that the data from the two states were analyzed separately, but reflected the same findings. Those statements to which students responded most favorably in Ohio were the same statements which students responded to most favorably in Virginia. Similarly, both Ohio and Virginia students had the most negative responses to the same item.

14. Further support for the effort of the intervention tutoring on students was provided by comments from parents, principals, and classroom teachers. Each of these groups was presented a questionnaire that asked for comments about the students' growth and about the program. There were no prompts within the questionnaire to mention student feelings, self-concept, or self-esteem. However, in 63 instances (more than one-third of the replies) parents, teachers, or principals commented about the effect of the intervention on student self-esteem.

15. Representative comments are listed in Table II. These comments appear to validate the students' positive responses to the scale. A total of twenty-two (22) parents commented about self-esteem and/or self-confidence. Thirty-six (36) classroom teachers and five (5) principals made similar comments.

16. It appears that an intensive instructional program which is effective in helping most students move from the lowest achievement group to the average performance level of their classroom peers creates positive self-esteem. While this is not surprising, it clearly suggests that the lowest students want to learn. Since the intervention stresses independent monitoring and self-correcting of errors which affect meaning, students are not responding to having a tutor make learning easy or "fun." Rather, they appear to learn that hard work achieves rewards of achievement and self-esteem. Earlier research (Pinnell et al., 1990) that successful students maintain their ability to achieve as well as the average of the class into fourth grade suggests that early learning of reading competence and self-esteem through independent work is long-term learning.

17. Teachers who work with first grade students know that, as Kronick (1981) suggests, self-esteem is inseparable from one's actions and ability to act. They know too that there is a point at which many bright children avoid reading rather than continuing to fail. Kronick sees the elementary school child at the mercy of teachers.

18.   The results of this study indicate that self-esteem feedback can be positively affected by early intervention. Teachers who respond to the positive aspects of reading behavior, including the positive aspects of errors, provide students a chance to recognize the effectiveness of their attempts at learning. Not only does this support help students increase their performance on reading tasks, but it also supports self-esteem.

References

Ahman, J. S., & Glock, M. D. (1981). *Evaluating student progress: Principles of tests and measurements* (6th ed.). Boston: Allyn and Bacon, Inc.

Clay, M. (1985). *The early detection of reading difficulties* (3rd ed.). Portsmouth, NH: Heinemann.

Hansford, B. C., & Hattie, J. A. (1982). The relationship between self-concept and achievement/performance measures. *Review of Educational Research, 52*, 123-142.

Harris, A. J., & Sipay, E. R. (1990). *How to increase reading ability* (9th ed.). New York: Longman.

Harris, J. E. (1986). *Clinical neuroscience: From neuroanatomy to psychodynamics.* New York: Human Sciences Press.

Kronick, D. (1981). *Social development of learning disabled persons.* San Francisco: Jossey-Bass Publishers.

Lerner, J. (1988). *Learning disabilities, theories, diagnosis and teaching strategies* (5th ed.). Boston: Houghton Mifflin Company.

Locklin, J. C. (1961-62). Word meaning and self description. *Journal of Abnormal and Social Psychology, 18*-34.

Minarik, E. H. (1957). *Little bear.* New York: Harper & Row.

Osgood, C. E., Succi, G. P., & Tannenbaum, P. H. (1971). *The measurement of meaning.* Chicago: University of Illinois Press.

Pinnell, G. S., DeFord, D. E., & Lyons, C. (1990). *Bridges to literacy.* New York: Teachers College Press.

Westman, J. C. (1990). *Handbook of learning disabilities: A multi-system approach.* Boston: Allyn and Bacon, Inc.

Factual Questions

1. What is the sample size?

2. What is the goal of Reading Recovery?

3. Were the questionnaires for principals, parents, and teachers designed to provide information about self-esteem?

4. The students gave the highest percentage of "yes" answers in response to which item?

5. The parents, teachers, and principals commented on the effect of the intervention on the students' self-esteem in how many replies?

Questions for Discussion

6. Describe in your own words the purpose of the study.

7. What is the independent variable?

8. Is the Reading Recovery program described in sufficient detail?

9. Students filled out the questionnaire anonymously. Was this a good idea? Explain.

10. What is your opinion on the items in Table I as a measure of self-esteem?

11. What is your opinion on the use of faces to represent the choices for the children? (See paragraph 8.)

12. This study is classified in this book as "pre-experimental." (See the table of contents.) Do you agree with this classification? Explain.

13. In a future study of this type, would it be desirable to include a control group? Why? Why not?

14. The comments in Table II were unsolicited. In your opinion, are these more valid than if they had been solicited? Explain.

15. In your opinion, would it be desirable to administer a reading achievement test in addition to the measures administered in this study in order to evaluate Reading Recovery?

16. Based on the data in this article, would you support increased funding to establish a Reading Recovery program in your local schools? Explain.

Quality Ratings

DIRECTIONS: Indicate your level of agreement with each of the following statements by circling a number from 5 for strongly agree (SA) to 1 for strongly disagree (SD). If you believe that an item is not applicable to this research article, leave it blank. Be prepared to explain your ratings.

A. The introduction establishes the importance of the research topic.
   SA   5   4   3   2   1   SD

B. The literature review establishes the context for the study.
   SA   5   4   3   2   1   SD

C. The research purpose, question, or hypothesis is clearly stated.
   SA   5   4   3   2   1   SD

D. The method of sampling is sound.
   SA   5   4   3   2   1   SD

E. Relevant demographics (for example, age, gender, and ethnicity) are described.
   SA   5   4   3   2   1   SD

F. Measurement procedures are adequate.
   SA   5   4   3   2   1   SD

G. The results are clearly described.
   SA   5   4   3   2   1   SD

H. The discussion/conclusion is appropriate.
   SA   5   4   3   2   1   SD

I. Despite any flaws noted above, the report is worthy of publication.
   SA   5   4   3   2   1   SD

ARTICLE 31

BENEFITS OF A PARENT EDUCATION AND SUPPORT PROGRAM IN THE FIRST THREE YEARS

Margaret Tresch Owen *Timberlawn Research Foundation*
Beverly A. Mulvihill *University of Alabama at Birmingham*

The effectiveness of a parent education and support program (Parents As Teachers [PAT]) was evaluated for middle-class participants by employing a quasi-experimental longitudinal design. Outcomes were assessed for mothers and fathers and for children at ages 1, 2, and 3 years. PAT homes were found to be more responsive and stimulating for children, and PAT parents perceived greater support from their communities than comparison group parents, but children's abilities were nearly identical in the two groups.

1. The family support movement (Zigler & Black, 1989) points to an increasing need among all American families for support, advice, and role models (Weissbourd & Kagan, 1989). Consequently, many parent education and support programs have encouraged the participation of all families, without regard to specified risk. By targeting all families, rather than low-income or otherwise at-risk groups, parent education and family support programs have achieved the broad-based backing necessary to underwrite statewide programs such as those in Minnesota and Missouri (Weiss, 1989). However, particularly in times of severe financial constraints, evaluations of community-based family support and education programs are essential to determine what works, how it works, and for whom it works. This study describes an evaluation of a parent education and support program offered to all parents of newborn children regardless of socioeconomic status in three independent school districts. Potential benefits to the parents and the children were examined longitudinally over the 3-year course of the program.

The Context

2. The Parents As Teachers (PAT) program was first implemented in Texas in three pilot sites. The Mental Health Association in Texas requested an outside evaluation of the pilot sites, thus providing an opportunity to study outcomes of this community-based parent education and support program.

3. The PAT curriculum, originally based on the work of Burton White (White, 1980), focuses on educating and supporting parents as their child's first and most influential teacher in language, cognitive, social-emotional, and motor development. The heart of the program is the home visit, in which educators provide information and guidance to parents to enhance the child's physical, social, and intellectual development. In these personalized home visits, the parent educators, who are certified by the PAT National Center, are required to follow a curriculum of developmental learning activities, model the activities with the child, and discuss age-appropriate expectations, parenting issues, and practices. Although the parent educators follow the same curriculum with each family, they are trained to individualize their strategies to suit each family's needs. Parent educators emphasize the parents' role as the primary decision makers for their children.

4. In addition to the home visits, the PAT program involves parents in group meetings with other parents to share parenting experiences and other topics of interest. A purpose of these group meetings, as well as the home visits, is to reduce the stress and increase the pleasures of parenting.

5. The program also includes periodic screening of the children in general development, language, hearing, and vision. Finally, the PAT educators are prepared to refer families to other community services, if needs for services beyond those offered by PAT become evident.

6. The programs are typically sponsored by school districts, and thus strengthen parents' support and awareness of the schools within their community before their children actually reach school age. PAT programs have also been adapted for sponsorship and delivery in some corporate day care centers.

7. Based on a nondeficit model of service delivery, the program assumes that most, if not all, parents benefit from informal and formal support systems for child rearing (Powell, 1988). Thus, when initiated in three pilot sites in Texas, the PAT program was open to all families with children from 0 to 3 years of age, regardless of specific need; emphasis was placed on recruiting parents of newborns who planned to stay with the program over its 3-year duration.

Methodological Concerns

8. There are multiple challenges associated with conducting evaluation studies of parent education and support programs (Gray & Wandersman, 1980; Seitz, 1987), including translating the goals of the program into researchable questions, the use of comparison groups, sample size, and sample attrition when assessing long-term intervention.

9. *Program goals and related hypotheses.* As with most home-based early intervention programs (Gray & Wandersman, 1980), the long-term goal of the PAT program is to increase the educability of the children and prevent school problems through strengthened early child

Owen, M. T., & Mulvihill, B. A. (1994). Benefits of a parent education and support program in the first three years. *Family Relations, 43*, 206-212. Copyright © 1994 by the National Council on Family Relations, 3989 Central Ave. NE, Suite 550, Minneapolis, MN 55421. Reprinted by permission.

This research was supported in part by a grant from the Hogg Foundation for Mental Health, Austin, Texas. It was conducted with cooperation from the Parents As Teachers (PAT) program and the Mental Health Association (MHA) in Texas. We gratefully acknowledge the assistance and support of Stella Mullins, Executive Director of the MHA in Texas; Elaine Shiver, PAT Program Director; directors and staff of the PAT programs in Allen, Fort Worth, and Garland, Texas; and the generosity of the parents and children who voluntarily participated in the study. We also thank John T. Gossett, who encouraged and contributed to all aspects of this research. We wish to thank Beth Bontempo, Maureen Crowley, Margaret Geiger, Julene Johnson, Carol Lewis, Cheryl Moody, Norma Muldoon, Virginia Austin Phillips, Ellen Wheatley, and, in particular, Ann Minnett and Kay Henderson for their assistance in conducting the study.

Margaret Tresh Owen is Associate Director of the Timberlawn Research Foundation, P.O. Box 270789, Dallas, TX 75227. Beverly A. Mulvihill is Research Assistant Professor at the Civitan International Research Center, University of Alabama at Birmingham.

development (Weiss, 1989). We identified three specific goals of the Parents As Teachers program: (a) to provide information and guidance to parents in the home environment in order to enhance the child's physical, social, and intellectual development; (b) to reduce the stress and increase the pleasures of parenting; and (c) to provide social support to the parents from their community and peers.

10. Four hypotheses were developed from the identified goals and tested in the evaluation study: (a) PAT participants would provide home environments that were more developmentally enriching to their children than would nonparticipants, (b) children in the PAT program would achieve higher scores on standardized tests of mental and social development than children whose parents did not participate, (c) PAT parents would perceive more community and peer support than nonparticipant parents, and (d) PAT parents would report less stress associated with parenting and child rearing than nonparticipants.

11. Thus, to evaluate effects of the PAT program, we employed an ecological model that targeted parent, parenting, and child outcomes (see Clewell, Brooks-Gunn, & Benasich, 1989). In addition, we addressed outcomes for fathers as well as mothers. Although mothers were the primary target in the PAT program, fathers were often involved in home visits and group meetings. Both family systems theory (e.g., S. Minuchin, 1974; P. Minuchin, 1985) and role theorists (e.g., Grams, 1960) emphasize that changing the behavior of one family member will influence other members. Within an ecological model, positive outcomes for the family system would be important information regarding the benefits of the program.

12. *Comparison group.* One of the primary concerns in the design of program effectiveness studies involves the selection of a comparison group. Community-based programs often have multiple constraints that preclude experimental evaluation of their programs, thus necessitating a quasi-experimental design. The PAT program was advertised and open to entire communities. A control group of families and children had to be chosen to allow a meaningful comparison of families and children who did and did not participate in PAT (Cook & Campbell, 1979).

13. For the comparison group, we sought to identify a pool of parents who were both demographically similar to those electing to participate in PAT and similarly motivated to seek information, but who were unlikely to have a PAT program in their local community. The comparison group was thus recruited from childbirth preparation classes held at a centrally located hospital in a large city. The PAT pilot

programs were located in two suburbs of the city and in a neighboring city. Baseline demographic, attitudinal, and parent knowledge data were collected to test the initial equivalence of the PAT and comparison groups.

14. *Sample size.* Often in community-based evaluation studies, the researcher has little control over the number of subjects that will constitute the sample. Long-term education and intervention programs are necessarily limited in the numbers they can serve. In addition, if policymakers wish to limit initial investment and the numbers of individuals served until an evaluation can demonstrate positive results, the ability to detect the true effects of a program is compromised to the extent that the sample size is small. The present evaluation was initiated after three different school districts committed to sponsor pilot PAT programs, thus assuring that a reasonable sample could be obtained for evaluation within the constraints of time, funding, and other available resources.

15. *Attrition.* The ability to draw conclusions from outcome evaluations of long-term intervention programs such as PAT is often weakened by attrition of participants over the course of the program and its study. Attrition rates of 30-40% (van Doornink, Dawson, Butterfield, & Alexander, 1980) to nearly 50% (Slaughter, 1983) have been reported in previous evaluations of intervention programs.

16. Multiple efforts were made to track subjects over the 3-year study and to minimize the burdens of data collection in order to diminish attrition from the evaluation study itself. When the causes for program attrition are examined, however, attrition rates can be used as an additional measure of program success. Dropout rates not due to family moves from the community or other indeterminable reasons can be used as one indication of participant dissatisfaction.

Evaluation Study Design

17. PAT parent education efforts have been previously evaluated in Missouri, where participant children surpassed comparison group children in cognitive, language, and social measures at the end of the program (Pfannenstiel & Seltzer, 1985). An evaluation of Missouri's second wave of programs, involving families from more diverse socioeconomic backgrounds than the first wave, did not include a comparison group but reported favorable assessments of participating children compared to national norms (Pfannenstiel, Lambson, & Yarnell, 1991). Because these studies focused only on 3-year outcomes, pre-program comparisons of potential differences between participant and control groups could

not be made, nor could the timing of effects be examined over the course of the 3-year program. The present study improved upon these earlier evaluations by collecting baseline data on both program participants and a comparison group of parents, followed by longitudinal assessments of both groups over the 3 years of program participation. In addition, the repeated comparisons of program and comparison groups ensured that both groups of children would have comparable experiences with the process of testing, a potential source of differences that could be unrelated to the program itself.

Method

Subjects

18. PAT participants from the three pilot program sites volunteered for an evaluation study of the Parents As Teachers program. The study sample was recruited over the course of 1 year, during which time PAT parent educators distributed information packets about the study to each family joining the PAT program. The PAT program requested that the study evaluators not contact the parents directly at this stage; therefore, parents decided to participate in the evaluation study solely on the basis of these information packets. Parents who chose to enter the study and provide baseline information mailed completed recruitment/baseline questionnaires directly to the independent evaluators. In this manner, PAT educators were unaware of which parents were in the evaluation study.

19. Approximately two thirds of the recruitment packets were returned, resulting in a PAT sample of 59 families. With the exception of one child who was 8 months old when the family was recruited, children in the PAT sample were 6 months old or younger; 81% enrolled when the children were 3 months old or younger, and 54% joined before the child's birth or immediately after. A group of parents ($N = 69$) was recruited to serve as the comparison group from childbirth preparation classes held at a hospital centrally located in a large city where a PAT program was not yet available to residents.

20. The pilot PAT programs served only first-time parents. The comparison group was also comprised solely of first-time parents. The two groups did not differ in parental age, education, or occupation. Education levels for both groups of parents ranged from high school graduate to professionally degreed. The typical profile was of a middle-class first-time parent who had attended college. Mothers' mean age was 28 years at the time of their first child's birth; fathers' mean age was 30 years. Only 7% of the

PAT participants and 8% of the comparison group were non-Caucasian. There were no single-parent families in the comparison group; 9% of the PAT group were single parents. Family socioeconomic status scores on the Hollingshead (1975) Four Factor Index of Social Status ranged from class 1 to class 5 (highest to lowest), but 85% of the PAT and 87% of the comparison families were in the upper two strata. There was no significant difference on SES scores between the groups.

Attrition

21. The cumulative subject attrition rate was 28.8% in the PAT group and 20.3% in the comparison group over the 3 years of the study. Subject attrition was primarily due to families moving out of the area (81% of those who did not complete the study). Of the 17 PAT dropouts, 11 left the program because of moves, 2 children died, and 4 discontinued participation for unknown reasons.

22. Demographic characteristics of the study-dropouts were compared to those who remained in the study. There were no significant differences between the dropouts and the remainder of the sample in marital status, age, education, or race of the mother.

Program Variability

23. All PAT home visitors are required to attend training and implement curriculum authorized by the Parents As Teachers National Center. The overall director of the Texas PAT program and the director of one of the pilot sites were trained at the PAT National Center in Missouri; they conducted all the training sessions for administrators and home visitors. Staff from the three pilot sites met monthly and attended frequent in-service training sessions. On-site supervision further assured compliance with expectations for implementation of the curriculum.

24. On average, families received 24 home visits and participated in 12 group meetings over the course of their involvement with the PAT program. An examination of the variability in program delivery for the individual participants found no significant differences between the pilot sites in program dosage as determined by number of home visits conducted, group parent meetings attended, or months in the program.

Procedure

25. Surveys contained in the initial information packets provided baseline information on the parents' knowledge of child development and attitudes toward parenting as well as the demographic information reported above. Whenever the packets were not returned in a timely manner, follow-up telephone calls were made. Subsequent assessments were made when the first-born child was 1, 2, and 3 years of age. The 1- and 2-year assessments were conducted entirely in the home. The home environment was chosen to reduce problems of getting participants to the lab and to ensure the comfort of the young children. At each assessment phase, self-report instruments were completed by the parents and returned by mail. At 3 years, the child assessments were conducted in two sessions, one in the home and one in the lab, to avoid overtaxing the child. The child language assessment was conducted in the home following the home environment observation, and the cognitive and social assessments occurred in the lab. Home visit and lab visit testers were blind to PAT participation except when PAT families occasionally volunteered such information.

Measures

26. *Child outcomes.* Following the rationale of the Missouri Evaluation Study (Pfannenstiel et al., 1991) and other recent policy statements on the assessment of young children (National Association for the Education of Young Children, 1987), multiple measures were used to evaluate the effect of the program on the children's development, with emphasis placed on standardized assessments of cognitive, language, and social development. Testers were extensively trained on all the standardized assessments employed. To assess cognitive development, the Bayley Scales of Infant Development (Bayley, 1969) were administered at age 1 and the Kaufman Assessment Battery for Children (Kaufman & Kaufman, 1983) at age 3. Language development was assessed with the Receptive-Expressive Emergent Language Scale (Bzoch & League, 1970) at ages 1 and 2, and the Preschool Language Scale (Zimmerman, Steiner, & Pond, 1979) was used at age 3. The Vineland Adaptive Behavior Scales (Sparrow, Balla, & Cicchetti, 1984) were used at ages 2 and 3 to assess social development.

27. *Parent knowledge of child development.* The Parent Knowledge Questionnaire (Research and Training Associates, 1985) was developed for the Missouri evaluation of PAT to determine whether PAT participation improved parents' knowledge of normal child development. The 34 items of the instrument included information from each of the seven phases of child development outlined by White (1975) and included in the PAT program. The questionnaire was filled out separately by mothers and fathers at the beginning of the study and again when the children were 3 years old. A sum of correct responses, as determined by three developmental psychologists, comprised the parent knowledge score. The measure was chosen to permit comparison of outcomes with those reported for the Missouri evaluation. Published reliability and validity information is not available on this scale.

28. *Parenting attitudes.* Attitudes of the mothers and the fathers toward issues of child rearing were measured by the Parent Attitudes Toward Childrearing (Easterbrooks & Goldberg, 1984) at three points in time: baseline, child age 1 year, and child age 3 years. Scores were determined for the four subscales of Parental Warmth, Encouragement of Independence, Strictness (the degree to which parents endorse attitudes espousing obedience, strict rules, control via punishment, and authority over the child), and Aggravation (how much bother the parents perceive the child will cause). Cronbach alphas ranged from .52 to .78 (median = .69) for the subscales across parent respondents and the three times of assessment.

29. *Parenting stress.* The Parenting Stress Index (Abidin, 1986) was administered to parents when their children were 1 year old and repeated when the children were 3 years old. This widely used instrument yields a total parenting stress score (with Cronbach alphas ranging from .87 to .90 for mothers and fathers across the two assessments), as well as separate scores for the stress due to parent characteristics (alphas ranged from .84 to .88) and the stress due to child characteristics (alphas ranged from .79 to .88).

30. *Perceptions of social support and parenting satisfaction.* The Inventory of Parenting Experiences (IPE; Crnic, Greenberg, Ragozin, Robinson, & Brasham, 1983) was used to assess parental perceptions of social support and parenting satisfaction and was administered at each of the postbaseline assessment ages. A single item was used to index satisfaction with parenting because the internal consistency of the 12-item subscale was low in this sample, especially for mothers. The social support questions address three sources of support: support received from intimate relations (4 items; alphas ranged from .59 to .78), friendships (3 items; alphas ranged from .56 to .77), and the neighborhood or community (2 items; alphas ranged from .40 to .55). The Intimate Support scale measured the availability of and satisfaction with such support. Friendship Support measured satisfaction with such contact, and Community Support measured satisfaction with involvement in the neighborhood and with support from organized groups.

31. *Quality of parenting and the home environment.* The quality of the child's home environment in terms of attributes of parenting and the availability of developmentally stimulating materials in the home was measured when the children were 1, 2, and 3 years of age using the Home Observation for Measurement of the Environment (HOME; Caldwell & Bradley, 1984). The 45-item infant version was used at the 1-year and 2-year home visits, and the 55-item preschool version was administered at the 3-year visit. Items in the inventory address qualities of parenting and the home environment, such as maternal vocal and verbal stimulation, maternal warmth expressed to the child, frequency and stability of adult contact, types of play materials, need gratification, avoidance of restriction in motor and exploratory behavior, and home characteristics indicative of parental concern with achievement.

32. Internal consistency of the total scale was acceptable but lower than the published level of .89. Cronbach alphas for the total score were .57, .60, and .68 at ages 1, 2, and 3, respectively. The restricted range in socioeconomic status of the present sample, as compared to the normative samples, and the very high percentage of scale items passed resulted in the lower than expected alphas (R. H. Bradley, personal communication, February 7, 1994). Because the

internal consistency of the subscales was generally lower than that of the total scale, ranging from .04 to .59, only the total scores were used in the analyses.

Results

Analytic Strategy

33. In this longitudinal evaluation, all measures were administered at least twice (see Tables 1 and 2 for a summary); repeated measures multivariate analyses of variance (MANOVAs) were used to test for effects of group (PAT versus control), time, and group X time. Conclusions regarding program effectiveness were made on the basis of either significant main effects of group or by significant time X group interaction effects. The ideal basis for concluding program effectiveness would be significant time X group effects (together with subsequent significant simple effects), indicating no initial baseline differences between groups together with increasingly better outcomes in the program than the comparison group over time. However, in the case of a parenting program such as PAT that begins before or near the birth of a child, no baseline, preprogram child outcome or parenting behavior measures can be

administered. Thus, for the majority of outcomes of interest, either a significant main effect of group or certain patterns of group X time interaction effects are used to indicate the effectiveness of the PAT program. Significant group effects are cautiously interpreted as evidence for program effectiveness when preprogram similarity between the groups is demonstrated or when preprogram differences potentially related to the outcomes are taken into account.

34. To specifically examine the initial comparability of the PAT and comparison groups, the baseline measures (demographics, parenting knowledge, and parent attitudes) were contrasted using *t* tests.

Child Outcomes

35. *Cognitive and language abilities.* Language measures, which differed at age 3 from previous assessments, were first standardized before they were analyzed. Repeated measures MANOVAs on the set of cognitive measures and on the set of language measures revealed no significant main effects of group or time and no group X time interaction effects. The similar mean scores are shown in Table 1.

Table 1   *Child measures: Means (M) and standard deviations (SD) at ages 1 year, 2 years, and 3 years*[a]

Measures	One Year PAT M	SD	Control M	SD	Two Years PAT M	SD	Control M	SD	Three Years PAT M	SD	Control M	SD
Cognition												
Bayley Scales of Infant Development (Mental)	118.2	10.6	118.1	11.3								
Kaufman-Assessment Battery for Children									108.8	11.7	108.0	11.8
Language												
Receptive-Expressive Emergent Language Scale	111.0	11.3	110.6	9.2	124.1	16.5	128.9	16.2				
Preschool Language Scale									47.5	7.0	46.8	7.1
Vineland Adaptive Behavior Scales					102.8	11.9	100.3	12.0	111.3	17.8	108.4	12.0

Note. PAT = Parents As Teachers program participants.

[a]Means are for all subjects who completed assessments at any point. Subjects without complete data at all assessment points were not included in the repeated measures analyses.

Table 2   *Parent Measures: Means (M) and standard deviations (SD) at baseline and ages 1 year, 2 years, and 3 years*[a]

Measures		Baseline PAT M	SD	Control M	SD	1 Year PAT M	SD	Control M	SD	2 Years PAT M	SD	Control M	SD	3 Years PAT M	SD	Control M	SD
Parent Knowledge Questionnaire																	
	M	25.32	3.02	23.84	3.01									26.40	2.47	22.23	3.12
	F	23.98	3.32	24.67	5.77									23.98	7.49	23.84	6.52
Parent Attitudes Toward Child Rearing																	
Warmth	M	5.45	.45	5.36	.34	5.54	.29	5.48	.38					5.37	.43	5.50	.30
	F	5.26	.36	5.22	.35	5.29	.38	5.31	.38					5.20	.40	5.24	.47
Independence	M	5.22	.47	5.20	.40	5.07	.46	4.97	.50					5.15	.52	5.09	.42
	F	5.02	.49	5.02	.45	4.87	.51	4.86	.57					4.92	.60	4.94	.48
Strictness	M	2.64	.46	2.63	.51	2.45	.61	2.50	.55					2.51	.41	2.56	.47
	F	2.91	.53	3.19	.55	2.82	.62	2.61	.54					2.80	.56	2.92	.49
Aggravation	M	2.99	.46	2.84	.45	2.85	.56	2.78	.51					2.80	.50	2.81	.52
	F	3.07	.59	2.94	.46	2.89	.55	2.77	.42					2.82	.50	2.81	.48
Parenting Stress Index																	
Child Stress	M					96.10	15.86	92.21	15.80					94.54	21.65	91.26	16.33
	F					96.73	18.69	94.38	14.37					96.26	17.23	94.44	15.83
Parenting Stress	M					108.22	21.14	107.68	19.97					106.97	24.81	108.60	21.02
	F					103.18	21.85	105.41	23.39					100.18	20.34	103.90	19.96
Total	M					204.29	33.74	199.89	31.68					201.51	43.58	199.55	33.57
	F					200.75	37.11	199.96	34.16					196.44	34.94	198.34	33.01
Inventory of Parenting Experiences																	
Parenting Satisfaction	M					1.73	0.57	1.70	0.65	1.77	0.57	1.74	0.60	1.31	0.70	1.39	1.00
	F					1.48	0.59	1.55	0.63	1.50	0.51	1.74	0.60	1.17	0.57	1.17	0.68
Intimate Support	M					10.41	1.64	10.53	1.75	10.39	1.17	10.16	1.46	14.88	3.01	14.86	2.22
	F					9.96	1.31	9.93	1.63	9.63	1.43	10.08	1.78	15.30	1.15	14.72	2.59
Community Support	M					3.88	1.09	3.40	1.05	4.00	1.06	3.34	1.12	6.48	1.75	6.06	1.22
	F					3.30	1.01	3.18	0.94	3.70	0.94	3.22	1.18	6.00	1.29	5.96	1.05
Friends Support	M					13.10	3.00	13.07	2.60	13.39	2.97	13.32	2.32	13.78	2.68	13.55	2.43
	F					11.11	3.14	12.36	3.22	11.53	3.81	12.08	3.33	13.08	1.98	12.90	2.39
Home Observation for Measurement of the Environment						40.20	3.20	38.40	2.80	39.60	2.90	39.30	3.50	48.50	3.50	46.60	3.90

Note: M = Mother, F = Father, PAT = Parents As Teachers program participants.

[a]Means are for all subjects who completed assessments at any point. Subjects without complete data at all assessment points were not included in the repeated measures analyses.

36. *Adaptive social behavior.* There were no significant group, time, or group X time interaction effects for adaptive social behavior measured at ages 2 and 3. Mean scores are shown in Table 1.

Parent Outcomes

37. *Parent knowledge.* At the initiation of the study, there was a significant difference between the PAT and comparison group mothers and fathers in parent knowledge about child development, with PAT mothers and fathers scoring higher. For mothers, the repeated measures MANOVA also found a significant group effect over both times of measurement [$F(1, 85) = 8.93, p < .01$] and a significant time effect [$F(1, 85) = 4.18, p < .05$]. The PAT group mothers had higher parent knowledge scores than comparison mothers (with mean scores of 26.07 for PAT and 24.13 for Control), and all parents increased in parent knowledge from baseline (mean score 24.38) to child age 3 (mean score 25.48), but there was no group X time interaction effect. There were no significant effects of group, time, or group X time indicated by the MANOVA of fathers' parent knowledge.

38. *Parent attitudes.* The two groups were highly similar in parent attitudes at baseline, and there were no significant effects of group, time, or group X time found in the repeated measures MANOVA.

39. *Quality of parenting and the home environment.* The mean scores of both the PAT and comparison groups were in the top quartile of the range of scores (37–45 for infants and toddlers; 46–55 for preschoolers) reported for the normative samples for the HOME (Caldwell & Bradley, 1984) at each assessment, indicating that the home environments of the children in the sample were high in quality relative to normative samples.

40. Despite the fact that both PAT and comparison group family home environments had high scores on the HOME, results of the repeated measures MANOVA indicated a significant main effect for group [$F(1, 89) = 9.77, p < .01$]. Overall mean scores were 42.76 for PAT compared to 41.28 for the comparison group. The differences across time were small but consistent in their direction. There were no significant time or group X time effects on this measure.

41. The baseline difference and overall differences found in parent knowledge of child development favoring the PAT group indicated that there were preexisting differences that could have mediated the group effect in the HOME scores. The HOME scores were therefore reanalyzed using the baseline assessment of mother's knowledge as a covariate.

Significant effects of PAT participation on the HOME scores were again found even after controlling for effects of initial parent knowledge.

42. *Parenting stress.* For both the PAT and comparison groups, the vast majority of the parents scored in the low- or moderate-risk range of the Parenting Stress Index, indicating little parenting stress. Whether marked by the overall stress score or subscales indicating stress due to the child or to parenting, there were no significant effects of group, time, or group X time on parenting stress.

43. *Perceptions of social support and parenting satisfaction.* Among the different social support and parenting satisfaction scales, there was a significant group effect for Community Support as perceived by mothers [$F(1, 79) = 6.2, p < .05$] and by fathers [$F(1, 71) = 5.5, p < .05$]. PAT mothers and fathers both reported more satisfaction with neighborhood involvement and support from community groups than the comparison group parents (for PAT and Control groups, respectively, mothers' mean scores were 4.70 and 4.23, and fathers' mean scores were 4.43 and 4.08). A significant effect for time [mothers: $F(2, 77) = 120.27, p < .0001$; fathers: $F(2, 70) = 101.85, p < .0001$] indicated that parents in both groups expressed increasingly greater satisfaction with support from the community as their children got older (at ages 1, 2, and 3, respectively, mothers' mean scores were 3.55, 3.64, and 6.14, and fathers' mean scores were 3.29, 3.44, and 5.99). The increase occurred primarily between child ages 2 and 3. There was no significant group X time interaction effect.

44. There was a significant decline over time in fathers', but not mothers', expressed satisfaction with parenting [$F(2, 66) = 9.26, p < .001$], with the decline evident between age 2 and age 3 (mean scores obtained at child ages 1, 2, and 3 were 1.57, 1.65, and 1.20, respectively). However, there were no significant group or group X time effects in parenting satisfaction for mothers or fathers. All parents expressed increasing satisfaction with support from intimate relationships over time, but there were no significant group or group X time effects. There were no group, time, or group X time effects found for parents' satisfaction with support from their friends.

45. *Parent satisfaction with PAT.* Parents expressed high levels of satisfaction with the PAT program: for example, 92% of the mothers and 88% of the fathers reported they had more confidence as parents and 95% and 94%, respectively, would recommend the PAT program to other parents. Clearly, the majority of the participants saw the program as helpful and supportive. On only one item did fewer than 70%

of mothers and fathers answer affirmatively: Forty-three percent of mothers and 27% of the fathers were unsure whether their child had increased abilities as a result of their participation in PAT. Only 7% of the PAT sample discontinued participating in the program for unknown reasons, perhaps related to dissatisfaction with the program. There was no significant change in program satisfaction from child age 1 to child age 3.

Discussion

46. There is a fundamental problem in detecting parenting and child outcome effects of intervention programs that begin at birth. Effects of intervention programs can be confidently discerned when there is a greater positive change from baseline, prior to initiating the program, in the program participant group than the control group. However, in evaluations of programs such as PAT, in which intervention begins prior to or near the birth of the child, baseline measurements of child-related outcomes cannot be obtained. In order to conclude that outcomes detected are indeed program related, outcome evaluation studies require baseline pretesting that addresses the initial equivalence of the groups in ways potentially related to the child or parenting outcomes examined.

47. All parents in this primarily middle-class sample scored highly in evaluations of the quality of parenting and the home environment, yet the PAT families were found to provide more developmentally stimulating environments for their children than the comparison group. It is possible that this group difference is not attributable to the program because differential changes from baseline cannot be tested for this measure, which requires a child of at least 3 months of age to be present. PAT and comparison groups were, however, highly similar in baseline demographic and attitudinal measures. Moreover, after controlling for baseline parent knowledge differences, the quality of the home environment was still higher for PAT participants. A reasonable explanation for the results, therefore, is that the PAT program was effective in increasing qualities of parenting and the home environment.

48. It should be noted, however, that the mean differences between the groups were small and perhaps developmentally insignificant. This conclusion is supported by the lack of differences between the groups of children in cognitive, language, or social development. These results add to those of other studies that have found little benefit from formal intervention among middle-class children (McGuire & Earls, 1991) or among children whose cognitive scores average 100 or better (e.g. Infant Health and Development Program, 1990; Scarr & McCartney, 1988).

49. Congruent with another tested goal, PAT mothers and fathers both reported higher levels of support from their communities than the comparison group parents. Levels of parenting stress were comparably low among both groups of parents, emphasizing the lack of parenting risk in the sample.

50. In the pilot implementation of the Texas PAT program, under the premise that all parents could benefit from the program, parents who might be considered at risk for providing inadequate parenting were not specifically targeted. The parents who participated in this phase of the program and the evaluation study fit the profile of successful parents with demographic characteristics indicative of later competence for their children (Finklestein & Ramey, 1980; Madden, O'Hara, & Levenstein, 1984). An equally important characteristic of these parents was the dedication they exhibited by participating for 3 years in the PAT program. By recruiting a comparison group from childbirth preparation classes, we identified another group of parents who similarly exhibited some commitment to seeking knowledge and who also were motivated to stay with a 3-year study of their children's development without financial remuneration. For parents with similar characteristics and resources, we predict that the PAT program would have modest effects similar to those reported here. On the basis of previously reported outcomes of the Missouri PAT program (Pfannenstiel et al., 1991), we speculate that the PAT program would demonstrate positive effects for children if it were to target families with demonstrable needs in the areas of parenting and parent stress. However, a longitudinal outcome evaluation, such as the present study, with attitudinal, parent knowledge, and demographic baseline testing of participant and comparison groups has not yet been conducted that has demonstrated these effects.

51. The higher quality of home environments found among the PAT participants in this evaluation may have later significance. Studies using the HOME instrument have found significant relations between the early home environment and children's later school performance (Bradley & Caldwell, 1984; Bradley, Caldwell, & Rock, 1988). Changes in the home environment have been shown to have lasting effects on children's achievement, with long-term benefits for children's abilities possibly even more likely than short-term benefits (Berrueta-Clement, Schweinhart, Barnett, Epstein, & Weikart, 1987; Bradley et al., 1988). This

indicates that there could be a sleeper effect of PAT participation on later child achievement that could not be discerned at age 3; however, the high levels of cognitive, language, and social abilities demonstrated by the children in the study may well preclude that possibility.

52. Proponents of the family support movement have argued that the need for support and education is universal among families today. Indeed, the PAT families expressed strong satisfaction with their participation in the PAT program and perceived greater support from their communities than comparison families. However, with no measurable benefits found in outcomes for these children compared to the early high level of ability found among the comparison group children, there is justification for questioning whether such publicly supported programs should continue to be made available to families who exhibit no known stresses or risks. It would be premature, however, to suggest that this program can be of little substantial benefit to the children of middle-class families in general. The present sample was comprised of committed parents exhibiting minimal stress from parenting. Middle-class families with low support, marital or parenting stress, and poor parenting abilities might well benefit from parent education and support efforts in a program such as PAT. Moreover, parents who are already practicing healthy and appropriate parenting may desire programs such as PAT for confirmation and reinforcement (Dembo, Sweitzer, & Lauritzen, 1985). The satisfaction with the program expressed by the PAT participants in this study indicates that they benefited from the program in this fashion.

Implications

53. The success of programs that intervene with the parents of infants and young children is often judged only by outcomes for the child. However, programs that work with the parents to influence the children, like the program examined here, should demonstrate effects on parents and children alike. Evaluation efforts that address effects for both and do so at multiple stages in the program are likely to provide information regarding not only whether the programs affect children but how they do so. Measuring child outcome alone may omit important information regarding the effectiveness of the program.

54. Another consideration is that parents' goals may differ from program goals. Parents' goals that may differ across economic and ethnic groups are important to consider. The high levels of parent satisfaction with this program and their reported increased confidence with parenting, despite evidence that program

participation did not enhance their children's development, indicates that the parents' goals may have differed from the program's emphasis on the children's achievements.

55. There was also evidence that the program achieved important goals with respect to parenting and the home environment. These results were sufficient to encourage continued efforts to make such parenting education and support programs available in more communities, and to increase efforts to reach out to greater numbers of parents with potentially greater needs for intervention. Current PAT programs in Texas have successfully attracted a much more diverse population of participants than the initial pilot programs: In 1993, 41% were teen mothers, 37% Hispanic, and 21% African American (Mental Health Association in Texas, 1993). With the likelihood that funds for family-oriented intervention will continue to be scarce, well-designed evaluation research with these diverse families is needed to study program effects at the child, parent, and parenting levels.

References

Abidin, R. R. (1986). *Parenting Stress Index*. Charlottesville, VA: Pediatric Psychology Press.

Bayley, N. (1969). *Bayley Scales of Infant Development*. New York: Psychological Corporation.

Berrueta-Clement, J. R., Schweinhart, L. J., Barnett, W. S., Epstein, A. S., & Weikart, D. P. (1987). *Changed lives: The effects of the Perry preschool program on youths through age 19*. Ypsilanti, MI: High/Scope.

Bradley, R. H., & Caldwell, B. M. (1984). The relation of infants' home environments to achievement test performance in first grade: A follow-up study. *Child Development, 52*, 708-710.

Bradley, R. H., Caldwell, B. M., & Rock, S. L. (1988). Home environment and school performance: A 10-year follow-up and examination of three models of environmental action. *Child Development, 59*, 852-867.

Bzoch, K. R., & League, R. (1970). *The Receptive-Expressive Emergent Language Scale for the measurement of language skills in infancy*. Gainesville, FL: Tree of Life Press.

Caldwell, B. M., & Bradley, R. H. (1984). *Home Observation for Measurement of the Environment*. Little Rock: University of Arkansas.

Clewell, B. C., Brooks-Gunn, J., & Benasich, A. (1989). Evaluating child-related outcomes of teenage parenting programs. *Family Relations, 38*, 201-209.

Cook, T. D., & Campbell, D. T. (1979). *Quasi-Experimentation: Design and analysis issues for field settings*. Chicago: Rand McNally.

Crnic, K. A., Greenberg, M. T., Ragozin, A. S., Robinson, N. M., & Brasham, R. (1983). Effects of stress and social support on mothers and premature and full-term infants. *Child Development, 54*, 209-217.

Dembo, M. H., Sweitzer, M., & Lauritzen, P. (1985). An evaluation of group parent education: Behavioral, PET, and Adlerian programs. *Review of Education Research, 55,* 155-200.

Easterbrooks, M. A., & Goldberg, W. A. (1984). Toddler development in the family: Impact of father involvement and parenting characteristics. *Child Development, 55,* 740-752.

Finklestein, N. W., & Ramey, C. T. (1980). Information from birth certificates as a risk index for educational handicap. *American Journal of Mental Deficiency, 84,* 546-552.

Grams, A. (1960). *Parent education and the behavior sciences* (Publication 379). Washington, DC: Dept. of Health, Education and Welfare Social Security Administration Children's Bureau.

Gray, S. W., & Wandersman, L. P. (1980). The methodology of home-based intervention studies: Problems and promising strategies. *Child Development, 51,* 993-1009.

Hollingshead, A. B. (1975). *Four factor index of social status.* New Haven, CT: Yale University.

Infant Health and Development Program. (1990). Enhancing the outcomes of low-birth-weight, premature infants. *Journal of the American Medical Association, 263,* 3035-3042.

Kaufman, A. S., & Kaufman, N. L. (1983). *Kaufman Assessment Battery for Children (K-ABC).* Circle Pines, MN: American Guidance Service.

Madden, J., O'Hara, J., & Levenstein, P. (1984). Home again: Effects of the Mother-Child Home Programs on mother and child. *Child Development, 55,* 636-647.

McGuire, J., & Earls, F. (1991). Prevention of psychiatric disorders in early childhood. *Journal of Child Psychology and Psychiatry, 32,* 129-134.

Mental Health Association in Texas. (1993, December). *Mental Health Advocate,* p. 3.

Minuchin, P. (1985). Families and individual development: Provocations from the field of family therapy. *Child Development, 56,* 289-302.

Minuchin, S. (1974). *Families and family therapy.* Cambridge, MA: Harvard University Press.

National Association for the Education of Young Children. (1987). *NAEYC position on standardized testing of young children 3 through 8 years of age.* Washington, DC: Author.

Pfannenstiel, J., Lambson, T., & Yarnell, V. (1991). *Second wave study of the Parents as Teachers program.* Jefferson City, MO: Research and Training Associates.

Pfannenstiel, J., & Seltzer, D. A. (1985). *New Parents as Teachers Project.* Jefferson City, MO: Missouri Department of Elementary and Secondary Education.

Powell, D. R. (1988). Challenges in the design and evaluation of parent-child intervention programs. In D. R. Powell (Ed.), *Parent education as early childhood intervention: Emerging directions in theory, research and practice* (pp. 209-227). Norwood, NJ: Ablex Publishing.

Research and Training Associates. (1985). *Parent Knowledge Questionnaire.* Jefferson City, MO: Author.

Scarr, S., & McCartney, K. (1988). Far from home: An experimental evaluation of the Mother-Child Home Program in Bermuda. *Child Development, 59,* 531-543.

Seitz, V. (1987). Outcome evaluation of family support programs: Research design alternatives to true experiments. In S. L. Kagan, D. R. Powell, B. Weissbourd, & E. F. Zigler (Eds.), *America's family support programs: Perspectives and prospects* (pp. 329-344). New Haven: Yale University Press.

Slaughter, D. (1983). Early intervention and its effects on maternal and child development. *Monographs for the Society for Research in Child Development, 48,* (4, Serial No. 202).

Sparrow, S. S., Balla, D. A., & Cicchetti, D. V. (1984). *Vineland Adaptive Behavior Scales.* Circle Pines, MN: American Guidance Service.

van Doornink, W., Dawson, P., Butterfield, P., & Alexander, H. (1980). *Parent-infant support through lay health visitors.* Denver: Parent-Infant Programs.

Weiss, H. B. (1989). State family support and education programs: Lessons from the pioneers. *American Journal of Orthopsychiatry, 59,* 32-48.

Weissbourd, B., & Kagan, S. L. (1989). Family support programs: Catalysts for change. *American Journal of Orthopsychiatry, 59,* 20-31.

White, B. L. (1980). Primary prevention: Beginning at the beginning. *Personnel and Guidance Journal, 58,* 338-343.

Zigler, E., & Black, K. B. (1989). America's family support movement: Strengths and limitations. *American Journal of Orthopsychiatry, 59,* 6-19.

Zimmerman, I. L., Steiner, V. G., Pond, R. E. (1979). *Preschool Language Scale.* San Antonio: Psychological Corporation.

Factual Questions

1. How many research hypotheses are explicitly stated? In which paragraph are they stated?

2. According to the authors, how can an examination of attrition rates help in the evaluation of a program?

3. Did the two groups differ in terms of the percentage of single-parent families? If yes, how?

4. Were the differences in cognitive effects for children statistically significant?

5. In Table 2, the letters *M* and *F* in the first column stand for what?

6. Did the PAT or control group mothers have a higher mean score on parenting stress at the end of three years?

7. Were the differences in parenting stress statistically significant?

8. The difference in community support as reported by fathers was statistically significant at what probability level?

Questions for Discussion

9. Is the PAT program described in sufficient detail in paragraphs 2 through 7? Explain.

10. The authors note in paragraph 12 that they had to use a *quasi-experimental design.* How is this different from a true experiment?

11. Is the fact that only two-thirds of the PAT participants volunteered to take part in the study a limitation of this evaluation? Explain.

12. How important is it to know the extent of compliance with expectations of the program? (See paragraph 23.)

13. The authors refer to *baseline information* in various places (for example, see paragraph 25). What does this term mean?

14. If you were a program administrator for PAT, would you be more interested in the child outcomes or the parent outcomes? Explain.

15. The authors discuss *internal consistency as measured by Cronbach alphas* in their discussion of the measures in paragraphs 26–32. What does this mean?

16. Do you think that the program might have had larger effects if applied only to parents at risk for providing inadequate parenting? Why? Why not?

17. In paragraph 1, the authors note the need to evaluate programs, particularly in times of severe financial constraints. Based on the results of this evaluation, would you recommend continued funding of the PAT program? Why? Why not?

18. If you were evaluating a PAT program in the future, what changes in research methodology, if any, would you make?

Quality Ratings

DIRECTIONS: Indicate your level of agreement with each of the following statements by circling a number from 5 for strongly agree (SA) to 1 for strongly disagree (SD). If you believe that an item is not applicable to this research article, leave it blank. Be prepared to explain your ratings.

A. The introduction establishes the importance of the research topic.

    SA   5   4   3   2   1   SD

B. The literature review establishes the context for the study.

    SA   5   4   3   2   1   SD

C. The research purpose, question, or hypothesis is clearly stated.

    SA   5   4   3   2   1   SD

D. The method of sampling is sound.

    SA   5   4   3   2   1   SD

E. Relevant demographics (for example, age, gender, and ethnicity) are described.

    SA   5   4   3   2   1   SD

F. Measurement procedures are adequate.

    SA   5   4   3   2   1   SD

G. The results are clearly described.

    SA   5   4   3   2   1   SD

H. The discussion/conclusion is appropriate.

    SA   5   4   3   2   1   SD

I. Despite any flaws noted above, the report is worthy of publication.

    SA   5   4   3   2   1   SD

LITERACY IN YOUNG CHILDREN: RESULTS FROM A THREE YEAR URBAN SCHOOL PROJECT

Jane A. Romatowski *University of Michigan–Dearborn*
Mary L. Trepanier-Street *University of Michigan–Dearborn*
Janice Peterson *Woodward Elementary School*

A three year Reading Club project was implemented in an urban school with kindergarten children for the purpose of promoting literacy. Results from this literature based project showed a positive influence on children's interest in books, reading comprehension, and home reading experiences.

1. Literacy, the ability to read and write and the preconditions for these abilities, has been the focus of attention for practitioners and researchers alike. Among these preconditions are language acquisition, an understanding of the uses of language, exposure to speech, exposure to print, development of the concept of "book," a sense of story, and an understanding of societal uses of print. It is argued that these experiences with language will or can lead naturally to the acts of reading and writing (Butler & Clay, 1979; Doake, 1989; Goodman, 1986; Holdaway, 1979; Sawyer & Sawyer, 1993; Strickland & Morrow, 1989; Teale & Sulzby, 1986). Both the home and the school play a vital role in whether these preconditions are met.

2. In *Becoming a Nation of Readers* (Anderson, Hiebert, Scott, & Wilkinson, 1985), the challenge to both home and school is the early development of positive attitudes toward reading. Numerous studies across several decades have continually found that early experiences with literature have a positive effect on attitudes toward reading and on learning to read (Bissett 1970; Cazden, 1981; Chomsky, 1970; Cohen, 1968; Cullinan, 1989; Durkin, 1966; Fields, Spangler, & Lee, 1991; Jewell & Zintz, 1990; Teale, 1978; Torrey, 1969; Trelease, 1982; Vacca, Vacca, & Gove, 1991). Early experiences with books helped children accumulate knowledge important for future learning; led to the expansion of vocabularies and the use of more sophisticated language structures; prompted an appreciation of books, the development of a sense of story, and the use of critical thinking skills. Concurrently, there was enhancement of the sense of self as a competent language user.

3. In the literature on early experiences with reading, some shared assumptions are operative. One assumption is that success in most school subjects is dependent on competency in reading. Another is that reading meaningfully in any subject will depend on prior experiences with the concepts in print. A third would be that the larger the store of lexical items, the more a reader can bring to the processing of print. Given these assumptions, the fourth flows rather naturally, i.e., the earlier the foundations of literacy are established the more opportunity children will have to grow in concept development in vocabulary acquisition, and in building a positive relationship with print and with reading. The compelling nature of the assumptions and the supportive research and literature on early literacy prompted the development of a project for kindergarten children in an urban school setting using university student volunteers.

Description of Project

4. The Reading Club (RC) project was a three year project which in its first year included children in kindergarten, first and second grades. Given the particular success with kindergarten children during the first year and the importance of early life experiences, the second and third years of the project included only kindergarten children. In this paper, the data from kindergarten children from all three years will be reported. Included in the study as RC members were 22 kindergartners (9 boys, 13 girls) year 1; 51 kindergartners (29 boys, 22 girls) year 2; and 46 kindergartners (20 boys, 26 girls) year 3. To be included as RC members, children had to attend a minimum of three reading sessions. As a comparison group, nonmembers were children who were in the same classrooms as the members but did not attend RC. There were 26 nonmembers (18 boys, 8 girls) year 1; 37 nonmembers (21 boys, 16 girls) year 2; and 14 nonmembers (9 boys, 5 girls) year 3. (Given the small number of nonmembers in year 3, any data for year 3 regarding nonmembers must be interpreted with caution.) All children (both RC members and nonmembers) attended the same elementary school located in a depressed urban area in a large Midwestern city. The school population was 99% African-American. Ninety-five percent of the students qualified for the federal free lunch program and many parents were receiving financial aid through the Aid to Families with Dependent Children program.

5. The general plan and format for RC was similar across the years. RC children were exposed to planned reading experiences and a culminating event. There were three reading sessions and a culminating event on Saturdays in year 1; six reading sessions and a culminating event on Saturdays in year 2; and six reading sessions and a culminating event after school on Thursdays in year 3. Each of the reading sessions consisted of an interactive experience with a book read by the university student volunteer followed by planned book activities implemented after children received their own copy of the book. At the culminating event, a book was read, a certificate of attendance was awarded, and additional books for summer home reading were given.

Romatowski, J. A., Trepanier-Street, M. L., & Peterson, J. (1995). Literacy in young children: Results from a three year urban school project. *Reading Improvement, 32*, 154-160. Copyright © 1995 by Project Innovation of Mobile. Reprinted by permission.

Acknowledgments are due the following persons for their assistance with the project: Dr. Louise Reid Ritchie and the Detroit Free Press Gift of Reading Program; grants from the University of Michigan–Dearborn; the University of Michigan–Dearborn student volunteers; and the administrators, teachers, parents and children at Woodward Elementary School.

A complete list of the children's books used in the project can be obtained from the authors at the School of Education, University of Michigan–Dearborn, 4901 Evergreen Road, Dearborn, MI 48128-1491.

6. Books used in the project were selected for their age appropriateness and their general appeal. From all the books reviewed, the final selection was made using several criteria among which were: predictable story and language patterns; lively plots; characters to whom children could relate; story problems which allowed for predicting, offering solutions, evaluating motive; and strong picture clues for future re-readings.

7. The reading session included a reading of the whole story by the university volunteer and various teaching strategies to encourage interaction between the listener and the story being read. Constructive rereading of the story and selective questioning techniques were used to promote critical thinking skills. Questions were asked which encouraged children to hypothesize, to make predictions about what might happen next, to justify their hypotheses and to identify clues which lead to their predictions. Other questions prompted children to describe the characters and to identify the characters' feelings and emotional states.

8. A number of different follow-up activities were prepared to engage the children in examining the book, the pictures, and the text. These included retelling the story from picture clues; finding repetitive language patterns and reading them or pointing to them while the volunteer read them; finding selected parts of the story in response to a stimulus question; choral reading especially of repeated language patterns or exciting story endings; expressive reading of dialogue where emotional states were clear, identifying one's favorite page and rereading it; and finding known words and phrases and reading them. Finally, children were encouraged to take their books home, to read the story to someone at home, or to have someone read the story to them. They were also informed that a copy of the book would be available in their classrooms.

Project Assessment and Results

9. Prior to the first reading club session, RC members as well as nonmembers were given an interest inventory (pretest). The same interest inventory (posttest) was given the week following the last reading club session. This represented a pretest to posttest time difference on the interest inventory of four weeks (year 1); one week (year 2); and one week (year 3). Children were tested on the interest inventory individually by their classroom teacher or by trained research assistants. In years 1 and 3, RC members were given an additional posttest (an interview) to assess interest in RC, the extension of the RC reading experience to the home, and comprehension and memory of a selected

Table 1 *Percentage of RC members giving the highest ranking to questions 1–3*

	1. Like book			2. Like storytime			3. Book present		
	Pre	Post	%Ch	Pre	Post	%Ch	Pre	Post	%Ch
Yr. 1									
Mem	73%	95%	22%	68%	91%	23%	68%	95%	27%
N/Mem	69%	69%	0%	77%	81%	4%	54%	54%	0%
Yr. 2									
Mem	73%	82%	9%	80%	68%	−11%	62%	77%	15%
N/Mem	81%	89%	8%	65%	65%	0%	70%	60%	−10%
Yr. 3									
Mem	91%	89%	−2%	63%	72%	9%	70%	78%	8%
N/Mem	100%	93%	−7%	67%	86%	19%	64%	29%	−35%

Note. Mem = members; N/Mem = Nonmembers; Pre = pretest; Post = posttest; %Ch = percentage of change from pretest to posttest.

RC book. Interviews were conducted one week after the culminating event and represented a time difference from the first reading of the selected RC book to the interview of 11 weeks (year 1) and three weeks (year 3). Trained research assistants scored the interest inventories and the interviews with an interrater reliability of 98% agreement across scorers.

Interest Inventory Results

10. The interest inventory consisted of eight questions. The first three questions required children to rate how much they liked books, how much they liked storytime, and how much they liked a book as a present. A three point rating scale ranging from a sad face (liking not at all), a neutral face (liking somewhat) to a happy face (liking a lot) was used. In question four, children were asked what they liked to do best. "Read a book" and "listen to stories" were the two relevant choices of the six choices given in years 2 & 3. In year 1, "read a book" was the only relevant choice of the five choices given that year. Next, children were asked what they would like to do best in school. "Read a book" and "listen to stories" were the two relevant choices of the six given in all three years. For questions six through eight children were given the following choices: clothes, a doll, a truck, a book, a game, or a Ninja Turtle, and asked the following three questions: Which would you like for a birthday present?, Which would you buy for a present for a girl your age? and Which would you buy for a present for a boy your age? Questions six through eight were asked twice requiring the children to give a first and a second choice. Comparisons of pretest and posttest interest inventories on each of the eight questions were made between RC members and nonmembers.

11. For the first three questions (the rating questions), the percentage of RC members and nonmembers giving the highest rating for each question can be seen in Table 1. The majority of children, members and nonmembers, tended to choose the highest rating. However, there were some differences between the pretest and posttest responses of members and nonmembers. The percentage of members choosing the highest rating tended to increase from the pretest to the posttest. The percentage of nonmembers choosing the highest rating tended to remain unchanged or decreased from the pretest to the posttest. As seen in Table 1, the percentage of positive change from pretest to posttest favors the members group.

12. A comparison of the percentage of RC members and nonmembers choosing, as a first or second choice, "reading" or "listening to stories" as a favored personal activity (question 4) or as a favored school activity (question 5) is reported in Table 2. When comparing pretest and posttest results, RC members' responses tended to show a pretest to posttest increase in choosing reading or listening to stories. In all but one instance (question 5, year 3) nonmember responses showed a decrease on the posttest. In response to questions about choosing a book, as a first or second choice, as a present for themselves (question 6), for a girl their age (question 7), or for a boy their age (question 8), the percentages are reported in Table 3. For both members and nonmembers, a book tended not to be a preferred choice for a present. However, members tended to show a positive pretest to posttest change, that is, the choice of a book

Table 2 *Percentage of respondents choosing reading or listening to stories as a favored activity on questions 4–5*

	4. Like to do best			5. Like to do in school		
	Pre	Post	%Ch	Pre	Post	%Ch
Yr. 1						
Mem	14%	36%	22%	44%	61%	17%
N/Mem	13%	6%	–7%	36%	28%	–8%
Yr. 2						
Mem	49%	78%	29%	74%	80%	6%
N/Mem	41%	22%	–19%	62%	32%	–30%
Yr. 3						
Mem	11%	25%	14%	26%	36%	10%
N/Mem	21%	7%	–14%	36%	71%	35%

Note. Mem = members; N/Mem = Nonmembers; Pre = pretest; Post = posttest; %Ch = percentage of change from pretest to posttest.

as a present tended to increase from pretest to the posttest. For nonmembers, the choice of a book as a present tended to remain the same or decrease in most instances. (In two of the three instances of positive change, the change represented one respondent only.) In summary, the data on the inventories as seen in Tables 1, 2, and 3 suggest that the responses of members showed an increase from the pretest to the posttest. With but a few exceptions, the responses of the nonmembers showed little change or a decrease from pretest to the posttest.

Interview Results

13. Interest in RC was assessed in years 1 and 3 by asking members whether they liked coming to RC and why. Interviewers used three prompts for the "why" question. Of those queried, the majority responded "yes" they liked coming to RC (100% year 1; 100% year 3). When asked why, members named reading or listening to stories as their first or second reason (100% year 1; 98% year 3).

14. In years 1 and 3 the extension of the RC experience to the home was assessed. When asked if they read the book at home, respondents often said "yes" (73% year 1; 67% year 3). When asked who read the book to them, mother was the most frequently cited reader (32% year 1; 48% year 3). Members reported that they read the book to someone at home (83% year 1; 83% year 3). The most cited person to whom the story was read was a sibling (46% year 1; 56% year 3).

15. In year 1 and year 3, RC members were assessed for their memory and comprehension of a selected RC book. Members were asked

"What was the big problem in this story?" and "What finally happened?" or "How did the story end?" Children responded to the questions without prompting by the interviewer. However, if a child mentioned a particular character by name, the interviewer, when appropriate, asked how the character felt. In year 1, 91% of the members and in year 3, 70% of the members identified the story problem accurately (the story for year 3 had a more complex story problem which included a subplot). In year 1, 73%, and in year 3, 65% were able to correctly identify the story ending.

16. Children's responses were also examined to determine the number of remembered story elements (events in story plot). In year 1, 91% of the members were able to remember between 3 to 6 elements in the story. In year 3, 85% of the members were able to remember between 3 to 6 elements in the story, with 28% remembering 6 or more.

17. Responses were also examined for the number of characters remembered and for the number of feelings or emotional states attributed to story characters. In year 1, given a 5 character story, 100% of the members named at least 1 character; 78% remembered 2 or 3 characters; 23% named 4 or 5. In year 3, given an 8 character story, 96% of the members named 3 to 6 characters; 19% remembered more than 6 characters.

18. Finally, responses were examined for the total number of feelings or emotional states (e.g., happy, sad, angry, scared, or mad) attributed to story characters by the RC members. In year 1, 68% remembered 3 to 5 feelings or emotional states; 92% remembered at least 1 or 2 emotional states. In year 3, 91% remembered 3 to 5 emotions; 37% remembered 6 or more.

Summary of Project Results

19. The results of this study suggest that the RC project was successful. The objectives of heightening awareness about the pleasures of reading, providing an opportunity for critical thinking and reading skills, and promoting literacy at home were achieved through the project. When interviewed about their RC experience, RC members reported that they definitely like coming to Reading Club because they could

Table 3 *Percentage of respondents choosing a book as a present on questions 6–8*

	6. Book for self			7. Book for girl			8. Book for boy		
	Pre	Post	%Ch	Pre	Post	%Ch	Pre	Post	%Ch
Yr. 1									
Mem	2%	14%	12%	0%	22%	22%	0%	9%	9%
N/Mem	0%	0%	0%	2%	0%	–2%	2%	0%	–2%
Yr. 2									
Mem	8%	22%	14%	16%	20%	4%	16%	26%	10%
N/Mem	13%	5%	–8%	11%	8%	–3%	8%	11%	3%
Yr. 3									
Mem	4%	9%	5%	1%	10%	9%	0%	4%	4%
N/Mem	0%	7%	7%	0%	0%	0%	0%	7%	7%

Note. Mem = members; N/Mem = Nonmembers; Pre = pretest; Post = posttest; % Ch = percentage of change from pretest to posttest.

listen to stories and read books. Posttest interest inventories for RC members showed an increase in liking books, liking storytime, and liking books as a present. Increases on the interest measure were seen in their choice of reading books and listening to stories as a favored personal activity and as a favored school activity. Also, some change toward selecting a book as a present for themselves or for a girl or boy their age was evident. On posttest interviews the majority of RC children reported that books from RC were read at home by them and by other family members. When interviewed about the selected RC book, RC members were able to describe the major problem in the story and the solution to that problem or the ending of the story. They remembered many story elements, story characters and accurately labeled the feeling or emotional states of the characters.

20. The results of the project were gratifying even though the project itself was limited in scope. The major goal of this service-oriented project was to have an impact on literacy for children whose homes were not print-rich environments. To that end, the results of this project affirmed what others have found regarding early experiences with books and stories. Studies have consistently supported the values of reading aloud to children and of helping children to interact meaningfully with books (Davidson, 1988; Johnson & Louis, 1987; Teale, 1978). Such early reading experiences have been shown to influence reading competency, cognition, language learning, and vocabulary acquisition (Froese, 1991). The work of others and the results of this Reading Club project suggest that literature-based programs can help lay a sound foundation in reading for young children on the brink of literacy.

References

Anderson, R. C., Hiebert, E. H., Scott, J. A., & Wilkinson, I. A. (1985). *Becoming a nation of readers. The Report of the Commission on Reading.* Washington, DC: National Institute of Education.

Bissett, D. (1970). The usefulness of children's books in the reading program. In J. Catterson (Ed.), *Children and literature.* Newark, DE: International Reading Association.

Butler, D., & Clay, M. (1979). *Reading begins at home.* Portsmouth, NH: Heinemann Educational Books.

Cazden, C. (Ed.) (1981). *Language in early childhood education.* Washington, DC: National Association for the Education of Young Children.

Chomsky, C. (1970). Stages in language development and reading. *Harvard Educational Review, 42,* 1-33.

Cohen, D. (1968). The effects of literature on vocabulary and reading achievement. *Elementary English, 45,* 209-213, 217.

Cullinan, B. E. (1989). *Literature and the child* (2nd ed.) New York: Harcourt, Brace, Jovanovich, Inc.

Davidson, J. (Ed.) (1988). *Counterpoint and beyond.* Urbana, IL: National Council of Teachers of English.

Doake, D. (1989). *Reading begins at birth.* New York: Scholastic, Inc.

Durkin, D. (1966). *Children who read early.* New York: Teachers College Press.

Fields, M. V., Spangler, K. L., & Lee, D. M. (1991). *Let's begin reading right.* New York: Macmillan Publishing Co.

Froese, V. (Ed.) (1991). *Whole-language: Practice and theory.* Needham Heights, MA: Allyn and Bacon.

Goodman, K. S. (1986). *What's whole in whole language?* Portsmouth, NH: Heinemann Educational Books.

Holdaway, D. (1979). *Foundations of literacy.* New York: Ashton Scholastic.

Jewell, M. G., & Zintz, M. V. (1990). *Learning to read and write naturally.* Dubuque, IA: Kendall/Hunt Publishing Co.

Johnson, T. D., & Louis, D. R. (1987). *Literacy through literature.* Portsmouth, NH: Heinemann Educational Books.

Sawyer, W. E., & Sawyer, J. C. (1993). *Integrated language arts for emerging literacy.* Albany, NY: Delmar Publishers, Inc.

Strickland, D., & Morrow, L. M. (Eds.) (1989). *Emerging literacy: Young children learn to read and write.* Newark, DE: International Reading Association.

Teale, W. H. (1978). Positive environments for learning to read: What studies of early readers tell us. *Language Arts, 55,* 922-932.

Teale, W. H., & Sulzby, E. (Eds.) (1986). *Emergent literacy: Writing and reading.* Norwood, NJ: Ablex.

Torrey, J. W. (1969). Learning to read without a teacher. *Elementary English, 46,* 556-559.

Trelease, J. (1982). *The read-aloud handbook.* New York: Penguin Books.

Vacca, J. L., Vacca, R. T., & Gove, M. K. (1991). *Reading and learning to read.* (2nd ed.) New York: HarperCollins Publishers.

Factual Questions

1. Why did the project include only kindergarten children during the second and third years?

2. In all, how many children were RC members?

3. According to the researchers, the data for which year should be interpreted with caution?

4. Was the number of reading sessions the same in all three years? Explain.

5. Were any of the changes for year 2 RC members on the first three questions negative? Explain.

6. In the year 1 group, what percentage remembered (named) at least one character?

Questions for Discussion

7. Is it reasonable to assume that children were assigned at random to be either RC members or nonmembers? If no, how do you think they acquired member or nonmember status? Is it important to know how this happened? Explain.

8. Is it important to know that RC members and nonmembers were in the same classrooms? (See paragraph 4.) Explain.

9. Although a majority of the RC members were girls, a majority of the nonmembers were boys. Is this important? Why? Why not?

10. What additional information, if any, would you like to know about the general plan and format for RC? (See paragraphs 5–8.)

11. Is it important to know that the interrater reliability was 98%? (See paragraph 9.) Explain.

12. In paragraph 11, the researchers summarize the data in Table 1. In your opinion, is their summary adequate? Explain.

13. Do the data in paragraph 14 indicate that the RC experience caused changes in students' behavior at home? Explain.

14. Different stories were used in different years of the project. Is this a strength or weakness? Explain.

15. To which population(s), if any, would you be willing to generalize the results of this study?

16. Do you believe that the results presented in this article justify extension of the RC project to other schools? If yes, should evaluations be conducted in those schools? Why? Why not?

17. This article is classified as an example of "program evaluation" in this book. (See the table of contents.) Would it be equally

appropriate to classify it as an example of experimental research? Why? Why not?

18. If you were evaluating this program, what changes, if any, would you make in the evaluation methodology?

Quality Ratings

DIRECTIONS: Indicate your level of agreement with each of the following statements by circling a number from 5 for strongly agree (SA) to 1 for strongly disagree (SD). If you believe that an item is not applicable to this research article, leave it blank. Be prepared to explain your ratings.

A. The introduction establishes the importance of the research topic.
SA   5   4   3   2   1   SD

B. The literature review establishes the context for the study.
SA   5   4   3   2   1   SD

C. The research purpose, question, or hypothesis is clearly stated.
SA   5   4   3   2   1   SD

D. The method of sampling is sound.
SA   5   4   3   2   1   SD

E. Relevant demographics (for example, age, gender, and ethnicity) are described.
SA   5   4   3   2   1   SD

F. Measurement procedures are adequate.
SA   5   4   3   2   1   SD

G. The results are clearly described.
SA   5   4   3   2   1   SD

H. The discussion/conclusion is appropriate.
SA   5   4   3   2   1   SD

I. Despite any flaws noted above, the report is worthy of publication.
SA   5   4   3   2   1   SD

ARTICLE 33

EVALUATING GANG RESISTANCE EDUCATION AND TRAINING (GREAT): IS THE IMPACT THE SAME AS THAT OF DRUG ABUSE RESISTANCE EDUCATION (DARE)?

Dennis J. Palumbo   *Arizona State University*
Jennifer L. Ferguson   *Arizona State University*

Gangs became a major concern of law enforcement and the public in the late 1980s and remain so in the first half of the 1990s. One response for addressing the problem has been the development and dissemination of a prevention program called Gang Resistance Education and Training (GREAT). This program is similar to the popular Drug Abuse Resistance Education (DARE) program of the 1980s. No published evaluations exist about GREAT although there have been numerous evaluations of DARE. The latter show that DARE has a very small effect on the drug behavior of children. This research reports an evaluation of GREAT in several sites in the United States that show that it also has a very small effect on children. However, as is the case with DARE, GREAT will continue because of the powerful symbolic political and public relations utility it has for various stakeholders.

1.   Gangs were not high on the public policy agenda very much prior to about 1985. There were relatively few newspaper stories about gangs before 1985 (see Figure 1). However, newspaper stories about gangs began to pick up in 1985 and greatly increased in 1988. Most of these stories, as well as television coverage, emphasized the violence associated with gangs (Jankowski, 1991).

2.   By the late 1980s, gangs had become a leading concern of law enforcement officers. A national survey of youth gang problems and programs conducted in 1988 and 1989 (Spergel et al., 1990) found that most local officials believed that the gang situation had worsened in their cities during the 1980s. In addition, participants attending a national gang conference held in Los Angeles in 1989 felt that the gang problem had gotten worse. Commander Lorne Kramer of the Los Angeles Police Department (LAPD) said that the growth of gangs in Los Angeles had been dramatic, especially between 1985 and 1988. Andrew Hague of the Dade County Attorney's Office said that the gang situation in Miami exploded in 1984.

3.   Efforts to control gangs and the violence associated with gangs include suppression by law enforcement and education and prevention programs aimed at elementary school students. The Gang Resistance Education and Training (GREAT) is one of the latter programs.

4.   This prevention program originated in Phoenix, Arizona, in 1991 under a grant from the Bureau of Alcohol, Tobacco and Firearms to the Phoenix Police Department. In 1993 it expanded to New Mexico and Hawaii, and in 1994 a number of other states also began GREAT programs.

5.   There are similarities between GREAT and the Drug Abuse Resistance Education (DARE) program. The latter was created in 1983 by the LAPD and it became a highly popular national program in the 1980s. Similar to DARE in emphasizing prevention, GREAT attempts to reduce involvement in gangs. The heart of this program is a curriculum taught by uniformed police officers to elementary school children. There are eight 45- to 60-minute sessions taught once a week primarily to seventh graders, although sixth graders are included at some sites. Officers who teach the GREAT curriculum are given 40 hours of training. All officers use the same curriculum.

6.   The GREAT program has a number of goals, but the most important is to get youths to resist joining a gang.

7.   The GREAT program emphasizes the acquisition of information and skills needed by students to enable them to act in their own best interest when facing high-risk or low-risk choices and to resist peer pressure and gang influences in making their personal choices. It also seeks changes in the violent behavior, attitudes, and self-esteem of middle school-age students.

8.   We worked closely with the police officials who supervised the GREAT program. Thus our measures reflect the objectives they thought were important.

9.   We present an evaluation of GREAT that was conducted at the end of its third year in selected sites in the United States.[1] Although DARE has been evaluated a number of times, there are no published evaluations of GREAT.[2] Because the two programs are similar in purpose and the way they are implemented, a short description of evaluations of DARE will be helpful because both programs have similar impacts.

10.   A few of the early evaluations of DARE found that it was popular and also appeared to enhance antidrug attitudes and knowledge among students while strengthening those social skills and behaviors relevant to resisting drug use (Nyre, 1984, 1984-85). However, DeJong's (1987) study, which focused on measures of self-concept, drug knowledge and attitudes, and self-reported drug usage among seventh-grade students in Los Angeles who had received the full-semester DARE curriculum in the sixth grade, found *no* difference in these variables when compared with a control group. Another study that replicated the DeJong study in Kokomo, Indiana, concluded that there is no one answer to the question of whether DARE is a success (Aniskiewicz and Wysong, 1990, p.

Palumbo, D. J., & Ferguson, J. L. (1995). Evaluating Gang Resistance Education and Training (GREAT): Is the impact the same as that of Drug Abuse Resistance Education (DARE)? *Evaluation Review*, 19, 597-619. Copyright © 1995 by Sage Publications, Inc. Reprinted by permission of Sage Publications, Inc.

Dennis J. Palumbo is the Regents' Professor of Justice Studies at Arizona State University. Author and editor of a number of books and articles in evaluation, public policy, and criminal justice, his most recent publication is "The Political Roots of Misuse of Evaluation" in *New Directions for Program Evaluation.*

Jennifer L. Ferguson is a doctoral student in justice studies at Arizona State University. She has been involved in various evaluations, including the Girl Scouts Behind Bars Program and the Community Partnership of Phoenix. She is currently working on a policy issues handbook relating to crime in America.

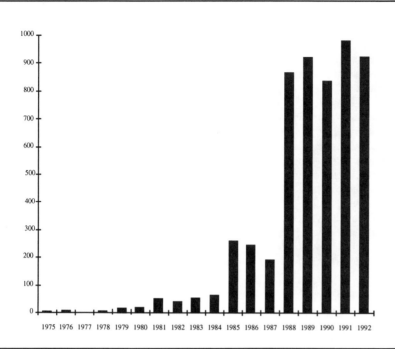

Figure 1   *Number of articles in the press about gangs, 1975–92.*
Source: Omni File Index and NEXIS Services

741). The authors found that DARE increased students' drug knowledge, willingness/ability to invoke drug-resistant coping skills and antidrug attitudes. However, they also found that the pre-DARE scores in Kokomo were very high; 80% of the 676 students gave appropriate responses in the pretest, and this increased to 90% in the posttest. According to Aniskiewicz and Wysong (1990), "this outcome may be the result of the prominent, general anti-drug social and political climate that has emerged in recent years" (p. 735). Most important, the authors believe that it is the symbolic appeal of DARE that is important, not its effectiveness in getting children to reject drugs.

11. A more recent meta-analysis of eight major evaluations of DARE showed the following conclusion:

> The results of this meta-analysis suggest that DARE's core curriculum effect on drug use relative to whatever drug education (if any) was offered in the control schools is slight and, except for tobacco use, is not statistically significant. Across the studies, none of the average drug use effect sizes exceeded .11. Review of several meta-analyses of adolescent drug use prevention programs suggests that effect sizes of this magnitude are small. (Ennett et al. 1994, p. 1398)

12. The evaluation of GREAT that we will now describe shows that its impact is similar to that of DARE: There is a slight increase among students in negative attitudes, resistance skills, and knowledge about gangs, and no impact on their self-esteem.

Method and Instrumentation

13. For this evaluation, a pre- and posttest design was used. The pre- and posttest measures of selected GREAT sites were conducted by a team of evaluators through the Arizona Prevention Resource Center at Arizona State University. The goal of these measurements was to evaluate the impact on the youths who participated in GREAT on their attitudes, self-esteem, self-reported gang and delinquent behavior, and knowledge of the GREAT curriculum. The design did not include a comparison group. The time constraints of the request to perform the pre-/posttests and focus groups precluded use of this element. The logistics of setting up the testing at the end of a school year and coordinating this with law enforcement agencies was another barrier. Therefore, a control group was not used in this study.

14. The lack of a control group prevents assessment of threats to internal validity. Therefore, it cannot be concluded that the results presented below were due to GREAT as opposed to other factors. Instead, the analysis focuses on the overall pattern of responses to the various measurements. If the pattern of responses to the questions about gang involvement and ability to resist peer pressure to join a gang is consistent among these measures and

with other items in the scales, then we may conclude that the results are related to GREAT, although not necessarily caused by GREAT. We stress that the research design is weak because of the conditions and time constraints under which the evaluation had to be conducted. Thus our conclusions are tentative. However, we believe that they contain useful information.

15. The pretest was a paper-and-pencil measure of self-reported behavior, attitudes, and knowledge that took approximately 45 to 50 minutes to complete. The tests were administered by individuals sent to each site by the Arizona Prevention Resource Center. Students' permission was obtained at the beginning of the sessions and their anonymity was guaranteed. Because we were dealing with seventh-grade children, we had to assure that their responses would not identify them in any way. Spanish and English versions of the questionnaires were used. Measures consisted of the attitude, behavior, and knowledge items that are described below.

Attitudes

16. Attitudes toward school, gangs, police, drugs, gang fighting, revenge, and weapons were measured using the "Feeling Thermometer." This is a valid and reliable instrument that has been used in a number of ways, including national opinion surveys by the Survey Research Center at the University of Michigan.

17. The nine-item scale measuring attitudes toward risky and delinquent behavior is part of a questionnaire called Knowledge, Attitudes, Behavior that is administered by the school system in Arizona. A factor analysis of the attitude items on this questionnaire has shown that the nine-item risk scale is a good predictor of self-reported drug use among elementary school children. Therefore, we assume that it also is a good predictor of gang involvement.

18. The third attitude measure is the Rosenberg Self Esteem Scale, a measure validated in previous research (Rosenberg, 1965). This is one of the most widely used measures in the psychological literature. The scale consists of 10 Likert-type (agree-disagree scale) items.

Knowledge

19. A 15-item test to assess knowledge of the GREAT curriculum was used to determine how much the students learned. This test consists of true-false questions and was constructed from the GREAT curriculum specified for 1993-1994.

20. The posttest design consisted of the items administered during the pretest and included focus groups along with the completion of questionnaires by classroom teachers and

GREAT officers. There were 8 to 12 children in each focus group. The purpose of the focus groups was to obtain relatively unstructured, qualitative impressions of the program and the problem of gangs in general. The discussions allowed participants to express themselves in their own words, with little or no guidance from the discussion leader. Focus groups are particularly useful for understanding how people perceive something and, in this design, helped explain the quantitative results. The focus groups were led by an evaluator who posed general, open-ended questions with prepared follow-up probes that were used as necessary.

21. A judgment sample was used to determine which students participated in the focus groups, so that they would reflect the makeup of the students in the GREAT program. The students were asked for their permission to have the interviews tape-recorded to assure accuracy in transcribing their responses. They gave their permission in all cases.

22. Thematic content analysis was used to analyze the interview data. This is a technique used for analyzing responses to open-ended interviews. Semantic, processual, and structural similarities were grouped together to create response typologies. In this manner a system was developed that summarized the responses.

23. The responses obtained from the pre-/post-survey were subjected to analysis of variance, t tests, chi-square analysis, and simple frequency counts. Other types of analysis, such as analysis of covariance, repeated measures, and regression analysis, were unable to be used because the subjects could not be identified. To protect the rights of the students, no identifiable indicators (e.g., name, social security number) were obtained and, as a result, there were no assurances that students responding to one scale in the survey (e.g., knowledge) were the same students responding to a different scale (e.g., self-esteem). Therefore, it was not possible to do analysis that required subjects to be identified.

Sample

24. The total sample size for the project was 2,029 for the pretest and 1,723 for the posttest and focus groups. For the posttest, attrition occurred with the Anglo population and, less considerably, for the Hispanic population. The other ethnic groups were more highly represented in the posttest, with the exception of the Asian students, who remained most consistently represented between pre- and posttesting.

25. There were 1,034 girls participating in the pretest and 995 boys. For the posttest, there were 860 girls and 863 boys. The overwhelming majority of the students were in the seventh grade. Family structure as measured by who the child lived with was a demographic variable that remained consistent between pre- and posttesting. Over half of the students (59.1% pretest and 58.4% posttest) lived with both their mother and father. A little more than 10% lived with a stepparent and parent families, and more than 20% lived in single-parent homes (most with mother). The category of "other" accounted for approximately 10% of youth. This category was intended to capture out-of-home placements (e.g., foster care) or other-relative placements, such as grandparents.

26. The differences between pre- and posttest on five measures were assessed. These included resistance, getting into trouble, gang membership, knowledge about the GREAT curriculum, and self-esteem. Each measure except self-esteem was also broken down to assess patterns in categories of gender, ethnicity, and family structure.

Results

Resistance Skills

27. Resistance skills of the students were fairly high both before and after their exposure to GREAT. The average of students who said that they could resist various kinds of peer pressure on the six-item scale before GREAT was 62.4% and after it was 64.3% (see Table 1). Thus there was some overall increase in resistance skills. However, this difference is not statistically significant at the .05 level. The largest increase was in resisting if a friend wanted the student to join a gang. It went from 59.2% to 67.1%, with students saying they definitely could resist if a friend asked them to join a gang. This is noteworthy because the percentage of those who said they could resist if their friend wanted to give them marijuana or cocaine declined rather than increased.

Gender

28. Girls had better resistance skills than boys at both the pre- and posttest. However, boys and girls both increased in resistance skills after GREAT in almost the same amount (about 3.3%). Significantly, for both boys and girls, the greatest increase was in the percentage of students who said they could tell their friend they did not want to if the friend wanted them to join a gang. This increased by 10.1% for boys and 7.7% for girls. This is especially noteworthy inasmuch as the percentage of boys who said they could resist either marijuana or cocaine went down in the posttest and for girls it remained about the same.

29. The overall resistance skills of the students was high. About two-thirds said they definitely could resist peer pressure on the six items. Furthermore, although the percentage of those who said they could resist marijuana and cocaine went down slightly from pre- to posttest, the percentage of those who could say no to these drugs is high as well—almost 80%.

Ethnicity

30. The increase in resistance skills among all ethnic groups was statistically significant after GREAT (see Table 2). Resistance skills increased most among Native Americans, followed by Asians, then African Americans, Hispanics, and, finally, Whites. However, Whites had slightly higher resistance skills at the pretest. Asians rose to the top at the

Table 1 *Resistance Skills*

Statement	% Saying They Definitely Could	
	Pretest	Posttest
I could go up to someone my age and start talking to that person.	21.4 (*n* = 457)	25.9* (*n* = 457)
If a friend wants me to do something that I don't want to do, I could tell my friend that I don't want to do it.	65.7 (*n* = 457)	69.9 (*n* = 1,230)
If a friend wanted to give me alcohol, I could tell my friend that I didn't want any.	71.2 (*n* = 1,524)	73.0 (*n* = 1,284)
If a friend wanted to give me marijuana, I could tell my friend that I didn't want any.	77.6 (*n* = 1,657)	76.7 (*n* = 1,349)
If a friend wanted to give me cocaine, I could tell my friend that I didn't want any.	81.3 (*n* = 1,737)	80.7 (*n* = 1,421)
If a friend wanted me to join a gang, I could tell my friend that I didn't want to.	59.2 (*n* = 1,264)	67.1* (*n* = 1,183)
Average	62.4	64.3
N	2,139	1,762

*Statistically significant difference pre- and posttest at the .05 level.

Table 2 *Ethnicity and resistance*

		% of Those Who Say They Definitely Could				
Statement		White	African American	Hispanic	Native American	Asian
I could go up to someone my age and start talking to that person.	Pretest	22.5 (n = 185)	17.9 (n = 84)	23.4 (n = 55)	18.4 (n = 7)	22.2* (n = 91)
	Posttest	25.5 (n = 137)	25.1 (n = 147)	26.5 (n = 39)	27.8 (n = 20)	26.3 (n = 90)
If a friend wants me to do something that I don't want to do, I could tell my friend that I don't want to do it.	Pretest	64.1 (n = 526)	71.4 (n = 334)	58.5 (n = 137)	69.2 (n = 27)	63.0 (n = 257)
	Posttest	67.5 (n = 363)	75.4 (n = 441)	57.8 (n = 85)	67.1 (n = 47)	69.0 (n = 236)
If a friend wanted to give me alcohol, I could tell my friend that I didn't want any.	Pretest	70.9 (n = 582)	75.5 (n = 354)	56.6 (n = 133)	66.7 (n = 26)	72.9 (n = 298)
	Posttest	71.3 (n = 381)	77.4 (n = 456)	58.5 (n = 86)	68.1 (n = 49)	83.6 (n = 342)
If a friend wanted to give me marijuana, I could tell my friend that I didn't want any.	Pretest	80.5 (n = 662)	77.1 (n = 361)	36.0 (n = 148)	66.7 (n = 26)	79.2 (n = 323)
	Posttest	79.7 (n = 428)	75.9 (n = 444)	61.9 (n = 91)	73.2 (n = 52)	80.5 (n = 273)
If a friend wanted to give me cocaine, I could tell my friend that I didn't want any.	Pretest	84.3 (n = 692)	79.5 (n = 373)	67.9 (n = 159)	71.8 (n = 28)	83.6 (n = 342)
	Posttest	82.3 (n = 441)	80.0 (n = 468)	70.1 (n = 103)	76.4 (n = 55)	85.1 (n = 291)
If a friend wanted me to join a gang, I could tell my friend that I didn't want to.	Pretest	60.1 (n = 493)	60.1 (n = 282)	50.4 (n = 118)	48.7 (n = 19)	59.3 (n = 242)
	Posttest	66.4 (n = 357)	67.7 (n = 396)	58.5 (n = 86)	68.1 (n = 49)	68.9 (n = 235)
Average	Pretest	63.7	63.5	53.3	56.9	63.4
	Posttest	65.5	66.9	55.6	63.7	67.4
Average Increase		1.8	3.3	2.3	6.8	4.0

*The differences in resistance skills among ethnic groups are statistically significant at the .001 level for each question and for all the questions combined at both the pre-and posttest.

posttest. Hispanic students are the group with the lowest resistance skills.

31. As with gender, the largest increase in resistance skills for all the ethnic groups was in telling a friend they did not want to join a gang if the friend asked. The greatest increase in the percentage of those who said they could tell a friend that they do not want to join a gang was among Native American students. However, the number of respondents here is fairly small, which might account for the fact that the increase went from 48.7% at the pretest to 68.1% at the posttest for them.

Family Structure

32. There was an increase from the pretest to the posttest in the resistance skills on all family structures except for those who lived with their father only; the latter's resistance skills decreased by 2.7%. The differences among the various family structures were relatively small. Thus resistance skills do not appear to be related very strongly to family structure. At the pretest, children living only with their father

had the highest resistance skills, but these dropped to the lowest at the posttest. The small number of students living with their father only might account for this drop. Children living with others (grandparent, foster care) had the highest resistance skills at the posttest, followed by children living with their mother and father. However, the difference between the two groups was not very great.

Getting Into Trouble

33. The percentage of students who got into various kinds of trouble decreased after participating in GREAT. The average percentage of students who got into trouble before GREAT was 22.25%, and it dropped to 21.55% after GREAT (see Table 3). The overall drop is not statistically significant at the .05 level; however, the drops in the percentage of students who fought with parents and who were involved in fighting with other groups are statistically significant at the .05 level. There was also a significant increase in the percentage of students who damaged school property.

Gender

34. With the sole exception of arguing or fighting with parents, boys are much more likely to get into trouble than are girls (see Table 4). For the pretest, there is a statistically significant relationship between gender and (a) getting into a fight at school or at home, (b) taking something not belonging to the respondent from another person, (c) taking something from a store without paying for it, (d) damaging school property, (e) taking part in a fight where a group of the respondent's friends was against another group, (f) going into a house or building when the respondent was not supposed to be there, and (g) getting into trouble with the police because of something the respondent did. Only in regard to arguing or fighting with parents are girls more likely to be involved. The same relationships existed in the posttest.

35. The correlations are also fairly high in regard to gender and the various trouble items. For example, the correlation between gender and getting into trouble with police is .47, for taking something from another person it is .24,

Table 3 *Getting into trouble*

	% Agreeing	
Statement	Pretest	Posttest
7. Got into a fight at school or home.	45.8 (n = 978)	42.5 (n = 756)
8. Stayed away from school because I was threatened.	3.5 (n = 74)	4.3 (n = 72)
9. Took something not belonging to me from another person.	24.8 (n = 529)	26.9 (n = 474)
10. Took something from a store without paying for it.	14.6 (n = 313)	15.1 (n = 283)
11. Damaged school property on purpose.	11.4 (n = 244)	13.4* (n = 242)
12. Argued or had a fight with either of my parents.	48.1 (n = 1,026)	43.3* (n = 760)
13. Took part in a fight where a group of my friends was against another group.	22.3 (n = 477)	19.3* (n = 339)
14. Went into a house or building when I was not supposed to be there.	17.7 (n = 378)	17.7 (n = 311)
15. Got into trouble with police because of something I did.	12.1 (n = 258)	11.5 (n = 208)
Overall	22.25 (N = 2,207)	21.55 (N = 1,821)

*Statistically significant difference pre- and posttest at the .05 level.

for taking something from a store it is .18, for damaging school property it is .15, for getting into a fight with another group it is .12, and for entering a house or building it is .16. Overall, boys are more likely to get into trouble than are girls.

Ethnicity

36. There does not seem to be a consistent pattern between the pre- and posttests for the various ethnic groups in regard to getting into trouble (see Table 5). For example, there were slight decreases in the percentages of those who got into trouble on six items, and slight increases in three items for the White students. The same is true for African American students; for Hispanic students there were slight decreases in the percentages of those who got into trouble for two items, but slight increases on the other seven items. Overall, there was a slight decrease in the percentage of White students who got into trouble on the nine items (.9%); a larger decrease in the percentage of African American students who got into trouble on the nine items (2.7%); but very small increases or no change for Hispanic, Native American, and Asian students. Thus we can conclude that there really was not any change in the students' behavior between the pre- and posttests.

37. However, there is a statistically significant difference among the ethnic groups in the percentage of those who say they got into various kinds of trouble. In general, a slightly higher percentage of African American, Hispanic, and Native American students got into trouble than did Whites or Asians. For example, on the pretest, the average percentage for who got into trouble on the nine items is as follows: 22.7% for White, 25% for African American, 23.4% for Hispanic, 24% for Native American, and 17.8% for Asian students. On the posttest, the equivalent figures are 21.8% for White, 22.3% for African American, 24.8% for Hispanic, 24.7% for Native American, and 17.8% for Asian. Thus the relative differences among ethnic groups remained about the same between

the pre- and posttests. Note also that, although differences among the ethnic groups are statistically significant, they are fairly small.

Family Structure

38. Students who live with their mother and father are less likely to get into various forms of trouble than are students who fit into any of the other categories (see Table 6). The type of living arrangements with regard to getting into trouble, ranked from least to most likely to get into trouble (on the posttest), is as follows: mother and father (20.3%), father only (21.2%), mother only (21.9%), stepparent and parent (23.0%), and other (26.6%).

39. The ranking changes from the pre- to the posttest: The category of children living with only their father had the lowest percentage of children who, on average, got into trouble on the nine items on the pretest, but dropped to second on the posttest because it had the largest percentage increase of children who got into trouble between the pre- and posttests. However, the latter may be due to the relatively small number of children in this category.

Gang Membership

40. The percentage of students who know gang members and who want to be gang members decreased slightly after students participated in GREAT (see Table 7). The largest decrease was in the percentage of those who said they wanted to be gang members. This declined from 9.9% before participating in GREAT to 8.2% after GREAT. It is likely that students belonging to gangs will not admit they are members of gangs, because gangs are not socially approved. The real figure is probably closer to the percentage of those who say their friends are gang members. In other words, prior to the program, 33.4% of students stated that their friends were in gangs, whereas 33.9% had friends in gangs following the program. Thus there was no change in the figure. Also, there

Table 4 *Gender and trouble (in percentages)*

	Pretest	
Statement	Male	Female
Got into a fight at school or home.	47.3	44.5
Took something not belonging to me from another person.	29.6	20.1
Took something from a store without paying for it.	17.4	12.0
Damaged school property on purpose.	13.0	9.4
Took part in a fight where a group of my friends was against another group.	24.4	19.9
Went into a house or building when I was not supposed to be there.	20.5	15.1
Got into trouble with police because of something I did.	17.3	6.4
Argued or had a fight with either of my parents.	43.5	53.9

Table 5 *Trouble and ethnicity (in percentages)*

Statement		White	African American	Hispanic	Native American	Asian	N
Got into a fight at school or home.	Pretest	45.9	50.2	49.6	43.6	38.3*	901
	Posttest	43.6	43.1	52.4	43.9	35.2*	714
Stayed away from school because I was threatened.	Pretest	2.9	3.4	7.2	7.7	2.2*	69
	Posttest	3.9	3.6	9.5	4.2	2.6*	68
Took something not belonging to me from another person.	Pretest	24.1	30.3	23.8	38.5	20.6*	495
	Posttest	23.6	31.4	25.2	33.3	23.4*	450
Took something from a store without paying for it.	Pretest	13.3	19.0	18.3	23.1	10.3*	292
	Posttest	12.3	19.3	17.0	23.6	14.4*	268
Damaged school property on purpose.	Pretest	9.4	15.2	14.0	7.7	9.8*	224
	Posttest	13.8	14.4	15.6	16.7	11.1*	231
Argued or had a fight with either of my parents.	Pretest	63.9	33.3	41.9	41.0	41.4*	961
	Posttest	56.9	31.4	44.9	40.8	39.9*	719
Took part in a fight where a group of my friends was against another group.	Pretest	19.2	31.6	23.9	20.5	16.1*	436
	Posttest	16.2	24.1	24.8	18.3	12.0*	318
Went into a house or building when I was not supposed to be there.	Pretest	15.6	25.8	17.1	17.9	13.2*	349
	Posttest	14.3	21.8	19.7	25.0	12.1*	291
Got into trouble with police because of something I did.	Pretest	10.2	15.8	14.9	15.4	8.6*	234
	Posttest	11.5	11.8	14.3	16.7	9.4	196
The average percent for each ethnic group that said they did the things in the nine statements.	Pretest	22.7	25.0	23.4	23.9	17.8	
	Posttest	21.8	22.3	24.8	24.7	17.8	
Amount of difference in average percent between pre- and posttests.		−0.9	−2.7	1.4	0.8	0.0	

*Statistically significant among the ethnic groups at the .05 level.

Table 6 *Who student lives with and getting into trouble (in percentages)*

Statement		Mother and Father	Stepparent and Parent	Mother Only	Father Only	Other	N
Got into a fight at school or home.	Pretest	42.4	51.7	49.0	40.0	54.0*	912
	Posttest	39.5	48.3	44.6	41.5	53.5*	730
Stayed away from school because I was threatened.	Pretest	3.2	4.3	3.9	2.3	3.0*	68
	Posttest	4.3	1.7	3.6	1.9	6.5*	69
Took something not belonging to me from another person.	Pretest	23.2	27.1	27.4	9.3	31.5*	497
	Posttest	26.4	28.3	26.4	24.5	27.1*	453
Took something from a store without paying for it.	Pretest	11.4	16.7	21.3	7.0	21.2*	292
	Posttest	14.7	15.6	16.4	22.6	21.1*	271
Damaged school property on purpose.	Pretest	10.2	13.3	13.0	9.3	10.4*	220
	Posttest	12.7	13.9	11.8	15.1	17.6*	225
Argued or had a fight with either of my parents.	Pretest	49.4	49.8	50.1	44.2	46.3*	978
	Posttest	44.1	52.8	38.4	28.3	43.8*	739
Took part in a fight where a group of my friends was against another group.	Pretest	19.6	25.1	24.9	23.3	27.1*	439
	Posttest	15.9	18.3	27.4	17.0	23.7*	324
Went into a house or building when I was not supposed to be there.	Pretest	16.1	19.1	20.0	9.3	23.6*	253
	Posttest	15.3	19.4	16.0	20.8	29.4*	297
Got into trouble with police because of something I did.	Pretest	9.4	16.6	12.2	9.3	15.3*	225
	Posttest	10.2	8.9	12.4	18.9	16.5*	193
The average percent for each category that said they did the things in the nine statements.	Pretest	20.5	24.9	24.6	17.1	25.8	
	Posttest	20.3	23.0	21.9	21.2	26.6	
Amount of difference in average percent between pre- and posttests.		−0.2	−1.9	−2.7	4.1	0.8	

*Statistically significant at the .05 level for differences among the categories of who the student lives with.

Table 7 *Gang membership*

Question	% Yes	
	Pretest	Posttest
Do you know any gang members?	54.2 (n = 1,159)	53.2 (n = 935)
Do any of your classmates wear colors, jewelry, flash hand signs, or display other things that may be gang related?	41.0 (n = 874)	46.9 (n = 824)
Is there more graffiti in your school or community than last school year?	50.6 (n = 1,086)	51.0 (n = 892)
Are there more weapons in your school than last year?	25.3 (n = 529)	25.0 (n = 436)
Do any of your friends dress like gang members?	43.4 (n = 926)	45.8 (n = 801)
Do any of your friends belong to gangs?	33.4 (n = 711)	33.9 (n = 597)
Do any of your family members belong to a gang?	14.1 (n = 300)	15.0 (n = 263)
Do you belong to a gang?	7.6 (n = 161)	8.0 (n = 141)
Do you want to become a gang member?	9.9 (n = 210)	8.2 (n = 142)

was a fairly large increase in the percentage of those who said fellow students wear gang clothes (from 41.0% before GREAT to 46.9% after GREAT).

41. There seems to be a slight pattern in these responses: There was a decrease in the percentage of students who said they wanted to be gang members, but the percentage of those who recognized other classmates wearing gang colors increased and the percentage of those who said they belonged to the gangs remained about the same. Thus there may not have been a drop in gang membership in the time between the pre- and posttests; however, because a smaller percentage said they wanted to be gang members, there could be a drop in gang membership if the survey were to be repeated in the future. As an aside, it should be noted that, although students recognized more classmates wearing gang colors, this does not necessarily mean that there was an increase in gang colors in schools. Rather, the curriculum of the GREAT program may be educating students in what are considered gang colors and, thus, they are able to recognize more easily and more frequently the display of gang colors by other classmates. The same argument could explain the increase in the number of students reporting their friends dressing like gang members.

42. Finally, overall, there was little change in the average percentage of those who said yes to the nine gang items (31.1% pre- and 31.9% posttest), but there was a 1.7% drop in the percentage of those who said they wanted to be a

gang member. Thus, although the message of GREAT may be getting through to some students, the increase is small.

Gender

43. Boys are more likely to know gang members or have friends that are gang members. Girls and boys are similar, however, in their recognition of gang colors or weapons in school, and both are similar in having gang members within their families.

Ethnicity

44. There is a statistically significant relationship among ethnic groups regarding whether or not the individual knew a gang member at the pretest. Forty-eight percent of Whites and Asians at the pretest said they knew gang members, whereas 63% of African Americans, 68% of Hispanics, and 64% of Native Americans said they knew gang members. These differences remained only for Hispanics in the posttest, whereas the percentage of African American students who said they knew gang members decreased quite a bit.

45. Overall, African Americans and Hispanics are more likely to (a) know gang members, (b) have classmates who wear gang colors, (c) have friends who dress like gang members, (d) have friends who belong to a gang, (e) have family members who belong to a gang, (f) belong to a gang themselves, or (g) want to become a gang member. Hispanic students are considerably more likely than are African American students to respond yes to these questions.

46. The average percentage of all ethnic groups who said they belonged to a gang at the pretest was 9.4%, and this dropped to 7% at the posttest. The average percentage of those who said they wanted to become gang members at the pretest was 11.8%; this dropped to 9.5% at the posttest. Thus, although there were decreases in the desired direction, the amount of the decrease was small.

47. The same pattern is evident in the percentage of those who say they have family members who belong to a gang and who have friends who belong to a gang. The pattern is not evident in the percentage of those who said they knew gang members, who have classmates who wear gang colors, and who said there are more weapons in school this year. Overall, when all eight items in the gang involvement scale are combined, the percentage of those who responded yes did not decrease except for Native Americans.

Family Structure

48. One finding stands out clearly in regard to whether a student knows someone who is a gang member, has classmates who wear gang colors, has friends who are in a gang, has friends who dress in gang colors, has a family member who belongs to a gang, the student belongs to a gang, or wants to be a gang member: Students who live with their mother and father are much less likely to say yes to these items than are students who are in any of the other categories. The most striking differences are in the categories of whether their friends or family members belong to a gang, and whether they are or want to be a member of a gang. Twice as many students who live with a stepparent answered yes to these four questions. The same pattern is evident if a student lived with a mother only, but not quite as great as when a student lived with a stepparent and parent. The pattern of knowing, having friends who know, belonging to, and wanting to be a member of a gang was not as great for students living with a father only.

Knowledge

49. The main question here is, Did students' knowledge about gang-related issues increase as a result of the program? There was a slight overall improvement in knowledge about the GREAT curriculum after students participated in GREAT (see Table 8). The largest increase was in the items concerned with the definitions of GREAT, victims, and values. The largest decrease was in response to the statement that "a gang is a group of people who only engage in criminal activities." The decrease in the percentage of students who answered this correctly may be due to their rejection of this statement.

Gender

50. There was an overall slight improvement in knowledge about the GREAT curriculum after students participated in GREAT. Girls improved more than boys, and girls also had higher scores before and after GREAT. However, overall, student knowledge about items on the GREAT curriculum was fairly high before GREAT and remained about the same after GREAT; there was a 0.6% increase for boys and a 0.8% increase for girls in the percentage of those who chose the correct answers.

Ethnicity

51. Each of the ethnic groups improved in its knowledge of the GREAT curriculum. Whites and Native Americans improved the most (2.4%), Asians the next (2.3%), and African American and Hispanics improved the least (.7% and .4%, respectively). Also, Whites had the highest score on both the pre- and posttests, followed by Asians, then African Americans, Hispanics, and Native Americans, on the pretest. The differences among ethnic groups were statistically significant at the .001 level. On the posttest the ranking changed slightly: Native Americans moved into third place, whereas the African American and Hispanic students dropped to fourth and fifth, respectively.

Family Structure

52. Students who live with their mother and father tended to do better on the knowledge test for the pretest than those in other family structures, but only very slightly better, and this slight amount disappears in the posttest. This is because responses to this item do not improve as much as they do for students who live with parent and stepparent and for those who live with mother only.

53. There was an increase in the percentage of students who chose the correct response for four of the five family structures and a large decline in the scores of the children who lived with father only. However, because the number of children who live with father only is small (an average of 35), this large drop could be due to this.

54. In contrast to gang involvement and getting into trouble items, family structure is only mildly related to knowledge and to improvements in scores. Nevertheless, the improvement in knowledge that exists is not statistically significant.

Self-Esteem

55. Self-esteem did not change after GREAT. Self-esteem was measured by 10 statements

Table 8 *Knowledge overview*

Question	% Correct	
	Pretest	Posttest
GREAT stands for "gangs reduce everyone's ability totally."	68.3 ($n = 1,497$)	83.9 ($n = 1,510$)
A victim is someone who suffers a loss, especially from a criminal act.	79.0 ($n = 1,712$)	89.3 ($n = 1,623$)
Culture is made up of beliefs and values.	77.6 ($n = 1,673$)	84.9 ($n = 1,534$)
Values only tell us what is wrong to do.	80.5 ($n = 1,730$)	80.5 ($n = 1,445$)
Discrimination is a way to treat people all the same.	83.4 ($n = 1,786$)	80.3 ($n = 1,451$)
Solving problems without fighting (called conflict resolution) is a way of solving problems without creating new problems.	79.9 ($n = 1,722$)	81.7 ($n = 1,483$)
A gang is a group of people who only engage in criminal activities.	44.3 ($n = 955$)	34.5 ($n = 625$)
Gangs are mostly made up of minority people (such as African Americans, Hispanics, or Asians).	70.9 ($n = 1,525$)	65.9 ($n = 1,194$)
All drugs are natural substances that change the way in which the human body works.	30.8 ($n = 660$)	27.8 ($n = 504$)
There is a relationship between gangs and drugs.	76.3 ($n = 1,633$)	80.8 ($n = 1,460$)
Getting in trouble with the law will not keep me from reaching goals I have set for myself.	50.6 ($n = 1,080$)	49.8 ($n = 904$)
A strong support system (people I trust, who care about me) will help me reach my goals.	87.1 ($n = 1,866$)	86.2 ($n = 1,560$)
Once you join a gang it is easy to get out.	88.4 ($n = 1,889$)	84.7 ($n = 1,527$)
When you join a gang you often inherit a lot of enemies.	84.8 ($n = 1,811$)	86.1 ($n = 1,559$)
It is possible to make a fresh start by getting out of a gang.	71.7 ($n = 1,528$)	71.7 ($n = 1,287$)

with which the respondent could agree, agree somewhat, disagree somewhat, disagree, or answer not sure. The average pretest score was 51.5 and the average posttest score was 51.4.

56. There are two things that should be noted about this finding. First, it is not surprising that self-esteem did not improve, because this is a fairly stable personality construct. Second, because self-esteem is a stable personality trait, only programs that are in effect for long periods of time could be expected to make a change in a student's self-esteem. Thus, because this program consisted of 1-hour visits for 8 weeks, it is not surprising that there were no significant changes in students' ratings of self-esteem.

57. A final area of attitudes relates to the feelings of students toward various items. The feelings of the students were fairly negative toward drugs, gang fighting, and weapons and were moderately low for revenge and fighting. On the other hand, students had positive feelings

toward police and school. It appears that the GREAT program had the greatest influence on students' feelings about revenge and fighting. In both cases, there were decreases in positive feelings toward these acts. In the pretest, the average revenge rating was 47.4, whereas in the posttest it was 42.4. The average rating for fighting was 38.2 in the pretest, which in the posttest the average was 34.1.

Discussion

58. The GREAT program shows some evidence of influencing the attitudes of its participants. In particular, students showed a slightly increased ability to resist joining a gang, especially if a friend asked them to join a gang. Given that the goal of the program is to get children to resist joining a gang, the increase in the percentage of those who said they could resist if their friend tried to persuade them to join a gang is a positive finding. At the same time, the increase was small, and this is similar to the results that Ennett et al. (1994) found for the DARE program. Moreover, if what Jankowski (1991) has found is correct, then we should not expect a program such as GREAT to have much impact. Jankowski says that youths will join a gang because it improves their chances of getting scant resources in a highly competitive environment. If it is true that the decision is a calculated choice, then there will be limits to the effectiveness of an antigang program in changing behaviors. Jankowski (1991) stated: "Because the decision has been made in a calculated manner, gang members resist outside attempts to convince them that gang membership is detrimental to them. They have already considered that possibility" (p. 29).

59. These findings are similar to those found in the evaluations of DARE. Ennett et al. (1994) found that the DARE program produced small mean effects for knowledge about drugs, social skills, attitudes toward the police, and attitudes about drug use and self-esteem. However, the mean effect on drug use was not significant, except for tobacco. These results suggest that the DARE program has limited effectiveness in changing the drug use behaviors of children. We believe that the impact of GREAT is similar. There is a slight increase in the desired attitude about gangs, but not much, if any, in actual gang behavior.

60. Both DARE and GREAT use law enforcement officers who assume a position of authority and are viewed as experts on the subject. In these situations information is merely disseminated to the students. Ennett et al. (1994) noted the limitations of this method. The limitations are supported also by comments made in focus groups with students in this research. Although students developed a more positive feeling toward police officers after GREAT, they did not always agree with the message presented. Some students in the focus groups criticized the program because they believed that gangs are not all bad. Gangs were viewed by many students as helpful and an important outlet for kids.

61. This evaluation has found that GREAT has only a small impact on students' attitudes and resistance skills, and no impact on the percentage of students who say they or their friends are members of gangs. Given the limitation of the research design that we were able to use, these conclusions should be considered somewhat tentative. However, no matter what evaluations find about programs such as GREAT and DARE, they will be continued because as Aniskiewicz and Wysong (1990) noted:

Because the program embodies goals and objectives that are nearly unassailable and attacks a problem that is widely viewed as a major threat to the society, it is laced with powerful symbolic qualities and thus has significant political, practical, and public relations utility for its stakeholders. (p. 741)

62. GREAT is a program that has the same political symbolism of the DARE program. Gangs are now considered to be a significant social problem, in part because of the attention given to them by the media since the late 1980s. Efforts by police to control gangs thus send a symbolic message that police are trying to do something about the problem. As a result, programs that are developed to address and reduce the gang problem will continue even if significant results are not produced.

Notes

1. This evaluation was conducted by the Arizona Prevention Resource Center of Arizona State University. The senior author conducted the data analysis for the evaluation.

2. At least none that we were able to find. However, the senior author participated in evaluations of GREAT in Phoenix, Arizona, in 1992 and 1993.

References

Aniskiewicz, R. E., and E. E. Wysong. 1990. Evaluating DARE: Drug education and the multiple meanings of success. *Policy Studies Review* 9:727-47.

DeJong, W. 1987. A short-term evaluation of Project DARE (drug abuse resistance education): Preliminary indicators of effectiveness. *Journal of Drug Education* 17:279-94.

Ennett, S. T., N. S. Tobler, C. L. Ringwalt, and R. L. Flewelling. 1994. How effective is drug abuse resistance education? A meta-analysis of Project DARE outcome evaluations. *American Journal of Public Health* 84:1394-401.

Jankowski, M. S. 1991. *Islands in the street: Gangs and American urban society*. Berkeley: University of California Press.

Nyre, G. F. 1984. *An evaluation of Project DARE (drug abuse resistance education)*. Los Angeles: Evaluation and Training Institute.

Nyre, G. F. 1984-1985. *Final evaluation report, 1984-1985: Project DARE (drug abuse resistance education)*. Los Angeles: Evaluation and Training Institute.

Rosenberg, M. 1965. *Society and the adolescent self-image*. Princeton, NJ: Princeton University Press.

Spergel, I. A., D. Curry, R. Chance, C. Kane, R. Ross, A. Alexander, E. Simmons, and S. Oh. 1990. *Youth gangs: Problem and response*. NYGIC Doc. No. D0026. Arlington, VA: National Youth Gang Information Center.

Factual Questions

1. According to the authors, is the impact of GREAT similar to the impact of DARE?

2. Did the researchers include a control group?

3. Do the researchers believe their research design is strong?

4. What types of choices are given in response to Likert-type items?

5. What was the purpose of the focus groups?

6. Was the difference between the two *averages* in Table 1 statistically significant?

7. According to Table 7, did the percentage who said they belong to a gang increase or decrease from pretest to posttest?

8. According to Table 8, the largest decrease in knowledge was in response to which question?

9. According to the authors, will programs to address the gang problem continue even if significant results are not produced?

Questions for Discussion

10. Is the GREAT program adequately described in the introduction? Explain.

11. Was it appropriate to review the impact of DARE in the introduction to this evaluation of GREAT? Explain.

12. What does the term "threats to internal validity" mean? (See paragraph 14.)

13. The researchers used measures of "self-reported behavior." (See paragraph 15.) Are there other ways behavior might have been measured in this evaluation? What are the advantages and disadvantages of each?

14. What do you think the term "judgment sample" means? Do you think it is random? (See paragraph 21.)

15. Could the differences between pretest and posttest scores be attributable to attrition? Explain. (See paragraphs 24–25.)

16. Are some of the questions in Table 7 more important than others for evaluating GREAT? Explain.

17. The authors question the percentages reporting that they want to be gang members. (See paragraph 40.) Do you agree with them?

18. The authors are silent on the question of the statistical significance of the differences in Tables 7 and 8. Are you willing to assume that none of the differences are significant?

19. The authors question the appropriateness of examining changes in self-esteem as an outcome variable for evaluating GREAT. (See paragraph 56.) Do you agree? Why? Why not?

20. Would you be interested in a more extensive report on the results obtained with the focus groups? (See paragraph 60.) Explain.

21. Consider the five types of outcomes measured (resistance, trouble, gang membership, knowledge, and self-esteem). Are any more important than others for evaluating GREAT? Explain.

22. In light of this evaluation, do you favor continued funding for GREAT? Explain.

23. If you were evaluating GREAT in the future, what changes, if any, would you make in the evaluation methodology?

Quality Ratings

DIRECTIONS: Indicate your level of agreement with each of the following statements by circling a number from 5 for strongly agree (SA) to 1 for strongly disagree (SD). If you believe that an item is not applicable to this research article, leave it blank. Be prepared to explain your ratings.

A. The introduction establishes the importance of the research topic.

    SA   5   4   3   2   1   SD

B. The literature review establishes the context for the study.

    SA   5   4   3   2   1   SD

C. The research purpose, question, or hypothesis is clearly stated.

    SA   5   4   3   2   1   SD

D. The method of sampling is sound.

    SA   5   4   3   2   1   SD

E. Relevant demographics (for example, age, gender, and ethnicity) are described.

    SA   5   4   3   2   1   SD

F. Measurement procedures are adequate.

    SA   5   4   3   2   1   SD

G. The results are clearly described.

    SA   5   4   3   2   1   SD

H. The discussion/conclusion is appropriate.

    SA   5   4   3   2   1   SD

I. Despite any flaws noted above, the report is worthy of publication.

    SA   5   4   3   2   1   SD

ARTICLE 34

A META-ANALYTIC VALIDATION OF THE DUNN AND DUNN MODEL OF LEARNING-STYLE PREFERENCES

Rita Dunn *St. John's University*
Shirley A. Griggs *St. John's University*
Jeffery Olson *St. John's University*
Mark Beasley *St. John's University*
Bernard S. Gorman *Nassau Community College*

Forty-two experimental studies based on the Dunn and Dunn Learning Style Model and conducted between 1980-1990 were identified to determine the value of teaching students through their learning-style preferences. The studies were rated according to Lytton and Romney's (1991) Quality Rating Scales. A jury determined that of the 42 studies, 6 studies evidenced serious threats to validity. The 36 remaining studies provided a database of 3,181 participants. Results were synthesized through meta-analysis. Eight variables coded for each study produced 65 individual effect sizes. The overall, unweighted group effect size value (r) was .384, and the weighted effect size value was .353 with a mean difference (d) of .755. Referring to the standard normal curve, this suggests that students whose learning styles are accommodated would be expected to achieve 75% of a standard deviation higher than students who have not had their learning styles accommodated. This finding indicates that matching students' learning-style preferences with educational interventions compatible with those preferences is beneficial to their academic achievement.

1. Learning style is the way in which individuals begin to concentrate on, process, internalize, and retain new and difficult academic information (Dunn & Dunn, 1992, 1993; Dunn, Dunn, & Perrin, 1994). Although some students learn when instruction is provided through strategies that do not complement their learning styles, significantly higher standardized achievement test scores resulted among previously failing students when they were taught with strategies that complemented their learning-style preferences. Those achievement gains were reported for students in elementary school (Andrews, 1990; Klavas, 1993; Lemmon, 1985; Stone, 1992), secondary school (Brunner & Majewski, 1990; Elliot, 1991; Gadwa & Griggs, 1985; Orsak, 1990), and

college (Clark-Thayer, 1987; Mickler & Zippert, 1987; Nelson et al., 1993).

2. A 4-year investigation by the U.S. Office of Education that included on-site visits, interviews, observations, and examination of national test data concluded that learning-styles-based instruction was one of the few strategies that had impacted positively on the achievement of classified special education students (Alberg, Cook, Fiore, Friend, & Sano, 1992). Similar gains were found by Stone (1992) with learning-disabled elementary students and by Brunner and Majewski (1990) with mildly handicapped high school students.

3. Critics of the learning-style movement (Curry, 1990; Kampwirth & Bates, 1980; Kavale & Forness, 1987; Snider, 1990; Ysseldyke, 1973) have neither reported findings of their own experimental studies with complementary and dissonant learning-style treatments nor analyzed the practitioners' reports describing students' achievement and attitude gains. Instead, critics have observed that (a) many diverse learning-style definitions and models exist (Curry, 1990); (b) certain models elaborate on only one or two variables on a bipolar continuum rather than on a comprehensive construct (DeBello, 1990); (c) two or more decades ago, disappointing results were reported with strategies designed to focus exclusively on remediating students' weaknesses (Snider, 1990); (d) there is an imbalance in the research available among the existing models (Curry, 1990; DeBello, 1990); and (e) studies that addressed special education populations' auditory and visual modalities revealed little improvement (Kampwirth & Bates, 1980; Kavale & Forness, 1987; Snider, 1990; Ysseldyke, 1973).

4. Kavale and Forness (1987) described few gains as a result of a meta-analysis of studies with different age, achievement level, and categories of special education students. However, their review neglected to discuss the following

limitations: inclusion of a majority of studies with serious design flaws; inclusion of, and no differentiation among, studies from extremely diverse models that used diverse identification assessments and student populations; omission of studies that focused on the specific variable they purportedly investigated (e.g., Carbo, 1980; Jarsonbeck, 1984; Kroon, 1985; Martini, 1986; Weinberg, 1983; Wheeler, 1983); misinterpretation of the magnitude of the effect sizes; misinterpretation of the increases in improved standardized test achievement for 55% to 59% of the special education pupils; and assumption that specific terms were defined and treated similarly by the many investigators whose studies were included in the meta-analysis.

5. For example, among the assessments used to define learning styles, some defined *auditory* as the ability to hear, whereas others defined it as the ability to remember what was heard, and still others defined it as preferring to learn by listening. When traits are defined, identified, and treated differently, conclusions concerning results cannot be generalized. Furthermore, because the Kavale and Forness (1987) meta-analysis averaged the findings of studies representing many different models without analyzing the similarities and differences among their variables and treatments, and also omitted studies representing the most researched model, accurately determining the effectiveness of

Dunn, R., Griggs, S. A., Olson, J., Beasley, M., & Gorman, B. S. (1995). A meta-analytic validation of the Dunn and Dunn model of learning-style preferences. *Journal of Educational Research, 88,* 353-362. Reprinted with permission of the Helen Dwight Reid Educational Foundation. Published by Heldref Publications, 1319 Eighteenth St., N.W., Washington, DC 20036-1802. Copyright © 1995.

Address correspondence to Rita Dunn, Division of Administrative and Instructional Leadership, St. John's University, 8000 Utopia Parkway, Jamaica, NY 11439.

learning styles as a construct may not have been possible.

6. Another critic (Curry, 1990) reported under "problems with the (research) evidence" that 4 of the 13 studies she referenced in that article that had used the Dunn and Dunn model showed "no discernable [*sic*] effect attributable to learning style variation" (p. 52). No explanation was provided for why only 13 of a possible 42 experimental studies were selected. However, among research reported as having no effects, Tappenden's (1983) study was correlational (*not* experimental); thus, no treatment existed and no effects could be computed. DeGregoris (1986) demonstrated the positive effects of different types of sound on sound-preferenced adolescents, although those adolescents who preferred quiet also performed well with soft background talking. However, DeGregoris's findings appear to corroborate those of Price (1980), who found that adolescents need significantly more sound and intake while concentrating than do elementary or adult populations. Only studies by Stiles (1985) and Cholakis (1986) revealed no effects. Therefore, of 13 experimental studies that Curry (1990) chose to cite, only 3 revealed no effects. Furthermore, 1 of those 3 revealed favorable effects for one of the two groups examined. Few researchers would refrain from experimenting further with a construct that yielded positive gains in three fourths of the school-based investigations conducted, particularly when those studies were administered by researchers in at least six different institutions using diverse instruments, populations, and treatments.

7. The research in learning styles is not flawless and is uneven across models. Some models are comparatively young; others have been developing over a quarter of a century. DeBello (1990) pointed out that at least two models were developed at universities by graduate faculty and doctoral students; a third model was developed by the National Association of Secondary School Principals (NASSP). He described some models as narrow in focus and others as comprehensive. DeBello also indicated that some models are called learning-style models but are not (one is a personality index and another is a lesson plan format that prescribes teaching all students in the same class with the same resources, in the same sequence, in the same way, at the same time, and in the same amount of time). Finally, the quality of learning-styles research varies from model to model and from study to study.

The Dunn and Dunn Learning Style Model
8. The Dunn and Dunn Learning Style Model focuses on identifying individuals' preferences for instructional environments, methods, and resources and is based on the following theoretical postulates:

1. Learning style is a biological and developmental set of personal characteristics (Thies, 1979) that makes identical instructional environments, methods, and resources effective for some learners and ineffective for others.
2. Most people have learning-style preferences, but individuals' learning-style preferences differ significantly.
3. Individual instructional preferences exist and the impact of accommodating these preferences can be measured reliably.
4. The stronger the preference, the more important it is to provide compatible instructional strategies.
5. Accommodating individual learning-style preferences through complementary instructional and counseling intentions results in increased academic achievement and improved student attitudes toward learning.
6. Given responsive (matched learning-style) environments, resources, and approaches, students attain statistically higher achievement and attitude test scores than students with dissonant (mismatched) treatments.
7. Most teachers can learn to use learning styles as a cornerstone of their instruction.
8. Most students can learn to capitalize on their learning-style strengths when concentrating on new or difficult academic material.
9. The less academically successful the individual, the more important it is to accommodate learning-style preferences.

9. In contrast with other models, the Dunn and Dunn model has elicited many practitioners' reports citing significantly increased achievement and attitude test scores as a result of its implementation with underachieving and special education students (Andrews, 1990; Brunner & Majewski, 1990; Elliot, 1991; Gadwa & Griggs, 1985; Klavas, 1993; Lemmon, 1985; Mickler & Zippert, 1987; Nelson et al., 1993; Orsak, 1990; Stone, 1992). The model has been implemented in urban schools (Quinn, 1994; The Buffalo Experience, 1993), suburban schools (Brunner & Majewski, 1990; Elliot, 1991; Gadwa & Griggs, 1985), and rural schools (Neely & Alm, 1992, 1993). It has generated extensive research by more than 100 institutions of higher education (*Research on the Dunn and Dunn Model*, 1995), in contrast with the minimal number of studies attributable to other learning-style models (*Annotated Bibliography of Research*, 1995).

10. Despite its attributes, the Dunn and Dunn model has not been reviewed comprehensively by the critics of learning styles. Therefore,

Sullivan (1993) performed a meta-analysis of the experimental studies conducted with this model between 1980-1990. She hypothesized that the research would reveal that accommodating individuals' learning-style preferences results in increased academic achievement and that specific moderators may affect the results.

11. The statistical methods used for the quantitative synthesis of the results of the studies analyzed were largely based on the work of Hunter, Schmidt, and Jackson (1982) and Hedges and Olkin (1985) and were carried out by a program developed by Schwarzer (1989). We anticipated that many different studies would demonstrate positive results when learning-style responsive treatments were provided. If substantiated, such results should have implications for teaching, counseling, and educational theory and practice. Through meta-analysis, researchers are able to transform the findings of separate, independent studies to form a common metric to provide summary estimates of the strength of hypothesized relationships and to test statistically the extent to which the studies collectively support, or fail to support, theoretical hypotheses.

12. In addition, meta-analysis provides a method for estimating the degree to which selected study characteristics account for variations in relationships obtained across studies. A second function of meta-analysis is the determination of homogeneity, described as sharing a common effect size. If a series of independent studies provide a homogeneous estimate of the population effect size, it is likely that the various studies are testing the same hypothesis (Wolfe, 1986). Thus, in this study we analyzed the hypothesis that accommodating individuals' learning-style preferences results in increased academic achievement, and we examined the moderators that may affect the results.

Method

Selection of Studies
13. A search was conducted of the studies that examined the effects of congruent versus dissonant treatments on learning-style preferences, as suggested by the Dunn and Dunn model. The search process began with the identification of descriptors for a computer-based search of the *Dissertation Abstracts International* and *Research in Education* from 1980 to 1990. Descriptors and key words were selected within the domains of learning style and the Dunn and Dunn model and then were screened by using the descriptor list for relevant studies from the ERIC databases and the titles of relevant dissertations from the *Dissertation Abstracts International* database, *Research on the Dunn and Dunn Model* (1992), and *Annotated*

Figure 1   *The Dunn and Dunn Learning Styles Model*

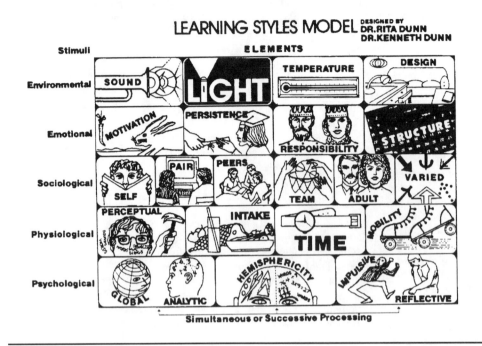

Bibliography of Research (1992). Descriptors included (a) instruments based on the Dunn and Dunn model (1992)—the *Learning Style Inventory* (Dunn, Dunn, & Price, 1975, 1989), *Productivity Environmental Preference Survey* (Dunn, Dunn, & Price, 1979, 1982), *Learning Style Inventory: Primary Version* (Perrin, 1983), and *Reading Style Inventory* (Carbo, 1982); (b) stimuli of the Dunn and Dunn Learning Style Model and individuals' *environmental* (sound, light, temperature, and design), *emotional* (motivation, persistence, responsibility [conformity versus nonconformity], and structure), *sociological* (learning alone, in a pair, with peers, with a teacher, and in a variety of social patterns), *physiological* (perception, intake while learning, chronobiological energy patterns, and mobility needs), and psychological processing characteristics (see Figure 1).

14. The search identified 138 studies, 42 of which employed an experimental design. Based on Lytton and Romney's (1991) rating scale for quality, a jury of several researchers used the following criteria to rate each of the 42 experimental studies: (a) appropriateness of operationalization of constructs; (b) degree of nonrestrictiveness of subjects; (c) degree of normalcy of testing, setting, and time; (d) carefulness of data collection and measure of reliability; (e) appropriateness of statistical analysis; and (f) degree of reporting of statistical information. Based on Campbell and Stanley's (1966) criteria, 6 of the 42 studies evidenced serious threats to both internal validity (i.e., instrumentation, selection, and mortality) and external validity (i.e., reactive effects of experimental arrangements and multiple treatment interferences) and thus were eliminated from the analysis.

Coding

15. The following information was coded for each study: (a) study characteristics (year of study and researcher affiliation); (b) instrument type (learning-style instrument form, degree of preference); (c) sample characteristics (sample size, number of groups, and mortality); (d) setting (school type, school level, grade, academic level, regional location, geographic position, socioeconomic level, ethnicity); (e) instructional factor (subject area, treatment, material); (f) methodological factors (assignment to groups, design, procedures); (g) outcome measure (type and number of independent and dependent variables); and (h) attitude (as determined by instruments or observations).

16. A letter and the present coding system were mailed to each researcher whose study was selected to ascertain reliability of the data included in each study and to request any data that may have been missing. Based upon the responses received, the researchers either verified or amended the coding characteristics. Responses to requests for additional information

that had not been included in the studies were examined and noted. In most instances, researchers reported that information excluded from their documents had not been collected and was unavailable. For example, when ethnicity, gender, or race had not been a component of a study, that information was rarely obtainable.

Calculation of Effect Sizes

17. We converted summary statistics (means, standard deviations, F ratios, t tests, and chi-squares) to a common measure of effect size. However, because many of the research studies did not provide appropriate statistics (e.g., numerous studies lacked standard deviations) for calculating a mean standardized deviation (MSD) statistic (d), we performed transformations to compute a correlation coefficient (r) as a measure of effect size. Using conversion formulas (i.e., Wolfe, 1986), we transformed r values to d statistics and analyzed them by Schwarzer's (1989) Meta-Analysis Computer Program. After individual effect sizes were derived, group effect sizes were calculated, and, as in other approaches (i.e., Hedges & Olkin, 1985), Schwarzer's program calculated the best estimate of the population effect size to be the weighted average of all correlations. Thus, when combining all effect sizes, more weight was assigned to studies with larger numbers of participants.

Tests for Homogeneity and Moderators

18. We used and rejected three indicators of homogeneity. First, the residual standard deviation (RSD) should be smaller than 25% of the population effect size. Second, if the percentage of observed variance accounted for by sampling error is at least 75%, sample homogeneity is indicated. Finally, we performed the chi-square test of homogeneity.

19. For each moderator subset, we performed separate meta-analyses. To classify as a moderator, the population effect size must vary across subsets, and the residual variance (RV) must average lower in the subsets than for the data as a whole (Hunter et al., 1982).

Results

20. The meta-analysis was designed to answer two questions: What statistical statement can be made about the overall effect size produced by the learning-style interventions of the 36 studies? What are the relationships among study characteristics and study effect results? The 36 experimental studies included in this meta-analysis provided a database of 3,181 participants. The studies produced 65 individual effect sizes or comparisons; each study included multiple variables.

21. The individual weighted effect sizes (WES), r, and MSD (d) of all 36 studies separated by learning-style stimuli, are reported in Table 1. When combined, the overall weighted effect size value r was .353, with a residual variance of .079. After conversion, an MSD (d) of .755 was calculated. According to Cohen's (1992) designations, these average effect sizes are in the medium to large range. Referring to the standard normal curve, this means that overall academic achievement of students whose learning styles have been matched can be expected to be three fourths of a standard deviation higher than that of students whose learning styles have not been accommodated. Given these data—a total sample size of 3,181, an alpha level of .01, and the general convention of .80 as a desirable level of power—the power of this study was estimated at .995. This finding seems to indicate that providing educational interventions that are compatible with students' learning-style preferences is beneficial.

Analysis of Homogeneity and Moderators

22. We rejected all three indicators of homogeneity. First, the residual standard deviation (RSD) was larger than 25% of the population effect size ($r = .353$; RSD = .282). Second, the percentage of observed variance accounted for by sampling error was computed to be 11.33%, which is much lower than the requisite 75%. Finally, the chi-square test of homogeneity was

Table 1 *Weighted effect sizes, total sample sizes, and residual variance (RV) for all analyzed studies, by learning-style stimuli*

Stimulus/author	WES(r)	MSD (d)	Sample size (N)	Stimulus RV
Complete model	.223	0.458	521	.035
Hutto (1982)	.256	0.530	163	
Rossman (1985)	.047	0.094	144	
Zippert (1985)	.792	2.594	17	
Garcia-Otero (1987)	.744	2.227	43	
Raviotta (1988)	.061	0.122	77	
Cook (1989)	.230	0.473	77	
Emotional	.259	0.536	140	.058
White (1981)	.030	0.060	80	
Napolitano (1986)	.565	1.370	60	
Sociological	.234	0.481	432	.009
Perrin (1984)	.356	0.762	56	
DeBello (1985)	.300	0.629	81	
Cholakis (1986)	.100	0.201	61	
Phelix (1987)	.033	0.066	90	
Miles (1987)	.510	1.186	40	
Giannitti (1988)	.272	0.565	104	
Environmental	.239	0.492	432	.026
Pizzo (1981)	.405	0.886	64	
Krimsky (1982)	.513	1.195	32	
Murrain (1983)	.278	0.579	76	
Shea (1983)	.491	1.127	32	
Hodges (1985)	.565	1.370	32	
Shaver (1985)	.057	0.114	60	
Stiles (1985)	.041	0.082	78	
DeGregoris (1986)	.037	0.074	58	
Physiological	.461	1.039	1656	.103
Lynch (1981)	.142	0.287	136	
Virostko (1983)	.756	2.310	286	
Della Valle (1984)	.727	2.118	40	
Freeley (1984)	.623	1.593	73	
Kroon (1985)	.395	0.860	38	
MacMurren (1985)	.809	2.753	40	
Martini (1986)	.640	1.666	30	
LaShell (1986)	.887	3.842	90	
Hill (1987)	.183	0.372	117	
Powell (1987)	.504	1.167	73	
Prince (1987)	.034	0.068	104	
Rowan (1988)	.996	22.294	166	
Zikmund (1988)	.171	0.347	149	
Ingham (1991)	.809	2.753	314	

Table 2 *Breakdown of meta-analytic results by seven potential moderators*

Moderator	MSD(*d*)	WES(*r*)	RV	*k*	*N*	Moderators' average RV
1. Strength of preference						.042
Strong	0.969	.436	.018	9	481	
Moderate	0.641	.305	.014	3	210	
Mixed	0.721	.339	.093	24	2,501	
2. Sample size						.056
Small	1.293	.543	.022	10	344	
Medium	0.597	.286	.057	16	1,154	
Large	0.678	.321	.088	10	1,583	
3. School level						.063
College/adult	0.907	.413	.115	8	894	
Secondary	0.314	.155	.008	5	373	
Elementary	0.782	.364	.067	23	1,914	
4. Socioeconomic status						.056
Lower	0.512	.248	.021	5	379	
Lower middle	0.782	.364	.080	6	473	
Middle	0.873	.400	.086	13	1,096	
Upper middle	0.523	.253	.006	7	566	
Mixed	0.782	.364	.109	7	920	
5. Academic level						.051
High	1.080	.475	.119	11	833	
Average	1.815	.672	.013	5	426	
Low	0.479	.233	.056	11	928	
Mixed	0.466	.227	.013	9	994	
6. Length of intervention						.061
>1 year	1.345	.558	.080	2	422	
Months	0.561	.270	.063	9	1,011	
Weeks	0.590	.283	.034	5	325	
Days	0.837	.386	.082	20	1,423	
7. Content area						.079
Mathematics	1.013	.452	.077	6	709	
Language arts	0.728	.342	.076	19	1,718	
Other	9.799	.371	.084	15	1,337	

greater impact than addressing their emotional, environmental, or sociological preferences, or combining their preferences.

24. We report in Table 2 the number of studies (*k*), total sample size (*N*), weighted effect size (*r*), weighted MSD (*d*), and RV for seven other variables that met the moderator criteria. These results indicated the following:

1. Students with strong learning-style preferences showed greater academic gains as a result of congruent instructional interventions than those students who had mixed preferences or moderate preferences.
2. Studies conducted with small sample sizes showed greater academic gains than those with large or medium sample sizes.
3. College and adult learners showed greater gains than elementary school learners or secondary school learners.
4. Examination of socioeconomic status indicated that middle-class students were more responsive to learning-style accommodations than were lower middle-class or upper middle-class or lower-class students.
5. Academic-level moderators indicated that average students were more responsive to learning-style accommodations than were high, low, or mixed groups of students.
6. Instructional interventions that were conducted for more than 1 year showed stronger results than those conducted for several days, weeks, or months.
7. The content area most responsive to learning-style accommodation was mathematics, followed by other subjects and language arts.

25. Moderators that did not meet the specified criteria included institutional affiliation of the researcher, learning-style instruments, geographic region, and ethnicity of participants. These findings have implications for teachers who plan to implement learning-style-based instruction in their classrooms. That is, the greatest achievement gains will probably be made in mathematics by academically average, middle-class students who have strong physiological preferences.

Educational Significance

26. According to Tallmadge (1977), an *r* effect size score of .33 may be educationally significant, as it accounts for 10% or more of the variance of outcomes. Educational significance refers to the point at which the incorporation of a specific treatment would be of practical benefit in the teaching and learning process.

27. The moderator subsets in this study contain 34 of the 49 unweighted effect sizes and 28 of 29 weighted effect sizes that reached an effect size greater than .33 and, therefore,

significant, χ^2 (35) = 365.43, *p* < .001, which also indicates the heterogeneity of the 36 sampled studies. Thus, there appeared to be a strong possibility that one or more variables actually mediated the effect size. We then conducted a number of searches to detect characteristics (moderators) that may have led to differences in effect sizes among the 36 studies included in this meta-analysis.

23. The total sample size (*N*), weighted effect size (*r*), transformed MSD (*d*), and residual variance (RV) for each stimulus subset are reported in Table 1. Because the average of the five subsets' RVs (.046) was much smaller than the RV of all 36 studies combined, we considered the learning-style stimulus to be a moderator. These results indicate that accommodating students' physiological preferences has a achieved educational significance. Accordingly, these moderate subsets would have importance and be of concern in educational practices.

Discussion

28. This research is not based on a variety of definitions and conceptualizations — only one. Limiting this meta-analysis to the Dunn and Dunn Learning Style Model should answer some of the concerns of learning-style critics. The Dunn and Dunn model is comprehensive and includes students' physiological traits of perceptual, time-of-day, mobility, and intake-while-concentrating preferences, as well as their environmental, sociological, emotional, and processing preferences. As reported by many practitioners, approaches to individualizing instruction by matching students' preferences have significantly increased achievement in diverse schools throughout the nation (Brunner & Majewski, 1990; Elliot, 1991; Gadwa & Griggs, 1985; Lemmon, 1985; Mickler & Zippert, 1987; Nelson et al., 1993; Orsak, 1990; Quinn, 1994; Stone, 1992). This meta-analysis provides support for those practitioners' reports and for the premise of modifying instructional strategies to match students' learning styles.

29. As discussed previously, Kavale and Forness (1987) performed a meta-analysis of studies resulting from a mixture of learning-style models that included only one master's thesis based on the Dunn and Dunn model. They found no association between strength of learning-style preference and effect size in their meta-analysis of studies from a variety of learning-style models. That result was not surprising, partly because of the flaws in the studies (Dunn, 1990), but also because it treated studies based on a variety of models as homogeneous. The homogeneity of studies based on the same model within the same meta-analysis addresses this criticism.

30. The concerns about learning-style models elaborated by both Curry (1990) and Snider (1990) are now largely irrelevant. They primarily raised questions about reliability and validity. However, in a comparative analysis of the conceptualizations of learning style and the psychometric standards of nine different instruments that measure learning-style preferences, Curry (1987) reported that the *Learning Style Inventory* (LSI) had good or better reliability and validity than other instruments that assess learning style. The results of this meta-analysis essentially answer concerns as they relate to the Dunn and Dunn model. That is, the instruments that operationalize this model are valid (De-Bello, 1990; Curry, 1987; Kirby, 1979) because they measure conditions or characteristics that

can be used to enhance academic performance. Given this validity, at least some amount of reliability is subsumed. In addition, both Miles's (1987) and Virostko's (1983) reliability studies, using the LSI, showed consistency of students' learning styles over time.

31. Furthermore, the quality studies included in this meta-analysis were conducted under the direction of 36 different researchers at 13 universities. Neither the identity of the researcher nor the researcher's university was a statistically significant moderator of the effects. This finding overcomes Curry's (1990) concern that learning-styles studies might be biased from being conducted under the direction of persons who developed the model. Moreover, by limiting analysis to experimental and quasi-experimental studies of the Dunn and Dunn Learning Style Model, we found that individualizing instruction to match learning-style preferences improved students' academic achievement and attitude toward learning.

Considerations for Future Research

32. Given the positive findings of this meta-analysis of experimental studies conducted with the Dunn and Dunn model, researchers should conduct a similar analysis of experimental studies with other models. It is possible that, when analyzing a body of research that involves multiple models, meta-analysis itself may obfuscate the impact of individual models. In addition, does the finding that small groups yielded larger effects than large groups did lead to research implications not previously considered and explored? Furthermore, does the finding that there were no significant differences between the St. John's University results and those of other universities suggest something positive about the portability of the Dunn and Dunn model?

33. In another vein, although Alberg et al. (1992), Andrews (1990), Perrin (1990), Stone (1992), and Quinn (1994) described the impact of matching instruction to the learning styles of low-socioeconomic underachievers, the Brunner and Majewski (1990), Elliot (1991), Gadwa and Griggs (1985), Lemmon (1985), and Nelson et al. (1993) populations were middle class and Orsak's (1990) sample comprised mixed socioeconomic levels. Because this meta-analysis sample of middle-class students revealed the largest effects, further study should be undertaken to determine whether differences in learning-style preferences are prevalent among, or tend to cluster within, high-, average-, or low-SES students. Conversely, despite the Alberg et al. (1992), Andrews (1990), Perrin (1990), Stone (1992), and Quinn (1994) reports of academic improvement

among underachieving and special education populations as a result of learning-style interventions, the sample of average students in this meta-analysis revealed the largest effects.

34. Thus, it seems appropriate to examine whether (a) specific instructional treatments impact more or less effectively on students of different academic levels and (b) differences in learning style exist among or tend to cluster within high-, average-, and low-achieving students. Similarly, do high achievers have fewer strong learning-style preferences than low achievers do, or are such students able to flex and thus accommodate instruction regardless of the match or mismatch?

References

Alberg, J., Cook, L., Fiore, T., Friend, M., & Sano, S. (1992). *Educational approaches and options for integrating students with disabilities: A decision tool.* Triangle Park, NC: Research Triangle Institute.

Andrews, R. H. (1990). The development of a learning styles program in a low socioeconomic, underachieving North Carolina elementary school. *Journal of Reading, Writing, and Learning Disabilities International, 6,* 307-314.

Annotated Bibliography of Research. (1992, 1995). New York: St. John's University Center for the Study of Learning and Teaching Styles.

Brunner, C. E., & Majewski, W. S. (1990, October). Mildly handicapped students can succeed with learning styles. *Educational Leadership, 48,* 21-23.

Campbell, D. T., & Stanley, J. C. (1966). *Experimental and quasi-experimental designs for research.* Chicago: Rand McNally.

Carbo, M. (1980). An analysis of the relationship between the modality preferences of kindergartners and selected reading treatments as they affect the learning of a basic sight-word vocabulary. (Doctoral dissertation, St. John's University, 1980). *Dissertation Abstracts International, 41,* 1389A.

Carbo, M. (1982). *Reading Style Inventory.* New York: Learning Research Associates.

Cholakis, M. M. (1986). An experimental investigation of the relationships between and among sociological preferences, vocabulary instruction and achievement, and the attitudes of New York, urban, seventh- and eighth-grade underachievers. (Doctoral dissertation, St. John's University, 1986). *Dissertation Abstracts International, 47,* 4046A.

Clark-Thayer, S. (1987). The relationship of the knowledge of student-perceived learning style preferences, and study habits and attitudes to achievement of college freshmen in a small urban university. (Doctoral dissertation, Boston University, 1987). *Dissertation Abstracts International, 48,* 872A.

Cohen, J. (1992). A power primer. *Psychological Bulletin, 112,* 155-159.

Cook, L. (1989). Relationships among learning style awareness, academic achievement, and locus of control among community college students.

(Doctoral dissertation, University of Florida). *Dissertation Abstracts International, 49*, 217A.

Curry, L. (1987). *Integrating concepts of cognitive or learning styles: A review with attention to psychometric standards.* Ottawa, Ontario: Canadian College of Health Services Executives.

Curry, L. (1990). A critique of the research on learning styles. *Educational Leadership, 49*, 50-52, 54-56.

DeBello, T. (1985). A critical analysis of the achievement and attitude effects of administrative assignments to social studies writing instruction based on identified, eighth grade students' learning style preferences for learning alone, with peers, or with teachers. (Doctoral dissertation, St. John's University, 1985). *Dissertation Abstracts International, 47*, 68A.

DeBello, T. (1990). Comparison of eleven major learning styles models: Variables, appropriate populations, validity of instrumentation, and the research behind them. *Journal of Reading, Writing, and Learning Disabilities International, 6*, 203-222.

DeGregoris, C. D. (1986). Reading comprehension and the interaction of individual sound preferences and varied auditory distractions. (Doctoral dissertation, Hofstra University, 1986). *Dissertation Abstracts International, 47*, 3380A.

DellaValle, J. (1984). An experimental investigation of the word recognition scores of seventh grade students to provide supervisory and administrative guidelines for the organization of effective instructional environments. (Doctoral dissertation, St. John's University, 1984). *Dissertation Abstracts International, 45*, 359A.

Dunn, R. (1990). A critical analysis of Kavale and Forness' report on modality-based instruction. *Exceptional Children, 56*(4), 354-356.

Dunn, R., & Dunn, K. (1992). *Teaching elementary students through their individual learning styles.* Boston: Allyn & Bacon.

Dunn, R., & Dunn, K. (1993). *Teaching secondary students through their individual learning styles.* Boston: Allyn & Bacon.

Dunn, R., Dunn, K., & Perrin, J. (1994). *Teaching young children through their individual learning styles.* Boston: Allyn & Bacon.

Dunn, R., Dunn, K., & Price, G. E. (1975, 1989). *Learning Style Inventory.* Lawrence, KS: Price Systems.

Dunn, R., Dunn, K., & Price, G. E. (1982). *Productivity Environmental Preference Survey.* Lawrence, KS: Price Systems.

Elliot, I. (1991). The reading place. *Teaching K-8. 21*(3), 30-34.

Freeley, M. E. (1984). An experimental investigation of the relationships among teachers' individual time preferences, inservice workshop schedules, and instructional techniques and the subsequent implementation of learning style strategies in participants' classrooms. (Doctoral dissertation, St. John's University, 1984). *Dissertation Abstracts International, 46*, 403A.

Gadwa, K., & Griggs, S. A. (1985). The school dropout: Implications for counselors. *The School Counselor, 33*, 9-17.

Garcia-Otero, M. (1987). Knowledge of learning styles and the effect on the clinical performance of nurse anesthesiology students. (Doctoral dissertation, University of New Orleans, 1987). *Dissertation Abstracts International, 49*(05B), 1602.

Giannitti, M. C. (1988). An experimental investigation of the relationships among the learning style sociological preferences of middle-school students (grades 6, 7, 8), their attitudes and achievement in social studies, and selected instructional strategies. (Doctoral dissertation, St. John's University, 1988). *Dissertation Abstracts International, 49*, 2911A.

Hedges, L., & Olkin, I. (1985). Statistical methods for meta-analysis. *Contemporary Education Review, 1*, 157-165.

Hill, G. D. (1987). An experimental investigation into the interaction between modality preference and instructional mode in the learning of spelling words by upper-elementary learning disabled students. (Doctoral dissertation, North Texas State University, 1987). *Dissertation Abstracts International, 48*, 2536A.

Hodges, H. (1985). An analysis of the relationships among preferences for a formal/informal design, one element of learning style, academic achievement, and attitudes of seventh and eighth grade students in remedial mathematics classes in a New York City junior high school. (Doctoral dissertation, St. John's University, 1985). *Dissertation Abstracts International, 45*, 2791A.

Hunter, J., Schmidt, F., & Jackson, G. (1982). *Meta-analysis: Cumulating research findings across studies.* Beverly Hills, CA: Sage.

Hutto, J. (1982). The association of teacher manipulation of scientifically acquired learning styles information to the achievement and attitude of second and third grade remedial students. (Doctoral dissertation, University of Southern Mississippi, 1982). *Dissertation Abstracts International, 44*(01A), 30.

Ingham, L. (1991). Matching instruction with employee perceptual preferences significantly increases training effectiveness. *Human Resource Development Quarterly, 2*, 53-64.

Jarsonbeck, S. (1984). The effects of a right-brain and mathematics curriculum on low achieving, fourth grade students. (Doctoral dissertation, University of South Florida, 1984). *Dissertation Abstracts International, 45*, 2791A.

Kampwirth, T. J., & Bates, M. (1980). Modality preference and teaching method: A review of research. *Academic Therapy, 15*, 597-605.

Kavale, K. A., & Forness, S. R. (1987). Substance over style: Assessing the efficacy of modality testing and teaching. *Exceptional Children, 54*, 228-239.

Kirby, P. (1979). Cognitive style, learning style, and transfer skill acquisition. Columbia, OH: The Ohio State University, National Center for Research in Vocational Education.

Klavas, A. (1993). In Greensboro, North Carolina: Learning style program boosts achievement and test scores. *The Clearing House, 67*(3), 149-151.

Krimsky, J. (1982). A comparative analysis of the effects of matching and mismatching fourth grade students with their learning style preference for the environmental element of light and their subsequent reading speed and accuracy scores. (Doctoral dissertation, St. John's University, 1982). *Dissertation Abstracts International, 43*, 66A.

Kroon, D. (1985). An experimental investigation of the effects on academic achievement and the resultant administration implications of instruction congruent and incongruent with secondary, industrial arts students' learning style perceptual preference. (Doctoral dissertation, St. John's University, 1985). *Dissertation Abstracts International, 46*, 3247A.

LaShell, L. (1986). An analysis of the effects of reading methods upon reading achievement and locus of control when individual reading style is matched for learning disabled students. (Doctoral dissertation, The Fielding Institute, 1986). *Dissertation Abstracts International, 48*(02A), 362.

Lemmon, P. (1985). A school where learning styles make a difference. *Principal, 64*(4), 26-29.

Lynch, P. K. (1981). An analysis of the relationships among academic achievement, attendance, and the learning style time references of eleventh and twelfth grade students identified as initial or chronic truants in a suburban New York school district. (Doctoral dissertation, St. John's University, 1981). *Dissertation Abstracts International, 42*, 1880A.

Lytton, H., & Romney, D. (1991). Parents' differential socialization of boys and girls: A meta-analysis. *Psychological Bulletin, 109*(2), 267-296.

MacMurren, H. (1985). A comparative study of the effects of matching and mismatching sixth-grade students with their learning style preferences for the physical element of intake and their subsequent reading speed and accuracy scores and attitudes. (Doctoral dissertation, St. John's University, 1985). *Dissertation Abstracts International, 46*, 3247A.

Martini, M. (1986). An analysis of the relationships between and among computer-assisted instruction, learning style perceptual preferences, attitudes, and the science achievement of seventh grade students in a suburban, New York school district. (Doctoral dissertation, St. John's University, 1986). *Dissertation Abstracts International, 47*, 877A.

Mickler, M. L., & Zippert, C. P. (1987). Teaching strategies based on learning styles of adult students. *Community/Junior College Quarterly, 11*, 33-37.

Miles, B. (1987). An investigation of the relationships among the learning style sociological preferences of fifth and sixth grade students, selected interactive classroom patterns, and achievement in career awareness and career decision-making concepts. (Doctoral dissertation, St. John's University, 1987). *Dissertation Abstracts International, 48*, 2527A.

Murrain, P. G. (1983). Administrative determinations concerning facilities utilization and instructional grouping: An analysis of the relationships between selected thermal environments and preferences for temperature, an element of learning style, as they affect word recognition scores of secondary students. (Doctoral dissertation, St. John's University, 1983). *Dissertation Abstracts International, 44*, 1749A.

Napolitano, R. A. (1986). An experimental investigation of the relationships among achievement, attitude scores, and traditionally, marginally, and under-prepared college students enrolled in an introductory psychology course when they are matched and mismatched with their learning style preferences for the element of structure. (Doctoral dissertation, St. John's University, 1986). *Dissertation Abstracts International, 47*, 435A.

Neely, R. O., & Alm, D. (1992, November/December). Meeting individual needs: A learning styles success story. *The Clearing House, 66*(2), 109-113.

Neely, R. O., & Alm, D. (1993). Empowering students with style. *Principal, 72*, 32-35.

Nelson, B., Dunn, R., Griggs, S. A., Primavera, L., Bacilious, Z., Fitzpatrick, M., & Miller, R. (1993). Effects of learning style intervention on college students' retention and achievement. *Journal of College Student Development, 34*, 364-369.

Orsak, L. (1990, July-September). Learning styles and love: A winning combination. *Journal of Reading, Writing, and Learning Disabilities International, 6*(3), 343-347.

Perrin, J. (1983). *Learning style inventory: Primary version.* New York: St. John's University's Center for the Study of Learning and Teaching Styles.

Perrin, J. (1984). An experimental investigation of the relationships among the learning style sociological preferences of gifted and non-gifted primary children, selected instructional strategies, attitudes, and achievement in problem solving and rote memorization. (Doctoral dissertation, St. John's University, 1984). *Dissertation Abstracts International, 46*, 342A.

Perrin, J. (1990, October). The learning styles project for potential dropouts. *Educational Leadership, 48*(2), 23-24.

Phelix, B. (1987). A comparison of two counseling approaches which are compatible versus incompatible with the sociological learning style preferences of black and Hispanic male adolescents on moral judgment issues. (Doctoral dissertation, St. John's University, 1987). *Dissertation Abstracts International, 48*(07A), 1962.

Pizzo, J. (1981). An investigation of the relationships between selected acoustic environments and sound, an element of learning style, as they affect sixth grade students' reading achievement and attitudes. (Doctoral dissertation, St. John's University, 1981). *Dissertation Abstracts International, 42*, 2475A.

Powell, L. (1987). An investigation of the degree of academic achievement evidenced when third and fourth grade students are taught mathematics through selected learning styles. (Doctoral dissertation, The University of Tennessee, 1987). *Dissertation Abstracts International, 48*(07A), 1654.

Price, G. E. (1980). Which learning style elements are stable and which tend to change over time? *Learning Styles Network Newsletter, 1*(3), 1.

Prince, W. (1987). Matching students' preferred learning time with the time of day tests are administered: An experimental study of effects on standardized reading in the fourth grade. (Doctoral dissertation, Columbia University Teachers College, 1987). *Dissertation Abstracts International, 48*(09A), 2236.

Quinn, R. (1994). The New York State compact for learning and learning styles. *Learning Styles Network Newsletter*, NY: St. John's University and the National Association of Secondary School Principals, *15*(1), 1-2.

Raviotta, C. (1988). A study of the relationship between knowledge of individual learning style and its effect on academic achievement and study orientation in high school mathematics students. (Doctoral dissertation, University of New Orleans, 1988). *Dissertation Abstracts International, 50*(05A), 1204.

Research on the Dunn and Dunn Model. (1992, 1995). New York: St. John's University's Center for the Study of Learning and Teaching Styles.

Rossman, M. (1985). Identified learning style characteristics and academic performance of selected freshman students. (Doctoral dissertation, North Texas State University, 1985). *Dissertation Abstracts International, 46*(11A), 3254.

Rowan, K. (1988). Learning styles and teacher in-service education. (Doctoral dissertation, The University of Tennessee, 1988). *Dissertation Abstracts International, 50*(02A), 418.

Schwarzer, R. (1989). *Manual for meta-analysis computer program.* Berlin, West Germany.

Shaver, S. (1985). Effects of matching and mismatching selected elementary students with their learning style preference for light as reflected by reading achievement scores. (Doctoral dissertation, Northwestern State University, 1985). *Dissertation Abstracts International, 46*, 3307A.

Shea, T. C. (1983). An investigation of the relationship among preferences for the learning style element of design, selected instructional environments, and reading achievement with ninth grade students to improve administrative determinations concerning effective educational facilities. (Doctoral dissertation, St. John's University, 1983). *Dissertation Abstracts International, 44*, 2004A.

Snider, V. E. (1990). What we know about learning styles from research in special education. *Educational Leadership, 48*(2), 53.

Stiles, R. (1985). Learning style preferences for design and their relationship to standardized test results. (Doctoral dissertation, The University of Tennessee, 1986). *Dissertation Abstracts International, 46*(9), 2551A.

Stone, P. (1992, November). How we turned around a problem school. *The Principal, 71*(2), 34-36.

Sullivan, M. (1993). A meta-analysis of experimental research studies based on the Dunn and Dunn learning-style model and its relationship to academic achievement and performance. Ed.D. dissertation, New York: St. John's University.

Tallmadge, G. K. (1977). *The joint dissemination review panel idea book.* Washington, DC: National Institute of Education and U.S. Office of Education.

Tappenden, V. J. (1983). Analysis of the learning styles of vocational education and nonvocational education students in eleventh and twelfth grades from rural, urban, and suburban locations in Ohio. (Doctoral dissertation, Kent State University, 1983). *Dissertation Abstracts International, 44*, 1326A.

The Buffalo Experience. (1993). Office of Special Education, Buffalo City Schools, NY.

Thies, A. P. (1979). A brain behavior analysis of learning style. In *Student learning styles: Diagnosing and prescribing programs.* Reston, VA: National Association of Secondary School Principals (pp. 55-62).

Virostko, J. (1983). An analysis of the relationships among academic achievement in mathematics and reading, assigned instructional schedules, and the learning style time preferences of third, fourth, fifth, and sixth grade students. (Doctoral dissertation, St. John's University, 1983). *Dissertation Abstracts International, 44*, 1683A.

Weinberg, F. (1983). An experimental investigation of the interaction between sensory modality preference and mode of presentation in the instruction of arithmetic concepts to third grade underachievers. (Doctoral dissertation, St. John's University, 1983). *Dissertation Abstracts International, 44*, 1740A.

Wheeler, R. (1983). An investigation of the degree of academic achievement evidenced when second grade, learning disabled students' perceptual preferences are matched and mismatched with complementary sensory approaches to beginning reading instruction. (Doctoral dissertation, St. John's University, 1983). *Dissertation Abstracts International, 44*, 2039A.

White, R. (1981). An investigation of the relationship between selected instructional methods and selected elements of emotional learning style upon student achievement in seventh grade social studies. (Doctoral dissertation, St. John's University, 1980). *Dissertation Abstracts International, 42*, 995A.

Wolfe, F. (1986). *Meta-analysis: Quantitative methods for research synthesis.* Beverly Hills, CA: Sage.

Ysseldyke, J. E. (1973). Diagnostic-prescriptive teaching: The search for aptitude-treatment interactions. In L. Hand and D. A. Sabin (Eds.), *First Review of Special Education* (Vol. 1), 5-31. Philadelphia: JSE Press.

Zikmund, A. B. (1988). The effect of grade level, gender, and learning style on responses to conservation type rhythmic and melodic patterns. (Doctoral dissertation, The University of Nebraska, 1988). *Dissertation Abstracts International, 50*(1), 95A.

Zippert, C. (1985). The effectiveness of adjusting teaching strategies to assessed learning styles of adult students. (Doctoral dissertation, The University of Alabama, 1986). *Dissertation Abstracts International, 47*(03A), 751.

Factual Questions

1. What is the researchers' criticism of Tappenden's study?

2. How are *sociological characteristics* defined?

3. Why were 6 of the 42 experiments excluded from the analysis?

4. What statistic was missing in numerous reports?

5. In all, how many participants (i.e., subjects) were in the 36 experiments analyzed in the meta-analysis?

6. Based on the normal curve, what is the meaning of the MSD (*d*) of .755?

7. Students at which academic level were more responsive to learning-style accommodations?

8. The authors note that an *r* of .33 accounts for 10% *or more* of the variance of outcomes. Calculate the exact percentage by squaring .33 and multiplying the result by 100. To one decimal place, what is the percentage?

Questions for Discussion

9. Is the Dunn and Dunn Learning Style Model adequately described?

10. The researchers included only studies that employed an experimental design. (See paragraph 14.) Was this a good decision? Explain.

11. Because the 36 studies were found to be heterogeneous (in their effects), the researchers analyzed the data to identify moderators (variables that might explain why the studies differed from each other). Are moderators of interest to you? Explain.

12. Speculate on why ethnicity of participants was not included in Table 2 as a moderator. (See paragraph 22.) Was this a good idea? Explain.

13. Some categories of the moderators in Table 2 are based on only a small number of studies. (Note that *k* in the table indicates the number of studies.) Is this a serious problem? Explain.

14. Is the fact that the studies included in the analysis were conducted by 36 different researchers important? Explain.

15. Meta-analysis provides a *statistical* summary of a collection of studies on a topic. An alternative is a traditional review of literature in which the methodology and results of studies are discussed with the aim of making sense of them. Are there advantages and disadvantages to each approach? Explain.

16. Has this study convinced you that the Dunn and Dunn model is important? Explain.

Quality Ratings

DIRECTIONS: Indicate your level of agreement with each of the following statements by circling a number from 5 for strongly agree (SA) to 1 for strongly disagree (SD). If you believe that an item is not applicable to this research article, leave it blank. Be prepared to explain your ratings.

A. The introduction establishes the importance of the research topic.
   SA   5   4   3   2   1   SD

B. The literature review establishes the context for the study.
   SA   5   4   3   2   1   SD

C. The research purpose, question, or hypothesis is clearly stated.
   SA   5   4   3   2   1   SD

D. The method of sampling is sound.
   SA   5   4   3   2   1   SD

E. Relevant demographics (for example, age, gender, and ethnicity) are described.
   SA   5   4   3   2   1   SD

F. Measurement procedures are adequate.
   SA   5   4   3   2   1   SD

G. The results are clearly described.
   SA   5   4   3   2   1   SD

H. The discussion/conclusion is appropriate.
   SA   5   4   3   2   1   SD

I. Despite any flaws noted above, the report is worthy of publication.
   SA   5   4   3   2   1   SD

APPENDIX A

READING RESEARCH REPORTS:
A BRIEF INTRODUCTION

David A. Schroeder
David E. Johnson
Thomas D. Jensen

1. To many students, the prospect of reading a research report in a professional journal elicits so much fear that no information is, in fact, transmitted. Such apprehension on the part of the reader is not necessary, and we hope that this article will help students understand more clearly what such reports are all about and will teach them how to use these resources more effectively. Let us assure you that there is nothing mystical or magical about research reports, although they may be somewhat more technical and precise in style, more intimidating in vocabulary, and more likely to refer to specific sources of information than are everyday mass media sources. However, once you get beyond these intimidating features, you will find that the vast majority of research reports do a good job of guiding you through a project and of informing you of important points of which you should be aware.

2. A scientific research report has but one purpose: to communicate to others the results of one's scientific investigations. To ensure that readers will be able to appreciate fully the import and implications of the research, the author of the report will make every effort to describe the project so comprehensively that even a naive reader will be able to follow the logic as he or she traces the author's thinking through the project.

3. A standardized format has been developed by editors and authors to facilitate effective communication. The format is subject to some modification, according to the specific needs and goals of a particular author for a particular article, but, in general, most articles possess a number of features in common. We will briefly discuss the six major sections of research articles and the purpose of each. We hope that this selection will help you take full advantage of the subsequent articles and to appreciate their content as informed "consumers" of social psychological research.

Heading

4. The heading of an article consists of the title, the name of the author or authors, and their institutional affiliations. Typically the title provides a brief description of the primary independent and dependent variables that have been investigated in the study. This information should help you begin to categorize the study into some implicit organizational framework that will help you keep track of the social psychological material. For example, if the title includes the word *persuasion*, you should immediately recognize that the article will be related to the attitude-change literature, and you should prepare yourself to identify the similarities and differences between the present study and the previous literature.

5. The names of the authors may also be important to you for at least two reasons. First, it is quite common for social psychologists to use the names of authors as a shorthand notation in referring among themselves to critical articles. Rather than asking, "Have you read 'Videotape and the attribution process: Reversing actors' and observers' points of view'?", it is much easier to say, "Have you read the Storms (1973) article?" In addition, this strategy gives the author(s) credit for the material contained in the article. Second, you will find that most researchers actively pursue programs of research that are specific to a particular area of interest. For example, you will eventually be able to recognize that an article written by Albert Bandura is likely to be about social learning processes, while an article by Leonard Berkowitz is probably going to discuss aggression and violence. Once you begin to identify the major researchers in each area, you will find that you will be able to go beyond the information presented within an article and understand not only how a piece of research fits into a well-defined body of literature but also how it may be related to other less obvious topics.

Abstract

6. The Abstract is a short (often less than 150 words) preview of the contents of the article. The Abstract should be totally self-contained and intelligible without any reference to the article proper. It should briefly convey a statement of the problem explored, the methods used, the major results of the study, and the conclusions reached. The Abstract helps to set the stage and to prepare you for the article itself. Just as the title helps you place the article in a particular area of investigation, the Abstract helps pinpoint the exact question or questions to be addressed in the study.

Introduction

7. The Introduction provides the foundation for the study itself and therefore for the remainder of the article. Thus it serves several critical functions for the reader. First, it provides a context for the article and the study by discussing past literature that is relevant to and has implications for the present research. Second, it permits a thorough discussion of the rationale for the research that was conducted and a full description of the independent and dependent variables that were employed. Third, it allows the hypotheses that were tested to be stated explicitly, and the arguments on which these predictions were based to be elucidated. Each of these functions will be considered in detail.

8. The literature review that is typically the initial portion of the Introduction is not intended to provide a comprehensive restatement of all the published articles that are tangentially relevant to the present research. Normally, a selective review is presented — one that carefully sets up the rationale of the study and identifies deficiencies in our understanding of the phenomena being investigated. In taking this approach, the author is attempting to provide insights into the thought processes that preceded the actual conducting of the study. Usually the literature review will begin by discussing rather broad conceptual issues (e.g., major theories, recognized areas of investigation) and will then gradually narrow its focus to more specific concerns (e.g., specific findings from previous research, methods that have been employed). It may be helpful to think of the Introduction as a funnel, gradually drawing one's attention to a central point that represents the critical feature of the article.

9.   Following the review of the past literature, the author typically presents the rationale for his or her own research. A research study may have one of several goals as its primary aim: (1) It may be designed to answer a question specifically raised by the previous literature but left unanswered. (2) It may attempt to correct methodological flaws that have plagued previous research and threaten the validity of the conclusions reached. (3) It may seek to reconcile conflicting findings that have been reported in the literature, typically by identifying and/or eliminating confounding variables by exerting greater experimental control. (4) It may be designed to assess the validity of a scientific theory by testing one or more hypotheses that have been deduced or derived from that theory. (5) It may begin a novel line of research that has not been previously pursued or discussed in the literature. Research pursuing any of these five goals may yield significant contributions to a particular field of inquiry.

10.   After providing the rationale for the study, the author properly continues to narrow the focus of the article from broad conceptual issues to the particular variables that are to be employed in the study. Ideally, in experimental studies, the author clearly identifies the independent and dependent variables to be used; in correlational studies, the predictor and criterion variables are specified. For those readers who do not have an extensive background in research methodology, a brief explanation of experimental and correlational studies may be in order.

11.   *Experimental studies.* An experimental study is designed to identify cause-effect relationships between independent variables that the experimenter systematically manipulates and the dependent variable that is used to measure the behavior of interest. In such a study, the researcher controls the situation to eliminate or neutralize the effects of all extraneous factors that may affect the behavior of interest in order to assess more precisely the impact of the

independent variables alone. In most instances, only the tightly controlled experimental method permits valid inferences of cause-effect relationships to be made.

12.   *Correlational studies.* In some circumstances the researcher cannot exert the degree of control over the situation that is necessary for a true experimental study. Rather than giving up the project, the researcher may explore alternative methods that may still permit an assessment of his or her hypotheses and predictions. One such alternative is the correlational approach. In a correlational study, the researcher specifies a set of measures that should be related conceptually to the display of a target behavior. The measure that is used to assess the target behavior is called the criterion variable; the measure from which the researcher expects to be able to make predictions about the criterion variable is called the predictor variable. Correlational studies permit the researcher to assess the degree of relationship between the predictor variable(s) and the criterion variable(s), but inferences of cause and effect cannot be validly made because the effects of extraneous variables have not been adequately controlled. Correlational studies are most frequently used in naturalistic or applied situations in which researchers must either tolerate the lack of control and do the best they can under the circumstances or give up any hope of testing their hypotheses.

13.   After the discussion of these critical components of the study, the author explicitly states the exact predictions that the study is designed to test. The previous material should have set the stage sufficiently well for you as a reader to anticipate what these hypotheses will be, but it is incumbent on the author to present them nonetheless. The wording of the hypotheses may vary, some authors preferring to state the predictions in conceptual terms (e.g., "The arousal of cognitive dissonance due to counter-attitudinal advocacy is expected to lead to greater attitude change than the presentation of an attitude-consistent argument.") and others preferring to state their predictions in terms of the actual operationalizations that they employed (e.g., "Subjects who received a $1 incentive to say that an objectively boring task was fun are expected to subsequently evaluate the task as being more enjoyable than subjects who were offered a $20 incentive to say that the task was interesting.").

14.   In reading a research report, it is imperative that you pay attention to the relationship between the initial literature review, the rationale for the study and the statement of hypotheses. In a well-conceived and well-designed investigation, each section will flow

logically from the preceding one; the internal consistency of the author's arguments will make for smooth transitions as the presentation advances. If there appear to be discontinuities or inconsistencies throughout the author's presentation, it would be wise to take a more critical view of the study — particularly if the predictions do not seem to follow logically from the earlier material. In such cases, the author may be trying to present as a prediction a description of the findings that were unexpectedly uncovered when the study was being conducted. Although there is nothing wrong with reporting unexpected findings in a journal article, the author should be honest enough to identify them as what they really are. As a reader, you should have much more confidence in the reliability of predictions that obtain than you do in data that can be described by postdictions only.

Method

15.   To this point, the author has dealt with the study in relatively abstract terms, and has given little attention to the actual procedures used in conducting it. In the Method section, the author at last describes the operationalizations and procedures that were employed in the investigation. There are at least two reasons for the detailed presentation of this information. First, such a presentation allows interested readers to reconstruct the methodology used, so that a replication of the study can be undertaken. By conducting a replication using different subject populations and slightly different operationalizations of the same conceptual variables, more information can be gained about the validity of the conclusions that the original investigator reached. Second, even if a replication is not conducted, the careful description of the method used will permit you to evaluate the adequacy of the procedures employed.

16.   The Method section typically comprises two or more subsections, each of which has a specific function to fulfill. Almost without exception, the Method section begins with a subject subsection, consisting of a complete description of the subjects who participated in the study. The number of subjects should be indicated, and there should be a summary of important demographic information (e.g., numbers of male and female subjects, age) so that you can know to what populations the findings can be reasonably generalized. Sampling techniques that were used to recruit subjects and incentives used to induce volunteering should also be clearly specified. To the extent that subject characteristics are of primary importance to the goals of the research, greater detail is presented in this subsection, and more attention should be directed to it.

17. A procedures subsection is also almost always included in the Method section. This subsection presents a detailed account of the subjects' experiences in the experiment. Although other formats may also be effective, the most common presentation style is to describe the subjects' activities in chronological order. A thorough description of all questionnaires administered or tasks completed is given, as well as any other features that might be reasonably expected to affect the behavior of the subjects in the study.

18. After the procedures have been discussed, a full description of the independent variables in an experimental study, or predictor variables in a correlational study, is typically provided. Verbatim description of each of the different levels of each independent variable is presented, and similar detail is used to describe each predictor variable. This information may be included either in the procedures subsection or, if the description of these variables is quite lengthy, in a separate subsection.

19. After thoroughly describing these variables, the author usually describes the dependent variables in an experimental study, and the criterion variables in a correlational study. The description of the dependent and/or criterion variables also requires a verbatim specification of the exact operationalizations that were employed. When appropriate and available, information about the reliability and validity of these measures is also presented. In addition, if the investigator has included any questions that were intended to allow the effectiveness of the independent variable manipulation to be assessed, these manipulation checks are described at this point. All of this information may be incorporated in the procedures subsection or in a separate subsection.

20. After you have read the Method section, there should be no question about what has been done to the subjects who participated in the study. You should try to evaluate how representative the methods that were used were of the conceptual variables discussed in the Introduction. Manipulation checks may help to allay one's concerns, but poorly conceived manipulation checks are of little or no value. Therefore, it is important for you as a reader to remember that you are ultimately responsible for the critical evaluation of any research report.

Results

21. Once the full methodology of the study has been described for the reader, the author proceeds to report the results of the statistical analyses that were conducted on the data. The Results section is probably the most intimidating section for students to read, and often the most difficult section for researchers to write. You are typically confronted with terminology and analytical techniques with which you are at best unfamiliar, or at worst totally ignorant. There is no reason for you to feel badly about this state of affairs; as a neophyte in the world of research, you cannot expect mastery of all phases of research from the start. Even experienced researchers are often exposed to statistical techniques with which they are unfamiliar, requiring them either to learn the techniques or to rely on others to assess the appropriateness of the procedure. For the student researcher, a little experience and a conscientious effort to learn the basics will lead to mastery of the statistical skills necessary.

22. The author's task is similarly difficult. He or she is attempting to present the findings of the study in a straightforward and easily understood manner, but the presentation of statistical findings does not always lend itself readily to this task. The author must decide whether to present the results strictly within the text of the article or to use tables, graphs, and figures to help to convey the information effectively. Although the implications of the data may be clear to the researcher, trying to present the data clearly and concisely so that the reader will also be able to discern the implications is not necessarily assured. In addition, the author is obligated to present all the significant results obtained in the statistical analyses, not just the results that support the hypotheses being tested. Although this may clutter the presentation and detract from the simplicity of the interpretation, it must be remembered that the researcher's primary goal is to seek the truth, not to espouse a particular point of view that may not be supported by the data.

Discussion

23. The Discussion section is the part of the manuscript in which the author offers an evaluation and interpretation of the findings of the study, particularly as they relate to the hypotheses that were proposed in the Introduction. Typically the author will begin this section with a brief review of the major findings of the study and a clear statement of whether the data were consistent or inconsistent with the hypotheses. The discussion will then address any discrepancies between the predictions and the data, trying to resolve these inconsistencies and offering plausible reasons for their occurrence. In general, the first portion of the Discussion is devoted to an evaluation of the hypotheses that were originally set forth in the Introduction, given the data that were obtained in the research.

24. The Discussion may be seen as the inverse of the Introduction, paralleling the issues raised in that section in the opposite order of presentation. Therefore, after discussing the relationship of the data with the hypotheses, the author often attempts to integrate the new findings into the body of research that provided the background for the study. Just as this literature initially provided the context within which you can understand the rationale for the study, it subsequently provides the context within which the data can be understood and interpreted. The author's responsibility at this point is to help you recognize the potential import of the research, without relying on hype or gimmicks to make the point.

25. The Discussion continues to expand in terms of the breadth of ideas discussed until it reaches the broad, conceptual issues that are addressed by the superordinate theoretical work that originally stimulated the past research literature. If a particular piece of research is to make a significant contribution to the field, its findings must either clarify some past discrepancy in the literature, identify boundary conditions for the applicability of the critical theoretical work, reconcile differences of opinion among the researchers in the field, or otherwise contribute to a more complete understanding of the mechanisms and mediators of important social phenomena.

26. Once the author has reached the goals that are common to most journal articles, attention may be turned to less rigorous ideas. Depending on a particular journal's editorial policy and the availability of additional space, the author may finish the article with a brief section about possible applications of the present work, implications for future work in the area, and with some restraint, speculations about what lies ahead for the line of research. Scientists tend to have relatively little tolerance for conclusions without foundation and off-the-cuff comments made without full consideration. Therefore authors must be careful not to overstep the bounds of propriety in making speculations about the future. But such exercises can be useful and can serve a heuristic function for other researchers if the notions stated are well conceived.

27. Finally, particularly if the article has been relatively long or complex, the author may decide to end it with a short Conclusion. The Conclusion usually simply restates the major arguments that have been made throughout the article, reminding the reader one last time of the value of the work.

28. As we suggested earlier, not all articles will follow the format exactly. Some latitude is allowed to accommodate the particular needs of the author and the quirks of the research being described. Given that the goal is effective communication of information, it would not be reasonable for the format to dictate what could and could not be included in a manuscript. We hope that this introduction will help to demystify research articles and provide you with some insights into what an author is trying to accomplish at various points in the report. Let us end with a word of encouragement: Your enjoyment of social psychology will be enhanced by your fuller appreciation of the sources of the information to which you are being exposed, and, to the extent that you are able to read and understand these original sources for yourself, your appreciation of this work will be maximized.

Reference

Storms, M. D. (1973). Videotape and the attribution process: Reversing actors' and observers' points of view. *Journal of Personality and Social Psychology, 27*, 165-175.

Factual Questions

1. What four elements should the Abstract contain?

2. If there is a research hypothesis, should it be explicitly stated in the Introduction?

3. Normally, should the literature review be selective or comprehensive in research reports?

4. Should the Introduction to a research report start with a narrow discussion of variables or with a discussion of broad conceptual issues?

5. What is a *criterion variable* in a correlational study?

6. The Method section usually begins with a description of what?

7. According to the authors, what is probably the most intimidating section of a research report for students?

8. How should the Discussion section of a research report typically begin?

Questions for Discussion

9. Name an area in which you are interested in identifying cause-and-effect relationships but in which a correlational study would probably be more appropriate than an experimental study.

10. Do you believe that *post hoc* explanations are ever acceptable in a research article?

11. Name some demographic information that might be of interest to you in a typical social science research article in addition to the examples given in paragraph 16.

12. Do you agree that possible applications and implications of the research should be discussed only if the editorial policy and space permit?

APPENDIX B

FUNDAMENTAL PRINCIPLES FOR PREPARING
PSYCHOLOGY JOURNAL ARTICLES

Harry F. Harlow *University of Wisconsin*

As retiring Editor of the *Journal of Compara-ve and Physiological Psychology,* I feel that I ave one remaining responsibility to my psy-hological colleagues. Having passed judgment n about 2,500 original manuscripts and almost s many revisions in my 12 years as Editor, I elieve I should bequeath to posterity some rinciples of scientific reporting that I have for-ulated only through countless hours of oonlighting.

Covering Letter

In plotting the publication of a manuscript he prospective author should think first about he covering letter. It is an unforgivable error to rite, "I am submitting a manuscript for your onsideration. . . ." This evasive method gets ou nowhere with editors. Even if the nondirec-ive technique works with many patients, there re some sick people who are best approached sing positive pressures.

There are a number of general principles nderlying a good covering letter, and they can e illustrated by example. I offer the following:

Dear Harry:

I am submitting the manuscript, "Creative Thinking by Paramecia," for publication in *JCPP.* My chairman has assured me that upon acceptance of this manuscript he will recommend me for promotion to associate professor. Two recipients of the Distinguished Psychologist Award have reviewed this paper and recommend it highly.

I am pleased to see that you are one of the five candidates for President of the American Psychological Association. As you know, I have nominated you for many years and will probably give you my support in the future.

Because of the unusual significance of these researches, I would like early publication, which I will finance from my National Institute of Mental Health grant.

Warm regards,

John Hopeful
Assistant Professor

The battle is now half won. You will get a air shake.

Introduction

Almost all scientific papers include an introduction even though large parts of it are frequently buried in the sections labeled Method and Results. However, the total omission of an introduction constitutes a glaring error, and, anyway, it is fun to write introductions—one is not constrained by facts.

One way to write an introduction is simply to state what the experiment is all about and make predictions about the outcome. Since the data will already have been collected and processed, you will have no difficulty in making insightful predictions. As all famous historians know, one can predict the past with great precision. However, prediction is one of the great booby traps into which young and inexperienced psychologists often fall. All their predictions are confirmed; older men know that this never happens. The proper technique is to select the prediction of minimum import, or throw in a completely extraneous one, and have this prediction fail. Honesty is the best policy.

Although some psychologists write simple, straightforward introductions, this is commonly considered to be *declasse.* In the sophisticated or "striptease" technique you keep the problem a secret from the reader until the very last paragraph. Indeed, some very sophisticated authors keep the problem a secret forever. Since I am interested in readers as well as authors, I advise that readers always approach introduction sections using the Chinese technique—begin at the end and read backward.

The function of the introduction is to impress your colleagues with your scholarship and erudition—academic appointments are seldom made on the basis of a Results section. Scholarly one-upmanship is attained with an unending number of nonspecific references, such as:

"The up-and-down effect was first discovered by _____ (1762), and this study led to many fruitful investigations (_____, 1804; _____, 1827; _____, 1844; _____, 1861; _____, 1874; _____, 1888; _____, 1894; _____, 1911; _____, 1917; _____, 1928;

_____, 1937; _____, 1944; and _____, 1952). Beyond these researches the broad implications of this discovery led to related studies on the in-and-out phenomenon (_____, 1829; _____, 1855; _____, 1888; _____, 1914; _____, 1927; and _____, 1950) and the around-and-about law (_____, 1884; _____, 1914; _____, 1933; _____, 1947; _____, 1952; and _____, 1960)."

Often, but not often enough, young and lazy authors are frightened away from this technique simply because they are appalled by the amount of work involved in reading the literature, especially if part is written in some foreign language. However, there is no excuse for this attitude; the author should remember that he is not reading the literature — just citing it. Anyway, he can always rely on some scholarly article in *Psychological Bulletin* as a secondary source to provide an impressive reference list with almost no effort.

Occasionally editors object to overly extended, striptease introductions and to long lists of nonspecific references. At this point the author should take the bull by the horns and write the editor a nasty letter accusing him of rigidity, illiteracy, and lack of scholarly interests. Editors are busy and editors are human. They can be broken—don't pamper them.

Method

To write a good Method section, one must be an idealist. If this section is to be understood, it must be clear, orderly, and systematic. The best way to achieve this is not to tell what really happened, or if you must tell, wait as long as is physically possible. Your four groups of *Ss* should always add to 20 or 30 each. If 7 *Ss* in Group 2 died of pneumonia and 19 *Ss* in Group 3 were suffocated, don't put it in the Method section. The death of these *Ss* was not planned but resulted, and the information obviously belongs in the Results. There is also good reason for putting this information in the

Reprinted from Harlow, H. F. (1962). *Journal of Comparative and Physiological Psychology, 55,* 893-896.

Discussion because you can then meditate on how different the results might have been had the *Ss* lived.

A mechanical problem that often creeps up in Method relates to the spelling and meaning of words such as "maize," "liman," and "maccaccuss resus." Fortunately there is a fundamental rule. Writing manuscripts is a tedious process and time means money. You must protect your time in every possible manner. If you cannot spell or do not know the meaning of a word, don't look it up in *Webster's Third International Dictionary*. If the word isn't in Thorndike and Barnhart, 95% of your psychological audience won't know the meaning of the word or how to spell it anyway. Moreover, that's the Editor's responsibility. Let well enough alone.

Results

The Results section comes in a very convenient place, and one way to start it is to put the procedures which you inadvertently omitted from the Method section — which you are too lazy to rewrite — at the very beginning of the Results.

If the Editor objects, point out that you are doing this for the sake of continuity. The next problem can only be resolved by reference to the Procedure. Reread the Procedure section and find out the order that you said you were going to follow; then, carefully rearrange that order in the Results. If you write succinctly and clearly, there is a real danger that the reader will only read your manuscript once, and every psychologist worth his salt recognizes the importance of overlearning. Then, too, if he has to struggle to understand it, he will naturally attribute the difficulties to the abstruseness of the problem.

The most important items in the Results will probably be the figures. Authors seldom realize the importance of figures and consequently fail to give them sufficient attention. It is absolutely imperative that the figures be of professional quality. This may cost a little money, but even with academic salaries what they are, the cost is cheap compared with the value of the man-hours spent in gathering and processing the data. The ordinate and abscissa should be boldly drawn and the curves should stand out like sore thumbs, which they frequently really are.

Now we are at a critical point. It is important to make sure that all legends, all numbers on the ordinate and abscissa, and all titles are completely unreadable. If you fail to do this, there is a real danger that editors and readers will compare the information given in the graph with what is written in the Results and

Discussion and call the discrepancies to your attention. Fortunately your figures can be made unreadable at a high academic level by following a few simple rules. Draw the figure on paper 2 ft. sq. and never purchase templates with letters more than 1/4 in. high. Then when the figures are reduced in size for Journal publication, the data will remain a personal secret. You can subsequently let out the data you are not trying to hide by personal correspondence.

Even authors who follow this rule — and the general principle is widely understood — frequently make a completely unforgivable error by sending glossy prints of their figures to the Editor. If the Editor has already recognized the fact that he has presbyopia and has purchased glasses, he may insist that the graphs be redrawn, and then the jig is up. However, if you send the original drawings and simply scratch out in pencil the copy for the carbon which some editors require, you have a high chance of success. A better technique is to send the carbon without figures. Most editors will relay this carbon to a consulting editor without checking for figures, and a single favorable review frequently insures publication.

Another good technique is to supplement the figures by presenting the data for individual animals in lengthy tables without means, medians, or standard deviations. No reader, and certainly no editor, will ever take the trouble to make the necessary computations to check your curves or statements of significance. The additional advantage is that long, detailed tables carry the implication that you engaged in an overwhelmingly complicated piece of research.

Discussion

Whereas there are firm rules and morals concerning the collection and reporting of data which should be placed in the Results, these rules no longer are in force when one comes to the Discussion. Anything goes — shoot the moon—the sky's the limit!

Even though one is going far afield, the endeavor should not be random, but the deception should be achieved with skill and grace. The most important fundamental guiding principle is to repeat the predictions made in the introduction—elaborating them if possible — and then to describe the importance of your work in broad generic terms and never get down to mundane fact. In Discussion sections one does not discover things about maze performance, minutes to run down a straight alley, 48 hr. of food deprivation, or the number of mechanical puzzle devices opened — one makes breathtaking discoveries about learning, drive reduction, motivation, and curiosity. After all, this is the way psychologists are going to talk when

they present and discuss their work at scientific meetings, and no man attains fluency in the jargon without practice.

Very occasionally some psychologist makes the mistake of saying what is worth saying in the Discussion and then stopping. This is interpreted by other psychologists as indicating that the person lacks verbal skill and creativity. Anyone can talk effectively about data which actually exist.

If your experiment has any merit whatsoever, and little is required, there is the likelihood that someone else will do it later and do it better. To save face it is important to engage in the alibi-in-advance technique. Endless Discussion pages can be consumed by describing how you would do the experiment if you were to do it over, and the joy of this device is that no data need be collected. You have the fellow who is going to be so cold and calculating as to check your results, on the run, and if you are smart enough, no matter what he obtains, it will be a dry run.

Even if you have only completed a single experiment you can greatly augment your data by several pages of descriptions of the results you would have obtained had you done a long series of related experiments. Furthermore, a clarity is achieved by describing the experiments that were not done instead of those that were because the results in the imaginary experiments come out in an integrated, orderly manner that is seldom achieved in the laboratory. Remember that data collection is a routine process and the brilliant scientist will rise above it when he comes to the Discussion.

Nothing is now left except to find a way to end the Discussion section, which has become so long and so confused that most readers will have forgotten what the original problem was about anyway. Discussion should be concluded in a friendly, charitable, and slightly condescending manner. First, say a few little things about the difficulties of doing research, particularly research in your chosen area. Then point out that there are a few little technical problems and research odds and ends that need to be picked up before your area of choice is completely neat and tidy. Finally, explain that once the research trail has been broken, less strong bodies can follow along.

Footnotes

Finally, one comes to the footnotes. Footnotes are always on a separate page (or pages) and there is a chance that the Editor will miss them, particularly if the typewritten material is single-spaced and turned upside down. Thus, here is an opportunity to introduce a couple of additional pages of complete trivia. If the Editor should discover them, nothing will be lost, for paper is cheap. Remember that this is your last chance to get in some padding, and never forget the fact that promotion is the prerogative of deans and final decisions are frequently weighed on other scales than those of justice.

Special attention should be given to one footnote — the acknowledgment. It is this one that separates the men from the boys. Since most experiments are not worth doing and the data obtained are not worth publishing, great care should be taken to protect one's reputation when one's name is associated with the conventional potboiler. This can be achieved by a simple and honest footnote.

"The author (or authors) had very little to do with this research. The idea was stolen from Dr. _____, the experimental design was proposed by my (our) statistical consultant, Dr. _____, the *Ss* were run by Mr. _____ and Miss _____, the data were processed by the mathematical computing center, and the paper was completely rewritten by Editor _____, on the basis of extensive notes and suggestions made by Consulting Editor _____, whose name was inadvertently left off the masthead of the *Journal of _____.*"

Editorial Policy

Faced with a mounting flood of uninspired researches and watching publication lag continuously mount despite multiple allotments of additional Journal pages, I came to realize that my editorial policies, even though rigid and unreasonable, were incomplete or else in error. For a long time I thought there was no solution, and then I realized that I was wrong. I established a new *JCPP* policy and formalized it with a rubber stamp, only to realize that my term as Editor had already expired. But at least I have the rubber stamp which I planned to use on a large number of manuscripts: "Not read but rejected."

CRITERIA FOR THE EVALUATION OF EDUCATIONAL RESEARCH

Suggested scale:

5 — Excellent (A model of good practice.)
4 — Good (A few minor defects.)
3 — Mediocre (Not good, not bad.)
2 — Poor (Some serious defects.)
1 — Completely incompetent (A horrible example.)

Title

1. Title is well related to content of article.

Problem

2. Problem is clearly stated.
3. Hypotheses are clearly stated.
4. Problem is significant.
5. Assumptions are clearly stated.
6. Limitations of the study are stated.
7. Important terms are defined.

Review of Literature

8. Coverage of the literature is adequate.
9. Review of literature is well organized.
10. Studies are examined critically.
11. Source of important findings is noted.
12. Relationship of the problem to previous research is made clear.

Procedures

13. Research design is described fully.
14. Research design is appropriate to solution of the problem.
15. Research design is free of specific weaknesses.
16. Population and sample are described.
17. Method of sampling is appropriate.
18. Data gathering methods or procedures are described.
19. Data gathering methods or procedures are appropriate to the solution of the problem.
20. Data gathering methods or procedures are used correctly.
21. Validity and reliability of data gathering procedures are established.

Data Analysis

22. Appropriate methods are selected to analyze data.

23. Methods used in analyzing the data are applied correctly.
24. Results of the analysis are presented clearly.
25. Tables and figures are effectively used.

Summary and Conclusions

26. Conclusions are clearly stated.
27. Conclusions are substantiated by the evidence presented.
28. Conclusions are relevant to the problem.
29. Conclusions are significant.
30. Generalizations are confined to the population from which the sample was drawn.

Form and Style

31. Report is clearly written.
32. Report is logically organized.
33. Tone of the report displays an unbiased, impartial, scientific attitude.

A Reader's, Writer's, and Reviewer's Guide to Assessing Research Reports in Clinical Psychology

Brendan A. Maher *Harvard University*

The Editors of the *Journal of Consulting and Clinical Psychology* who served between 1974 and 1978 have seen some 3,500 manuscripts in the area of consulting and clinical psychology. Working with this number of manuscripts has made it possible to formulate a set of general guidelines that may be helpful in the assessment of research reports. Originally developed by and for journal reviewers, the guidelines are necessarily skeletal and summary and omit many methodological concerns. They do, however, address the methodological concerns that have proved to be significant in a number of cases. In response to a number of requests, the guidelines are being made available here.

Topic Content

1. Is the article appropriate to this journal? Does it fall within the boundaries mandated in the masthead description?

Style

1. Does the manuscript conform to APA style in its major aspects?

Introduction

1. Is the introduction as brief as possible given the topic of the article?
2. Are all of the citations correct and necessary, or is there padding? Are important citations missing? Has the author been careful to cite prior reports contrary to the current hypothesis?
3. Is there an explicit hypothesis?
4. Has the *origin* of the hypothesis been made explicit?
5. Was the hypothesis *correctly* derived from the theory that has been cited? Are other, contrary hypotheses compatible with the same theory?
6. Is there an explicit rationale for the selection of measures, and was it derived logically from the hypothesis?

Method

1. Is the method so described that replication is possible without further information?

2. *Subjects:* Were they sampled randomly from the population to which the results will be generalized?
3. Under what circumstances was informed consent obtained?
4. Are there probable biases in sampling (e.g., volunteers, high refusal rates, institution population atypical for the country at large, etc.)?
5. What was the "set" given to subjects? Was there deception? Was there control for experimenter influence and expectancy effects?
6. How were subjects debriefed?
7. Were subjects (patients) led to believe that they were receiving "treatment"?
8. Were there special variables affecting the subjects, such as medication, fatigue, and threat that were not part of the experimental manipulation? In clinical samples, was "organicity" measured and/or eliminated?
9. *Controls:* Were there appropriate control groups? What was being controlled for?
10. When more than one measure was used, was the order counterbalanced? If so, were order effects actually analyzed statistically?
11. Was there a control task(s) to confirm specificity of results?
12. *Measures:* For both dependent and independent variable measures—was validity and reliability established and reported? When a measure is tailor-made for a study, this is very important. When validities and reliabilities are already available in the literature, it is less important.
13. Is there adequate description of tasks, materials, apparatus, and so forth?
14. Is there discriminant validity of the measures?
15. Are distributions of scores on measures typical of scores that have been reported for similar samples in previous literature?
16. Are measures free from biases such as
    a. Social desirability?
    b. Yeasaying and naysaying?
    c. Correlations with general responsivity?
    d. Verbal ability, intelligence?

17. If measures are scored by observers using categories or codes, what is the interrater reliability?
18. Was administration and scoring of the measures done blind?
19. If short versions, foreign-language translations, and so forth, of common measures are used, has the validity and reliability of these been established?
20. In correlational designs, do the two measures have theoretical and/or methodological independence?

Representative Design

1. When the stimulus is human (e.g., in clinical judgments of clients of differing race, sex, etc.), is there a *sample* of stimuli (e.g., more than one client of each race or each sex)?
2. When only one stimulus or a few human stimuli were used, was an adequate explanation of the failure to sample given?

Statistics

1. Were the statistics used with appropriate assumptions fulfilled by the data (e.g.,

Maher, B. A. (1978). A Reader's, Writer's, and Reviewer's Guide to Assessing Research Reports in Clinical Psychology. *Journal of Consulting and Clinical Psychology, 46,* 835-838. Published by the American Psychological Association. This material may be reproduced in whole or in part without permission, provided that acknowledgment is made to Brendan A. Maher and the American Psychological Association.

Copyright 1978 by the American Psychological Association, Inc. 0022-006X/78/4604-0835$00.75

Many detailed responses to a first draft were reviewed. Particular acknowledgment is due to Thomas Achenbach, George Chartier, Andrew Comrey, Jesse Harris, Mary B. Harris, Alan Kazdin, Richard Lanyon, Eric Mash, Martha Mednick, Peter Nathan, K. Daniel O'Leary, N. D. Reppucci, Robert Rosenthal, Richard Suinn, and Norman Watt.

Requests for reprints should be sent to Brendan A. Maher, Department of Psychology and Social Relations, Harvard University, Cambridge, Massachusetts 02138.

normalcy of distributions for parametric techniques)? Where necessary, have scores been transformed appropriately?

2. Were tests of significance properly used and reported? For example, did the author use the *p* value of a correlation to justify conclusions when the actual size of the correlation suggests little common variance between two measures?

3. Have statistical significance levels been accompanied by an analysis of practical significance levels?

4. Has the author considered the effects of a limited range of scores, and so forth, in using correlations?

5. Is the basic statistical strategy that of a "fishing expedition"; that is, if many comparisons are made, were the obtained significance levels predicted in advance? Consider the number of significance levels as a function of the total number of comparisons made.

Factor Analytic Statistics

1. Have the correlation and factor matrices been made available to the reviewers and to the readers through the National Auxiliary Publications Service or other methods?

2. Is it stated what was used for communalities and is the choice appropriate? Ones in the diagonals are especially undesirable when items are correlated as the variables.

3. Is the method of termination of factor extraction stated, and is it appropriate in this case?

4. Is the method of factor rotation stated, and is it appropriate in this case?

5. If items are used as variables, what are the proportions of yes and no responses for each variable?

6. Is the sample size given, and is it adequate?

7. Are there evidences of distortion in the final solution, such as single factors, excessively high communalities, obliqueness when an orthogonal solution is used, linearly dependent variables, or too many complex variables?

8. Are artificial factors evident because of inclusion of variables in the analysis that are alternate forms of each other?

Figures and Tables

1. Are the figures and tables (a) necessary and (b) self-explanatory? Large tables of nonsignificant differences, for example, should be eliminated if the few obtained significances can be reported in a sentence or two in the text. Could several tables be combined into a smaller number?

2. Are the axes of figures identified clearly?

3. Do graphs correspond logically to the textual argument of the article? (E.g., if the text states that a certain technique leads to an *increment* of mental health and the accompanying graph shows a *decline* in symptoms, the point is not as clear to the reader as it would be if the text or the graph were amended to achieve visual and verbal congruence.)

Discussion and Conclusion

1. Is the discussion properly confined to the findings or is it digressive, including new post hoc speculations?

2. Has the author explicitly considered and discussed viable alternative explanations of the findings?

3. Have nonsignificant trends in the data been promoted to "findings"?

4. Are the limits of the generalizations possible from the data made clear? Has the author identified his/her own methodological difficulties in the study?

5. Has the author "accepted" the null hypothesis?

6. Has the author considered the possible methodological bases for discrepancies between the results reported and other findings in the literature?